PRAISE FOR
DEFEAT INTO VICTORY

"Here is a great book worthy to set beside Churchill's *War Memoirs*."
—*Evening News* (London)

"Slim's lessons are valuable: They teach the leadership of men."
—*The New Yorker*

"A dramatic story, a well-knit and exciting narrative with a sound, strong plot. . . . The boundless scope of this man shines from every page of this book."—*New York Times*

"The best general's book of World War II. Nobody who reads [Slim's] account of the war, meticulously honest yet deeply moving, will doubt that here is a soldier of stature and a man amongst men."—*London Standard*

"[*Defeat into Victory*] is something rare—an autobiography of command and revelation at the same time of as decent and attractive a man as one could meet. . . . Slim writes with grace, humor and verve." —*New York Herald Tribune Books*

"A vivid and deeply moving story of endurance and heroism "
—*Observer*

"Of all the world's greatest records of war and military adventure, this story must surely take its place among the greatest. It is told with a wealth of human understanding, a gift of vivid description, and a revelation of the indomitable spirit of the fighting man that can seldom have been equaled—let along surpassed—in military history."—*The Field*

Defeat into Victory

Battling Japan in Burma and India, 1942–1945

Field-Marshal Viscount William Slim

KG, GCB, GCMG, GCVO, GBE, DSO, MC

With a New Introduction by David W. Hogan Jr.

Cooper Square Press

First Cooper Square Press edition 2000

This Cooper Square Press paperback edition of *Defeat into Victory: Battling Japan in Burma and India, 1942–1945* is an unabridged republication of the edition originally titled *Defeat into Victory* first published in London in 1956, with the addition of a new introduction by David W. Hogan Jr. It is reprinted by arrangement with the author's estate.

Published by Cooper Square Press,
An Imprint of Rowman & Littlefield Publishers, Inc.
150 Fifth Avenue, Suite 911
New York, New York 10011

Distributed by National Book Network

Library of Congress Cataloging-in-Publication Data

Slim, William Joseph Slim, Viscount, 1891–1970.
Defeat into victory : battling Japan in Burma and India, 1942–1945 / William Slim. — 1st ed.
   p.   cm.
Includes index.
ISBN 0-8154-1022-0 (pbk. : alk. paper)
1. World War, 1939–1945— Campaigns— Burma. 2. World War, 1939–1945— Campaigns— India.   I. Title.

D767.6 .S55 2000
940.54'25— dc21   99-055963

⊖™ The paper used in this publication meets the minimum requirements of American National Standard for Information Sciences— Permanence of Paper for Printed Library Materials, ANSI/NISO Z39.48-1992.
Manufactured in the United States of America.

To

AILEEN

*a soldier's wife who followed the drum
and
from mud-walled hut or Government House
made a home*

INTRODUCTION

Today, Field Marshal Sir William Slim is almost unknown in the United States and only slightly more renowned in Great Britain. The British general who rebounded from the Burma catastrophe of 1942 to form and lead the multinational army that won overwhelming victory over the Japanese in 1944 and 1945 usually receives a few obscure paragraphs in most World War II histories and almost no recognition among the Anglo-American public. Among those who study the war in Burma, however, Slim has earned acclaim as one of the great generals of World War II, and his memoir, *Defeat into Victory,* has gained plaudits as one of the classics of its genre—possibly, as one reviewer put it, "the best general's book of World War II."

Why has Slim received so little notice? To be sure, Burma's status as a "forgotten theater" has been a bit overplayed, given the attention devoted to the region in Allied councils and the American media's fascination with Lt. Gen. Joseph W. "Vinegar Joe" Stilwell and "Merrill's Marauders." But much of this attention began to decline after early 1944, as the Allies advanced in Europe and the Pacific and prospects for an enhanced Chinese contribution to the common effort faded. Also, when Americans have looked at the theater, they have tended to focus their attention on the campaign in North Burma, where the vast majority of their troops were and where they were trying to build a new supply route to China, and not on Slim's offensive in Central and South Burma, which they viewed as a drive to regain Britain's Asiatic colonies. Then too, Slim has often been eclipsed by other more arresting figures. The campaigns and personality of Field Marshal Sir Bernard L. Montgomery, the British general Americans love to hate, has left almost every other British military figure of World War II in his shadow. With regard to Burma, the colorful Stilwell has similarly dwarfed all other contenders, especially in American accounts. Of British generals in Burma, the eccentric Maj. Gen. Orde C. Wingate, leader of the Chindit raiders, has been the only individual to receive anywhere near the attention lavished on Stilwell.

INTRODUCTION

As of early 1944, about the time the Burma theater began to
recede in the consciousness of the Allied public, Slim's career gave
little promise of great success. Born to a lower middle-class family
in Bristol in 1891, he was a schoolteacher and later a junior clerk
in Birmingham before receiving a commission at the start of World
War I. He was badly wounded at Gallipoli and again in Mesopota-
mia, and then was invalided to India. Facing little opportunity in
the postwar British Army, he transferred to the Indian Army,
where he commanded Gurkha units, saw combat on the North-
west Frontier, served as a staff officer, and attended and taught at
various staff colleges. He displayed a capacity for analysis in these
assignments but gained no special notoriety. At the outbreak of
World War II, he was promoted to brigadier and command of the
10th Indian Brigade along the Ethiopia-Sudan border. He badly
mishandled the brigade's attack on the Italian fortress at Metema,
but, through good fortune, ended up commanding the 10th Indian
Division, where he fared better. In March 1942 he arrived in
Burma, in time to lead the Burma Corps in its disastrous defeat and
debilitating withdrawal to India. By 1943, Slim was associated with
a long string of defeats. Perhaps Prime Minister Sir Winston
Churchill was recalling those events when he remarked in 1944,
"I cannot believe that a man with a name like Slim can be much
good."

Such adversity forged the essential humanity that so many have
noted in Slim's memoir. As Duncan Anderson stated, "The reader
looked in vain for a 'Great Captain' striding across the stage of
history, deploying his divisions in accordance with some brilliantly
conceived and implemented masterplan." Instead, Slim freely
admits his frequent mistakes in the first Burma campaign: his damaging delay in ordering the withdrawal to the Imphal plain, his
near-fatal underestimation of the enemy's ability to infiltrate to
Kohima, and the success of the Mandalay offensive in spite of
seeing every assumption with which he had started the campaign
proved wrong. He repeatedly attributes his successes to others, notably the support of his superiors, the hard work of his staff, and the
"resourcefulness of my subordinate commanders and the stubborn
valour of my troops." He finds numerous opportunities to laugh
at himself, from his account of a Gurkha sergeant guffawing over
his futile efforts to look brave when caught under enemy fire, to
his efforts to cheer his staff after a defeat with the remark, "It might

be worse—it might be raining," only to have the skies open two hours later. Slim is even willing to concede that, in the grand picture, other theaters might have had greater claims to scarce manpower and resources. The contrasts with Montgomery and General of the Army Douglas MacArthur cannot be more striking.

Slim also could admit frequent struggles with self doubt, as his justifiably famous retrospective on the 1942 defeat shows.

> The only test of generalship is success, and I had succeeded in nothing I had attempted. . . . The soldier may comfort himself with the thought that, whatever the result, he has done his duty faithfully and steadfastly, but the commander has failed in *his* duty if he has not won victory—for that *is* his duty. He has no other comparable to it. He will go over in his mind the events of the campaign. 'Here,' he will think, 'I went wrong; here I took counsel of my fears when I should have been bold; there I should have waited to gather strength, not struck piecemeal; at such a moment I failed to grasp opportunity when it was presented to me.' He will remember the soldiers whom he sent into the attack that failed and who did not come back. He will recall the look in the eyes of men who trusted him. 'I have failed them,' he will say to himself, 'and failed my country!' He will see himself for what he is—a defeated general. In a dark hour, he will turn in upon himself and question the very foundations of his leadership and his manhood.
>
> And then he must stop! For, if he is ever to command in battle again, he must shake off these regrets, and stamp on them, as they claw at his will and self-confidence. He must beat off these attacks he delivers against himself, and cast out the doubts born of failure. Forget them, and remember only the lessons to be learnt from defeat—they are more than from victory.

Few memoirs by notable leaders have ever reached such a level of honesty and self-revelation as Slim achieved in this passage. At the same time, one finds none of the self-indulgence or self-pity characteristic of so many reminiscences. Through the self evaluation, moral courage, and mental discipline shown in this extraordinary section, Slim managed to ward off the demons that beset a defeated general and prepared himself for the challenges facing his successful return to Burma.

Those challenges were real enough. As described by Slim, the Fourteenth Army's area of operations consisted of "some of the world's worst country, breeding the world's worst diseases, and having for half the year at least the world's worst climate." The theater lay at the end of long lines of communication extending halfway around the world from Britain and the United States. That, and strategic priorities, resulted in shortages of nearly every item of supply. Within the theater, operations were hampered by inadequate railroads, poor roads, and a shortage of rolling stock and motor transport. Slim's army would encounter steep, densely wooded mountain ranges cut by streams and, crossing their line of advance, the Chindwin and Irrawaddy, two of the world's great river systems. Planners had to take into account the monsoon season, torrential rains that began in May and lasted two to three months, as well as the problem of disease, including malaria, dysentery, and typhus. Most of the population in Burma was indifferent or hostile to the Allied armies. Finally, the Allies themselves were divided by suspicion and diverging interests. The Nationalist Chinese were distrustful of Westerners and eager to preserve their forces for the postwar showdown with the Communists. The British were concerned about the defense of India and recovery of their colonies from the Japanese, while the Americans were suspicious of British imperial designs and eager to build China into a major factor in the war against Japan.

In *Defeat into Victory*, Slim cites as the "foundations of victory" building up the theater's logistical infrastructure and supply reserves, maintaining the army's health, and rebuilding the army's morale. None of these would sound especially unusual to the military professional, but in the Burma context, they each assumed special importance. With regard to logistics and health, Slim, of course, faced obstacles common to Western armies operating on the Asian mainland in the mechanized age. He was well aware of the importance of administration and logistics to his success, notably in the case of the decisive battle for Imphal, where he could rely on good lines of communication while the Japanese suffered from elongated and exposed lines of supply. His conscientious attention to logistics and health issues paid dividends to the Fourteenth Army throughout the campaign.

To meet the logistical challenge, Slim preached frugality and self-reliance, reminding his troops that "God helps those who help themselves." His resourceful logisticians improvised material for all-weather road surfaces and assembled a flimsy but effective collection of vessels for reconnaissance and support of river and sea-coast operations. Air supply in particular made his operations possible, as the Allies developed a highly efficient system of air drops, transport, and evacuation to maintain the Fourteenth Army in the field. Indeed, so great was the demand for parachutes for air drops that his supply officers, lacking enough silk, used jute, common in the Bengal region, to manufacture serviceable chutes. In his memoir Slim acknowledges the crucial role of air transport in his operations but is also careful to point out air supply's dependence on air supremacy, the key role of the Army as well as the Air Force in arranging deliveries, and air supply's limitations in sustaining an encircled force over long periods of time.

In *Defeat into Victory* Slim also remarks, "The most important thing about a commander is his effect on morale." Again, this is one of those shibboleths familiar to those steeped in military affairs, but its application is not always so easy. What impresses the reader about Slim is the methodical yet insightful way in which he approaches the subject. He notes the psychological ascendancy that the Japanese held after the 1942 campaign, exacerbated by the hardships of the theater, the sense of distance from home, and, in the case of Commonwealth troops, the lack of enthusiasm to die for the British Empire. Developing a program aimed at the spiritual, intellectual, and material foundations of morale, Slim managed to convince his troops that they were part of a larger team whose mission was to destroy the embodiment of evil, the Japanese Army. Through thorough training, tactical adjustments, and carefully planned operations, his troops became convinced that they could maneuver in the jungle and defeat the Japanese.

Slim's personality was crucial to the rebuilding of morale. He displayed a natural talent as a manager of men, choosing the right people and providing steadfast support while allowing them the leeway to do their jobs. Although the reader cannot get the full sense of his personal impact from the memoir, plenty of accounts exist of Slim's common touch in his frequent personal visits to the troops—the way in which his physical presence and bulldog jaw inspired confidence, and, not least, the effect of his ability to speak English, Gurkhali, or whichever other dialect the occasion demanded. Raymond Callahan describes an astonished British soldier near Meiktila who encountered the army commander, "virtually unaccompanied, carbine slung on his shoulder," telling him and his companions, without Montgomery's stagecraft or Lt. Gen. George S. Patton's histrionics, that the sooner they took Rangoon, the sooner they would be on the "big ships" home. He quickly won the affection and admiration of his men, who called him "Uncle Bill."

In his comments about his allies outside his own army, Slim is surprisingly more guarded in his comments on the Americans than on the Chinese, although he praises individuals of all nationalities. While noting the Chinese disregard for time, their bent for theft, and their obsession with "face," he effusively extols the courage, endurance, and eye for terrain of the Chinese soldier. In contrast, even though he pays tribute to the American logistical effort in constructing the Ledo Road, he points out that "the Americans had available a quantity of machinery that made our mouths water." One senses, in his account, irritation at the extravagant claims of American ingenuity in the construction of the road at a time when his own troops were building roads in terrain as difficult with much less equipment. Part of his irritation, too, may be attributed to the American focus on building the road through northern Burma at the expense of support for a southern offensive that, in the British view, would have opened a really effective link with China. Slim condemns as a distortion the American suspicion that the British hoped to regain their empire with American lives, but he must have recognized how plausible such a suspicion would be to Americans.

Notwithstanding his disagreements with Stilwell on many points of strategy, Slim actually appears to like the acerbic American. To be sure, he clearly finds Stilwell to be a bit of a caricature with his stubbornness, his unnecessary prejudices, and his efforts to maintain for press and public the image of a rugged foot soldier, uninterested in the trappings of command. But Slim was impressed with Stilwell's mental and physical toughness, determination, sincerity, and courage. He evaluates Stilwell as "not a great soldier in the highest sense, but he was a real leader in the field; no one else I know could have made his Chinese do what they did." Obviously, Slim was flattered that Stilwell, after making a long and tenacious argument against coming under the British general who served as Commander-in-Chief of Allied Land Forces for Southeast Asia, suddenly offered to place himself under Slim, his junior and a mere army commander. Stilwell's action revealed the high regard in which he held Slim as a fighter, a regard he displayed for few other British officers. As early as March 1942, during the disastrous first Burma campaign, Stilwell had written in his diary, "Good old Slim. Maybe he's all right after all."

Slim's reaction to Wingate was nowhere near as positive as his reaction to Stilwell. While acknowledging the great moral benefits of the Chindits' first mission and the courage and endurance of the raiders, he denounces the raid as an expensive failure. His regard for Wingate slipped even further during the opening phases of the second great Chindit raid in March 1944, when Wingate, over-wrought by reports of obstacles on one of the three crucial Chindit landing zones, became fearful that his troops would be ambushed and thrust on Slim the responsibility for continuing the operation. Part of Slim's dislike might have come from a discomfort with strongly egotistical, missionary personalities like Wingate and Mac-Arthur, both of whom receive little praise in the memoir. Looking back on the Chindit operations, Slim concludes that special forces are wasteful, taking men and resources that would find better service in more orthodox formations. He insists that he was not opposed to Wingate and indeed agreed with many of the man's ideas, but most of his discussion gives precisely the opposite impression.

His animosity toward the Japanese is even more evident. From the time he arrives in Burma, in the best tradition of Sun Tzu, he makes it his business to know his enemy. He praises their fighting qualities and what seems to him to be an almost innate aptitude for night fighting, a skill that comes harder for his white troops from urban backgrounds. But he also finds the Japanese, particularly their leaders, to be predictable and inflexible, at a loss when their initial plans do not work. From a Chinese officer, Slim gains the insight that if one can only hold against the initial Japanese on-slaught, waiting until they exhaust their meager supplies, one can eventually counterattack, a lesson Slim used to good advantage at Imphal. One senses, in his view of the Japanese, not only a personal antipathy but also a lack of comprehension, arising not just from the atrocities that the enemy perpetrated against his troops but also their fanatical discipline and seeming penchant for suicide missions. Even when complimenting the Japanese fighting man, Slim views him as essentially subhuman, as in his description of the individual Japanese soldier as "the most formidable fighting insect in history." Contrary to MacArthur's wishes, he forces his Japanese counterparts at war's end to give up their swords, thereby driving home the realization of defeat.

It took Slim years to receive the recognition he deserved. Even Imphal, though it earned him a knighthood, did not spare him criticism for cautious, unimaginative tactics. In the ensuing drive into Burma during 1944 and 1945, including his brilliant crossing of the Irrawaddy and thrust to Meiktila, he displayed plenty of imagination, even genius. Still, after Slim returned home following the surrender, he received a lukewarm reception. Montgomery and Field Marshal Sir Harold Alexander were the heroes of the hour. Even Churchill gave more credit for the Burma victory to Admiral Lord Louis Mountbatten and Alexander than he did to Slim. In 1947, Slim retired to become deputy chairman of British Railways, but he received a measure of recognition when—over the objections of his predecessor Montgomery—he returned to active duty in 1948 as Chief of the Imperial General Staff. Five years later, he became Governor General of Australia. While he was serving in that post, in 1956, Cassell and Company published his *Defeat into Victory*. The work became an immediate sensation, selling out the first edition of 20,000 within a few days. Slim became a military hero, and his memoir won applause as the classic account of the Burma campaign.

Although Slim has returned to near anonymity among the general public, *Defeat into Victory* has retained its luster over the years, as generations of military historians who have read it can attest. It stands as a monument to a great soldier and a better man. Cooper Square Press is to be applauded for making available once more this timeless account, which reminds the reader once more that human beings fight wars and, moreover, that "nice guys" can finish first.

DAVID W. HOGAN, JR.
Washington, D.C.
June 1999

PREFACE

GENERAL who has taken part in a campaign is by no means best fitted to write its history. That, if it is to be complete and unbiased, should be the work of someone less personally involved. Yet such a general might write something of value. He might, as honestly as he could, tell of the problems he faced, why he took the decisions he did, what helped, what hindered, the luck he had, and the mistakes he made. He might, by showing how one man attempted the art of command, be of use to those who later may themselves have to exercise it. He might even give, to those who have not experienced it, some impression of what it feels like to shoulder a commander's responsibilities in war. These things I have tried to do in this book.

It is a personal narrative, written from the standpoint of a corps or army commander in the field, whose outlook was often limited by his own surroundings. It is based on a short account I wrote at the time, a skeleton diary, some contemporary papers, and my recollection. For any inaccuracies and, of course, for its opinions and judgments I only am responsible.

If in places I have noticed by name individuals, units, and formations, that is usually because I happened to be near them at a particular time and they caught my eye. I am very conscious that for every one I mention, there were a hundred others whose doings were just as worthy of record. Named or unnamed, I shall always be proud to have served with them. Victory in Burma came, not from the work of any one man, or even of a few men, but from the sum of many men's efforts. We all, even those among us who may have seemed to fail, did our best. Luckily, that combined best proved good enough.

W. J. SLIM
F.-M.

Canberra,
1st December 1955

CONTENTS

BOOK I
Defeat

BOOK II
Forging the Weapon

BOOK III
The Weapon is Tested

BOOK IV
The Tide Turns

CONTENTS

BOOK V
The Decisive Battle

BOOK VI
Victory

MAPS

BOOK I

Defeat

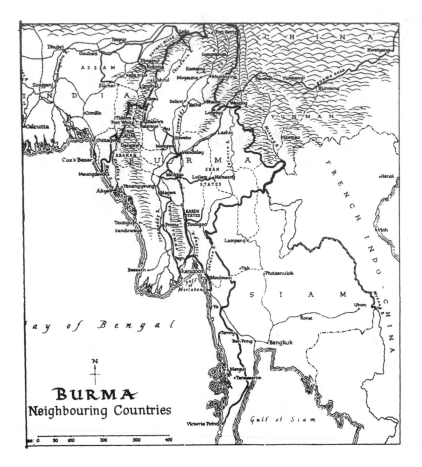

N

BURMA
Neighbouring Countries

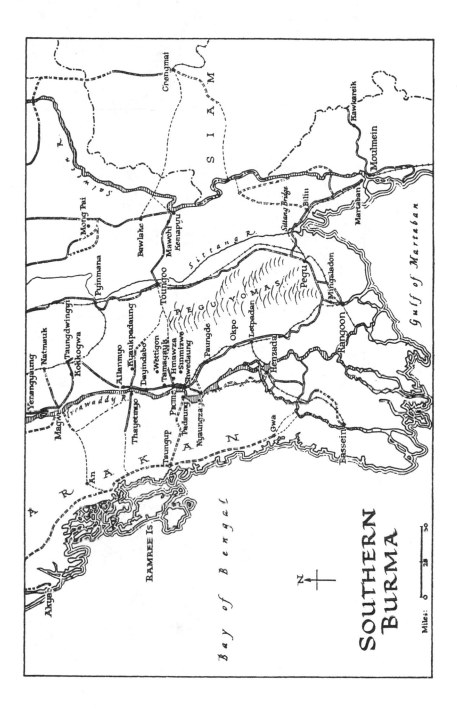

SOUTHERN
BURMA

Miles: 0   25   50

N

Bay of Bengal

Gulf of Martaban

ARAKAN

BAMREE IS.

Akyab

An

Taungup

Gwa

Bassein

Ngaungza

Padaung

Prome

Thayetmyo

Irrawaddy R.

Magwe

Yenangyaung

Natmauk

Taungdwinggyi

Kokkogwa

Allanmyo

Dayindabo

Kyaukpedaung

Wettigon

Tamagauk

Hmawza

Sinmizwe

Shwedaung

Paungde

Okpo

Leepadan

Henzada

Pyinmana

Toungoo

PEGU YOMAS

Mingaladon

Rangoon

Pegu

Sittang R.

Sittang Bridge

Bilin

Martaban

Moulmein

Kawkareik

Crengmai

S I A M

Y O M A S

Mawchi
Kemapyu

Bawlake

Mong Pai

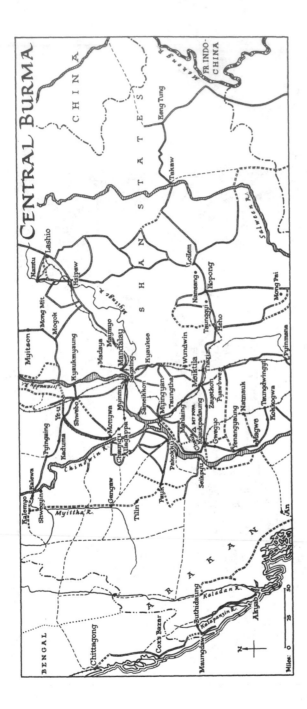

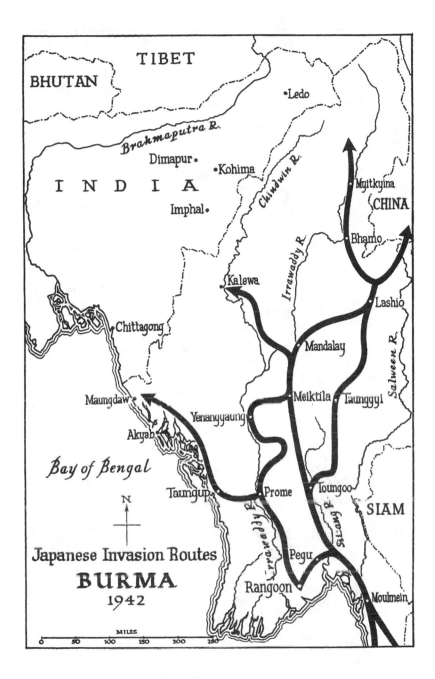

TIBET

BHUTAN

•Ledo

Brahmaputra R.

Dimapur•

•Kohima

I N D I A

Imphal•

Chindwin R.

•Myitkyina

CHINA

•Bhamo

•Kalewa

Irrawaddy R.

•Lashio

•Chittagong

Mandalay•

Salween R.

Maungdaw•

•Meiktila

Taunggyi•

Yenangyaung•

Akyab•

Bay of Bengal

N

Taungup•

•Prome

Toungoo•

SIAM

Irrawaddy R.

Sittang R.

Japanese Invasion Routes

•Pegu

BURMA

Rangoon•

•Moulmein

1942

MILES

0   50   100   150   200   250

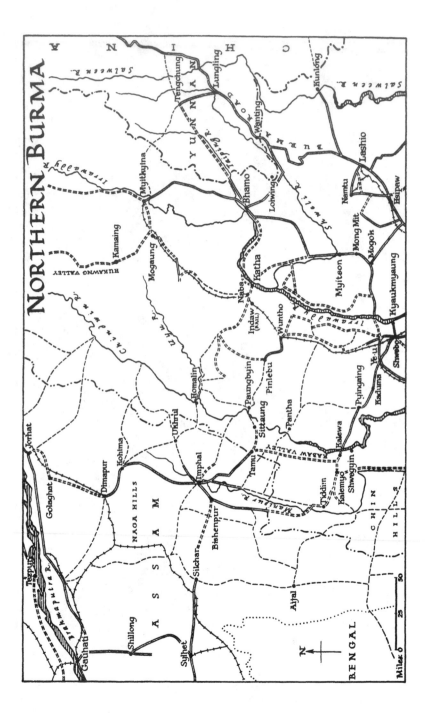

CHAPTER I

INTO BURMA

IT was good fun commanding a division in the Iraq desert. It is good fun commanding a division anywhere. It is one of the four best commands in the Service—a platoon, a battalion, a division, and an army. A platoon, because it is your first command, because you are young, and because, if you are any good, you know the men in it better than their mothers do and love them as much. A battalion, because it is a unit with a life of its own; whether it is good or bad depends on you alone; you have at last a real command. A division, because it is the smallest formation that is a complete orchestra of war and the largest in which every man can know you. An army, because the creation of its spirit and its leadership in battle give you the greatest unity of emotional and intellectual experience that can befall a man.

It was especially good to be commanding the 10th Indian Division. We had, as a division, found ourselves. We had scrambled through the skirmishes of the Iraq rebellion, been blooded, but not too deeply, against the French in Syria, and enjoyed unrestrainedly the *opéra bouffe* of the invasion of Persia. We had bought our beer in Haifa and drunk it on the shores of the Caspian. We could move, we could fight, and we had begun to build up that most valuable of all assets, a tradition of success. We had a good soldierly conceit of ourselves. Now, in March 1942, in spite of dust storms, equipment shortages, obsolete armament, and an overdose of digging strong-points, it was stimulating to be at what we all felt was a critical spot, waiting for the threatened German invasion of Turkey. If it came and the Panzer divisions rumbled over the pearl-tinted horizon, we should be the soft-skinned orange flung in front of the steamroller, but meanwhile it was exhilarating to go bucketing about the desert, a hundred miles a day, sweeping our field-glasses round a great

3

circle of bare sand. The desert suits the British, and so does fighting in it. You can see your man.

So, when I was called to the telephone at my headquarters in the wrecked flying-boat station at Lake Habbaniyeh, to speak to the Army Commander in Baghdad, and was told to fly to India within the next three days, my heart slumped.

'Am I sacked?' I asked.

'No, you've got another job.'

'But I don't want another job. I want to stay with my division.'

'A good soldier goes where he's sent and does what he's told!'

And the telephone rang off in my ear.

Constant sandstorms held up my departure for a few days and prolonged the unhappiness of saying good-bye, but at last I was chuffing out into Habbaniyeh Lake to the flying-boat. Through the sand, still blowing and stinging my face, I watched the half-dozen figures of my divisional staff who had come to see me off fade quickly into the haze, and I felt as forlorn as they looked, hunched against the driving sand. The flying-boat loomed up; I scrambled on board, bumped my head in the low entrance, as I nearly always do, and heard the crew discussing whether it was too thick to take off. However, the pilot decided it was not and up we roared. I cheered myself with the thought of the cable I had sent telling my wife to meet me at Delhi, but I was feeling glum enough at leaving my division.

We came down next day on the shrinking lake outside Gwalior and, after a tedious train journey, I met my wife at Delhi station. Next morning at General Headquarters, India, no one seemed able, or at any rate willing, to tell me what my job was to be. The only thing that was definite was that I was to fly to Burma almost at once with Lieut.-General Morris, the Chief of the General Staff in India, who was visiting the front to get a first-hand view of a not too bright situation. Why I should go in addition I did not know, but this time I was a good soldier, went where I was sent, did what I was told, and asked no questions.

We left early, spent the night in Calcutta, and then flew on to Akyab, a little port on the Arakan coast of Burma. It seemed a very pleasant, peaceful seaside town, much cleaner and better kept than similar places in India—as indeed were all Burmese towns and villages. We sat up late discussing the situation with Air

Vice-Marshal Stevenson, the Air Officer Commanding in Burma. Rangoon had fallen on the 9th of March, a few days before, and the British force had extricated itself with difficulty, but was now clear and reorganizing. The position, both on the ground and in the air, was an anxious one.

In the air, we had, in the face of great enemy superiority in numbers, been undoubtedly more successful than we had been on land. The importance of air power in any theatre is obvious, but in Burma it was from the very start a dominating factor. In plans for the defence of Burma, made before the Japanese attack, great reliance had been placed on the ability of air forces to stop, or at least greatly delay, the advance of enemy columns. In effect, too much was expected, for, as both we and the Japanese discovered over the next three years, air attack alone never succeeded in *stopping* the movement of either side. Even if it could, the British-American air forces in Burma were, in 1942, never on a scale seriously to attempt it. Burma was last on the priority list for aircraft, as for everything else, and in December 1941 the air forces in Burma were almost negligible. They consisted of only one R.A.F. squadron equipped with Buffaloes, a flight of the Indian Air Force with a few obsolete machines, and the Third Squadron of the American Volunteer Group with P40 Tomahawks. There should also have been an R.A.F. bomber squadron, but the aircraft had been kept in Malaya and only the men reached Burma.

The American Volunteer Group, under the dynamic command of Colonel Chennault, had the task of protecting the Burma–China road. Its base was Kunming in China, but Generalissimo Chiang Kai-shek, impressed with the importance of Rangoon as the only door opening on that road, had sent the Third Squadron there for its defence. These A.V.G. airmen were hand-picked from the American Air Force, had had considerable experience against the Japanese before the United States entered the war, and were as good a collection of fighter pilots as could be found anywhere. With our own R.A.F. pilots, they had gained a personal ascendancy over their Japanese opponents that was very marked. But the Anglo-American Forces were contending against great odds.

It had been estimated that fourteen fighter squadrons, apart from bombers, would be required to meet the Japanese over

Burma. Yet, when the Japanese attack began, there were only two fighter, one bomber, and two army co-operation squadrons in the country. Later, three squadrons of Hurricanes, mostly worn-out Mark I's, and a Blenheim bomber squadron arrived. The shortage of spares was acute. Against this small force the enemy, working from Siamese airfields, produced one hundred and fifty operational aircraft.

Speaking generally, all the Japanese fighters were inferior in performance to the Hurricane and the P40, with the exception of the Navy 0, which was approximately equal to them. The Navy 0 was, however, more vulnerable as neither it nor the Japanese bombers had self-sealing tanks or armour for the pilot. The Japanese, however, had a considerable advantage in range, which was of great service to them in a country where distances were vast. The Navy 0, for example, had a radius of two hundred and fifty miles, or five hundred with jettisonable tanks, compared with the one hundred and thirty-five miles of the Hurricane II. We were thus denied the power of retaliating with fighters against the enemy machines on their airfields.

Nor were the superior numbers and range of the Japanese aircraft the only handicaps from which we suffered. With the odds against us, an efficient warning system, which would enable us to defend our own airfields, was essential if our machines were to escape destruction on the ground. Yet the layout of the Burma airfields made this impossible. They had almost all been sited in a long north–south line facing the Siamese frontier, and running from Victoria Point in the extreme south, through Mergui, Moulmein, Rangoon, Toungoo, Heho, and Namsang to Lashio. These main airfields, unless our troops advanced far into Siam, which was never contemplated, did not allow of any adequate warning. They should, of course, have been sited in the Irrawaddy Valley, where instead we had only the subsidiary airstrips at Magwe, Meiktila, Shwebo, and Myitkyina. The Burma Public Works Department had done a very fine job in constructing these all-weather airfields so rapidly and with such small mechanical resources, and it was not their fault that they had been told to put them in the wrong place. Add to the unfortunate location of our main airfields the facts that we possessed only *one* radio direction-finding set, a meagre complement of anti-aircraft artillery, and that the newly raised and hurriedly trained Burma Observer

Corps had no wireless, and was thus tied to the scanty civil telephone and telegraph system, and it is easy to picture the disadvantage at which our tiny air force operated.

Rangoon had suffered heavily from bombing, but the two and a half British squadrons and one American squadron defending the city, in meeting thirty-one day and night attacks in the first two months, destroyed one hundred and thirty enemy aircraft with sixty probables, and compelled the Japanese to abandon the attacks after the end of February. The majority of the enemy fell to the A.V.G., who not only had in the P40 the better fighter, but were more experienced than most of the British pilots. It was thus possible for the last convoys of reinforcements to enter Rangoon and for the demolitions and final evacuation to be completed without serious air interference. At the same time, P40's and Buffaloes—the range was too great for Hurricanes—attacked any enemy airfield within reach, and our few bombers ranged far into Siam. Rarely can so small an air force have battled so gallantly and so effectively against comparable odds.

Such an effort could not be maintained. On the 31st January 1942, our operational strength was thirty-five aircraft, against one hundred and fifty Japanese. Appeals for reinforcements were refused; Malaya and the Dutch East Indies still had first call. Singapore fell on the 15th February, and at once the Japanese air forces began to receive heavy additions. By mid-March, there were fourteen regiments of the Japanese Air Force deployed against Burma, a total of some four hundred aircraft with a daily effort of two hundred and sixty. Against this we could produce a daily operation average of under forty-five. The odds were growing too heavy, even for British and American airmen.

Much of this we heard that evening, sitting over our drinks at Akyab. We learnt, too, that with the fall of Rangoon the Air Force had had to be withdrawn into Central Burma. What was left of it had been split into two mixed Wings, one at Magwe, one at Akyab. The split was forced upon us largely for administrative reasons—my first acquaintance with the overriding force of supply and maintenance factors in Burma. With Rangoon gone, the Air Force, like the Army, must live almost wholly on its hump. No supplies or reinforcements could reach Central Burma overland or by sea; only a tiny trickle might come by air.

7

The whole of the Air Force maintenance resources and reserves in Burma were surveyed and calculation of what these could maintain was made. That decided the strength of the force at Magwe. The remainder went to Akyab, where it was hoped to maintain them by sea from India. As a result the Wing at Magwe was composed of:

> Improvised Wing H.Q.
> One Hurricane Squadron, R.A.F.
> One Bomber Squadron, R.A.F.
> A detachment Army Co-operation Flight, R.A.F.
> Pursuit Squadron, A.V.G.
> R.D.F. Station.

The A.V.G. Squadron was by now very weak and our one ewe lamb of an R.D.F. station on its last legs.

There were left for Akyab:

> An improvised H.Q.
> One Hurricane Squadron (obsolete Mk. I).
> A General Reconnaissance Flight.
> A detachment Communication Flight.

Magwe had been chosen for the Burma Wing, known as 'Burwing', for the following reasons:

> (i) It was covered by two lines of telephone, one down the Sittang, the other down the Irrawaddy Valley, along which the Burma Observer Corps could be stationed. Some warning might thus be obtained.
> (ii) There was no airstrip south of Magwe big enough for modern bombers or fighters to operate from.
> (iii) It was the only airfield from which the army retreating up the Irrawaddy could be covered.

With all its faults, Magwe was, therefore, the best, and in fact the only, choice.

We also learnt that, in addition to the Air Marshal's responsibilities in Burma, he had been ordered by the Air Officer Commanding, India, under whose command he was, to organize the air defence of Calcutta, of the industrial centres of Bengal and Bihar, and of the oil installations at Digboi in Assam. He was to continue offensive bombing from India in support of the Burma Army and to reconnoitre and attack enemy vessels in the Bay of Bengal. This new directive would compel him to set up his H.Q. in Calcutta, and he proposed to move there in a few days.

Sixteen months before, in the Sudan, I had learnt a sharp lesson on the necessity for the headquarters of the land forces and of the air forces supporting them to be together. I was, therefore, rather dismayed to find that for the Burma campaign Air Headquarters at Calcutta and Army Headquarters at Maymyo, near Mandalay, were to be five hundred miles apart by air and unconnected by land. Even the Burwing at Magwe was about two hundred miles from Army Headquarters, and until 1945 this pull between the defence of Calcutta and the Burma campaign continued. It was, with the paucity of resources, unavoidable, but it hampered the free movement of air support in the theatre, and air commanders were compelled to keep looking over their shoulders.

Next day we went on from Akyab to Magwe, now our main air base in Burma. We flew over the Arakan Yomas, and I had my first sight of the jungle-clad hills of Burma. Flying over them you can realize what an obstacle they are to vision, but you cannot really appreciate what an obstacle they are to movement. To do that you must hack and push your way through the clinging, tight-packed greenery, scramble up the precipitous slopes and slide down the other side, endlessly, as if you were walking along the teeth of a saw. I often wished afterwards that some of my visitors, who measured distances on small-scale maps, and were politely astonished at the slowness with which I proposed to advance, had walked to my headquarters instead of flown. But all that was to come later. Now, as we roared over these endless, razor-edged ridges, covered to their very summits with the densest jungle, they gave the impression of a thick-piled, dull green carpet, rucked up into fold after fold. It was a relief to me, my eyes for the past year attuned to the bare desert, to come out suddenly on to the Irrawaddy with its narrow strip of comparatively open country on each side of the river.

At Magwe, after a talk with a very confident local air force commander, Morris and I flew, in a smaller plane, to Mandalay, landing, after some hesitation, on a very rough strip cleared among rice fields, a few miles from the town. Here we sat, rather forlorn, until eventually a station wagon appeared, and we drove up the winding road to Maymyo, the summer capital of Burma. It was a delightful spot, with English houses in the best Surrey stock-broker style, each in its own spacious garden.

Army Headquarters, Burma, was moving in, after its hazardous escape from Rangoon, and it was quite evident that some of it had been considerably shaken by that experience. To begin with, Army Headquarters, Burma, was neither organized, manned, nor trained as a mobile headquarters to command fighting formations in the field. It was, in fact, a miniature peacetime War Office on the Delhi-Whitehall model. Hurried additions and expansions had been made to meet the sudden onset of invasion, but it was very far from being a suitable instrument for the direct control of a campaign. The unfortunate Lieut.-General Hutton, who took over command in Burma just as the Japanese attack started, was, as commander in the field, terribly hampered by having to work through a cumbersome headquarters designed for quite different purposes. Given a little time, I have no doubt that Hutton, with his great organizational powers, would have evolved a more suit-able instrument, but he was plunged at once into a critical tactical situation when such reforms became wellnigh impossible. One need not be unduly surprised or indignant that we entered the war with no superior field headquarters in this theatre. Burma had seemed less likely to be attacked than Britain, and Britain had only a War Office until crisis forced the appointment of a Commander-in-Chief, Home Forces, with an adequate head-quarters. However, an unsuitable headquarters was only one of several crippling handicaps under which Hutton and his forces started their war.

In Burma our unpreparedness when the blow fell was extreme, and we paid for it. The basic error was that not only did few people in Burma, and no one outside it, expect that it *would* be attacked, but there was no clear or continuous decision as to who would be responsible for defence preparations or for its actual defence if it *were* attacked. Burma, while politically separated from India in 1937, was in every way physically linked to it for defence. Burma was, in fact, a defensive outwork of India; it would depend on India for the bulk of its troops and India would be its base. It was essential that the closest ties should be kept without interruption between the two countries. Up to 1937 Burma had been part of India, and its defence, as all its other activities, had been a matter for the Indian Government. Then with political separation from India, Burma was made fully responsible for its own military forces. A change came with the outbreak of war with Germany. In September 1939, Burma's forces were placed for operational purposes under the British Chiefs of Staff, but remained for finance and administration under their own Government. Suddenly, in November 1940, operational control was transferred to the recently formed Far Eastern Command in Singapore, while administrative responsibility was divided between the Burma Government and the War Office in London, which now contributed substantially to the defence budget of Burma. Both Singapore and London had more urgent matters on their doorsteps than the needs of distant Burma, and to separate operational from administrative responsibility is to break a rule that I have never seen violated without someone paying a heavy penalty. Indeed, it had been quite obvious, and very understandable, that neither of its new masters was taking much interest in Burma, and local commanders and successive Commanders-in-Chief in India pressed for its return to India. Just over a year later, on 12th December 1941, when a Japanese attack was seen to be imminent, it was at last passed back to India, but not for long. On the 30th of the same month, just as the Japanese attack really started, it was, in spite of protests locally and in India, tossed to yet another rather reluctant master—this time to the new A.B.D.A., as with our passion for initials the South-West Pacific Command was called. Under this organization, the Burma front was to be operationally controlled from Java and administered from Delhi. With the rapid break-up of A.B.D.A. following the Japanese invasion of the Dutch East Indies, back Burma came again to India. Thus in the space of about sixteen vital months there had been five separate superior headquarters in turn responsible for the defence of Burma, and for practically the whole of that time administrative had been separated from operational control. These changes alone would have ensured delay, neglect, confusion, and a lack of understanding of local difficulties. They led also to little or no progress being made in linking up India and Burma by road, so that when war came there was no overland communication between them.

Added to this was the usual chronic shortage of troops, and of

DEFEAT

equipment for even the troops we had. The 17th Indian Division, newly arrived with its brigades hurriedly collected from other formations, had been trained and equipped, like all Indian Army divisions, for desert warfare in the Middle East. Its transport was mechanical and except in open country it was incapable of operating off a road. There are few roads in Burma. The other formation, the 1st Burma Division, contained a high proportion of Burmese units, untried, many raised in a last-minute scramble and as yet without tradition. Neither division had battle experience. Their allotment of artillery was far below that of normal divisions and often of obsolete type. An anti-tank battery, for example, was equipped with Austrian 77-mm. guns, captured by the Italians in 1918 and in turn taken by us twenty-two years later from the Italians in the Western Desert. These museum pieces were, it is interesting to note, without dial sights and had one hundred and twenty rounds per gun as their total ammunition supply. Reinforcements promised from England and Africa had been diverted to Singapore in an eleventh-hour effort to save the fortress or, as in the case of the Australian divisions, diverted to hold Ceylon, itself under threat of overwhelming Japanese sea power. As a result, in the Japanese first thrust our two ill-prepared divisions, one Indian, one Burmese, supported by the tiny British-American Air Force, were pitted against superior and well-equipped veteran forces of jungle-trained troops and against a vastly preponderant air power.

Geographically, from the first clash we suffered from the fact that our main line of communication, the railway from Rangoon to Mandalay, ran from south to north, parallel and near to the Siamese frontier, liable almost everywhere to attack from the east. The original plan of defence, for this reason, tied a large portion of our scanty forces, including most of the Burma Division, to the southern Shan States, as it was expected that the main Japanese attack would come via Kengtung direct on to this vulnerable route. Another cause of dispersion was the long thin tail of Burma, Tenasserim, running four hundred miles to the south, with an average width of about forty miles. It would, from the Burma point of view, have been better to have abandoned this strip of territory, but the airfields in it had a twofold importance. First, they were needed for the air route to Singapore or the Dutch East Indies, and, second, in enemy hands they would be a most serious

12

threat to Rangoon. An attempt was, therefore, made to hold it by small scattered garrisons.

The main Japanese thrust came, not as expected through the Shan States, but over the Kaw Kareik Pass and through Tenasserim on to Moulmein. For fear of offending the neutral susceptibilities of the Siamese, we had not been allowed to set up any intelligence organization in that country, and our ignorance of Japanese movements was profound. The attack broke through the detachment holding the Pass, and after a fight the enemy advancing from the south took Moulmein, the main body of the 17th Division falling back northward on Bilin. There it fought a gallant action against superior numbers, but under threat of encirclement was compelled again to withdraw. Meanwhile the small garrisons in Tenasserim, attacked by air and land, had been evacuated by sea. Then followed, on the 22nd and 23rd February, the disaster at the Sittang River. The 17th Division, retreating by the jungle track to the river and tied to that track by its motor transport, found that strong Japanese forces moving round the flank had cut in between the leading brigade, now across the river, and the remainder of the division. Desperately and gallantly the two brigades still east of the river fought to break through to the great Sittang railway bridge, held by their comrades, their only hope of getting their vehicles, and indeed themselves, over the six-hundred-yard-wide stream. Then came tragedy. The Divisional Commander was roused in the night to be told that the small bridgehead on the east bank could hold out no longer; that the Japanese were almost on the bridge itself. He had to decide whether to risk the bridge falling intact into the enemy's hands, when they could sweep on to Rangoon, or to blow it up, leaving a large part of his force cut off on the other side, but with the great obstacle still between the Japanese and the capital. He gave the order to blow. The bridgehead garrison was withdrawn to the west bank and the bridge destroyed. It is easy to criticize the decision; it is not easy to make such a decision. Only those who have been faced with the immediate choice of similar grim alternatives can understand the weight of decision that presses on a commander.

The sound of the explosion was a signal for a sudden lull in battle. Both sides knew what it meant: the Japanese that however fiercely they attacked they could not capture the bridge; the

British that they were in desperately hard case. With a final effort they broke through to the bank. In horror they saw the broken bridge; it was hopeless to attempt to get vehicles or guns across. These were, as far as possible, destroyed, and men and officers individually and in parties stripped themselves and took to the water. A few managed to cross with their arms on rough rafts or petrol tins; the majority had to swim for it, helped only by bamboos. It was impossible for any man, even a powerful swimmer, burdened by equipment or arms to get over. Numbers were drowned; some were shot while crossing. By the afternoon of the 24th, all that had reached the west bank out of the eight battalions that had been cut off was under two thousand officers and men, with five hundred and fifty rifles, ten Bren guns, and twelve tommy-guns between them. Almost all were without boots, and most were reduced to their underwear.

This was the decisive battle of the first campaign. After it, however gallantly our troops fought, there was little hope of holding Rangoon. And when Rangoon went, as it did on the 9th March, the whole army in Burma was cut off from the outside world almost as effectively as had been the two brigades on the east bank of the Sittang.

No wonder then that when at Maymyo I first met General Alexander, newly, and by sheer luck, arrived from Rangoon, he was, while as calm as ever, obviously worried about the situation. Hutton, his predecessor and now his Chief of Staff, struggling to bring order out of complications and difficulties that threatened chaos, looked far from fit. For the last two months he had been under tremendous strain and only a short while before he had been in a particularly nasty air crash in which his pilot had been killed and he himself knocked about to an extent that would have put a less courageous man into hospital for weeks. He was, I think, still feeling the effects of that accident. The plain fact was that first Hutton, and then General Alexander who replaced him, had each in turn found himself in the normal position of a British general at the start of a war—called upon to carry out a task impossible with the means provided.

A moment ago, I wrote that General Alexander had escaped from Rangoon by sheer luck. And it was that. The whole British force from Rangoon, and with it General Alexander and his headquarters, would have been destroyed had it not been for the

typically rigid adherence to the letter of his orders by a Japanese
divisional commander. Coming from the east, by paths through
hills and jungle in a swoop on the city, he had been told to by-pass
it to the north and, swinging round, to attack it from the west,
the unexpected direction. To cover his flank as he crossed north
of Rangoon, he put out a strong block on the main Prome road.
He thus completely bottled up the British force as it tried to get
away. Several attacks were made on the road-block, but Japanese
tenacity proved a match for British and Indian valour. The
obstacle remained. All the Japanese commander had to do then
was to keep his road-block in position and with the rest of his
troops attack the forty-mile column strung out along the road.
Nothing could have saved the British, tied as they were by their
mechanical transport to the ribbon of road. Luckily for them, as
soon as his main body had crossed on its march west, considering
that his flank guard had served its purpose, he withdrew the road-
block. The Japanese division thus entered Rangoon from the
west, according to plan; the British, finding the cork removed,
flowed on, bag and baggage, to the north, also according to
plan.

My interview with General Alexander did not last long. He left
to attend a conference with the Governor. I doubt if it can have
been a very cheerful one, for the civil picture was no brighter
than the military. The people of the country were quite un-
prepared for invasion and, as the British suffered defeat after
defeat and the Japanese swept forward, they were stunned at the
collapse of a Power they had always thought, if they thought
about it at all, invincible and part of nature. The vast majority
had no feeling that the war was their business; they wished only
to avoid it. A small minority, mostly soldiers and officials, were
actively loyal; about the same number, nationalist politicians, the
relics of the old rebels of 1924, students, and some political pongyis
(Buddhist priests) were actively hostile. These elements were
rendered more formidable by the leadership of Japanese trained
Burmans, imported with the invading army, and by the flocking
to their standards of numbers of dacoits and bad characters
attracted by the prospect of loot. As the Japanese advanced,
desertion among the police, the subordinates of all services, and
clerical staffs began to spread. The air raids on towns, with their
heavy casualties and great destruction by fire, and the swarms of

Indian refugees, flying not so much from the Japanese as from the Burmans among whom they lived, all helped in the breakdown of control and communications. The civil administration was crumbling ahead of the Japanese.

There was, however, one bright gleam on the otherwise murky scene—the Chinese. At Christmas 1941, Generalissimo Chiang Kai-shek had generously offered the Chinese V and VI Armies to co-operate in the defence of Burma. General Wavell had accepted at once the 93rd Division of VI Army, the most readily available, and moved it into the Shan States; the 49th Division of the same army was to be brought through Lashio to the Salween at Takaw. The third division, the 55th, which was scattered and not as ready as the others, was to concentrate at Wanting, there to equip and train. At the end of January, when arrangements for their maintenance had been hurriedly made, the Generalissimo, at Hutton's request, agreed that V Army should take over the Toungoo area. This army consisted of the 22nd, 96th, and 200th Divisions, and was considered the best-equipped and trained force in China. During February, the Chinese troops, much hampered by lack of transport, moved forward into Burma.

A great deal of criticism has been directed against the British command for not at once accepting the whole of the Chinese forces offered, but it was then decided, with a great deal of justification, that as these armies expected to subsist entirely on the country and had practically no supply or transport services, it would be impossible to move or maintain very large numbers until some organization to do so had been improvised. With transport for their move so short and only one road available, it is very doubtful, even if all the Chinese divisions had been accepted at once, whether they would have arrived in Burma any quicker than they did. Their maintenance would certainly have been most precarious. In any case, the move of the 22nd and 96th Divisions was delayed on the orders of the Generalissimo, while he changed his mind over the command of Chinese troops in Burma. By mid-March 1942, only one division of V Army, the 200th, had reached Toungoo in the Sittang Valley, the rest of the army was slowly following up, with VI Army behind it. This would in due course allow General Alexander to transfer the 1st Burma Division from Toungoo across to the Irrawaddy Valley to join 17th Indian Division. He would then have two groups, a

Chinese and a British, separated by the tangled, jungle-covered hills of the Pegu Yomas.

To add to General Alexander's difficulties, command in the Chinese group was somewhat uncertain. In mid-March, the American commander, Lieut.-General Stilwell, arrived, in the double capacity of commander of all Chinese forces in Burma and Chief of Staff to the Generalissimo. In the first, he was subordinate to General Alexander, but not, of course, in the second. Stilwell was much hampered by inadequate staff and signals. Moreover, there was a Commander-in-Chief of the Chinese Expeditionary Force, General Lo Cho Ying, through whom all his orders had to go to the Army Commanders. These officers evinced considerable independence in selecting which of the orders they would accept, and even divisional commanders at times showed a tendency to pick and choose. They were able to back up their refusals with some show of legality as Chiang Kai-shek had not actually given Stilwell his official seal as Commander-in-Chief. And, if this were not enough, there was, seated at Lashio with a Chinese mission, a General Lin Wei, who as the Generalissimo's direct representative blandly disclaimed all operational responsibility, but, as he modestly put it, 'exerted influence'. Such was this 'influence' that no Chinese Army Commander would carry out an Alexander-Stilwell-Lo order unless it had been passed by him.

A Chinese 'army' corresponded to a European corps and consisted usually of two or three divisions. The division itself was not only much smaller than its British or American equivalent, having a strength of from seven to nine thousand, but only two-thirds of the men were armed; the other third replaced the absent animal or motor transport and acted as carriers. As a result the rifle-power of a Chinese division at full strength rarely exceeded three thousand, with a couple of hundred light machine-guns, thirty or forty medium machine-guns, and a few three-inch mortars. There were no artillery units except a very occasional anti-tank gun of small calibre, no medical services, meagre signals, a staff car or two, half a dozen trucks, and a couple of hundred shaggy, ill-kept ponies. Nevertheless, the Chinese soldier was tough, brave, and experienced—after all, he had already been fighting on his own without help for years. He was the veteran among the Allies, and could claim up to this time that he had held back the Japanese more successfully than any of the others. Indeed, he registered his arrival in the forward areas by several minor but marked successes against enemy detachments.

In Maymyo, I had talks with many staff officers, often old friends with whom I had served in years gone by, and attended several conferences, including one with a Chinese general who had played a great part in the only real victory the Chinese had won against the Japanese up to that time—Changsha. I drew him on one side and listened very carefully, through an interpreter, to his account of the tactics of that battle. His experience was that the Japanese, confident in their own prowess, frequently attacked on a very small administrative margin of safety. He estimated that a Japanese force would usually not have more than nine days' supplies available. If you could hold the Japanese for that time, prevent them capturing your supplies, and then counter-attack them, you would destroy them. I listened to him with interest— after all he was the only Allied commander I had heard of who had defeated the Japanese in even one battle. There were, of course, certain snags in the application of this theory, but I thought its main principles sound. I remembered it and, later, acted on it.

I was still quite ignorant as to why I had been brought to Burma, and again no one seemed willing to enlighten me. My secret fear was that I was going to be told to take over Chief of Staff to General Alexander in place of Hutton, who was going back to India. General Alexander would have been a charming and unselfish master to work for, but, apart from the fact that I could never be in the same class as Hutton as a staff officer—he was outstanding in that capacity—I had never fancied myself in that line at all. I had been a second-grade general staff officer in India ten years before, and for a short time in early 1941 I had been a Brigadier, General Staff. I had had enough experience, anyway, to convince me, and I think others, that whatever I was like as a commander I was certainly worse as a staff officer.

A day at Mandalay while we waited for an aircraft gave us an opportunity to look around. We saw a number of units and details that had been withdrawn for various reasons from the fighting to reform or be used as reinforcements. Gunners who had lost their guns—the most pathetic people in the world—staffs of broken-up formations and evacuated camps, a hotchpotch of bits and pieces, odd groups and individuals. The British looked worried, the Indians puzzled, and the Burmese sulky. I had a suspicion that, unless someone very quickly took hold pretty tightly, a rot might set in behind the front.

We started on our return journey to India still without my future being revealed, and I began to fear an even worse fate—I might be destined for some staff job in India. However, it was no good worrying. I should have to be told soon. I got no farther than Calcutta. There, immediately after breakfast on the day of my arrival, in the gloomy and, I suspect, insanitary Government House, I was sent for by General Wavell. He was standing in one of the visitors' sitting-rooms, in his usual firmly planted attitude. He had seen swept away, in overwhelming disaster, Malaya, the Dutch East Indies, the Philippines, and Allied sea and air power in the Far East. He held at that moment the most difficult command in the world—India and Burma. Yet it gave one confidence to look at him. I had seen him at the height of dazzling success, and he had stood and looked calmly and thoughtfully at me in the same way as he looked at me now. He asked some questions on what I had seen in Burma. When I had answered, he said, 'I see', and we lapsed into silence. He broke it by saying without any preliminaries, 'I want you to go back to Burma to take command of the corps that is to be formed there.'

My heart gave a thump. This was better than a staff job! But I knew enough now to realize that a command in Burma was more likely to be a test, and a tough one, than a triumph.

As if he knew my thoughts, he went on, 'Alexander has a most difficult task. You won't find yours easy.' Another pause, and then, 'The sooner you get there the better.'

'I'll start tomorrow morning,' I assured him.

'I see.'

A pause.

Emboldened, I asked him why Singapore had fallen as it did. He looked steadily at me for a moment and then told me. He wished me luck. We shook hands and I left.

Back in my room, I sat under a slow-moving electric fan, and thought. There was a good deal to think about—what I had heard and seen in Burma and what General Wavell had told me about Singapore. With a map on my knees I reflected how little I knew about Burma. I did what I always do in such circumstances—reduced the map to a rough diagram with the distances between

DEFEAT

the main places marked. When you have got such a diagram into your head you have a skeleton of the terrain and can cover it with the flesh and features of further knowledge without distortion. I reflected also how very ignorant I was of the Japanese, their methods and their commanders. In 1938, when I was commanding the 2/7th Gurkhas, I had taken the Japanese as enemy in my annual battalion training in the hills round Shillong. I had also used some officers and men of the Assam Rifles, a military police force who controlled the tribes of the Eastern Frontier, to give us instruction in jungle fighting. Sitting in Government House, I thought with a little spasm of conceit that my unit had been one of the very few in the British Empire that had done *some* jungle training, and I smiled, wryly, when I thought of it now in the desert with my old 10th Indian Division. It *is* a bit hard always to train British forces for the *next* war as so many voluble advisers urge us! I tried to recall the Japanese organization as I had learnt it for that battalion training, but my knowledge had only been sketchy and my recollection was hazy. I really did know very little.

Then more immediate personal details forced themselves to my attention. I had been travelling light, with not more than twenty or thirty pounds of kit. My baggage with all my camp equipment and the rest was somewhere between Baghdad and Bombay. I got hold of an A.D.C. and asked him to produce me an Indian tailor. Within half an hour the *darzi* had run the tape over me, noted my measurements on the edge of a newspaper, and departed with an order to produce three khaki drill bush shirts, three pairs of slacks and shirts by five o'clock the next morning. He swore he would —and he did, by dint of sitting up stitching all night.

That evening, after dinner in the great dining-room of Government House, we went in a party to an air-conditioned cinema. Watching the usual inane picture seemed rather a stupid way of spending one's last evening in civilization, but the resources of the city for intelligent recreation were limited, and I did not feel that more thinking in my room would get me anywhere.

I rose early, packed the fruits of the tailor's labour in my valise, and prepared to set out. However, as so often happened, an inquiry by telephone made it clear that my aircraft would not be ready at the time originally given. I spent a couple of hours, therefore, in shopping for a few extras, accompanied by the helpful A.D.C. This young man worked hard on me, using all his

20

charm—and he had a lot—to persuade me to take him to Burma. Apart from a reluctance to rob my kind host, the Governor, of an A.D.C., I discovered that the boy had by no means recovered from a serious wound got in North Africa. But his heart was all right.

At the revised time I went to Dum Dum aerodrome, on the outskirts of Calcutta. It was an infuriating place for a passenger, and remained so until Air Marshal Coryton put it in order in 1945. After the usual difficulty in finding anyone who knew anything about one's projected journey, or indeed about anything at all, I eventually located the pilot and the Lysander that were to take me to Burma. The pilot was a cheerful young Sikh of the Indian Air Force, who strangely enough had flown me once or twice in Iraq. We strapped on our parachutes and climbed into our seats. The aircraft then refused to start. It went on refusing for half an hour. At the end of that time my Sikh, cheerful as ever, started off to find another Lysander. Eventually he did, and we transferred to it and took off.

Petrol capacity compelled us to proceed by a series of hops. At Chittagong swarms of coolies had to be cleared before we could land, and I thought my light-hearted Sikh would write a few of them off and possibly us too. But I need have had no fears, he was a most skilful pilot. Time was getting on when, after a cup of tea, we took off again, and flew on over what seemed interminable jungle. The sun had set and petrol was getting a bit low when suddenly we saw the glistening Irrawaddy, and crossed it by a white pagoda that showed up in the dusk. My pilot's navigation had been excellent; he had struck the river just opposite our destination, the airfield at Magwe. We circled, waiting for a signal from the ground, but no lamp flickered, so we landed and taxied up the runway. No one emerged to guide us, and we halted at the end of the strip. Still no one appeared. Darkness was falling rapidly, and all around us parked closely together were aircraft. I got out and walked towards some huts, which were evidently the control station. The door of the first was open. It was an office, but empty; so were the others. My pilot joined me, but, as far as we could discover, the airfield and the bulk of the British aircraft in Burma were completely deserted. The Sikh found a telephone but failed to get any response from the other end, wherever that was. While he still hopefully went on ringing,

I wandered to the road that skirted the airfield, and at last a truck with some Burma Rifles in it came along. I hailed it, got the pilot, and we drove into R.A.F. Wing H.Q. in Magwe, some two or three miles away. There I found everyone in good heart and cheer. When I suggested that it was a bit rash to leave so many aeroplanes on a deserted airfield in the midst of a not too reliable population, I was told that it was the Army's business to look after their safety. Although I knew warning had been sent from India, I never discovered whether I had really been expected or not. It was a strange arrival, and not too reassuring as to either the standard of staff work in Burma or the safety of our precious aircraft.

CHAPTER II

FIRST IMPRESSIONS

NEXT morning, the 13th March 1942, I flew south to Prome, and there met General Alexander and the two divisional commanders, who had been called in for a conference. The 1st Burma Division was under Major-General Bruce Scott; the 17th Indian Division under Major-General 'Punch' Cowan. By a trick of fate for which I shall always be very thankful, Scott, Cowan, and I all came from the 1st Battalion, 6th Gurkhas. We had served and lived together for twenty-odd years; we—and our wives—were the closest friends; our children had been brought up together in the happiest of regiments. I could not have found two men in whom I had more confidence or with whom I would rather have worked. The fact that we were on these terms was more than a help in the tough times ahead. It meant that we understood one another, that each knew how the others would react and that the most searching tests would still find us a team. I have never heard of any other occasion on which the corps commander and both his divisional commanders came not only from the same regiment but from the same battalion. So unique a coincidence demanded that the corps should be brilliantly successful. Alas, we were thoroughly defeated, but whatever the reasons for that, they were certainly not in the divisional commanders. Both had distinguished themselves as young officers in the First World War and they had seen much and successful active service between the two world wars. They were now veterans in fighting the Japanese, and Cowan especially, both as Second-In-Command to Smyth and later as his successor in command of the division, had, I suppose, more experience of their methods and tactics than any other British senior officer. I was fortunate in finding at the heads of my divisions such examples of the able, highly trained, and truly professional younger leaders that the British and Indian Armies

23

had quietly produced in surprising numbers, while their country-men were laughing at cartoons of 'Colonel Blimp'.

General Alexander, finding it unnecessary to introduce me to my divisional commanders, began without preamble to issue his directive to 1 Burma Corps. I had driven straight to the conference from the airfield and had only a very general idea of what my corps was, where it was, and of the actual situation. Most of the place-names even were unfamiliar to me, and I groped over the map for them. However, I still had the rough diagram I had made in Calcutta two days before fairly well in my head, and that helped.

The situation briefly was that the 17th Division, not yet by any means fully re-equipped or reorganized after the Sittang disaster, was re-forming some thirty miles south of Prome, and was at the moment out of touch with the enemy. The 1st Burma Division was about Toungoo, some eighty miles to the east and the other side of the jungle hills of the Yomas, holding the Sittang Valley. The Chinese V Army was moving in to relieve it, so that it could be transferred to the Irrawaddy front. As the Chinese would not go south of Toungoo, 1 Burma Corps would cover Prome. Thus the Allied army would hold a roughly level front right across Burma, while the Chinese assembled and my corps collected together.

The conference was a short one, and General Alexander left by air immediately after lunch. I had a few words with Scott, who had been completely surprised to see me, and asked him to get his division over to join the 17th as quickly as the arrival of the Chinese would let him. Then I turned to have a first look at my corps headquarters.

It consisted of a handful of officers collected mainly from Burma Army Headquarters, a few clerks, and a small, very small, detachment of Burma Signals with four wireless sets. Altogether not more than about sixty officers and men, sitting on their valises and kitbags. I asked about office equipment, messing arrangements, tentage, and transport. There was ludicrously little of any of these for the normal set-up of any unit let alone a corps head-quarters. The only thing that really reassured me was the Chief of Staff, Brigadier 'Taffy' Davies, who had been with Hutton in the same capacity. I had known him for a long time, and he had commanded a battalion in my brigade at the beginning of the

24

war. He left me to be a staff officer, in Iceland of all places, returned from there to India, and so to Burma. If I had been lucky in my divisional commanders I was equally fortunate in my B.G.S. Taffy Davies was something more than a brilliant staff officer; he was a character in his own right. His tall, bony figure grew more and more emaciated as the retreat dragged on while he gave himself no rest, either physical or mental. But he got—and kept—that scratch headquarters working. From nothing and almost with nothing, he formed, organized, and infused it with his own spirit. It never reached one-fifth the size of any other corps headquarters I have seen, or had one-tenth of its equipment but, possibly because we could not issue or keep much paper, it was I believe really efficient. We were never out of touch with our formations; we quickly knew their dispositions and movements, we never failed to feed and ammunition them to the extent possible, and we never failed to get our orders to them in time. We were, of course, a tactical battle headquarters only—the whole of our 'G' branch, for instance, moved on two jeeps, one truck, and a couple of motor-cycles—and orders were more often than not verbal. We issued, I think, only four written directives. All things considered, that headquarters was a surprisingly good effort, but it could not have continued for more than a few months at the pressure under which it worked; officers and men could not have stood the strain indefinitely. I had got with Davies a small group of key officers who rivalled even him in energy, unselfishness, ability, and devotion. Simpson, who as 'A.Q.', was responsible for a nightmare of improvised administration, Patterson-Knight his right-hand man, whom nothing ever flurried or dismayed, Montgomery the G.2 who never seemed to need sleep, Wilson the Engineer who achieved miracles and died of sheer exhaustion as we reached India. One of the greatest attributes a commander can have is the ability to choose his staff and commanders wisely, but I can claim no credit for the staff I got at Burcorps; that I suspect should belong to Hutton. Whoever was responsible, I am grateful to him.

As I left with Punch Cowan to visit his division, Taffy Davies was shepherding my headquarters into the Prome Law Courts, while the redoubtable Patterson-Knight proceeded to rustle up an officers' mess by the simple expedient of collecting cooking-pots, crockery, and cutlery from abandoned European bungalows, and a mess staff from the roadside. A ceaseless stream of Indian refugees of all types and classes was pouring into the town. When a man passed who looked as if he might have been a servant, he was grabbed, interrogated, and, if suitable, installed as cook, waiter, washer-up, or sweeper. Most of these poor creatures were only too glad to become once more part of some organization that would look after them, protect them, and give them someone to whom they could turn. Incidentally, it was thus that Anthony, our mess butler, was procured. I doubt if the British forces would have got out of Burma at all without Anthony. Corps H.Q. certainly could not have kept going. He ran a reasonably decent senior officers' mess in circumstances of incredible difficulty, and we owed him a great deal. I think he made sure we paid him, but who would grudge him that?

The 17th Division was moving into an area just south of Okpo, and Cowan drove with me there in his armoured wheeled carrier. As we travelled down the main Rangoon road he told me something of what had befallen his division in the campaign up to then. The fact that he had anything left that could be recognized as a division at all was a great tribute to his troops and above all to him. When we arrived at Divisional Headquarters, in the stilt-raised houses of a Burmese village, almost the first man I met was Brigadier Welchman. I had said good-bye to him in the hospital at Khartoum where we had both been taken from Eritrea, after being shot up in the same truck. He had commanded the artillery regiment in my brigade group in East Africa and been my second-in-command, adviser, and chief support. Here he was, cheerful as ever, and still carrying the spear that had always accompanied him in Africa. 'Welcher' was, next to Punch Cowan himself, the greatest morale-raiser I had ever met. I thought it wrong that one divisional headquarters should have both of them, and as I lacked a commander for the corps artillery, of which incidentally there was extremely little, and Welcher was a superb gunner, I deprived Cowan of him.

We saw a good many of the troops of the 17th Division, British, Indian, and Gurkha. They looked tired, as well they might, and I was shocked at their shortages of equipment and the state of their boots and clothing, but considering all they had gone through recently their spirit was surprisingly good. The strengths of units, while they had been made up to some extent after the Sittang battle by calling up our last reinforcements, were still disturbingly low, and it was a disquieting thought that, with Rangoon gone, there was no hope of further reinforcements.

Brigadier Anstice's 7 Armoured Brigade was also under Cowan's command, and I was delighted to see it and note its condition. Its two regiments of light tanks, American Stuarts or Honeys, mounting as they did only a two-pounder gun and having very thin armour which any anti-tank weapon would pierce, were by no means ideal for the sort of close fighting the terrain required. Any weakness in the tanks, however, was made up by their crews. The 7th Hussars and 2nd Royal Tank Regiment were as good British troops as I had seen anywhere. They had had plenty of fighting in the Western Desert before coming to Burma and they looked what they were—confident, experienced, tough soldiers. Their supporting units, 414 Battery R.H.A., 'A' Battery 95 Anti-tank Regiment and the 1st Battalion West Yorkshire Regiment were up to their standard. After seeing as many troops and meeting as many officers, some of them old friends, as I could, I returned to my headquarters.

This was not the first, nor was it to be the last, time that I had taken over a situation that was not going too well. I knew the feeling of unease that comes first at such times, a sinking of the heart as the gloomy facts crowd in; then the glow of exhilaration as the brain grapples with problem after problem; lastly the tingling of the nerves and the lightening of the spirit, as the urge to get out and tackle the job takes hold. Experience had taught me, however, that before rushing into action it is advisable to get quite clearly fixed in mind what the object of it all is. So now I sat down to think out what our object should be. We had our immediate task—the formation of two groups, Chinese on the Sittang, British on the Irrawaddy, and the stabilization of a front across Burma from Prome to Toungoo but what was the object behind that, the overall aim? Were we going somewhere to stage a last-ditch stand to hold part of Burma? Or were we, now that Rangoon was lost, going to concentrate on getting the army, by a series of planned withdrawals, back to India intact? Were we hoping that the Chinese, added to the resources we had left, would give us strength enough to counter-attack successfully? On the answers to these questions would depend very much how we carried out any intermediate operation; all would be conditioned

27

by the overriding object of the campaign. What that was we
did not know. Indeed, it was never, until the last stages, clear,
and I think we suffered increasingly in all our actions from
this.

Still, whatever our eventual purpose, delay, holding, or
advance, from all points of view it was necessary, somehow or
other, to wrest the initiative from the Japanese. That meant we
must hit him, and hit him hard enough to throw him off balance.
Could we do it? I thought so. As far as we could make out, our
17th was opposed by the Japanese 33rd Division with possibly
some attached units, and an unknown number of hostile Burmese.
When the 1st Burma Division joined us we should, therefore, for
the first time be in at least equal, perhaps superior, strength on our
front. The Japanese, judging by their form up to date, were
bound to attack, and almost certainly at the same time to make
a turning movement round our left through the Yomas. If we
could collect a mobile reserve, let them commit themselves to the
attack, and then strike back in real strength, either at the turning
movement as it issued from the jungle or straight down the road
at their vitals, we might give them a considerable jar. I made up
my mind, therefore, that our object in Burma Corps should be to
concentrate our two divisions with a view to counter-attacking
at the earliest possible opportunity.

Within the next day or two, as I moved about among the
troops or sat in the judge's gloomy room, lined with heavy law
books, which was my office, several factors—none of them
reassuring for the success of our plans—made themselves obvious:

(i) *Our intelligence was extremely bad*
    There was no Burmese intelligence organization to give
    us news from behind the enemy's lines or even from our
    own territory. Air reconnaissance was of necessity scanty
    and from the nature of the country almost always negative
    and therefore unreliable. We had taken no prisoners. Our
    only source of information was identification of enemy
    units by their dead and by documents found on them.
    Exploitation of even this source was limited because in the
    whole corps there was only *one* officer who could speak
    and read Japanese reasonably well. He laboured day and
    night, but the inevitable delay in translation often made

what he discovered stale news. It is no exaggeration to say that we had practically no useful or reliable information of enemy strength, movements, or intentions. Our first intimation of a Japanese move was usually the stream of red tracer bullets and the animal yells that announced their arrival on our flank or rear. We were like a blind boxer trying to strike an unseen opponent and to parry blows we did not know were coming until they hit us. It was a nasty feeling.

(ii) *We were ill-trained and ill-equipped for jungle warfare*

The Japanese were obviously able to move for several days at a time through jungle that we had regarded as impenetrable. This was not only because they had local Burmese guides, but they travelled lighter than we did and lived much more off the country. Nearly all our transport was mechanical, and this stretched our columns for miles along a single road through the jungle, vulnerable everywhere from air and ground. Our British, Indian, and Gurkha troops were a match for the Japanese in a stand-up fight, but, invariably, this being tied to a road proved our undoing. It made us fight on a narrow front, while the enemy, moving wide through the jungle, encircled us and placed a force behind us across the only road. The Japanese had developed the art of the road-block to perfection; we seemed to have no answer to it. If we stood and fought where we were, unless the road were reopened, we starved. So invariably we had turned back to clear the road-block, breaking through it usually at the cost of vehicles, and in any case making another withdrawal.

(iii) *Combat units were becoming much below strength in men and equipment*

Casualties, especially in the 17th Division, had been heavy; sickness was on the increase; and there was a fear that the Burmese units, if we were compelled to withdraw farther, would desert at an increasing rate. Obviously, these and future losses could not be made up. There was no communication now with India except by air, and we had a negligible number of transport aircraft. If a battalion went into action today two hundred men short and lost fifty, it would go into action tomorrow two hundred and fifty men short, and so on until it was reduced to impotence. We suffered from an incurable wasting disease.

(iv) *The local inhabitants were not being helpful*

There was nothing in the nature of a Burmese Home Guard or even an organization to provide guides or civil transport. I gathered that little had been done to prepare the people to co-operate against the invader because it had been feared to create alarm, despondency, and possibly disaffection by admitting the possibility of British withdrawal. The hill tribes were almost all actively loyal, but the Burman of the plains, where the bulk of the fighting would take place, was, generally speaking, apathetic and out to avoid getting involved on either side. A small minority was actively hostile under Japanese officers or agents. The civil administration behind our front was showing signs of collapse; although British officials, and most senior Burmese, stuck to their posts, their subordinates were melting away.

(v) *There was a wide gap between our forces in the Sittang Valley*
    and those on the Irrawaddy

The 1st Burma Division about Toungoo, and the Chinese who were replacing them, were separated from the 17th Division in the Prome area by the eighty-mile stretch of the Pegu Yomas. Through these broken and jungle-covered hills there were no roads, and few tracks. Transfer of forces from one to the other would be difficult and slow, yet the gap, unless held, would leave the Japanese an opportunity for their favourite tactics of encirclement.

(vi) *Morale was threatened*

This was the most serious danger of all. The troops had fought well, but they had had no success. Constant retreats, the bogy of the road-block, the loss of Singapore and Rangoon, and the stories of Japanese supermen in the jungle, combined with the obvious shortages of every kind, could not fail to depress morale. At this stage, the effects of the Sittang disaster on the fighting troops were evident but not irremediable, but morale in the administrative areas in our rear did not impress me as good. There were a lot of badly shaken people about.

It is one thing to know what is wrong; it is another to put it right. I have no doubt whatever that Hutton, if he had been given even a few months in which to prepare, would have corrected much of this and a lot more too. But I was to find, as he had, that to retrieve the past in the midst of a fierce and relentless present is no easy matter.

The first thing to get right was the intelligence organization. Until we could rely on a reasonable degree of warning and information about Japanese moves we could not hope successfully to hold off the enemy, let alone judge the moment to strike or even the direction of our blow. Cowan, in the 17th Division, had realized this, too, and had begun the formation of an intelligence screen to cover the front, which he christened the 'Yomas Intelligence Service'. The guiding spirit in this enterprise was Bill Gunn, a senior member of one of the big Burma trading firms, whom Cowan had very early made his divisional intelligence officer. Scattered all over the forests of the area were numbers of Burmans who in happier times had been engaged in cutting and extracting timber for Gunn's and other firms. The overseers and more senior men among these became the framework on which we built. Officers we found among the keen young British employees. We began to extend this screen across the Yomas, and we were in great hopes of having something at last that would give reliable warning of any Japanese manœuvre on our flank. To the employees of these firms we added government forest officers and rangers, but when I would have introduced certain other civilians I found I had stumbled on a hornets' nest. X and Y refused point-blank to serve under Z! They didn't like him, had never liked him, and he had been a blight on their otherwise idyllic peacetime life. They had some excuse for frayed nerves, but in war these squabbles were silly, unworthy, and most irritating. I am afraid I was a little brusque with one or two, but an appeal to everyone's sense of duty prevailed and the work went on. I only refer to it as an instance of the many and varied difficulties of military-civil improvisations under pressure. Actually, I should say, as a class our best intelligence officers were not the government civilians, but the outside up-country members of the business firms who had a closer knowledge of the country and its people. It was noticeable that parliamentary government, which had progressed far in the central government and in local administration, seemed

31

to have forced officials to become more and more office-bound. Business, too, seemed among all grades in Burma to have been a better training than government service for initiative.

The transformation of these young civilians into officers was a simple matter. There was no time for training, nor was it practicable to submit their names through the usual channels and await their publication in the *Gazette of India*. We needed them now. So my divisional commanders and I told them they were officers and allotted them temporary ranks, second-lieutenant, lieutenant, or even captain, as we thought suited to their age and standing. Such was our poverty of resources that we were hard put to it to provide them with rank badges. One of the young men himself solved this problem by producing his black evening socks—which he was not likely to require for some time—and cutting small squares out of them, which, sewn on his shoulder-straps, adequately indicated his new status. We adopted this as our general method. As may be imagined, there were later certain difficulties over the pay of these somewhat irregularly appointed officers, but in the end all was well.

Our improvised intelligence screen had considerable weaknesses. First it required time to establish itself, secondly it had no means except runners, or at the best ponies, of getting its news back to a roadhead, and thirdly it had to stay put. Whether we advanced or retreated, we should lose almost all the Burmans in it because they worked from their homes. Even those who would come with us would not be anything like as useful in a new area. Still, if we had a little time and as long as we remained in the area it would be invaluable.

We, of course, asked urgently for more Japanese-speaking officers or men. We were told that numbers were just starting to learn the language in universities and classes in England and India; as soon as they were proficient we should get them. I am afraid the Japanese got us out of Burma quicker than the brightest students got out of their universities!

Training for jungle fighting was almost as difficult to improve as intelligence. The Japanese ability to move through jungle more freely than we could, added to our road-bound mechanical transport system, gave them every advantage—advantages which they had earned and deserved. The remedies were for us to learn how to move on a light scale, to become accustomed to the jungle, to do without so much transport, to improve our warnings of hostile movements, and above all to seize the initiative from the enemy. All our tactics up to the present had been dominated by the Japanese road-block, which had already become a nightmare to our troops. A solution to this problem I thought might be found by keeping back a reasonably strong reserve placed where it was likely the enemy would try to plant his road-block, so that he could be attacked at once before he had time to dig in. When the troops were available this proved as good an answer as we could get until we were jungle mobile, but often, with our weakening numbers, we were so pressed in front that such a reserve could not be found.

The major difficulty in training was opportunity. If troops are to be trained, they must be pulled out of the fight, even if only for a month. We could not do that. Every fighting man we had was needed, more and more pressingly, at the front. Experience taught a good deal, but with the Japanese as instructors it was an expensive way of learning. The Jungle Warfare School run by Army Headquarters turned out a few theoretically trained officers and men, but they all went to form small 'commando' units. It would have been better, I think, to have sent them to ordinary infantry battalions to raise the general standard, especially in patrolling—a crying need. The problem of lightening our equipment was to some extent solving itself. Men and units were jettisoning more and more as they realized that mobility and survival were synonymous. We could not, however, shake loose from the tin-can of mechanical transport tied to our tail, until we were both trained to move and live much more lightly and until we had more animal transport. We thought fleetingly of air supply; it was an obvious solution, but still in the dim future awaiting aircraft. Divisional and brigade commanders worked strenuously to devise and inculcate new tactical methods. The standard of jungle craft rose a little, but not really appreciably. I do not know to this day what more we could have done in the time and the circumstances.

Few problems are insoluble, but our wasting strength was one. The most we could hope was to slow up the decline. We combed out combatants or potential combatants behind the line but, in a theatre where almost all administrative personnel were Burman or lower-grade Indian, little could be scraped up from this source.

Army Headquarters co-operated and we speeded up the return of men from hospital and of convalescents, but this is a method not without danger. Our medical services were much below what they should have been in establishment, and, even working as devotedly as they did, could not reduce the sickness rates. The tendency was, in fact, for sickness to rise as medical supplies grew scantier and men suffered more from prolonged strain, fatigue, and privation.

In East Africa, where, through the night, we had beaten the Ethiopian emperor's rallying call on his royal drums to summon his subjects from the Italian regiments back to their allegiance, I had thought, 'How terrible to be an Italian officer and wake each morning to find more of your men gone.' Now I was learning what it was like. Reports of desertions from Burmese units increased. The Indian soldier has three loyalties: to his home, to his religion, and to his regiment and his officers. The Burman soldier, too often, had not had time to develop the third, so the fear of leaving their families unprotected in a Japanese-held Burma, made men slink off along the jungle paths for home. There was no way of putting that right except by victory and advance.

As we could not hope to find enough troops to hold the dangerous gap between ourselves and the Chinese, we attempted, in addition to our 'Yomas Intelligence Service', to produce a few mobile units of the mounted infantry type. The mounted portion of the Burma Military Police, whose men were Indians domiciled in Burma, were to form the nucleus, but there was a great shortage of ponies. I remember discussing on one occasion the provision of these ponies with an elderly, tired, and depressed civilian who, in other matters, it seemed to me, had shown no great nerve. On this subject, however, he roused himself and became positively animated, 'Ah!' he volunteered. 'Ponies! The man you should have gone to was X. He could lay his hand on any number of ponies, exactly the sort you want!'

'Grand!' I said, thrilled that we were at last getting somewhere. 'Where is he? Fetch him along.'

'Alas!' answered my civilian, dropping back to his usual lugubrious tones. 'Poor X! He died three years ago!'

These mounted infantry detachments were to be pushed out along such tracks as there were to form watching-posts and centres to which the Yomas Intelligence Service could send their reports by runner. It would then be the duty of a despatch rider to get the news back at the gallop while the rest of the post, calling its supports to its assistance, delayed the Japanese columns by all possible means. This for the moment was the best we could devise to close, or at least watch, the gap.

Hard things have been said and sometimes written about the Civil Services and of the collapse of the administration in Burma. My general impression was that many of the British senior government officials were too old, too inflexible in mind, and too lacking in energy and leadership really to cope with the immense difficulties and stark realities of invasion. But before soldiers criticize too much, I think they would be well advised to remember that in the defence of Burma, right from the start of the war with Germany, the vital decisions were made by the Fighting Services. It was the Chiefs of Staff who decided what forces should be allotted to Burma and the roles they should play, and the various Commanders-in-Chief and their local commanders who decided how these forces should be used. The Civil Services could at the best only conform to these decisions and co-operate in them. No doubt some civilians failed, but were the military results achieved such as to allow us soldiers to forget the proverb about people who live in glass houses? My experience was that, with very few exceptions, British civilians, both governmental and commercial, and many Burmans stood to their posts with courage and devotion. Nor did we always realize the extent to which, in the districts, the civil officials were hamstrung by the defection of their subordinate Burmese staffs. An inspector of police whose constables have mostly disappeared, the president of a municipality whose clerical and public utility staffs have taken to the jungle, a deputy commissioner whose subordinates have gone on indefinite leave on urgent private affairs, is liable to appear ineffective to a soldier, who, however difficult the situation, still has somebody who will take his orders. It can, of course, be argued that the fact that policemen, clerks, scavengers, and minor officials desert is itself proof of something very wrong with their superiors. Nevertheless, when all is said, the real reason the Burman civilian, like his soldier brother, left his post was because he doubted that we, the soldiers and airmen, could hold back the Japanese. The only thing we could do to help the civil administration was to keep the closest touch with them so that we could

35

pool our information, give warning of our demands, and provide such help as we could in the maintenance of order, the control and evacuation of refugees, and a thousand other things. I asked for a senior but active civil officer to be attached to Corps Headquarters to assist this co-operation. I received Mr. Denis Phelips, who was invaluable, not only in the work for which he was appointed, but in the effect his courage, energy, resource, and devotion to duty had on all of us. He was invariably cheerful, but with the cheerfulness that, far from irritating when things are black, raises the spirit. His laugh was like a battle-cry to us, and, I am sure, to the Japanese too, for they must often have heard it. Phelips was the embodiment of the highest tradition of the Indian Civil Service; he was an example to us soldiers.

Our last and most fundamental danger would be a collapse of morale in our own troops. Morale depends on so many things: spiritual, intellectual, and material. Success is of course the easy foundation on which to build and maintain morale—if you have it. Even without success, confidence in their leaders will give soldiers morale. Difficult as it is to attain without the glamour of victory, we were better off here. The Army Commander was a great name after Dunkirk, to the British element at least. He showed himself forward freely and lived up to his reputation for personal bravery. The greatest assets for morale that we had, however, were the two divisional commanders, who had and held the confidence and indeed affection of their troops, British, Indian, and Gurkha, in a remarkable degree. The hard test of battle had brought forward some excellent brigadiers, like Jones and Cameron, who were real leaders, and they too played a noble part in keeping up tails that had every reason to droop.

The most important thing about a commander is his effect on morale. I was known to a number of the more senior officers, especially those of the Indian Army from the rank of battalion commanders upwards, but little to the troops. As far as morale was concerned, I therefore started pretty well from scratch, which is not a bad thing to do. It has often happened in war that a fresh commander has taken over after a period of ill-success just as the reinforcements, improved armament, and increased supplies arranged by his predecessor are beginning to arrive in the theatre. This, of course, in no way detracts from the skill the new leader may show in the use he makes of the increased resources, but it does help him enormously in the fundamental matter of morale. The troops naturally identify him with the improved conditions, and he finds a ready-made foundation on which to start building until he can give them a victory, and thus, in the only permanent way, consolidate their morale. This advantage neither General Alexander nor I would have. We had to expect the exact opposite. The loss of Rangoon meant not only that our resources and amenities would be progressively and drastically reduced, but, combined with the fall of Malaya, that a tide of Japanese reinforcements would sweep in through the port. Clearly I must get about among the troops and see and be seen. Luckily there was no public relations department at my headquarters to greet my arrival with the clumsy beating of the big drum. A commander, if he is wise, will see that his own troops know him *before* the Press and other cymbal-clashers get busy with his publicity. All that can be most helpful *afterwards*.

The broad conclusion of my survey of the situation was the not very brilliant or original one that what was required for morale and for all our other troubles, was a good recognizable victory. We had a chance of getting this, I thought, if we could bring over the 1st Burma Division, reorganize the 17th, and carry out the overdue maintenance of our tanks, so that we could hit back with a united corps. If neither the pressure of the Japanese on our front nor events elsewhere forced us to undertake comparatively large-scale operations before we had managed to do these things, we might reasonably hope that the enemy would offer us an opportunity.

Our first task was to get the 1st Burma Division into the Prome area as soon as possible. Its move was, of course, dependent on the arrival of the Chinese to replace it. During January the Chinese VI Army (98th, 49th, 55th Divisions) had come into the Shan States; the V Army was now moving in south of it, but it would not go beyond Toungoo. This was most unfortunate as it meant that the 1st Burma Division, which had been conducting successful offensive operations well to the south, had to pull back, leaving open to the enemy a considerable stretch of the lower Sittang Valley. For supply reasons, also, the loss of one of the best rice production areas was serious. The 1st Burma Division had earlier sent some of its units to reinforce the hard-pressed 17th Division, and this withdrawal, for which the troops could see little reason,

37

had a depressing effect, especially on the Burmese soldiers, many of whom found themselves abandoning their home districts. The Japanese followed up closely; rearguards fought stoutly and inflicted heavy losses, but the division arrived at Toungoo considerably exhausted. Here it passed through the newly arrived Chinese V Army, and on the 22nd March received orders from me to concentrate in the Dayindabo-Kyaukpadaung-Allanmyo area in the Irrawaddy Valley, some fifty miles north of Prome. I chose this area, rather than Prome itself or its immediate neighbourhood, for administrative reasons and because it was desirable that the division, which must of necessity arrive piecemeal, should be able to collect without interruption. The last thing I wanted was to commit any portion of it to action before the whole was ready. It was difficult to get a firm date for the completion of its concentration, but ten days to a fortnight was the estimate.

Meanwhile, the 17th Division showed its spirit. On the 17th March a young major, Calvert, afterwards to become the best known of Wingate's column commanders, led a daring raid by river on Henzada, a port thought to be much used by the enemy. His scratch party of commando men and Royal Marines inflicted heavy losses on a force of hostile Burmese under Japanese officers who were holding the town. The 1st Gloucesters, at about the same time, surprised a Japanese battalion in billets in the small town of Letpadan, eighty miles south of Prome, inflicted severe losses on it, and chased it into the jungle—a most sprightly affair. There was obviously a great deal of fight in the 17th Division.

After seeing Cowan I decided to pull his division and the armoured brigade closer in to Prome. I did this to get them nearer to 1st Burma Division and to ease the transport situation. I was of the opinion, too, that it would lessen the chance of their flanks being turned from either the river or the Yomas, and that the country immediately south of Prome would be equally suitable for tanks. I rather hoped, also, that the move would throw out or delay any plans the enemy had for an attack. I was anxious at this stage to gain time for the corps concentration. I think I made a mistake. I should have done better to leave the 17th Division forward and to concentrate the 1st Burma Division about Prome. Apart from all else it was a mistake to begin my command by a withdrawal if it could have been avoided. However that may be, the 17th Division pulled in. One brigade (63) in Prome itself

38

covered the main road from the south, another (16) in Sinmezwe-Hmawza held the south-eastern approaches, and the third (48) was echeloned back in the Wettigan area as reserve and to meet any hostile move round the flank. In rear was 7 Armoured Brigade with the reserve brigade, hoping to find an opportunity for tank maintenance. The left flank was protected by the Yomas Intelligence screen, and detachments of the Burma Frontier Force; the right by the Marines in their river craft and commando parties on the west bank of the Irrawaddy working with them. Corps Headquarters in Prome was now perhaps rather near the actual front, but I had no intention of going back if we could avoid it, so it remained.

Prome was bombed by Japanese aircraft, usually not in much strength, every other day or so, invariably at breakfast-time. I had been bombed often enough before, but never in a town, and I found it much more frightening than in the desert or the bush. We had difficulty in controlling the fires that broke out, and, even when there were no air raids, fires still occurred. These mysterious fires in towns we occupied became an annoying feature of the campaign. Sometimes we caught Burmans in the act of starting them, and they got short shrift, but to the end it was one of the favourite activities of the fifth columnists of whom there appeared to be plenty. Prome was, unfortunately, the centre of an area that was notable for its hostility. What with air raids, fires, and refugees, it was, in spite of its attractive situation, its bungalows and gardens, not a comfortable place. The thousands of wretched Indian refugees, many with smallpox and cholera, bivouacked all over its streets and river wharfs, waiting to cross the Irrawaddy and to trudge down the Taungup track to the Arakan coast, were in pitiable case. They were, in addition, quickly reducing the town and its water supply to a state that threatened an epidemic among the troops. The civil authorities with such help as our administrative staffs and units could give—which was not much —worked devotedly and passed thousands over the river to eventual safety in Bengal. The cleaning of the streets was a problem, as the municipal conservancy services had melted away under air attack. We solved it to a considerable extent by taking gangs of convicts from the local jail and giving them liberty in return for a few days' work as street-cleaners. We began with the least criminal and gradually worked up the scale of guilt. The residue of really bad men, the violent criminals, we finally shipped up-stream for confinement in Mandalay. The barge on which they were being towed was, however, attacked by Japanese aircraft. Convicts and warders took to the water together; some of the criminals were shot, some drowned, but none, I think, reached jail in Mandalay or anywhere else. I hope the survivors were a great trouble to the Japanese during their occupation; I fear they must have been to their fellow-countrymen.

CHAPTER III

A CHAPTER OF MISFORTUNES

WHILE we had registered only a couple of minor offensive scores on the ground, the Royal Air Force in Burma had achieved a more notable success. Reconnaissance on the 20th March reported fifty Japanese aircraft, part of the heavy reinforcements now arriving from other fronts, on the airfield at Mingaladon, near Rangoon, and an attack by all available aircraft from Akyab and Magwe was staged next morning. The small force of nine British bombers and ten Hurricanes was intercepted by Navy 0 fighters some seventy miles from Rangoon, but fought its way in, bombed and machine-gunned the airfield, and fought its way out again. Eleven Japanese fighters were destroyed in the air and sixteen of their aircraft on the ground. All our bombers were hit but all returned; our total loss was one Hurricane.

Thoroughly pleased with itself, as it had every reason to be, our air force was preparing to repeat the dose the same afternoon, the 21st March, when Magwe airfield was suddenly attacked by Japanese fighters and bombers in overwhelming strength. During the course of the next twenty-five hours six attacks came in. In all, nearly two hundred and fifty enemy aircraft were employed, of which about one hundred and fifty were medium and heavy bombers. There is doubt as to what, if any, warning was received of the first raids; none was obtained of the later ones. When the first enemy wave came over there were twelve serviceable Hurricanes on the landing-ground. Some of these got up, intercepted the Japanese and shot down four of them, but the weight of the attack got home. By nine o'clock on the 22nd, after successive attacks, only three P40s of the A.V.G. and three Hurricanes were flyable, and of these only the Hurricanes were fit to fight. We paid heavily for our failure to provide pens and dispersal areas for our aircraft. The A.V.G. commander reported that, owing to the absence of warning and the scale of attack, he had no option but to withdraw such of his aircraft as could still fly, and during the afternoon they left for Loiwing. At half-past three the last three Hurricanes went up to intercept an enemy reconnaissance machine. At about half-past four, just after they had landed again, a Japanese attack by about fifty bombers in two waves with a strong fighter escort came in. This final attack completed the destruction of almost the whole of our aircraft. Those that could still fly left for Akyab during the late afternoon, and early next morning, the 23rd March, Burwing H.Q. and the personnel of its squadrons left rather hurriedly for Lashio and Loiwing. On the 23rd March, and again on the 27th, the Japanese repeated the Magwe attacks on Akyab, with the same results. Akyab was abandoned. The last of the R.A.F. had left Burma.

Some hard things were said by the angry soldiery when the Air Force disappeared, especially about the speed and disorder of the abandonment of Magwe. But they would have done well to remember that this same small Anglo-American air force had already destroyed 233 Japanese machines in the air and 58 on the ground, of which the A.V.G. accounted for 217 and the R.A.F. 74 at a cost to us of 46 in the air and 51 on the ground, or a ratio in the air of five-to-one in our favour. Even on the ground, with all the odds of range and warning against them, they had destroyed plane for plane.

From then onwards my corps was totally without air reconnaissance, defence, or support. Any aircraft we saw in the sky was hostile—and we were to see many. We were even blinder than before, forced more and more to move at night, and by day to greater dispersion. Buildings became death-traps to be avoided; we took increasingly to the jungle. The actual casualties to fighting troops inflicted by the Japanese air force, even after it had absolute freedom of the skies, were surprisingly small. The effect on morale, while not as great as might have been expected, at first was serious, but later the troops seemed in some way to become accustomed to constant air attack and to adjust themselves to it.

Now great wedges of silver bombers droned across the sky, and one after another the cities of Burma spurted with flame and vanished in roaring holocausts. Prome, Meiktila, Mandalay, Thazi, Pyinmana, Maymyo, Lashio, Taunggyi, largely wooden towns, all of them crumbled and burned. The Japanese used pattern bombing, coming over in faultless formation, giving themselves a leisurely dummy run or two, and then letting all their bombs go in one shattering crump. They were very accurate. We always said they had in each formation only one leader capable of aiming, and all took the time from him. It was certainly effective, but I personally preferred it to the methods of the Italians when they also had no air opposition. They had cruised round, dropping a few sticks at a time, and keeping one in suspense. With the Japanese it was all over quickly; you had either had it or were alive till next time. Whatever the method, it was effective enough with the civil population. The police, hospital staffs, air-raid precaution units, public services, and railways collapsed. Labour vanished into the jungle; towns were evacuated. Only a few devoted British, Anglo-Burmans, and Burmese carried nobly on.

We were told that occasionally bombers from Calcutta or elsewhere in India had attacked Rangoon, but that only raised in the troops what stage directions call a 'bitter laugh'. General Wavell had decided that the only sound course was to retain in India such air forces as he could scrape together, so as to build up something capable of defending that country when the time came. To commit his pathetically meagre resources on the Burma front, without a warning organization and against overwhelmingly superior strength, would inevitably be to destroy them. The Army in Burma must struggle on without an air force. There is no doubt that this was a right decision. But it was cold comfort to us—and it made our chances of taking the initiative by counter-attack much more slender.

With the news of the disappearance of our air force came further disturbing tidings which were to affect not only the plans of Burma Corps but the whole campaign. The Chinese 200th Division of their V Army in Toungoo, which up to the present had scored several minor successes, was on the 24th March suddenly cut off by the Japanese 55th Division and other troops. The nearest regiment of the Chinese 22nd Division, which was following up the 200th Division, was then at Pyinmana, sixty miles away; the rest of the division was in Lashio, over three hundred miles distant. The third division, the 96th of V Army, was only just approaching the Burmese frontier. The single road, difficulty in passing through VI Army en route, and other troubles had delayed V Army's move south. The Chinese in Toungoo resisted stoutly, while the 22nd Division pressed on to relieve them. The

43

situation was critical. On 28th March, General Alexander, urged
by the Generalissimo, ordered me to take the offensive at once in
order to relieve pressure on the Chinese. Two of Stilwell's staff
came to see me, also, with a message stressing his need.

It was quite contrary to the whole idea on which our local
intentions were based thus to attack before the corps was concentrated. It was doubtful, too, if anything we could do at such short
notice would really divert forces already engaged against the
Chinese, although it might possibly keep additional troops from
being sent to their front. However, General Alexander was in a
much better position to judge the effects than I was, and it was up
to us to do all we could to help our ally.

Our information was not good enough to stage an offensive
properly; this fighting blind was a terrible handicap. Nor was my
corps yet assembled, while even the 17th Division was still trying
to re-equip. The best I could do to carry out General Alexander's
directive was to order Cowan, with the strongest force he could
make mobile, to:

(i) Advance astride the main road and railway on Okpo, some
sixty miles south-east of Prome.
(ii) Establish a detachment at Zigon, fifteen miles north of
Okpo to act as a lay-back and to watch the east flank.
(iii) Secure Nyaungzaye, on the Irrawaddy, twenty-three miles
south of Prome, to protect the west flank and prevent the
enemy crossing the river.
(iv) Destroy all enemy encountered in these advances and
exploit any local successes.

The only help I could give him, as he already commanded
practically all fighting troops in the area, was to organize a small
detachment of Marines, commandos, and Burma Frontier Force
to operate on the west bank of the Irrawaddy. There had been a
report of a Japanese-Burmese force at Tonbo on that side of the
river some twenty-five miles south of Prome. We hoped that our
detachment, plus the small armed flotilla on the river itself and
the boom we had built with difficulty under air attack below
Prome, would prevent hostile forces crossing behind Cowan to
the east bank. There was danger of this and of our shipping being
shelled from the far side, but we had few troops to spare.

I had given Cowan rather a vague task, but he tackled it with

44

his accustomed energy. On the day the order was issued the Gloucesters, in one of their bold strikes, had attacked and taken Paungde, a big village thirty miles south of Prome, killing a number of the enemy. As it was isolated, Cowan had recalled the battalion, but when he received the corps order, he formed a striking force of a regiment of tanks, a battery, three infantry battalions and a field company of sappers and miners, under the command of Brigadier Anstice, and directed them to reoccupy Paungde, as a preliminary to advancing on Okpo. It was an improvised force, as his division was still sorting itself out, and its battalions were each only the strength of two companies. While approaching Paungde, Anstice received a report of a Japanese detachment advancing towards the road behind him. Some of his troops were detached to deal with this threat while the remainder attacked Paungde and found it strongly held. A confused fight followed, during which our troops had a partial success, entering Paungde, and inflicting heavy casualties, but ultimately being driven out of the village again. A liaison officer returning from Anstice to divisional headquarters received a shock when he found Shwedaung, a town on the main road about ten miles south of Prome, full of Japanese, who appeared to have arrived from the south-west. Other parties also were infiltrating behind Anstice, and Cowan ordered him to withdraw. To help Anstice out he sent two Indian battalions to clear Shwedaung from the north.

Shwedaung straggles astride the road for two miles, spreading out for about a mile on each side. It was necessary to force a way through it as there was no other road by which vehicles could go. Just after six o'clock in the evening, Anstice's advance guard attacked a road-block at the southern end of the town, while the two battalions attacked the northern outskirts. Both attacks were held up by heavy fire from houses and bamboo groves. During the night, another attack was put in by Anstice in greater strength, but after making some progress it was stopped by the main road-block inside the town. At seven o'clock this attack was renewed, and during the morning our troops burst through the block. Transport began to pass, but was held up by the block at the north end of the town and vehicles jammed up along the road. Shwedaung was now burning fiercely, many trucks took fire, and to make matters worse Japanese aircraft continuously

45

machine-gunned the column. The two battalions attacked from the north again, and then the tanks from the south crashed through the block, followed by a string of trucks and ambulances loaded with wounded, but many vehicles, disabled by air attack, burnt, or jammed by others, had to be abandoned. Several hundred Japanese and rebel Burmans were caught and killed while trying to escape from the burning town.

Meanwhile, the detachment of Marines, commandos, and Burma Military Police sent to secure the west bank of the Irrawaddy had occupied Padaung village. The villagers welcomed them and brought food. A patrol sent out reported no enemy for eighteen miles to the south. Actually, a Japanese force was all the time concealed in the village, and it surprised our men as they were resting. They put up a desperate but hopeless resistance. Some escaped, many were killed on the spot by the Japanese or treacherous inhabitants, but twelve British soldiers and Marines, all wounded, were kept till next day when they were tied to trees and used by the Japanese to demonstrate bayonet fighting to the admiring villagers. This was only one instance of many bestial outrages committed by the Japanese Army against helpless prisoners, British, Indian, Gurkha, and Chinese, throughout the campaign. The fate of a prisoner in the field depended largely on the caprice of the officer into whose hands he fell. He might be tortured and brutally murdered, shot or killed by the sword, or merely maltreated, starved, bound, and beaten. There were even instances when a prisoner was not seriously maltreated, but these were very rare and almost unknown with British prisoners. The Japanese conduct to prisoners in the field and in their prison camps will always remain a foul blot on their record, which those who fought against them will find it hard to forget.

With the loss of our detachment on the west bank, the enemy began to cross the river in large numbers. Several hundreds of them were Burmans in the blue uniform of the puppet Burma National Army, organized into units under Japanese officers. At first they fought in and around Shwedaung fanatically, believing themselves to be invulnerable to bullets, but their ardour cooled as they found their error. Nevertheless they were an aggravation to the troubles of our withdrawing force. Casualties on both sides in this action at Shwedaung were heavy. We lost ten tanks, two guns, numerous vehicles, and over three hundred and fifty killed and wounded in the infantry alone. These were losses, which at our reduced strengths and without hope of replacement, we could not afford.

Unpleasant as they were, the effects of the Shwedaung fight were nothing like as serious as the loss of Toungoo on the Sittang front which occurred at about the same time. The Chinese 200th Division, cut off in the town, put up a really stout resistance, but first two reserve regiments of the Chinese V Army and then their 22nd Division disregarded Stilwell's orders to attack. There is little doubt this refusal cost us Toungoo, for when the efforts of the 22nd Division failed to relieve it, there was no alternative to starvation or surrender except for the garrison to cut its way out. This the 200th Division did, but it had to abandon all vehicles, guns, and most of its equipment, and suffer over three thousand casualties while the remnants in small parties made their escape. A general Chinese withdrawal towards Pyinmana followed. The loss of Toungoo was in fact a major disaster, second only to our defeat at the Sittang bridge.

It was now a question whether we should continue to hold Prome. The eastern half of the line across Burma had gone; the town itself, stretching a couple of miles along the river bank with scrub jungle all about it, would need a big perimeter to defend it, and even then could easily be cut off. Already the Japanese were working close up to our positions and had occupied parts of the opposite west bank. The state of the town itself was desperate. It had been almost completely burnt after a particularly heavy air raid, cholera among refugees was increasing, and there had even been a few cases among the troops. Had it not been for the large dumps of stores, mainly rice, lying on the riverside quays, there would have been little object—and a good deal of danger—in hanging on. Army Headquarters appeared to think so, too, as in the last days of March we received orders to back-load all surplus stores. There was no railway out of Prome to the north, our available road transport was negligible, and so we had to rely entirely on the river. In normal times Prome handled a vast river traffic, including thousands of tons of rice, but now it was more difficult. Civilian steamer crews were not unnaturally loath to come so far south. The river was abnormally low, thus rendering night navigation dangerous, while by day the Japanese air force made it infinitely more so. Frequent air raids had dispersed all

47

DEFEAT

labour. However, thanks to the energy and ability of Goddard, General Alexander's chief administrative officer, who paid us frequent visits, and of my own staff, considerable progress was made.

My headquarters moved to Allanmyo on the river, some thirty-five miles north, as Prome was now obviously too much in the front line. At Allanmyo on the 1st April I had a visit from Generals Wavell and Alexander. After a review of the whole situation, General Wavell decided that a further withdrawal was necessary. I was ordered to speed up the back-loading of stores and to concentrate the corps in the area Allanmyo-Kyaukpadaung-Thayetmyo, to defend the oilfields and Upper Burma. I was glad the decision had been taken. Apart from being nervous about the 17th Division's position, I did not think that, even when the corps was concentrated, we should have as good a chance of staging a counter-offensive from Prome as we should from Allanmyo. The 1st Burma Division was coming in as fast as Scott could urge it, but it was unavoidably arriving in bits and pieces which had to be put together. I was horrified at its low scale of equipment. It had never been up to even the standard of the 17th Division in this respect—the whole division, for instance, could only muster one improvised carrier platoon, instead of one per battalion. It was shockingly short of artillery. A considerable proportion of its infantry and administrative units was Burmese. Although the division had acquitted itself well, there had already been numerous desertions, and, in spite of many good British and Burmese officers, things were not getting better. As the enemy threat on the west bank was increasing, it was necessary to split the division, a thing I disliked doing very much, by sending 2 Burma Brigade over the river to hold south of Thayetmyo, the town opposite Allanmyo.

On the evening of the day of General Wavell's conference at Allanmyo, the 1st April, the Japanese made their contribution to the question whether we should hold Prome. The 17th Division was disposed in three brigade groups, one (63) in the town and south of it; another (48) about Hmawza, four miles to the east; a third (16) around Tamagauk, five miles north. The first Japanese attack was delivered against the Indian battalion holding south of the town. It was repulsed. A second followed, and during it numbers of enemy infiltrated between our positions into the town. Finding

48

itself apparently surrounded in the dark, the battalion fell back into the town, where among the houses it lost cohesion. Attacks on other sectors of the brigade had failed, but the gap to the south was used by the Japanese to pour into the town and take the other defenders in rear. After confused fighting, the whole 63 Brigade pulled out of the town and fell back towards 16 Brigade at Tamagauk. Meanwhile 48 Brigade had been heavily attacked, but had bloodily repulsed its assailants.

The enemy pushed through Prome and pressed on, while another strong force was apparently now trying to pass round to the east of Hmawza. 48 Brigade caught this force in flank and inflicted heavy losses on it, but shortly afterwards Cowan ordered the brigade to move across to the main road to stop the enemy advancing from Prome. 7 Armoured Brigade and 16 Brigade were sent forward to cover 63 Brigade and the divisional transport as they fell back on Tamagauk. At 1030 hours that morning Cowan rang me up from his headquarters in the Reserve Forest on the Prome–Allanmyo road, to say that he had received reliable reports of a strong enemy force moving round his left on Dayindabo, sixteen miles north behind him, which would cut him off. Was he to hold on where he was or to fall back on Allanmyo? I had not a great deal of time in which to think, but if a Japanese force got in between Cowan and me there was nothing to stop it going on to Yenangyaung, except the two weak brigades of the 1st Burma Division. My object still was to concentrate the corps; Japanese between its two divisions would not help. I knew the area where Cowan was and there was little to be said for holding it either from the point of view of ease of defence or value, and I had already been directed to bring back the corps to Allanmyo. Accordingly I ordered him to continue the retirement to that place and sent 1 Burma Brigade to Dayindabo to hold it if threatened and to help the 17th Division through. The brigade was in position by the late afternoon, the 2nd April.

Cowan's men had a trying march. They had been fighting all night and much of the day. It was very hot, very dusty, and there was no water on the route. In addition, the Japanese air force gave them no respite, strafing and bombing them constantly. In spite of this, they passed under the wing of the 1st Burma Division on the 3rd April, complete and in not too bad shape. We were lucky the exhausted Japanese had not pressed the pursuit. In spite of the eyewitness statement of an officer's patrol, it later appeared that no Japanese force had threatened Dayindabo. No great damage was done by my acceptance of the report, but it was one of many instances when the total lack of air reconnaissance made it impossible to check rapidly such information.

My corps was now concentrated, not *where* I had hoped originally, or, for that matter, *how* I had hoped. Still, concentrated it was, and it now remained to decide how I should carry out my task of denying the oilfields to the enemy and defending Upper Burma. The first thing was to choose where we should stand and fight. A reasonable defensive line could have been found running from Allanmyo up into the higher ground to the west, but this would have left a gap of many miles between us and the Chinese. To avoid this, General Alexander had ordered me to hold Taungdwingyi in strength as the junction point where the Chinese front would meet mine. To hold both banks of the Irrawaddy at Allanmyo and a line to Taungdwingyi fifty miles to the north-north-east would mean stretching my two very weak divisions—now not equal in strength to one full one—over some sixty or more miles. It seemed to me that I must shorten my front in the only way I could, by moving farther up the Irrawaddy until I was nearer to Taungdwingyi. I decided, therefore, to fall back to just south of Magwe and to hold to the south of the west-east Magwe-Taungdwingyi lateral road. I did not like the idea of another withdrawal; we were fast approaching the dangerous state when our solutions to all problems threatened to be retreat, but I hoped this would be the last.

We held south of Allanmyo long enough to demolish the small oilfield on the opposite bank of the river, evacuated the town on the 8th April, and withdrew through a lay-back position to the final line. The Japanese did not follow up in strength and only minor skirmishes occurred when we got on to the new line. It was clearly no use sitting down, strung out in this way, waiting for the enemy to attack; we had somehow to collect a striking force for counter-attack. This was by no means easy. One brigade had to be west of the river and two weak divisions, less this detachment, on a forty-mile front held out little hope that we could scrape together for the counter-attack anything really effective. I, therefore, strongly pressed the Army Commander to make the Chinese, who were now in and north of Pyinmana, take over the eastern end of my line. He agreed, and Stilwell ordered General Tu, commander of the V Army, to relieve me with a regiment, and later a division, in the Taungdwingyi area. These were my first active contacts with Stilwell, who had arrived in Burma a few days after me. He already had something of a reputation for shortness of temper and for distrust of most of the rest of the world. I must admit he surprised me a little when, at our first meeting, he said, 'Well, General, I must tell you that my motto in all dealings is "buyer beware",' but he never, as far as I was concerned, lived up to that old horse-trader's motto. He was over sixty, but he was tough, mentally and physically; he could be as obstinate as a whole team of mules; he could be, and frequently was, downright rude to people whom, often for no very good reason, he did not like. But when he said he would do a thing he did it. True, you had to get him to *say* that he would, quite clearly and definitely—and that was not always easy—but once he had, you knew he would keep to his word. He had a habit, which I found very disarming, of arguing most tenaciously against some proposal and then suddenly looking at you over the top of his glasses with the shadow of a grin, and saying, 'Now tell me what you want me to do and I'll do it.' He was two people, one when he had an audience, and a quite different person when talking to you alone. I think it amused him to keep up in public the 'Vinegar Joe, Tough Guy' attitude, especially in front of his staff. Americans, whether they liked him or not—and he had more enemies among Americans than among British—were all scared of him. He had courage to an extent few people have, and determination, which, as he usually concentrated it along narrow lines, had a dynamic force. He was not a great soldier in the highest sense, but he was a real leader in the field; no one else I know could have made his Chinese do what they did. He was, undoubtedly, the most colourful character in South-East Asia—and I liked him.

The Burma Corps had now entered the 'Dry Belt'. The country, instead of being green and thickly covered, was brown and bare, with occasional patches of parched jungle. The water-courses, worn through the low undulating hills, were dry, and the general effect was of heat and dust. Yet the terrain was too cut up by nullahs and stony hills for the free movement of motor transport off roads. We had, as far as we were able, reorganized our fighting troops' transport. Infantry brigades were now partly on a pack basis, and vehicles with divisions had been reduced to meet only their more essential needs. The vehicles thus saved had been formed into a corps pool of mechanical transport, which was held back and allotted as required. Apart from tactical reasons, if we were to continue to supply the troops, this reorganization would have been forced on us by our losses in vehicles by air attack, destruction in battle, and above all through lack of proper repair facilities and spares. The greater flexibility in rear thus obtained, combined with the increased pack element forward, would, we hoped, enable our striking force, when we had collected it, to attack in flank any Japanese columns that might penetrate the front.

Relying on the Chinese to take over the Taungdwingyi end of the front, we planned to have as striking force under H.Q. 1st Burma Division, 13 Brigade of that division, 48 Brigade of the 17th Division, and 7 Armoured Brigade. Limited water supplies compelled their location in two somewhat widely separated groups. 48 Brigade and 7 Armoured Brigade at Kokkogwa, ten miles west of Taungdwingyi, 13 Brigade at Thityagauk, eight miles farther west still. The 'line' would have to be held by the rest of the corps, the 17th Division, less its 48 Brigade, on the left and the two remaining Burma brigades astride the Irrawaddy. Pushed out in front to give warning of hostile approach were detachments of the Burma Frontier Force. The final disposition could not be taken up, nor could the striking force be collected until the Chinese arrived at Taungdwingyi. We waited expectantly for them.

We waited in vain. I kept my headquarters in Taungdwingyi in the attempt to make direct contact with the Chinese. Messages via Burma Army H.Q. and Stilwell brought vague answers. The regiment was on its way. It would arrive next day, two days hence. It was held up by supply difficulties; if we would send rice it would come. Officers were sent out to look for it. It was reported here, there; the reports were then cancelled. At last *some* Chinese were actually contacted and disappeared again. This was repeated. It was rather like enticing a shy sparrow to perch on your windowsill. We dumped supplies of rice. Chinamen appeared, collected them, and melted away again. We dumped the rice a little nearer Taungdwingyi each time and at last a Chinese unit did appear there. But, alas, it was not the promised regiment, only what was called a 'guerrilla battalion' and a very small one at that, quite insufficient and quite inadequately equipped to take over by itself any part of the line. So the 17th Division had to remain in and about the town, which was made into a real stronghold. Large parts of it were levelled by controlled burning, not only to improve fields of fire and increase freedom of movement, but to avoid the complete destruction such as had befallen Prome. It was as well this clearing was done as air attacks became frequent and heavy.

One raid occurred as divisional commanders and others were assembling at Corps Headquarters for a conference. Some of us were just finishing breakfast when the alarm went. In a group we walked towards the slit-trenches, I still carrying a cup of tea. Looking up, we could see the usual tight wedge of twenty or thirty bombers coming straight over. The mess servants and others saw them too and began to run for shelter. I had been insistent on stopping people running at these times as it had led to panic, so continuing our move at a slow and dignified pace, I called out to them to stop running and walk. I remember shouting in Hindustani, 'There's plenty of time. Don't hurry!' a remark that almost qualified for the Famous Last Words series. At that instant we heard the unmistakable scream of bombs actually falling. With one accord two or three generals and half a dozen other senior officers, abandoning dignity, plunged for the nearest trench. Scott, being no mean athlete, arrived first and landed with shattering impact on a couple of Indian sweepers already crouching out of sight. I followed, cup of tea and all; the rest piled in on top, and the whole salvo of bombs went off in one devastating bang.

Poor Scott, crushed under our combined weight, feeling warm liquid dripping over him, was convinced that I had been blown into the trench and was now bleeding to death all over him. His struggles to come to my assistance were heroic, but almost fatal to the wretched bottom layer of sweepers. We hauled ourselves and them out, and, slightly shamefacedly, returned to our conference.

On the 8th April, I moved Corps Headquarters to Magwe, on the other flank, a much better communication centre and not quite so much in the front line, though equally annoyed by air attack. It was also on the main road and much nearer to Yenangyaung, where the oilfields were now being prepared for demolition. I spent a good deal of my time on the lateral road from Magwe to Taungdwingyi which ran just behind our front, and I do not think I have ever disliked a road more. It was, for most of its course, unshielded from the air, and throughout the hours of daylight the Japanese kept a constant patrol of two or three fighters over it. A jeep was the safest vehicle; from it you had a clear view of the sky, and it was easy to spring in one bound from your seat to the ditch. One often did! Once when I was visiting his area, Curtis who commanded 13 Brigade, went ahead in a closed car with the colonel of the Inniskillings beside him. A Japanese fighter swooped and riddled the back of their car. The colonel was killed instantly, and when we came up we found Curtis bleeding from three wounds, all luckily superficial. Bandaged but completely unshaken, he took me round his positions without any further reference to the incident. I have rarely seen a better instance of steady nerves.

It soon became evident that the Japanese were preparing a strong push for the oilfields. From such indications as we were able to get, it looked as if their main thrust would come directly up the east bank of the river. Japanese reinforcements, we knew, had been pouring in through Rangoon. Their old formations would have been made up in strength again and there would almost certainly be new ones added. The blow, when it came, would be heavy. All this made me more anxious to pull the 17th Division out of Taungdwingyi, even if only to free 48 Brigade for the striking force. The promised Chinese regiment, however, showed no signs of turning up, and Army Headquarters were very insistent that the corps should keep a strong force in the town. True, it should have been the point of junction between the Allied Armies, but I ought, I think, when I could not persuade Army Headquarters to agree to weakening the garrison, to have done it myself.

The expected enemy advance began on the 10th April, covered by numerous small parties of hostile Burmans and Japanese, disguised as peaceful villagers. These tactics were difficult to counter, as the countryside was covered by numbers of genuine refugees trying to escape from the battle area. It was always a toss-up for our men whether the group of Burmese men,

54

women, and children, wandering past their positions with their creaking bullock carts, were what they seemed or Japanese with concealed machine-guns.

Early on the 11th, the advanced posts of 1 Burma Brigade were in touch with large, formed bodies of the enemy. A little later, 13 Brigade south of the main road was engaged with a Japanese regiment, while 48 Brigade was dealing with parties, sometimes trying to pass as Chinese, attempting to infiltrate north. There was heavy fighting that night when the Japanese real attack was fiercely pushed home against both 1 Burma Brigade on our right and 48 Brigade at Kokkogwa. Both attacks were repulsed. That against 48 Brigade was one of the bitterest fought actions of the whole campaign. The enemy attacked fanatically and in strength. It was a pitch-dark night, lightened fitfully by violent thunderstorms. By dawn on the 12th, after fierce hand-to-hand fighting that had swayed back and forward in attack and counter-attack, the Japanese were flung back and the tanks moved out to a good killing. Unfortunately, while these attacks, both on 1 Burma Brigade and on 48 Brigade, were being repulsed, other considerable Japanese forces infiltrated between our groups and established themselves in positions from which they could fire on the road. Throughout the day, pressure up the east bank increased and hostile aircraft constantly struck at any movement.

I took General Alexander with me when I visited both divisional headquarters, and we saw something of the start of the battle. We were machine-gunned from the air at Scott's headquarters, which although well hidden in a big clump of forest were betrayed, I think, by tracks leading into the trees, or perhaps by Burmese agents. General Alexander, as usual, was quite unperturbed and refused to take shelter in a trench, as I did very briskly, preferring to stand upright behind a tree. I was very annoyed with him for this, not only because it was a foolhardy thing to do, but because we had been trying to stop the men doing it. We had lost a number in this way. It was all right as long as the hostile aircraft did not come from more than one direction and if they did not drop the small anti-personnel bombs some of their fighters carried. If, as often happened, they did either of these things, results were apt to be unpleasant for everyone not in a trench or flat on the ground. This was not the only time I found the Army Commander's courage above my standard.

Returning from Taungdwingyi late that afternoon, we found 48 Brigade had just cleared the main road of a big Japanese infiltration party that had tried to put a block across it. Our car was held up as the fight was still going on about eight hundred yards south of the road, and the enemy, with what appeared to be a single infantry gun, were shelling a bridge over which we had to pass. Their shooting was not very effective, but they might score a bull in time, so I whistled up a couple of light tanks that were standing by and suggested to General Alexander that he got into one and I into the other to cross the bridge.

'What about my car and the driver?' he asked at once.

'Oh, he'll have to stand on the gas and chance it,' I replied.

'But it'll be just as dangerous for him as it would be for me!'

'Yes, but he's not the Army Commander.'

'All right,' said Alexander. 'You go in a tank. I'm staying in the car!'

So, of course, we both went in the car.

During the night, 12th/13th April, the Japanese resumed their attacks. 48 Brigade again heavily repulsed the one on their front, but we were not so fortunate on our 1 Burma Brigade flank. During the 12th, Scott, expecting this attack, had ordered the reinforcement of the forward troops on the river bank while he prepared to strike the enemy assault in flank next morning with his main mobile reserve. Unfortunately, his division was lamentably short of signal equipment, especially wireless, while telephone cable was constantly cut by saboteurs and agents. As a result, orders went astray and moves were delayed. Meanwhile, in the dark, Japanese dressed as Burma Rifles and as civilians surprised the Burma Rifles and Burma Frontier Force dug in on the river bank. Strong Japanese forces followed up and when our delayed reinforcements, not knowing this had happened, approached next morning they were ambushed. Although they rallied, counter-attacked, and rescued some of the prisoners taken in the night, they were compelled to fall back, leaving the way to the north open. Japanese pressure against 1 Burma Brigade increased, there was considerable infiltration by strong enemy parties, and certain of our units gave way. The striking force, moving down to counter-attack, became involved in a series of fights with enemy

56

groups, and exhausted itself by marching and counter-marching to deal with them. Finally 1 Burma Brigade, in much confusion, fell back to the main road, exposing the whole of our right flank and giving the enemy a clear run for Magwe.

The first news we had at Corps Headquarters was a warning from Scott that the situation on the river bank was obscure, but that he feared something unpleasant had happened. This was quickly followed by the arrival of certain fugitives, who, as is the way of fugitives, described the heroic fight they had put up and assured us they were the sole survivors. I had enough experience to know that things are never quite as bad—or as good—as first reports make them, but this was obviously serious. Something had to be done at once to reconstitute our right flank. There was very little available; nothing, in fact, except a handful of exhausted units we had pulled out for a short rest. These, hurriedly organized into some sort of a force, were sent off. First, in mechanical transport, the 2nd King's Own Yorkshire Light Infantry, now very weak in numbers indeed, to hold Myingun and block the enemy advance along the river bank; following them the 1st Cameronians, also only a skeleton battalion, and one of our Indian Mounted Infantry detachments. I also brought a battalion from 2 Burma Brigade back across the river to form a fresh reserve.

Corps Headquarters, somewhat hampered by a couple of air raids, packed rather hurriedly and stood by for a move. It was on these occasions, far too frequent, that we congratulated ourselves on the smallness of our staff and lightness of our equipment.

By the morning of the 14th April it was clear that there was a wide gap between our two divisions, the road from Magwe to Taungdwingyi was completely cut, and very strong Japanese forces were astride it between 13 Brigade and 48 Brigade. Neither of these brigades was now on the offensive; both were fighting hard defensive battles against superior numbers. I agreed with Scott that there was no prospect now of getting his striking force going again. For this reason and because the failure of communication made it practically impossible for Burma Division to control it, I reverted 48 Brigade to the 17th Division. Immediately south of us the improvised force sent to reconstitute the flank was heavily engaged. The Yorkshiremen were, indeed,

surrounded—they eventually most gallantly cut their way out—
and the remaining units had not the strength to hold the Japanese.
There was nothing for it but to pull back this flank to the deep,
dry water-course of the Yin Chaung, which, starting just north
of Taungdwingyi, meandered from east to west to enter the
Irrawaddy some eight miles south of Magwe, and to try with the
1st Burma Division to hold that obstacle. If we could not, then
our next halt would for reasons of water supply have to be on
the Pin Chaung, north of Yenangyaung. In other words, we
should lose the oilfields.

It was, in fact, now evident that unless we quickly reunited
our two divisions, we could hardly hope to hold the enemy. I was
sure the time had now come when it was imperative to draw in
the 17th Division, but General Alexander was loath to do anything that might adversely affect the Chinese. He still insisted on
keeping the 17th Division in Taungdwingyi. Luckily, while
Corps Headquarters had still been there, we had, by removing
the lines and planking the bridges of the railway that ran north
out of the town to Kyaukpadaung, turned its earth formation
into a rough road. Had this not been done, it would have been
impossible, when the Magwe road was cut, even to maintain the
17th Division. The conversion of a railway to a road had been
a fine bit of work by the sappers who carried it out under frequent
air attack.

For the next two days the 1st Burma Division pulled back,
devotedly covered by tanks of 7 Armoured Brigade, to the Yin
Chaung. On the night of the 16th/17th April, the Japanese
attacked 1 Burma Brigade along this obstacle. At first the brigade
resisted stoutly and inflicted considerable losses by ambushing the
leading enemy units, but a battalion of Burma Rifles gave way,
thus allowing an Indian battalion to be surrounded. The Indians
fought their way out, but the whole front was broken. It must be
remembered that at this time units were very weak, few battalions
having as many as three hundred men, and those tired, ill-fed, and
lacking equipment. The 1st Burma Division had no option but
to save what it could by ordering a retirement of both 1 and
13 Brigades across country to the Magwe–Yenangyaung road.

We had already sent the bulk of our administrative units and
a portion of Corps Headquarters back to Yenangyaung. When a
mountain battery started firing from just behind my headquarters

I went out and asked what range they were firing at. An officer told me, 'Two thousand yards', but when he added, 'We're just reducing to fifteen hundred', I thought it time for the rest of Corps Headquarters to go.

The retreat through the oilfields had begun.

CHAPTER IV

DISASTER

IT was a great disappointment that our efforts to stage a counter-blow on the Magwe–Taungdwingyi line had failed so badly, and I drove into Yenangyaung to check the final arrangements for demolition in no very happy frame of mind. I had watched other oilfields in Syria and Iraq prepared for denial, but the luck had been with us there, and the order for destruction had never been given. Here I knew it was inevitable. Everything was ready for the word to blow. Forster, a senior oil company official, and his staff had done their melancholy work, not only with the highest technical skill but with admirable devotion. They knew as well as I did how threatening was the situation; they saw the back-wash of an army streaming past, but every gallon of petrol was precious now, and in spite of air attacks, alarms and rumours, they kept up some production until the last moment. They were among the last to leave, and their behaviour was an example to all in coolness and courage.

The forced retirement of the 1st Burma Division on its right and the withdrawal north of the Chinese on its left, exposed the 17th Division, in and around Taungdwingyi, on both flanks. The fact that the Japanese were not pressing it, but were by-passing it, only made its situation more dangerous. I wished to abandon Taungdwingyi, leave a detachment at Natmauk, some twenty-five miles north, to cover our communications with Mandalay, and to bring the division by the main road to Magwe. It would thus cut right across the line of communication of the enemy following up the 1st Burma Division and could attack them in rear. There were many risks about this scheme, but the 17th Division was still full of fight and quite pleased with itself over the Kokkogwa encounter. I think it would have got to Magwe, and once there altered the state of affairs considerably. However, Army Headquarters still insisted that Taungdwingyi must be held in strength. This, dangerous as it might be to my corps, was understandable, as the Chinese VI Army in the hills between the railway and the Sittang River was already in difficulties. The 17th Division was not in touch with the Chinese, but its move west at this juncture might have been interpreted as the abandonment of our allies. All I could do, therefore, was to order Cowan to strike with mobile columns from Taungdwingyi and Natmauk at the flank and rear of the Japanese south of Yenangyaung. This he did with some success, but the effects were, of course, nothing like as great as would have resulted from the retaking of Magwe by the whole division.

Burma Corps Headquarters halted among low scrub-covered hillocks, which gave some cover from air observation, on the bank of the Pin Chaung, just north of Yenangyaung. Here I heard that General Alexander was sending me the 38th Chinese Division from the newly arrived LXVI Army, and I asked for it to be concentrated at Kyaukpadaung as soon as possible. It was generous of Stilwell to make no protest at the move of this division as he cannot have been happy about his own VI Army. I had already brought one battalion of Burma Rifles of 2 Burma Brigade, from the west to the east bank of the Irrawaddy; I now pulled over a second, an Indian battalion, leaving the brigade with only two weak Burma battalions and a Burma Frontier Force detachment. Both battalions from the west bank were put in to reconstitute 1 Burma Brigade which was by now badly reduced and much shaken. Throughout the day, Burma Division made its way up the road towards Yenangyaung. It was a melancholy march. They started very tired. There was no water on the route, and, although the corps engineers had by a great effort put in and filled a few water tanks beside the road, the troops suffered greatly from thirst and heat, while Japanese aircraft bombed and machine-gunned them frequently. 7 Armoured Brigade again covered the withdrawal; what we should have done without that brigade I do not know. We managed to pass the rear echelons of Burma Division's mechanical transport safely through the oilfields and collect them at Gwegyo, twenty-five miles north of Yenangyaung.

After visiting Yenangyaung at 1300 hours on the 15th April, I gave orders for the demolition of the oilfield and refinery. It was essential that they should not fall intact into Japanese hands.

Our information of enemy moves from ground sources, though far from full, was ominous, and from the air non-existent, so that I could risk no further delay. The power-house was exempt from destruction as from it we still ran the small subsidiary oilfield at Chauk, and I wished to cling to production as long as possible. Forster at once put the denial scheme into operation. A million gallons of crude oil burned with flames rising five hundred feet; the flash and crash of explosions came as machinery, communications, and buildings disintegrated; over all hung a vast, sinister canopy of dense black smoke. It was a fantastic and horrible sight.

On the 16th, we moved Corps Headquarters from the Pin Chaung back to Gwegyo, a much better position both from the point of view of air cover and of communications. It was as well we did so, for, soon after dark that night, the Japanese, disguised in Burma Rifles uniforms, suddenly pounced on the road at the exact spot we had left. When we got the news the only troops within reach of Corps Headquarters were a detachment of Burma Frontier Force. Colonel Pryce, the indefatigable officer on my staff whom I had put in charge of all Frontier Force units, was luckily available to lead them. They put in a brisk counter-attack in the dark, and after some very rough fighting cleared the Japanese off the road, although elusive snipers and light machine-gunners kept working their way back and giving trouble. In spite of them transport again began to come through. Some anti-aircraft guns covering the road were ambushed and, after a fight, captured by the enemy. A counter-attack, helped by passing tanks, retook them, and the Japanese tried to set them on fire. I met them coming out, one of the guns with its tyres still burning. The British gunners were smoke-blackened, but cheerful; nor was their shooting affected, for they brought down seven aircraft later in the day. There was no lack of targets.

South of the Pin Chaung, the enemy infiltrated into Yenan-gyaung itself and attacked the guard on the power-house. The 1st Burma Division, wearily making its way up the road and still south of Yenangyaung, heard in the early hours of the 17th that the Japanese were ahead of it in the town. Scott began to concentrate his men, tired and thirsty, on the southern outskirts during the night, while his leading troops went on and reinforced the detachment at the power-house. It was blown up at midnight on the 16th April, thus completing the destruction of the whole oilfield.

North of the Pin Chaung, at the old Corps Headquarters location, the enemy had reappeared in greater strength and had re-established their block. This time, in addition to Pryce and his Frontier Force Gurkhas, there were available some West Yorkshires and a few tanks coming up from the south. A concerted attack again cleared the road, inflicting heavy casualties, the Japanese leaving many bodies in our uniforms. Transport then moved over the ford again, but numbers of vehicles had been lost by air attack during the enforced halt. More enemy appeared south of the cleared block, about a thousand of them being shelled by our artillery with effect, but again they established a block, this time near the ford. The situation was not encouraging, and I was greatly relieved to hear that 113 Regiment of the Chinese 38th Division was just arriving at Kyaukpadaung. I dashed off in my jeep to meet their commander and give him his orders.

Apart from the guerrilla battalion that had so reluctantly come to us at Taungdwingyi, this was the first time I had had Chinese troops under me. I found the Regimental Commander in the upstairs room of one of the few houses still standing in Kyaukpadaung village. He was a slight but tough-looking little Chinaman, with a real poker face, a pair of field-glasses, and a huge Mauser pistol. We were introduced by the British liaison officer with the regiment, who spoke perfect Chinese. We shook hands, and got down to business with a map. As I described the situation, the Chinese colonel struck me as intelligent and quick to grasp what I wanted. This was to bring his regiment, in lorries which I had ready, down to the Pin Chaung at once, and then send back the transport to fetch the next regiment as quickly as possible. I explained that it was my intention to attack with those two regiments, or, if possible, with the whole division, across the Pin Chaung early on the 18th in co-operation with a break-out by the 1st Burma Division. Having explained all this fully I asked him, through the interpreter, if he understood. He replied that he did.

'Then let's get moving,' I said cheerfully. The translation of this remark brought a flow of Chinese. He could not, he said, budge from Kyaukpadaung until he had the orders of General Sun, his Divisional Commander.

'But,' I explained, 'General Sun has been placed under my orders. If he were here I should tell him to do what I have told you to do, and he would do it. Isn't that right?'

'Yes,' agreed my Regimental Commander readily.
'All right, then let's get going.'
'But I cannot move until I get the orders of General Sun.'

And so it went on for an hour and a half, at the end of which I could cheerfully have shot the colonel with his own pistol. At last, just when I was feeling desperate, he suddenly smiled and said, 'All right, I will do it!'

Why he changed his mind I do not know. I suspect some of the Chinese of various ranks who had flowed in and out of the room throughout our interview must have brought a message from Sun, telling him to do whatever I wanted. Once he got moving, I had no complaints about my Chinaman. Indeed within the next few days I got to like him very much.

In fact, I got to like all, or almost all, my Chinese very much. They are a likeable people and as soldiers they have in a high degree the fighting man's basic qualities—courage, endurance, cheerfulness, and an eye for country. In dealing with them I soon discovered that we got on very well, if I remembered three things about our allies:

(i) Time meant nothing to them. No plan based on accurate timing had a hope of success. Whether it was attacking the enemy or coming to dinner, eight o'clock might mean four or just as likely twelve.

(ii) They would steal anything that came near them: stores, rations, lorries, railway trains, even the notice-boards from our headquarters. It was no good getting fussed about this or even finding it extraordinary. After all, if I had belonged to an army that had been campaigning for four or five years without any supply, transport, or medical organization worth the name and had only kept myself alive by collecting things from other people, I should either have had much the same ideas on property or have been dead.

(iii) The most important thing to a Chinaman was 'face'. I suppose 'face' might be defined as the respect in which one Chinaman is held by others. In practice, if a proposal can be put to a Chinaman so that carrying it out will enhance his prestige among his associates he will almost invariably accept it. Whatever 'face' is, and however annoying its repercussions may be to an Occidental, it is well to remember it is a very human thing. The Chinese are not the only people who bother about what the neighbours think.

Later in the day Lieut.-General Sun Li Jen, commanding the 38th Division, arrived. He was a slight but well-proportioned, good-looking man, who might in age have been anything from twenty-five to forty-five. He was alert, energetic, and direct. Later I found him a good tactician, cool in action, very aggressively minded, and, in my dealings with him, completely straightforward. In addition, he had the great advantage that he spoke good English with a slight American accent, having, as he was rightly proud to tell, been educated at the Virginia Military Academy. The Academy could be proud of Sun; he would have been a good commander in any army.

I discussed with him the details of the attack next morning. He was suspicious, having, I think, been warned somewhere to look out for the slick British trying to put one over him. All our allies at first suspect us of being terribly clever; it is flattering, but a bit disconcerting. I was impressed by Sun and it was essential to gain his confidence. His division had no artillery or tanks of its own, and I was therefore arranging that all the artillery we had this side of the Pin Chaung and all available tanks should support his attack. I decided there and then that these arms should not be 'in support of' but 'under command of' his division. Long-suffering Brigadier Anstice, commanding 7 Armoured Brigade, threw me the look of a wounded sambhur when he heard me give this out, but as always he rose to the occasion and he and Sun got on famously together. I had in fact arranged privately with Sun, as I would have done with a British divisional commander inexperienced with tanks, always to consult with Anstice before employing them. Sun, being an extremely sensible man, did so. He was, as far as I know, the first Chinese general to have the artillery and armoured units of an ally placed actually under his command, and his 'face' with his own people was accordingly vastly enhanced. The gunners and tank crews, as is the way of British soldiers, soon got on good terms with their new comrades, and, in spite of language difficulties of an extreme kind, co-operation was, I was assured by both sides, not only close but mostly friendly.

The rearguard of the 1st Burma Division closed up on Yenan-gyaung during the night of the 17th/18th. They were still almost without water as the Japanese were now between them and the Pin Chaung, and, having arrived by boat, held the river bank as well. My only link with Scott was by radio from Tank Brigade Headquarters to the small tank signals detachment he had with his one squadron. We used, as far as we could, code for our talks, and here again I found it a tremendous advantage to have a close friend as divisional commander. Our speech was so interlarded with references to things like our various children's ages, the numbers of the bungalows we had lived in in India, and other personal matters, to say nothing of being carried on largely in Gurkhali, that he would have been a very clever Japanese who could have made much of it. In this way we co-ordinated the attack for next morning. The only thing that the Japanese seemed to get hold of was the recognition signal we had arranged to distinguish Chinese from Japanese. We had already had trouble from Japanese passing themselves off as Chinese; it was very necessary not to have our Chinese taken for Japanese. The identi-fication signal had to be simple and easily seen. I told the Chinese to put their caps on the muzzles of their rifles and raise them above their heads as soon as they saw any Indian, Gurkha, or British. This message was sent in cipher, but whether the enemy inter-cepted and decoded it, or whether they saw the Chinese giving the signal, jumped to its meaning, and copied, they were certainly giving it at times by next evening.

The plan was roughly for the 1st Burma Division to break out north while the Chinese came down to the Pin Chaung, cleared up the road-block at the ford, and took in rear the Japanese trying to hold the Burma Division. I was still a little doubtful whether my friend the Chinese Regimental Commander, who was to lead the attack, would be quite as pushing as he should or whether some scruple might not delay him as it had yesterday. I mentioned this to Sun, who at once said, 'Let's go and see.' Off we went to Regimental Headquarters, where the Colonel, as far as I could see, had his battalions all ready for the attack. The Colonel knew what I had come for, and so, with something of a twinkle in his narrow eyes, he said:

'We will now go to a battalion.'

We went.

At the Battalion Headquarters, which was well forward, the Commanding Officer, through Sun, told me his company dispositions. Feeling quite sure that our allies meant business, I announced my satisfaction, and prepared to go back; but I was not to get away so easily. The Colonel, twinkling even more pronouncedly, said:

'We will now go to a company.'

I was not sure that a company, just as the attack was starting, was where I wanted to be, but it was a question of 'face' for me now. So, not liking it very much, I went on, dodging along shallow nullahs to a company command post. We had not been there long when the attack went off. There was no hesitation about these Chinese soldiers. I think a lot of them must have had experience under fire, as they used ground skilfully. The Japanese made a lot of noise as the Chinese broke cover, but, as usual, their shooting was high and bad. The Colonel turned to me. For one awful moment I thought he was going to say, 'We will now go to a platoon!' but he did not. Instead, he looked at me and grinned. Only a good and seasoned soldier can grin at you like that when bullets are about.

The Chinese attack we had watched reached the Pin Chaung and cleared the north bank, but failed to take the strongly held road-block at the ford. Even the tanks, prevented from closing by the soft sand of the river bed, could not drive out the defenders. Sun got busy preparing another attack, but with communications as bad as his were and with the units by now rather mixed up, I did not think he could renew the assault as quickly as he hoped.

Meanwhile, the Burma Division had begun in real earnest the Battle of the Oilfields. And a brutal battle it was. The temperature that day was 114 degrees; the battlefield was the arid, hideous, blackened shale of the oilfield, littered with wrecked derricks, flames roaring from the tanks, and shattered machinery and burning buildings everywhere. Over it all hung that huge pall of smoke. And there was no water.

At 6.30 in the morning, the Burma Division attacked. Progress was made, under cover of artillery, but the guns were running short of shells. Then some Burman troops faltered. In spite of this a by-pass road was cleared and a good deal of transport got down almost to the Pin Chaung itself, only to be held up by Japanese on the south bank. The British and Indian troops of the division fought doggedly over low ridge after ridge, the Japanese defending each one to the last man. A detachment of the Inniskillings struggled through to the Pin Chaung and enthusiastically greeted the troops it found there, believing them to be Chinese. They were Japanese who lured the Irishmen into an ambush. The tanks made a last attack on the road-block, but it was defended by several anti-tank guns, and the tanks, bogged in the soft sand, became sitting targets. The attack, like that of the Chinese from the other side, petered to a standstill.

More Japanese were coming in from the east and were reported on the river. The situation was grave. At half-past four in the afternoon, Scott reported on the radio that his men were exhausted from want of water and continuous marching and fighting. He could hold that night, he thought, but if he waited until morning his men, still without water, would be so weakened they would have little or no offensive power to renew the attack. He asked permission to destroy his guns and transport and fight his way out that night. Scott was the last man to paint an unduly dark picture. I knew his men were almost at the end of their strength and in a desperate position. I could not help wishing that he had not been so close a friend. I thought of his wife and of his boys. There were lots of other wives, too, in England, India, and Burma whose hearts would be under that black cloud a couple of miles away. Stupid to remember that now! Better get it out of my head.

I thought for a moment, sitting there with the headphones on, in the van with the operator crouching beside me, his eyes anxiously on my face. Then I told Scott he must hang on. I had ordered a Chinese attack again with all available tanks and artillery for the next morning. If Burma Division attacked then we ought to break through, and save our precious guns and transport. I was afraid, too, that if our men came out in driblets as they would in the dark, mixed up with Japanese, the Chinese and indeed our own soldiers, would fail to recognize them and their losses would be heavy. Scott took it as I knew he would. He said, 'All right, we'll hang on and we'll do our best in the morning, but, for God's sake, Bill, make those Chinese attack.'

I stepped out of the van feeling about as depressed as a man could. There, standing in a little half-circle waiting for me, were a couple of my own staff, an officer or two from the Tank Brigade, Sun, and the Chinese liaison officers. They stood there silent and looked at me. All commanders know that look. They see it in the eyes of their staffs and their men when things are really bad, when even the most confident staff officer and the toughest soldier want holding up, and they turn where they *should* turn for support—to their commander. And sometimes he does not know what to say. He feels very much alone.

'Well, gentlemen,' I said, putting on what I hoped was a confident, cheerful expression, 'it might be worse!'

One of the group, in a sepulchral voice, replied with a single word:

'How?'

I could cheerfully have murdered him, but instead I had to keep my temper.

'Oh,' I said, grinning, 'it might be raining!'

Two hours later, it was—hard. As I crept under a truck for shelter I thought of that fellow and wished I *had* murdered him.

Throughout the night, as we sat inside a circle of laagered tanks just above the Pin Chaung, we could hear and see the crump and flash of Japanese shells and mortar bombs flailing Scott's wretched men. His guns did not reply. They were down to about twenty rounds per gun now, and he was keeping those for the morning. Time and again the Japanese put in infantry attacks, attempting to infiltrate under cover of darkness and shelling. These attacks, one after the other, were beaten off, but certain of the Burma troops panicked and abandoned their positions, throwing extra strain on the British and Indians.

The day began for me before dawn with a severe blow. The Chinese attack across the Pin Chaung to take Twingon, a village about a mile south of the ford, which I had hoped would start soon after daylight, could not be got ready in time. After a good deal of talk it was promised for twelve-thirty as the earliest possible hour. I was then faced with the problem of either telling Scott to hold his attack, which was due to go in at seven o'clock, or to let it go as arranged. I decided to let it go, rather than keep his men and transport sitting cramped and waterless under artillery, mortar, and air attack.

At seven o'clock the Burma Division resumed the attack, but a reinforced Japanese defence held it after it had made some progress. Meanwhile, on the north bank, while still urging the Chinese to hurry their preparations, we had managed to scrape up a small British force which attacked and, during the morning, actually got a squadron of tanks and some of the West Yorkshire Regiment across the Chaung. This small success might have been expanded had not one of those infuriating mishaps so common in battle occurred. An officer some distance in rear, received a report that strong enemy forces were advancing to cut off the transport assembled about Gwegyo. Without realizing the situation forward, and still less that the threatening forces advancing on him were not Japanese but Chinese, he ordered back the tanks and accompanying infantry to deal with this new but imaginary danger.

Burma Division was once more halted in a tight perimeter and was being heavily shelled. The heat was intense, there was still no water, the troops were exhausted and they had suffered heavy casualties, their wounded, of course, being still with them. At this stage the Burma battalions, in spite of the efforts of their officers, really disintegrated. 1 Burma Brigade reported that the bulk of their troops were no longer reliable; even 13 Brigade said that some of theirs were shaky. It was hardly to be wondered at; their ordeal had been terribly severe.

The Chinese attack, promised for 1230 hours, had now been postponed to 1400 hours. Just before that time it was again put back to 1600 hours. We managed, however, to get it off at 1500 hours instead. These delays were of course maddening, but I had not then learned that time means little to the average Chinaman. Actually, with their lack of signal equipment, of means of evacuating wounded and of replenishing ammunition, and their paucity of trained junior leaders, it was not surprising that to sort themselves out, reform, and start a fresh attack took time. The trouble was not with Sun, who was all energy and desire to attack, but with so many of his subordinates, who promised but did not perform, and in the delays and errors that occurred in getting his orders to them. One of their troubles, and a real one, was water. They could not attack until water had been replenished, and they had no means of fetching it up except a few petrol tins slung in pairs on a bamboo and carried, willow pattern plate fashion, across a man's shoulder. We got one of our few remaining water lorries and ran it up nearly to their front line, with orders to make continuous trips backwards and forwards. It went the first time and did not return. Eventually the British driver appeared on foot. He said, with soldierly embellishments, that having emptied the tank of water, the Chinese, in spite of his protests, emptied the radiator also, and, when he left to get help, were trying to empty the petrol tank as well! Sun dealt with that incident; we got the water lorry back and it ran regularly. Even so, when I was at one of the forward Chinese headquarters, a large and very fat Chinese officer protested volubly that it was impossible to attack as none of his men had water. He was deeply moved about it. I noticed that all the time he was so passionately describing the sufferings of his men he had a very large water bottle hanging from his belt, and that even at his most gesticulatory moments it lay snug against his ample posterior. I walked quietly up to him, lifted it, and shook it. It was full to the cork. There was a pause in his flow of language, and a moment's hush among the spectators. Then all shouted with laughter—in which the fat officer joined. Without more ado he agreed they could attack by 1500 hours, and they did.

Unhappily, before that time communication with Scott had ceased and his last desperate effort to break out could not be co-ordinated with the Chinese attack. His squadron of tanks had found and cleared a rough track, leading east, down to the Pin Chaung, over which it was hoped vehicles could move. Scott himself formed up the column, guns in front, wounded in ambulances and trucks next, followed by such vehicles as had survived the bombardment. With a spearhead of tanks and infantry the column lurched down the narrow, uneven path, through the low hillocks. But the trail turned to sand; the leading ambulances were bogged and the column stopped. As many wounded as possible were piled on the tanks, and Scott gave the order to abandon vehicles and fight a way out on foot across the Pin Chaung. This his men did, some in formed bodies, some in small groups, and on the other side they met the Chinese. At the sight of the water in the Chaung the mules which had come out with them went mad, and the men flung themselves face downwards into it. The haggard, red-eyed British, Indian, and Burmese soldiers who staggered up the bank were a terrible sight, but every man I saw was still carrying his rifle. The two brigades of the division had reached Yenangyaung at a strength of not more than one; there they had lost in killed and wounded twenty per cent of that small number, with a considerable portion of their guns, mortars, and vehicles. None of these losses, either in men or equipment, could be replaced. After its ordeal the division would be of no fighting value until it had rested, and, as best it could, reorganized. We collected it that night about Gwegyo.

When the Chinese did attack they went in splendidly. They were thrilled at the tank and artillery support they were getting and showed real dash. They took Twingon, rescuing some two hundred of our prisoners and wounded. Next day, the 20th April, the 38th Division attacked again and with tanks penetrated into Yenangyaung itself, repulsing a Japanese counter-attack. The fighting was severe and the Chinese acquitted themselves well, inflicting heavy losses, vouched for by our own officers. Sun now expected a really heavy Japanese attack at dawn on the 21st. I discussed this with him and agreed that he should come out of the town, back to the Pin Chaung. His division had done well and I did not want it frittered away in a house-to-house dog-fight for the shell of Yenangyaung. In spite of the stories I had heard from American sources, of Chinese unwillingness to fight, I had remembered how enthusiastic officers, who had served with our own Chinese Hongkong regiment, had been about their men, and I had expected the Chinese soldier to be tough and brave. I was, I confess, surprised at how he had responded to the stimulus of proper tank and artillery support, and at the aggressive spirit he had shown. I had never expected, either, to get a Chinese general of the calibre of Sun.

As I talked this over with Davies, my Chief of Staff and my mainstay in these difficult times, we thought we saw a chance of striking back at the 33rd Japanese Division. True, our 1st Burma Division, never really a division in either establishment or equipment, was at the moment incapable of action, but it was definitely recovering in the peace of Mount Popa, where we had sent it. In a week or two we might hope to have it back in the field at a strength of, say, a brigade. If we could get the 17th Division, still in Taungdwingyi, we might, with the Chinese 38th Division and anything else we could scrape up, try a counter-stroke. We were always building up our house of cards, Davies and I, and seeing it fall down—but we went on. So we renewed our attempts to persuade Burma Army to let us take the 17th Division from Taungdwingyi. Meanwhile the 38th Division and, as usual, 7 Armoured Brigade covered the 1st Burma Division as it lay gasping but not dying.

A number of our badly wounded had of necessity been left in the ambulances when the Burma Division had finally broken out. A young gunner officer volunteered to go back to discover their fate. Under cover of darkness he did so. The ambulances were still standing on the track, but every man in them had had his throat cut or been bayoneted to death.

We were not alone in our misfortunes. While the battle of Yenangyaung was in progress the Japanese attack on the Chinese VI Army in the Shan States was causing anxiety. In fact, the final phase of the campaign had opened. When the V Army had been driven out of Toungoo north towards Pyinmana, the VI Army was occupying the hills between the Mandalay–Rangoon railway and the Sittang River. The country was wild and broken, pierced by only one road from west to east, that from Toungoo to Mawchi, and one from south to north, the Mawchi–Bawlake–Loikaw road. The 55th Chinese Division was spread out from Loikaw in depth along the Mawchi road, with the other divisions of VI Army, the 49th still farther north and 93rd as far away as Kengtung. Detachments of the Japanese 56th Division, amounting to about a brigade group, commenced to push up towards Mawchi at the beginning of April. The British-led Karen Levies, newly raised and partially trained, tried to delay them, but they and the Chinese were swept away and the town, with some of the most valuable wolfram mines in the world, fell into Japanese hands. The Chinese withdrew to strong positions in the Bawlake–Kemapyu area. The commander of the 55th Chinese Division appealed for reinforcements, and the 93rd Division and one regiment of the 49th Division were ordered to Loikaw. One regiment was, however, retained at Mong Pai, ten miles north-west of Loikaw. Through bad staff work, failure to use properly the transport allotted, and the normal difficulties of moving a Chinese force, these reinforcements were delayed, and the forward troops of the Chinese 55th Division again fell back. A Japanese frontal attack was held, but on the 16th April an outflanking movement, after heavy casualties to both sides, compelled a further withdrawal to Bawlake. Next day the enemy cut the road west of Bawlake, thus isolating a large part of the 55th Division. Throughout the 18th, the Chinese fought hard to open the escape road but failed. Suddenly all telephone and wireless communication with the 55th Division ceased. It had been overrun and scattered. Early

73

on the 18th, Japanese armoured cars appeared only nine miles south of Loikaw; VI Army hurriedly evacuated the town, leaving only partially organized rearguards. Moving rapidly by side tracks, the Japanese cut the main Thazi–Loilem–Kengtung road behind the VI Army, which scattered and fell back pell-mell without demolishing bridges *en route*. On the 20th April its remnants were halted on a position twelve miles east of Hopong, eighty miles north of Loikaw.

We were aware that this was roughly the actual position on the VI Army front, when General Alexander, Stilwell, and I met on the 19th April to decide what should be done next. We planned on the basis that the VI Army, while being pressed, was in extremely good defensive country and should be able to hold anything the Japanese could bring against it, even if it had to give way a little. On the V Army front, the Japanese, after capturing Toungoo, had attacked and taken Yedashe, fifteen miles farther north, on the 5th April, and the Chinese had fallen back slowly on Pyinmana, where General Tu had hoped to stage another 'Changsha' battle. It was for this reason that he had ignored Stilwell's orders to send a division to take over Taungdwingyi, but Japanese air reconnaissance and spies had discovered his trap and the enemy refused to walk into it. Tu still had three divisions in the area and the enemy showed no signs of staging an attack here. The Chinese LXVI Army had its 28th Division in Mandalay and its 29th still moving into Burma at this time. Thus Stilwell was, or rather thought he was, able to dispose of three armies totalling seven or eight divisions, the ninth division—the 38th —being under my command.

There had already been a good deal of talk among officers and men about giving up any idea of holding even Northern Burma and, instead, concentrating on getting out to India and China what could be saved from the armies in Burma. As a precautionary measure, in case it should be decided to do this, outline plans had been prepared in Burma Army Headquarters at the end of March. The method then proposed was:

(i) *Chinese VI and LXVI Armies*
   Troops east of the Salween to return by direct route to China; those west of river also to return to China via Hsipaw and Lashio.

74

(ii) *Chinese V Army*
   To China via Lashio.
(iii) *British*
   (a) 7 Armoured Brigade and one brigade group of the
   17th Division to Lashio with V Army for China.
   (b) 17th Division (less one brigade group) via Mandalay–
   Shwebo–Katha–Hukawng Valley to India.
   (c) 1st Burma Division via Kalewa–Tamu to India.

The objects of this plan were, first, to cover the exits from
Burma into China and India, and, second, by sending a British
force with the Chinese to ensure their remaining active allies.
Personally I did not like this plan at all. Above all, I disliked
sending any British formations into China. Their administration
in a famine-stricken area would be practically impossible, they
would arrive in a shocking state and be no advertisement for us,
while the men, both British and Indian, would be horribly
depressed at the prospect. I urged that, if my corps had to come
out, it should do so intact through Kalewa into India. It would
then be of some value for the defence of India. I also asked
that the 38th Chinese Division should come out that way with
us, the remainder of the Chinese armies going via Lashio to
China.

I still thought there was a chance that even now we might turn
the tables on the Japanese and thus avoid abandoning Burma. I
had come to the conference armed with a suggestion, worked
out by Davies and myself, to take advantage of the exposed
position of the Japanese 33rd Division in Yenangyaung, to attack
and destroy it. To do this I hoped to get on loan for a short time
another, or, if possible, two more Chinese divisions to join my
38th. With these I proposed to attack Yenangyaung from the
north and east, while the 17th Division, at last released from
Taungdwingyi, swept up through Magwe and fell on the enemy
rear from the south. With the reconstituted 1st Burma Division
to hold various 'stops', I felt we had a good chance, if we acted
quickly, of smashing the 33rd Division. When we had done that,
and I calculated it would take a week from the time the attacking
divisions reached Yenangyaung, we should be in a position to
move over to the Sittang and take the Japanese opposite V and VI
Chinese Armies in flank and rear. A little ambitious, I know, but

75

still a chance and, as both Stilwell and I recognized, about our last chance. I found him, as he always was, ready to support an offensive move and prepared to go a long way to help me. He was naturally anxious also to do anything that would prevent any further withdrawal of my corps to the north, as that would expose V Army to flank attack from the Japanese Irrawaddy forces. He promised me the 200th Chinese Division from V Army, and I asked for it at Kyaukpadaung as soon as possible. I had some hopes too of his sending another from Mandalay to follow it, though I could not get this firm. General Alexander gave this transfer of a Chinese division his blessing, but he still refused to sanction the withdrawal of the 17th Division from Taungdwingyi as he felt that to do so would expose the Chinese flank. This, of course, took a good deal of the sting out of our plan, but I felt the main thing was to get the Chinese to Kyaukpadaung. Then we would see what would happen to the 17th Division. I returned to my headquarters at Gwegyo more cheerful than I had been for some time, and Davies got down to preparing our masterpiece—Burma Corps Directive No. 5, which was to put paid to our account with the redoubtable Japanese 33rd Division. Alas, it was never issued!

Events on the Chinese front were moving to a climax. By the 21st April, their VI Army had practically disintegrated. The Japanese, moving swiftly in relatively small columns with motorized infantry, tanks, and armoured cars, had constantly hooked round and cut off the Chinese forces trying to hold main roads on narrow fronts. On that day, the Japanese reached Hopong; the next, the 22nd, they drove the Chinese out of positions to the east of it and towards Loilem on the road to China. Loilem itself was bombed from the air and burnt, while the Chinese again tried to hold astride the road, some eight miles west of it. Another hook, and the Japanese had Loilem, and General Kan, the Chinese Army Commander, with three hundred men, all that was left to him, was a fugitive on the Lashio road. The Chinese 93rd Division had advanced from Kengtung to within twenty miles of Loilem, when it heard the Japanese were in the town. It turned and withdrew. General Kan with his remnant came across country to Kengtung, where he joined what was left of the 49th and 93rd Divisions and the stragglers of the 55th Division. Having collected these, he, and with him the last

76

traces of VI Army, moved into China. Kengtung was then occupied by Siamese forces under Japanese control. The road north to Lashio was open to the enemy.

All unconscious of these disasters, we at Burma Corps were very pleased at the speed with which Stilwell carried out his promise to send us the 200th Chinese Division from the V Army. In spite of difficulties in finding transport, it reached Meiktila, and the leading regiment began to roll in by lorry to Kyaukpadaung. From the look of it I thought the 200th would be nearly as good as the 38th Division. I had come back to our headquarters in the evening of the 20th after spending some time seeing Chinese soldiers debussing, and Davies and I were sitting after dinner putting the finishing touches to our famous Directive No. 5, when a staff officer came in and said 'Do you know that all the Chinese at Kyaukpadaung are packing up and going back again?' And they were!

Stilwell, at last having received something approaching accurate information of the VI Army débâcle, had recalled the 200th Division for a desperate attempt to retrieve the situation. Any message he sent saying he was doing so never reached Burma Corps, but with his makeshift staff arrangements and Chinese signals that was not surprising. When the Japanese had driven the VI Army out of Loilem they had also occupied Taunggyi, to the west of it, on the main Loilem–Thazi road. A further advance on Thazi would place the Japanese behind V Army, still about Pyinmana, and would threaten them with the same fate as had befallen VI Army. Collecting the 200th Division and one regiment of the 22nd Division, Stilwell himself led them to the recapture of Taunggyi, which he attacked on the 23rd April and took on the 24th. He was again greatly handicapped by the Chinese reluctance to obey his orders, and it was only by offering the stimulus of a considerable cash reward that vigour in the attack on the town could be assured. Pushing on eastward, the 200th Division drove the enemy out of Hopong on the 25th, killing some five hundred, and occupied Loilem. It was a magnificent achievement and only made possible by Stilwell's personal leadership with the very front units. Gallant as it was, this could only be a last effort; the disintegration of the Chinese forces had gone too far. VI Army had vanished, now the bulk of V was involved in scattered, confused fighting against small Japanese

77

forces over a wide area. Stilwell himself, without staff or signals, had to command local minor engagements until he was needed so badly at his headquarters that he had to return, and the counter-stroke petered out. Left to themselves, the Chinese moved north up the Loilem–Lashio road.

Headquarters of LXVI Army with the 28th Division (less a regiment) and part of the 29th Division were sent to hold the Lashio area. They arrived there between the 26th and 29th April, probed a little south, but, coming in contact with a Japanese column, withdrew again to Lashio. Meanwhile transport and armoured vehicles of V Army, which had also met with disaster as the Japanese turned on it, were pouring through Lashio on the way to China. These would have been invaluable to General Chang, commander of the LXVI Army, trying to organize some resistance to the advancing enemy. However, such was the lack of co-operation and the jealousy of the Chinese commanders, coupled with the failure of higher control, that he could obtain none. Dumps of stores and ammunition in Lashio were now destroyed, though much was left to fall into Japanese hands. On the 29th April, the enemy attacked Lashio and, after what was described as heavy fighting, took it. The Japanese forces engaged amounted to thirty light tanks, a few armoured cars, twelve guns, and only two battalions of lorry-borne infantry. Chang withdrew from Lashio with only three thousand men, fought a couple of small rearguard actions, and made his way out into China. The Japanese pressed on for Bhamo. They rushed the Shweli River bridge, imperfectly guarded by a local Burmese battalion, before it could be demolished and swept on unhindered. They were in Bhamo on the 4th May and Myitkyina on the 8th.

The 200th Division and the regiment of the 22nd Division which Stilwell had led to Taunggyi reached Hsipaw on the Mandalay–Lashio road, and finding Lashio occupied by Japanese went back to Maymyo. They then wandered north again to Mogok, where they found the regiment of the 28th Division left behind when the rest of that formation went to Lashio. The combined party then made its way out to China. The only Chinese troops now left in Burma were the remains of V Army and my 38th Division.

Pressure against V Army had increased while we were holding our conference on the 19th April, and next day the Chinese were forced out of Pyinmana. The 96th Division fell back some twelve miles, but was again bundled off its positions and one of its regiments cut off, surrounded, and dispersed. The 22nd Division, less the regiment that Stilwell had taken to Taunggyi, was holding Pyawbwe behind it, but this division in turn was outflanked on the 25th April and forced to evacuate that night. Its motor transport had already, in a *sauve qui peut* dash, made Lashio, adding to the confusion of LXVI Army, also trying to reach that area. By this time both the 96th and 22nd Divisions had ceased to be fighting formations and were streaming back in disorganized groups through Thazi towards Mandalay. These divisions, especially the 22nd, had fought well, but the Japanese hooking tactics had been too much for them.

The events of the first three weeks of April had made it necessary to recast Burma Army's plans, and on the 23rd April a revised directive was issued to Stilwell and me, which was not to be put into force unless the Chinese lost Meiktila. Under this, the 17th Division and what was left of the 1st Burma Division were to stand astride the Chindwin to cover Kalewa; 7 Armoured Brigade with the 38th Chinese Division was to hold from the Mu River to the Irrawaddy; the Chinese V Army, with the 22nd, 28th, and 96th Divisions in and south of Mandalay, was to defend the crossings over the Myitnge River. All other Chinese to the east of the Mandalay–Rangoon railway were to make for Lashio, and reorganize there. It was still the intention that, if the evacuation of Burma became necessary, some British forces, including 7 Armoured Brigade, would accompany the Chinese into China. I was, of course, not in a position fully to assess what would be the political effects of this, but I was more than ever convinced that to send any of our British units in their present state to China would be a grave military and political error.

On the 25th April, General Alexander and I met Stilwell, just returned from the taking of Taunggyi, at Kyaukse, twenty-five miles south of Mandalay. The complete disappearance of the VI Army and the rapidly spreading disintegration of the other two Chinese armies were the dominating facts of a grim situation. There was no longer any chance of staging a counter-offensive; the Japanese were about to seize Lashio and with it would go our hopes of holding Northern Burma. With the Chinese rapidly passing out of the picture, realism demanded that we should now decide to get out of Burma as intact as we could, with as much as we could. Recognizing this, the Army Commander ordered a general withdrawal north of Mandalay, and, as the Chinese were no longer able to protect themselves during such a move, he ordered my corps to extend to its left and act as rearguard to the fugitive Chinese V Army as it made north along the Meiktila–Mandalay road and railway. The retirement was to begin at once; indeed, as far as the Chinese were concerned, it was already in full disorderly swing.

There was no time to be lost if we were to stop the Japanese pouring over the Irrawaddy at Mandalay on the heels of the fleeing Chinese, and 7 Armoured Brigade was ordered at once with all speed to Meiktila. Back once more at Corps Headquarters, Davies and I, instead of our precious, stillborn Directive No. 5, issued orders for:

(i) The 38th Chinese Division to cover Kyaukpadaung.
(ii) The 1st Burma Division (less its 2 Brigade on the west of the Irrawaddy) to complete its reorganization and be ready to move on Taungtha.
(iii) The 17th Division to evacuate Taungdwingyi, move rapidly to the area Mahlaing–Meiktila–Zayetkon, and, with 7 Armoured Brigade, cover the withdrawal of the Chinese V Army.

On the evening of the 25th, tanks of 7 Armoured Brigade interposed east of Meiktila between the Chinese and the pursuing Japanese. They surprised an enemy armoured and mechanized column, shot it up, and dispersed it with considerable loss. The corps, terribly stretched out, was now on the line Seikpyu (on the west bank of the Irrawaddy)–Chauk–Kyaukpadaung–Zayetkon–Meiktila. The 17th Division, having evacuated Taungdwingyi and Natmauk, was firmly established in the Meiktila–Zayetkon area, supporting 7 Armoured Brigade in its thrusts against Japanese columns advancing astride the main road and railway. There were many small parties of fugitive Chinese scattered over the country, and these were passed back and directed on Kyaukse. Several small engagements between our troops and the enemy took place around Meiktila. A typical example was when a detachment of our tanks and infantry caught a small Japanese motorized column infiltrating north and engaged it. The Japanese at once

80

took refuge in one of the numerous villages, scattered over the plain, and our infantry prepared to attack, but were delayed by machine-gunning enemy aircraft. On the disappearance of these the attack was resumed and the village taken. In hand-to-hand fighting, one hundred and fifty Japanese were accounted for and twelve lorries and one gun captured, while we lost two tanks, ten men killed, and some wounded.

As the Chinese were now clear of the Meiktila area, I ordered Cowan to fall back on Wundwin, which he was to hold until 1600 hours on the 27th and then to withdraw through Kyaukse. His 63 Brigade, around Wundwin, was bombed almost continuously throughout that day, while our tanks held off strong Japanese infantry and artillery groups which tried to force their way up the main road. A number of Japanese light tanks appeared but, when engaged by ours, hurriedly withdrew behind the shelter of their own guns. 63 Brigade remained in Wundwin until midnight, 26th/27th April, when it fell back through 48 Brigade, now established in Kyaukse, and occupied positions covering the road and railway bridges over the Myitnge River south of Mandalay. I was extremely pleased at the way the 17th Division and 7 Armoured Brigade were carrying out the difficult rearguard tasks so hurriedly thrust upon them.

Throughout this time, it was very difficult to get any reliable information of the locations of Chinese troops of the V Army. Obviously both the 96th and 22nd Divisions had disintegrated and were making their way back in leaderless parties as best they could. All higher control seemed to have disappeared and neither the Chinese nor American headquarters could give any reliable estimate of the position or when the fugitives would be over the Myitnge River. An occasional Chinese officer appeared fleetingly at Corps or 17th Division Headquarters with appeals, usually for transport, or with requests for information about his own troops. On one occasion a Chinese colonel, whose men were to entrain at one of the stations north of Wundwin to which a few trains had been sent by night, asked for our troops to be posted on and close to the railway station. If this were not done, he feared that the first Chinese troops to arrive would panic, rush the trains, and drive off, leaving the others behind. In answer to his request, a small detachment from the 17th Division was sent back and duly occupied obvious positions on and around the station. Some of

General Stilwell's staff, vainly trying to get order into the retreat, arrived at the station, saw our troops there and jumped to the conclusion, no doubt confirmed by the Chinese, that this was the rearmost portion of the British rearguard. Knowing many Chinese were still well to the south, the harassed Americans reported that the British were beating the Chinese in the race north. Stilwell, infuriated, sent me a message accusing me in emotional terms of having failed to carry out my duty as rearguard. I dare say my nerves were nearly as stretched as his—we were neither of us having a very good time—and I was furious at this injustice to my troops who were at that moment fighting briskly far to the south of his Chinese. I replied with a very astringent refutation of the charge. This was the only time Stilwell and I fell out, but a few days later he sent me a message withdrawing the accusation and coming as near to an apology as I should think he ever got.

On the 28th April, with Lashio about to fall and little or nothing to stop a Japanese dash for Bhamo and even Myitkyina, I received from General Alexander directives for the final withdrawal to India. Recognizing that our hold on the Mandalay-Irrawaddy line could only be temporary, the plan, given in some detail, was:

(i) Two brigades to fall back astride the Chindwin, delaying the enemy as far south as possible.

(ii) A strong detachment to be left in the Myittha Valley which runs north, roughly parallel to, and some thirty miles west of, the Chindwin.

(iii) The remainder of the corps to move via Ye-u on Kalewa, leaving a detachment to cover this route, and to see out of Burma by the Shwegyin track all administrative, civil, and other refugees not escaping by other routes.

(iv) The 38th Chinese Division and possibly other Chinese troops to accompany Burma Corps.

I had pressed hard that the 38th Chinese Division should come with my corps into India. Sun had welcomed the idea, and I was glad to see that General Alexander now intended the division to march out with me. The remainder of the Chinese were, as far as I could judge, already making their way as best they could to China.

82

It was not easy to arrange this withdrawal while we were closely engaged in a rearguard action, with the Irrawaddy, one of the great rivers of the world, crossed by only one bridge, behind us. Burma Army had directed the corps to cross by the ferries at Sameikkon and west of Mandalay. I was a bit doubtful about these ferries as we had already experienced the difficulty there was in keeping the civilian crews who manned them at work under air attack and the threat of the Japanese advance. I made a hurried reconnaissance with Swift, my Chief Engineer. It was as well we did so. One ferry consisted of nothing at all, another of one dumb barge aground some yards from the bank, and the third of a small craft capable of taking one or two vehicles at a time. I do not doubt Army Headquarters had made preparations, but it was becoming increasingly difficult to hold administrative detachments in place and our prospects of getting three divisions, with the Japanese on their heels and no air cover, over by these ferries did not look too promising. However, Swift and the Chief Engineer of the 1st Burma Division were not easily defeated. The river fleet of the Irrawaddy Flotilla was being sunk in Mandalay. Swift rushed there, seized some of the vessels and brought them downstream to the ferries, barges were pulled off sandbanks, approaches improved, and ferries of a sort provided. We christened the provision of ferries by Burma Army the 'Blanket' system of administration, from the old story, 'And we says to 'im, "Jump, and we'll 'old the blanket." And 'e jumped. And there worn't no blanket!' Luckily we looked before we leapt.

On the 28th April, Corps orders were issued directing:

(i) 1st Burma Division to cross the Sameikkon ferry and move to Monywa. There 13 Brigade was to cross to the west bank of the Chindwin to secure the town from the south and south-west.

(ii) 1 Burma Brigade to move from Monywa to Kalewa by boat.

(iii) 2 Burma Brigade (now on the Irrawaddy west bank) to withdraw via Pauk and Tilin into the Myittha Valley, to deny that route to the enemy and eventually make touch with the rest of the 1st Burma Division west of Kalewa.

(iv) 17th Division (less 63 Brigade) to cross and hold the north bank of the Irrawaddy from Myinmu to Allagappa.

(v) 63 Brigade of the 17th Division to cover the road thence to Monywa.

(vi) 38th Chinese Division and 7 Armoured Brigade to hold the river from Sagaing to Ondaw.

The Ava bridge had been allotted to the Chinese V Army, for the crossing of the Irrawaddy, but I obtained permission from Burma Army Headquarters to use it also for 7 Armoured Brigade. It appeared to me, however, that if the 17th Division was to cover the last of the Chinese over the bridge they might as well follow themselves before destroying it. The 17th Division was therefore ordered to hold Kyaukse until all V Army were north of the Myitnge River, then follow with 7 Armoured Brigade, cross, and destroy the Ava bridge.

Having seen the 1st Burma and 38th Chinese Divisions well started on their way to the Irrawaddy, with the Japanese showing little inclination to follow too closely, but being very annoying from the air, I started off on the 27th to visit the more dangerous 17th Division flank. On the west to east secondary road to Kyaukse we ran into increasing evidences of attacks and atrocities by gangs of Burmese against Indian refugees, Chinese stragglers, and, in one case, Indian troops who had been trying to repair a signal wire. We were fortunate enough to fall in with a mobile column from the 17th Division just in time to bring down a just retribution on the gang responsible for the last outrage, and to rescue two sepoys, one of whom was badly mutilated. The country was by no means safe for solitary vehicles, despatch riders, or signal linesmen.

In Kyaukse, we found 48 Brigade settled into a strong defensive position. The small town had been badly bombed and burnt out; many of its inhabitants with their cattle were lying dead in the streets. It was surrounded by paddy fields giving a good field of fire, but there were banana groves and some thick jungle on the banks of the river that ran round the southern and western outskirts. Brigadier Cameron, commanding 48 Brigade, had four weak battalions of Gurkhas, twelve guns, a troop of anti-tank two-pounders, and some Sappers, in all about eighteen hundred men. He was not strong enough to occupy the whole of the long pagoda-dotted ridge that ran out from the town to the east, but in true mountain warfare style he had placed picquets along it. While we were there, the last of the Chinese, footsore stragglers, were being passed through. Cameron had infantry in lorries and a few tanks well to the flanks and to the south to help bring in 63 Brigade, due that night, and to ambush any Japanese who might follow. I left feeling 48 Brigade would give a good account of itself. It did.

During the night, 63 Brigade with its tanks came through and moved on to hold the Myitnge crossings. Early on the 29th, flank patrols had brushes with armed Burmans and rescued more Indian refugees, but not before some had suffered atrocities. There was a brisk little action between our own and Japanese tanks, some ten miles down the main road, in which one enemy tank was destroyed and ours were bombed from the air. However, with the arrival of large Japanese reinforcements, our detachments fell slowly back to Kyaukse. At 2200 hours in bright moonlight, the Japanese launched a fierce attack on our positions astride the road. The Gurkhas held their fire until their yelling assailants were a hundred and fifty yards away and then let them have it. The attack withered away, leaving many dead. At midnight, a Japanese column of motor transport and bullock carts blundered almost on to our defences, and was heavily shelled and mortared. Half an hour later another attack was met with close-range fire and destroyed. At 0515 hours next morning in pitch darkness, a third attack was flung back in confusion. At dawn on the 30th April, tanks and Gurkhas sallied out and cleared a burnt-out village in front of our lines. Many Japanese in it were killed and several mortars and light automatics captured. The Gurkhas were particularly pleased at trapping thirty-eight of the enemy who had taken refuge in a culvert under the road. The enemy belonged to the 18th Division—one we had not previously met. The general opinion in 48 Brigade was that, compared with their old opponents, the 33rd Division, these newcomers were much inferior in both courage and fighting skill. The Japanese throughout the day shelled our positions heavily but not very effectively, except Brigade Headquarters which they appeared to have located exactly. It was clear during the 30th that the whole 18th Division was deploying for a renewal of the attack and that the usual out-flanking movements were starting. The brigade was, therefore, ordered to withdraw through 63 Brigade that night. At 1530 hours yet another attack was repulsed, at 1700 hours our men were dive-bombed but suffered no casualties, and at 1800 hours they pulled out covered by one battalion and some tanks. 48 Brigade embussed in the dark a few miles up the road and then went straight through, across the Ava bridge to Myinmu. The action at Kyaukse was a really brilliant example of rearguard work. It not only enabled the last of the Chinese to cross the Ava bridge without molestation and gave us all a breathing space, but it inflicted heavy casualties on the enemy at extremely small cost to ourselves.

On the night of the 27th, I returned to Corps Headquarters, now at Sagaing. Mandalay was full of dumps, stores, and camps of every kind—almost all of them deserted. A few officers and men of the administrative services and departments remained, but there had been a general and not very creditable exodus. We were to find more and more that demoralization behind the line was spreading. From now on, while the fighting troops, knowing that their object—to get out intact to India—was at last clear, actually improved in morale and fighting power, the amorphous mass of non-fighting units on the line of communication deteriorated rapidly. In its withdrawal the corps was from now on preceded by an undisciplined mob of fugitives intent only on escape. No longer in organized units, without any supply arrangements, having deserted their officers, they banded together in gangs, looting, robbing, and not infrequently murdering the unfortunate villagers on their route. They were almost entirely Indians and very few belonged to combatant units of the Army. Most of them were soldiers only in name, but their cowardice and their conduct brought disrepute on the real Indian soldiers who followed. It was not to be wondered that as we retreated we found villages burnt and abandoned and such inhabitants as were not in hiding frightened and unfriendly.

It was impossible to guard all the stores lying unattended in Mandalay. On one dump—of special octane petrol for our tanks—we did, however, put a small guard. We were growing greatly anxious about fuel supply for tanks, and the find was a godsend, but when the tanks arrived next day to refill they found nothing but twisted and blackened drums. A senior staff officer, alleged to be from Burma Army, had appeared and ordered it to be destroyed, and so, with the help of the guard, it was. In the growing confusion, mistakes of this kind were almost inevitable, but none the less damaging.

Numbers of V Army Chinese were collected in Mandalay, and attempts were being made to get them away to the north by train. At the same time I was anxious to rescue some of the more important items such as rifles, bren guns, ammunition, medical stores, and boots, without which we could not continue to fight. With this object, two or three small trains were being loaded under the direction of a few stout-hearted British and Anglo-Burmese railway officials who set a magnificent example of devotion to duty. My Chinese of the 38th Division came one afternoon and told me that a certain Chinese general had discovered these trains and was coming that night with his troops to seize them and to escape north. I was in a quandary. I had not enough troops to guard them against the numbers who would appear, nor did I want a fight with our allies. I sent warning to our railway friends and asked them to steam the engines ten miles up the line. In due course the Chinese arrived, piled themselves in, on, and all over the wagons. The general ordered the trains to start. He was then told there were no engines, as on my orders they had all been taken away. There was nothing for my Chinese friend to do but to call off his men and think of some other way of stealing a train. Eventually he succeeded in doing so and got away, but it was not one of my trains. I met him frequently afterwards in India. We never mentioned trains, but I noticed that he regarded me with an increased respect.

The corps, with the exception of 63 Brigade, that still held the approaches to the Ava bridge on the south bank, was now all safely over the Irrawaddy. There had been an anxious moment with the tanks. I found a line of them halted on the south side of the bridge with officers in consultation. A Stuart tank weighs some thirteen tons, and a notice warned us that the roadway running across the bridge on brackets each side of the railway had a maximum capacity of six tons. I asked who had built the bridge and was shown a tablet with the name of a well-known British engineering firm. My experience has been that any permanent bridge built by British engineers will almost certainly have a safety factor of one hundred per cent, and I ordered the tanks to cross, one by one. I confess I watched nervously to see if the roadway sagged under the first as it made a gingerly passage, but all was well. Good old British engineers! At last even the Chinese C.-in-C. agreed that all his men were over, and so 63 Brigade was withdrawn across the bridge. With a resounding thump it was blown at 2359 hours on the 30th April, and its centre spans fell neatly into the river—a sad sight, and a signal that we had lost Burma.

CHAPTER V

EVACUATION

THE whole of the Burma Corps had crossed the Irrawaddy by the Ava bridge and the ramshackle ferries with much less trouble than I had expected. The vigorous Japanese follow-up at Kyaukse was not repeated against the 1st Burma Division farther west, and there, what might have been a very hazardous operation, was interfered with only by air attack. By the evening of the 28th April, the 38th Chinese Division, 7 Armoured Brigade, and the bulk of the 17th Division were in position along the north bank of the river from Sagaing to Allagappa. The 1st Burma Division was also over the river and about to move to Monywa. I made a quick tour of the river line and returned to my headquarters, now in a monastery near Sagaing. I was relieved that the crossing had gone so smoothly and reassured by the condition of the 17th and 38th Divisions.

There was still, however, plenty to cause anxiety. It was clear that, with the Chinese armies in the state they were and with the Japanese pushing so rapidly north on the east of the Irrawaddy, our positions along the river west of Mandalay could not be held for long. Apart from this tactical consideration, the next stage of our long retreat must start soon to avoid the monsoon rains. Our road would run through Ye-u to Kaduma, twenty miles to the north-west, and there it would plunge into the jungle for a hundred and twenty miles until it reached the Chindwin at Shwegyin. For that distance the route was no more, and often less, than an unbridged, earth cart track, with frequent sharp bends, steep gradients, and narrow cuttings. Long stretches, sometimes as much as thirty miles, were completely without water. It crossed several wide stream-beds of soft sand, difficult enough now for vehicles, and, when rain came, likely to be unfordable rivers. When Shwegyin was reached, the track ended and there was a six-mile river journey up-stream to Kalewa. Then came the long trek up the malaria-infested Kabaw Valley, through dense jungle to Tamu to reach the unmetalled road that we hoped was being built from Imphal in Assam. Whatever happened it would be an arduous march; if the monsoon rains came before we had completed it, it could be an impossible one. The consensus of informed opinion was that the monsoon could be expected to start in earnest about the 20th May but, of course, there might well be heavy rain before that.

I was, from what I heard of the route, doubtful if, even without rain, our heavier and bulkier vehicles could be got through. To test this and to discover where the track must be improved, I ordered a reconnaissance party with engineers to take a column consisting of one of each type of large vehicle, tank, anti-aircraft gun, lorry, etc., and go over the route to check its feasibility. Burma Army Headquarters were now working as hard as they could to improve the track and to stock it with supplies and, where needed, with water, while General Headquarters, India, were, we were told, working similarly from the other end. But time was short and the way would be long and hard.

I was sitting outside my headquarters at Sagaing, musing on these things, when I was surprised to see a civilian motor-car drive up and disgorge half a dozen Burmese gentlemen, dressed in morning coats, pin stripe trousers, and grey *topis*. There was a definitely viceregal air about the whole party. They asked to see me. They were a deputation of influential Burmese officials from the large colony who had taken refuge in the Sagaing hills in the bend of the Irrawaddy opposite Mandalay. They submitted a neatly typed resolution duly proposed, seconded, and passed unanimously at a largely attended public meeting. This document stated that the Burmese official community had received an assurance from His Excellency the Governor that no military operations would take place in the Sagaing hills, a locality held in particular veneration by the Burmese people. Trusting in this, they and their families had removed themselves there. Now to their dismay Chinese troops had entered the hills and were preparing defences, even siting cannon. They therefore demanded that I, as the responsible British commander, should order out the Chinese and give a guarantee that, in accordance with His Excellency's promise, no military operations should take place in the Sagaing hills.

90

I was terribly sorry for these people. They were all high officials of the Burma Government, commissioners, secretaries, judges, and the like; their world had tumbled about their ears, but they still clung to the democratic procedure of resolutions, votes, and the rest that we had taught them. They brought me their pathetic little bit of paper as if it were a talisman. When I told them that, as far as I was concerned, I had no wish for military operations in their hills—I might have added truthfully, nor anywhere else at that moment—but that the Japanese general was equally concerned and not likely to be so obliging as to agree, they departed polite but puzzled. The impressiveness of the proceedings was somewhat marred by one gentleman who came back and asked could he not be issued with a six-months' advance of pay? I do not blame him—it would be a long time before he would draw his British pay again.

The only Chinese now left as organized formations were our 38th Division, which was in better state than when it joined us, and the 22nd Division, which had been badly mauled but still held together. I think the 38th Division had enjoyed its time with us, for, as far as supplies, ammunition, artillery, tank support, and transport had been concerned, it had been on the same footing as our other two divisions. This would not have seemed a very generous scale to most armies, but to the Chinese it was luxury. We had developed a real affection for Sun and for the brave, cheerful, uncomplaining rascals he commanded. We had been told that they would remain part of the corps and that we should go out to India together. We were therefore the more disappointed when Stilwell asked for them to be returned to him to act as rearguard to the remaining Chinese struggling north, and General Alexander agreed. Sun would have liked to come with us, but there was nothing for it. He assured me he would not move his division until we were ready, and we arranged to concert our movements as long as we could. 7 Armoured Brigade was also left temporarily as rearguard to the Chinese, but with orders to rejoin us later.

On the 30th April, the 17th Division was still in position along the river bank from Sagaing to Allagappa, but my headquarters had moved back through Monywa, and was now established some miles north of the town, in a grove of trees around a small Buddhist monastery. Monywa itself was garrisoned only by a

91

weak detachment of the Gloucesters, some Royal Marines of the river patrol, and a few Sappers. The town had been quite peaceful as we came through and the civil authorities were still functioning. The headquarters of the 1st Burma Division was encamped four miles south of Monywa, and two of its brigades, 1 and 13, were plodding along the main Sagaing–Monywa road about twenty miles south. These brigades, after crossing the Irrawaddy on the 28th, had been delayed for twenty-four hours by lack of transport and exhaustion. It had been my intention to send one of them across to the west bank immediately on arrival at Monywa to replace 2 Burma Brigade which was under orders to begin its March to the distant Myittha Valley on the night of the 28th/29th April. Very foolishly, although I knew the Burma Division would be at least twenty-four hours late at Monywa, I did not stop the march of 2 Brigade. As a result, the approaches to Monywa on the west bank were left without protection from the night of the 28th/29th. My only excuse was that news was coming in of hostile Burmese gatherings in the Myittha Valley which, especially if some Japanese were with them, could quite easily cut our escape route to India west of Kalewa. Threats were growing in many directions with competing claims on our slender resources. Forgetting the speed with which the Japanese might come up the river by boat, I chose to meet the wrong one, and we paid heavily for my mistake.

We were sitting, after our rather meagre dinner, in the twilight under the trees—Davies, one or two others, and myself. We had just received a visiting staff officer from Army Headquarters, and I was behaving rather badly to him. I was, in fact, telling him what I thought about the 'Blanket' system of administration. I was being quite unjust, because Goddard, General Alexander's chief administration officer, had done an astounding job in circumstances of fantastic difficulty, and in any case the victim before me was not responsible. But tempers were frayed, and one or two things had that day annoyed me—more were going to! So, really enjoying myself, I was relating the administrative enormities that had been perpetrated against my long-suffering corps. At the end of each catalogue of crimes of commission and omission, I said, 'And you can tell Army Headquarters *that!*' My litany was still in full swing when looking up I saw, standing in the gloom, two or three white-faced officers whom I did not know.

'And what do you want?' I asked, still in a bad temper.
One of them stepped forward.
'The Japs have taken Monywa,' he said, 'and if you listen you will hear them mortaring!'
A deathly pause fell on the gathering. Then sure enough, softened by distance but unmistakable, came the *Wump, wump, wump*! of Japanese mortars. The silence was broken by Taffy Davies.
'And you can tell Army Headquarters *that*!' he said.
The situation was a nasty one. We knew that, except for the very small garrison of Monywa itself, the only troops near were the headquarters of the 1st Burma Division just south of the town. Scott's headquarters would have with it only a platoon of Burma Rifles, and we were hardly in any better shape for defence than they were. Something had to be done. Burma Division was called up on the wireless, an officer's patrol sent off at once to investigate, and all available troops were collected. These consisted only of a Burma Frontier Force detachment, the remains of the Cameronians at about the strength of a company, and some Burma Mounted Police—a very scratch force, amounting to about three hundred men. Under the command of the redoubtable Lieut.-Colonel Thomas of the Cameronians, who was by now becoming used to dealing with such emergencies, it was sent down the road with instructions to hold any Japanese as far south as possible. Orders were sent to the 1st Burma Division to concentrate its two brigades, 1 and 13, at Chaungu on the road fifteen miles south of Monywa. At the same time, I ordered the 17th Division to send by rail under cover of darkness 63 Brigade to join the Burma Division at Chaungu. With these three brigades Scott was to advance in the morning and retake Monywa. I also told the 17th Division to send back a brigade as soon as possible to hold Ye-u. The situation as we knew it was reported to Army Headquarters with an urgent request for the return of some, at least, of the tanks which we had left to cover the Chinese. General Alexander immediately sent me two squadrons, one to Ye-u, the other to Chaungu. I then ordered Corps Headquarters to pack.
Having taken all these steps, there was little we could do except wait. It was a toss-up, if the Japanese had really taken Monywa, whether they would turn north or south from the town. If south it would probably be unpleasant for Headquarters 1st Burma

Division; if north, for us. We had the scanty transport of our
headquarters formed up ready to get on to the road, the men
sleeping alongside the vehicles, with our Burmese Defence
Platoon, stiffened by a few British clerks, out as sentry posts. We
had no great faith in the reliability of this Defence Platoon which
had suffered a great deal from desertion. Our doubts were justified; a few days later the whole platoon disappeared in the night.
I tried to get some sleep lying on the hard wooden platform that
had been the abbot's bed in the upper room of the small monastery round which our headquarters was grouped. My thoughts,
listening to occasional distant explosions and the faint chatter of
machine-guns, were not very cheerful. If the Japanese had a force
of any size in Monywa, there was considerable danger that they
had cut me off from almost the whole of my corps. Our timing
had gone badly wrong. I reproached myself bitterly for having
allowed 2 Burma Brigade on the west bank to continue its march.

Actually the Japanese had not at this time taken Monywa,
although we believed they had. The first alarm had come just
after seven o'clock in the evening, when machine-gun and mortar
fire had suddenly opened from the west bank on to the town
river front. Firing continued throughout the night, under cover
of which a party of enemy crossed and established a road-block
between the headquarters of 1st Burma Division and the town.
More Japanese followed, and at 0500 hours on the 1st May a
considerable force including many armed Burmans attacked 1st
Burma Division H.Q. Some Indian Engineers with the British
and Indian clerks and staff officers, under Scott, the Divisional
Commander, put up a stout fight and fell back towards Chaungu.
Several officers and men were killed or wounded; all kit and most
of the equipment of the headquarters were lost, but they succeeded
in getting away their ciphers and secret papers. It says much for
their spirit and toughness that within a few hours they were
functioning again as a divisional headquarters.

Early on the same day several large Japanese naval launches
came up river and embarked six or seven hundred troops from
the west bank. Our small garrison in Monywa opened fire with
every weapon it had and inflicted numerous casualties as the ships
were crossing, but the heavy Japanese artillery and mortar retaliation overwhelmed our few posts on the river front. The enemy
landed, were reinforced, and cleared the town.

During the morning of the 1st May, 63 Brigade arrived by rail, detrained eight miles from Monywa, and at once advanced. They were held up about the old Burma Division Headquarters, where, in a village, the enemy had considerable strength. During the late afternoon one squadron of tanks and 13 Burma Brigade joined them outside Monywa, and 1 Burma Brigade reached Chaungu. The division laid on an attack by all three brigades for next morning.

Meanwhile, reports had been reaching Corps Headquarters confirming the loss of Monywa, the overrunning of Burma Division Headquarters, and the attempted move up-stream by Japanese naval craft. Owing to the break of communication with the 1st Burma Division which continued most of the morning, we had no news of the arrival of their brigades. I decided therefore as a precautionary measure to send back the bulk of Corps Headquarters to Ye-u. After they had left, some excitement was caused by Burma Mounted Police galloping into us with stories that Thomas's force had been overwhelmed by thousands of Japanese. As, however, we were in touch with him by officers' patrols and despatch riders we were not unduly alarmed. I collected about twenty of the policemen and, having told them what I thought of them, I kept them under my eye. However, something called me away, and as soon as my back was turned they had vanished, to become, I suppose, another gang of looters ahead of us.

On the 1st May, General Alexander and Stilwell were both in Ye-u, where my rear headquarters and the headquarters of the 17th Division were arriving. In view of the seriousness of the loss of Monywa, the Army Commander ordered the withdrawal from the Mandalay–Irrawaddy line to begin. He also brought the remainder of 7 Armoured Brigade from the Chinese back to Burma Corps. Accordingly, the 17th Division, less the brigade at Chaungu, was ordered to Ye-u, while Stilwell proposed to withdraw the 38th Chinese Division and remnants of the V Army to Katha and thence probably to India. This was, I think, the last time General Alexander and Stilwell met. That evening I sent the rest of my headquarters, with the exception of a small tactical group, into Ye-u.

The attack by the 1st Burma Division to recover Monywa went in on the 2nd May with two brigades up and one in support.

DEFEAT

One talks of brigades, but they were by now sadly depleted and the whole force did not amount in numbers to much more than one normal brigade group. The Japanese defence was stubborn as our troops fought their way into the town. There was a particularly bitter struggle around the railway station, which changed hands three times. By 1500 hours we were well into the town, thanks to a vigorous attack by 1 Burma Brigade, fighting well after its reconstitution with two Indian battalions. Another Japanese attempt to push naval launches up the river was frustrated by our mortar fire. All was going well when 13 Brigade received a message purporting to be from 7 Armoured Brigade to the effect that a withdrawal to Alon, north of Monywa, was ordered. 13 Brigade passed this to the 1st Burma Division who, after some doubt, accepted it as genuine, and ordered the whole division to pull out. Later it was discovered that the original order was given by an officer of 7 Armoured Brigade who said he had had it from the Army Commander. Communications in the Burma Division were most meagre and they relied to a great extent on relaying via tanks. It must have been in some such way that the message came through and was accepted as genuine. This was not found out until much later, and at the time we all believed that the message was a false one put out by the Japanese, probably using code captured when Burma Division Headquarters was overrun. Disappointing as a withdrawal was, just when Monywa was about to be retaken, the effect was not really great. All transport had already by-passed the town and reached Alon; the rest of the division collected there during the 3rd May, covered by a rearguard and 7 Armoured Brigade. It then moved to Ye-u followed by the enemy, who that night were given a smart rap by the rearguard. The two brigades of the 17th Division from the Irrawaddy reached Ye-u by the 3rd May when the whole corps was concentrated in that area.

We were by this time accustomed to serious situations, but I could not admire too much the coolness with which my staff took every fresh crisis as it rushed upon us. We were faced with one now. The Japanese moving by the Chindwin were clearly making a great effort to cut us off from India. If they forestalled us either at Shwegyin, where our escape track reached the river, or at Kalewa or Kalemyo, they would cut our only road to India. We should then be in a desperate position. It was essential for us

96

to get to all these places first. During the night of 2nd/3rd May, and next day, we pushed 16 Brigade of the 17th Division in lorries down the Shwegyin track as hard as we could to hold all three towns. It arrived in time and put a battalion each into Shwegyin and Kalemyo and two into Kalewa.

My headquarters and those of the 17th Division outside Ye-u were within a couple of miles of one another. During the night of the 3rd/4th May some Japanese parties infiltrated through the covering troops and attacked the 17th Division Headquarters with grenades and light machine-gun fire. An enemy jitter party also made noises and threw grenades round Corps Headquarters, while we, bereft of our defence platoon, stood-to half the night. The proceedings were further enlivened by an agitated British sergeant suddenly dashing into our midst, staggering up to Welchman, my chief gunner, and gasping out, 'The battery's overrun. They're all dead and the guns lost.' He then fainted gracefully but heavily into the brigadier's arms. Of course the battery was all right. The sergeant had been wakened from an exhausted sleep by a bang as someone threw a grenade or firework, and, still asleep, had panicked. Men's nerves were wearing thin. I do not altogether wonder that I said myself at this time, 'If somebody brings me a bit of good news, I shall burst into tears!' I was never put to the test.

Sun from the 38th Division visited me at Ye-u. He would still have liked to rejoin us and come out via Kalewa. I should have been very glad to have him, but I could not give him any encouragement as we both had our orders. He was then anxious, and rightly so, that we should not leave Ye-u until he was well to the north. I agreed to do my best to cover his flank and sent him on to General Alexander, who then ordered me to hold Ye-u until Sun's rearguard was north of Shwebo. I was very willing to do this as, apart from wanting to help Sun, I saw little likelihood of clearing Ye-u and Shwebo, where we had many refugees, including European women and children, and over two thousand wounded, before Sun was away. He was doing a very difficult job and doing it well.

We gave up as much of our precious transport as we could for refugees and wounded, but I am afraid the wounded had a bad journey. There were few ambulances left, and we were compelled to pack the casualties into lorries and a few civilian buses that we picked up. The rough dusty track in these ill-sprung vehicles was a nightmare, and I fear many did not survive.

The 1st Burma Division, with one regiment of tanks, held a rearguard position on an arc south of Ye-u, while the 17th Division moved off to provide lay-backs at Kaduma, the entrance to the jungle track, Pyingaing, known always as Pink Gin, about half-way along it and at Shwegyin. On the evening of the 5th May, the Chinese being then out of Shwebo, we withdrew from Ye-u. Our going was delayed at the last minute by the discovery of a number of wounded who had been overlooked. Thanks to the energy, courage, and resource of MacAlevey, the chief medical officer of the 17th Division, they were got out just in time.

While we were waiting at Ye-u we pushed ahead some of our Sapper units to improve the track, and organized a part of the transport of 7 Armoured Brigade for ferrying troops. We also put in additional water-points, dumps of rations, and evacuating posts for sick, with an improvised traffic control system. Many of the water-course crossings were difficult because of soft sand, and all labour we could collect was turned on to laying corduroy tracks across them. It was as well this was done; otherwise the march, difficult enough, would have been much worse. Corps Headquarters moved to 'Pink Gin'. From there, in order to reduce the congestion at Shwegyin river crossing that was already causing trouble, I sent 1 Burma Brigade, without any vehicles, north-west across country, to strike the Chindwin well north of Kalewa at Pantha, to cross there and make for Tamu. After an arduous march, it arrived on the 16th May. I should have done better had I risked the congestion and sent it to help defend Shwegyin. A scratch force of commando men and two companies of Gurkhas was at the same time sent south-west to the river, where a tributary entered it, to guard against a Japanese attempt to strike inland up the water-course and cut us off.

We now had three major anxieties. First, that the Japanese might cut us off and get a strong force between us and India. Second, that our food supplies might run short. We had been retiring down our line of communication until we got to Mandalay, and it was comparatively easy to draw from dumps or bases en route. Now we were no longer doing this but falling back away from our supplies. We had therefore to move stores long distances and try to build up supplies along the track. We did our best, but were haunted by the fear that we might not have enough in these dumps. As a precautionary measure, rations were still further reduced. Our third fear was the monsoon. This was the worst danger of all. If it came while we were still struggling hundreds of miles from safety, the track would turn to the most glutinous mud, vehicles would be bogged, and all movement practically impossible. Immobilized, we should be in imminent danger of starving. Even a heavy shower or two might have disastrous consequences. The odds were we might escape either the Japanese, the failure of our supplies, or the monsoon, but our chances of avoiding all three were slender. Actually, it was the Japanese who got us first.

To begin with, the withdrawal went reasonably well. 63 Brigade of the 17th Division came through, ferried in lorries. All of the 1st Burma Division passed safely over the Chindwin, its 13 Brigade crossing on the 9th May and marching for Tamu. The division, having by now shed most of its Burmese, besides suffering heavy casualties, was pitifully reduced in numbers. The first echelon of 7 Armoured Brigade arrived at Shwegyin, passed the bulk of its men and some of its wheeled vehicles over, and harboured its tanks under cover along the track to await calling forward as ships became available. The rearguard of the 17th Division, 48 Brigade, and the rest of 7 Armoured Brigade, was at 'Pink Gin', having covered forty miles in thirty hours. To avoid our three enemies, Japanese, hunger, and monsoon, speed in crossing the Chindwin was essential.

But speed was not easy to attain. Shwegyin was one huge bottle-neck. There had been originally six river steamers, each of which would take five or six hundred men packed tight, but not more than one lorry, two or three guns, and a couple of jeeps. Loading was slow from the single rickety improvised pier, which incidentally was submerged by a sudden rise in the river in the midst of our exodus, and had to be rebuilt. There was no direct crossing. Steamers leaving Shwegyin had to proceed six miles up-stream to Kalewa, unload, and return, a round trip of several hours. Nor was there even a cart track on either bank; from Shwegyin to Kalewa everything, except a man walking or a mule, had to go by river. The difficulties of embarkation were greatly increased by the hundreds of derelict civilian cars dumped by

99

refugees, regardless of obstruction, in all the scanty open spaces and approaches to the ferry, and by numbers of Indian refugees hoping to cross the river.

The road to the pier ran for about the last fifteen hundred yards in the 'Basin'. This was a horseshoe-shaped, flat space about a thousand yards wide, mostly open but with small clumps of jungle, surrounded on three sides by a steep two-hundred-foot escarpment, almost precipitous on the inside, but not so steep on the outside slopes which were covered with jungle. From the edge of this escarpment the whole of the 'Basin' was displayed at one's feet. Looking down, one felt it could be a death-trap, and now it was literally full of soldiers, refugees, animals, motor vehicles, guns, and tanks. It was obvious that if we were to get all these to Kalewa we should require the uninterrupted use of all six steamers for several days. Patterson-Knight of the Corps 'Q' staff and several officers from Burma Army Headquarters, left behind for the purpose by Goddard, were working heroically to load steamers throughout the twenty-four hours but, try as they might, it was a terribly slow business. Every gun had to be man-handled on to a deck where stanchions, railings, and fittings seemed specially designed and sited to make stowage difficult. Lorries and trucks had to be manœuvred most delicately; one slight misjudgment and a vehicle jammed on the gangway or hanging into the river might mean hours of delay. I had already ordered only four-wheel-drive vehicles to be shipped; if we were, as seemed likely, only going to get out a portion of our transport we had better have what would be most useful. The embarkation of men was, of course, easy, as they had no kit to worry about except their arms. Before embarking all men had to cut wood for fuel and as they filed on board each man, as if in payment for his trip, threw a log on to the pile for the engine.

Burma Army Headquarters, when organizing the withdrawal of themselves, the administrative units, and refugees that preceded us, had installed Brigadier Ekin with a small staff as area commandant at Shwegyin. This was most helpful as it saved us from having to detach a brigade headquarters from one of the divisions, and gave a much needed continuity of control. The defence of the 'Basin' was not easy as it was surrounded by dense jungle, running, on the outside, right to the top of the escarpment. We had already pushed forward the Gurkha commando detachment to watch the most likely approach from the river. In addition, to prevent the passage of Japanese naval craft, a floating boom had been built from bank to bank about two miles south of Shwegyin, where a battalion and the small Marine flotilla were disposed to cover both sides of the river. The close-in defence of the 'Basin' along the escarpment was entrusted to another Indian battalion, and some detachments. Units were so weak that the defence was thin, but there were almost always troops waiting in the 'Basin' to embark who formed a reserve. We relied on our outlying· defence screen for enough warning to give time to get these into position. To guard against air attack, which was a terrible danger in a place like this, we concentrated all our available anti-aircraft artillery—an amount that in any other theatre would have been regarded as pathetic.

Everyone—staff, Sappers, Marines, Irrawaddy Flotilla officials —was working all-out and considerable progress was being made when on the 7th and 9th May the Japanese put in several heavy air attacks on what must have been an ideal target. Casualties were not as heavy as one would have expected, for the troops by now, without waiting for orders, automatically dug slit trenches, though a good many vehicles were destroyed or damaged. The boom was broken twice, but replaced at night. It was great good fortune that none of the steamers was hit, but the bombing, not unreasonably, proved too much for many of the civilian Indian crews. They deserted in large numbers, and those that stayed refused to bring their ships downstream of Kalewa. We put guards of soldiers on board to force them to work, but it was impossible to prevent the lascars from slipping overboard. It was only owing to the courage of the British ships' officers and of a few stout-hearted Indian subordinates that any of the steamers at all could be got to the Shwegyin jetty. The number of ships and the rate of turn-round both decreased alarmingly.

On the evening of the 8th May, Cowan and his rearguard of 48 Brigade and a regiment of tanks, to avoid the congestion that would have resulted from coming into the 'Basin', halted two miles down the track north-east from Shwegyin. Very wisely on the 9th he sent forward the 7th Gurkhas to reinforce the troops holding the escarpment. The battalion arrived after dark and bivouacked in the 'Basin'.

At my headquarters in the jungle just outside Kalewa I was

very worried at the delays caused by air bombing, and the fear
that either the Japanese or the monsoon would be on us before
we could complete the crossing. Having collected the officer
responsible for river transportation, and assured myself that he had
done all a man could at the Kalewa end, I started off in the dark
by launch early in the morning of the 10th May to visit Shwegyin
and see what could be done there. My A.D.C. and I reached the
jetty at about 0530 just as it was getting light. A steamer was
alongside but loading for the moment was interrupted while the
Sappers repaired the pier damaged by a lorry. Followed by my
A.D.C., I walked across the steamer's deck on to the jetty. Just
as I set my foot on it a stream of red tracer bullets cracked
viciously overhead and at once, from the south side of the
escarpment to my right, a terrific din of rifle, machine-gun,
mortar, and some artillery fire broke out. It was the most unpleasant welcome I have ever had. Obviously something quite
big in attacks was starting and it was already close. What had
happened to our outer defences I had no idea; they must have
been either by-passed or overrun.

I was now by myself, my A.D.C. having decided rather
sensibly that, whatever was happening, I should want breakfast
and that he had better fetch the box containing it. Rather put off
by my reception, I walked up the track from the jetty, past a
number of parked tanks, and turned off right towards Ekin's
Brigade Headquarters. A lot of stuff was coming over, all too
high to be dangerous, but, judging by the noise, just ahead a
proper fight seemed to be developing. I found myself crossing
one of the larger open spaces, where, crouching behind every
little mound and bush that dotted it, were men of the 7th
Gurkhas, the battalion that had arrived the previous night. My
inclination to run for cover, not lessened by a salvo of mortar
bombs that came down behind me, was only restrained by the
thought of what a figure the Corps Commander would cut,
sprinting for safety, in front of all these little men. So, not liking
it a bit, I continued to walk forward. Then, from behind a bush
that offered scant cover to his bulky figure, rose my old friend,
the Subadar Major of the 7th Gurkhas, his face creased in a huge
grin which almost hid his twinkling almond eyes. He stood there
and shook with laughter at me. I asked him coldly what he was
laughing at, and he replied that it was very funny to see the

General Sahib wandering along there by himself *not knowing what to do*! And, by Jove, he was right; I did not!

It is a funny thing how differently the various races react to such a situation. A British soldier would have called out to me to take shelter and would have made room for me beside him. The average Indian sepoy would have watched anxiously, but said nothing unless I was hit, when he would have leapt forward and risked his life to get me under cover. A Sikh would have sprung up, and with the utmost gallantry dramatically covered me with his own body, thrilled at the chance of an audience. Only a Gurkha would stand up and laugh.

But it was no use standing there being laughed at by a braver man than I was. So I went on a little farther to Brigade Headquarters. There I found Ekin and alarm, but no panic. It was clear—only too clear—that somehow a considerable force of Japanese with mortars and infantry guns had got through our outer guard and was now attacking the Indian battalion holding the escarpment in its southern sector nearest the jetty. This attack seemed to be being held—but only just.

What had actually happened, although we did not, of course, know it at the time, was that the previous afternoon some seven hundred Japanese, with guns and mules, had landed from naval craft about eight miles south of Shwegyin. The landing craft had immediately turned round and brought in more during the evening and night. At the same time a larger force had come ashore on the west bank about six miles south. The party on the east bank moved inland to avoid the battalion defending the boom and ran into the Gurkha commando party, whose only wireless set failed to get in touch with the Brigade Headquarters at Shwegyin. For some reason the commander of the party did not attack the Japanese column, but attempted to withdraw, keeping his men between the enemy and the 'Basin'. In the dark, the Gurkhas lost touch with one another and broke up into small groups, which made their way back as best they could. The officer himself was drowned trying to swim the Chindwin to escape capture. Some of his men arrived mingled with the Japanese, others made their way back individually, a large number were lost—and no warning was given.

While I was at Brigade Headquarters a second and heavier attack came in, rather more to the east, and after making some progress was beaten back, but the Japanese were now heavily mortaring the 'Basin'. Their mortar, the equivalent of our three-inch, was their most effective weapon, and they handled it boldly and skilfully. A high proportion of our casualties in most of our engagements came from it. Fortunately its shell was not as powerful or lethal as our own or the effects would have been more serious, but it was unpleasant and trying enough for troops penned in a narrow space. Some time after the second attack, or more probably during it, numbers of Japanese infiltrated between our rather widely spaced posts and got on to the forward edge of the escarpment, dominating the eastern side of the 'Basin'. The Gurkhas, with my old friend the Subadar Major well to the fore, then put in a very spirited counter-attack, right up the cliffs. There followed very confused fighting in which the Gurkhas and the Indians, who were still clinging in places to their positions, savagely clashed with large numbers of enemy in the precipitous jungle around the 'Basin's' edge. The situation was restored, but enemy snipers continually crept forward and made themselves a nuisance. At one moment the Japanese brought up to the rim of the escarpment an infantry gun—the small field-piece that their battalions had—and proceeded to fire at point-blank range. A Bofors gun of an Indian light anti-aircraft battery engaged it and a duel ensued. It was quickly over; the Bofors scored several direct hits on the gun, turned it over, and wiped out its crew. Japanese aircraft flew over frequently, but did not attempt any actual attack, probably because from the air it was impossible in that close fighting to distinguish British from Japanese.

After the Gurkha counter-attack I returned to the neighbour-hood of the jetty to try and get in touch through the tank signals with Cowan and 48 Brigade. I could not get Cowan himself, but learnt he was already on the move towards the 'Basin'. A steamer was alongside the jetty, its skipper, an official of the Irrawaddy Flotilla, holding it there by sheer will-power and courage, in spite of its crew. The twenty-five-pounders of 7 Armoured Brigade were being embarked and as the guns were brought down to the water's edge they were kept firing until the last moment. Wounded were coming down the track in a trickle and being carried on board, while certain administrative troops filed across the gangways. The loading went on steadily, but at the highest pressure, and there was no sign of panic. Even a crowd of about a hundred Indian refugees, cowering in the shelter of a bank, did as they were told and huddled there in mute misery. One poor woman, near the tank from which I was speaking, lay propped against the side of the track dying in the last stages of smallpox. Her little son, a tiny boy of four, was trying pathetically to feed her with milk from a tin a British soldier had given him. One of our doctors, attending wounded at the jetty, found time to vaccinate the little chap, but nothing could be done for his mother. She died and we bribed an Indian family with a blanket and a passage on the steamer to take the boy with them. I hope he got through all right and did not give smallpox to his new family. At the last minute, when the steamer was fully loaded and casting off, I let the rest of the refugees scurry on board, to cling precariously to rails and fill every crevice in the ship. It was no longer possible, as enemy pressure increased, to get ships alongside the jetty. Another and fiercer attack broke into the 'Basin' itself and penetrated towards the track. Everyone who could be scraped up was pushed out to hold back this vital thrust. Patterson-Knight, my 'Q' staff officer, who had been at Shwegyin for some days supervising embarkation and was a conspicuous figure in his exquisitely cut, but by now somewhat soiled, jodhpurs, took a tommy-gun and went into the fray. About an hour later he came back and exchanged the tommy-gun for a rifle, explaining that, 'The little yellow baskets are a bit farther off now!'

Ekin had handed over to Cowan, who had fought his way into the 'Basin', losing his A.D.C. wounded at his side in the process. Thinking with his arrival that this was no place for a Corps Commander and that I should be of more use if I could get some of the ships lying up-stream to come down again, I took to my launch and visited them. Three extremely gallant skippers, two civilians of the Irrawaddy Flotilla (their names, I think, Murie and Hutchinson), and Lieut.-Commander Penman of the Burma Naval Volunteer Reserve, in turn brought their ships inshore a few hundred yards above the jetty, under a cliff which gave shelter from mortar fire. Here they embarked wounded and administrative units for the last trips. After that no crews, whatever their skippers did to induce them, would come downstream again. That was an end to the last chance of getting anything out of Shwegyin except mules and men and what they could carry over the roughest and steepest of paths.

At about 1400 hours a desperate attempt by the 7th Gurkhas to dislodge a strong Japanese party that still held a hill commanding the 'Basin' failed. All embarkation had stopped, and Cowan, who had my authority to do so, made the only possible decision —to get out before more Japanese arriving finally cut him off. Rearguards were laid out covering the track along the east bank, guns were ordered to waste down their ammunition, and all non-essentials started off up the track. At about eight o'clock that evening all guns put down a concentration on the escarpment as the Gurkhas and Indians holding it withdrew. It was by far the heaviest artillery concentration we had put down in Burma; for the first time the gunners were not stinting their ammunition, and they fired all they had in twenty minutes. Under cover of this barrage the last troops passed through the rearguard, leaving the 'Basin' lit by flames and explosions as guns, tanks, and vehicles were destroyed. It was a sad ending to all the effort that had brought them so far, but at this stage it was better to lose material than risk the destruction of the whole force. We had saved about one-third of the guns, and a fair portion of the best mechanical transport, the four-wheel-drive lorries, but the loss of the tanks was a terrible blow. True, they were worn out and in any case obsolete, but even they would be hard to replace in India, and they held such a sentimental place in our esteem for what we owed to them and heir crews that it was like abandoning old and trusted friends to leave them behind.

The march along the track to Kaing, opposite Kalewa, was arduous for weary, burdened men. The path was narrow, in places precipitous and everywhere rough, but the Japanese did not follow up. Their losses had been heavy and they were busy trying to salvage what they could in the smoking 'Basin'. Although we did not then know it, we had fought the last action of the campaign. 48 Brigade and some other units were taken upstream from Kalewa to Sittaung, whence they marched through the hills to Tamu, while the steamers that carried them were sunk to avoid capture. The rest of Burma Corps marched from Kalewa, ninety miles through the Kabaw Valley, well-termed Death Valley on account of its virulent malaria, to Tamu—a grisly march!

While the main body of Burma Corps was suffering these vicissitudes, 2 Burma Brigade, which had withdrawn up the west bank of the Irrawaddy and turned north-west to follow the Myittha Valley, had plodded steadily on. It had several skirmishes with large bands of armed Burmans, but had not been followed by Japanese. The brigade had supplemented its scanty pack transport by locally impounded bullock carts which carried its wounded and sick. Its feelings may be imagined, therefore, when an officer of the line of communication services, retiring ahead of the corps, demolished the only bridge over the wide Manipur River while 2 Brigade was still south of it. The carts had to be abandoned and the brigade with difficulty ferried itself across. It rejoined us at Kalemyo, west of Kalewa, tired, hungry, and angry.

Even then we were not without further alarms. Our greatest danger was that the Japanese coming up-river in their naval craft might land south of Kalewa and, moving across country, cut the track between Kalewa and Kalemyo. Sure enough, one day we received apparently reliable and circumstantial news that the worst had happened. The Japanese, in strength, had established a road-block between Corps Headquarters, then just north of Kalemyo, and our rearguard, a few miles east of Kalemyo. The rearguard was cut off. In one of our few remaining jeeps I at once returned to Kalemyo, where a couple of battalions of the 1st Burma Division were bivouacked. As I looked round the gaunt, ragged men, lying exhausted where they had dropped at the end of the day's march, my heart sank. I thought, 'Nothing can rouse them. They have reached the end of endurance!' Yet, when their no less weary officers called on them, they struggled into their equipment, once more grasped their weapons, formed their pitifully thin ranks, and, turning their backs on safety, tramped doggedly off to another fight.

There was, thank God, no fight. We had not gone far when the officers I had sent ahead to reconnoitre returned and told us that the alarm was false. There were no Japanese and no road-block. A staff officer, seeing from a distance our own troops making a traffic-control barrier across the road, and hearing at the same time the noise of a Japanese fighter strafe in the neighbourhood, had in his tired imagination combined the two into an enemy road-block. The troops were turned about, and, muttering curses on generals who disturbed them without cause, went back to their broken rest. I sent for the officer responsible for the alarm and told him what I thought about him in a way which, I fear, showed that my nerves were little better than his.

Next day we resumed the march. The track through the jungle seemed unending. We had only fifty lorries and these we used to ferry troops forward, but, of course, the bulk did the distance, as they had done so many weary miles, on their feet. In too many cases literally *on* their feet, for their boots had given out. Clothing was in rags, officers and men had only what they stood up in. Beards were common as shaving kit had grown scarcer and scarcer. I had tried growing a beard myself at one time in the retreat when it was becoming rather fashionable, but mine appeared completely *white*, and the probable effect on the troops of having a Corps Commander who looked like Father Christmas was such that I resumed shaving with the relic of a blade.

While Burma Corps had been thus laboriously and perilously making its way back to India, the remnants of V Chinese Army, covered by Sun's 38th Division, fell back from Shwebo to the north. V Army Headquarters with parts of the 22nd and 96th Divisions, after great hardships, eventually staggered out through the Hukawng Valley. Their conduct on this terrible retreat was, perhaps understandably, not such as to endear them to either local inhabitants or fellow fugitives. They seized trains, ejecting our wounded and refugees, women and children, took all supplies on evacuation routes, and looted villages. Their necessities knew no law and little mercy. General Stilwell with the American portion of his headquarters remained at Shwebo until the 1st May when, any further effort to control the V Army being obviously useless, he moved to Wuntho on the railway a hundred miles farther north, with a view to reaching Myitkyina and flying out. There he learnt that he could not reach the airport before the Japanese, and he was compelled to strike west, by car as long as the road lasted, then on foot with some pack transport to the Chindwin about Homalin, and through the hills to Imphal. It was a gruelling march and the party owed its survival to the astringent encouragement of the elderly general himself, who proved the stoutest-hearted and toughest of the lot. His party reached Assam on the 15th May.

Meanwhile, the 38th Division, still intact and now operating without any superior command, followed V Army to Naba, fifty miles north of Wuntho, on the Myitkyina railway. There, learning that it would be impossible to reach Myitkyina ahead of the Japanese, Sun turned south again back to Wuntho, where he met the Japanese now in occupation and had a skirmish. With his 113 Regiment as rearguard he then struck across the hills to the Chindwin at Paungbyin where on the 14th May he collided with a Japanese force coming up the river in the attempt to cut off Burma Corps. He held them off, crossed the river, and reached Imphal on the 24th May. Unfortunately, 113 Regiment of his division was cut off and almost destroyed. Nevertheless Sun's withdrawal was a bold and skilful one and he was the only Chinese commander who brought his troops out, starving and in rags, it is true, but still a fighting formation.

We had already had one or two heavy showers to give us a foretaste of what the monsoon would do to us, when, on the 12th May, it burst in full fury. On that day our rearguard was leaving Kalewa and our main body toiling up into the hills. From then onwards the retreat was sheer misery. Ploughing their way up slopes, over a track inches deep in slippery mud, soaked to the skin, rotten with fever, ill-fed and shivering as the air grew cooler, the troops went on, hour after hour, day after day. Their only rest at night was to lie on the sodden ground under the dripping trees, without even a blanket to cover them. Yet the monsoon which so nearly destroyed us and whose rain beat so mercilessly on our bodies did us one good turn—it stopped dead the Japanese pursuit. As the clouds closed down over the hills, even their air attacks became rare.

A couple of marches south of Tamu we received our first helping hand from India. An Indian mechanical transport company met us, but its recruit drivers had been so scared by the stories fugitives from Burma had told them and by the perils of the half-made road, that many of them would not drive any farther south. When ordered to do so they took their lorries into the jungle and hid. This difficulty was overcome by putting beside each driver a man from 7 Armoured Brigade who saw to it that they went where they were told—a last service of this magnificent formation. Then the company was of inestimable value in ferrying wounded and sick and sometimes whole units forward.

On the last day of that nine-hundred-mile retreat I stood on a bank beside the road and watched the rearguard march into

India. All of them, British, Indian, and Gurkha, were gaunt and ragged as scarecrows. Yet, as they trudged behind their surviving officers in groups pitifully small, they still carried their arms and kept their ranks, they were still recognizable as fighting units. They might look like scarecrows, but they looked like soldiers too.

CHAPTER VI

AFTERMATH

THE men of Burma Corps, when they reached Imphal, were physically and mentally very near the end of their strength. They had endured casualties, hardships, hunger, sickness, and, above all, the heart-breaking frustration of retreat to a degree that few armies have suffered and yet held together as armies. They were, even at the last, as I had proved, ready if called upon to turn and fight again, but they had been buoyed up by the thought that once over the border into India, not only would other troops interpose between them and the enemy to give them relief from the strain they had supported so long, but that welcome and rest would await them.

Instead, they found that the only forces India had been able to provide on this threatened frontier were a single infantry brigade of raw troops, with a promise of the gradual arrival of the remainder of a division. Instead of rest behind covering troops, they were harshly told to do the covering themselves. They did not expect to be treated as heroes, but they did expect to be met as soldiers, who, even if defeated, were by no means disgraced. Yet the attitude adopted towards them by certain commanders and their staffs was that they were only to be dragooned into some show of soldierly spirit by hectoring and sarcasm. Apart from its lack of comradely feeling, this was profoundly bad psychology. How much wiser was the treatment of the troops who escaped from Dunkirk. Their hardihood in the face of great material odds was generously recognized, their courage in retreat and defeat acclaimed; at once they were received as if they had won a great victory, not suffered a disaster. My men had endured a longer ordeal with at least equal courage; they deserved an equal welcome. The one they got, intensely resented by commanders and troops, would have had more serious consequences had it not been for the efforts of Scott and Cowan, the divisional commanders, on one side, and of Major-General Savory commanding the 23rd Indian Division, which provided the troops from India, on the other. Savory was a tough, war-experienced, and successful leader, proved in the Middle East, who understood the handling of men. Although he had troubles enough of his own with his raw division, he was always ready to help the less fortunate troops of Burma Corps, and to his soldierly understanding they owed a great deal.

Savory recognized at once that the fighting troops of Burma Corps, who came out in their disciplined ranks, every man with his weapons but little else, were very different from the hotchpotch of improvised units, rear organizations, non-combatants, civil and military deserters, officerless men, refugees, and riff-raff that had swarmed out ahead of them. Others did not, and my soldiers suffered for the sins of those who had preceded them; nothing could have been more galling to tired, exasperated fighting men, who knew they had done their duty.

If our welcome into India was not what we expected, the comfort provided was even less. As the wasted units marched wearily into Imphal, through the sheets of monsoon rain, they were directed into areas of jungle on the steep hill-sides and told to bivouac there. It seemed to them that no preparations at all had been made for their reception. They had arrived with nothing but the soaked, worn, and filthy clothing they stood up in; they had no blankets, no waterproof sheets, no tentage. Nor did they find any awaiting them. On those dripping, gloomy hill-sides there was no shelter but the trees, little if any clothing or blankets, no adequate water or medical arrangements. As Taffy Davies, indefatigable in labouring to ease the sufferings of our troops, wryly said, 'The slogan in India seems to be, "Isn't that Burma Army annihilated yet?"'

The men were bitter, and who could wonder at it, but it was not fair to criticize too fiercely the material failure of India to be ready to receive us. Imphal was a thousand miles from Calcutta at the extreme end of a most rickety line of communication, stretched to breaking-point. India itself was deficient of everything, and it was impossible to get forward over that distance at short notice what a destitute corps required. The fault was a lack of foresight, months before, when preparation should have begun. Yet here, as everywhere, the frequent changes and divisions in the higher responsibility for the Burma campaign had prevented any smooth, long-term development of Assam as a base for an army. The administrative and medical staffs on the spot made super-human efforts to cope with the tragedy, but they had not a tenth of the resources required. If we had come out of Burma a fully equipped corps, with our proper complement of transport, tent-age, and medical supplies, we might have managed, but we had not. We had practically nothing—even if that, as was pointed out to us, *was* our own fault. Still, the effect of such a reception on tired men, keyed up by the expectation of something very different, can be imagined. Many lost the will to fight longer against the malaria, dysentery, and exhaustion that attacked them. I should estimate that eighty per cent of the fighting men who came out of Burma fell sick, and many died.

Obviously the whole Burma Army should have been sent on leave or to hospital in India as fast as the transportation system would allow. Unfortunately, the slow arrival of reinforcements from India and the possibility of a Japanese advance against Imphal, compelled the retention of the whole of the 17th and of some units of the 1st Burma Division. Actually, although one would not have gambled on it at the time, the monsoon effectively put a stop to any further Japanese follow-up, and the two armies settled down for some months out of touch with one another.

The 17th Division, while very reduced in numbers, was still capable of functioning as a division. The 1st Burma Division had at various stages toward the end of the retreat sent to their homes most of its Burmese. Each man was given his rifle, fifty rounds, and three months' pay, told to go to his village, wait for our return, and be ready to join any organization we should start to fight the Japanese in Burma. These men, mainly Kachins, Chins, Karens, and other hillmen, almost without exception did so, and in due course formed the backbone of the resistance movements that grew in strength as the Japanese occupation continued. Their loss and the casualties its British and Indian units had suffered made it no longer possible for the 1st Burma Division to continue as a division. Its headquarters and the bulk of its remaining units were gradually returned to India and absorbed into the 39th Indian Division, which became a training formation.

Of the 150 guns of all kinds that Burma Corps had possessed at one time, 74 had reached the Chindwin, but of these only 28 had crossed into India. The total mechanical transport of the corps on arrival at Imphal was 50 lorries and 30 jeeps. Our casualties had been some 13,000 men killed, wounded, and missing, besides, of course, those evacuated sick. The Japanese losses had been only a third of this—4,600 killed and wounded. I kept a record of all we had lost in men, guns, tanks, and vehicles. Some day I hoped to balance the account with perhaps a little interest added.

On 20th May, I handed over all my troops to 4 Corps, and Burma Corps ceased to exist. There was then nothing more for me to do in Imphal. I said good-bye to Scott and Cowan and to as many units as I could reach. I had a horrible feeling I was deserting them, and the friendship and loyalty that officers and men showed me when I bade them farewell only made it worse. To be cheered by troops whom you have led to victory is grand and exhilarating. To be cheered by the gaunt remnants of those whom you have led only in defeat, withdrawal, and disaster, is infinitely moving—and humbling.

Burma Corps Headquarters left for India a few days ahead of me. We had handed in all transport, including my own jeep, so I tried to make the journey to railhead at Manipur Road in a civilian refugee car found derelict on the roadside and tinkered into some sort of mobility by my faithful Cameronian body-guard. By luck and with nursing we got it to Kohima, but there its tired engine gave out. We coasted down the hill to within a few miles of the railway where a rise finally stopped us, and we finished the journey ignominiously in a passing lorry. Even then we had a day to wait for a train, as the railway had been bombed and most of the staff had vanished. At last some military railway operating officials arrived with a train which had to stop at the points outside the small junction. A colonel and a major of Engineers, with a couple of senior railway officials, assembled in the signal cabin and an earnest debate took place as to which lever should be pulled to allow the train to enter the station. At last the fateful decision was made. We watched the colonel seize the lever and fling it over with a professional crash. No signal moved, no point shifted. The wires had been cut, and so we never discovered if it was the right lever after all.

I slept sitting up nearly all the long crowded journey to Calcutta, and on to Ranchi in Bihar where Burma Corps Head-quarters had preceded me. I found it pathetically reduced. Malaria had taken a heavy toll, starting with Taffy Davies, and running right through the party. It was a particularly virulent type of cerebral malaria which struck a man down, sent his temperature rocketing into delirium, and often killed him in three or four days. It was noticeable that the older men, the forty-fives and upwards, seemed to suffer less from disease and exhaustion than the younger ones. In fact, almost the only members of my staff to escape hospital were these presumably well-salted veterans. We tried to pretend it was because we were a tougher generation, but it was actually due, I think, to the greater care we took of ourselves, and the greater docility with which we obeyed medical instructions.

I had now an opportunity for a few days to sit down and think out what had happened during the last crowded months and why it had happened. The outstanding and incontrovertible fact was that we had taken a thorough beating. We, the Allies, had been outmanoeuvred, outfought, and outgeneralled. It was easy, of course, as it always is, to find excuses for our failure, but excuses are no use for next time; what is wanted are causes and remedies.

There were certain basic causes for our defeat. The first and overriding one was lack of preparation. Until a few weeks before it happened, no higher authority, civil or military, had expected an invasion of Burma. They were all grievously pressed in other quarters, and what was held to be the comparatively minor responsibility of the defence of Burma was tossed from one to another, so that no one held it long enough to plan and provide over an adequate period. The two great errors that grew from this were the military separation of Burma from India and the division of operational from administrative control. An army whose plan of campaign is founded on fundamental errors in organization cannot hope for success unless it has vast superiority over the enemy in numbers and material. Another fatal omission, springing from the same cause, was that until too late no serious attempt was made to connect India and Burma by road, so that when Rangoon fell the army in Burma was for all practical purposes isolated.

A most obvious instance of the lack of preparation was the smallness and unsuitability of the forces provided to defend Burma. Two ill-found, hurriedly collected, and inexperienced divisions, of which one had been trained and equipped for desert warfare and the other contained a large proportion of raw and unreliable Burmese troops, were tragically insufficient to meet superior Japanese forces in a country of the size and topography of Burma. The arrival of the Chinese adjusted the numerical balance in favour of the Allies, and, if they could have been got up to the front in strength before Rangoon fell, they might, in spite of their lack of almost all the necessities of a modern army, have changed the result. It is perhaps doubtful if, with the transport and supply resources available, their forward concentration could have been achieved; the pity is it was not tried. Even if it had been, the refusal of the Chinese to obey Stilwell's orders would probably have ensured defeat.

The completely inadequate air forces and their total elimination in the campaign were most grievous disadvantages to the Army. Had we, however, had enough well-trained and suitably-equipped divisions I do not think this handicap, serious as it was, would have been fatal; we could still have beaten the Japanese. Nor would a superior air force have enabled us to defeat the Japanese with the troops we had. It would have helped greatly and relieved the Army of a terrible strain, but we had to outfight the enemy, soldier for soldier, on the ground.

In Burma we ought, whatever our strength, to have had one great advantage over the Japanese—we should have been fighting in a friendly country. The inhabitants should have been not only on our side, but organized and trained to help us. They were not. It is easy to say the Burmans disliked British rule and were therefore hostile to us, but I do not think that was actually so. A very small minority was actively and violently hostile. I should estimate it as certainly not more than five per cent—a figure that compares favourably with the number of collaborators in many European countries. These were drawn mainly from the intensely nationalist youth of the towns and the remnants of the old rebels of the 'twenties. Naturally, in a country like Burma, notorious always for its dacoits, they were joined by considerable numbers of bad characters as soon as our defeats and withdrawals gave opportunities for looting. A larger section of the Burmese population was actively loyal as long as it seemed we should hold their native districts, while many of the hill tribes remained faithful to the British at great cost to themselves even during the Japanese occupation. The fact was that to the main mass of the peasant population the invasion was an inexplicable and sudden calamity;

116

their only interest was, if possible, not to become involved in it and to avoid the soldiers of both sides.

Up to December 1941, even the military regarded the likelihood of invasion as remote, so it was not surprising that the civil government did not take comprehensive measures to educate and prepare the population for it. When it became evident that war was imminent, the civil authorities were reluctant to organize evacuation schemes, refugee control, intelligence machinery, the militarization of railways, or anything in the nature of a Home Guard. There was a fear, which seems often to afflict other administrations than the Burman, that if the people were told unpleasant things about an unpleasant situation they might become depressed and panic. As a result, no one was prepared for war and the series of British reverses was a stunning surprise.

The Burmese fighting forces themselves were affected in much the same way as their civilian brethren. They were hurriedly expanded with raw recruits who had no military tradition, and had incorporated in them civil armed corps such as the Burma Frontier Force and the Burma Military Police who were neither equipped nor trained for full-scale war. The position of their families was what really undermined the reliability of the Burmese soldiers, the police, and the lower grades of all the civil services. As we retreated their homes were left in the dangerous no-man's-land between the lines or in the crudely and brutally administered Japanese-occupied territory. Small wonder that many Burmans deserted to protect their families. Indians in the Burmese services, and there were many, were in an even worse plight, for their families not only suffered all the dangers that the Burmese did, but in addition were liable, without British protection, to the savage hostility of Burmans, only too ready to seize an opportunity to vent their hatred. If the families of Indians, Anglo-Indians, and Anglo-Burmese in government employ could have been evacuated to India at the start of the campaign it might have caused some despondency among the local population, but it would have increased the reliability of the Burmese military and civil services very considerably.

In spite of all these disadvantages we could have, if not defeated the Japanese, at least made a much better fight of it with even the small force of reliable troops we possessed, had they been properly trained. To our men, British or Indian, the jungle was

117

a strange, fearsome place; moving and fighting in it was a nightmare. We were too ready to classify jungle as 'impenetrable', as indeed it was to us with our motor transport, bulky supplies, and inexperience. To us it appeared only as an obstacle to movement and to vision; to the Japanese it was a welcome means of concealed manoeuvre and surprise. The Japanese used formations specially trained and equipped for a country of jungle and rivers, while we used troops whose training and equipment, as far as they had been completed, were for the open desert. The Japanese reaped the deserved reward for their foresight and thorough preparation; we paid the penalty for our lack of both.

To me, thinking it all over, the most distressing aspect of the whole disastrous campaign had been the contrast between our generalship and the enemy's. The Japanese leadership was confident, bold to the point of foolhardiness, and so aggressive that never for one day did they lose the initiative. True, they had a perfect instrument for the type of operation they intended, but their use of it was unhesitating and accurate. Their object, clear and definite, was the destruction of our forces; ours a rather nebulous idea of retaining territory. This led to the initial dispersion of our forces over wide areas, an error which we continued to commit, and worse still it led to a defensive attitude of mind.

General Alexander had been confronted with a task beyond his means. He had been sent to Burma with orders to hold Rangoon, presumably because it was obvious that, if Rangoon fell, it was almost inevitable that all Burma would be lost. On his arrival he found the decisive battle of the campaign, the Sittang Bridge, had already been lost, and with it the fate of Rangoon sealed. The advent of the Chinese may have roused a flicker of hope that its recovery was possible, but the loss of Toungoo and the state of the Chinese armies soon quenched even that glimmer. It was then that we needed from the highest national authority a clear directive of what was to be our purpose in Burma. Were we to risk all in a desperate attempt to destroy the Japanese Army and recover all that had been lost? Ought we to fight to the end on some line to retain at least part of Burma? Or was our task to withdraw slowly, keeping our forces intact, while the defence of India was prepared? Had we been given any one of these as our great overall object it would have had an effect, not only on the major tactics of the campaign, but on the morale of the troops.

No such directive was ever received. In the comparatively subordinate position of a corps commander, immersed in the hour-to-hour business of a fluctuating battle, I could not know what pressures were being exerted on the local higher command, but it was painfully obvious that the lack of a definite, realistic directive from above made it impossible for our immediate commanders to define our object with the clarity essential. Whoever was responsible, there was no doubt that we had been weakened basically by this lack of a clear object.

Tactically we had been completely outclassed. The Japanese could—and did—do many things that we could not. The chief of these and the tactical method on which all their successes were based was the 'hook'. Their standard action was, while holding us in front, to send a mobile force, mainly infantry, on a wide turning movement round our flank through the jungle to come in on our line of communications. Here, on the single road, up which all our supplies, ammunition, and reinforcements must come, they would establish a 'road-block', sometimes with a battalion, sometimes with a regiment. We had few if any reserves in depth—all our troops were in the front line—and we had, therefore, when this happened, to turn about forces from the forward positions to clear the road-block. At this moment the enemy increased his pressure on our weakened front until it crumbled. Time and again the Japanese used these tactics, more often than not successfully, until our troops and commanders began to acquire a road-block mentality which often developed into an inferiority complex.

There was, of course, nothing new in this idea of moving round a flank; it is one of the oldest of stratagems, and there were many answers to it. The best answer would have been to do the same to the Japanese before they did it to us, but we, by reason of our complete dependence on motor transport and the unhandiness of our troops in the jungle, could not carry out these hooks successfully in any strength. They were only possible for forces trained and equipped for them. Another counter would have been to have put in the strongest possible frontal assault on the enemy while the flanking force was still distant in the jungle and he was divided. Japanese tenacity in defence and our lack of artillery, however, was such that before our assault had made much progress the flank blow was likely to be delivered. If we could have arranged our forces in more depth we might have held off the hook when it approached the road, but we never had enough troops to allow this. In any case, if we had, we could have employed them more profitably offensively. Lastly, there was at least a partial answer in supply by air, which would, temporarily at any rate, have removed our dependence on the road, but that needed aircraft and we had literally none. Equipped and trained as we were in 1942, we had no satisfactory answer to the Japanese road-block.

The most infuriating thing was that, while we guessed these movements round our flanks were almost certainly going on, we could never get warning of them. Contrary to general belief, these columns did not move fast through the jungle; their progress was steady but slow, almost leisurely. They did not start very early, halted during the midday heat, and allowed themselves ample time to cook before a full night's rest. They took few precautions, often moving in dense columns without protective detachments. For warning of our proximity they relied largely on Burman informers, and for their routes on local guides. Apart from the absence of air reconnaissance and the lack of co-operation of the inhabitants, we felt terribly the want of light, mobile reconnaissance troops, who could get out into the jungle, live there, and send back information. Our attempts to form such units did not have much success. The extreme inefficiency of our whole intelligence system in Burma was probably our greatest single handicap.

As to the two corps commanders, neither Stilwell nor I had much to boast about. His difficulties were greater than mine, and he met them with a dogged courage beyond praise, but his Chinese armies were, as yet, not equal to the Japanese. He was constantly on the look-out for an aggressive counter-stroke, but his means could not match his spirit. He could not enforce his orders nor could his inadequate staff and communications keep touch with his troops. When he saw his formations disintegrate under his eyes, no man could have done more than and very few as much as Stilwell, by personal leadership and example to hold the Chinese together, but once the rot had set in the task was impossible.

For myself, I had little to be proud of; I could not rate my generalship high. The only test of generalship is success, and I had succeeded in nothing I had attempted. Time and again I had tried to pass to the offensive and to regain the initiative and every time I had seen my house of cards fall down as I tried to add its crowning storey. I had not realized how the Japanese, formidable as long as they are allowed to follow undisturbed their daring projects, are thrown into confusion by the unexpected. I should have subordinated all else to the vital need to strike at them and thus to disrupt their plans, but I ought, in spite of everything and at all risks, to have collected the whole strength of my corps before I attempted any counter-offensive. Thus I might have risked disaster, but I was more likely to have achieved success. When in doubt as to two courses of action, a general should choose the bolder. I reproached myself now that I had not.

In preparation, in execution, in strategy, and in tactics we had been worsted, and we had paid the penalty—defeat. Defeat is bitter. Bitter to the common soldier, but trebly bitter to his general. The soldier may comfort himself with the thought that, whatever the result, he has done his duty faithfully and steadfastly, but the commander has failed in *his* duty if he has not won victory—for that *is* his duty. He has no other comparable to it. He will go over in his mind the events of the campaign. 'Here,' he will think, 'I went wrong; here I took counsel of my fears when I should have been bold; there I should have waited to gather strength, not struck piecemeal; at such a moment I failed to grasp opportunity when it was presented to me.' He will remember the soldiers whom he sent into the attack that failed and who did not come back. He will recall the look in the eyes of men who trusted him. 'I have failed them,' he will say to himself, 'and failed my country!' He will see himself for what he is—a defeated general. In a dark hour he will turn in upon himself and question the very foundations of his leadership and his manhood.

And then he must stop! For, if he is ever to command in battle again, he must shake off these regrets, and stamp on them, as they claw at his will and his self-confidence. He must beat off these attacks he delivers against himself, and cast out the doubts born of failure. Forget them, and remember only the lessons to be learnt from defeat—they are more than from victory.

BOOK II

Forging the Weapon

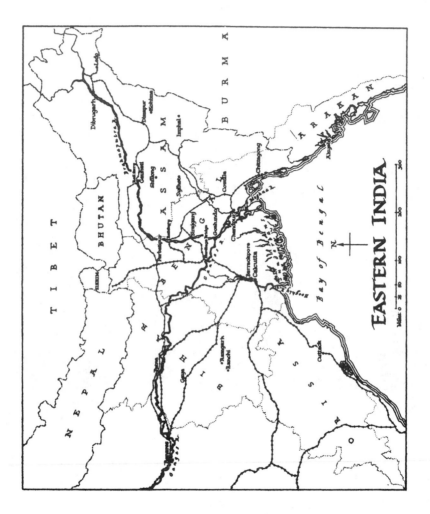

EASTERN INDIA

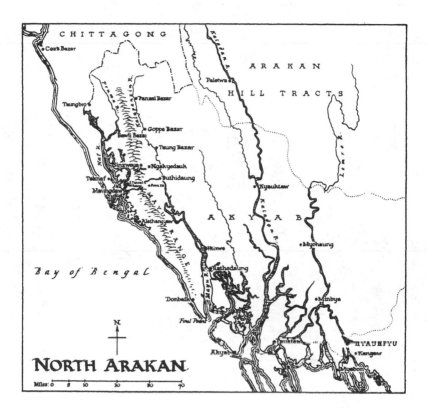

CHITTAGONG

ARAKAN

HILL TRACTS

Cox's Bazar

Paletwa

Taungbro

Panzai Bazar

Goppe Bazar

Bawli Bazar

Taung Bazar

Sinzweya

Ngakyedauk

Teknaf

Buthidaung

Kyauktaw

Maungdaw

Point No

Nhila Tunnel

Razabil

Nathangaw

A K Y A B

Htizwe

Myohaung

Bay of Bengal

Rathedaung

Donbaik

Minbya

Foul Point

Akyab

Myebon

KYAUKPYU

Kangaw

NORTH ARAKAN

Miles: 0   5   10   20   30   40

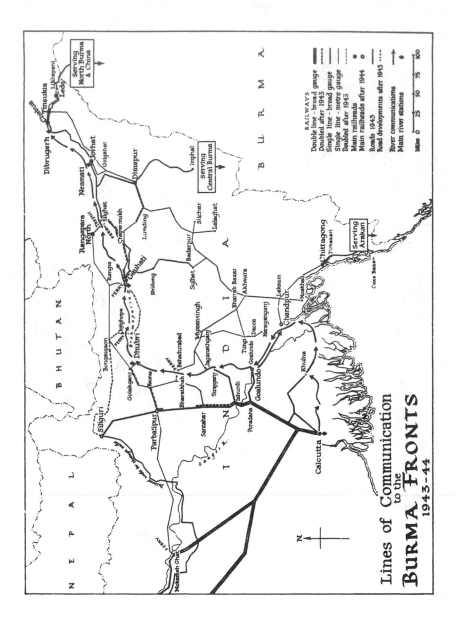

Lines of Communication
to the
BURMA FRONTS
1943-44

RAILWAYS.
Double line - broad gauge
Doubled after 1943
Single line - broad gauge
Single line - metre gauge
Doubled after 1943
Main railheads
Main railheads after 1944
Roads 1943
Road developments after 1943
River communications
Main river stations

Miles 0   25   50   75   100

Serving
North Burma
& China

Serving
Central Burma

Serving
Arakan

BURMA

BHUTAN

NEPAL

INDIA

Ledo
Lekhapani
Tinsukia
Chabua
Dibrugarh
Jorhat
Golaghat
Neamati
Dimapur
Imphal
Rangapara
North
Tezpur
Silghat
Chaparmukh
Rangia
Gauhati
Lumding
Badarpur
Silchar
Lalaghat
Shillong
Sylhet
Bongaigaon
Dhubri
Golakganj
Jogighopa
Bahadurabad
Mymensingh
Jagannathganj
Bhairab Bazar
Akhaura
Leksam
Noakhali
Chittagong
Tezhnazari
Cox's Bazar
Chandpur
Narayanganj
Dacca
Tungi
Goalundo
Khulna
Siliguri
Parbatipur
Amnura
Bharatkhali
Santahar
Saraganj
Teliamura
Teburdi
Goalundo
Poradaha
Calcutta
Mokameh Ghat
Ganges

N

CHAPTER VII

THE THREE V's

APART from my not too cheerful musings on the past campaign, I had little to occupy me for the few days I was in Ranchi, except visits to hospitals. These visits were as depressing as my thoughts. No one had expected the proportion of sick among the returning troops to be so appallingly high. The hospital provision was inadequate. Inadequate in amount, in accommodation, staff, equipment, and in the barest amenities. To supplement the few existing hospitals new ones were being improvised, and hurriedly raised medical units swept up from all parts of India to man them. Schools and other large buildings were requisitioned, the medical staffs arriving barely ahead, sometimes indeed after, a swarm of patients. It was no unusual thing to find a desperate hospital staff frantically organizing the unloading of their equipment and the clearing and cleaning of rooms left by previous occupants in no very sanitary state, while the sick lay on verandas and under trees awaiting admission. I saw many of my staff and hundreds of my officers and men lying grievously sick or wounded, some dying, in the squalid discomfort of these places. It was months before the hospitals of Eastern India reached even a reasonable standard of comfort. That they were able to function at all in the summer of 1942 was due to the superhuman exertions of commanding officers and their matrons and to the devoted, unceasing labour of their staffs, British and Indian. The European civil population rallied to our help. Its women worked in the wards, kitchens, and offices; they opened their homes to convalescents and they made up in sympathy and energy what they lacked in numbers. Their menfolk, nearly all over middle age, left office, tea-estate, mill, and colliery at the end of a full day's work to lend a hand in canteens and rest centres. I have read in English newspapers bitter criticism of the alleged indifference of the British civilian community in India. I can only speak of

Eastern India, but there, from my own observation, I would say British residents, official and non-official, did as much in direct service to the troops as any community of their size in the Empire. It is worth remembering, too, that they were the only community who *asked* for conscription to be imposed on them. There were no other conscripts in India.

At the moment there was little for me to do, so although quite fit, even if a stone or two lighter, I asked for, and got, a couple of weeks' leave. Just as I was off to join my family in Simla, I was ordered to Calcutta to take over the newly formed 15 Indian Corps whose sign, the three V's for fifteen and victory, gives its name to this chapter. I travelled down to Calcutta with General Broad, who commanded Eastern Army, of which the corps was part, and after a hurried take-over entered on a series of fresh tasks and problems.

The situation in June 1942 was an anxious one, likely at short notice to become critical. Eastern Army, with its headquarters at Ranchi in Bihar, was responsible to General Headquarters, India, at Delhi, for the internal security and external defence of all Eastern India, which included, of course, the conduct of the war in Burma. The forces at its disposal were meagre and of necessity spread over a vast area. In Army Reserve, about Ranchi, were the 70th British Division and 50 Armoured Brigade. To safeguard strategic railways and to support the various provincial civil administrations, a number of small garrisons were scattered at great distances from one another. Forward, the Army had two corps deployed to hold the Burma frontier against the Japanese and to safeguard the Bengal–Orissa coastline. 4 Corps, with its headquarters at Imphal in Assam, faced the enemy roughly along the northern portion of this frontier. It contained the newly arrived 23rd Indian Division and what was left of the troops who had come out of Burma in the 17th Indian Division, not yet re-equipped, fever-ridden, and much below strength, but still, wonderful to relate, with fight in them.

South of 4 Corps, in the jumbled mass of forest-covered hills on each side of the Indo-Burmese border, was a gap of nearly a hundred miles before the left of 15 Corps in Arakan was reached. This gap, although quite unguarded, was not at the moment as dangerous as it might appear because the monsoon was in full blast, and even the Japanese at this season could hardly bring any appreciable force through such country. Still, it was a disquieting factor, and would become a real danger when the rains stopped.

To hold the southern Burma front, 15 Corps had only the 14th Indian Division under Major-General Lloyd, who had outstandingly distinguished himself as a fighting brigadier in the Middle East. The division was complete and mobile on a mixed animal and mechanical transport basis, but it was not yet battle-tried and its jungle training left much to be desired. It was concentrated mainly about Comilla, east of the Meghna River, with detachments at Chittagong and a rather nebulous forward line of outposts watching the Japanese. My other division, the 26th Indian, located mostly around Calcutta, had as its tasks the internal security and coastal defence of Bengal and Orissa. It was not then a mobile or battle-worthy division at all, being woefully short of all forms of transport; nor could it, by any stretch of the imagination, be regarded as a trained formation. Besides its two divisions, the corps had a few other combat units, such as the Calcutta garrison, tied to the soul-destroying duties of internal security in a great city. My only armour was one Indian States Forces armoured car regiment.

Two infantry divisions, only one of which was operable, were not much with which to face an increasing Japanese army, to control an uneasy area as large as a major European country, with a population of millions, and to defend against probable invasion seven hundred miles of coast, uncovered by any naval force. The supporting air force, recovering as it was from the disasters of the Burma retreat, was far too small and ill-equipped to meet the demands that might be made on it. Help, if it came at all, would not be great, and it might take some time to come—gloomy thoughts that could only be dispelled by action.

In the steamy heat I began, with my Chief of Staff, to assess my three tasks. The first, the southern Burma front, did not present an immediate anxiety. The Japanese Army seemed as little prepared as we were to advance during the monsoon, and we might reasonably look for a breathing space, during which we could build up the 14th Division for a limited offensive after the rains. The internal situation, my second responsibility, was not, however, reassuring. The Congress Party, by far the most powerful political party in India, was rapidly working up anti-Allied feeling.

It not only urged all Indians to refrain from the war effort, but its agents conducted a campaign against recruiting, and attempted to suborn sepoys from their allegiance. Many of its leaders seemed to have the naïve idea that, if the Japanese Army were allowed to enter India, it would at once set them up as the Government and gracefully withdraw, leaving India to the Indians, or rather to the Congress. The fate of half China was not held to have any bearing on the matter. The Moslem League, the next most important political body, a little more realistic, did not adopt an actively hostile attitude, but, rather shamefacedly, refused co-operation in defence. The immediate results of all this were not serious; recruiting and the loyalty of Indian troops were not affected. There was, however, developing in the civil population of Eastern India, a restlessness, which, fanned by fantastic rumours and worked on by unscrupulous propaganda, might at any time break out in violence. In the event of invasion, there would be an extremist minority which would take every advantage of the inevitable panic to hamper and confuse the Allied defence and to aid the enemy. The Non-Congress Government of Bengal, a coalition of Indian politicians, would on the first signs of Japanese invasion have collapsed. It showed the feebleness of its moral and administrative standards in the terrible famine that afflicted Bengal shortly afterwards. The fact that all our communications to the Burma fronts ran for hundreds of miles through Bengal and Bihar did not lessen anxiety, which remained and mounted, but was not immediate.

As things appeared then, it seemed to me that the most serious danger, and the one we were least prepared to meet, was invasion from the sea. The Japanese could send a battle fleet into the Bay of Bengal, secure in the knowledge that we had no naval forces of any size nearer than East Africa, and that even these were incapable of challenging it. Our air forces would be hard put to it to meet a concentration of enemy land planes based on the Burmese airfields, especially if the enemy added a carrier force at sea. The monsoon made landings on open beaches too hazardous, but the coast is so indented that quite large vessels might in places steam some distance inland before disembarking troops, while the Japanese in China had shown a disconcerting ability to land in places and at times that our experts had declared impossible. In any case, there would be favourable conditions for a large-scale attempt as soon as the monsoon subsided, and we were in no state to meet it.

The most likely Japanese approaches were a landing at the mouth of the Hoogly with a direct thrust at Calcutta, or infiltration through the Sunderbans, which if successful would cut off our forces in Assam and threaten Calcutta from the rear. The Sunderbans, a complicated delta of waterways through which the combined Ganges and Brahmaputra, on a front of two hundred miles, reach the sea, was an invitation to amphibious penetration. The 26th Division had neither troops enough to hold even the main channels nor road or water transport enough to make mobile a useful striking force. In addition, our intelligence system here was extremely weak. We depended on civilian coast watchers, who, however willing, were most inadequately trained to identify either ships or aircraft. There were no telephones in most of the area, and reports, hurriedly written in imperfect English, went by boat or runner to the nearest civil telegraph office. There, the local telegraph clerks transmitted them to Calcutta and they were eventually delivered to my headquarters. No wonder that delays and mutilations were common. The last straw was when a sweating messenger arrived at the telegraph office with a report of alleged hostile shipping, only to be told that, as it was Sunday, and he had not the extra fee with him, the signal could not be sent. With our shortages of signalling equipment and lack of trained personnel, what was surprising was not that these things happened, but that we had a watching organization that worked at all. As its strength grew, we relied more and more for warning on the R.A.F., and the chance of any large collection of ships approaching unreported steadily lessened. But the risk of the Japanese coming, observed or unobserved, remained.

There were two answers to the problem of the Sunderbans—an overwhelming air force or a flotilla of river craft. The first was, at this stage, out of the question, so we fell back on the second. We turned to the Navy. Our requests followed a descending scale. We asked first for a force of light naval craft. It was regretted they were not available. A few coastal motor-boats? The same answer. All right, we would provide the ships; but could we have some naval officers and ratings to man them? Alas, not one. Finally, with memories of the gallant detachment

I had in the Retreat, we asked for a few Royal Marines. None could be spared. So we settled down to raise our own navy. We based its organization on three functions:

(i) Reconnaissance—fast, light motor-boats.
(ii) Fighting—small steamers as heavily armed and protected as we could make them.
(iii) Support—several larger steamers, enough to carry up to a brigade group to land and form road and river blocks.

Few, if any, of the river craft we obtained were really fitted for their roles. Most were old, worn out, and generally ill-found. It often seemed a toss-up which would happen first—their cardboard-thick boilers blow up or rock loose on their seatings and go through the fragile sides of the ships. Nevertheless, based on the existing Army Inland Water Transport Service, which carried supplies on the rivers, we formed our fleet of over a hundred vessels.

We manned it by enrolling the civilian crews of the ships in the I.W.T.; a process that only partially turned them into disciplined Servicemen. Our officers were volunteers, merchant seamen, amateur yachtsmen, marine engineers of sorts. These, with the stalwarts already in the I.W.T., formed the navigational crews. For manning the armament and for signalling, we fell back on the medieval expedient of drafting soldiers on board. We found an ideal commander for our flotilla, Lieut.-Colonel Featherstonhaugh, a Regular soldier, who had sailed before the mast, got a coastal mate's certificate, and had his wings as an airman. He had led commandos in Norway and was just the man to handle such a military-nautical set-up and, it must be confessed, the sometimes queer types that gravitated towards it. The main armament of our fighting ships was the two-pounder anti-tank gun; for anti-aircraft defence we relied on Bren guns. Dockyard maintenance, a big item in so decrepit a fleet, was undertaken by workshop companies of the I.W.T. which we established at various river ports. They did noble work, but lacked much essential machinery. For major repairs, we had, therefore, to rely on civil firms in Calcutta.

In spite of all difficulties, we were able, in July 1942, to stage a grand combined exercise with the flotilla and the R.A.F. Our fleet, steaming down the winding channels to the sea, was an impressive sight—especially its smoke. At the conclusion of the exercise we felt that, combined with the fighters of the R.A.F., our flotilla gave us a reasonable hope, not only of discovering Japanese infiltration, but of seriously delaying and even checking it. The spirit of its men was that of the young soldier ship commander who sent the signal, '*Large Japanese submarine reported off mouth of Meghna River. Am proceeding to sea to engage.*' His heaviest armament was a two-pounder, his speed, with the safety valve screwed down, eight knots, and his rickety river steamer was never meant to venture to sea, least of all in the monsoon. The submarine would do eighteen knots on the surface and have a four-inch gun. But he went to look for it! Later the officers and men of the flotilla gave many examples of high courage and initiative in Arakan. When the time came for serious landings on that coast, however, more orthodox forces were available. All the same, we were proud of our flotilla; anyway it was *ours*—no one had helped us much in the making of it.

To prepare for invasion there was a great deal to be done besides raise our flotilla. The rather primitive coastal batteries defending the Hoogly had to be made and kept as ready as chronic shortages of equipment would allow. There was a vast amount to be done in co-operation and liaison with the civil authorities and provincial governments. Above all, we had to press on with the training of the troops, especially with that of the 26th Division, and with improving its mobility. We passed full days and some anxious nights when scares of invasion called us from our beds. We know now that the Japanese never seriously contemplated a seaborne invasion of India, but at the time it loomed constantly over us. Other British commanders have devoted energy and resources, badly needed for what would have been more profitable enterprises, to preparations against invasions that never came, yet who knows to what extent rumours of those preparations, exaggerated probably, caused the enemy to hesitate? There can be no doubt that the preparations themselves, and the determination they bred, did much to raise our morale. It is a simple rule that the worse the situation the more the troops should be kept fully and actively employed.

A first step was to get my headquarters out of Calcutta to Barrackpore, a suburb a few miles farther up the Hoogly. Here we installed ourselves in Government House, Lord Wellesley's country residence. The site itself, with a spacious Georgian house, supplemented by huts and bungalows in the park, was a good one, although its approach from Calcutta was through some of the most sordid slums it has been my misfortune to see or smell. Indeed, the horrible thing about Calcutta was the contrast of the blatant wealth of some of its citizens with the squalid misery, beyond mere poverty, at their very doors.

My headquarters was the successor to the old Presidency and Assam District Headquarters, which in various forms had functioned in Calcutta Fort since the days of Clive. As I watched the loads of files, books, and papers being moved, I could well believe it. When I looked at some of the staff, too, I realized that it had indeed been a static headquarters. It is hard to ask men, whose lives had for years been a matter of routine, to change not only the tempo of their work but their whole scale of values in it. Some can and do. Then their experience and their sense of duty are invaluable. Some cannot. The only thing then is to find some niche where they can still be useful; a mobile, live, fighting head-quarters is no place for them. Once again, through no merit of my own, I was fortunate in the Chief of Staff I inherited. Brigadier Tony Scott, with his judgment, energy, and dash of the dramatic, was just the man to act as yeast in a rather lumpy headquarters and get it moving, physically and mentally.

We shared Government House, Barrackpore, with Air Head-quarters for Bengal and Burma. The A.O.C. was responsible for the whole of Burma and Eastern India; I dealt only with Bengal, Bihar, Orissa, and the Arakan front. He should therefore, by rights, have been with Eastern Army who were responsible for the same areas as he was, not with 15 Corps. However, the arrangement suited us admirably, and we began at once to build up the close and friendly co-operation that was a marked feature of later operations. Soon after our arrival, Air Vice-Marshal Bill Williams was appointed A.O.C. He was an inspiring commander for his own Service and an understanding and unselfish colleague to us. I never quite shared his belief that, owing to the success of air action, every Japanese soldier was already starving, but there is no doubt Bill Williams was the man who laid the foundations of the air supremacy we later gained, and on which everything else was built.

Although we had moved our headquarters from Calcutta, the city remained for us a fourfold problem. We had to:

(i) Ensure its tranquillity.
(ii) Defend it from land, sea, and air attack.
(iii) Organize it as the main base of the Burma war.
(iv) Clean it up and make it a proper leave centre for British, American, and Indian troops.

At the moment, the swarming city was peaceful enough, but, apart from the eternal communal tension between Hindus and Mohammedans, the activities of the Congress Party were almost certain to lead to disturbances. All this meant constant vigilance and the tying down of troops that were needed to get on with the war. The only defence, apart from a few anti-aircraft and coastal guns, against sea or air attack was the R.A.F., whose fighters used the wide roads of the Calcutta Maidan, or Park, as their runways. If invasion occurred, the city would be one of the enemy's first objectives. Our plan was to hold the Japanese advance with the 26th Division and the flotilla, until the Eastern Army reserve from Ranchi, and anything else that could be raked up, came to fight the decisive battle. Movement would be complicated by hordes of refugees, estimated to number three millions, and plans had to be made to deal with them.

There had been one incursion of Japanese naval forces into the Bay of Bengal, when we had lost a large number of merchant ships. Alarms were frequent, usually at night, and we had our anxious moments. So thin was our defence at this time that full arrangements were made to destroy, if necessary, the many installations in Calcutta that would have been invaluable to an invader had they fallen intact into his hands.

The organization of Calcutta as a base was the responsibility of G.H.Q. India, but, as the local formation, much of the actual work fell on us. A first essential was to keep the docks working. Not so easy, when the smallest Japanese raid sent the dock labour streaming back to its villages. Almost equally urgent was the need to expand and convert to war purposes the industrial resources of Eastern India. From Tatas, the largest and at this time the most modern steel works in the British Empire, to the smallest Bengal workshop, the hum of industry was rising to a crescendo. It was the 'Box Wallahs', the commercial community, who in those hot, anxious months by their energy, efficiency, and above all by their calmness, turned Eastern India into a base and workshop not only for Burma but for the Allies in every theatre of South-East Asia and the Middle East. They deserved well of their country and of India; if they made a profit, they earned it.

The modern British or American Serviceman is a townsman, and, especially after a spell in the jungle, he yearns for the once familiar distractions of the city. Calcutta alone in Eastern India could offer these. It had cinemas, restaurants, and clubs equal to those of the great cities of Europe, but it offered also less reputable relaxations, running down the whole scale of vice from doubtful dance halls to disease-ridden dens of perversity. The problem was to provide wholesome amusements in such abundance that the soldier would not be lured into these darker by-ways. In this we got no help from home; we were thrown back on our own ingenuity and on what the civilian community could do to help us—and that, considering their limited resources, was a great deal. To them we owed our first theatrical companies, who performed for us when the stars of Ensa were as distant and aloof as their celestial counterparts. They ran, too, leave hostels—the one at the race-course was a model—supper bars, clubs, lectures, dances.

Parallel with these activities, we conducted an energetic campaign to clear up the worst of the plague spots. British and American Military Police—there was a rapidly increasing influx of American Air Force and administrative units—co-operated closely with the Calcutta Police. The work of the joint Anglo-American police patrols was effective and not without a humorous aspect. During a fracas, involving both British and American soldiers, one such patrol sailed into the mêlée and sorted out each its own nationals. One American G.I., however, proved particularly truculent. A burly American policeman drew his night-stick, removed the soldier's cap, and slugged him hard on his bare head. As the man subsided unconscious to the floor, the policeman carefully replaced the cap. 'Why,' asked an admiring British colleague, 'did you take off his cap? The way you hit him it wouldn't have mattered if you'd left it on!' 'Say,' was the reply, 'that hat is the property of Uncle Sam. Don't you respect Government property in the Royal British Army?'

For some time the statistics of venereal disease and of absence without leave were high in Calcutta, but, with increasing speed, the tightening of our discipline and the close alliance of the Army with all decent elements in the city brought about improvement. It was not so very long before Calcutta was reasonably satisfactory as a leave centre.

The training of the formations in Bengal and of their staffs was pushed on at high pressure, under conditions more suitable to ducks than to men. Mobile columns were formed and exercised, some of them in boats, and tactical schemes carried out. Many of the Indian units were newly raised, several from races that had no tradition of military service and could not, therefore, provide their own N.C.O.s or Indian officers. For the bulk of the British troops this was their first experience of India, and there are better introductions to the glamorous East than being marooned in mildewed Bengali towns and dumped in sodden paddy fields. They took it all very well, and I wish I could have been easier with them, but they had to be trained. I am afraid, also, that a number of commanders and staff officers for various reasons failed to make the grade, and were removed. They took that very well too.

I was, of course, much occupied simultaneously with current operations in Arakan, and with preparations for an advance, but what befell there I leave to the next chapter. In July, however, Lieut.-General Irwin, who had succeeded Broad as Eastern Army Commander, told me that he wished himself to exercise direct control of the forthcoming Arakan offensive, and for this and other reasons his headquarters and mine would shortly change places. He would take direct command of the 14th and 26th Divisions, and I should form and train a new 15 Corps at Ranchi. Whether it was wise to eliminate a corps headquarters in the chain of command to the Arakan I doubt, but Barrackpore was certainly a better location for Army Headquarters. It put the equivalent land and air commands together, and was an incomparably better communications centre.

Before the date of our move arrived, internal trouble, so grave as to be in effect an organized rebellion, broke out in Bengal and Bihar. The Cripps Mission had ended in failure, and Gandhi had proclaimed civil disobedience throughout India with the avowed object of driving out the British. No government at any time, and certainly not in war, with the enemy at its gates, could ignore such a challenge. Gandhi and the Congress chiefs were arrested

135

and imprisoned, but their subordinate leaders plunged into the struggle, translating Gandhi's order 'to do or die', in the only way they understood—incitement to violence. Widespread disturbances broke out. In Calcutta, the students, joined by the large numbers of hooligans always ready to take advantage of any weakening or preoccupation of the forces of order, came into the streets and serious rioting began. One of the first symptoms was, as is usual in a Calcutta riot of any kind, the burning of trams. More annoying to us were the attacks on Government motor transport, attempts to decapitate motor-cycle despatch riders by stretching wires across roads, and the cutting of telegraph and telephone cables. At first it looked as if we might have really serious trouble in the city, but when the rioters realized, as they quickly did, that the troops were not prepared to stand as Aunt Sallies under showers of bricks but would hit back, they revised their ideas. With practically no casualties among the troops and very few indeed among the rioters, the disturbances in Calcutta petered out.

Those in the countryside were much more serious. Here, especially in Bihar, they took the form of concerted attacks on strategic rail communications. Large gangs, numbering often several hundreds, armed with primitive but effective weapons and some fire-arms, assaulted railway stations all over the country. Signalling instruments were destroyed, station buildings burned and looted, lines torn up over considerable distances, and European passengers dragged from trains to be hacked to pieces. The flow of supplies to the Burma front was cut off for days at a time, the large cities of Patna, capital of Bihar, and Gaya were isolated, and Calcutta itself was left little better off. Requests for troops to restore order and reopen communications flowed in from all sides. The police in many districts were besieged in their own police stations; large areas passed out of control of the civil authorities.

The urgent need was to reopen the main railways so that we could move troops as required to deal with the disturbances and restart supply to the Burma front. Eastern Army wisely relieved 15 Corps of responsibility for most of Bihar, and the British 70th Division, scattered through the worst areas of that province, quickly began to restore the situation. We, with all Bengal and Orissa left as our responsibility, had to bear in mind the possibility that the rebellion was concerted with the Japanese and that an invasion might be attempted simultaneously, or at least some desperate airborne support given to the rebels. There was no definite indication of such a link up between Congress and the Japanese, but the public utterances of its leaders and the systematic wrecking of strategic communications lent colour to the idea. Enough, at any rate, to make us hesitate to disperse all the 26th Division in detachments to restore order. So it was with one eye on possible Japanese intervention, that we proceeded to clear up our area. Before we had finished we were reduced to any expedient to get more troops. First we emptied reinforcement camps, improvising units from the soldiers in them. Then those in convalescent depots were turned out to replace fit men in more static defence duties. When my last available battalion had been sent north of the Ganges to reopen the railway to Assam—and incidentally itself been cut off with the line both ahead and in rear of it uprooted—I was reduced to the expedient of forming my final and only reserve from the venereal patients in the Calcutta and Barrackpore hospitals. A route march or two, and guard duties, had a very good effect on them.

After an anxious two or three weeks, the situation in Bengal was well in hand, although that in Bihar was still far from happy. The Japanese had made no move, for in actual fact they had heard little or nothing of the disturbances until long afterwards. It would have been a great relief to me to have known that, but at the time, I am afraid, we rather overestimated the efficiency of the Japanese intelligence. By the end of August we were able to carry out our exchange of locations with Eastern Army Headquarters, and we moved to Ranchi without incident.

The Ranchi plateau was almost ideal for the training we needed. Its climate was vastly preferable to the steaming heat of Bengal, malaria was much less, and the tawdry distractions of Calcutta were absent. There were great areas of jungle, wide stretches of more open country, and rivers and streams of all sizes. Here, as the first instalment of the new 15 Corps, we took over the 70th British Division, 50 Armoured Brigade, and some corps units. The division was still spread about Bihar dealing with the rebellion, which, though it kept on flaring up in odd places, was coming increasingly under control. The civil administration of the province had been badly shaken. While some of the district officials had tackled a most alarming situation with resolution, others had allowed their areas to slip completely out of their grasp. The police, too, on whom so much depended, gave me the impression of having been grievously neglected. Even their uniforms were in such a state that I gave them some hundreds of pairs of khaki shorts. A policeman with his shirt showing through the seat of his trousers is at a disadvantage in his attempts to uphold the majesty of the law. Apart from this the lot of the Indian policeman was a particularly unhappy one. He was called upon to suppress and jail the very people whom he shrewdly and rightly suspected would tomorrow be the Government and have absolute control of his and his family's fate. The astonishing thing is, not that there were some mutinies and troubles in the police, but that so many remained true to their salt.

Gradually the rebellion subsided into sporadic attacks on isolated stations and attempts to derail trains. A practical preventive to these outrages was found by enforcing village responsibility under which the inhabitants living along the railway guarded their own local stretches of line. They were willing to do this provided there were troops in the neighbourhood and that they were rewarded promptly for any success they achieved. British soldiers, as usual, proved the best of peace-makers. In spite of one or two nasty incidents in which a few of them were murdered, they kept their tempers admirably and were soon on good terms with the population. Civil power was slowly re-established, still rather shaky in places, and the 70th Division collected again for training.

Meanwhile, we had really got down to training ourselves—the Corps Headquarters. As a battle fighting headquarters it was neither mobile nor efficient, and we had to make it both. I think we got most fun from making it mobile. First we had to make the individuals who composed it, staff officers, signallers, cooks, clerks, mess waiters, and menials, themselves mobile. Physical training started the day, with route marches increasing in length and toughness as time went on, varied by a little brisk drill under selected instructors from the 70th Division. At first, protests, mainly from the Indian clerical establishment, were indignant and vigorous. Our worthy *babus* averred that:

(1) In many years of honourable service they had never been subjected to such an indignity as parades.

(2) The drill instructors were harsh men who used rude words.
(3) The exhaustion consequent on these warlike goings-on rendered them incapable of performing their clerical duties.
(4) If compelled to continue this violent exercise, all the internal organs of their bodies—enumerated with unblushing detail—would cease to function and they would indubitably die.
(5) Their boots would wear out.

On the third morning before a route march the whole of the Indian clerks of one section of the headquarters paraded sick, complaining of divers obscure but incapacitating aches, pains, and distresses. I told the doctor attending them that, whatever was or was not the matter with them now, I relied on him to see that they really did feel ill within the next couple of hours. What dismal drench he administered I do not know, but, pale and shaken, they were on parade next morning. When I asked how they felt and inquired whether they would not like to see the doctor again, they assured me most earnestly that they were in no further need of medical attention.

It had been vividly impressed on me during the Retreat from Burma that in the jungle there are no non-combatants, so, with this physical toughening, we introduced weapon training for everybody. The whole headquarters from the Corps Commander downwards went through qualifying courses in rifle, pistol, Bren gun, bayonet, mortar, and grenade. I was not much good with the Bren gun, but kept my end up with the other weapons. My Gurkha orderly, Bajbir, when I ordered him to parade at the rifle range protested:

'What *me*!'

'Yes, you.'

'Me! On a *range* to shoot at a paper *target*?'

'Yes, on a range, at a target.'

'But I've killed *five* Japs!'

All the same he paraded with the rest of us. He was a superb shot, and, having scored near possibles in all positions, at all ranges, and with all weapons, he was mollified by being made an instructor.

After the first month there were no attempts to avoid parades, and everyone took a pride in toughness and soldierly skill. The efforts of some, handicapped by nature and years of soft and sedentary living, may have been pathetic, but they were gallant. As one of the British N.C.O.s said of a *babu*, "Is feet's horful, sir, but 'is 'eart's all right!' The physical effect on the men was plainly noticeable; not only did they look cleaner, fitter, and healthier, but they moved with the brisk and confident carriage of men sure of themselves. We began to get a very good feel about headquarters.

Having got the individuals mobile, it remained to achieve the mobility of the headquarters as a unit. The first step towards this was to limit the number of lorries allotted to each section for its baggage, tentage, office equipment, and messes, to an essential minimum. Heartrending appeals to increase these allotments were sternly refused. The next step was to order everything to be packed in 'yakdans', those leather-covered boxes, fitted with rings and chains, that can be slung one on each side of a pack saddle. This ensured that, not only was no superfluous equipment carried, but that all the impedimenta of Corps Headquarters could, without repacking, be loaded at once on to either trucks, boats, aeroplanes, or even mule transport. We were, I knew, likely to use all these, and change rapidly from one to the other. The accumulation of paper at any headquarters has to be seen to be realized. Every fortnight each section was ordered to sort its papers and destroy everything not essential. My order, rigidly enforced, was, 'When in doubt, burn.' We constantly practised moving until the drill for it was thoroughly mastered; we could pack in a couple of hours and open up a properly camouflaged working headquarters in the bush in less. A large part of headquarters I kept permanently in tents and we frequently moved out into the jungle for several days at a time. At last, even Tony Scott was compelled to admit we were mobile. If we were, it was largely thanks to him.

Making ourselves mobile, essential as it was, was only one step towards being operationally efficient. Most of our junior staff officers were only partially trained, our clerks had a lamentably low standard of efficiency, our mess staff left much to be desired, and our signals needed a great deal of attention. Courses were held for staff officers, classes for clerks. Those of us who had wives in India were able to get them to Ranchi, and they at once set to work, in hospitals, canteens, or at any job required, including instruction in shorthand and typewriting.

The operational efficiency of our organization was based on two nerve centres—the War Room and the Information Room. In the War Room, where the Second Grade Operational Staff Officer reigned supreme, there were throughout the twenty-four hours always on duty an operational and an intelligence officer. The War Room had also, either present or at immediate call, an administrative staff officer and a Royal Air Force representative. All signals both in and out came straight to the War Room, where one copy was posted on the appropriate board, others went direct to the branches of the staff concerned for action, and, unless really secret or not of general interest, a final copy went to the Information Room. Admission to the War Room was, of course, restricted to the principal staff officers and heads of branches, who could at any time bring themselves completely up to date on the situation and the activities of other departments from the signals and the marked maps. The Information Room, on the other hand, was open to all ranks. It was divided into two sections, one dealing with the operations of the corps, and its immediate neighbours, the other with more distant fronts and the war in general. It played a large part in keeping even the most subordinate in touch with events. I had long ago decided that any risk of leakage from such a source was more than outweighed by the increased keenness and intelligence developed by this feeling of being in the know. There was nothing very original in any of this, although we had to work out most of it for ourselves by experiment. We tested our system pretty thoroughly in exercises and manœuvres and assured ourselves it worked. I doubt if any headquarters ever had harder or more intensive training, and I am sure no body of men could have responded to it more wholeheartedly and effectively. Within three months we were a mobile and efficient fighting headquarters, very different from the static and rather stodgy crowd who had left Calcutta.

As the 70th Division, under Major-General George Symes, reassembled around Ranchi, I was able to get to know it well. It was one of the best British formations I have met, with a magnificent battle-hardened spirit gained in the Middle East. It was a tragedy that it was never allowed to fight in Burma as a division. I found also in Ranchi many of the Indian units that had been in the 1st Burma Division of the Retreat, now formed into the 39th Indian Division. Not long afterwards, however, this division

was taken from 15 Corps to become a training division. We had,
too, a Special Training brigade used to test new organizations and
tactics suggested by the experiences of 1942. It had a battalion of
Indian infantry mounted on ponies and another in jeeps, in the
attempt to solve the problem of jungle mobility. Eventually it
abandoned its experimental role and joined a normal division.
50 Tank Brigade, equipped with Valentines, was the corps
armoured formation, and I liked the look of it very much. With
these four formations, and an increasingly alive Corps Headquarters, we began serious training.

This training was based on a short memorandum I had drawn
up, giving what I considered to have been the tactical lessons of
the 1942 campaign. The chief of these were:

(i) The individual soldier must learn, by living, moving, and
exercising in it, that the jungle is neither impenetrable nor
unfriendly. When he has once learned to move and live in
it, he can use it for concealment, covered movement, and
surprise.

(ii) Patrolling is the master key to jungle fighting. All units,
not only infantry battalions, must learn to patrol in the
jungle, boldly, widely, cunningly, and offensively.

(iii) All units must get used to having Japanese parties in their
rear, and, when this happens, regard not themselves, but
the Japanese, as 'surrounded'.

(iv) In defence, no attempt should be made to hold long continuous lines. Avenues of approach must be covered and
enemy penetration between our posts dealt with at once
by mobile local reserves who have completely reconnoitred the country.

(v) There should rarely be frontal attacks and never frontal
attacks on narrow fronts. Attacks should follow hooks and
come in from flank or rear, while pressure holds the enemy
in front.

(vi) Tanks can be used in almost any country except swamp.
In close country they must always have infantry *with* them
to defend and reconnoitre for them. They should always
be used in the maximum numbers available and capable of
being deployed. Whenever possible penny packets must
be avoided. 'The more you use, the fewer you lose.'

(vii) There are no non-combatants in jungle warfare. Every unit and sub-unit, including medical ones, is responsible for its own all-round protection, including patrolling, at all times.

(viii) If the Japanese are allowed to hold the initiative they are formidable. When we have it, they are confused and easy to kill. By mobility away from roads, surprise, and offensive action we must regain and keep the initiative.

These were the lessons I had learnt from defeat and I do not think I changed them in any essential throughout the rest of the war. There was, however, one big omission, as I gave them to 15 Corps. I did not mention air supply. This was intentional. Most of us had long ago recognized that air transport could solve some of our worst problems, but as yet we had no transport aircraft. My experience was—and is—that it only does harm to talk to troops about new and desirable equipment which others may have but which you cannot give them. It depresses them. So I made no mention of air transport until we could get at least some of it.

The troops lived in tents or *bashas*, the bamboo huts, thatched with leaves, that were so familiar to us. Reasonably cool and certainly airy, they were pleasant enough in dry weather, but far from waterproof in wet. The aboriginal tribes of the Ranchi plateau were a friendly race of excellent physique. Their men made our roads, and their young women provided most of the labour for our camps. On my first visit to a camp under construction, I was startled to find, working among the troops, gangs of these cheerful girls, most of whom wore nothing above the waist. I was more than a little apprehensive of the results of such a display of dusky but by no means unattractive femininity. It says much for both parties, the girls and the soldiers, that there was practically no trouble of any kind. Later a Bihar regiment was raised, and when I inspected it in Burma, where it did well, and complimented the men on their appearance, one of them laughingly replied, 'Ah, but, sahib, you should see our women!' I told him I had and admired them. A friendly, cheerful, free people who deserve to remain so.

In our training we had as neighbours our old friends, the Chinese. Sun's sorely tried 38th and the remnants of Liao's

143

22nd Chinese Division had been collected after the Retreat at Ramgarh, some forty miles from Ranchi. In spite of their reduced state, Stilwell, indomitable as ever, planned to raise on this nucleus, a strong, well-equipped Chinese force of several divisions that would re-enter Northern Burma and open a road to China. Only Stilwell believed that was both possible and worth the resources it would demand. The Chinese themselves were by no means enthusiastically co-operative; the Indian Government, not without justification, felt considerable apprehension at the prospect of thousands of Chinese about the countryside. With a few notable exceptions, the Americans had little confidence in anybody—in the Chinese, in the British, or in Stilwell.

Stilwell was magnificent. He forced Chang Kai-shek to provide the men; he persuaded India to accept a large Chinese force, and the British to pay for it, accommodate, feed, and clothe it. The American 'Ferry Command' then flew thirteen thousand Chinese from Kunming over 'The Hump', the great mountain range between Assam and China, to airfields in the Brahmaputra Valley, whence they came by rail to Ramgarh. This was the first large-scale troop movement by air in the theatre and was an outstanding achievement. The young American pilots of the Hump should be remembered with admiration and gratitude by their countrymen and their allies.

The two Chinese divisions were reconstituted. Good food, medical care, and regular pay achieved wonders. I have never seen men recover condition as quickly as those Chinese soldiers. Intensive training, under picked American instructors, began on mass-production methods, which were most effective. I was very impressed by the rapid progress of the infantry who were converted to artillery, and who in an astonishingly short time were turned into serviceable pack batteries. No doubt they were apt pupils, but the major credit went to their teachers, under Colonel Sliney, one of the best artillery instructors any army has produced. Everywhere was Stilwell, urging, leading, driving.

I saw a good deal of Sun and Liao, as well as a number of Chinese regimental and battalion commanders whom I had met in Burma. The mass system of instruction left these senior Chinese officers little to do but watch their men being trained by the American experts, and they feared a loss of face. Sun, I think, especially felt this, but when I advised him to make the best of it and reap the benefit later, he was too sensible not to agree. If it surprised us to see our Chinese friends coming on at such a rate, it had an even greater effect on the Americans themselves, an effect which spread even to their headquarters in Delhi. At last they began to catch some of Stilwell's faith and to believe that the Chinese could, with training, equipping, and leadership, be made fit to fight the Japanese.

Some weeks later another division, the 7th Indian, joined 15 Corps. It had not been tried in war, but there was a freshness and a keenness in all it did, which received an imaginative lead from its new commander, Major-General Frank Messervy. He had been chief staff officer of the 5th Indian Division when I had been a brigade commander in it, and later with his audacious Gazelle Force in East Africa he had made a great name for hunting the Italians. He had had his ups and downs as a divisional commander in the Middle East, but I welcomed him as an offensively minded leader, steadied by experience and misfortune in a hard school.

Shortly afterwards, the 5th Indian Division itself arrived from the Middle East. It had been overseas since August 1940 and had seen as much and as varied fighting as any division. It had a spirit and a self-reliance that come only from real fighting. It owed much to its commander, Major-General Briggs, and like all good divisions—and bad ones—reflected its commander's personality. The war had found him in command of a battalion in this division; a battalion that in some extraordinary way was always where it was wanted, that always did what was wanted, and was ready to go on doing it. So Briggs got a brigade. His brigade was just as steadily successful as his battalion had been. It went into the toughest spots, met the most difficult situations, and came out again, like its commander, still unperturbed and as quietly efficient as ever. So, while others fell by the wayside, Briggs got his division. I know of few commanders who made as many immediate and critical decisions on every step of the ladder of promotion, and I know of none who made so few mistakes.

Towards the end of our stay in Ranchi another new Indian division, the 20th, joined the corps. It was commanded by Douglas Gracey, a fellow Gurkha, whom I had known for many years, and who, as a brigade commander, had co-operated with

my 10th Division against the French in Syria in 1941. Full of
energy and ideas, he had a great hold on his Indian and Gurkha
troops.

I was indeed fortunate in these three divisional commanders.
Messervy, Briggs, and Gracey all served with me later in Burma.
Messervy became an inspiring corps commander, Briggs a most
successful commander-in-chief in Burma during the trying time
after the war, and Gracey, after brilliantly commanding his
division, carried out in an outstanding manner a most difficult
military-political task in Indo-China.

My stay in Ranchi was interrupted by two visits to Arakan;
once by myself, and once with most of my headquarters, as I shall
relate. In spite of this, training in Ranchi was continuous and
progressive. There were infantry battle schools, artillery training
centres, co-operation courses with the R.A.F., experiments with
tanks in the jungle, classes in watermanship and river-crossing,
and a dozen other instructional activities, all in full swing. Our
training grew more ambitious until we were staging inter-
divisional exercises over wide ranges of country under tough
conditions. Units lived for weeks on end in the jungle and learnt
its ways. We hoped we had finally dispelled the fatal idea that
the Japanese had something we had not.

As I went from division to division and saw their keenness,
their toughness, their jungle-craft, and their speed of movement,
I began to feel that, when the time came, we should live up to the
15 Corps sign of the three V's, for fifteen and victory.

CHAPTER VIII

THE FIRST ARAKAN CAMPAIGN

WHEN we withdrew, rather precipitately, from Akyab Island in April 1942, chaos and civil war spread throughout Arakan. First, the local inhabitants fell on the wretched Indian refugees, who were still in thousands trying to escape by the coastal route. This exodus was followed by a bitter internecine struggle for land and power between the Arakanese and the Maughs, two sections of the population. The Maughs got the worst of it and many were driven across the Naf River to take shelter in territory still held by us, there to make yet another refugee problem. Faction fights among the victorious Arakanese then became the order of the day, until the Japanese, pushing up to Buthidaung, restored some sort of uneasy peace.

This was the position when I took over 15 Corps, a command that carried with it the responsibility for the Arakan front. Our information of Japanese movements and intentions was meagre. The first necessity was to improve it, and to this end we began the organization of 'V' Force in Arakan. It already existed on the Central front and was slowly spreading out to cover the gap between us and 4 Corps. 'V' Force was primarily an intelligence organization, much on the lines of our old 'Yomas Intelligence Service' of lamented memory. A number of selected British officers, where possible those with local knowledge, was sent into the most forward areas. There they collected round them a small escort of inhabitants, and built up a network of agents who operated behind the Japanese front, bringing and sending back information. Japanese intelligence officers had built up much the same spy system on their side, and the collection of information developed into a duel between the rival organizations. I think our officers, being much more intelligent and enterprising than their opposite numbers, had, after a time, the better of the exchanges. On both sides the agents used were without training in observation

147

and without any military knowledge, but they did begin to produce some sort of information, and their standard gradually improved. As was bound to happen, many of the agents worked for both the enemy and ourselves, but on the whole this was to our advantage as they quickly came to prefer our officers and their methods to those of the Japanese. Later, along the whole front, 'V' Force became an important and very valuable part of the intelligence framework. It later extended its activities to include minor raiding operations, and frequently fought successful actions with Japanese patrols and detachments, but in July 1942 an attempt to bolster up the Arakanese in our area by issuing fire-arms of various sorts was judged premature and abandoned.

Our most forward outposts at Cox's Bazaar and Teknaf were held, I discovered, only by armed police, borrowed from the Civil Government, who, not unreasonably, regarded this as a role more suited to troops than to them. Actually for this work, police, with their local knowledge and contacts, were better than soldiers, but obviously we had to get at least patrols of the 14th Division forward, if only to inspire confidence among the police. The bulk of Lloyd's forces were still north of Chittagong, and he was, as yet, reluctant to stretch so far south. However, G.H.Q. India and Eastern Army, to say nothing of 15 Corps, were all contemplating a minor offensive in Arakan at the end of the monsoon, and, whether we made it or remained on the defensive, a proper reconnaissance screen well ahead of the main force was clearly essential. I, therefore, pressed Lloyd to get his patrols moving.

Visits to his division showed that it was becoming a better-knit fighting force, and I sympathized with Lloyd's wish to keep it concentrated as long as possible for training, but, as I pointed out, as long as the enemy remained quiescent, it could train rather more realistically farther south. Lloyd agreed and preparations for the move forward were put in hand. I had every confidence in Lloyd and was sure he would be well supported by his staff under Colonel Warren, whom I had taught at the Staff College and knew well. Warren concealed a quiet and determined character beneath a deliberate manner, and he had the priceless gift of imperturbability which was later to stand him and his commanders in good stead.

My first inspection of Chittagong, the only port of consequence on the whole coast and therefore of primary importance in any advance, was not reassuring. The Japanese had bombed it once or twice, not very seriously, but some partially trained non-Regular Indian troops, who formed its garrison, had not stood even that light introduction to warfare well; there was a distinctly jumpy feel about the place. Its wide perimeter could not be held by merely static defence. All the more reason, therefore, to get the 14th Division moving.

Towards the end of July, G.H.Q. India became firm in the intention to order an Arakan offensive. Its modest objects were to clear the enemy out of Mayu Peninsula and to take Akyab Island. Prospects of success were good. As far as we knew, the Japanese had only four divisions in Burma, though more were believed to be coming. Of the four, one was in the far north-east watching the Yunnan Chinese; two were on the Assam front and in Central Burma; one, the 55th, was in Western Burma, and of this only one regiment with some divisional units was in Arakan. The rest of this division was guarding the long coastline and in South Burma. An advance on Akyab should not, at first, meet more than four battalions and some divisional troops. Lloyd would, therefore, have a handsome margin of superiority, at any rate in the opening exchanges.

There were, as always in war, other factors besides numbers. The ground was one—the most important. The Mayu Peninsula is some ninety miles long and about twenty wide at its northern end, whence it tapers to a point just short of Akyab Island. Down its centre runs the Mayu Range, a razor-sharp ridge, from one to two thousand feet high, almost precipitous but jungle covered. The lower slopes, in a tangle of broken spurs, approach to within a thousand yards or so of the sea on one side and of the Mayu River on the other. The narrow strips of flat ground on each side are split by innumerable streams or *chaungs*, which on the west especially are tidal with treacherous banks of mud at low tide. Such a terrain would afford, at frequent intervals, ideal positions for defence, and gravely hamper the deployment of an attacking force.

Before Eastern Army had decided to control the offensive direct, and while we had thought that, if it came, we at 15 Corps would be responsible for it, we had, of course, begun the consideration of a plan. Leaving out a full-scale amphibious assault,

which lack of resources made impossible, there were three ways
of advance on Akyab:

(a) A methodical approach straight down the peninsula.
(b) A series of hop, skip, and jump minor amphibious operations working down the coast in hooks behind the successive
Japanese positions.
(c) A long-range penetration expedition of the type for which
Wingate's brigade was now training. This, swinging out
well to the east, could reach Akyab by the back door.

We felt that a straightforward advance, even with superior
force, would be slow and costly and, knowing the Japanese
tenacity in defence, might be held up. The amphibious hooks
would at the best be weak, and our flotilla, owing to Japanese air
attacks could only work at night, so that the hooks would be
very short ones. The long-range penetration method we liked
very much, but it could not be effective by itself. Our final
answer, as far as we got to an answer before we were called off,
was a combination of all three. The main advance by the 14th
Division down the peninsula; a couple of battalions, scraped up
from internal security and trained with the flotilla, for the hooks;
and Wingate's brigade for a simultaneous strike at Akyab or
beyond.

Eastern Army had straight away to give up the idea of using
Wingate's brigade. General Wavell had rightly decided to use
that in the north, to co-operate with a Chinese advance from
Yunnan. Eastern Army had very understandable doubts of the
value of our cherished flotilla for even small landing operations.
I admit it did look a bit Heath Robinsonish, but I think we could
have found places to land by night where there was no enemy,
and the R.A.F., if we were willing to risk it, might have welcomed the chance to draw out the Japanese airmen. However,
Eastern Army came down in favour of the orthodox direct
advance overland, relying, with what seemed good reason, on
their preponderance of strength.

This, our first offensive in the theatre, was never intended to
accomplish more than the very limited objective of taking Akyab.
Its most important effects would not be the minor improvement
in the tactical situation that the possession of Akyab would give,
but the moral effect that *any* successful offensive would have on

world opinion, on our allies, and, most important of all, on our own troops. Morale in places was not too high and we badly needed a victory of some sort. It was a mistake to blazon the advance as an invasion of Burma. Even if the limited success aimed at were attained, it would not come up to the expectations raised, and, if we failed, the depression would be the greater. It is better to let a victory, if it comes, speak for itself; it has a voice that drowns all other sounds. If it does not come—and victory is never certain—the less preliminary drum-beating there has been the better.

From Ranchi, to which we had moved in August, we watched with growing anxiety the progress of the Arakan offensive, now no longer our responsibility. The weather, difficulties in collecting supplies and equipment, and other reasons, delayed its start, and it was not until mid-December that the 14th Division began in earnest its ninety-mile move on Akyab. The advance was made on both sides of the Mayu Range, along the sea-coast and astride the Mayu River, with a flanking detachment still farther east in the Kaladan Valley. The central spine of the range was not occupied; it was judged too precipitous and too thickly jungle-covered to be passable. For most of the way, therefore, it effectively separated the two prongs of the advance.

To begin with, all went well. The little port of Maungdaw on the estuary of the Naf River, and the town of Buthidaung were taken against slight opposition. The west to east road between them, which pierced the range by two tunnels—relics of a vanished railway—was occupied, giving us the only lateral road in the peninsula. The last days of 1942 found Lloyd's troops, on the right of the range in the coastal plain just short of Donbaik, ten miles from the tip of the peninsula; and on his left, approaching Rathedaung in the Mayu River Valley, about fifteen miles from Foul Point. A carrier patrol even reached that point, separated by only a narrow channel from Akyab Island, and returned to report no enemy seen.

An unfortunate pause in the advance until the 6th January then occurred, which gave the Japanese time to bring up reinforcements and to dig in at both Donbaik and Rathedaung. Our left attack on Rathedaung, gallantly pressed, was repulsed; two set-piece frontal attacks on the right across the paddy fields on Donbaik also failed disastrously. The Japanese held Donbaik with

151

little more than a battalion, with other troops in reserve, yet so skilfully were their positions sited and hidden that an attack on the restricted front between the ridge and the sea failed to dislodge them. For the first time we had come up against the Japanese 'bunker'—from now on to be so familiar to us. This was a small strong-point made usually of heavy logs covered with four or five feet of earth, and so camouflaged in the jungle that it could not be picked out at even fifty yards without prolonged searching. These bunkers held garrisons varying from five to twenty men, plentifully supplied with medium and light machine-guns. They were quite impervious to bombardment by field-guns and even the direct hit of a medium bomb rarely penetrated. They were sited in groups to give mutual support, so that it was impossible for assaulting troops to reach a bunker without coming under fire from at least two others.

Some reports and many rumours of these set-backs in Arakan spread through the Eastern Army. The high hopes inspired by the drum-beating that had preceded the offensive died down and heads began to be shaken. Reinforcements were sent from India to give renewed impetus to the attack, until eventually four fresh Indian brigades and one British brigade had been added. The 14th Division now had nine brigades and it was, I think, the largest that ever went into action. To overcome the bunker difficulty, 15 Corps was ordered to send one troop of Valentine tanks to Arakan. The tank brigade commander protested against such a small detachment and I supported him, as it was against all my experience in the Middle East and Burma. 'The more you use, the fewer you lose.' I argued that a regiment could be deployed and used in depth even on the narrow front chosen for attack. We were overruled on the grounds that more than a troop could not be deployed and that the delay in getting in a larger number across the *chaungs* was more than could be accepted. Reluctantly we sent the troop, and the secret of its move was admirably kept. This and the gallantry of the crews were the only admirable things about the episode.

The third assault on Donbaik went in, but the handful of tanks was knocked out almost at once, and the attack again failed. After a pause to bring up fresh troops a fourth attack on the same frontal model, but now without tanks, was made on the 18th February. By sheer gallantry, Punjabi troops penetrated to the bunkers, but were eventually thrown back after suffering very heavily. The Japanese technique was, when our troops reached the enemy positions, to bring down the heaviest possible artillery, mortar, and machine-gun concentrations on them, irrespective of any damage they might inflict on their own men. Actually, as the Japanese defenders were mostly in bunkers they suffered little, while our troops, completely in the open, had no protection from this rain of projectiles.

In the second week of March, I was summoned to Calcutta by the Army Commander, General Irwin, who told me he wished me to visit Lloyd in Arakan. I asked him if, now so many brigades were operating there, he intended to send my headquarters with me to take over control. He replied that he did not want me to take any operational command, nor did he think a corps headquarters necessary at this time, but he might decide to send us there later. All I was to do now was to look around, get into the picture, and report to him.

I reached Lloyd's headquarters, near Maungdaw, on the 10th March, and spent some days there and with forward brigades. My first impression was that the force, nine brigades with a very large and difficult line of communication area, was much too big for a divisional headquarters, even if augmented, to command and administer. My second, that in many units morale was very definitely on the down-grade. There was every night a great deal of panicky firing which on one occasion developed into a full-scale battle—at least in ammunition expenditure—between two adjacent parts of the force. Warren, Lloyd's chief staff officer, remarked dryly the next morning, 'At least we won *that* battle!' Lloyd had been ordered to make yet another attempt to break through the Donbaik position, and had been given 6 Brigade, four battalions strong, from the 2nd British Division for the purpose. The plans for this attack seemed to me very like those of its predecessors—a direct frontal attack. Lloyd assured me that there was no other way; he had no ships for a hook down the coast and his patrols had reported repeatedly that the ridge and its jungle were impassable to a flanking force. He was confident that with this fresh British brigade, improved covering fire by artillery and aircraft, and the increased knowledge he had gained of the Japanese defences, he would this time succeed. I told him I thought he was making the error that most of us had made in

1942 in considering any jungle impenetrable and that it was worth making a great effort to get a brigade, or at least part of one, along the spine of the ridge. He replied that he had given a lot of thought to this and had decided it was not feasible and his brigadiers agreed. Looking at the densely covered and almost perpendicular slopes of the Mayu Range, it was difficult to question this. In any case, I had no operational control over Lloyd, and, as he pointed out, plans were so far advanced that the date of the attack could not be put back to allow of changes, if time were to be left to stage the capture of Akyab. Wrongly I left it at that, flew back to Calcutta, and made my report to the Army Commander. He, also, having studied the question and heard the opinions of subordinate commanders, was compelled to believe that a flanking move via the ridge was impossible. He did not say so, but I judged he was not altogether enthusiastic over another attack on Donbaik, but that he was being pushed from Delhi to undertake it. I had some time before asked for ten days' leave in Simla, where my wife and daughter were living, and, on the assurance that I should not be required, I left.

Meanwhile, as I paused in Delhi to attend a General Headquarters exercise on air co-operation, the final attack on Donbaik took place on the 18th March. 6 Brigade made a desperate attempt to break through the strengthened Japanese defences. Advancing again, straight in the open, over the dead of previous assaults, they got among and even on the tops of the bunkers; but they could not break in. Like the Punjabis, they were caught by the merciless Japanese counter-barrage and bloodily driven back. It was a magnificent effort, and it was the last. Donbaik remained impregnable, and all hope of taking it was abandoned.

Now, having brought us to a standstill, it was the Japanese turn to attack. A strong enemy column, which had marched from Central Burma, suddenly fell upon our flank detachment in the Kaladan and scattered it. Other Japanese detachments led by a Colonel Tanahashi, afterwards to become only too well known to us, broke into the Mayu Valley and struck behind 55 Brigade opposite Rathedaung. After fierce fighting, the brigade extricated itself and, badly shaken, fell back up the Mayu River. Lloyd reacted by a counter-attack, but the Army Commander, who had hurried to the front on the news of disaster, relieved him, took command of the division himself, and redisposed the forward troops to hold any further Japanese advance. For a short while it appeared as if the front was stabilized and the Army Commander, handing over to Major-General Lomax, who arrived to replace Lloyd, returned to Calcutta.

At four o'clock in the morning of the 5th April at Gaya, I was awakened by a banging on the door of the railway carriage in which my wife and I were returning from Simla to Ranchi. I was told by a railway official that I was wanted urgently on the telephone and the train would be held up for me. In my pyjamas I staggered over the recumbent figures that invariably litter every Indian platform at night to the station-master's office. Here I heard Tony Scott speaking from Ranchi. Dramatically he proclaimed, 'The woodcock are flighting!' 'Woodcock' was the code name for the move of Corps Headquarters to Arakan. I was to go straight on in the train to Calcutta; my wife would be picked up at the junction for Ranchi; Scott would be off that morning for Chittagong with the Corps Headquarters.

At dawn on a dismal station platform I said good-bye to my wife and left her rather forlorn, hoping that someone *would* come and take her to Ranchi. We had had too many partings of this kind in the last twenty years, but this was, I think she would agree, one of our most hurried and most miserable. Late in the morning I arrived in Calcutta and spent some hours with General Irwin, getting his view of the situation as it was known to him and receiving his instructions. Things in Arakan were obviously again going wrong; but how seriously was not clear. I was to set up Corps Headquarters in Chittagong as soon as possible, but I was not to take operational control until told to do so by him. I was not, even when I assumed operational command, to have administrative control; that would remain with Army Headquarters, who on all such matters would deal direct with the division. I was, therefore, to leave almost the whole of my administrative staff behind in Ranchi. I did not like this separation of operational and administrative control, especially as a corps could have relieved the overworked division of much of its administrative burden, but the Army Commander was insistent. The situation in Arakan was further complicated as at this juncture the 26th Division Headquarters from Calcutta was in process of replacing the 14th Division Headquarters, which, together with certain brigades, it was intended to bring back to India. That night I dined with

Lloyd, the dismissed commander of the 14th Division, and heard his side of the story. He was quite without bitterness and took misfortune as well as I had seen him take success. His death some time later in the Middle East was a great loss, as, in spite of a failure in Arakan for which he was by no means wholly responsible, he would, had he lived, have regained his place in the group of brilliant divisional commanders the Indian Army produced.

Early next morning I flew to Chittagong, where I picked up a fighter escort as Japanese aircraft were busy, and landed on a forward airstrip near Divisional Headquarters. I had never met Lomax, the new divisional commander, but I was at once impressed by his calm level-headedness. He would have had plenty of excuse for nervousness had he shown it. The situation as far as it could be discovered was fantastically bad. Lomax, barely arrived, had just begun to study the dispositions he had inherited from General Irwin, was learning the names of his brigadiers, and meeting a completely strange staff, when the Japanese struck again. Using not very large forces with the greatest boldness and rapidity, they had crossed the Mayu River in the night, fallen on the flank of 47 Brigade which had been extended to cover the eastern side of the range, and rolled it up. The brigade disintegrated and, losing practically all its equipment, struggled out over the hills in small starving parties. As far as we knew at Lomax's headquarters that brigade had ceased to exist—as, indeed, it had —and his left flank was crumbling, if not already gone. The Japanese, without pause, had exploited to the full the opportunity this gave them. Straight over the Mayu Range they came, following or making single file tracks through the jungle and over the precipitous slopes that we had complacently considered impassable. On the night of the 5th, while Lloyd and I were dining in the Bengal Club, Japanese infantry and pack-guns, debouched from the foot-hills on to the coastal strip, west of the range. They struck into the rear of 6 Brigade as it pulled back from Donbaik. The Brigade Headquarters was rushed by howling Japanese streaming out of the darkness, most of the staff were killed, and the Brigadier, Cavendish, was captured, only to be killed a little later either by his guards or by our own artillery fire. Everywhere the units of 6 Brigade found Japanese in between them, behind them, and around them. It says much for the stubborn courage of the British soldier, that, in these conditions, with control temporarily gone, battalions, companies, and batteries rallied, cleared their immediate localities with the bayonet and began to fall back, holding off a fanatical enemy, delirious with success.

The position as Lomax and I looked at it next day was grim, so grim as to have almost a comic element. With the left flank, east of the range, gone, the right along the coast looked like a Neapolitan ice. First and farthest south, so far as we could discover, were some British artillery, then a wad of Japanese, next half 6 Brigade minus its headquarters, again more Japanese, and lastly the rest of 6 Brigade.

For myself, I was in a strange position, which was new to me, and which I did not like. I have rarely been so unhappy on a battlefield. Things had gone wrong, terribly wrong, and we should be hard put to it to avoid worse. Yet I had no operational control and, even if I had, no troops in hand with whom I could influence events; Lomax already commanded everything. In spite of all this I would have had no hesitation in assuming tactical command at the front, as General Irwin had done with Lloyd and as I had done myself on occasion, but for one thing—Lomax. I did not know him; I had been with him only a matter of hours, but they were testing hours. Never had a divisional commander, immediately on taking over a strange formation, in a new type of war, been confronted with a more desperate situation. I was filled with admiration for the way in which he took hold. Wherever he went he inspired confidence by his steadiness, decision, and obvious competence. Was this his true form? Would it last? I was prepared to bet it was and would. In fact, I did not flatter myself that I could handle the immediate situation any better than he could. On the other hand, I did know there were a hundred ways in which, at Corps Headquarters behind him, I could take some of the strain.

Quietly, without fuss, Lomax regrouped his rear brigades to cover the vital Maungdaw–Buthidaung road, and reorganized the units already shattered. In this latter task I did what I could to help. There was no doubt that the disaster had tragically weakened morale in a number of units, British and Indian. Those of 6 British Brigade, in spite of the hammering they had taken, were an exception. They had not liked it, but they were still staunch.

Not the least of Lomax's difficulties was that the tired but efficient headquarters of the 14th Division had been replaced by the untried staff of the 26th Division, newly arrived, unacquainted with most of the brigades, and finding the contrast between a fast-moving battle and the static life of Calcutta only too painful. The rapid recoil of our front made it necessary to move back Divisional Headquarters, and it was evident from the resulting confusion that, if it found it so difficult to move itself, it was not likely to be very efficient at getting others to move. With my concurrence, Lomax made a clean sweep of several of the divisional staff, whom I replaced for him by the temporary loan of officers from Corps Headquarters. In a few days we managed to produce as G.1, or chief staff officer for the division, Colonel Cotterill-Hill. He and Lomax made a splendid pair, and from the day of his arrival the 26th Division Headquarters began to sort itself out. Lomax was, at the same time, relieved of the strain of reorganizing the headquarters himself and could devote his energies more freely to the proper functions of a commander in battle.

I stayed with Lomax for a few days and I hope he did not find my presence a handicap. My original opinion of his leadership was confirmed, indeed I never changed it throughout the war. When things at the front were rather more under control I rejoined Corps Headquarters.

Chittagong was a melancholy place. It had not been badly knocked about, but the light bombing it had suffered had driven out a large part of its inhabitants. Those who remained, the poorest, were menaced by approaching famine. The railway workshops, formerly the chief industry of the town, had been dismantled when it looked as if the Japanese would advance into Bengal, and even the roofs had been removed. The docks, whose demolition had been stopped just in time, were a brighter spot. Under the energetic drive of Hallet, the naval officer in charge, and of some devoted civilians, the quays were beginning to show great activity. In peace, Chittagong must have been the most attractive of the larger towns of Bengal; now, its general air of neglect, stagnation, and apprehension was depressing.

Scott had installed Corps Headquarters in part of a large college where it was ready to function, even if, without its administrative half, only one-sidedly. A few days later, on the 14th April, Eastern Army handed over operational control. In Chittagong we found 224 Group, R.A.F., under Air Commodore Gray, and

THE FIRST ARAKAN CAMPAIGN

with him and his squadrons we at once began the close and friendly co-operation that lasted between the corps and the group until the end of the war. The Army in Arakan already owed a great debt to 224 Group, which had achieved marvels of sustained effort to cover the recent withdrawals. More than once the troops could not have extricated themselves without this cover.

I continued to visit Lomax and his troops every few days, and so was well in touch with the situation. He had, temporarily at least, stabilized his front on both sides of the Mayu Range and had at last got troops into position along its spine. It was quite evident that the Japanese would not rest satisfied with what they had achieved so far with such ease. They had made one or two tentative passes at 6 Brigade, now dug in across the coastal strip and in the foot-hills, but had shown no intention of delivering a real attack here. Perhaps they had too healthy a respect for this British formation in spite of their successes against it. With a second brigade in depth behind it, Lomax was reasonably secure on this flank. All indications were that the push would come east of the ridge. It would, I was sure, be a strong attempt to get across the lateral Maungdaw–Buthidaung road. If it succeeded we should certainly have to abandon Buthidaung—its supply would be impossible—and our hold on Maungdaw would become precarious.

Lomax had no intention of sitting down waiting for this to happen, and, with my full approval, he planned a counter-stroke in the nature of a trap. The Japanese striking force was to be shepherded into a box. When it was well in, the lid was to swing to behind it with a bang. One side of the box was two battalions on the ridge itself, the other was two more along the Mayu River. The bottom of the box, its northern end, was yet again two battalions holding the hills south of the Maungdaw–Buthidaung road. The lid was a mobile striking force of a brigade less a battalion, placed behind the river side of the box, ready to swing in. That all sounds nicely geometrical and simple, but translated into tired troops, many of them badly shaken, holding positions among tangled jungle hills and streams, it was not so tidy, and much less simple. I was more than a little anxious as to the outcome. It would all have been so easy if we could only have washed out the last four months of defeat and frustration. Then the troops would have been mentally and physically fit for this sort of battle,

159

but time is the one thing you cannot regain in war. I had no doubt the Japanese would walk into the trap. They did. Their attack began as we expected and, according to plan—our plan. Feeling stiff opposition on their flanks, they pressed rapidly forward in the centre and flowed into the box. So far, so good. Now was the time to crash down the lid. Lomax was just giving the order for this when the bottom fell out of the box, and out of our plan. The two battalions south of the lateral road failed to hold. First one, then the other gave way. The Japanese broke through and seized the Point 551 feature which dominated the eastern half of the Maungdaw–Buthidaung road. In the confused fighting that followed, we not only failed to retake Point 551, but were pushed back, and the Japanese got astride the road. That meant we could no longer maintain a force in Buthidaung, as the road was its only means of access. Even more serious, it put paid to most of the wheeled transport east of the range. We had now no route by which to get it away, and when the troops pulled out of Buthidaung by jungle tracks over the hills they destroyed their vehicles. It was too much like 1942 over again, with the added bitterness that this time we had been defeated by forces smaller than our own.

It was no use crying over spilt milk. In war you have to pay for your mistakes, and in Arakan the same mistakes had been made again and again until the troops lost heart. I got very angry with one or two units that had not behaved well, and said some hard things to them, but thinking it over I was not sure the blame was all theirs. In any case, what was wanted now was not recriminations, post mortems, and witch hunts, but some clear —and quick—thinking.

Could we hang on to the tunnels area and the western part of the lateral road? Could we hold Maungdaw? If not, where should we go back to? Bawli Bazaar, Cox's Bazaar, Chittagong? Frankly, the troops that had been in action for the past weeks were fought out and many of them could not be relied on to hold anything. I had asked for the 70th Division from Ranchi to enable me to send back to India the bulk of worn-out formations, and it was coming in bit by bit, but less than a brigade had yet arrived. It would have taken a month or two to stock up Maungdaw, while ships coming in would have to run a Japanese gauntlet. To hang on to Maungdaw as a matter of prestige—and it had now no

THE FIRST ARAKAN CAMPAIGN

other value—would have been to invite a siege and a disaster. I urged its abandonment. The Army Commander was naturally reluctant, but I was quite sure, whatever the effects in Delhi, we must get out, and he finally agreed. Our only hope of stabilizing the front, if the Japanese really pushed us, was to hold the rice-field country. Our men were still untrained for the jungle and they feared it more than they did the enemy. We had to select areas where we could give our troops reasonable fields of fire and open manœuvre. The first place where this could be done was about Cox's Bazaar, and here we planned a layout for a division of three or four brigades, astride the main line of advance to Chittagong. Bawli we would hold as what amounted to an out-post position. It was very galling to be thrown back on these defensive tactics, but at the moment there was no alternative.

I was constantly flying between Lomax's and my headquarters. On one occasion, when seeking a forward brigade, I got a bad fright through landing on an airstrip we had already abandoned, but which luckily the Japanese had not yet taken over. The situation was not improved by the pilot of my Lysander stopping his engine before we realized where we were, and then being unable to restart it! Before he got it going again I was sweating with more than the heat.

With great skill and very little loss Lomax broke contact with the Japanese. On 11th May we evacuated Maungdaw and pulled back to the new positions. The rain came and the enemy, almost as tired as we were, sat down on his gains at Buthidaung, the Tunnels, and Maungdaw, making no serious attempt to follow us to Bawli.

Here we were back where we had started, a sad ending to our first and much heralded offensive. Our actual losses in killed, wounded, and missing were not high, about two thousand five hundred, and, while we had not inflicted as many on the enemy, he had suffered too. Malaria had taken a heavy toll, far above our battle casualties, and we had lost a good deal of equipment. Neither these serious losses nor the abandonment of territory was as damaging as the loss of morale. It was no use disguising the fact that many of the British and Indian units which had fought in Arakan were shaken and depressed. As so often happens, too, the troops in the rear areas, who greatly outnumbered those at the front, suffered an even greater decline in morale. It was plain that our main task during the respite of the monsoon must be to rebuild that morale. At this critical time, two men, each almost the antithesis of the other, one indirectly, the other directly, came to our help. The first was Brigadier Orde Wingate; the second, General Sir George Giffard.

I had first met Wingate in East Africa, when we were both fighting the Italians, he with his Abyssinian partisans, whom in those days we impolitely called *Shiftas* or brigands, and I with my more orthodox Indian Infantry Brigade. I had already in 1941 and 1942 had several lively discussions with him on the organization and practice of guerrilla warfare. With many of his ideas I was in agreement, but I had doubted if methods based on his Abyssinian experience would succeed equally well against a tougher enemy and in country not so actively friendly. Wingate was a strange, excitable, moody creature, but he had fire in him. He could ignite other men. When he so fiercely advocated some project of his own, you might catch his enthusiasm or you might see palpable flaws in his arguments; you might be angry at his arrogance or outraged at so obvious a belief in the end, his end, justifying any means; but you could not be indifferent. You could not fail to be stimulated either to thought, protest, or action by his sombre vehemence and his unrelenting persistence.

Just at this time he had returned from his first raid into Burma.

Passing through the 4 Corps outposts along the Chindwin, his brigade in a number of columns, all supplied by air, had pushed two hundred miles eastwards into Japanese-held Burma. They had blown up bridges and cuttings on the Mandalay–Myitkyina railway that supplied the Japanese northern front, and attempted to reach across the Irrawaddy to cut the Mandalay–Lashio line. Exhaustion, difficulties of air supply, and the reaction of the Japanese, prevented this, and the columns breaking up into small parties made for the shelter of 4 Corps. About a thousand men, a third of the total force, failed to return. As a military operation the raid had been an expensive failure. It gave little tangible return for the losses it had suffered and the resources it had absorbed. The damage it did to Japanese communications was repaired in a few days, the casualties it inflicted were negligible, and it had no immediate effect on Japanese dispositions or plans. The abandonment of a projected enemy offensive through the Hukawng Valley was not due to this raid, but to the fact that the Japanese

55th Division, which was to take part in it, had to be diverted at the end of 1942 to meet the British threat in Arakan. If anything was learnt of air supply or jungle fighting it was a costly schooling.

These are hard things to say of an effort that required such stark courage and endurance as was demanded of and given by Wingate and his men. The operation was, in effect, the old cavalry raid of military history on the enemy's communications, which, to be effective against a stout-hearted opponent, must be made in tactical co-ordination with a main attack elsewhere. Originally, Wingate's raid had been thus planned to coincide with an advance by Chinese forces from Yunnan. Later, although it was clear that this Chinese move would not materialize, General Wavell sent Wingate's force in alone. It was a bold decision, and as it turned out, it was justified, not on military, but on psychological grounds. It cannot be judged on material results alone. Whilst, like the Arakan offensive, it was a failure, there was a dramatic quality about this raid, which, with the undoubted fact that it had penetrated far behind the Japanese lines and returned, lent itself to presentation as a triumph of British jungle fighting over the Japanese. Skilfully handled, the press of the Allied world took up the tale, and everywhere the story ran that we had beaten the Japanese at their own game. This not only distracted attention from the failure in Arakan, but was important in itself for our own people at home, for our allies, and above all for our troops on the Burma front. Whatever the actual facts, to the troops in Burma it seemed the first ripple showing the turning of the tide. For this reason alone, Wingate's raid was worth all the hardship and sacrifice his men endured, and by every means in our power we exploited its propaganda value to the full.

On the 21st May, I heard that General Giffard had replaced General Irwin as Commander-in-Chief, Eastern Army. Except for a brief visit to my headquarters ten days earlier, I had not met him. He called me to Calcutta at the end of the month and we had a very full discussion on the Arakan situation. The new Army Commander had a great effect on me. A tall, good-looking man in the late fifties, who had obviously kept himself physically and mentally in first-class condition, there was nothing dramatic about him in either appearance or speech. He abhorred the theatrical, and was one of the very few generals, indeed men in any position, I have known who *really* disliked publicity. The first impression he gave was of courtesy and consideration, and this was a lasting impression because it was based on thought for others.

But there was much more to General Giffard than good taste, good manners, and unselfishness. He understood the fundamentals of war—that soldiers must be trained before they can fight, fed before they can march, and relieved before they are worn out. He understood that front-line commanders should be spared responsibilities in rear, and that soundness of organization and administration is worth more than specious short-cuts to victory. Having chosen his subordinates and given them their tasks, he knew how to leave them without interference, but with the knowledge that, if they needed it, his support was behind them. I returned to Calcutta—with some difficulty, as the weather forced back my aircraft twice—feeling that the new Army Commander was a man I could work with, and for, wholeheartedly.

Within a few days General Giffard came with me on an Arakan tour. He visited the forward troops, my own headquarters, and the rear areas. He met officers and men and spoke to them. He was at his best talking to individuals. As a speech-maker he was neither eloquent nor picturesque, but he had two things that impressed soldiers—he knew his stuff and he was dead honest. *The* quality that showed through him was integrity, and that was the quality which, as much as any other, we wanted in our Army Commander. Without any shouting from the house-tops or organized publicity stunts, belief in the new Army Commander spread, and with it spirits began to revive. Those who, like myself, commanded under him, built on the foundations he laid in morale and organization, and later, when we succeeded him, often received credit that should justly have been his.

After a few weeks tidying up Arakan, getting tired formations out, building up supplies, and doing the hundred and one things necessary to give the troops in their sodden trenches and leaky *bashas* as much comfort as possible, Corps Headquarters, leaving Lomax and his 26th Division to hold the front, returned to Ranchi. General Giffard's instructions to me were to have the divisions already at Ranchi, and those he would send me later, fit for a real offensive immediately after the monsoon.

With him I discussed the forthcoming Arakan offensive, which he was entrusting to 15 Corps. For it, I was to have the 5th and 7th Divisions. The 20th Division was to go to 4 Corps at Imphal;

the 70th Division would remain in Army Reserve. The 26th Division, when relieved by either 5th or 7th, would remain in Arakan, as reserve for that front. The old Sunderbans flotilla had by now largely reverted to transport duties, and though we had hoped for landing craft and naval forces for a minor landing, they were not yet available. We should thus again be reduced to a straightforward advance overland with only amphibious feints. I was anxious to avoid the old move on a narrow front, and I asked for an additional formation to send down the Kaladan River on the left flank, always the dangerous spot in Arakan. This would be independent of the main advance, and would have to be supplied entirely by air. General Giffard accordingly made available for me the 81st West African Division, less one brigade, and provided enough air transport from our growing resources to supply it.

This was the first time a normal formation such as a division was to be committed to complete air maintenance. General Giffard's staff with mine worked out the organization required. We very soon realized that if we were going to make the best use of this great new weapon of air supply we must, with our limited resources in aircraft, provide a simple, flexible organization of control and operation, that would suit any normal formation without elaborate preparation. We approached the problem from the starting-point that transportation by air was no more extraordinary than movement by road, rail, or boat; it was merely one method of moving things and men. There is indeed only one test of airmindedness, and that is not whether you can fly an aeroplane, but whether you regard it as a vehicle. If you do, you are airminded; if you regard it as anything else—a weapon, a sporting adjunct, or a bag of tricks—you can be an air marshal, but you are not airminded.

The 81st West African Division was training in the jungle near Bombay, and I flew down to spend a few days with them. Their discipline and smartness were impressive, and they were more obviously at home in the jungle than any troops I had yet seen. They had neither animals nor vehicles with their fighting units, but were organized on a man-pack basis. In order to see what this meant, I did what I have often found very enlightening with a new organization. I had a formal parade. A battalion and a battery at war establishment were drawn up for inspection, with every man in his place. I was at once struck by two things. First, by the horde of unarmed porters who were needed to carry supplies, ammunition, baggage, and the heavier weapons, and secondly by the large number of white men in a unit, fifty or sixty to a battalion. Accustomed as I was to Indian battalions in the field with usually only seven or eight Europeans, it struck me as an unnecessarily generous supply. I never changed that view and later experience confirmed it. This I know is rank heresy to many very experienced 'coasters'. I was constantly told that, far from being too many, with the rapidly expanded African forces, more British officers and N.C.O.s were needed. But these large British establishments in African units had great drawbacks. The only way to fill them was to draft officers and N.C.O.s willy-nilly to them, and this did not always give the right kind. The European who serves with native troops should be, not only much above average in efficiency and character, as he must accept greater responsibility, but he should serve with them because he wants to, because he likes them. Another effect of so many British was to stifle the initiative of the Africans. All commanders, even down to seconds-in-command of platoons, were British; the African N.C.O. thus had, at least during training, a white man always at his elbow to whom he could turn for orders. Naturally he did so, and when in battle the Britisher became a casualty or for some other reason the African was left on his own, he was lost. The Sudan Defence Force units, the only other African troops I had, up to then, commanded, seemed to me even after their expansion to have got a better answer, with their few but picked British officers and their Sudanese officers and N.C.O.s, temperamental perhaps, but trained to be full of initiative.

As the monsoon drew to a close, our divisions slipped quietly away from Ranchi. The 5th and 7th went to Arakan, where they took over the front from the 26th Division, which went into Corps Reserve at Chittagong. The 81st West African Division was already collecting for its move down the Kaladan, when early in October, 15 Corps Headquarters was established in the jungle a few miles south of Bawli. On 6th October I left Ranchi, and, after a day with the Army Commander, flew to my new headquarters and took command of the Arakan front. Our plans for the offensive had been made, and all that was required at the moment were the usual final checks.

I had hardly had time to make a tour of the front by air, launch, and jeep, when I was summoned to Calcutta to act for General Giffard as Commander-in-Chief, Eastern Command. Lieut.-General Sir Philip Christison, whom I knew very well, having been a fellow instructor at Camberley Staff College, was to replace me at Corps. I left with many regrets, not only at parting from my staff, who had served me so very well and for all of whom I had, and still have, a real affection, and from the troops, but at not having had the chance of wielding with my own hand the weapon I had seen forged.

I flew to Calcutta on 15th October 1943, without even an A.D.C. Nigel Bruce, who held that thankless post, had broken his leg immediately on arrival in Arakan, and I missed him badly. My aircraft, piloted by Air Commodore Gray, who had insisted on paying me this compliment, made an unexpectedly quick trip, and I arrived considerably ahead of time. No one was at Dum Dum airfield to meet me—I never did have much luck there—and so I wandered off rather forlornly to try and find a car. Eventually I forced a protesting Indian driver, who said he was waiting for a brigadier, to take me. A mile or so outside the airfield I met Brigadier Steve Irwin, the Chief of Staff of Eastern Command, coming to meet me at the correct time, and changed cars. I hope the other brigadier was not kept waiting too long.

As we drove out to Barrackpore, I watched an army commander's black-and-red flag fluttering over the bonnet of the car, and wondered where I was really going.

CHAPTER IX

THE FOUNDATIONS

IT was strange to find myself back at Barrackpore as an army commander, in the same room, at the same desk, I had left a few months before as a corps commander. The scene was little altered, except that the rooms were more congested with staff officers and clerks, there were now huts all over the grounds, and more despatch riders noisily came and went under the windows. Yet great changes were in progress.

The army of which I took command was still the old Eastern Army of India, and I was thus, at the moment, under General Auchinleck, who had recently succeeded General Wavell as Commander-in-Chief, India. However, in August 1943, the British and United States Governments had formed a new South-East Asia Allied Command to control all forces in Burma, Ceylon, Malaya, the Dutch East Indies, Siam, and Indo-China. Admiral Mountbatten was appointed Supreme Commander, with, under him, three Commanders-in-Chief, for Sea, Land, and Air. General Sir George Giffard was to be the land C.-in-C. at 11th Army Group, and I, as Commander of the newly formed Fourteenth Army, should serve under him. This reorganization dividing South-East Asia Command from India was carried out during the next two months. It entailed splitting my headquarters between the new Fourteenth Army and the revived Indian Eastern Command, and it gave me one immediate advantage—it relieved me of all responsibility for Bihar, Orissa, and most of Bengal, an immense weight off my shoulders.

I do not believe in the system, so popular in the war, of commanders when promoted taking with them from the formations they leave, the cream of their staffs. These travelling circuses, grouped round particular generals, cause a great deal of heartburning and confusion. Not only is the subordinate headquarters skimmed of its best officers, but in the higher, a number of efficient and worthy officers are abruptly thrown out to make room for newcomers. I am not at all sure either that the practice is good for the generals concerned themselves. So, as usual, I arrived at Eastern Army without a following, and took over the complete staff as I found it.

Again, through no merit of my own, I was lucky. I soon found that Steve Irwin, who had recently been appointed Brigadier General Staff was an outstanding staff officer, with a first-class brain that grasped, and what was more important held to, the essentials of any plan or organization. Unruffled by crisis, he had a dry, keen wit in the summing-up of people and affairs that I found refreshing. The transfers to other headquarters that now had to be made, did, however, give me an opportunity to introduce some officers of my own choosing. Chief among these was 'Alf' Snelling, to whom I had said good-bye in the sandstorm on Lake Habbaniyeh eighteen months before. He came to me now as my Major-General in charge of Administration. I knew that the campaign in Burma would above all be a supply and transport problem, and I was determined to get the best possible man to take charge of that side of it for me. I think I did.

Immediately on taking over I found myself confronted by three major anxieties—supply, health, and morale.

Supply was, of course, largely a matter of communications. The Fourteenth Army was deployed on a seven-hundred-mile front, from the Chinese frontier beyond Fort Hertz to the Bay of Bengal. Along the Indo-Burmese border, in a shallow curve, sweeps the wide belt of jungle-clad, precipitous hills, railless, roadless and, for six months of the year during the monsoon rains, almost trackless. Sparsely populated by wild tribes, disease-infested, and even unmapped in places, much of this great area had been penetrated only by occasional Europeans and then only in the dry season. It could fairly be described as some of the world's worst country, breeding the world's worst diseases, and having for half the year at least the world's worst climate. To move even small pack caravans by the few dry-weather tracks from Burma to India was so difficult that no proper trading route existed. To supply, move, and fight great armies in or through the mass of jumbled hills had for so long been regarded as impossible that no serious defence measures had ever been taken on India's eastern frontier. Nor had any effective communications either for trade or war been built. Such roads, railways, and navigable rivers as there were stopped abruptly each side of the mountain barrier, a couple of hundred miles apart.

From the Indian side, the fighting areas could be reached—but only circuitously—by railway and river; there were no through roads. From Calcutta the broad-gauge railway, for about half of the distance a single track, ran for 235 miles to Parbatipur. Here, hordes of coolies unloaded the wagons and noisily transferred the contents to the ramshackle metre-gauge train that, if all had gone well, would be waiting. This then wandered up the Brahmaputra Valley to the ferry at Pandu, 450 miles from Calcutta. The coaches and wagons were uncoupled and pushed, with much clanking and banging, on to barges. A slow river crossing and the laborious process was repeated in reverse on the opposite bank. Over at last and reassembled, the train rattled monotonously on to Dimapur, the terminus for the Central front, over 600 miles from Calcutta. If bound for the Northern front, it continued its journey, even more slowly, to Ledo, more than 800 miles from Calcutta.

The line had been built mainly to serve the Assam tea gardens, and in peace its daily capacity had been only 600 tons. By the time the Fourteenth Army was formed, this had risen to 2,800, but even this was quite inadequate to supply both British forces at Imphal and the Chinese at Ledo, and the ever-rising tonnage required on the American airfields for the traffic to China. Plans for increasing capacity were in hand, but it was obvious that India could produce little more in the way of railwaymen, and there was no possibility of getting British. The American Army came to the rescue with the offer of six battalions of Railway troops, some 4,700 fully trained railwaymen. Early in 1944 these troops took over the operation of the line, and by October they had raised capacity to 4,400 tons and by 1st January 1946 to 7,300 tons a day. This was possible owing to the large additional American staffs—on the lengths of line normally in charge of two British or Indian officers, the Americans were able to put twenty-seven officers, all professional railwaymen—because of the arrival of more powerful locomotives from America and Canada, and because of the drive and energy put into the task. Thus to treble the capacity was a great achievement without which the vast and mounting air supply to China could not have been undertaken. But this is anticipating. We had in the summer of 1943 to work on 2,800 tons capacity, and this would not nearly meet demands for stocking the bases at Dimapur and Ledo, the construction of the American airfields and the Ledo road, the lift for China, and the move of reinforcing formations, all added to normal maintenance. This railway, until we took Rangoon, remained our chief transportation link, and for the next year at least was a terribly limiting factor, indeed something of a nightmare. I remember once saying, 'Well, that railway's been washed away by floods, put out by bombing, swept away by landslides, closed by train wrecks; there's not much more that can happen to it.' But there was. We had an earthquake that buckled rails and shifted bridges over a hundred miles of it.

It was also possible to reach almost to the Northern front by river. Leaving Calcutta by a winding route through the Sunderbans, the main stream of the Brahmaputra was reached and followed to Dibrugarh, a distance of 1,136 miles by water. For the Central Assam front, the river-head was Gauhati, near Pandu, but the capacity of this route was limited by the bottle-neck of the metre-gauge railway, already overloaded, between Gauhati and Dimapur. The Southern front in Arakan was reached by a tortuous combination of broad-gauge, river-steamer, and metre-gauge, which ended at Dohazari railhead, thirty miles south of Chittagong.

To bridge the gaps between the railheads and the fighting lines, main all-weather roads were under construction in the autumn of 1943—from Ledo to the Chinese front, from Dimapur to the Central front and from Dohazari, south of Chittagong, for Arakan. The most important of these was that serving the main front, which climbed through the hills from Dimapur to Imphal and then wound down again almost to the Burmese frontier. This road, a truly magnificent engineering achievement, was of a quality and permanence beyond any other on the Burma front. There was something splendid in its sweep through jungle, along mountain flanks, and over torrents. Day and night without break thousands of lorries swung round its curves, and ground in low gear up its gradients. Then from this main artery, at Imphal, branched off that crazy road to Tiddim, 180 miles away in the Chin Hills, zigzagging up cliffs, meandering through deep valleys, soaring again literally into the clouds. The making of this road was hardly a more wonderful feat than keeping it open against the spates, subsidences and the great landslides of the monsoon. The Arakan road had its own difficulties to overcome. It did not cross the great mountains of the others, but it encountered innumerable *chaungs*, tidal creeks running up inland from the sea. It went through a country that produced no stone for road metal, and it was impossible to bring in the thousands and thousands of tons that would be required. My engineers proved equal to the need. They built the road with bricks, millions and millions of them. Every twenty miles or so was a great brick kiln, looking in the distance rather like a two-funnelled ship. We imported skilled brickmakers from India, brought the necessary coal by rail, boat, and lorry, and baked our bricks. A brick road is terribly apt in rain to sink into the earth, but, constantly having fresh bricks relaid, it held, a monument to ingenuity and determination.

These three roads were pick, shovel, and basket roads, made by human labour, with an almost laughable lack of machinery. The men who built them worked under the most arduous conditions of climate and with the most elementary scale of accommodation, often with the enemy within striking distance. The whole of the labour, many thousands, was Indian, and much of it came from the Indian Tea Association, which organized, officered, and controlled some forty thousand of its own workers. Without this contribution we should never have built either the roads or the airfields that were vital for the Burma campaign and for the supply of China.

Pushing forward also at this time, under the vigorous direction of American engineers, was the Ledo road, intended eventually to link up with the old China–Burma road via Myitkyina. This road was, in its standards, even more ambitious than the Imphal one. For its construction the Americans had available a quantity of road-making machinery that made our mouths water—and they knew how to use it. With Indian labour and American machinery, the road, covered by the Chinese divisions, was at this time, the winter of 1943, beginning to nose its way south.

Inadequate railways, shortage of motor transport, few roads and those at the mercy of climate, to say nothing of enemy action, made the movement of men and supplies a constant anxiety. Our immediate worry, however, was not only inadequate transportation but an actual lack of supplies, especially of certain items. Our ration strength was well over half a million, mainly, of course,

Indian. Only a fraction of the total were fighting men, the larger proportion were the labour, administrative, technical, and non-combatant units, unavoidable in a country where every road, airfield, and camp had to be made from virgin jungle or rice-field. We were a very mixed party, and Snelling's problems were not simplified by there being some thirty different ration scales in the Fourteenth Army. Among the Indians, these were based partly on religion, partly on district of origin, and partly, in such cases as the Indian Tea Association labour, on the special contract of their service. These scales were all reasonably adequate—the question was, 'Were the men, especially in the forward areas, getting them?' The answer was, as I had suspected, 'No.'

Meat is one of the main items on which a soldier fights. The British soldier without it cannot fight. Even the Indian, who in his village is often almost a vegetarian for economic reasons, as a soldier needs a regular ration of meat twice a week if he is to reach his full physical and intellectual vigour. Meat was one of our greatest difficulties. On the Assam front, owing to the complete lack of cold storage facilities and of insulated wagons, the British troops in Imphal were receiving only half an issue a week of fresh meat; those forward of Imphal, that is, almost the whole of the fighting troops, got none. Instead they received bully beef, a good enough food in itself, but terribly monotonous and very unattractive in hot weather when it flows half molten from the tin. There were no stocks of alternatives to bully beef, no tinned or dehydrated meat, and no combined meat and vegetable rations, such as were available in other theatres. To make matters worse, except for a rare issue of tinned herrings or bacon, there were no 'breakfast meats' at all. No animals could be purchased locally, there were no sheep or goats, and the only cattle were needed for the plough. To have slaughtered those would have given only a momentary relief and would have left us with another starving population on our hands. As a result, the average British soldier on the Assam front went month after month without tasting fresh meat. In Arakan, where the transport difficulties for live goats were not so impossible and where there were some local slaughter cattle, the British soldier was better off and received one or two fresh meat issues a week. For the rest, like his comrade in the north, he had to be content with bully beef.

The Indian soldier fared much worse. Near railheads and in

Arakan he got up to two issues of meat a week, but forward of that he got none. The sepoy, whether Hindu or Mohammedan, does not eat tinned meat and, therefore, when fresh was not obtainable he went without meat altogether. This would not have been so serious were the authorized substitutes, additional issues of milk, and *ghi* (clarified butter), available. They were not. In Assam the total stock of *ghi* allowed for only thirteen days of normal issue, the arrival of further supplies was uncertain, and obviously no extra issues could be made. For milk it was much the same. Our stocks of tinned milk were very low. One reason for this is interesting. To guard against disruption of milk supplies by bombing in the United Kingdom, the Government had wisely laid in large stores of tinned milk in various parts of the country. The tins were sent from America in cardboard cartons. When demands for large quantities of milk for India were received the crisis in England was not so acute, and the Food Controller very sensibly decided to take the opportunity of turning over his store. So the milk was shipped to India. The cartons, already weakened by long storage and handling, rapidly deteriorated during the tropical voyage round the Cape, the tins rusted, and the cartons turned into pulp, making it impossible to pack them safely for the long rail journey across India with its interminable bumping and shunting. The wagons when opened on their final arrival at advanced railheads contained often a heap of battered, rusted tins and disintegrated cardboard. The unhappy Supply Officer was lucky if he rescued half in a still usable state, but, even so, gone was his chance of issuing a substitute for the non-existent meat.

Vegetables ranked with meat as an almost insoluble problem. Fresh vegetables could be grown in great quantity in Bengal and around Shillong in Assam, but the week or more's journey in lorries and steel railway wagons in great heat resulted usually in a putrid mass on arrival that could not be thrown away quickly enough. It was of course a little better in the cold weather, and again the troops in Arakan fared better, being nearer the sources of supply, but the almost complete lack of fresh vegetables in so many men's diets had a serious effect on health. The substitutes should have been tinned vegetables, tinned fruit, dried fruit, or dehydrated vegetables, but there were practically none of these in the forward supply depots. Stocks even of such basic commodities as rice and *atta* (Indian wholemeal flour) were a cause for anxiety. On the main front at Dimapur, we should have had 65,000 tons of supplies for the troops already based on that depot, even without regard to the increased numbers expected. The actual stock, I found, was only 47,000 tons, a deficiency of twenty-seven per cent. This was bad enough, but made much worse by the unbalanced state of the reserves with their almost complete lack of certain essential commodities. The supply situation was indeed so serious that it threatened the possibility of any offensive.

Although General Giffard had already set up his 11th Army Group Headquarters in Delhi, he had not yet had time nor had he the staff to take over administration from India. I, therefore, seized the opportunity of a visit by General Auchinleck to my headquarters to represent the dangers of the supply situation to him. He had only recently taken over in India and its seriousness was new to him. He summoned me to a conference with him and his principal supply officers in Delhi. On the 3rd November 1943, this meeting took place. Snelling was with me, armed as usual with all the facts and figures.

It appeared that to a large extent the Indian peacetime system of financial control still operated in the procurement of supplies. For example, when large quantities of dehydrated vegetables were ordered from Indian contractors, demands placed on the United Kingdom for tinned vegetables were, in accordance with peacetime rules, cancelled. The scale of issue of dehydrated vegetables is one-quarter that of tinned, so, for every hundred tons of dried ordered in India, four hundred tons of tinned ordered in England were cancelled. The quantities ordered in India, and the deliveries promised, were hopelessly optimistic so when the dehydrated failed to appear we were left without any vegetables at all. Again, it had been ruled that supplies for formations either being raised or coming into India could not even be ordered until the troops had actually been raised or arrived. Not all our troubles, however, were due to a financial control intended for peace. The alarming shortages in such staples as rice and flour were caused by the failure of the Food Department to deliver as promised, which in turn rose largely because some provincial governments could not supply their quotas.

Whatever the causes, it was clear that the supply situation was critical, and equally obvious that something vigorous would have to be done to avoid disaster. Luckily, General Auchinleck was the man to do it. There was a considerable and prompt injection of ginger into the Indian administrative machine, military and civil. Even at the beginning of 1944 the results of Auchinleck's drive began to show. Gradually, with now and then a temporary setback, our rations and our reserves climbed up and up. It was a good day for us when he took command of India, our main base, recruiting area, and training ground. The Fourteenth Army, from its birth to its final victory, owed much to his unselfish support and never-failing understanding. Without him and what he and the Army in India did for us we could not have existed, let alone conquered.

Our shortages were, unfortunately, not limited to supplies. In ammunition, for instance, we fell seriously below even the modest reserves calculated for jungle warfare, and they were much below those of any other theatre. Some typical shortages were:

Rifle	26 per cent
Sten- and tommy-gun	75 per cent
2- and 3-inch mortar	25 per cent
25-pounder H.E.	42 per cent
5.5-inch H.E.	86 per cent

Generally speaking, the ammunition we needed was in India, but that was a thousand miles from where we wanted it, and to bring it forward was a slow and laborious business. It was rather irritating, too, to find that some people had the habit of reckoning ammunition as on our charge the moment an order for its issue from an arsenal in India left Delhi, irrespective of the fact that it would be several months before it reached the Fourteenth Army depots. We were not only deficient of the ammunition but also of the guns to fire it. We were below our needs in most forms of equipment, notably vehicles, wireless sets, ambulances, and medical stores. In fact, we were short of everything.

Snelling's task was an immense one, and, having discussed it fully with him and selected the key men to work under him, I gave him a very free hand to carry it out. Soon, under his energetic direction, there were signs of improvement, and, while my anxieties on the supply side remained, I could see for myself wherever I went that our difficulties were being grappled with throughout the army and that we were getting increasing understanding and help from India.

My second great problem was health. In 1943, for every
man evacuated with wounds we had one hundred and twenty
evacuated sick. The annual malaria rate alone was eighty-four
per cent per annum of the total strength of the army and still
higher among the forward troops. Next to malaria came a high
incidence of dysentery, followed in this gruesome order of
precedence by skin diseases and a mounting tale of mite or jungle
typhus, a peculiarly fatal disease. At this time, the sick rate of men
evacuated from their units rose to over twelve per thousand per
day. A simple calculation showed me that in a matter of months
at this rate my army would have melted away. Indeed, it was
doing so under my eyes.

In anxious consultation with Snelling and my senior medical
officers I reviewed our resources. To start with, I discovered that
for some reason the medical establishments of the Fourteenth
Army were lower than those of other British armies in Africa or
Europe, and that actual strengths were gravely below even this
reduced establishment. We were short of units, doctors, nurses,
and equipment. Our hospitals had been of necessity expanded to
take twenty-five per cent more patients than they were designed
to hold. We now had twenty-one thousand hospital beds, all
occupied. To nurse these seriously sick or wounded men we had
a total of four hundred and fourteen nursing sisters, less then one
nurse to fifty beds throughout the twenty-four hours, or in
practice one to one hundred beds by day or night.

Demands for more nurses from home met with the answer that
there were none to spare from other fronts and that, anyway,
India should provide the nurses for Indian troops who formed the
bulk of my army. We might just as well have been told that
India must provide the aircraft for the air force. Aircraft were not
made in India; nor were nurses. The Indian Military Nursing
Service, struggling heroically against prejudice and every kind of
handicap, was in its infancy and could only grow very slowly. In
spite of all our efforts, and although General Auchinleck milked
the hospitals of India to danger-point to help us, it was clear that
any increase in our medical strength would be grievously slow.

I knew we had to beat Germany first. I was even ready to
accept the fact that the Fourteenth Army was the Cinderella of
all British armies, and would get only what her richer sisters in
Africa and Europe could spare. I would not grumble too much

177

if we came last for men, tanks, guns, and the rest, but I would protest, and never cease from protesting, that we should be at the bottom of the list for medical aid. That was not fair, nor, I believe, wise.

However, as we had long ago discovered, it was no use waiting for other people to come to our help. Nor was it much use trying to increase our hospital accommodation; prevention was better than cure. We had to stop men going sick, or, if they went sick, from staying sick. We tackled this problem on four main lines:

(i) The practical application of the latest medical research.
(ii) The treatment of the sick in forward areas instead of evacuation to India.
(iii) The air evacuation of serious casualties.
(iv) The raising of morale.

The prevention of tropical diseases had advanced immensely within the last few years, and one of the first steps of the new Supreme Commander had been to get to South-East Asia some of the most brilliant research workers in this field. Working closely with medical officers who had had experience of practical conditions, they introduced new techniques, drugs, and methods of treatment. Gradually the new remedies became available, although for long we lagged behind in their supply. Sulphonamide compounds, penicillin, mepacrine, and DDT all appeared later than we liked but still in time to save innumerable lives. Without research and its results we could not survive as an army.

It was, however, forward treatment that brought the first visible results. Up to now, when a man contracted malaria, he had been transported, while his disease was at its height, in great discomfort hundreds of miles by road, rail, and boat to a hospital in India. Before he reached there he had probably been reinfected several times, and while his first bout would be over he was booked for a relapse. In any case he would not return over the congested line of communication for, on the average, at least five months. Often enough he was employed in India and never returned. To avoid all this we organized M.F.T.U.s, Malaria Forward Treatment Units. They were, in effect, field hospitals, tented or more often in bashas, a few miles behind the fighting lines. A man reached them within twenty-four hours of his attack of malaria and he remained there for the three weeks or so it took to cure him. He was back

178

fit with his unit again in weeks instead of months, the strain on the line of communication was lightened, and he avoided the often terrible discomforts of the long journey. M.F.T.U.s had one other advantage. When morale was not high some men welcomed malaria and took no precautions to avoid it, reasoning that a bout of malaria was a cheap price to pay for getting away from the Burma front. If it only took them half a dozen miles from the front and brought them briskly back it was not so attractive.

For the wounded, forward surgical teams were introduced on an increasing scale. Working almost in the midst of the battle, specially selected surgeons, including some of the leading professors of our medical schools, performed major operations within a few hours of a man being wounded. Their work was brilliant, but it should be remembered that where the surgeon saved the individual life, the physician, less dramatically, saved hundreds by his preventive measures. We also sent nurses—when we had them —farther into the battle area than had been usual. There were some diseases, like mite typhus, for which we had then no proved treatment, in which the patient's chance of survival depended more on the nurse than on the doctor. The extra danger and hardship these nurses cheerfully endured were repaid in lives many times over.

Air evacuation, in the long run, probably made the greatest difference of all to the wounded and sick. Only those who have suffered the interminable anguish of travel over rough ground or tracks by stretcher or ambulance and the long stifling railway journey for days on end, with broken limbs jolting and temperatures soaring, can realize what a difference quick, smooth, cool transport by aircraft can mean. In November 1943 we had for all transport purposes, other than the maintenance of the 81st West African Division in Arakan, only some one hundred and twenty air sorties a month, but the number was rapidly growing and with it our technique of air evacuation. Later, light aeroplanes of the Moth, Auster, or L5 type picked up the casualties on airstrips hurriedly cut out of jungle or rice-field within a mile or two of the fighting. Each little aircraft carried one lying or two sitting patients and flew them to the supply strip, anything from ten to forty miles farther back. Here the casualties were transferred to Dakotas returning empty from the supply run and flown direct to a general hospital. There were, I remember, heated arguments

179

as to where these hospitals should be situated. Roughly, there was the choice between putting them in such hot sticky places in the plains as at Comilla or in the cool of the hills as at Shillong. I plumped for the plains, because there we could have an airstrip almost alongside the hospital; to reach the hills would have meant long and trying road journeys. So our casualties went almost direct from the battlefield to the hospital and later as convalescents by road from the plains to the hills. There was some shaking of heads among the more orthodox, but the results justified it. One such hospital took in during 1944 and 1945 over eleven thousand British casualties straight, in their filthy, blood-soaked battledress, from the front line. The total deaths in that hospital were twenty-three. Air evacuation did more in the Fourteenth Army to save lives than any other agency.

Good doctors are no use without good discipline. More than half the battle against disease is fought, not by the doctors, but by the regimental officers. It is they who see that the daily dose of mepacrine is taken, that shorts are never worn, that shirts are put on and sleeves turned down before sunset, that minor abrasions are treated before, not after, they go septic, that bodily cleanliness is enforced. When mepacrine was first introduced and turned men a jaundiced yellow, there was the usual whispering campaign among troops that greets every new remedy—the drug would render them impotent—so, often the little tablet was not swallowed. An individual medical test in almost all cases will show whether it has been taken or not, but there are a few exceptions and it is difficult to prove for court-martial purposes. I, therefore, had surprise checks of whole units, every man being examined. If the overall result was less than ninety-five per cent positive I sacked the commanding officer. I only had to sack three; by then the rest had got my meaning.

Slowly, but with increasing rapidity, as all of us, commanders, doctors, regimental officers, staff officers, and N.C.O.s, united in the drive against sickness, results began to appear. On the chart that hung on my wall the curves of admissions to hospitals and Malaria Forward Treatment Units sank lower and lower, until in 1945 the sickness rate for the whole Fourteenth Army was one per thousand per day. But at the end of 1943 that was a long way off.

My third great anxiety, intimately involved with health as with every aspect of efficiency, was morale. There was no doubt that the disasters in Arakan, following an unbroken record of defeat, had brought morale in large sections of the army to a dangerously low ebb. Morale was better in the forward combat formations, as most of the shaken units from Arakan had been withdrawn. 4 Corps in the centre, and, I flattered myself, 15 Corps in the south were staunch enough. It was in the rear areas, on the lines of communication, in the reinforcement camps, amid the conglomeration of administrative units that covered the vast area behind the front, that morale was really low. Through this filter all units, drafts, and individuals for the forward formations had to percolate, and many became contaminated with the virus of despondency. In the summer of 1943 there was a depressingly high incidence of desertion from drafts moving up the line of communication. Right back into India rumours were assiduously spread picturing the Japanese as the super bogy-men of the jungle, harping on their savagery, their superior equipment and training, the hardships our men suffered, the lack of everything, the faults in our leadership, and the general hopelessness of expecting ever to defeat the enemy. Such stories were brought even by drafts from England. It was an insidious gangrene that could easily spread. Whether morale went up or down, and with it hope of victory, was an issue that swayed in the balance.

On our side we had the somewhat phoney propaganda that followed Wingate's raid and the more solid influence of General Giffard's character. Against us was that record of defeat, the lack of even elementary amenities, the discomfort of life in the jungle, and worst of all the feeling of isolation, with all the heart sickness of long separation from home. The British soldier, especially, suffered from what he felt was the lack of appreciation by his own people and at times of their forgetfulness of his very existence. The men were calling themselves a 'Forgotten Army' long before some newspaper correspondent seized on the phrase. It was an understandable one. After all, the people of Britain had perils and excitements enough on their own doorsteps and Burma was far away. Its place in the general strategy was not clear, nor did what happened there seem vital. Much more stirring news was coming out of Africa. It was no use belly-aching because the Fourteenth Army was not in the headlines of the home papers; so far, we had not done anything to put us there. When we had won a victory or two we should be in a better position to complain. All the same, this feeling of neglect, of being at the bottom of all priority lists, had sunk deep. There was a good deal of bitterness in the army, and much too much being sorry for ourselves.

So when I took command, I sat quietly down to work out this business of morale. I came to certain conclusions, based not on any theory that I had studied, but on some experience and a good deal of hard thinking. It was on these conclusions that I set out consciously to raise the fighting spirit of my army.

Morale is a state of mind. It is that intangible force which will move a whole group of men to give their last ounce to achieve something, without counting the cost to themselves; that makes them feel they are part of something greater than themselves. If they are to feel that, their morale must, if it is to endure—and the essence of morale is that it should endure—have certain foundations. These foundations are spiritual, intellectual, and material, and that is the order of their importance. Spiritual first, because only spiritual foundations can stand real strain. Next intellectual, because men are swayed by reason as well as feeling. Material last—important, but last—because the very highest kinds of morale are often met when material conditions are lowest.

I remember sitting in my office and tabulating these foundations of morale something like this:

1. *Spiritual*
   (a) There must be a great and noble object.
   (b) Its achievement must be vital.
   (c) The method of achievement must be active, aggressive.
   (d) The man must feel that what he is and what he does matters directly towards the attainment of the object.
2. *Intellectual*
   (a) He must be convinced that the object *can* be attained; that it is not out of reach.
   (b) He must see, too, that the organization to which he belongs and which is striving to attain the object is an efficient one.
   (c) He must have confidence in his leaders and know that whatever dangers and hardships he is called upon to suffer, his life will not be lightly flung away.

3. *Material*

(a) The man must feel that he will get a fair deal from his commanders and from the army generally.

(b) He must, as far as humanly possible, be given the best weapons and equipment for his task.

(c) His living and working conditions must be made as good as they can be.

It was one thing thus neatly to marshal my principles but quite another to develop them, apply them, and get them recognized by the whole army.

At any rate our spiritual foundation was a firm one. I use the word spiritual, not in its strictly religious meaning, but as belief in a cause. Religion has always been and still is one of the greatest foundations of morale, especially of military morale. Saints and soldiers have much in common. The religion of the Mohammedan, of the Sikh, of the Gurkha, and of the fighting Hindu —and we had them all in the Fourteenth Army—can rouse in men a blaze of contempt for death. The Christian religion is above all others a source of that enduring courage which is the most valuable of all the components of morale. Yet religion, as we understand it, is not essential to high morale. Anyone who has fought with or against Nazi paratroops, Japanese suicide squads, or Russian Commissars, will have found this; but a spiritual foundation, belief in a cause, there must be.

We had this; and we had the advantage over our enemies that ours was based on real, not false, spiritual values. If ever an army fought in a just cause we did. We coveted no man's country; we wished to impose no form of government on any nation. We fought for the clean, the decent, the free things of life, for the right to live our lives in our own way, as others could live theirs, to worship God in what faith we chose, to be free in body and mind, and for our children to be free. We fought only because the powers of evil had attacked these things. No matter what the religion or race of any man in the Fourteenth Army, he *must* feel this, feel that he had indeed a worthy cause, and that if he did not defend it life would not be worth living for him or for his children. Nor was it enough to have a worthy cause. It must be positive, aggressive, not a mere passive, defensive, anti-something feeling. So our object became not to defend India, to stop the

Japanese advance, or even to occupy Burma, but to destroy the Japanese Army, to smash it as an evil thing.

The fighting soldier facing the enemy can see that what he does, whether he is brave or craven, matters to his comrades and directly influences the result of the battle. It is harder for the man working on the road far behind, the clerk checking stores in a dump, the headquarters telephone operator monotonously plugging through his calls, the sweeper carrying out his menial tasks, the quartermaster's orderly issuing bootlaces in a reinforcement camp—it is hard for these and a thousand others to see that they too matter. Yet every one of the half-million in the army—and it was many more later—had to be made to see where his task fitted into the whole, to realize what depended on it, and to feel pride and satisfaction in doing it well.

Now these things, while the very basis of morale, because they were purely matters of feeling and emotion, were the most difficult to put over, especially to the British portion of the army. The problem was how to instil or revive their beliefs in the men of many races who made up the Fourteenth Army. I felt there was only one way to do it, by a direct approach to the individual men themselves. Not by written exhortations, by wireless speeches, but by informal talks and contacts between troops and commanders. There was nothing new in this; my corps and divisional commanders and others right down the scale were already doing it. It was the way we had held the troops together in the worst days of the 1942 retreat; we remained an army then only because the men saw and knew their commanders. All I did now was to encourage my commanders to increase these activities, unite them in a common approach to the problem, in the points that they would stress, and in the action they would take to see that principles became action not merely words.

Yet they began, as most things do, as words. We, my commanders and I, talked to units, to collections of officers, to headquarters, to little groups of men, to individual soldiers casually met as we moved around. And we all talked the same stuff with the same object. Whenever I could get away from my headquarters, and that throughout the campaign was about a third of the time, I was in these first few months more like a parliamentary candidate than a general—except that I never made a promise. One of the most successful of British commanders once told me

that you could make an appeal to these higher things successfully
to officers, but not directly to the rank and file. He under-
estimated his countrymen, and he had forgotten history. His
dictum was not true of the England of the Crusades, of Cromwell,
of Pitt, nor of Churchill. It was not true of my army, of either the
British, Indian, Gurkha, or African soldier. I made a point of
speaking myself to every combatant unit or at least to its officers
and N.C.O.s. My platform was usually the bonnet of my jeep
with the men collected anyhow round it. I often did three or four
of these stump speeches in a day. I learnt, or perhaps I had already
learnt in 15 Corps, the various responses one got from the
different nationalities. Even the British differed. A cockney battalion saw the point of a joke almost before it came, a north country
unit did not laugh so easily but when it did the roar was good to
hear. All responded at once to some reference to their pride in the
part of Britain they came from or in their regiment. A lot more
could be made of this local pride; it is a fine thing. All the British
were shy of talk of the spiritual things. This was most marked in
the English; the Welsh and Irish had fewer inhibitions on these
subjects, and the Scots, who are reared more on the romance of
their history, least of any. While Indian races differed in almost
everything, they all were more ready than the British to respond
openly to direct appeals on these more abstract grounds. They
had not only a greater feeling for personal leadership, but their
military traditions, their local patriotisms, and their religions were
much more part of the everyday fabric of their lives than such
things are with us. Their reaction was immediate and often
intense. The Gurkha, bless him, made the most stolid of all
audiences. He had a tendency to stand or sit to attention and his
poker face never changed its expression until it broke into the
most attractive grin in Asia at a rather broad jest. With the
African I was handicapped by language but, speaking without
deep knowledge, I should say that, allowing for his greater lack
of sophistication, he responded much as an Indian.

Language was a difficulty. The Indian Army now contained
many recruits who had not had time to learn Urdu and some units
such as the Madras ones had hardly any Hindustani speakers.
However, I managed somehow, though it was only the innate
good manners of the Indian soldier that on many an occasion
prevented laughter at some gaffe I made. I remember one day

I spoke to a Gurkha battalion, drove a mile or so, and addressed
an Indian one. My talk in substance was the same to both of them.
When I had finished what I thought was a particularly eloquent
Urdu harangue to the Indians, I turned to my A.D.C. and said
with some pride, 'That was a pretty good effort, wasn't it?'
'Quite, sir,' he replied crushingly, 'but I suppose you know that
after the first two sentences you relapsed entirely into Gurkhali!'

I learnt, too, that one did not need to be an orator to be
effective. Two things only were necessary: first to know what
you were talking about, and, second and most important, to
believe it yourself. I found that if one kept the bulk of one's talk
to the material things the men were interested in, food, pay,
leave, beer, mails, and the progress of operations, it was safe to
end on a higher note—the spiritual foundations—and I always did.

To convince the men in the less spectacular or less obviously
important jobs that they were very much part of the army, my
commanders and I made it our business to visit these units, to
show an interest in them, and to tell them how we and the rest
of the army depended on them. There are in an army, and for that
matter any big organization, very large numbers of people whose
existence is only remembered when something for which they
are responsible goes .vrong. Who thinks of the telephone operator
until he fails to get his connection, of the cipher officer until he
makes a mistake in his decoding, of the orderlies who carry papers
about a big headquarters until they take them to the wrong
people, of the cook until he makes a particularly foul mess of the
interminable bully? Yet they *are* important. It was harder to get
this over to the Indian subordinates. They were often drawn
from the lower castes, quite illiterate, and used to being looked
down upon by their higher-caste fellow-townsmen or villagers.
With them, I found I had great success by using the simile of a
clock. 'A clock is like an army,' I used to tell them. 'There's a
main spring, that's the Army Commander, who makes it all go;
then there are other springs, driving the wheels round, those are
his generals. The wheels are the officers and men. Some are big
wheels, very important, they are the chief staff officers and the
colonel sahibs. Other wheels are little ones, that do not look at all
important. They are like you. Yet stop one of those little wheels
and see what happens to the rest of the clock! They *are* important.'

We played on this very human desire of every man to feel

himself and his work important, until one of the most striking things about our army was the way the administrative, labour, and non-combatant units acquired a morale which rivalled that of the fighting formations. They felt they shared directly in the triumphs of the Fourteenth Army and that its success and its honour were in their hands as much as anybody's. Another way in which we made every man feel he was part of the show was by keeping him, whatever his rank, as far as was practicable in the picture of what was going on around him. This, of course, was easy with staff officers and similar people by means of conferences held daily or weekly when each branch or department could explain what it had been doing and what it hoped to do. At these conferences they not only discussed things as a team, but what was equally important, actually *saw* themselves as a team. For the men, talks by their officers and visits to the information centres which were established in every unit took the place of those conferences.

It was in these ways we laid the spiritual foundations, but that was not enough; they would have crumbled without the others, the intellectual and the material. Here we had first to convince the doubters that our object, the destruction of the Japanese Army in battle, was practicable. We had to a great extent frightened ourselves by our stories of the superman. Defeated soldiers in their own defence have to protest that their adversary was something out of the ordinary, that he had all the advantages of preparation, equipment, and terrain, and that they themselves suffered from every corresponding handicap. The harder they have run away, the more they must exaggerate the unfair superiority of the enemy. Thus many of those who had scrambled out of Burma without waiting to get to grips with the invader, or who had been in the rear areas in 1943, had the most hair-raising stories of Japanese super-efficiency. Those of us who had really fought him, believed that man for man our soldiers could beat him at his own jungle game, and that, in intelligence and skill, we could excel and outwit him.

We were helped, too, by a very cheering piece of news that now reached us, and of which, as a morale raiser, I made great use. In August and September 1942, Australian troops had, at Milne Bay in New Guinea, inflicted on the Japanese their first undoubted defeat on land. If the Australians, in conditions very

187

like ours, had done it, so could we. Some of us may forget that of all the Allies it was Australian soldiers who first broke the spell of the invincibility of the Japanese Army; those of us who were in Burma have cause to remember.

But all this could not be convincingly put over by talking and education alone. It had to be demonstrated practically. This is what my predecessors had tried in Arakan, but they had been, amongst other things, too ambitious. A victory in a large-scale battle was, in our present state of training, organization, and confidence, not to be attempted. We had first to get the feel through the army that it was we who were hunting the Jap, not he us.

All commanders therefore directed their attention to patrolling. In jungle warfare this is the basis of success. It not only gives eyes to the side that excels at it, and blinds its opponent, but through it the soldier learns to move confidently in the element in which he works. Every forward unit, not only infantry, chose its best men, formed patrols, trained and practised them, and then sent them out on business. As was to be expected, the superior intelligence of our officers and men told. These patrols came back to their regiments with stories of success, of how the Japanese had walked into their ambushes, how they had watched the enemy place their observation posts day after day in the same place, and then had pounced on them, how they had followed their patrols and caught them asleep. Our men brought back a Japanese rifle, an officer's shoulder-straps, a steel helmet. Sometimes they brought back even more convincing exhibits, as did the Gurkhas who presented themselves before their general, proudly opened a large basket, lifted from it three gory Japanese heads, and laid them on his table. They then politely offered him for his dinner the freshly caught fish which filled the rest of the basket. The buzz went round each unit. 'Have you heard about Lieutenant Smith's patrol? Cor, they didn't 'alf scrag the Nips . . .!' 'We rushed them as they were cooking, Havildar Bhupsingh bayoneted three. . . .' 'Rifleman Gingerbir crept up *luki-luki* behind him with his *kukri*. The Yellow-belly's head bounced three times before it stopped rolling!' The stories lost nothing in the telling, and there was no lack of competition for the next patrol. It went out with new men but under an experienced leader, and came back with more tales of success. Even if it returned with little to report, it had stalked its quarry without finding him, and that is one way to whet a hunter's appetite. In about ninety per cent of these tiny patrol actions we were successful. By the end of November our forward troops had gone a long way towards getting that individual feeling of superiority and that first essential in the fighting man—the desire to close with his enemy.

This recovery had already been accomplished to a very large extent in the two divisions, the 17th and 23rd, which held the Assam front during the monsoon of 1943, before I took over command of the whole Burma front. All I did was to see that this became an army method and was carried on in all formations.

Having developed the confidence of the individual man in his superiority over the enemy, we had now to extend that to the corporate confidence of units and formations in themselves. This was done in a series of carefully planned minor offensive operations, carried out as the weather improved, against enemy advanced detachments. These were carefully staged, ably led, and, as I was always careful to ensure, in greatly preponderating strength. We attacked Japanese company positions with brigades fully supported by artillery and aircraft, platoon posts by battalions. Once when I was studying the plan for an operation of this kind submitted by the local commander, a visiting staff officer of high rank said, 'Isn't that using a steam hammer to crack a walnut?' 'Well,' I answered, 'if you happen to have a steam hammer handy and you don't mind if there's nothing left of the walnut, it's not a bad way to crack it.' Besides, we could not at this stage risk even small failures. We had very few, and the individual superiority built up by successful patrolling grew into a feeling of superiority within units and formations. We were then ready to undertake larger operations. We had laid the first of our intellectual foundations of morale; everyone knew we could defeat the Japanese, our object *was* attainable.

The next foundation, that the men should feel that they belonged to an efficient organization, that Fourteenth Army was well run and would get somewhere, followed partly from these minor successes. At the same time the gradual but very noticeable improvements that General Giffard's reorganization of the rear areas and Snelling's and the line of communication staff's almost incredible achievements within the army itself were making themselves felt. Rations did improve, though still far below what they

189

should be; mail began to arrive more regularly; there were even signs of a welfare service.

An innovation was to be the publication of a theatre newspaper—*Seac*. One day I was told its editor designate was touring the army area and had asked if I would see him. A hefty-looking second-lieutenant was ushered into my office and introduced as Frank Owen. I had strong views on Service newspapers, and sat the young man down for ten minutes, while I explained to him exactly how his paper should be run and what were an editor's duties. He listened very politely, said he would do his best, saluted, and left. It was only after he had gone that I learned he had been one of the youngest and most brilliant editors in Fleet Street and had characteristically thrown up his job to enlist at the beginning of the war. *Seac* under his direction—and Admiral Mountbatten wisely gave him complete editorial freedom—was the best wartime Service journal I have seen. It—and Owen himself—made no mean contribution to our morale.

One of the greatest weakeners of morale had been the state of the rest and reinforcement camps. In these camps on the line of communications all reinforcements to the various fronts were held often for weeks until required or until transport was available to take them forward. Almost without exception I found these places depressing beyond words. Decaying tents or dilapidated *bashas*, with earth floors, mosquito ridden and lacking all amenities, were the usual accommodation; training and recreation were alike unorganized; men were crowded together from all units. No wonder spirits sank, discipline sagged, and defeatist rumours spread. Worst of all, the commandants and staffs, with a few notable exceptions, were officers and N.C.O.s who were not wanted by units or who preferred the rear to the front. This lamentable state of affairs had to be taken in hand at once. The first step was to choose an officer with energy, experience, and organizing ability to take overall charge. I found him in Colonel Gradige of the Indian Cavalry. The next was to select really good officers to command and staff the camps. Fighting unit C.O.s were naturally reluctant to spare their best, but when the need was explained, and in some cases a little pressure applied, they produced them. General Giffard was the first to appreciate the need and he gave us every possible help from the still meagre equipment and resources he had. Each camp was allotted to a

forward division. That division provided its officers and instructors; the divisional flag was flown and its sign worn. Divisional
commanders were encouraged to visit their camps, and from the
moment a man arrived he was made to feel that he belonged to
a fighting formation in which he could take pride. Training
became real, discipline was reasserted, and in a few months the
Fourteenth Army reinforcement camps, although still on a scale
of accommodation and amenities much below what I could wish,
were clean, cheerful, active parts of the army. Although Gradige
controlled on an average fifty thousand men I was never allowed
to give him even the acting rank of brigadier. Few colonels did
more for the success of the Fourteenth Army than he.

Behind these camps, Generals Auchinleck and Giffard had
established two training divisions, the 14th and 34th, who drew
their commanders and instructors from battle-experienced officers
and N.C.O.s of the Fourteenth Army. Here, recruits who had
completed their elementary training passed on to practical jungle
work. Within a few months the quality of the reinforcements
reaching us from these divisions through the camps had completely changed, not only in skill but, above all, in morale.

In the main, as always, the men judged the efficiency of their
show by the qualities of their leaders. Corps and divisional
commanders had their men's confidence to the full; they were
capable, experienced, and above all they were known to their
troops. Our brigadiers and unit commanders had been carefully
weeded and were an active, tough bunch of professional fighting
soldiers. We kept them such. I was often throughout the campaign pressed to take straight into appointments as brigadiers or
battalion commanders, sometimes even as divisional commanders,
officers from home or India without war experience in command.
I always resisted this. I would take them as seconds-in-command
of brigades or battalions for a period of trial and instruction, but
it would not have been fair, whatever their peacetime or training
records, either to the men they were to command or to the
officers themselves to have thrust them raw into a jungle battle.
Let them win their spurs. Most of them did, but some did not. It
was as well to find out first.

The setting up of South-East Asia Command, divorced from
India, was itself a promise of better things, of new drive, new
resources. When Admiral Mountbatten, the new Supreme

Commander, appeared these hopes were confirmed. Youthful, buoyant, picturesque, with a reputation for gallantry known everywhere, he talked to the British soldier with irresistible frankness and charm. To the Indian he appealed equally. The morale of the army was already on the upgrade; he was the final tonic.

I met him for the first time on the brick-floored airfield at Barrackpore near my headquarters. He was an hour or so late, and I sat in my car, chatting to an American air general. There had been some confusion between the markings on Japanese aircraft, the single round red blob, and on our own, the R.A.F. red, white, and blue roundel, with its red centre. As a result the R.A.F. in the Burma theatre had repainted their markings to do away with their red centre and we had issued orders that an aircraft with any red on it was an enemy and could be shot at. The first thing I noticed, as Mountbatten's large transport aircraft came in to land, was the conspicuous red centres of the roundels on its wings and fuselage. Luckily no one was trigger happy, and he landed without incident.

His visit was very brief. He came to our headquarters, met the commanders and staff of the R.A.F., the U.S.A.A.F., and my chief staff officers, and gave us a short speech on what he intended to do. It seemed a lot, but we were all for it. I gathered from this talk and from the few minutes we had together that ideas of taking Burma from the north were off. The main offensive was now to come from a landing in the south. This seemed to be eminently sensible. It had often been discussed before, but was hopeless until we got the necessary naval covering forces and landing craft. When I asked him if these would be forthcoming, 'We're getting so many ships,' he told us, 'that the harbours of India and Ceylon won't be big enough to hold 'em!' We saw him off in his aircraft for Delhi—the red roundels would not matter much inside India —and went back to our work all the better for his visit and with confidence that the Burma front was at last moving up the priority list. We began to feel that we belonged to an efficient show, or what was going to be one, and that feeling spread.

A most potent factor in spreading this belief in the efficiency of an organization is a sense of discipline. In effect, discipline means that every man, when things pass beyond his own authority or initiative, knows to whom to turn for further direction. If it is the right kind of discipline he turns in the confidence that he will get sensible and effective direction. Every step must be taken to build up this confidence of the soldier in his leaders. For instance, it is not enough to *be* efficient; the organization must *look* efficient. If you enter the lines of a regiment where the Quarter Guard is smart and alert, and the men you meet are well turned out and salute briskly, you cannot fail to get an impression of efficiency. You are right; ten to one that unit *is* efficient. If you go into a headquarters and find the clerks scruffy, the floor unswept, and dirty tea mugs staining fly-blown papers on the office tables, it *may* be efficient, but no visitor will think so.

The raising of the standard of discipline throughout the army, which, especially in many of the newly formed units, had deteriorated, was taken vigorously in hand by all commanders. We tried to make our discipline intelligent, but we were an old-fashioned army and we insisted on its outward signs. In the Fourteenth Army we expected soldiers to salute officers—and officers to salute in return—both in mutual confidence and respect. I encouraged all officers to insist whenever possible, and there were few places where it was not possible, on good turn-out and personal cleanliness. It takes courage, especially for a young officer, to check a man met on the road for not saluting properly or for slovenly appearance, but, every time he does, it adds to his stock of moral courage, and whatever the soldier may say he has a respect for the officer who does pull him up. I would have made only one exception to the rigid enforcement of saluting. I would have declared Calcutta a non-saluting area. That city was crowded with officers and men on leave; they had no mufti clothing, and to walk down Chowringhee, Calcutta's main street, was a weariness for all of us. Either one saluted every five steps or one was constantly checking soldiers for failing to salute. However, I was not successful in persuading my superiors to accept this innovation.

With growing confidence in the possibility of defeating the Japanese, the lift that the establishment of South-East Asia Command gave to our hopes, and the rapid improvement in discipline, the intellectual foundations of morale were laid. There remained the material. Already the greater backing we were getting from Auchinleck's India, the steady improvement in transportation, and the general toning up of all rearward services were having their effect. Material conditions, though lamentably low by the standards of any other British army, were improving.

Yet I knew that whatever had been promised to the Supreme Commander from home, it would be six months at least before it reached my troops. We would remain, for a long time yet, desperately short. In my more gloomy moments—and in private I had plenty—I even doubted if we should ever climb up the priority list. There was only one thing to do if the hearts of my men were not to be sickened by hope deferred—admit to them the shortages, already only too obvious, but impress on them that:

(i) The Germans in Europe had to be beaten first. The Germans had a much higher scale of equipment than the Japanese. In fairness and common sense, therefore, the armies fighting them, however hard it was on us, should have first call on new equipment.

(ii) Within this limit every responsible commander would do his utmost to get what we needed.

(iii) If we could not get everything we wanted issued to us, we would either improvise it ourselves or do without.

(iv) We should be short of many things but I would not ask the troops to do anything unless there was at least the minimum of equipment needed for the task.

These things were frankly put to the men by their commanders at all levels and, whatever their race, they responded. In my experience it is not so much asking men to fight or work with inadequate or obsolete equipment that lowers morale but the belief that those responsible are accepting such a state of affairs. If men realize that everyone above them and behind them is flat out to get the things required for them, they will do wonders, as my men did, with the meagre resources they have instead of sitting down moaning for better.

I do not say that the men of the Fourteenth Army welcomed difficulties, but they grew to take a fierce pride in overcoming them by determination and ingenuity. From start to finish they had only two items of equipment that were never in short supply: their brains and their courage. They lived up to the unofficial motto I gave them, 'God helps those who help themselves.' Anybody could do an easy job, we told them. It would take real men to overcome the shortages and difficulties we should be up

THE FOUNDATIONS

against—the tough chap for the tough job! We had no *corp d'élite* which got preferential treatment; the only units who got that were the ones in front. Often, of course, they went short owing to the difficulties of transportation, but, if we had the stuff and could by hook or crook get it to them, they had it in preference to those farther back. One of the most convincing evidences of morale was how those behind—staffs and units—accepted this, and deprived themselves to ensure it. I indulged in a little bit of theatricality in this myself. When any of the forward formations had to go on half rations, as throughout the campaign they often did, I used to put my headquarters on half rations too. It had little practical effect, but as a gesture it was rather valuable, and it did remind the young staff officers with healthy appetites that it was urgent to get the forward formations back to full rations as soon as possible.

The fair deal meant, too, no distinction between races or castes in treatment. The wants and needs of the Indian, African, and Gurkha soldier had to be looked after as keenly as those of his British comrade. This was not always easy as many of our staff officers, having come straight from home, were, with the best will in the world, ignorant of what these wants were. There were a few, too, who thought that all Indian or African troops required was a bush to lie under and a handful of rice to eat. The Indian soldier's needs are not so numerous or elaborate as the British's, but his morale can be affected just as severely by lack of them.

In another respect we had no favourites. I was frequently asked as the campaign went on, 'Which is your crack division?' I always replied, 'All my divisions are crack divisions!' This was true in the sense that at some time or other every division I ever had in the Fourteenth Army achieved some outstanding feat of arms, and it might be any division that at any given period was leading the pack. The men of each division believed that their division was the best in the whole army, and it was right they should, but it is very unwise to let any formation, however good, be publicly recognized as better than the others. The same thing applies to units, and this was especially important where we had fighting together battalions with tremendous names handed down from the past, newly raised ones with their traditions yet to make, men of recognized martial races and others drawn from sources that had up to now no military record. They all got the same treatment

195

and they were all judged by results. Sometimes the results were by no means in accordance with accepted tables of precedence.

The individual, we took pains to ensure, too, was judged on his merits without any undue prejudice in favour of race, caste, or class. This is not always as easy as it sounds or as it ought to be, but, I think, promotion, for instance, went by merit whether the officer was British or Indian, Regular or emergency commissioned. In an army of hundreds of thousands many injustices to individuals were bound to occur but, thanks mainly to officers commanding units, most of the Fourteenth Army would, I believe, say that on the whole they had, as individuals, a reasonably fair deal. At any rate we did our best to give it them.

In these and in many other ways we translated my rough notes on the foundations of morale, spiritual, intellectual, and material, into a fighting spirit for our men and a confidence in themselves and their leaders that was to impress our friends and surprise our enemies.

BOOK III

The Weapon is Tested

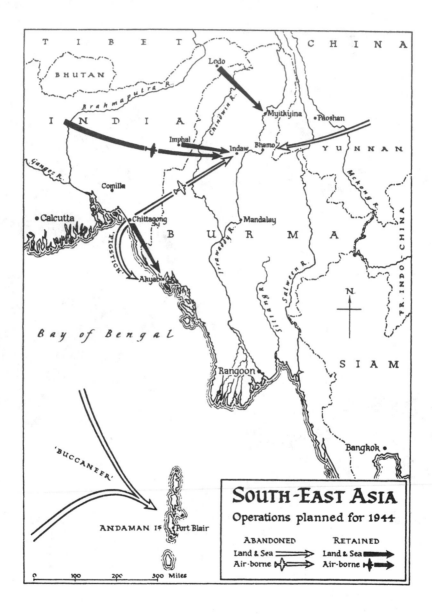

TIBET

CHINA

BHUTAN

Brahmaputra R.

INDIA

Ledo

Chindwin R.

Myitkyina • Paoshan

Imphal

Indaw Bhamo

YUNNAN

Ganges R.

Comilla

Mekong R.

• Calcutta

Chittagong

Mandalay

B U R M A

PIGSTICK

Akyab •

Irrawaddy R.

Sittang R.

Salween R.

FR. INDO-CHINA

Bay of Bengal

N.

S I A M

Rangoon •

'BUCCANEER'

Bangkok •

ANDAMAN IS Port Blair

0   100   200   300 Miles

SOUTH-EAST ASIA

Operations planned for 1944

ABANDONED	RETAINED
Land & Sea ⟶	Land & Sea ⟹
Air-borne ⊫⟹	Air-borne ⊪⟹

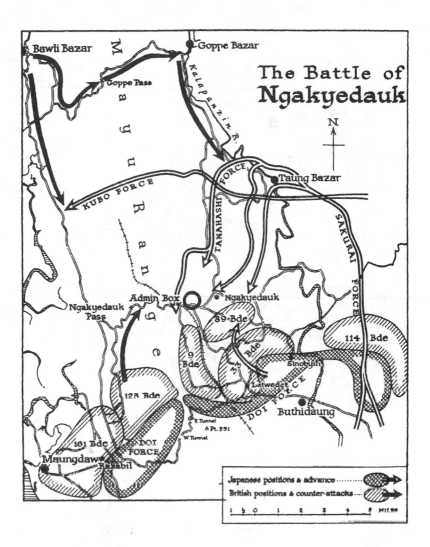

Bawli Bazar

Goppe Bazar

Goppe Pass

Kalapanzin R.

The Battle of
Ngakyedauk

N

M a y u   R a n g e

KUBO FORCE

TANAHASHI FORCE

Taung Bazar

SAKURAI FORCE

Admin Box

Ngakyedauk
Pass

Ngakyedauk

89 Bde

114 Bde

9 Bde

33 Bde

Sinohyin

Letwedet

DOI FORCE

123 Bde

Buthidaung

E.Tunnel

Pt. 551

W Tunnel

101 Bde

DOI
FORCE

Maungdaw

Razabil

Japanese positions & advance ....

British positions & counter-attacks ....

MILES

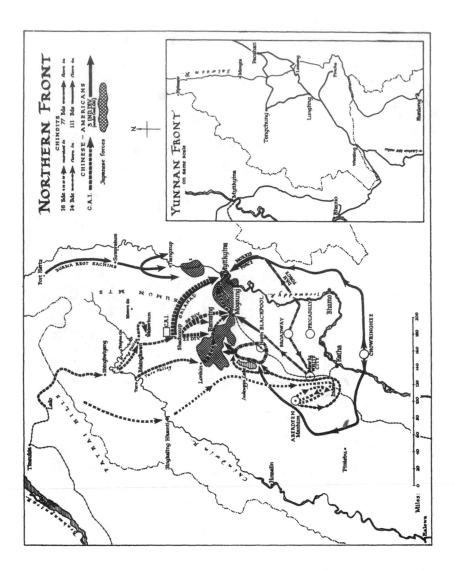

CHAPTER X

THE BEST-LAID PLANS

HAVING set things in motion to deal with the three great internal problems of supply, health, and morale, I next turned my attention to the location of my own headquarters. As a place, I intensely disliked Barrackpore. Its sordid slums depressed me, as did the faded splendours of the pre-Mutiny buildings in which we worked and lived. The distractions of Calcutta were on our doorstep and were not good for us or for our work; worst of all, it was too far from the fighting areas. Air travel, the only practicable way of getting round the fronts, reduced time, but it by no means annihilated distance. By air, Barrackpore to Imphal was about four hundred miles, the fighting was from a hundred to a hundred and fifty miles beyond that, and the northern Chinese front farther still. It was as if I were controlling from London a seven hundred mile battle front in the Italian Alps, only the roads and railways of Europe did not exist and the telegraphic and wireless communications were comparatively rudimentary. It was obviously necessary from every point of view to get my headquarters moved forward and, if possible, more centrally placed.

Choice was limited. Army Headquarters needed a considerable amount of accommodation, preferably in buildings, with good communications and at a site equally suitable for the air forces. I was determined that, wherever we went, my headquarters and that of the air forces working with me should be together. They, indeed, were already pressing for a move to Comilla, a largish town some two hundred miles east of Calcutta. For Bengal, its rail and road communications were good; it was capable of development into an air centre, as the capital of a district, it had a number of large administrative buildings, and it was at least no more unhealthy than Barrackpore. So to Comilla we decided to go. The Sappers and Signallers were soon at work, and preparations to receive both Army and Air Headquarters were now pressed on most vigorously.

At the end of October, with Bill Williams, the A.O.C., I made a final reconnaissance to allot accommodation between us. I should have liked to build a new Army Headquarters on slightly higher ground a few miles out of the town, but that would have taken too long, so we reserved this high ground for hospitals and wireless transmitters and went into the town itself. A Bengali town, its walls mildewed and stained by past monsoons, is invariably depressing, but Comilla had a sideline in melancholy all its own—its most noticeable features were the memorials erected to British civil and police officers, who, with monotonous frequency, had been murdered in the town by Bengali terrorists. My office windows would give me a good view of one such monument.

My next task was to get round my front. Arakan could wait. I was well acquainted with it and with what was going on there, but the main front in Assam I had not visited since June 1942, so I went there first. A lot had happened since the Retreat, not so much in the way of fighting as in administrative development. I found Lieut.-General Geoffry Scoones, who commanded on that front, a little worried about the dispersion of his corps on a two-hundred-mile stretch. However, I felt that if the local situation on the Japanese side remained much as it was, if our intentions continued offensive, and, above all, if plans for a major amphibious operation were going to be realized, we need not be unduly anxious about the rather scattered dispositions of 4 Corps.

From the Assam front I was called to Supreme Headquarters to attend conferences on the forthcoming general offensive. It was a sudden change from the jungle *bashas*, bivouacs, and worn green battledress of 4 Corps to the decorative interiors of New Delhi, thronged by all known, and some unknown, types of Allied uniform, male and female. New Delhi, the most beautiful and romantic official capital in the world, spacious as it is, was overcrowded. Apart from the wartime expansion of the Civil government, there were three great military headquarters competing there for space—General Headquarters India, Supreme Headquarters South-East Asia, and 11th Army Group Headquarters. I could sympathize with Admiral Mountbatten's desire to move his headquarters to some less congested spot and one within his own command.

The conferences themselves were impressive affairs. They took place in the red sandstone secretariat building, where, as a junior staff officer, I had worked fifteen years before. The room in which they were held was large, and it was full. I had never seen so many people at a planning conference, but then, I reminded myself, I had never before seen a planning conference on this level. At the head of a very long table flanked by big windows sat the Supreme Commander, Admiral Mountbatten; down each side were ranged his commanders-in-chief and his principal staff officers, while at the foot a scurry of secretaries of two nations and six Services ran a note-taking marathon. On ranks of chairs filling the rest of the room were American generals, Chinese admirals, British air marshals, Dutchmen, Indians, and what seemed to me a very large number of officers of all ranks and kinds.

The men who impressed me most in these gatherings were General Wheeler, the American Chief Administrative Officer, obviously a man of great ability, and, what was even more important, experienced common sense, and my own Commander-in-Chief, General Giffard, who, although not at his best in debate of this sort, kept to the fore the element of practical soldiering. I was surprised to find that the conference often occupied itself with minor matters of equipment, moves of units, and a dozen things that might have been thrown to staff officers to handle. A good many hares were put up and enthusiastically chased. At times we seemed to be thinking more of the effects of our proposed action on Whitehall and Washington than on Tokyo. The truth was I had not been accustomed to the large staffs that had become popular in Europe and Africa, nor did I make allowances for the inevitable teething troubles of a great headquarters.

This was the first conference I had sat through at S.E.A.C. Headquarters, and I found it a little bewildering. I attended many in the next two years, and it was interesting to see how rapidly they became more business-like and effective as Admiral Mountbatten learnt the job of Supreme Commander. Because he had to learn it. No Englishman ever got much opportunity to practise high command in peace, and none to be a supreme commander. Admiral Mountbatten's career as a naval officer, his command of a destroyer flotilla, and later an aircraft carrier with the quick-thinking, instant decisions and direct control of men that such tasks call for, were the finest possible training for tactical command. His period as Chief of Combined Operations gave him an insight into the organization and working of the other two Services that was of tremendous value to him; but the tactical planning of combined operations involves, more than any other, attention to and concentration on detail, in contrast to the broader, long-term considerations that are the province of a supreme commander. It was as a member of the Chiefs of Staffs Committee for Combined Operations, where he came into contact with the wider direction of the war as a whole, that he served his apprenticeship for supreme command.

His comparative youth—he was ten years younger than I and twenty years younger than Stilwell—was something of a stimulant to most of us, and certainly to our troops. There may have been a few in the Navy, where they are more stripe conscious, who found it hard to forget that they were admirals when he was a commander, but in the Army we are more tolerant in these matters. We are too accustomed to the vagaries of acting and temporary rank. My substantive rank when I became Army Commander was still Colonel, but I do not think that bothered anyone very much. From the very start, no one could fail to like the Supreme Commander—even Stilwell, in a picturesque phrase, once admitted that to me—and his quick brain, backed by a remarkable memory and tireless vitality, enabled him to grasp the intricacies of the whole vast organization of which he was the head. He came more and more to concentrate on essentials and to look farther ahead, until he was in every sense a real supreme commander.

I found Supreme Headquarters a fascinating place to wander through. It was full of interesting people, not least persuasive young men interested in selling short cuts to victory, of which they held the rights of way. These 'racketeers', as I called them, were of two kinds, those whose acquaintance with war was confined to large non-fighting staffs where they had had time and opportunity to develop their theories, and tough, cheerful fellows who might be first-class landed on a beach at night with orders to scupper a sentry-post, but whose experience was about the range of a tommy-gun. I liked talking to them and they were very willing to oblige me. Few of them had anything really new to say, and the few that had, usually forgot that a new idea should have something to recommend it besides just breaking up normal organization.

While the new headquarters was quickly getting into its stride, there arose in Delhi one disturbing feature—a growing danger of serious friction between Supreme Headquarters, South-East Asia, and General Headquarters, India. Many of the newly arrived staff had no knowledge of India, its limitations or its capabilities, and sometimes they showed the arrogance of ignorance. The old hands at Indian Headquarters in their turn were too ready to resent their displacement in control of operations and to be sensitive to criticism of their past efforts. It was only the admirable good sense of the commanders themselves that avoided the catastrophe of a split into two factions, the pro-Mountbatten and the pro-Auchinleck. They set their faces firmly against any encouragement of this rivalry, and, in spite of the many real difficulties, co-operated fully and unselfishly. Had they not, success in South-East Asia would have been longer delayed.

All this time, planning was proceeding at high pressure, and in what might justly be termed two camps—the 'Sac' and the 'Cic', the Supreme Allied Commander's planners and the Commanders-in-Chief's planners. It was rather like a game of tennis. One set of planners tossed up a plan and served it to the others, who amended it and sent it back over the net. These returns went on for quite a time, until Sac or Cic eventually ended the rally by a triumphant smash that bounced the unfortunate plan right out of court. Early in the proceedings the Supreme Commander himself became aware of this, and it was not long before he organized a machine that really worked, by the simple expedient of placing the Cs.-in-C.'s planners and his own in one joint body under the chairmanship of his senior planner.

The first directive from the Combined British and American Chiefs of Staff laid down two tasks for the Allied Forces in South-East Asia. First, they were to engage the Japanese as closely as possible so as to divert enemy formations from the Pacific theatre, where the Americans were staging an offensive, and, second, they were to expand our contacts with China by developing the air route and by building a road through North Burma to connect with the old China–Burma route. Full advantage was to be taken of our increasing superiority at sea and in the air to seize some area which would induce a powerful reaction from the enemy. Mr. Churchill had for this purpose strongly urged an amphibious operation against Sumatra, and the first task of the planners had been to consider this. It was, however, decided that, with the resources available, it could not be undertaken. This was reported to the Chiefs of Staff, who replied that no more could be sent to Burma at this stage of the war. There was then no alternative but to abandon the Sumatra project.

Nothing daunted, the planning teams set to work to discover something less ambitious in the way of an amphibious operation. The Andaman Islands were obviously a second choice, but the best within the scope of the forces available. The capture of these islands, combined with operations in Burma itself, would, it was hoped, fulfil the directive. By the end of November these plans had crystallized into a series of connected offensives which were to take place in 1944. They were:

(i) The capture of the Andaman Islands by 33 Corps in an amphibious operation.

(ii) The occupation of the Mayu Peninsula in Arakan by 15 Corps, as a preliminary to an amphibious assault on Akyab.

(iii) An advance across the Chindwin by 4 Corps on the Central front, with the object of drawing off the main Japanese forces from (iv).

(iv) An advance by General Stilwell's Chinese from Ledo to Myitkyina to cover the building of a road to China.

(v) To help Stilwell's advance, a long-range penetration operation behind the Japanese opposing him, by Wingate's Special Force.

(vi) An airborne operation by the Indian Parachute Brigade and an Indian division to seize the Rail Indaw area, first to help Stilwell's advance and, second, to co-operate with (vii).

(vii) An offensive by the Chinese Yunnan armies into the Lashio-Bhamo area.

This programme, in addition to the Andamans assault, entailed a widespread offensive over the whole of the Burma front. The operations proposed were within the compass of the land forces and strategically well integrated. Obviously, however, as they included one major and one lesser amphibious operation, and at least two large airborne or air-supplied campaigns, to say nothing of other air transport commitments, the whole plan depended for its practicability on large numbers of naval landing craft and considerable air transport formations being available. Everyone at S.E.A.C. Headquarters appeared confident that these forces would be forthcoming from those already in or firmly allotted to the theatre. I had the pleasant feeling that now we really were on the map in Whitehall and Washington.

The first difficulty that arose was over command of the operations in Burma. It had originally been intended that Stilwell would command the Ledo advance and the Chinese Yunnan forces as soon as they entered Burma. At this time, November 1943, his command was in effect only a small corps, but it was hoped to bring in more Chinese divisions to join the Ledo force, and, when the large but amorphous Yunnan armies were added, Stilwell would have under him the rough equivalent of an army. The other Burma operations, in Arakan, on the Central front, and the two airborne landings behind the Japanese would be under Fourteenth Army. Stilwell and I would each act as army commanders, under General Giffard, the Commander-in-Chief of 11th Army Group, who would thus have two fairly well-balanced armies in his group. This would have been the logical and militarily sound organization of the command. Stilwell, however, bitterly resisted it, and when that old man resisted anything it was a dour business. Dour, yet not without its humorous side. To watch Stilwell, when hard pressed, shift his opposition from one of the several strong-points he held by virtue of his numerous Allied, American, and Chinese offices, to another, was a lesson in the mobile offensive-defensive.

Finally, to settle this matter of command, the Supreme Commander held a conference—wisely not so large a one as usual. There were present, besides the Supreme Commander and his chief staff officers, American and British, General Giffard, Stilwell, and myself. The proceedings opened by Admiral Mountbatten very politely suggesting that as he had a military Commander-in-Chief for an Army Group, and as his own headquarters was not designed to deal direct with subordinate formations, Stilwell should come under General Giffard's command. Stilwell at once pointed out that, as C.-in-C. of the Chinese forces in Burma, he

THE WEAPON IS TESTED

had to obey the Generalissimo's order that these formations must remain under his direct command, subject only to the overall control of the Supreme Commander. After some brisk argument around this contention, Stilwell came out as the commanding general of the American China–Burma–India theatre. Giffard, he said, was not an Allied but a British Commander-in-Chief, and, as an American general, he had not the President's authority to put himself or his forces under a purely British commander. A good deal more time was occupied in arguing that. Then the redoubtable old man changed hats again and appeared in another role. As Deputy Supreme Commander he was, anyhow, senior to any group commander and could not, therefore, fittingly be put under General Giffard! The more Admiral Mountbatten, showing infinite patience, reasoned with him, the more obstinate and petulant the old man became. The real trouble lay in the unfortunate personal antipathy that had existed between Giffard and Stilwell from their first contacts. While each had basic qualities that should have appealed to the other, they were such poles apart in manner, upbringing, outlook, and methods, that neither could or would conceal his opinion of the other.

The temperature of the meeting rose. Stilwell fell back on a surly obstinacy that showed him at his worst. I, of course, said nothing, as I was only there to accept such decision as would be reached; neither did General Giffard, who in spite of considerable provocation, behaved, as he always did, with dignity. The American officers were in a peculiarly uncomfortable position— and they looked it—for, although of Admiral Mountbatten's staff, they realized clearly that Stilwell was very much the senior American general, and the Americans have a respect for seniority only equalled by our Navy. He would have been a brave American who would have stood up to Joe Stilwell to his face. Admiral Mountbatten was growing, understandably, more and more exasperated. He had, as one of the powers granted him by both the American and British Chiefs of Staff, the right to remove any Allied officer in his command if he thought fit, and thus held the final card if he cared to use it. It looked as if there could be no solution to the deadlock but a flat order from the Supreme Commander to his Deputy.

Suddenly, with one of those unexpected gestures that I had seen him make more than once, Stilwell astonished everyone by saying, 'I am prepared to come under General Slim's operational control until I get to Kamaing!' With great relief, this surprising solution was hastily seized upon as a way out of the impasse. Actually it created an even more illogical situation. By it, I took command of all land operations on the Burma front, but I was responsible to my Army Group Commander for only the Fourteenth Army portion of my force. For Stilwell's formations I was theoretically responsible only to the Supreme Commander, thus by-passing my own Commander-in-Chief. Rather rashly, Admiral Mountbatten inquired how Stilwell and I proposed to work this military nonsense. With one accord we asked to be allowed to discuss that together. The conference broke up, and Stilwell and I went straight to his Delhi headquarters, where he functioned as Commanding General of the American China–Burma–India theatre. He was, while determined on certain things, by no means uncompromising. Luckily he and I were determined on the same things—to get more Chinese divisions for the Ledo force, to push hard for Myitkyina, and to use Wingate's Chindits to aid that push. After my experience with Sun's 38th Chinese Division in the Retreat, I had always agreed with Stilwell that his Chinese, given a fair chance and a superiority in numbers, could beat the Japanese, and that he was the man to see they did. Tactically we were in agreement and, wisely, we avoided strategic discussion. He told me how he proposed to launch his offensive and what his objectives were. I assured him that, as long as he went on those lines, he would not be bothered by a spate of orders and directives from me, that Wingate's force would be used to help him, and that my operations on the Assam front would keep the main enemy strength engaged. We shook hands; he went back to his headquarters and I to mine.

In practice, this illogical command set-up worked surprisingly well. My method with Stilwell was based on what I had learnt of him in the Retreat to send him the minimum of written directions, but, whenever I wanted anything, to fly over and discuss it with him, alone. Stilwell, talking things over quietly with no one else present, was a much easier and more likeable person than Vinegar Joe with an audience. Alone, I never found him unreasonable or obstructive. I think I told him to do something he did not approve of on only two or three occasions, and on each he conformed, I will not say willingly, but with good grace.

I was told that the command organization, especially the fact that Stilwell was under my operational control, was not to be made public. Whether this was face-saving for Stilwell, on the lines of our Chinese allies, or to avoid the criticism that such an illogical set-up was bound to provoke, I do not know—both, probably. In any case it did not affect me, and I was careful at all times to observe the condition. Generalissimo Chiang Kai-shek had at the end of November agreed to Stilwell and his Chinese army coming under my control, but had made it clear that this was a concession that applied only and personally to me. As he had never seen me, I cannot help thinking that, had Stilwell held other views, he might as easily have persuaded the Generalissimo to accept General Giffard.

After these conferences I flew from Delhi to Comilla, where Fourteenth Army Headquarters were now established. Thanks to Steve Irwin and Alf Snelling, I found the various offices and departments all settled in and working smoothly, while the Signals under Brigadier Bowen, my Chief Signal Officer, had accomplished marvels. It is not often realized what a volume of traffic the Signals of an army headquarters have to deal with— more than that of a large town—and to be ready to accept and transmit on that scale so soon was a great achievement. I never met anyone who could make a piece of wire stretch as far as Bowen could. Strangely enough we had first met years before when as subaltern he had joined my Gurkha company. His technical knowledge and interest in wireless had led him to transfer to the Royal Corps of Signals, and I found him in 1942 Chief Signals Officer in Burma. I seized the chance to get him in the same position when the Fourteenth Army was formed.

Our organization at Army Headquarters was basically the same as I had used for 15 Corps. I never adopted the 'Chief of Staff System', which, following the German and American lead, had been introduced in some British armies. Under this system the Chief General Staff Officer not only co-ordinates the work of the whole staff, but is the mouthpiece of the commander to the other principal staff officers and heads of Services, interpreting to them his Commander's intentions and wishes. I preferred to stick to the old British method of the Commander dealing directly himself with his principal staff officers. Command is the projection of the commander's personality and, as such, is an extremely individual matter. What, therefore, suits one commander may not suit another, and, in practice, whatever system is theoretically laid down, individual commanders will, as they quite easily can by altering the emphasis within the organization, produce a headquarters which responds to their personality. It is not that one system is so much better than another, but that a wise commander chooses the one that enables him best to instil his will into every part of his force. The real danger is that generals may slavishly model their personal behaviour and their organization on those of some outstandingly successful commander, when they are quite unlike him in character, mental qualities, and perhaps physical appearance. Imitations are never masterpieces.

In Fourteenth Army, while I relied on my Brigadier General Staff to co-ordinate the complex working of the headquarters, my senior staff officer was actually my major-general in charge of administration. For an army engaged in a campaign in Burma this was logical, as administrative possibilities and impossibilities would loom large, larger than strategical and tactical alternatives. In any case the immense supply, transport, medical, and reinforcement organizations that we were beginning to build up more than justified a major-general's rank.

The principles on which I planned all operations were:

(i) The ultimate intention must be an offensive one.
(ii) The main idea on which the plan was based must be simple.
(iii) That idea must be held in view throughout and everything else must give way to it.
(iv) The plan must have in it an element of surprise.

My method of working out such a plan was first to study the possibilities myself, and then informally to discuss them with my Brigadier General Staff, Major-General Administration, and my opposite number in the Air Force. At these discussions we would arrive at the broadest outline of possible alternative courses of action, at least two, more often three or four. These alternatives the B.G.S. would give to our team of planners, specially selected but comparatively junior officers, representing not only the general and administrative staffs, but the air staff as well. They would make a preliminary study, giving the practicability or otherwise of each course and its advantages and disadvantages. They were quite at liberty to make new suggestions of their own, or to devise permutations and combinations of the originals. The results of the planners' examination of the proposals were put up to me as a short paper, largely in tabular form, and from it I decided on the main features of the plan to be followed. At this stage I usually discussed with the intelligence officer whom I had selected to represent the Japanese command at my headquarters —a key appointment—what the enemy's reactions to this plan were likely to be. I was, of course, kept daily in the picture of the Japanese actions, intentions, and dispositions, as far as we knew or could surmise them, but I intentionally waited until I had selected my plan before considering the enemy response to it, as I intended him to conform to me, not me to him. A consideration of these possible Japanese counter-moves never, I think, caused a major alteration in a plan, but they did affect such things as the location and expected tasks of reserves. After that I would talk it over with the A.O.C., who would already be acquainted with the work of the planners through his representative in their team. As few of our plans were not dependent on air support and air transportation, this was the stage at which general agreement between us had to be reached. This done—and thanks to the generosity and unselfishness of the air commanders, British and American, with whom I was lucky enough to work, it always was done—the next step was a meeting of my principal staff officers. At this, besides the Major-General Administration and the B.G.S., would be present my chief gunner, engineer, signaller, doctor, ordnance and R.E.M.E. officers. To them I would put over my plan, meet or override any special difficulties they might have, and send them off to their own staffs to hold their own conferences and to get the thousand and one things required moving. Meanwhile the B.G.S. and the Senior Air Staff Officer got down to the dovetailing of the land and air aspects on which so much would depend. There was still more for the B.G.S. to do. He had to produce the operation order or directive for the corps and other commanders who were to carry out the operations. This he prepared in conjunction with the administrative staff and the Services.

I suppose dozens of operation orders have gone out in my name, but I never, throughout the war, actually wrote one myself. I always had someone who could do that better than I could. One part of the order I did, however, draft myself—the intention. It is usually the shortest of all paragraphs, but it is always the most important, because it states—or it should—just what the commander intends to achieve. It is the one overriding expression of will by which everything in the order and every action by every commander and soldier in the army must be dominated. It should, therefore, be worded by the commander himself.

The next step was to take the operation order myself to the subordinate commanders who were to act on it. On principle, in the field, it is better to go forward to them, than to call them back; to give them their orders at their headquarters rather than at your own. That applies whether you command a platoon or an army group.

In November 1943, about one-third of the combat aircraft were American, the remaining two-thirds British, but the proportion of American, especially transport aircraft, was increasing. Throughout the campaign the total number of British squadrons exceeded that of American, but in transport aircraft the Americans rapidly increased until they held a large majority. At first the whole of the American air force was under the direct command of Stilwell, not of Peirse, the British Air Commander-in-Chief; but, very wisely, Admiral Mountbatten, against Stilwell's wishes, enforced the integration of the two air forces and made Peirse the Allied Air Commander-in-Chief. As his second-in-command, the United States Major-General Stratemeyer was placed in command of what was called Eastern Air Command, which contained all Allied air formations operating on the Burma front—in other words, practically all the air forces in the theatre. His command in the air, as long as I held operational control of all land forces on the Burma front, thus corresponded to mine on the ground. Eastern Air Command was organized as:

(i) The Third Tactical Air Force.
(ii) The Strategic Air Force.
(iii) Troop Carrier Command.
(iv) The Photographic Reconnaissance Force.

Air Marshal Baldwin commanded the Third Tactical Air Force, which in turn was subdivided into:

(i) The American Northern Air Sector Force whose task was to support Stilwell's Chinese and to protect the air-ferry route over the Hump to China.

211

(ii) 221 Group R.A.F., with its headquarters at Imphal, responsible for the support of 4 Corps on the main central front.

(iii) 224 Group R.A.F., with its headquarters at Chittagong, supporting 15 Corps on the Arakan front.

Stratemeyer's headquarters was set up in a huge jute mill near Barrackpore, while Baldwin's Third Tactical Air Force Headquarters was alongside mine at Comilla. Brigadier-General Old, the commander of the joint American and British Troop Carrier Command, also established his headquarters there. In actual practice we, Fourteenth Army, Third T.A.F., and Troop Carrier Command, worked to a considerable extent as a joint headquarters. We pooled intelligence resources, our planners worked together and, perhaps most effective of all, the three commanders and their principal staff officers lived in the same mess. We even reached the stage when the Americans contracted the tea-sipping habit and the British learnt to make drinkable coffee. With this intimate contact between Baldwin, Old, and myself and our staffs, direct references to Eastern Air Command from Fourteenth Army became less frequent, although occasionally Stratemeyer and I issued joint directives. I also found it less cumbersome to place demands on Brigadier-General Davidson's Strategic Air Force through Baldwin, who in effect became my opposite number in the air. Fourteenth Army owed an especial debt to Third Tactical Air Force, to Troop Carrier Command, to the Strategic Air Force and to their commanders. We grew into a very close brotherhood, depending on one another, trusting one another, and taking as much pride in each other's triumphs as we did in our own. The difficulties overcome and the successes obtained on the Burma front were a joint achievement.

Life at the headquarters followed a daily routine. At six-thirty I got up; at seven, saw the important messages received during the night; at seven-thirty to eight, breakfasted with the air commanders and our principal staff officers. I attended the joint air and land intelligence conference, known as 'morning prayers' at eight-thirty, when the events of the past twenty-four hours were related and commented on and those for the next described to a considerable audience by British and American army and air officers. I then dealt with any urgent matters with my B.G.S. and

Major-General Administration, and saw to the multifarious business that comes to an army commander for decision. We all met again at lunch and usually talked shop through the meal. I left my office at about three, read a novel for an hour, had tea, and went for a walk in the cool with one of my staff; dined at seven-thirty, talked at the bar of the mess till half-past nine, visited my operations' room for a final look at the latest reports, and was in bed by ten. If, between then and six-thirty, when my faithful Gurkha orderly, Bajbir, roused me, anyone disturbed me for anything short of a real crisis, he did so at his peril. I had seen too many of my colleagues crack under the immense strain of command in the field not to realize that, if I were to continue, I must have ample leisure in which to think, and unbroken sleep. Generals would do well to remember that, even in war, 'the wisdom· of a learned man cometh by opportunity of leisure.' Generals who are terribly busy all day and half the night, who fuss round, posting platoons and writing march tables, wear out not only their subordinates but themselves. Nor have they, when the real emergency comes, the reserve of vigour that will then enable them, for days if necessary, to do with little rest or sleep.

I had not long been back at my headquarters when events began which threatened to upset some, and then most, of the plans I had brought with me from Delhi. The seven offensive operations, scheduled for 1944, had been approved by the Combined Chiefs of Staff at the Cairo Conference at the end of November 1943. Only a week later, however, at Teheran, Marshal Stalin promised to enter the war against Japan if all Anglo-American efforts were directed first to defeating Germany. Roosevelt and Churchill accepted the condition, and, as part of this concentration against the main enemy, more than half the amphibious resources of South-East Asia were ordered back to Europe. As this rendered impossible the sea assault on the Andaman Islands, it was planned to use what remained for a landing behind the Japanese in Arakan. The Generalissimo had made the move of his Yunnan armies into Burma conditional on the Allies carrying out an amphibious operation against the Japanese in South-East Asia. When he was informed that the contemplated attack on the Andamans had been abandoned but that a smaller landing would be carried out, he refused to regard this as fulfilling the agreement made at Cairo and withdrew his orders for the advance of the Yunnan force. This, in turn, would make the airborne landing of an Indian division in the Indaw area to co-operate with the expected Chinese advance from Yunnan useless, and indeed likely to be disastrous. So *that* operation, too, had perforce to be cancelled. However, in spite of this, plans and preparations for the Arakan landing were pushed on, and I held several conferences with the commanders and staffs detailed for the operation. Then, at the end of December, the Chiefs of Staff informed the Supreme Commander that, as the Generalissimo did not accept the Arakan landing as a substitute for the attack on the Andamans, amphibious operations in South-East Asia would be cancelled and *all* landing craft returned forthwith either to England or the Mediterranean. So that was that.

As our schemes, one by one, each with its picturesque code name, went the way of the ten little nigger boys, the planners worked manfully, and at times frantically, to adjust projects to melting resources. It was no fault of theirs or of the Supreme Commander's, who had been subjected to such sudden and violent cuts in the forces firmly promised, that our operations were thus whittled away. It says a good deal for his resilience and for the spirit of the troops, that they took these disappointments and all the wasted effort they entailed, philosophically and good-humouredly. Even the poor planners, in a whirl of feverish activity, could laugh at themselves, and one of them found time to put into verse something of the turmoil of plans, modifications, substitutes, cancellations, and code names in which they existed as:

> Plan followed plan in swift procession.
> Commanders went; commanders came,
> While telegrams in quick succession
> Arrived to douse or fan the flame.

The practical result of all this was that the projected operations in South-East Asia for 1944 were reduced from seven to four:

(i) The overland advance of 15 Corps in Arakan.
(ii) The advance of Stilwell's Chinese on Myitkyina.
(iii) A long-range penetration operation by Wingate's force to help Stilwell.
(iv) An advance on the main front in Assam by 4 Corps to the Chindwin.

The correct strategy, that of a landing in Southern Burma, had thus perforce to be abandoned, and we fell back on this four-pronged invasion. As I thought over the coming campaign, I was confirmed in my belief that, in spite of this, it should be possible to re-enter and reconquer Burma from the north; but there were disturbing features in our latest plan. The Japanese, we knew, were being steadily reinforced. On both the Northern front, as more Chinese divisions came into action, and on the Southern in Arakan, with its shorter and easier communications, we could count on concentrating superior strength to the enemy. In Assam, however, on the Central front, where the decisive battles would have to be fought, the most optimistic calculations cast doubt on our ability to move and maintain, over so precarious a line of communication, forces even equal to those the Japanese could muster against us. To be frank, too, at this stage, much as our troops had improved in training and morale, I did not want the first big clashes to be on equal terms, division for division. I wanted superior strength at the decisive point for the opening of the struggle; after one victory to confirm the spirit of the Four-teenth Army, I should not worry so much about the odds against us.

I racked my brains and bullied my administrative staff to discover some means of getting even one more division on to the Central front, but without avail. With the transportation we had at that time, and with the vast numbers of non-combatants needed to build roads and airfields for an advance, to squeeze in another fighting formation would have been to take a grave administra-tive risk. It was a risk, however, which I think I should have insisted upon, but I did not. Had the campaign taken place as planned we should have suffered from my failure to do so. I became a better judge of administrative risks later.

There was, of course, an attractive alternative by which the odds could be turned in our favour. If we could somehow seriously weaken the Japanese Army *before* we plunged into Burma, the whole picture would be changed. The only way this could be done was, at an early stage, to entice the enemy into a major battle in circumstances so favourable to us that we could smash three or four of his divisions. The thought of how to do this constantly nagged at my mind, but my generalship was not enough to find a way to provoke such a battle. I devoted myself, therefore, to ensuring that our offensive as planned should be successful.

Three of my commanders, Stilwell, Scoones, and Christison, had already discussed their plans with me, and had them vigorously in hand. There remained only the plans for Wingate's operation in support of Stilwell to be finally settled. Wingate and I, in Delhi and elsewhere, had discussed at length the principles on which his force should be used, its training, its composition, and his plan for its use. On the whole, Wingate and I agreed better than most people expected, perhaps because we had known one another before, or perhaps because we had each in our own way arrived at the same conclusions on certain major issues, the potentialities of air supply, the possibility of taking Burma from the north, and in our estimates of the strengths and weaknesses of the Japanese. Of course we differed on many things. It was impossible not to differ from a man who so fanatically pursued his own purposes without regard to any other consideration or person.

His force, known for deception reasons as the 3rd Indian Division, had in it British, Gurkhas, Burmese, and Africans, but no Indians. It had finished its training in India, and was now placed under my command. I called Wingate to Comilla to clear up several matters about the forthcoming operations on which there might be misunderstanding, and to give him his orders.

The proposed employment of Wingate's force had, like that of all others in the theatre, to be repeatedly modified and changed as resources available waxed and waned. He was, however, fortunate compared with others, in that while for them there was more waning than waxing, his resources had, thanks to the power and brilliance of his advocacy in Whitehall and Washington, greatly increased. He had, first of all, taken over complete the 70th British Division that had formerly been part of my 15 Corps at Ranchi. This was done after the separation of Fourteenth Army from India, when the division, which had remained behind, was no longer under my command. I was not, therefore, consulted on the change; had I been, I would have opposed it as strongly as I could. I was convinced—and nothing I saw subsequently caused me to change my mind—that a battle-tried, experienced, well-knit British division, like the 70th, would have more effect against the Japanese than a special force of twice its size. Moreover, the

70th Division was the only British formation trained in jungle warfare. It was a mistake to break it up. With it Wingate's force now had an infantry strength of over two divisions and an elaborate staff and administrative set-up. In addition it had the unique luxury of its own air force. Admiral Mountbatten, fired by Wingate's burning enthusiasm, had in turn persuaded General Arnold, head of the United States Army Air Force, to provide the 3rd Indian Division with an American force, known as No. 1 Air Commando, containing not only fighters and light bombers for close support, but transport aircraft, gliders, light planes for inter-communication and evacuation of wounded, and the necessary maintenance organization. The pilots were carefully chosen and the commando raised and commanded by Colonels Cochrane and Alison, both outstanding fighting aces, and, what is not always the same thing, first-class organizers and leaders. One of the first difficulties that Wingate's force posed was this very air component. It was represented very strongly by the air staffs, American and British, that it was uneconomical permanently to lock up what was an appreciable proportion of our total air strength in Burma in support of one subsidiary operation. While I agreed in principle with this argument—private air forces are no less wasteful than private armies—I felt strongly that the air commando must remain part of Wingate's force. It had been generously given with that intention, it had wholeheartedly identified itself with the force, and to take it away now, apart from provoking heated squabbles with all sorts of people, would depress and upset the men just as they were about to embark on a most hazardous and arduous venture.

The next difficulty was with Wingate himself. I do not think he ever confided his intentions or ambitions fully to anyone, certainly not to his own staff or to his superior commanders, and it was evident to me from our discussions that there had been a considerable development in his views. His original idea had been that of a force, which, penetrating behind the enemy lines, would operate in comparatively small, lightly-equipped columns to harry his communications and rear establishments, while our main forces struck the decisive blows elsewhere. From this, as he increasingly appreciated the possibilities of air supply and transportation, he had gradually swung to the view that the main force should be the penetrating one, the subsidiary forces those that would remain, comparatively static, on what might be called the perimeter. This entailed, first, a great increase in the penetrating force, and, second, demanded for it a much heavier scale of armament as it would be required, not only to hold landing-ground bases against major attacks, but to assault strongly defended positions. As usual, I found Wingate stimulating when he talked strategy or grand tactics, but strangely naïve when it came to the business of actually fighting the Japanese. He had never experienced a real fight against them, still less a battle. The Japanese, unlike the Italians, with whom he had dealt in East Africa, were not to be frightened into a withdrawal by threats to their rear; they had first to be battered and destroyed in hard fighting. Wingate's men were neither trained nor equipped to fight pitched battles, offensive or defensive. The strategic idea that a penetration formation, operating behind the enemy, could be the decisive force was by no means new or unsound—I used it myself in the great Mandalay–Meiktila battle of 1945—but what would have been unsound was to attempt it with his present force and with our present air resources. At one stage of South-East Asia planning, when it was intended to fly in a standard Indian division to the Indaw area where it would form the central core of an advance by the Yunnan Chinese, we were approaching the idea; but even when that operation had been abandoned, Wingate still hankered after a large force. I did not blame him; all commanders do.

His first demand to me was that I should give him Lomax's 26th Indian Division, which had originally been earmarked and trained for the Indaw landing. I refused. He already had more troops than we should be able to lift and supply by air. The division was the only reserve I had in my whole army; it would have been madness to break it up on the off-chance that Wingate might use it next year. Besides, I knew that if there were ever the chance of the decisive battle I hoped for, the division would be vitally needed.

However, Wingate was, as all good commanders should be, a most determined and persistent fellow, and he had set his heart on expanding his command. When he found argument failed, he turned to sterner measures. Such had been his romantic success with the Prime Minister that he claimed the right to send him messages direct, with his views and recommendations, irrespective of whether Admiral Mountbatten or any other superior

commander agreed with them or not. I had been told this extraordinary arrangement existed, so when Wingate began by saying
that, while he held a personal loyalty to me, there was a loyalty
above that to an immediate commander, I knew what was
coming. I asked him to whom it was. He replied, 'To the Prime
Minister of England and to the President of the United States.'
He went on to say that they had laid on him the duty of reporting
direct to them whenever any of his superiors, in his opinion, were
thwarting his operations. With the greatest regret he felt that this
was such an occasion, and he must, whatever the consequences to
me, so report to the Prime Minister. I pushed a signal pad across
my desk to him, and told him to go and write his message. He
did not take the pad but he left the room. Whether he ever sent
the message I do not know, nor did I inquire. Anyhow that was
the last I heard of his demand for the 26th Division.

Wingate was back next day, and we resumed our study of his
operations. The original plan had been much on the lines of his
first raid but in two waves. Three of his brigades were to have
entered Burma and reached their operational areas by long jungle
approach marches across the Chindwin and through the Japanese
front. After some two or three months, the next wave of three
brigades was to go in on foot to relieve the first. When the
transport aircraft of No. 1 Air Commando, however, became
available, Wingate wished to fly one brigade to Paoshan in China
and introduce it, across the Salween River, into Burma from the
east. The rest would cross the Chindwin as already proposed. By
this time, however, I was getting reports from 4 Corps that all
crossings along the river were closely watched by the enemy, and
in Scoones's opinion, with which I agreed, it would be impossible
to get the brigades across without their being intercepted. As it
was essential that columns should reach their operating areas without serious interference, this plan was abandoned and we settled
down to calculate the possibility of flying them in direct. This
had the additional advantages of saving fatigue and giving more
time for effective operations. We were already committed to the
air supply of the 81st West African Division in Arakan and other
projects, and, even if we used the air commando gliders for troops
instead of heavy equipment, we found we should still be short of
the minimum air lift. However, by supplementing the air commandos, at peak periods, from the meagre resources of Troop

Carrier Command, we calculated we could lift two brigades in March and two later. The Paoshan idea, attractive as it appeared, was therefore discarded and we decided that in each wave two brigades should fly and one march. Wingate, of course, knew that the fly-in of the 26th Division to Indaw was no longer contemplated, and I made it quite clear that I could allot him no more aircraft and no more troops, beyond an extra Gurkha battalion and some artillery that I gave him.

Wingate was dissatisfied with the rate of fly-in, and so was I. Still, as it was impossible to increase it without cancelling operations already begun, which I would certainly not do, or by taking aircraft off the Hump route to China which even the Supreme Commander had not the power to do, I had to stand firm on that too. He made one last attempt to make me change by saying he could not accept the order I had drafted. I gave him an unsigned copy of the draft, told him to take it away, sleep on it that night, and come back at ten o'clock the next morning, when I would give him the same order signed. I told him I had never had a subordinate officer refuse an order, but if one did, I knew what to do. General Giffard happened to be visiting my headquarters, and I asked him to be in my office next day when Wingate came. I rather expected trouble, but, as soon as Wingate was seated in the chair on the other side of my desk, I passed the signed order across to him and, with a slightly wry smile, he accepted it without comment.

We set up Wingate's headquarters at Imphal alongside that of 4 Corps. He was now developing his 'stronghold' technique, the method by which airstrips as bases for his columns would be held. This demanded ever-increasing scales of defensive equipment, artillery, anti-aircraft guns, mines, machine-guns, sandbags, and the rest. I went over with him his ideas of the defence of one of these strongholds, and found that he had little appreciation of what a real Japanese attack would be like. I told him to get Scoones's ideas on the 'floater model' of defence as practised in 4 Corps, by which each garrison had a satellite mobile column to operate against the rear of any enemy attacking formation. Scoones must have been a little amused to find this appear as a new Wingate method of defence. Meanwhile the first wave of the Special Force, as we usually called the 3rd Indian Division, moved up into the forward areas from which it would fly or march into Burma.

Thus for the moment ended our orgy of planning, but in war it is not only one side that plans. I had throughout been conscious that, improving as our intelligence was since 1942, it was far from being as complete or accurate as that in other theatres. We never made up for the lack of methodically collected intelligence or the intelligence organization which should have been available to us when the war began. We knew something of the Japanese intentions, but little of the dispositions of their reserves, and practically nothing about one of the most important factors that a general has to consider—the character of the opposing commanders. I had all the information I could obtain about Lieut.-General Kawabe, my opposite number, who as Commander-in-Chief, Burma Army Area, controlled all Japanese land and air forces in Burma, but it did not amount to much on which to build up a picture of how his mind would work. At this time, from what I had seen of his operations, I could only expect him to be, like most Japanese commanders I had met, a bold tactical planner of offensive movements, completely confident in the superiority of his troops, and prepared to use his last reserves rather than abandon a plan. Many years before, when I was working for the Staff College examination, I had studied the Russo-Japanese War, and one thing about that campaign I had always remembered. The Russians never won a battle. In almost every fight they accepted defeat while a considerable portion of their forces, in reserve, was still unused. On the other hand, the Japanese were prepared to throw in every man, and more than once tipped the scales of victory with their very last reserves. The Japanese generals we were fighting had been brought up on the lessons of that war, and all I had seen of them in this convinced me that they would run true to form and hold back nothing. This was a source of great strength to them, but also, properly taken advantage of might, in conjunction with their overweening confidence, be a fatal weakness.

I did, however, manage to get a photograph alleged to be that of Kawabe. It showed what might have been a typical western caricature of a Japanese; the bullet head, the thick glasses, and prominent teeth were all there. To these attractions he added a long waxed moustache, extending well beyond his cheeks. I pinned this picture to the wall of my office, opposite my desk. When I needed cheering I looked at it and assured myself that, whichever of us was the cleverer general, even I was, at any rate, the better looking.

At the end of December I visited Stilwell's Northern Combat Area, and his base at Ledo. I found the old man in good heart, as he had every reason to be. His advance, after some initial stickiness by the Chinese which he had overcome with characteristic vigour, had gone well. I saw a number of my old American and Chinese friends and left well satisfied with their progress and with my admiration for Stilwell's drive and power of personal leadership confirmed.

Then, my other fronts well under way, I turned my attention to Arakan, where I expected the first really serious clashes of the campaign to occur.

CHAPTER XI

PATTERN FOR VICTORY

A S our wider visions of amphibious operations on the Arakan coast faded with the withdrawal of the resources necessary for them, we were thrown back on our original plans. These were certainly modest in their scope—a limited advance down the Mayu Peninsula to secure, first, the tiny port of Maungdaw and then the road running from it, through the central spine of the Mayu Range, to Buthidaung in the valley of the Kalapanzin River. Having got these we could, by using the Naf River and Maungdaw, supply our forward formations in Arakan largely by sea, while the road would give us the essential lateral communications to support forces on the east of the range. Thus firmly established on both its sides, we should be in a position later to stage a more formidable offensive with Akyab and beyond as its objective.

We were careful in our plan to guard against the fatal errors of the 1943 campaign—attacks on narrow fronts and the neglect of an enemy outflanking counter-stroke. The intention was to advance with two divisions, not only on both sides of the Mayu Range, but along its spine as well, while the 81st West African Division, moving down the Kaladan Valley well to the east, would provide a flank guard and would, I hoped, be in its turn a threat to the Japanese flank and their west to east communications.

During November, 15 Corps completed its assembly for the advance. The 26th Indian Division, which had held the front throughout the monsoon, was brought back into Army Reserve at Chittagong. Its place was taken by the 7th Indian Division under Messervy, followed by Briggs's 5th Indian Division, both from Ranchi. The 81st West African Division, commanded by Major-General Woolner, now entered the theatre of war for the first time. The division was concentrated about Chiringa, some

223

fifty miles south of Chittagong, and ordered to get itself into the Kaladan Valley. In a month the West Africans had built the 'African Way', a jeep track that ran for seventy-five miles through most difficult country to debouch at Daletme on the Kaladan River. The Africans' first task was to build airstrips along the river bank. Adepts at bush clearing, this they did with great rapidity, and the division was launched—the first normal formation to rely completely on air supply. It was not until the 20th January that they met the Japanese when, in their opening engagement, they overran an enemy post. Thereafter, meeting stubborn resistance from small detachments, they began to push steadily down the valley for Paletwa and Kyauktaw. In these encounters the Africans showed great dash in the attack.

Tanks, on account of the country, could not be got to the 81st West African Division, but I was determined that this time the *main* advance should have adequate armoured support. When all the old arguments about the impossibility of getting more than a few tanks into Arakan, or of using them when there, were again trotted out, I gave Colonel 'Atte' Persse, of the Indian Armoured Corps, an assignment. I told him that, whatever else happened, he was to see that a complete regiment of Lee-Grant medium tanks, the 25th Dragoons from Ranchi, with the necessary maintenance, was to be ready in November to go forward with the leading infantry. He had my permission to use my name, to send what signals he liked to whom he liked, and was to report to me only when the job was done. I knew Persse and his qualities well, having had him in command of a cavalry regiment under me. He lived up to his reputation for drive, pertinacity, and ingenuity, and also, it must be confessed, for making himself a nuisance to all and sundry until he got what he wanted. In spite of few landing-craft, bridges unable to carry a tank, tidal *chaungs*, swamps, quicksands, jungle, and Japanese aircraft, the tanks were there on time.

Nor were tanks our only anxiety. In whatever way our plans developed there would be great demands on air supply. The 81st Division, Wingate's force, and half a dozen other commitments would moreover call for a large measure of dropping, as distinct from landing, supplies. For this we should need vast numbers of parachutes. Just as the 81st Division was committed I received the unwelcome news that the dispatch of parachutes from India would be much less than we had been led to expect, and would indeed fall far short of our requirements. It was useless to hope for supplies from home. We were bottom of the priority list there, for parachutes as for everything else. The position was serious. Our plans were based on large reserves of parachutes for supply dropping; if we had not got them we risked, if not disaster, at least a drastic slowing up and modification of those plans. I went for a walk in the comparative cool of the evening and did some hard thinking.

Next morning I assembled Snelling and one or two of his leading air-supply staff officers and explained the position. If we could not get proper parachutes of silk or other special cloth we must make them of what we could get. I believed it possible to make a serviceable supply-dropping parachute from either paper or jute. There are great paper mills in Calcutta; all the jute in the world is grown in Bengal and most of it manufactured there. I despatched officers forthwith to Calcutta to explore possibilities. The paper parachute, although I still believe it quite practicable, we could not obtain, because the manufacturers could not produce the kind of paper required in the time. With jute we were more fortunate. My assignment officer visited some of the leaders of the British jute industry in Calcutta, told them our difficulty, and asked their help. He warned them that to save time I had sent him direct and that my need was my only authority. I hoped they would be paid, but when or how I could not guarantee. The answer of these Calcutta business men was, 'Never mind about that! If the Fourteenth Army want parachutes they shall have them!'

And have them we did. Within ten days we were experimenting with various types of 'parajutes' as we called them. Some fell with a sickening thud; others had a high percentage of failure. By trial and error we arrived at the most efficient shape and weave for the cloth. In a month we had a parajute that was eighty-five per cent as efficient and reliable as the most elaborate parachute. It was made entirely of jute—even the ropes—and was of the simplest design. It dispensed with the vent at the top of the normal parachute as the texture of the jute cloth was such that the right quantity of air passed through it to keep the parajute expanded and stable. Instead of having one large vent it had innumerable tiny ones. It would have been risky to drop a man

225

in a parajute, or a particularly valuable or fragile load such as a wireless set, but for ordinary supplies it worked admirably. It had in addition another advantage. The cost of a parajute was just over £1; that of a standard parachute over £20. As we used several hundreds of thousands of parajutes we saved the British taxpayer some millions of pounds, and, more important even than that, our operations went on. My reward was a ponderous rebuke from above for not obtaining the supply through the proper channels! I replied that I never wanted to find a more proper channel for help when in need than those Calcutta jute men.

My intelligence staff estimated in November that the Japanese had in Arakan a force amounting to just over a division. Of this two regiments (brigades) were forward of Akyab and one in or around Akyab Island itself, with a detachment from the division, including its cavalry regiment, in the Kaladan Valley to oppose the West Africans. This estimate proved to be remarkably accurate as to strength and location; the actual force being the complete 55th Division with two extra battalions. A little later we discovered that behind the 55th Division, another, the 54th, was moving into Arakan and had its headquarters for the moment, we thought, at Prome. Thus, to deal with, at the most, two Japanese divisions we were concentrating three (less a brigade) with one in near reserve; but, apart from the fact that we should need a preponderance in strength if we were to attack, I had no intention, if I could avoid it, of pitting my army division for division against the Japanese on their own ground. I hoped that the Arakan campaign would be the first step towards building up a tradition of success, and I did not intend to take more risks than I had to at this early stage. Later we would take on twice or thrice our number in Japanese divisions—but not yet. At this time all my plans were based on ensuring a superiority in numbers and force at the decisive points.

During the monsoon, patrols had constantly gone out to probe the Japanese defences and from them we had learned that the enemy had only outpost detachments forward, while their main positions were just north of the Maungdaw–Buthidaung road. Air reconnaissance told us little; the enemy dispositions were too well hidden under the carpet of trees.

By the end of October, the leading division of Christison's 15 Corps, the 7th, under Messervy, had relieved the 26th Division all along the front on both sides of the Mayu Range, and was in close contact with the enemy outposts. During November the 5th Division, under Briggs, arrived and took over the range itself, the foothills, and the narrow coastal plain which formed the western half of the front. This allowed Christison to concentrate the 7th Division to the east of the range on both banks of the Kalapanzin River. Here it was maintained over the Goppe Pass by laborious mule and porter columns and then by boat on the river. Our engineers introduced yet another form of transport by erecting a rope-way, last used in the Khyber on the North-West Frontier of India, to carry loads to the top of the pass. Creaking in every joint the old rope-way tugged valiantly away and saved the situation—another and ancient monument to the versatility of our Fourteenth Army Sappers.

On the last night of November 1943, Christison began his advance. The 7th Division, east of the range, pushed in the Japanese outposts and broke through into the Letwedet area. On the 20th December the 5th Division in its turn punched through to the Maungdaw plain facing Razabil. Against minor opposition, which nevertheless furnished some brisk small engagements, the two divisions pushed on. As they approached the Maungdaw-Buthidaung road the pattern of the enemy defence was picked out by many a daring patrol.

Roughly half-way between the villages the sixteen-mile-long metalled road passed literally through the Mayu Range, over a thousand feet high here, by means of two tunnels, relics of a light railway built to link Maungdaw with the rice-fields of the Kalapanzin. This line had been bought out and dismantled by a river steamer company, who much preferred trade to follow rivers rather than go burrowing from one valley to another. The road followed the formation of the old railway, and provided the only lateral communication fit for wheels until the Taungup-Prome road was reached, nearly two hundred miles to the south. The Japanese positions in the precipitous jungle hills covered the road continuously, but in three places they grew to an elaborateness and strength that justified the term fortresses. These were, first, at the tunnels themselves, and then in two great buttresses, one each side of the range at Letwedet on the east and Razabil on the west, which thrust forward to guard the approaches. All three positions were of the greatest strength. The Japanese had

227

tunnelled far into the hills, with living accommodation, store-rooms, and dug-outs twenty or thirty feet below the surface. There were innumerable mutually supporting machine-gun posts and strong-points subterraneously linked. The extent of their preparation and the extreme formidableness of the defences were not, of course, then fully known to us, but it was obvious that they would be hard nuts to crack.

Christison's plan, worked out in great detail, was a methodical advance up to the main positions, a complete mopping up of all enemy in front of them, the capture of both buttresses, followed by the isolation and reduction of the tunnels fortress. The 5th Indian Division was to take Razabil, while the 7th Indian Division, moving round behind Letwedet, was to take Buthidaung and then attack the eastern buttress from the rear. Meanwhile the 81st West African Division would advance down the Kaladan River, capture Kyauktaw and go on to cut the Kanzauk–Htizwe road, the enemy's main line of communication between Kaladan and Kalapanzin Valleys.

It now became necessary, if an attack on Letwedet was to be made, to pass vehicles, guns, and tanks across to the 7th Division. A footpath crossed the range, some five miles north of the Maungdaw–Buthidaung road, through the wild and winding Ngakyedauk Pass. It had been declared that this route could not in any conceivable circumstances be converted into a road; but a road there had to be and, poor as it was, this pass was the only hope of making one. Luckily the path was in our hands. On his first arrival, Messervy, seeking a better way than the Goppe Pass by which to move and maintain his division, had told one of his Brigadiers, Roberts, to find, if possible, an alternative. Roberts, who had an excellent eye for country, decided the Ngakyedauk was the only answer. He took measures at once to strengthen our hold on the pass, and when, soon after, the Japanese, realizing its importance, attacked, a detachment of Punjabis of his brigade were ready for them, and in an all-night fight beat them off. Had it not been for Brigadier Roberts's initiative, the story of Ngakyedauk might have been very different. While other troops held the enemy in his positions just to the south, the 7th Divisional Engineers set about driving their road. With the exception of two or three bulldozers they had only the field equipment of divisional engineers, but in an incredibly short time, right under the snub noses of the Japanese, they built, first a jeep track, and then, before Christmas, a real road, unmetalled of course, but capable of taking tanks and medium artillery. Over this pass, christened the 'Okey-doke' by the British soldiery, flowed the vehicles, stores, and equipment needed for the 7th Division's assault on Letwedet fortress. We, too, now had our lateral road connecting directly the 7th Division on the east of the range and the 5th on the crest and to the sea.

The assault on Razabil began. The Japanese positions were in a series of low but steep hillocks grouped round a main horseshoe-shaped hill, known as Tortoise. On the last day of 1943 the artillery preparation began, but it took a week to reduce the outlying positions—a week of hard, fierce fighting. Then our troops slipped past Tortoise and took Maungdaw. I visited what was left of the village next day—a tangle of burnt beams, riddled galvanized-iron sheeting, and smashed dock equipment, the whole overgrown with grass and weeds and plentifully laced with mines and booby traps. Loofah plants had spread every-where and there were enough of these useful bathroom adjuncts to furnish us for years. The 'docks', never much to boast about, looked incapable of restoration, but by the time the troops had cleared the mouth of the Naf River of Japanese snipers, the 5th Divisional Engineers, emulating their brethren in the 7th, had the 'port' cleared of mines, a couple of steamer berths prepared, and were ready to unload ships. Although the mouth of the river was still under long-range enemy artillery fire, the little coastal steamers crept past in the dark. Many familiar faces from the old Sunderbans flotilla of happy memory appeared, and Maungdaw sprang once more to life as much of the maintenance of 15 Corps rattled over its ramshackle wharves.

With Maungdaw safely in the bag, Briggs and his 5th Indian Division set about the keep of Razabil fortress—the Tortoise. This was the first time we had assaulted an elaborate, carefully prepared position that the Japanese meant to hold to the last, and we expected it to be tough. It was. The attack was preceded by heavy bombing from the strategic air force and dive-bombing by R.A.F. Vengeances, directed by smoke shells from the artillery. After this pounding, which left the Japanese apparently unmoved, medium and field artillery took up the task and pumped shells from their accumulated dumps into the smoking, burning, spouting hill-sides. Then the guns suddenly paused and the Lee-Grant tanks roared forward, the infantry, bayonets fixed, yelling their Indian war cries, following on their tails. The Dismal Jimmies who had prophesied, one, that the tanks would never get to the line, two, that they could never climb the hills and, three, if they did the trees would so slow them up that the Japanese anti-tank guns would bump them off as sitting targets, were confounded. The tanks, lots of them—'the more you use, the fewer you lose' —crashed up the slopes and ground over the dug-in anti-tank guns. All was going well, but as the infantry passed ahead of the armour for the final assault the guns of the tanks had to cease firing for fear of hitting our own men. In that momentary pause the Japanese machine-gunners and grenadiers remanned their slits and rat-holes. Streams of bullets swept the approaches and a cascade of bombs bounced down among our infantry.

The attacks of the first three days shaved the Tortoise bare and cost us many casualties, but they did not shift the Japanese, burrowed deep into the hill, with their cunningly sited, wonderfully concealed, and mutually supporting machine-guns. It was the old problem of the First World War—how to get the infantryman on to his enemy without a pause in the covering fire that kept his enemy's head down. It was solved in Arakan—and copied throughout the Fourteenth Army—by the tanks firing, first, surface-burst high explosive to clear the jungle, then delay-action high explosive to break up the faces of the bunkers thus exposed, and lastly solid armour-piercing shot as the infantry closed in. With no explosion, the last few yards were safe, if you had first-class tank gunners and infantrymen with steady nerves, who let the shot whistle past their heads and strike a few feet beyond or to one side of them. We had such tank gunners and such infantrymen—and they had the confidence in one another, even when of different races, that was needed. Gradually, bit by bit, Tortoise was nibbled away, until only in its very heart a few desperate Japanese, with a courage that, fanatical or not, was magnificent, still held out.

At this stage Christison swung his punch to the other side of the Mayu Range. Here, in the Kalapanzin Valley, the 7th Indian Division had pushed on until one of its battalions, the King's Own Scottish Borderers, had audaciously seized a hillock overlooking the main lateral road between the tunnels and Buthidaung.

Neither savage counter-attacks nor the point-blank fire of a 155-mm. gun from the tunnels area could dislodge them or the Gurkhas who relieved them. The time had come to seize Buthidaung, preparatory to the attack on the Letwedet bastion. Over the Ngakyedauk Pass tramped a brigade of the 5th Division to relieve the right brigade of the 7th, and thus provide Messervy with a striking force. Behind it trundled the guns of a medium regiment and the tanks of the Dragoons, leaving behind at Razabil their reserves, to make the enemy believe the armoured regiment was still west of the range. Where the Ngakyedauk Pass road debouched into the valley, a maintenance area for the troops in the Kalapanzin was laid out, with supply depots, ammunition dumps, vehicle parks, and main dressing stations—the famous 'Administrative Box'.

While 15 Corps thus methodically pounded forward, the Japanese, true to form, were not content to remain on the defensive. Christison and I had been quite sure that sooner or later, and almost certainly before they lost the tunnels fortress, the enemy would stage a counter-attack. For some time now, the signs had been becoming clearer that this would not be a local affair, intended merely to relieve pressure in Arakan, but a much more ambitious and more widely spread effort—something in the nature of a general offensive on the Burma front.

Another factor was appearing in the overall strategy of the theatre. While the resources allotted to us in South-East Asia had been reduced by recalls to Europe, it was becoming evident that the Japanese were greatly increasing their forces in Burma. Throughout the monsoon of 1943 their strength had been four divisions, plus, of course, a considerable number of army and line-of-communication troops. Then a fifth, the 54th from Java, began, as already related, to move into Arakan. A sixth, the 31st, had, we now heard, arrived from Malaya. In November we received intelligence that a seventh, believed to be the 15th, was marching from Siam over the Takaw Ferry on the Salween River. In addition there were indications of other formations being transferred from the Pacific. At the end of January my intelligence staff, with considerable accuracy as it afterwards appeared, placed the Japanese formations as:

H.Q. Burma Army Area (Lieut.-General Kawabe): Rangoon
54th Division—In and *en route* Arakan.

55th Division—Arakan, with detachment in Kaladan Valley.
15th Division—Entering Burma from Siam.
5th Air Division—Rangoon and other airfields.

H.Q. 15 Army (Lieut.-General Mutaguchi): Maymyo
56th Division—Yunling facing Yunnan Chinese.
18th Division—Myitkyina facing Ledo Chinese.
31st Division—Wuntho ⎱ facing 4 Corps in Assam.
33rd Division—Kalewa ⎰

These increases were, from the global strategy point of view,
satisfactory to us, as they automatically fulfilled the Combined
Chiefs of Staff directive to draw off the Japanese forces, and, at
least, prevented these divisions being used to reinforce the Pacific
theatre. From my point of view as Commander in Burma,
however, it began to look as if I was not the only one staging offensives. Lieut.-General Kawabe, my opposite number, who commanded all enemy land and air forces in Burma, was not likely
to have his army practically doubled for purely defensive purposes. It would be unlike the Japanese to reinforce anywhere on
that scale unless they intended seriously to attack. Other indications were soon forthcoming, which showed that the enemy
offensive, when it came, would not be confined to the 15 Corps
front, but would involve also 4 Corps on the Central front.

In Arakan itself the signs multiplied. Captured documents told
us that a formation of the Indian National Army, the force raised
by the Japanese from Indian civilians and prisoners of war under
Bose's puppet government, had been brought up close to the
front, east of the Mayu Range. This was significant, as it indicated
an intention to advance into India, where the renegades would be
used to rouse the population to rebellion. We learnt, also, of the
formation of a new Japanese Army Headquarters, the 28th, under
Lieut.-General Sakurai Seizo, to control operations in Arakan.
Most of this intelligence was collected by our fighting patrols
who were showing great skill in surprising Japanese minor headquarters. Conspicuously successful were the raids behind the
enemy lines delivered by the Reconnaissance Regiment of the
81st West African Division. This unit developed to a high degree
the technique of small amphibious commando operations. One
of its coastal raids in January identified what up till then had been
the missing regiment of the Japanese 55th Division which we had

thought to be in the Pacific. Its arrival from that theatre was another pointer to enemy intentions in Burma.

About the middle of January I flew to Arakan, landing on a newly-made advanced airstrip. As hostile aircraft had been reported, I had an escort of four Hurricanes which circled round as my plane taxied to shelter. Suddenly one of them fired a burst into the Hurricane ahead of it. The pilot was killed and the machine crashed. The airman who had fired had shot down one of his best friends and could give no explanation except that he saw the other machine in his sights, and, forgetting that he had a gun instead of a camera, pressed the trigger. I wonder there were not more of these tragic accidents when our young pilots were under such strain.

I spent several days going round the Arakan front, watching the operations of both divisions, inspecting the Administrative Box, and discussing the future with Christison and his commanders. It was clear that the enemy counter-stroke in Arakan would not be long delayed, and, while it was difficult to judge in what strength it would come, we both agreed it would take the form of an outflanking attack on the 7th Division's left. Christison was at the time beginning the transfer of his weight to the east of the range. This reinforcing of the 7th Division suited well with our ideas of the enemy's intentions and it was continued. At the same time Christison warned the V Force posts screening the left to be particularly alert, and for patrolling on that flank to be intensified to obtain warning of any hostile moves. Christison and I agreed that if any 15 Corps troops were cut off they would stand fast. I promised that, when necessary, they would be supplied by air and that they would be relieved by our counter-attacking forces, with whom they were to co-operate by taking the offensive themselves at the first opportunity.

When I left Messervy's headquarters east of the range, and drove through the Ngakyedauk Pass on my way to the airstrip at 15 Corps at the end of my visit, Japanese fighters were beginning to come over in formations of up to a hundred at a time. This challenge to our air force was clearly the opening move of the enemy counter-stroke. It was heartening to see how our fellows took it up. Our Spitfires, much inferior in numbers, fairly laced into the Zeros and began most effectively to knock them out of the sky. While these whirlwind dog-fights streaked about high in the clear air, our reconnaissance Hurricanes kept up their steady patrols. I was impressed by the conduct of a reconnaissance squadron of the Indian Air Force. Flying in pairs, the Indian pilots in their outmoded Hurricanes went out, time and again, in the face of overwhelming enemy fighter superiority. I looked in on the squadron just at a time when news had come in that the last patrol had run into a bunch of Zeros and been shot down. The Sikh squadron leader, an old friend of mine, at once took out the next patrol himself and completed the mission. His methods, rumour had it, were a little unorthodox. It was said that if any of his young officers made a bad landing he would take them behind a *basha* and beat them. Whatever he did, it was effective; they were a happy, efficient, and very gallant squadron.

At Chittagong I warned Lomax and his 26th Division that they would probably be needed—and needed in a hurry. Then on to my headquarters at Comilla to meet General Giffard on his way, in his turn, to visit Arakan. I found him in complete agreement with my estimate of the situation and the measures we were taking. He also cheered me very much by telling me that he would order the 36th British Division from Calcutta into Chittagong to replace the 26th Division if I had to move it south. He went on to Christison and I checked over with Snelling, my chief administrative officer, Old, commanding the Troop Carrier Command, and Baldwin, of the 3rd Tactical Air Force, the arrangements for air supply to 15 Corps, should it be required. The joint air force and army organization which had been supplying the 81st West African Division had already been adjusted to meet possible new demands. Snelling quietly warned the air supply units and organizations at the Comilla and Agartala airstrips to go full out on the prearranged packing programme and to stand by for twenty-four hours' a day working. The supply units were reinforced by Indian Pioneers who took over most of the non-technical work, additional transport was allotted to airfields, British reinforcement camps were told to earmark men to help supervise packing, and we called for volunteers to fly with the aircraft as 'kickers-out', whose task it was to push the stores out of the aircraft. The complete maintenance of over a division for several days, everything that it would require, from pills to projectiles, from bully beef to boots, was laid out, packed for dropping, at the airstrips. We were as ready as we could be.

Yet when the Japanese struck I am ashamed to say it was a surprise. On the 1st February, Frank Festing, the commander of the 36th British Division, arrived at my headquarters just ahead of his division. On the 2nd, General Giffard returned from his tour of Arakan and left again for Delhi next day. He had had a narrow escape when shot up by Zeros in the Ngakyedauk Pass. On the morning of the 4th, not feeling too bright myself, as I had just had my ninth daily emetine injection for dysentery, I was out at a reinforcement camp a few miles from Comilla watching a demonstration of the, to us, new lifebuoy flame-thrower, when a motor-cycle despatch rider roared up with a message. It told me that the Japanese had suddenly swept down out of the blue and rushed Taung Bazaar, five or six miles in rear of the 7th Division. The situation was obscure, said the signal, but it was clear that the enemy were in considerable strength.

The only thing I can think of more depressing than the effect of a series of emetine injections is the receipt of a message such as this. I had expected ample warning of the Japanese move, but this meant they had passed right round the 7th Division unobserved, and were within two or three miles of the Ngakyedauk Pass and the Administrative Box, which I knew was prepared for nothing more than raids. I was angry and disappointed that all our precautions had failed to give warning of the enemy move, but, trying not to look as anxious as I felt, I quickly got back to headquarters and telephoned Christison. He could tell me little more, except that Messervy's reserve brigade was engaged in heavy fighting somewhere south of Taung Bazaar. It was a real Japanese break-through and looked nasty. This was not cheerful news. I rang up Lomax at Chittagong and warned him to be ready to move at short notice. Meanwhile my principal staff officers had assembled and I gave them the news, reminding them that things are never as bad—or as good—as they are first reported.

On the 5th February, I gave Lomax orders to move to join Christison at Bawli Bazaar and General Giffard flew to my head-quarters. Some commanders-in-chief I would not have welcomed at such a moment, but General Giffard had the invaluable knack of not interfering, yet making one feel that he was there, calm, helpful, and understanding, if required. Early on the 6th, I flew to Chittagong, saw Lomax just off to Christison, and watched the last of 26th Division, workmanlike and cheerful, moving out.

235

Then I saw Festing of the 36th Division, the brigadier commanding the Chittagong Area of the line of communication, and Air Commodore Gray, commanding 224 Group of the R.A.F. Everything was working smoothly, there was no flap, and 36th Division was taking 26th Division's place in Army Reserve. Next day, after a conference with Baldwin and Old of the Troop Carrier Command and a talk on the phone with Christison, I told Snelling to put the 7th Division on to air supply. The switchover, as far as I was concerned, was simple, thanks to the preparation that Fourteenth Army, Third Tactical Air Force, and Troop Carrier Command together had made—it required only the word 'Go!' I made one attempt to interfere with Snelling's arrangements. 'Wouldn't it be a good idea,' I said, 'to put a case of rum in every fourth or fifth plane so as to make sure that when the stuff is shoved out the chaps will really search for it?' Alf Snelling looked at me in the slightly pitying way professionals look at amateurs. 'Sir,' he said, 'I have *already* given orders that a case of rum should be put in *every* plane!'

It might not have been so simple. The first flight of Dakotas had to turn back to avoid enemy fighters. Old himself at once took the pilot's seat in the leader of the next flight, and led it in to drop on 7th Division. The Spitfires and Hurricanes of 3rd T.A.F. swept up, the Zeros tumbled out of the sky or scuttled back. Air supply for 15 Corps was on, and, as long as needed, never faltered. Snelling himself, and in turn his administrative staff officers, flew with the supplies. When an unfortunate crash during taking-off destroyed three Dakotas and killed several of the British soldiers who were kickers-out, it only brought a new rush of volunteers. The pilots, American and British, flew three or four sorties a day, or more usually a night, as most of the supply dropping was done after dark to avoid the Japanese fighters, who still occasionally slipped in between our air cover. Day and night the army supply units continuously packed for dropping whatever was required, delivered it on the airstrips, and loaded it into the aircraft. All round the clock, in the sunshine or by the light of flares and car lamps, the ground-crews snatching their broken rest on the airstrip, worked to turn round the Dakotas.

On the 8th, I flew down to Christison's headquarters, which had been subjected to several jitter raids by parties of infiltrating Japanese. With my approval he pulled his headquarters back a couple of miles to Bawli Bazaar behind the river, where it was easier to protect. He was going to have a tough battle to fight, and it would not help if he and his staff were standing to alarm posts half the night. I knew only too well what that meant.

The situation was now fairly clear. Thanks to the Japanese habit of carrying orders and marked maps into action, we had an almost complete picture of their general plan. It was, as we would expect from them, tactically bold and based on their past experience of the effects of cutting our communications. They intended to destroy 15 Corps and capture Chittagong as, it seemed, the first stage of an invasion of India.

The Japanese 55th Division, reinforced, and with detachments of the Indian National Army under its command, had been divided into three parts. The first or main striking force under Colonel Tanahashi, who had proved himself the most formidable of the enemy leaders in our 1943 Arakan disasters, was formed round his 112 Regiment and was about seven thousand strong. Its task was to move secretly through the jungle, between the left of our 7th Division and the right of the 81st West African Division, and seize Taung Bazaar from the east. It was then to turn south, overrun the Administrative Box and cut the Ngakyedauk Pass, thus isolating the 7th Division. The second smaller force, a battalion group under Colonel Kubo, was to move even wider than Tanahashi, block the track south from Goppe Bazaar and, turning west over the range, cut the main road to Maungdaw just south of Bawli Bazaar. This would isolate our 5th Division. The outflanking operations were under the direct command of Major-General Sakurai Tohutaro, the commander of the infantry of the 55th Division, not to be confused with Lieut.-General Sakurai Seizo, 28th Army Commander. The third Japanese force, known as Doi Force, consisting of the remainder of the 55th Division and some other troops, was to put in holding attacks from the south on both our 5th and 7th Divisions. Overall command of the whole Arakan offensive was in the hands of Lieut.-General Hanaya, commander of the 55th Division.

The basic idea was that the British divisions, when thus cut off, would behave as they had in the past, and, deprived of all supplies, turn to fight their way back to clear their communications. The 7th Division would be destroyed as it tried to scramble to safety

237

through the Ngakyedauk Pass. All the Japanese forces would then turn on the wretched 5th Division and annihilate it as it struggled to escape across the Naf River. Chittagong would be the next stop for the victorious Sakurai. There the local population, rallied by the Indian National Army, would rise and Bengal would lie open to the invader. The much heralded 'March on Delhi' had begun.

The operation was planned to a strict time-table under which the total destruction of the British forces was billed to be completed in ten days. The Japanese administrative arrangements were based on capturing our supplies and our motor transport by that time, and thence onwards using them. So confident of success were they that they brought with them, in addition to a considerable artillery, units of gunners without guns to take over ours. None of our transport was to be destroyed; it was all wanted intact for the March on Delhi. The Japanese radio had evidently been issued with a copy of the programme, as for the first ten days of the battle it announced the destruction of our forces strictly in accordance with the time-table.

Sakurai's outflanking operations began smoothly enough. With its local guides, Tanahashi Force, large as it was, succeeded in evading our posts and patrols, and in the early morning of the 4th February burst into Taung Bazaar, scattering the few administrative troops located there. Sakurai's supply column, following up, was not so fortunate. The 7th Division caught it as it tried to get by, destroyed its escort, captured a considerable quantity of gun ammunition, much rice, and a complete field ambulance, so that the Japanese supply arrangements, already rather sketchy, were further imperilled. The porters of this column were Arakanese Mohammedans and Maughs. All dropped their loads and the Arakanese made off into the jungle, but the Maughs, two hundred of them, preferred wisely to be captured rather than have their throats cut by the local Arakanese as they attempted to escape. These prisoners, fed off the supplies they had been carrying, made and maintained an airstrip from which, during the operations, American L5 aircraft evacuated over two hundred badly wounded men. They also did most of the picking up of airdrops for one of our brigades.

Having gained Taung Bazaar, without pause Tanahashi turned on the rear of the 7th Division, but here the Japanese met the second hitch in the great plan. When 9 Brigade of the 5th Indian Division had been sent through the pass a few days before to free the 7th Division for its attack on Buthidaung and Letwedet, a brigade (89) of the latter with the 25th Dragoons had been taken into divisional reserve. Messervy at once launched this brigade and the tanks in a counter-attack to the north against Sakurai Force. The attack, especially the tanks whose presence east of the range had not been expected by the enemy, severely jolted the exultant Japanese, but it did not stop them. They swept on round its flanks and, wading through the breast-high dawn mist of the 6th, overran Messervy's divisional headquarters. A fierce dog-fight ensued among the camouflaged tents and dug-outs of the headquarters and along the jungle paths through it. Clerks, orderlies, signallers, and staff officers threw back yelling rush after rush, but when the Japanese mortars made the area untenable, Messervy gave the order for the whole headquarters to fight its way through the Japanese to the Administrative Box. After destroying equipment, ciphers, and documents, they broke out in several groups, one led by the general himself. Casualties were numerous, but the bulk reached the Box, and Messervy had a reduced headquarters working and himself in control of his division again by the evening. The enemy swarmed round the Administrative Box, and to strengthen it Messervy called inside its perimeter two additional infantry battalions from certain out-lying positions, for use as counter-attack troops. The brigades of 7th Division and 9 Brigade of the 5th Division, in accordance with the orders given for such a situation, dug in for all-round defence on their position, and beat off attacks, frontally from Doi Force and in rear from Tanahashi's troops. On the 7th, patrols of the 7th Division moving up the Ngakyedauk Pass from the east were ambushed and had to turn back. On the 8th, patrols of the 5th Division from the west found a well-dug-in road-block across the road, for on that day Doi Force and Sakurai's men had joined hands. The 7th Division was surrounded.

Meanwhile Kubo Force pushed north towards Goppe Bazaar, and, dropping a detachment to close the road south, turned directly west to cross the Mayu Range. There was no track; the ridge was almost precipitous for a thousand feet. The Japanese, ant-like, dragged their mortars and machine-guns up the cliff and lowered them the other side, until they burst out on the main

Bawli–Maungdaw road, much to the surprise of certain administrative units peacefully pursuing their daily tasks. Bridges were blown up, camps fired on, 15 Corps Headquarters harried, and for forty-eight hours the 5th Division was, like the 7th, cut off from all access by road. Well might Sakurai congratulate himself on the success of his blow, while Tokyo Rose crooned seductively on the wireless that it was all over in Burma.

Actually it was just starting. The leading brigade of Lomax's 26th Division, which I had placed under Christison, crossed the Goppe Pass into the Kalapanzin Valley, reoccupied Taung Bazaar, and began to press on Sakurai's rear. On the same day the rest of the division, relieved in the Bawli area by Festing's 36th British Division, followed. Briggs, with the 5th Division, although he had only two of his three brigades left, thinned out along his front, in spite of Doi Force demonstration attacks, and began to push up the Ngakyedauk Pass towards the 7th Division. At the same time, hurriedly organized forces from the 5th Division and corps reserve attacked from both sides the road-block that Kubo Force had established south of Bawli Bazaar.

The Japanese knew they *had* to destroy the 7th Division in the next few days and they were going to spare nothing to do it. As their reinforcements arrived they flung them to the attack on the Administrative Box or against our entrenched brigades. The fighting was everywhere hand-to-hand and desperate. The Administrative Box was our weak spot. Commanded from the surrounding hills on all sides at short range, crowded with dumps of petrol and ammunition, with mules by the hundred and parked lorries by the dozen, with administrative troops and Indian labour, life in it under the rain of shells and mortar bombs was a nightmare. Yet the flimsy defences held, held because no soldier, British, Indian, or Gurkha, would yield; they fought or they died where they stood. How some of them died will be for ever a black blot on the so often stained honour of the Japanese Army. in the moonless dark, a few hundred yelling Japanese broke into the Box and overran the main dressing station, crowded with wounded, the surgeons still operating. The helpless men on their stretchers were slaughtered in cold blood, the doctors lined up and shot, the Indian orderlies made to carry the Japanese wounded back and then murdered too. A counter-attack next morning exacted retribution, but found the hospital a shambles, the only survivors a few wounded men who had rolled into the jungle and shammed dead.

Such an outrage only steeled the resolve of our men. Typical was the spirit of a battery of medium artillery pent up in the Box. An air pilot reported he had seen their five-inch guns firing at a range of four hundred yards as the enemy pressed home an attack. He thought their situation desperate. A wireless signal was sent to the gunners asking how things were with them. 'Fine,' was the answer, 'but drop us a hundred bayonets!' The bayonets were dropped—and used.

Messervy now ordered his brigades to send out strong offensive detachments to harry and cut the tracks by which the enemy's mule and porter columns were trying to replenish their forces. The Japanese were beginning to suffer from their optimistic time-table. The ten days allowed were almost up; they had captured none of our guns or supplies; the British were showing no signs of the panic retreat expected. Instead, it was the Japanese themselves who, more and more, were becoming the encircled force. Sakurai made desperate efforts to bring in reinforcements, supplies, and ammunition; but his convoys were ambushed in the jungle, and his boats shot up from the air as they tried to creep up the rivers, while commando raids and demonstrations by light craft along the coast behind him held down the troops that might have helped him. The West African advance down the Kaladan Valley, which now threatened Kyauktaw and was approaching a position from which it might menace the Japanese right rear, was a growing threat to the whole Japanese position in Arakan. In spite of this, Hanaya, with commendable resolution, refused, until the third week in February, when the result of his main battle was beyond doubt, to send any help to his hard pressed and outnumbered Kaladan detachment. Meanwhile Sakurai's losses were heavy, and they were not being replaced. His wasting battalions were growing hungry. Hanaya should by this time have realized that his blow had failed and saved what he could by retreat. Instead, with typical dull Japanese ferocity, he continued to push his now increasingly disorganized units to the attack.

The 36th British Division under Festing now went into action. It had only two brigades, one of which began to advance south down the main road on the west of the range, while the 26th Division on the east pushed south from Taung Bazaar. The plan by which Sakurai Force would be caught and crushed between the 5th and 7th Divisions and the 26th and 36th was moving steadily to its climax.

My time was spent between my own headquarters and Christison's, with occasional visits to the troops. It was good to see how the attitude had altered from that of 1943. Now confidence and the offensive spirit reigned in everyone. There were, of course, anxious moments; we had some over air supply. The American and British transport aircraft available were proving too few to meet our increasing demands. In Arakan not only were the whole of the 7th Division, part of the 5th, and most of the 26th on air supply, but the 81st West African also. This total, formidable as it was, we might have managed, but another large demand had to be met. The time for the fly-in of Wingate's force was approaching, and, unless the whole operation was to be postponed or perhaps abandoned, it was necessary to divert aircraft first for its training and rehearsals, and later for its maintenance. This difficulty was met by Admiral Mountbatten obtaining the permission of the Combined Chiefs of Staff to borrow aircraft from the Hump. Twenty-five Commandos (C46) were lent for three weeks, thus enabling Dakotas to be sent to Wingate's force to tide over the peak demand.

In the first days of the battle, the Japanese Air Force tried hard to wrest superiority from us. The biggest air fights yet seen in Burma took place in the Arakan sky and went decisively in our favour. The R.A.F. shot down the Tojos and Zeros at the rate of ten for one Spitfire, until the enemy returned only on an occasional tip-and-run raid against our transport aircraft. Indeed, anti-aircraft fire from the ground was soon a greater danger to our aerial supply line than air attack. Luckily the Japanese were always unskilful anti-aircraft gunners, and, as most of the dropping was now done at night, their fire, though at times considerable, was strangely ineffective. Air supply went steadily on.

Watching Snelling's men at work, meeting the demands of the fighting troops, I was surprised at the range and flexibility of his ground organization for air supply. All the standard items—rations, ammunition, mail, petrol for tanks, grain for animals, and the rest—went largely on a regular schedule, but the emergency and fancy demands made were also met with the promptitude and exactness of the postal order department of a first-class departmental store. Blood plasma, instruments, and special drugs for the doctors, spare parts for guns and tanks, boots of unusual size, the daily issue of S.E.A.C. newspaper, typewriter ribbons, cooking pots to replace those destroyed by shellfire, socks, even spectacles to replace those lost—nothing was too unusual, too trivial, or too fragile to be found and packed by the supply units or delivered by the airmen. As an example, when Messervy's headquarters took refuge in the Administrative Box it arrived minus all such domestic items as spare clothing, bedding, razors, soap, tooth brushes, and the rest. All these items were replaced within forty-eight hours, and would have been delivered earlier had not the first drop unfortunately gone to the Japanese. One item, however, even Snelling could not replace. Messervy's red-banded general's hat had been left behind and not another of the size was available. However, even that loss was recovered a couple of weeks later, when in a party of Japanese, ambushed while trying to escape, one was found to be wearing the general's hat! It was duly returned, the temporary wearer having no further use for a hat of any kind. When I congratulated Snelling on the excellence of his organization he told me he regarded the Arakan show as merely a rehearsal for bigger things. How right he was!

By the middle of February, the Japanese had shot their bolt; a week later Hanaya accepted defeat and, too late, attempted to pull out his disorganized units. Under cover of suicide detachments, who hung on to the last, Sakurai Force broke up into small groups and took to the jungle. But our 7th Division had already passed to the offensive, the 5th was battering through the Ngakyedauk Pass, which was fully opened on the 24th, and from the north swept down, on both sides of the ridge, the 26th and 36th Divisions. The hammer and the anvil met squarely, and the Japanese between disintegrated. Kubo Force, among the cliffs and caves of the Mayu Range, was destroyed to the last man in a snarling, tearing dog-fight that lasted days, with no quarter given or expected. Of Sakurai's seven thousand men who had penetrated our lines, over five thousand bodies were found and counted, many more lay undiscovered in the jungle; hundreds died of exhaustion before they reached safety; few survived. The March on Delhi via Arakan was definitely off!

The spirit and cohesion of 15 Corps were shown by the fact

that it resumed its general offensive, interrupted by the Japanese counter-stroke, on the 5th March. The enemy, bringing up strong reinforcements, resisted desperately. Our advance was slowed up also because drastic reductions were made in the air supply to 15 Corps. Not only had the borrowed aircraft to be returned to the Hump, and others sent to Wingate's force, but Baldwin and I were growing increasingly anxious for the squadrons to have at least a short rest after their magnificent achievements, before the obviously approaching major test on the main Assam front again called on them for prolonged intensive effort. Road and water transport replaced air, and the advance went on. Buthidaung, a shattered wreck of a village, was taken on the 11th March, after a series of deliberate assaults on the defences covering its approaches. In these attacks Christison made use of really heavy artillery bombardments; in one of them his corps artillery put down seven thousand shells in ten minutes on a five-hundred-yard objective. Luckily our Arakan line of communication could now bear the strain. After Buthidaung, the reduction of the formidable Letwedet fortress was begun, and achieved, bit by bit, in savage fighting.

The Japanese made one desperate bid to hold up this attack. On the 25th March, they infiltrated a suicide force of some four hundred men into the neighbourhood of the Administrative Box. The attempt had no effect on our operations; the troops in reserve quickly and with relish liquidated the lot. By the end of March the whole Buthidaung–Letwedet area was in our hands, although a few Japanese stragglers still survived, dodging about in the mass of tiger grass and the scrub-covered hillocks until the monsoon obliterated them.

Meanwhile, on the west of the range, Briggs's 5th Division had again set about the keep of Razabil fortress which still held out. One brigade, Warren's, cut in between Razabil and the tunnels area; the Japanese positions, pounded out of recognition, were rushed and their last defenders bayoneted as they crouched deep in the hill-sides. It was then the turn of the 36th British Division to attack the last enemy stronghold defending the Maungdaw–Buthidaung road, the tunnels fortress. This they did with *élan* and skill. The Japanese resisted and counter-attacked at every step. Their reinforcements were, we knew, pouring in to refill the depleted ranks of the 55th Division and to build up the 54th behind it, but Festing's men were not to be denied.

On the 27th March, a Welsh battalion supported by tanks assaulted the defences of the western tunnel. In the mêlée a tank fired a shell directly into the tunnel mouth. Ammunition stored inside blew up, in a series of stunning explosions, and in the confusion the Welshmen rushed the enemy and the tunnel was ours. On the 1st April, another battalion, the Glosters, attacked the eastern tunnel positions and took a beating; but, with true West Country doggedness, they had another go on the 4th. This time the Japanese had had enough and did not wait for them. The tunnel itself was taken on the 6th April.

The final step to clear the tunnels area and to free the road for our use was the capture of the dominating hill known as Point 551, which overlooked a stretch of the road. It was under attack throughout April, during which the 26th Division delivered three separate assaults on it. Its capture on the 3rd May, at the fourth attempt, was the toughest fighting of the whole tunnels battle. I was glad it fell to Lomax and his 26th Division, for it was here in 1943 that the bottom had fallen out of our box and of our plan to hold the Maungdaw–Buthidaung road. It was the first time we had won a battle on a spot where we had previously lost one; later we were to do this again and again, and it always gave me an especial satisfaction. Revenge *is* sweet. 15 Corps had now achieved all the tasks I had set it.

It was only in the Kaladan Valley that our plans were not completely successful. Here the 81st West African Division had contributed to the general victory by a rapid advance, brushing aside opposition, to Kyauktaw and on to Apaukwa, both taken early in March. The enemy, appreciating what a threat the division was becoming, then concentrated against it a column of about four battalions under a Colonel Koba, a regimental commander of the 54th Division, who carried out a brilliant counter-attack which rightly earned him promotion to Major-General. The West Africans, rather dispersed in their advance, were caught by surprise, and they proved not so steady in defence as they were dashing in attack. They were thrown into confusion and pushed back again to the north-west of Kyauktaw. The division, having been rallied, collected in the area of Kaladan village, while its transport withdrew north up the river. It then moved on a pack-and-porter basis to the Kalapanzin Valley, near Taung Bazaar on the flank of the main battle, while a detachment retired slowly up the Kaladan River covering the transport. Koba followed up this detachment, attacked it fiercely, and eventually drove it out of the Kaladan Valley into that of the Sangu.

Before the battle in Arakan was over it was clear that the enemy was about to take the offensive on the main front in Assam. Both my reserve divisions, the 26th and 36th, were committed and it was imperative that I should collect a fresh Army Reserve. For this purpose I began to withdraw the 5th Indian Division to the Chittagong area to rest and refit. Its place was taken by the 25th Indian Division which General Giffard sent me from India, under Davies, my old Chief of Staff in 1942. This enabled me to warn Christison that the 7th Division, in turn, would follow the 5th into Army Reserve. The intention was to transfer these reserves, if necessary, partly by air and partly by rail, from Chittagong to Imphal.

As the monsoon approached and the Japanese offensive on the main front developed, it became imperative to reduce as much as possible any demands, especially for air supply, that might come from Arakan. For this reason, and in order to avoid sickness, General Giffard had agreed to my proposal that 15 Corps should pull back its forward troops from Buthidaung, which was un-healthy, low-lying, and difficult to hold. In May, therefore, Christison drew back to a line which could be held by a minimum of troops, avoided the most unhealthy areas, and was not likely to require air supply. A firm hold was kept on Taung Bazaar, the high ground west of Buthidaung, on the tunnels area, on Maungdaw, and on the mouth of the Naf River by which it was approached.

This Arakan battle, judged by the size of the forces engaged, was not of great magnitude, but it was, nevertheless, one of the historic successes of British arms. It was the turning-point of the Burma campaign. For the first time a British force had met, held, and decisively defeated a major Japanese attack, and followed this up by driving the enemy out of the strongest possible natural positions that they had been preparing for months and were determined to hold at all costs. British and Indian soldiers had proved themselves, man for man, the masters of the best the Japanese could bring against them. The R.A.F. had met and driven from the sky superior numbers of the Japanese Air Force equipped with their latest fighters. It was a victory, a victory about which there could be no argument, and its effect, not only on the troops engaged but on the whole Fourteenth Army, was immense. The legend of Japanese invicibility in the jungle, so long fostered by so many who should have known better, was smashed. I could not help feeling an especial pride that it had been my old 15 Corps that had done it. Under Christison's leadership they had earned at least one of the three V's I had taken as their badge.

CHAPTER XII

THE NORTHERN FRONT

THE Northern was the most isolated of the Burma fronts. To reach it by rail—there was no road—you left Dimapur and continued your seemingly interminable journey through the tea-garden area of Assam. As you crept northward, it was impossible to avoid a growing feeling of loneliness, which even the sight of the increasingly busy airfields of the Hump route, strung along the line, failed to dissipate. At last Tinsukia, the junction for the Assam oilfields, was reached and your train turned wearily into the branch for Ledo. Ledo, in December 1943, seemed rather like the end of the world. Instead, it was the start of the road to China, the road that, if it were ever built, would replace the one from Rangoon, so effectively closed in early 1942.

Many people at this time, Americans no less than British, doubted if the Ledo road *could* be built. They doubted if the Chinese divisions would ever be able to drive back the Japanese and clear the route. They doubted if the Ledo railway would carry and maintain the troops, labour, equipment, and material required. They doubted if any road builders could overcome the monsoon climate combined with the extreme difficulty of the terrain. Many, even of those who believed it possible, did not think that the Ledo road would ever repay the expenditure in men and resources that would have to be devoted to it. Indeed, at this time, Stilwell was almost alone in his faith that, not only could the road be built, but that it would be the most potent winning factor in the war against Japan. His vision, as he expounded it to me, was of an American-trained and -equipped Chinese force, of some thirty divisions to begin with, maintained, except for what was available in China, by the road from Ledo. This new model army, under his command, would drive through China to the sea and then with the American Navy strike at Japan itself.

I agreed with Stilwell that the road could be built. I believed that, properly equipped and efficiently led, Chinese troops could defeat Japanese if, as would be the case with his Ledo force, they had a considerable numerical superiority. On the engineering side I had no doubts. We had built roads over country as difficult, with much less technical equipment than the Americans would have. My British engineers, who had surveyed the trace for the road for the first eighty miles, were quite confident about that. We were already, on the Central front, maintaining great labour forces over equally gimcrack lines of communication. Thus far Stilwell and I were in complete agreement, but I did not hold two articles of his faith. I doubted the overwhelming war-winning value of this road, and, in any case, I believed it was starting from the wrong place. The American amphibious strategy in the Pacific, of hopping from island to island would, I was sure, bring much quicker results than an overland advance across Asia with a Chinese army yet to be formed. In any case, if the road was to be really effective, its feeder railway should start from Rangoon, not Calcutta. If it had been left to me, on military grounds, I would have used the immense resources required for this road, not to build a new highway to China, but to bring forward the largest possible combat forces to destroy the Japanese army in Burma. Once that was accomplished, the old route to China would be open; over it would flow a much greater tonnage than could ever come via Ledo, and the Allied forces in Burma would be available for use elsewhere.

This became the fundamental difference between the American and the British outlook in Burma. To the Americans, the reconquest of Burma was merely incidental to the reopening of land communications with China, and need be pursued only to the limited extent necessary for that purpose. To the British, the reoccupation of Burma was not only an end in itself—the liberation of British territory—but, by the capture of Rangoon, the best means of opening up a really effective link with China. Both points of view were understandable and, with national backgrounds, almost inevitable. Unfortunately, they could easily be distorted, until some Americans could accuse the British of hoping to regain by the efforts of the Americans the Empire they had lost, and the British could retaliate by alleging that several Chinese divisions and great logistical resources, devoted to an unsound and largely political American objective, were being held by one Japanese division, while the British fought the main enemy forces. These differences of approach had no serious effect on the relations between the troops, but they did lead in 1943 and early 1944 to a mutual lack of appreciation of their respective efforts.

The main trouble as far as we, the fighting formations, were concerned was due, more than anything else, to the segregation of the various fronts. The British could not see the Americans and Chinese fighting and enduring in the Hukawng Valley, any more than the Americans could see us waging desperate battles in Imphal and Arakan. Actual contact between the troops of both nations would have soon cured it. Indeed it did. It was noticeable that, when the American light aeroplane pilots began to help in the fly-out of thousands of British and Indian wounded, and the American Field Service Ambulance units were attached to our divisions, a strong sense of comradeship grew up between these magnificent Americans, who never spared themselves in their work of mercy, and our troops. Squabbles between allies are hard to avoid, especially when both have suffered disaster as we did in 1942, but, as the tide of war turned and the fronts drew closer together, the troops forgot them, and rejoiced in one another's successes.

In fact, more actual and determined opposition to Stilwell's strategic ideas came from Americans, who, like Chennault, thought all resources should be devoted to building up a great American air force in China rather than to creating a powerful Chinese army. Their theory was that the Japanese in China could be defeated by air power, with such support as local Chinese forces could provide. Stilwell, for personal and military reasons, bitterly opposed this idea. As soon as the American air force became a real nuisance to the Japanese, he affirmed, they would retaliate by an advance against its airfields. Then, unless there were a well-found Chinese army to protect them, they would be overrun and the air force put out of action. Stilwell was undoubtedly right, but the controversy inflamed the rivalry and jealously between the two leading Americans. Their enmity did not help the Allied cause; still less did the activities of their publicity merchants.

However, it was not for me to decide the merits or demerits of the Ledo road. The Anglo-American Combined Chiefs of Staff had told Admiral Mountbatten to make the road, and so, in every way possible, even to devoting half the total transport lift and large British ground forces to the Northern front, we in Fourteenth Army got down to helping Stilwell in what we knew was a tough assignment.

Before he came under my operational control, Stilwell had received orders from Admiral Mountbatten to occupy Northern Burma up to the Mogaung–Myitkyina area, so as to cover the building of the road, and to increase the safety of the air route to China. Obviously, in view of the relative value of Chinese and Japanese divisions, he would not be able to do this unless the main Japanese forces on the other fronts were engaged so hotly that they could not seriously reinforce their 18th Division opposing him. This was arranged, and in addition, to give him overwhelming odds, it was decided that Wingate's Special Force would be used to cut the communications of the enemy's Northern front. Everything was also to be done to persuade the Generalissimo at the same time to order the advance of the Chinese armies from Yunnan towards Lashio, though, wisely, no dependence was to be placed on this occurring.

In accordance with these plans, in October 1943, the Chinese 38th and 22nd Divisions under Sun and Liao were brought from Ramgarh to Ledo. Behind them, in India, the 30th Chinese Division and an American regiment of three battalions, originally intended for Wingate, were made ready to follow.

Stilwell had also a Chinese tank group armed with American light tanks and an irregular force of a few hundred Kachin raiders, local tribesmen led by American officers. Away on his left flank, completely cut off from all but air supply, was the small British garrison of Fort Hertz, consisting of Kachin levies stiffened by a battalion of Burma Rifles. The task of this detachment was to cover an airstrip which served as an emergency landing ground on the Hump route, and to prevent Japanese infiltration. At first, Fort Hertz was directly under Fourteenth Army, but later I transferred it to Stilwell's command as it would have to act in co-ordination with his main force. To support him, Stilwell had the American Northern Air Sector Force. The whole Chinese-American force was known, rather clumsily, as the Northern Combat Area Command or N.C.A.C. At this time the Ledo road stretched only thirty miles towards China.

Opposing the N.C.A.C. was the 18th Japanese Division, our old opponents, who had been so roughly handled by the Gurkhas at Kyaukse in 1942. This division had its headquarters at Myitkyina. One of its regiments was held as a reserve for either the Yunnan or the N.C.A.C. front. The other two were in depth at the head of the Hukawng Valley, with detachments forward in touch with the 38th Chinese Division. It was not likely that the 56th Japanese Division, which was watching the Yunnan Chinese, could spare any of its troops for other purposes, and so Stilwell would have a comfortable superiority in numbers even if, as was probable, the whole 18th Division were concentrated against him. I was as anxious that we should have this superiority here as I was to have it in Arakan. It was on the N.C.A.C. front and in Arakan that the first real clashes would come, and a lot would depend on their results.

Stilwell was not only the Deputy Supreme Commander; he was responsible for the actual Chinese fighting front, the training of Chinese armies, advice to Chiang Kai-shek, supply to China, Lease Lend to the Allies, and command of all American forces in the China-Burma-India theatre. When he announced that he would take personal command in the field, there were not wanting those who thought that, instead of acting as a corps commander, he should have delegated that to some more junior general and placed himself at Supreme Headquarters, where he might properly perform at least some of his other functions. Personally, I think he was right. The most important thing of all was to ensure that the American-trained Chinese not only fought, but fought successfully. No one could do that as well as Stilwell himself. Indeed, he was the only American who had authority actually to command the Chinese. At that time, while there were several able American staff officers in S.E.A.C., I do not think there was one sufficiently experienced to take command of a corps in battle. From my point of view, too, I much preferred to have Stilwell himself under me. I knew that any other American officer would refer all instructions to him, wherever he was, and I did not want a repetition of the Chinese Command set-up of 1942.

In October 1943, the 38th Chinese Division began the advance from Ledo against slight opposition, but early in November the Japanese defence stiffened, and the Chinese, reverting to their old methods, sat down and dug in. Stilwell was away at the Cairo Conference, and Boatner, his deputy, in despair at failing to get them to move, sent a signal to Delhi reporting that the Chinese refused to advance. This had a depressing effect in headquarters from Delhi to Cairo, and produced a good many 'I told you so's' from both British and Americans. I was very disappointed when I heard, but consoled myself with the twofold thought that most troops are a bit sticky at times and that Stilwell was on his way back. He reached the N.C.A.C. front on 21st December. On 22nd and 23rd, he toured the Chinese positions, injected ginger into the senior officers, both Chinese and American, and laid on an attack in superior force on the Japanese detachment blocking the way. On the 24th, he saw the attack go in and stayed with the troops until the 30th, by which time the enemy had been completely cleaned up. On the 31st, Stilwell flew to Delhi for the conference at which he placed himself under my operational control, and was back again a few days later to repeat the performance at the next hold-up. After two or three of these minor successes, the Chinese began really to get their tails up. For the first time they were attacking and defeating a modern enemy—something that had never before happened in the history of China.

The Chinese were now firmly established at Shingbwiyang in the Hukawng Valley, and pushing for their next objective, Shaduzup, at the head of the Mogaung Valley. By 27th December, the road had reached Shingbwiyang, a hundred and three miles from Ledo—a magnificent achievement by the American engineers under Brigadier-General Pick and the heterogeneous labour force of Indians, Kachins, and Nagas that they controlled. To get this far, the road had been driven over the formidable Patkoi mountains, the most difficult section of the whole route. At Shingbwiyang the Chinese struck the fair-weather road the Japanese had built and this was, of course, a tremendous help in the construction of the new road, which generally followed the Japanese trace.

By 1st February, the 38th Chinese Division had, after a series of small actions, occupied Thipha Ga, while a regiment of the 22nd Division, moving wide on the right flank, cleared the Japanese from the Taro Valley, which lay on the east bank of the Chindwin, separated from the Ledo road in the Hukawng Valley by a range of rugged jungle hills. This was the 22nd Division's entry into the campaign, and they did well. In all these actions Stilwell had kept a close hand on the Chinese troops, steadying them when they faltered, prodding them when they hesitated, even finding their battalions for them himself when they lost them. He was one of the Allied commanders who had learnt in the hard school of the 1942 retreat. His tactics were to press the Japanese frontally while the real attacks came in through the jungle from the flank, with probably a road-block well behind the enemy. In this way, by a series of hooks round and behind the Japanese, he pushed forward. He, also, was an advocate of the sledge-hammer to crack a walnut, at this stage. He saw to it that if a Japanese company was to be liquidated, it was attacked by a Chinese regiment.

At the beginning of March I visited Stilwell at Thipha Ga just as he was launching up to then his biggest attack for the capture of Maingkwan, a large village and the capital of the Hukawng Valley. Besides his two Chinese divisions, he now had with him the American Long-Range Penetration Regiment. Stilwell had changed its original commander for Brigadier-General Merrill, whom I had known well and liked. After him, the regiment was christened 'Merrill's Marauders'. Merrill was a fine, courageous leader who inspired confidence, and I congratulated myself that I had restrained my Gurkha orderly, that day in 1942, when he would have tommy-gunned a jeep-load of men wearing un-familiar helmets. If he had, the Marauders would have had another commander, and that would have been a pity.

Stilwell's plan for the Maingkwan battle was for the 22nd Division (less one regiment) to continue its push straight down the road for the village, while its third regiment came in over the hills from Taro on the Japanese left rear. Simultaneously, the 38th Division was to make a closer wheel round Maingkwan and strike the enemy right. For the first time the Chinese tank group was to take part in a major engagement. The Marauders were to sweep wide and cut the road well south of the Japanese on both sides of the next large village, Walawbum, and hold their road-blocks until the Chinese advancing beyond Maingkwan joined them.

Stilwell met me at the airfield, looking more like a duck hunter than ever with his wind-jacket, campaign hat, and leggings. As always, he told me fully what was going on tactically, and explained his plan. Like most commanders I have known on the

254

eve of a battle, he was concealing a certain jumpiness. He had had bad luck with the weather recently; there had been unseasonably heavy showers. Rain now would make things very difficult. He was depending, too, on co-ordinated timing between Chinese forces and, as he knew better than I did, there was risk in this. But the plan was sound, the Chinese in good fettle, and the Americans out to mark their entry into the campaign. In addition to his dispositions for the immediate battle, Stilwell surprised me by showing me on a map his idea for a sudden dash at Myitkyina, which he thought might be brought off by an outflanking march over the Daru Hkyet Pass and sudden descent on the town from the north-west, while the Japanese were concentrating on the defence of Mogaung. Naturally he could not forecast a date for this. As he said, it depended on how things went and when he got Shaduzup, his next objective after Maingkwan. This was the first I had heard of anything approaching a plan for the seizure of Myitkyina, and I do not know whether he had even discussed it with his staff. At any rate he asked me very solemnly not to speak of it to *anyone*, and made it quite clear that that included not only my staff but my superior commanders. He gave as his reason that if his intentions got to Delhi there would be leakage, and that would be fatal to his plan. Actually there was, judging by experience, much more likelihood of leakage through Chinese channels than through S.E.A.C. or 11th Army Group, and I thought the real reason was that, if the operation did not come off or misfired, he did not want anyone to be able to say he had had a failure. I understood this feeling and, as the project depended on a good many intervening ifs, I gave him my assurance I would mention it to no one.

In any case I had not come to discuss the tactical conduct of Stilwell's campaign—I had every confidence in his handling of that and it was his business, not mine. The fly-in of Wingate's Special Force, due to commence on the 5th March, was intended primarily to help the American-Chinese advance, and I wanted to make sure he was completely familiar with the final arrangements.

Stilwell was always rather prickly about Wingate's force. To begin with, Mountbatten and Wingate between them had persuaded the American Chiefs of Staff to send United States troops, even if only a regiment, to the Burma front, when he himself had

255

failed to get them. Further, he felt passionately that all American troops in the theatre should be under his direct command, and had been angered when they were allotted to Wingate. Stilwell had pressed for them to be transferred to him, and confessed quite frankly to me that he had been very surprised when Mountbatten yielded to his request. Nevertheless he did not seem particularly grateful to the Supreme Commander and some bitterness remained. Nor did he approve of Wingate's long-range penetration methods; he preferred the short-hook tactics. He now professed doubts as to the value of Wingate's operation, but had to admit, when I put it to him, that if he were the commander of the Japanese 18th Division and suddenly found ten thousand troops sitting across his rear, cutting his communications, he would not feel too happy about it. At last, he grinned at me over his glasses, and said, 'That'll be fine if Wingate does it and stays there; if he goes in for real fighting and not shadow boxing like last time.' I told him that my only doubt was, not that Wingate's people would shadow box, but that with his new stronghold technique they might get too pinned down. I promised that whatever happened we would cut the Japanese line of communication for him and keep it cut for quite a time. No commander could ask more than that.

I was struck, as I always was when I visited Stilwell's headquarters, how unnecessarily primitive all its arrangements were. There was, compared with my own or other headquarters, no shortage of transport or supplies, yet he delighted in an exhibition of rough living which, like his omission of rank badges and the rest, was designed to foster the idea of the tough, hard-bitten, plain, fighting general. Goodness knows he was tough and wiry enough to be recognized as such without the play acting, for it was as much a bit of stage management as Mountbatten's meticulous turn-out under any conditions, but it achieved its publicity purpose. Many people sneer at generals who wear quaint head-dress with too many or too few badges, carry odd sticks, affect articles of civilian attire in uniform, or indulge in all sorts of tricks to make themselves easily recognizable to their troops or to anybody else. These things have their value if there is a real man behind them, and, for the rest, his countrymen should forgive almost anything to a general who wins battles. His soldiers will. Stilwell, thank heaven, had a sense of humour, which some who practise these arts have not, and he could, and did, not infrequently laugh at himself.

By this date we had won our battle in Arakan and I was able to give Stilwell an account of the first real victory of the Burma campaign. He followed that success up with one of his own within the next few days. The Maingkwan-Walawbum battle, while it did not, as we had hoped it would, destroy the Japanese 18th Division, was a triumph for the Chinese and a personal one for Stilwell. His tactical plan for the battle was bold but sound. Merrill's Marauders, after an outflanking move, duly captured Walawbum, thus cutting off the main Japanese force; but the Chinese advance to link up with them was slow and over-cautious. Indeed, at one stage in the afternoon it stopped altogether while a division was issued with a leisurely meal. Meanwhile the Marauders had been turned out of Walawbum, and it was with some difficulty that American officers with the Chinese persuaded some of their tanks and infantry to go on again. They found Walawbum only lightly held by the enemy and entered it, but withdrew again when darkness fell. Next morning, however, another formation finally occupied the village, but by then the bulk of the Japanese 18th Division had extricated itself from the trap.

The Chinese, in spite of the dilatoriness of some of their formations, had, when put to it, fought well, and inflicted some hundreds of casualties on the enemy. My old friends, the 38th Chinese Division, bore the brunt of the fighting, and the Chinese tanks, in this their first serious action, especially distinguished themselves. With their escorting battalion they suddenly encountered two Japanese battalions, concealed in tall elephant grass, waiting to counter-attack. The Chinese, although raw troops, flung themselves on the enemy and routed them. Walawbum was an undoubted victory. It just missed complete success because Stilwell himself could not be everywhere at once, and at this time his actual presence was the only thing that would impart real drive to his troops. Nevertheless, although it escaped almost intact, the Japanese 18th Division was roughly handled and had hurriedly to retreat, leaving a large part of the Hukawng Valley in our hands. Now we had won a battle handsomely on each flank of the Burma front.

From the N.C.A.C. I flew back to my Comilla headquarters

for a day, and then on to Lalaghat and Hailakandi where the two brigades of the first wave of Wingate's Special Force were ready to fly into Burma. Of this wave, 16 Brigade which was to march in was already well on its way. Starting from Ledo on the 8th February, it had pushed steadily southward, supplied by air through extremely difficult hill and jungle country, to the Chindwin near Singkaling Kamti. Here the rafts the troops had built were supplemented by rubber boats dropped by No. 1 Air Commando, and the brigade crossed to continue its arduous march through almost uninhabited country. In response to a request from Stilwell, the brigade raided Lonkin, some fifty miles south of Maingkwan, but found it practically empty of enemy. No opposition except a Japanese-led Burmese patrol or two was encountered. Passing the great Indawgyi Lake by the end of March, 16 Brigade had established itself in a stronghold christened 'Aberdeen', some twenty-five miles from the Rangoon–Myit-kyina railway, which was the main supply route for the Japanese 18th Division fighting Stilwell, and their 56th Division watching the Yunnan Chinese. The brigade had covered four hundred and fifty miles of about the most difficult country in the world in just over six weeks—a magnificent feat of endurance.

On the morning of Sunday, March 5th, I circled the landing ground at Hailakandi. Below me, at the end of the wide brown airstrip, was parked a great flock of squat, clumsy gliders, their square wing-tips almost touching; around the edges of the field stood the more graceful Dakotas that were to lift them into the sky. Men swarmed about the aircraft, loading them, laying out tow ropes, leading mules, humping packs, and moving endlessly in dusty columns, for all the world like busy ants round captive moths.

I landed and met Wingate at his temporary headquarters near the airstrip. Everything was going well. There had been no serious hitch in the assembly or preparation for the fly-in, which was due to begin at dusk that evening. For some days previously our diversionary air attacks had been almost continuous on the enemy's airfields and communication centres to keep his air force occupied. Meanwhile, ostentatious air reconnaissances over the Mandalay district had been carried out in the hope of convincing the enemy that any airborne expedition would be directed against that area. The attacks on airfields were useful in keeping Japanese aircraft out of the sky, but the false reconnaissances, as far as I ever discovered, had little effect.

Just a month earlier, cn 4th February, Stratemeyer, the American commander of the Eastern Air Command, and I had issued a joint directive to Wingate and Cochrane, the American commander of No. 1 Air Commando. In this, Wingate's force was ordered to march and fly in to the Rail Indaw area (*Rail* Indaw to distinguish it from another Indaw not on the Mandalay–Myitkyina railway), and from there to operate under direct command of Fourteenth Army, with the objects of:

(i) Helping the advance of Stilwell's Ledo force on Myitkyina by cutting the communications of the Japanese 18th Division, harassing its rear, and preventing its reinforcement.

(ii) Creating a favourable situation for the Yunnan Chinese forces to cross the Salween and enter Burma.

(iii) Inflicting the greatest possible damage and confusion on the enemy in North Burma.

The tactical plan for getting the force into position behind the enemy was based on four assembly places:

'Aberdeen', 27 miles north-west of Indaw.
'Piccadilly', 40 miles north-cast of Indaw.
'Broadway', 35 miles east-north-cast of Indaw.
'Chowringhee', 35 miles east of Indaw.

These places were all away from roads and uninhabited. They were selected because there was enough flat ground to make the building of an airstrip possible in a short time and because there was water in the immediate vicinity. They were in fact fancy names written on the map, within striking distance of Indaw.

It was intended that in the first wave 16 Brigade should march to Aberdeen, 77 Brigade fly in two halves to Piccadilly and Broadway, and 111 Brigade land at Chowringhee. The remaining three brigades, 14, 23, and 3 West African, were to be held for the second wave which it was expected would be required to relieve the first in two or three months.

As the afternoon wore on, the atmosphere of excitement and suspense at Hailakandi grew—the old familiar feeling of waiting to go over the top, intensified by the strangeness and magnitude

259

of this operation. Everyone, even the mules, moved about calmly, quietly, and purposefully. Except perhaps for those patient beasts, it was, all the same, obvious that everyone realized that what was, up to this time, the biggest and most hazardous airborne operation of the war was about to begin.

During the morning the gliders had been loaded with supplies, ammunition, engineer equipment, signalling stores, and men's kits. In the late afternoon the first wave, 77 Brigade Headquarters, the leading British and Gurkha infantry, and a small detachment of American airfield engineers emplaned. Each Dakota was to take two gliders. This was a heavy load, and, as far as I know, never before had these aircraft towed more than one. There had been a clash of opinion among the airmen themselves on its practicability. Cochrane, in charge of the gliders, was confident it could be done; Old, whose Combat Cargo planes would provide the tugs, maintained it was unsound. Various airmen, British and American, took sides and argument was heated. Eventually, after experiments, Wingate agreed with Cochrane, and then Baldwin and I accepted the double tow. Now as I watched the last preparations I was assailed by no doubts on that score. The Dakotas taxied into position. The tow ropes were fixed. Everyone was very quiet as the roar of engines died down and we waited for zero hour. I was standing on the airstrip with Wingate, Baldwin, and one or two more, when we saw a jeep driving furiously towards us. A couple of American airmen jumped out and confronted us with an air photograph, still wet from the developing tent. It was a picture of Piccadilly landing ground, taken two hours previously. It showed almost the whole level space, on which the gliders were to land that night, obstructed by great tree-trunks. It would be impossible to put down even one glider safely. To avoid suspicion no aircraft had reconnoitred the landing grounds for some days before the fly-in, so this photo was a complete shock to us. We looked at one another in dismay.

Wingate, though obviously feeling the mounting strain, had been quiet and controlled. Now, not unnaturally perhaps, he became very moved. His immediate reaction was to declare emphatically to me that the whole plan had been betrayed—probably by the Chinese—and that it would be dangerous to go on with it. I asked if Broadway and Chowringhee, the other proposed landing places, had been photographed at the same time.

I was told they had been and that both appeared vacant and unobstructed.

Wingate was now in a very emotional state, and to avoid discussion with him before an audience, I drew him on one side. I said I did not think the Chinese had betrayed him as they certainly had no knowledge of actual landing grounds, or, as far as I knew, of the operation at all; but he reiterated that someone had betrayed the plan and that the fly-in should be cancelled. I pointed out that only one of the three landing grounds had been obstructed, and that it was the one which he had used in 1943 and of which a picture with a Dakota on it had appeared in an American magazine. We knew the Japanese were nervous of air landing and were blocking many possible landing sites in North and Central Burma; what more likely than they should include a known one we had already used, like Piccadilly? He replied that, even if Broadway and Chowringhee were not physically obstructed, it was most probable that Japanese troops were concealed in the surrounding jungle ready to destroy our gliders as they landed. With great feeling he said it would be 'murder'. I told him I doubted if these places were ambushed. Had the Japanese known of the plan I was sure they would have either ambushed or obstructed all three landing grounds. Wingate was by now calmer and much more in control of himself. After thinking for a moment, he said there would be great risk. I agreed. He paused, then looked straight at me: 'The responsibility is yours,' he said.

I knew it was. Not for the first time I felt the weight of decision crushing in on me with an almost physical pressure. The gliders, if they were to take off that night, must do so within the hour. There was no time for prolonged inquiry or discussion. On my answer would depend not only the possibility of a disaster with wide implications on the whole Burma campaign and beyond, but the lives of these splendid men, tense and waiting in and around their aircraft. At that moment I would have given a great deal if Wingate or anybody else could have relieved me of the duty of decision. But that is a burden the commander himself must bear.

I knew that if I cancelled the fly-in or even postponed it, when the men were keyed to the highest pitch, there would be a terrible reaction; we would never get their morale to the same peak again. The whole plan of campaign, too, would be thrown out.

THE WEAPON IS TESTED

I had promised Stilwell we would cut the communications of the enemy opposing him, and he was relying on our doing it. I had to consider also that one Chindit brigade had already marched into the area; we could hardly desert it. I was, in addition, very nervous that if we kept the aircraft crowded on the airfields as they were, the Japanese would discover them, with disastrous consequences. I knew at this time that a major Japanese offensive was about to break on the Assam front, and I calculated on Wingate's operation to confuse and hamper it. Above all, somehow I did not believe that the Japanese knew of our plan or that the obstruction of Piccadilly was evidence that they did. There was a risk, a grave risk, but not a certainty of disaster. 'The operation will go on,' I said.[1]

Wingate accepted my decision with, I think, relief. He had by now recovered from his first shock and had realized that the obstruction of one landing site need not hold all the implications he had imagined. We walked back to the group of officers and, with Baldwin's concurrence, I announced that the fly-in would proceed, adding that as Piccadilly was obviously out, it was for Wingate as the tactical commander to decide what changes should be made. He stated the case for continuing the operation clearly and calmly, and directed that the troops allotted to Piccadilly were to be diverted to Chowringhee. Although this was strictly Wingate's business and not mine, I very much doubted the wisdom of this. Chowringhee was on the east of the Irrawaddy; the railway and road to be cut were on the west. Before the troops could be effective, therefore, they had to cross the river, and I questioned if this could be done as quickly or as easily as Wingate thought. I asked Calvert, the commander of 77 Brigade, and I found him strongly against Chowringhee. Cochrane also opposed it for the very sound reason that the layout there was quite different from Piccadilly and Broadway and there was little time to re-brief pilots. Baldwin, who as commander of the Third Tactical Air Force, had the overall responsibility for the air side

---

[1] In an account of this incident written shortly afterwards, but which I did not see until after his death, Wingate reversed his role and mine. In it he stated that he used these arguments to urge that the fly-in should go on and that I accepted them and agreed. That is not my recollection of his first reactions, nor in accordance with my notes made nearer the time. In any case the point is of little consequence, as whether Wingate persuaded me, or I him, the responsibility for ordering the operation to continue and for all its consequences could not be his, but must be Baldwin's and mine.

of the operation, was emphatic that Chowringhee could not be used by Piccadilly aircrews, and that settled it. Wingate saw the force of these opinions and accepted that the fly-in would take place as originally planned, with the exception that the troops for Piccadilly would go to Broadway.

Cochrane collected the Piccadilly Dakota and glider pilots, whose destination was now changed, to re-brief them. Curious to see how he would break the news of the alteration and a little anxious lest so obvious a hitch at the start might have a rather depressing effect on them, I followed to listen. Cochrane sprang on to the bonnet of a jeep. 'Say, fellers,' he announced, 'we've got a better place to go to!'

The leading Dakota, with its two gliders trailing behind, roared down the runway just after six o'clock, only a few minutes behind scheduled time. The moment it was clear the others followed at about half a minute intervals. The gliders took the air first, one or two wobbling nervously before they took station behind, and a little above, the towing aircraft. More than once I feared a Dakota would overrun the strip before the gliders were up, but all took off safely and began the long climb to gain height to cross the hills. The darkening sky was full of these queer triangles of aircraft labouring slowly higher and higher into the distance. Eventually even the drone of engines faded and we were left waiting.

And an unpleasant wait it was. Sixty-one gliders had set off. The full complement for Broadway and Piccadilly had been eighty, but we had agreed that sixty was about the most we could hope to land on one strip in the hours of darkness, so the rest had been held back. I sat in the control tent, at the end of the airstrip, to which all messages and signals came. At the rough table with its field telephones was Tulloch, Wingate's chief staff officer, who proved himself quick, reliable, and cool in crisis, and Rome, another admirable staff officer. As the moon came up, in spite of hurricane lanterns and one electric lamp, it was almost lighter outside than within. There was a pause. Then came a report of red flares, fired from the air a few miles away. That meant a tow in distress—ominous if difficulties were beginning so soon. I took a turn outside and thought I saw a red Very light fired high up in the distance. I returned to the tent to find more rumours of gliders down or tows returning before they had crossed our lines.

Not so good. Then another long wait. We looked at our watches. The leading aircraft should be over Broadway now with the gliders going in. We ought to get the first wireless message any minute. Still it did not come. Wingate prowled in and out, speaking to no one, his eyes smouldering in a pallid face. Tulloch sat calmly at the phones. A garbled report over the telephone from another airfield told us that a tow pilot had seen what looked like firing on the Broadway strip. It was the time when doubts grow strongest and fears loom largest. Then, just after four o'clock in the morning, the first signal from Broadway, sent by Calvert, came in plain language, brief, mutilated, but conveying its message of disaster clearly enough—'Soya Link'. The name of the most disliked article in the rations had been chosen in grim humour as the code word for failure. So the Japanese *had* ambushed Broadway! Wingate was right and I had been wrong. He gave me one long bitter look and walked away. I had no answer for him.

Then more signals, broken, hard to decipher, but gradually making the picture clearer. Gliders had crashed, men had been killed, there were injured and dying lying where they had been dragged to the edge of the strip—but there was no enemy. There had been no ambush. A great weight lifted from me as I realized that this was going to be like every other attack, neither so good nor so bad as the first reports of excited men would have you believe. We had to recall the last flight, as Broadway was too obstructed by smashed gliders to accept them. The situation was still far from clear to us as I left the control tent after dawn, but I was confident that if only the Japanese did not locate them for the next twelve hours, the Chindits would have the strip ready for reinforcements by nightfall.

Of the sixty-one gliders dispatched, only thirty-five reached Broadway. The airmen who said that one Dakota could not tow two gliders had been right. In practice the steep climb to cross the mountains, so close to the start, put too great a drag on the nylon ropes and many parted. It also caused overheating in the aircraft engines and unexpected fuel consumption, with dire results. Many gliders and a few aircraft force landed, some in our territory, nine in Japanese. There was a brisk battle near Imphal between the Chindits of a crashed glider, convinced they were behind the enemy lines and determined to sell their lives dearly, and our own troops rushing to their rescue. Gliders by chance came down near a Japanese divisional headquarters and others beside a regimental headquarters far from Broadway. These landings confused the enemy as to our intentions and led to a general alert for gliders and parachutists through all his units.

Long afterwards we discovered that it was not the Japanese who had obstructed Piccadilly but Burmese tree-fellers, who had, in the ordinary course of their work, dragged teak logs out of the jungle to dry in the clearing. The firing reported at Broadway was a nervous burst from a shaken glider pilot.

Even without the enemy, that night at Broadway was tragic and macabre enough. One or two of the leading gliders, circling down to a half-seen gap in the jungle, had crashed on landing. The ground control equipment and its crew were in a glider that failed to arrive so that, until a makeshift control could be improvised, it was impossible to time landings. Some gliders hurtled into the wrecks, others ran off the strip to smash into the trees or were somersaulted to ruin by uneven ground concealed under the grass. Twenty-three men were killed and many injured, but over four hundred, with some stores, and Calvert, the Brigade Commander, landed intact. Most of the engineering equipment did not arrive, but the small party of American engineers, helped by every man who could be spared from patrolling, set to work with what tools they could muster to drag the wreckage clear and prepare the ground. Never have men worked harder, and by evening a strip was fit—but only just fit—to take a Dakota.

Next night the fly-in continued. Fifty-five Dakotas landed at Broadway and the first flights reached Chowringhee, where also there was no sign of enemy. By the 11th March the whole of Calvert's 77 Brigade and half Lentaigne's 111 Brigade were at Broadway, Lentaigne's Brigade Headquarters and the other half with 'Dahforce', a body of Kachins with British officers for use in raising the local tribes, were safely at Chowringhee. Between the 5th and 10th March, one hundred glider and almost six hundred Dakota sorties flew in nine thousand troops and eleven hundred animals. In addition, Fergusson's 16 Brigade had reached Aberdeen after its long march, so that Wingate now had nearly twelve thousand troops well placed, as he put it, 'in the enemy's guts'.

It was clear that the initial operation had been a success and, as a minor consequence, there was the usual fuss about publicity. I was in favour of saying nothing and letting the Japanese find out what they could for themselves, but that was quickly overruled. A fierce controversy then arose as to whether Wingate's name should be mentioned. It was decided not to, on what grounds I was never quite clear, but to Wingate this was *Hamlet* without the Prince of Denmark, and he was furious. He protested, with a good deal of reason, that all formations wanted if possible to see their names in the papers, and that to refer to his Chindits as 'troops of the Fourteenth Army' would gain nothing and miss a chance of giving their morale a boost. I agreed because I thought the Japanese were much more likely, if Wingate's name were given, to take this expedition as merely a repetition of his minor and ineffective raid of 1943, and not be too urgent in concentrating strong forces against it. What we wanted was no interference until we were well established. After a certain amount of the silly temper on both sides that such matters always seem to evoke, Wingate's name was announced.

The Japanese reaction to the landings was surprisingly slow. It is true they had been nervous of airborne attack, but not in the rather inaccessible places we had chosen. Their major offensive towards Imphal was on the point of being launched and all troops were, as we had calculated, either massed on the eastern border for this or moving towards it. The number of our aircraft passing over, night after night, must have been some indication of the size of our force, but Kawabe and his army commanders decided —and kept to the decision—not to divert any considerable number of troops from the main Imphal battle. They took some time collecting and organizing into scratch formations a number of lines of communication and other odd units to deal with the Chindits. The only action taken against the landings was an air attack on Chowringhee on the 10th March, a couple of hours after Lentaigne had marched off, leaving only derelict gliders behind him. Three days later thirty enemy fighters attacked Broadway which was humming with activity. The Japanese pilots met with a surprise. By that time, not only was a troop of light anti-aircraft artillery in position, but a flight of Spitfires from 221 Group R.A.F. was stationed on the strip—the first time an operational airfield had been established *behind* the enemy. The Japanese lost from guns and Spitfires over half their strength.

The slowness of the enemy reaction on land gave our troops the chance to strike first. Calvert's 77 Brigade marched west and on the 16th March attacked a small enemy garrison near Mawlu on the Mandalay–Myitkyina railway, some fifty miles from Broadway. The Japanese detachment was destroyed and the brigade established an airstrip and a stronghold which they christened 'White City', from the supply parachutes that soon draped the trees. Thus, eleven days after the beginning of the fly-in, Special Force's first task had been accomplished—both the main road and rail communications to the Japanese fighting Stilwell had been cut. It was impossible for the enemy to ignore this. The 53rd Japanese Division was at this time arriving piece-meal in Burma and, based on the Divisional Headquarters, under Lieut.-General Kawano, and one regiment of the division, a group known as Take Force, which never much exceeded six thousand in strength, was formed to deal with the airborne invasion. The force was an improvised one and suffered, as such expedients always do, from a lack of cohesion, transport, support-ing arms, signals, and administrative staff. Kawano himself was a sick man—he died soon afterwards—and was replaced by Lieut.-General Takeda. The first serious action was an attempt by Take Force to capture White City and destroy 77 Brigade. The Japanese delivered a series of ferocious assaults, day and night, which were everywhere beaten back in hand-to-hand fighting of the bloodiest kind. British and Gurkhas (my old regiment the 6th Gurkhas won two V.C.s here) proved themselves man for man the superior of the enemy. Take Force, having suffered heavily, withdrew badly shaken from White City, and they never took it.

From Chowringhee one of our columns had struck east to the Chinese frontier and then turned north towards Myitkyina, cutting the important Bhamo Myitkyina road. Lentaigne's 111 Brigade, uniting the portions that had landed at Chowringhee and Broadway, moved well to the west of Indaw. These opera-tions did not, as I had hoped they would, seriously disorganize the Japanese communications with the Assam front. Their chief effect, as far as the battle there was concerned, was to delay for a couple of months two infantry and one artillery battalions of the Japanese 15th Division on their way to take part in the offensive against Imphal.

This offensive was now in full swing and dominated the whole Burma campaign. It was obviously the decisive factor, and it at once confronted me with two problems on Wingate's front. The first was whether to fly in his second wave. The Imphal battle was putting a heavy strain on our air transport resources. If we were to fly in more of Wingate's brigades we could only do so at a reduced rate and even then at some risk to the main front. All reports showed me that 16 Brigade, after its long march, while fit for possibly one more operation, would need early relief. Wingate was also pressing for larger garrisons for his strongholds. After weighing things up, I decided, in spite of the anxious tactical situation now developing about Imphal and Kohima, to fly in, at the best rate compatible with not seriously affecting the move of reinforcements to Assam, Wingate's 14 Brigade and his West African Brigade. The fly-in to Aberdeen began on 22nd March. 14 Brigade under Brodie were in by the 4th April, and by the 12th the West Africans split up into battalions were garrisoning various strongholds.

The second and greater problem was whether I should change Wingate's main object from helping Stilwell to helping 4 Corps, now hard pressed about Imphal. The alteration had obvious advantages as it would use Special Force in direct tactical co-ordination with the main battle. Besides, Stilwell, who would get indirect aid from Wingate, had a considerable superiority over the 18th Japanese Division opposing him, and was in no dire need of help. However, I decided to adhere to my original plan, and Special Force continued to direct its efforts to the north rather than to the west. In this I think I was wrong. Imphal was the decisive battle; it was there only that vital injury could be inflicted on the Japanese Army, and I should have concentrated all available forces to that end. I fear I fell into the error of so many Japanese, and persisted in a plan which should have been changed.

No sooner had these decisions been taken than Special Force suffered a tragic loss. Wingate, flying from Imphal to his new headquarters at Lalaghat in a Mitchell bomber, crashed by night in the wild tangle of hills west of Imphal. He, and all with him, were instantly killed. The cause of the accident cannot be definitely stated. The wreckage was eventually found on the reverse side of a ridge, so it was unlikely that the aircraft had flown into the hill. The most probable explanation is that it had suddenly entered one of those local storms of extreme turbulence so frequent in the area. These were difficult to avoid at night, and once in them an aeroplane might be flung out of control or even have its wings torn off.

I was at Comilla when the signal came in that Wingate was missing. As the hours passed and no news of any sort arrived, gloom descended upon us. We could ill spare him at the start of his greatest attempt. The immediate sense of loss that struck, like a blow, even those who had differed most from him—and I was not one of these—was a measure of the impact he had made. He had stirred up everyone with whom he had come in contact. With him, contact had too often been collision, for few could meet so stark a character without being either violently attracted or repelled. To most he was either prophet or adventurer. Very few could regard him dispassionately; nor did he care to be so regarded. I once likened him to Peter the Hermit preaching his Crusade. I am sure that many of the knights and princes that Peter so fierily exhorted did not like him very much—but they went crusading all the same. The trouble was, I think, that Wingate regarded *himself* as a prophet, and that always leads to a single-centredness that verges on fanaticism, with all its faults. Yet had he not done so, his leadership could not have been so dynamic, nor his personal magnetism so striking.

There could be no question of the seriousness of our loss. Without his presence to animate it, Special Force would no longer be the same to others or to itself. He had created, inspired, defended it, and given it confidence; it was the offspring of his vivid imagination and ruthless energy. It had no other parent. Now it was orphaned, and I was faced with the immediate problem of appointing a successor. This was one of those cases in which seniority should not be taken much into account. To step into Wingate's place would be no easy task. His successor had to be someone known to the men of Special Force, one who had shared their hardships and in whose skill and courage they could trust. I chose Brigadier Lentaigne. He not only fulfilled all these requirements, but I knew him to be, in addition, the most balanced and experienced of Wingate's commanders. It is an interesting sidelight on a strange personality that, after his death, three different officers each informed me that Wingate had told him he was to be his successor should one be required. I have no doubt at all that they were speaking the truth.

Under Lentaigne the Chindits did not slacken their activity. Rail Indaw was the centre of a Japanese maintenance area of scattered ammunition and supply dumps. It had, also, one of the best airfields in North Burma, which it had always been intended Wingate should take. Ferguson's 16 Brigade, supported by part of Brodie's 14 Brigade, moved out of Aberdeen and attempted to seize Indaw by surprise. Although the Japanese garrison was not large, it was well dug in, and the Chindits without artillery were too lightly equipped to dislodge it. They were compelled to abandon the attempt and fell back. 16 Brigade were now so exhausted by their march and this final abortive effort that there was nothing for it but to get them out as soon as we could. They were flown back in the empty aircraft returning from taking supplies and reinforcements to Aberdeen. Even without them Lentaigne had three mobile brigades, operating in a large number of columns, besides considerable numbers of 'stronghold' troops. The Japanese communications to their 18th Division were effectively cut. The railway was completely blocked and it was only on rare occasions that an enemy road convoy was able to sneak through. The Japanese, while still refraining from diverting any formation from their vital Assam front, swept up more odds and ends of units to add to Take Force, including part of a regiment of their 2nd Division, newly arrived in Burma. Lentaigne's columns roamed the area north of Indaw on both sides of the railway, fighting many minor engagements with Japanese detachments groping for them. In May the concentration against White City grew too threatening. The Chindits quietly slipped out, to strike again on the railway at several places, and then, after an eighty-mile march across mountains, early in May established another stronghold block at 'Blackpool', just north of Hopin.

While Wingate's brigades had been flying in and operating round Indaw, Stilwell to the north of them had been driving his Chinese southwards. Using his American Marauders in short hooks to strike in behind the Japanese, much as they had done against him in 1942, Stilwell, after a tough fight at Jambu Bum on March 19th, his sixty-first birthday, broke into the Mogaung Valley which leads to the town of that name.

The old warrior was well pleased with his progress and he had cause to be. Not only were the Chinese, under his skilful prodding, fighting well, but, reinforced by Admiral Mountbatten's appeals to the Generalissimo, he had succeeded in extracting two more divisions from China. The 50th Chinese Division was now flying in to northern Assam and it was to be followed by the 14th Division. This, early in May, would bring Stilwell up to five Chinese divisions and the American contingent. If the main Japanese strength could be kept engaged on the other fronts, the chances of their already somewhat battered 18th Division, with its line of communication cut by Lentaigne, holding this over-whelming force should be slight. Myitkyina was no longer a distant vision but a practicable objective.

Then, just as Stilwell felt the prize coming within his grasp, he saw it about to be snatched away by failure elsewhere. I could forgive him bitterness—and he was bitter even for Vinegar Joe—and some uncharitableness, when he saw, or thought he saw, that happening.

The great Japanese offensive against 4 Corps had begun in the second week of March. With ominous rapidity Kohima was besieged and Imphal cut off. To Stilwell, as he so justly described it, 'out on a limb' to the north, the threat to his only line of communication up the Brahmaputra Valley, through Dimapur, was a stark danger that no commander in his position could ignore. If the Japanese in strength broke through at Kohima and burst into the plain, all he could do would be to trek out over the hills into China. Knowing this only too well, and receiving, through sources far removed from the actual fighting, alarming reports of the situation around Imphal, he suggested to me that he should stop his advance, which had by now reached Shaduzup, well down the Mogaung Valley, and pull out the 38th Chinese Division, so that I could use it to help restore the position on his line of communication.

On the morning of 3rd April I flew to Jorhat to meet Stilwell. There was an atmosphere of gloom throughout the large American air force contingent located there—and a certain jumpiness. I have on several occasions noticed this in our own and other airmen, when there is threat of attack on the ground. I can sympathize with their feeling. They are not half as frightened of being attacked on the ground as I, a soldier, am of being attacked in the air. It is a matter of what you are used to. They seemed to have an idea that Japanese hordes might appear on the edge of the strip at any moment, and, knowing I had refused requests for troops to defend the American airfields—any resources I had were infinitely better employed going for the Japanese at Kohima—the 'Limey general' was not over popular.

The usual crowd of photographers, which dogs the steps of every American general, was present and, to cheer them up, when they wanted my photograph I said I would like to have it taken shaking hands with an American private soldier. I warned them laughingly that, from what I had seen of their air force, it would be a little difficult to find a private—officers and sergeants yes, but privates not so easy. So we started off to visit the nearest sentry group that, rather self-consciously, was patrolling the huts and immediate approaches. Sure enough, they were all sergeants; the nearest we got was a two-striper, but never a simple private. We returned to the mess in much better spirits and on very friendly terms after this little bit of nonsense, in time to meet Stilwell who had just flown in.

He looked tired and older, but he greeted me with friendliness and, I think, understanding. Within a few minutes he led me outside where we were alone, and repeated his offer of the 38th Division. He explained that it would mean stopping his advance, probably withdrawing, and certainly not getting Myitkyina before the monsoon. He was obviously bitterly disappointed, but he made no criticisms and uttered no reproaches. I had the impression that, apart from his own troubles, he was genuinely out to help me in mine. I was most reluctant to hold up his advance at this moment, when the whole of the Japanese striking forces were irretrievably committed to battle against 4 Corps, when my reinforcements for the Imphal battle were beginning to come in, and our troops were fighting so well. With his preponderance in numbers and the effect of Lentaigne's Special Force behind the Japanese 18th Division opposing him, I was sure this was Stilwell's great opportunity. I, therefore, told him to retain the 38th Division and the other Chinese divisions now arriving and to push on for Myitkyina as hard as he could go. He asked me if I would guarantee that his line of communication would not be cut. I said I could not promise that Japanese detachments would not elude us and get down into the Brahmaputra Valley, but that I would guarantee that his line of communication would not be interrupted for more than ten days. I said we were in for a really hard fight around Kohima and Imphal, that it was the decisive battle of the campaign, and I was confident of the eventual result. He accepted this and said it was what he had hoped I would say.

To give a feeling of security to the American airfields, as I could not spare troops for the purpose, he would sent a regiment of one of his new divisions to Dinjan where, in addition, it would be well placed for a fly-in if Myitkyina were taken. I asked him if he still had his plan for seizing Myitkyina and when he would do it. He replied that he had and, if all went well and there was not too much rain, he hoped to be there about the 20th of May. He again asked me to tell no one of his plan or of the proposed date of its execution. I agreed I would not. After all, everyone knew he had been ordered to take Myitkyina, and whatever his motives in this secrecy I was prepared to humour him. After lunch, Admiral Mountbatten, Lentaigne, Stopford, and others arrived and the Supreme Commander held a conference at which he approved the instructions I had given Stilwell.

Meanwhile the small force of Burma Rifles and British-officered Kachin levies, isolated far out on Stilwell's left, had struck south from Fort Hertz and seized Sumprabum, the first great triumph of their little private war. The main Chinese forces were pressing hard towards Kamaing and, if Stilwell was to get Myitkyina before the monsoon, his dash for it could not be long delayed. In great secrecy he organized his striking force. It consisted of the three battalions of American Marauders, each joined with two Chinese battalions, to form three mixed brigades. On the 28th April, Merrill set out on his hazardous expedition; and hazardous it was. He had to lead his men nearly a hundred miles through the wildest country; to cross a mountain range six thousand feet in height by tracks that had to be hacked out of the hill-sides before the pack mules could pass over. Then at the end he would have to attack an enemy whose strength could not be accurately assessed.

No sooner had the striking force started than it rained, trebling the difficulties of their march and tormenting Stilwell with anxiety. Luckily it was not the monsoon, but merely warning storms, and the weather cleared again. On the 14th May, Merrill reported he was within forty-eight hours of his objective; on the

15th, within twenty-four, and the follow-up Chinese were warned for the fly-in.

On the 17th May, Merrill's force, brushing aside slight opposition, rushed the airfield at Myitkyina. The surprise had been complete, and the Japanese with a total strength of about eight hundred withdrew into the town itself. During the afternoon the fly-in of the first of the Chinese reinforcing regiments began, followed quickly by another. The Marauders and the Chinese who had marched in with them were exhausted with their effort, much as Ferguson's Chindits had been after a similar march, and, thinking that the enemy in Myitkyina were in strength, contented themselves with consolidating about the airfield. Actually the Japanese garrison in Myitkyina was small, consisting as it did of the headquarters of 114 Regiment of the 18th Division, two very weak battalions, some aerodrome defence troops, and about three hundred administrative details. In addition, there was the 18th Divisional Field Hospital, containing several hundred patients, many of whom were, in accordance with Japanese custom, at once turned out to fight.

The newly arrived Chinese regiments attacked the town on the 19th. They were going into action for the first time, and they were not very well led, nor had they had much time, since getting out of their planes, to orientate themselves. After a little progress, they were held up. In the confusion one body of Chinese fired into another, panic ensued and the attack fell back in disorder. The Japanese reacted quickly to the threat to Myitkyina by calling in to its help all units in the neighbourhood. By the end of May there were in the town elements of both the 18th and 56th Divisions, which with the hospital patients, line of communication and administrative troops, made up a strength of some three thousand five hundred men. Colonel Maruyama of 114 Regiment was in command until Major-General Mizukami, from the 56th Division, reached the town on 2nd June and took over from him. Both these officers proved themselves to be of outstanding courage and determination, while the heterogeneous garrison fought with fanatical desperation.

Unfortunately, Merrill had collapsed soon after arrival at Myitkyina, and the officers sent to replace him were inexperienced and unaccustomed to the strain of actual command in the field. The fact was that Stilwell had no one, at this time, except himself, on whom he could rely either to direct or push through an operation, and he could not be in two places at once.

Reinforcements continued to pour into the original Myitkyina airfield and the other strips that were quickly made near it, until over thirty thousand Chinese were collected there. Still their attacks lacked sting and made little progress. In desperation Stilwell changed his commanders and flew in Pick's American Combat Engineers to replace the Marauders, now decimated by sickness; but most of the Engineers had not had even elementary training as infantry—it was rash to pit them against the Japanese. The fighting round Myitkyina, so brilliantly begun, settled down to an untidy, uninspired, ill-directed siege.

While Stilwell was launching his dash at Myitkyina, Lentaigne's main force was fighting hard to hold Blackpool, the block across the Japanese road and rail communications near Hopin, and 'Morrisforce', composed of part of 111 Brigade and the Kachins of Dahforce, was moving north up the Bhamo road. Hopin was only forty miles south of Kamaing, Stilwell's next objective, while Morrisforce might expect to be close to Myitkyina in a week or so. It was obvious that, as Special Force came up from the south and the Chinese pressed down from the north, the need for intimate and daily tactical co-ordination between Lentaigne's and Stilwell's forces would become urgent. On the 17th May, therefore, I placed Special Force under Stilwell's direct command. He now had an American brigade, five Chinese divisions, the three mobile Chindit brigades, and their stronghold troops, a large force approximating now more to the size of an army than a corps. Opposing it was only the sorely battered but still indomitable Japanese 18th Division with a few odds and ends of their 56th Division pulled in from the Yunnan front, and Take Force.

But even the Yunnan front, so quiescent for two years, had now sprung to violent life. The Generalissimo, at last yielding to Allied importunities, had in the latter half of April ordered the long-hoped-for offensive on the Salween. On the night of the 10th/11th May, forty thousand Chinese troops crossed the river at three main points between Hpimaw in the north and Kunlong in the south, a front of nearly two hundred miles. A fourth attempt at Kunlong itself failed. Within a few days twelve Chinese divisions, under General Wei Li Huang, amounting to some seventy-two thousand men, were on the west bank. Holding the passes through the mountains against them was only the Japanese 56th Division with a strength of about twelve thousand. The country was ideal for defence; the Japanese, although vastly outnumbered and without air support, fought skilfully and tenaciously. The first real clashes came as the Chinese forced their way into the mountains north of Mengta, about Lameng, where a Japanese infantry battalion and an artillery unit were wiped out, and at Pingka. At Kunlong, in the south, the Japanese continued to hold the river crossing, but on the rest of the front, during May and early June, they were pushed slowly back to the main road that ran from Wanting to Tengchung. As the Chinese seeped through by mountain tracks, the hard-pressed 56th Division withdrew gradually, converging on Lungling, leaving a regimental headquarters, a battalion, and some detachments in Tengchung to cover the concentration. An unexpected Chinese advance from the north, however, surrounded Tengchung. The garrison held out with fanatical valour until the 21st September when Tengchung fell to overwhelming assault and every Japanese in it died.

Meanwhile the main body of the 56th Division around Lungling was fighting the most desperate battle of the Yunnan front against six Chinese divisions. The Chinese were handicapped by the elementary state of their supply organization, the immense difficulties of their long line of communications, and the monsoon climate against whose wet and cold their soldiers had little protection. Admiral Mountbatten had wisely transferred from the Central front, although I could ill spare it, a squadron of American Dakotas. This, with such help as the 10th and 14th Air Forces could give, was only enough to provide air supply for a very small part of Wei Li Huang's force.

The Lungling battle raged from the end of June until the end of August. Lieut.-General Matsuyama, the Japanese commander, conducted this defensive battle with great skill. He managed throughout to counter every attempt at encirclement and to keep open the road south to Wanling. In this he was helped by a piece of good fortune that occurred in May. A Chinese transport plane in cloud mistook Tengchung for a friendly airfield and landed. In it were three Chinese staff officers, carrying not only complete details of all the formations taking part in the offensive, but the new cipher for their army. Matsuyama was after that the only commander on either side in Burma who had advance information

276

of enemy movements and intentions. He made good use of it. The Japanese hurried up reinforcements and then, with the bulk of their 2nd Division and a regiment of their 49th, staged a fierce counter-attack in August which, for the time being, stopped the Chinese advance dead in most places, and reduced its subsequent resumption to a crawl. The Chinese losses were heavy, not only from disease and privation, but because their training, armament, and leadership, which were much below those of Stilwell's troops, made them no match for the Japanese. Nor were their losses being replaced from China. Wei Li Huang had no easy task. His only real advantages were numbers and air support from American fighters and medium bombers which lost much of its value in these wild mountains.

Still, this mass, pressing in on their right flank, however slowly it moved, was a menace to the Japanese front in North Burma. Indeed, even towards the end of May, their whole position there was rapidly becoming precarious. The 18th Division was beginning to crack. Stilwell's main force was closing in on Kamaing. In addition to the large Chinese force attacking Myitkyina, the Fort Hertz detachment was approaching from Sumprabum and Morrisforce was operating against the town from the east of the Irrawaddy. The fall of Myitkyina, although it no longer seemed imminent, could be only a matter of time.

A brigade of Lentaigne's Special Force held Blackpool, near Hopin, against constant attack for three weeks, cutting the enemy's main line of communication at a critical time. The Japanese concentrated most of Take Force, including a regiment of the 53rd Division, against the Chindits here and bombarded them heavily with field and medium artillery. Worst of all, they established anti-aircraft guns in range of the landing ground. In spite of that, the British and American Dakota pilots, unable to land as the strip was under direct fire, continued to drop their loads, but supply was intermittent and there was no evacuation of wounded. Then the weather broke badly and, as the Japanese closed in, so did the clouds. Air supply and air support both ceased. On the 25th May the Chindits, carrying their wounded, broke out of Blackpool and plodded north-west towards the Indawgyi Lake, around which other columns of Lentaigne's men were collecting. The rain had made it impossible to keep earth airstrips in action and there seemed little hope of getting out the increasing number

of sick and wounded that were being laboriously brought in by
their comrades. The R.A.F. found the answer in two Sunderland
flying-boats, which, as a change from submarine hunting in the
Indian Ocean, flew from Colombo to this fifteen miles by five
miles stretch of water in the heart of Burma. Working throughout
some of the worst monsoon weather, they flew out nearly six
hundred casualties.

During the first weeks of June, Stilwell's Chinese had kept up
their drive down the Mogaung Valley. Fighting with increasing
confidence and boldness, they destroyed the Japanese who tried
to bar their way at Shadazup and Laban. Then on the 16th June
the Chinese 22nd Division took Kamaing, and on the 20th
Calvert's 77 Brigade of Lentaigne's force stormed Mogaung, just
ahead of the Chinese 38th Division coming from the north. By
this time, too, the great battles around Imphal had definitely
turned against the Japanese. Such reinforcements as he could
scrape up, Kawabe, the enemy Commander-in-Chief, was sending there to cover his withdrawal. His two northern fronts were
crumbling and there was little he could do to bolster them up.
He was by now plainly reduced to fighting merely a delaying
campaign in North Burma.

Negotiations had been going on between Admiral Mountbatten
and Generalissimo Chiang Kai-shek for Wei Li Huang's Yunnan
armies to come under South-East Asia Command when they
crossed the Burma border. As seemed inevitable, however, where
Chinese were concerned, there was considerable mystification
about the command of these troops. To begin with, the Sino-
Burmese frontier was not marked in these outlandish hills. British
maps showed it in one place, the Chinese several miles farther
west. In any case, whatever the line, it was likely that at times
some parts of the same Chinese formation would be on each side
of it—a hopeless complication. The Generalissimo kept a tight
hand on these Yunnan troops, and Stilwell's control, exercised
through an American mission, was, I gathered from him, pretty
nebulous. Still, whether he commanded them or not, Stilwell's
own force now amounted to about seven divisions and the agreement had been that when Kamaing was taken he should pass
from my command. It was only logical to regard him as an army
commander on the same footing as myself and place him, like me,
under 11th Army Group, but once again Stilwell refused to serve

under General Giffard. He insisted on coming directly under Admiral Mountbatten, although there was no organization at South-East Asia Command Headquarters to deal direct with an army.

When I visited Stilwell on his passing from my command he said, with his frosty twinkle, 'Well, General, I've been a good subordinate to you. I've obeyed all your orders!' That was true enough, but so was my retort, 'Yes, you old devil, but only because the few I did give you were the ones you wanted!'

The long-drawn-out siege of Myitkyina was a great disappointment to Stilwell, and it was at this period that he really lived up to his nickname, Vinegar Joe. He was extremely caustic about his unfortunate American commanders, accusing them of not fighting, and of killing the same Japanese over and over again in their reports. He was equally bitter against the Chindits, complaining that they did not obey his orders, had abandoned the block at Hopin unnecessarily, and had thus let strong Japanese reinforcements into the Kamaing–Myitkyina area. He asked for British parachute troops to restore the situation, but, apart from the fact that the small parachute formation available was already in the thick of the fighting at Imphal and could not have been extricated, there was no doubt he took a much too alarmist view of the position on his front. Lentaigne retaliated to the accusations hurled at him by complaining that Stilwell was demanding the impossible and that, by continually setting simultaneous tasks for all his columns, was making it impossible to give any part of his force the time essential for reorganization and evacuation of casualties without which they could not operate effectively. Relations between the two commanders became strained, and finally, at the end of May, Stilwell asked Admiral Mountbatten to withdraw Special Force. As a result, early in June, although I was no longer in command of this front, I was sent to N.C.A.C. to adjudicate between Stilwell and Lentaigne and to attempt to heal the breach.

I found Stilwell bitter and Lentaigne indignant, both obviously and very understandably suffering from prolonged strain. One or the troubles was that Stilwell, in his then mood, would not meet Lentaigne and really discuss things with him. There was too much of the Siege of Troy atmosphere, with commanders sulking in their tents. However, with me, Stilwell, after one or two

279

outbursts, was reasonable and explained his charges against the Chindits. I had already seen Lentaigne and heard his version. Stilwell's orders on the face of it were sound enough and it was quite obvious that the Chindits had not carried all of them out. It was equally clear that in their present state of exhaustion, after the casualties they had suffered and in the rain which made movement so difficult, unless given some chance of reorganization they were physically incapable of doing so. Stilwell replied to this by pointing to his Marauders who, he said, were still operating effectively. Without belittling their efforts, I pointed out that Lentaigne's men had endured the strain of being actually behind the enemy's lines for longer periods than Merrill's and that their incidence of battle casualties, as compared with sick, was much higher. As far as his complaints against Morrisforce on the east of the river were concerned, I told him I thought it was a bit hard to reproach a few hundred men for not doing what thirty thousand had failed to do on the other bank. Finally, looking at me over the top of his glasses, he said, 'What do you want me to do?' I said, 'See Lentaigne, talk things over with him, give his columns a chance to get out their casualties and reorganize, and keep his force on until Myitkyina falls.' He agreed, and I returned to headquarters.

I had hoped that Myitkyina would fall by the middle of June, but at the end of the month it was still apparently as far from capture as ever. It then became obvious that the remains of Special Force were not fit to continue operating throughout the monsoon. Admiral Mountbatten himself this time visited Stilwell and an arrangement was made by which two of Lentaigne's brigades that had been longest in the field should be medically examined and all unfit men flown out at once—the remainder to operate for a short time further and then follow them. The last of Special Force would remain until the 36th British Division, which was refitting at Shillong in Assam, began to come into Stilwell's command, when they too would be taken out.

Actually it would have been wiser to take the whole of the Chindits out then; they had shot their bolt. So, too, for that matter had the Marauders, who a little later packed in completely. Both forces, Chindits and Marauders, had been subjected to intense strain, both had unwisely been promised that their ordeal would be short, and both were asked to do more than was possible.

On the afternoon of the 3rd August, after a siege of two and a half months, Myitkyina fell. Some days before, Mizukami, the Japanese commander, had ordered what was left of the garrison to break out. He had then committed suicide. Maruyama, the original commander, had again taken over, and under his leadership the Japanese attempted to escape by night on rafts down the river. Most of them were intercepted and killed, but Maruyama himself and a couple of hundred did get away.

The capture of Myitkyina, so long delayed, marked the complete success of the first stage of Stilwell's campaign. It was also the largest seizure of enemy-held territory that had yet occurred. Throughout the operations the Allied forces, Chinese, British, and American, had been vastly superior to the Japanese on the ground and in the air, even without including the Chinese Yunnan armies. This superiority was only achieved because the main Japanese forces were held locked in the vital Imphal battle, and any reinforcements they could rake up were fed into that furnace. The Japanese had the advantages of position and communications, but even their desperate courage and defensive skill could not hold back such a numerical preponderance. Yet, when all was said and done, the success of this northern offensive was in the main due to the Ledo Chinese divisions—and that was Stilwell.

BOOK IV
The Tide Turns

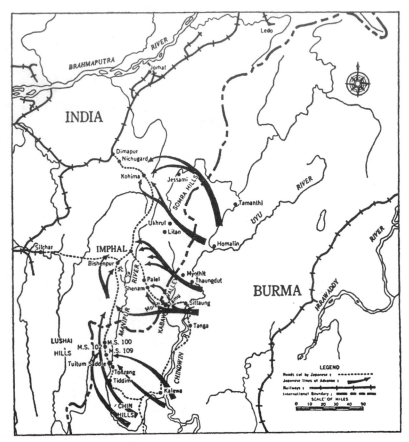

JAPANESE INVASION ROUTES, BURMA 1944

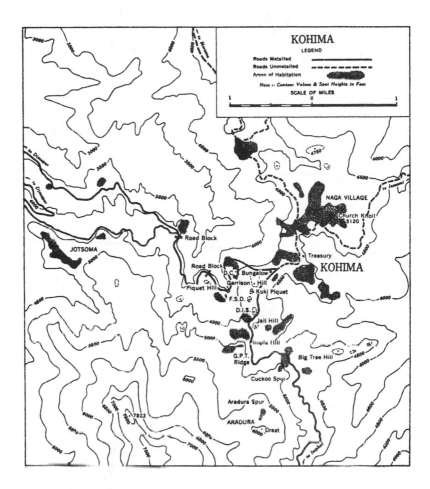

KOHIMA

LEGEND

Roads Metalled
Roads Unmetalled
Areas of Habitation

Note :- Contour Values & Spot Heights in Feet

SCALE OF MILES

IMPHAL AREA

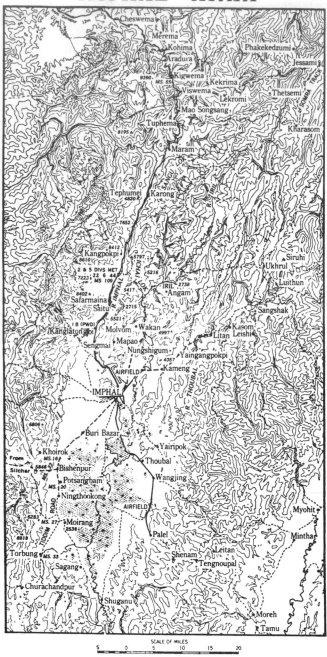

SCALE OF MILES

5   0   5   10   15   20

Contour interval 1000 feet

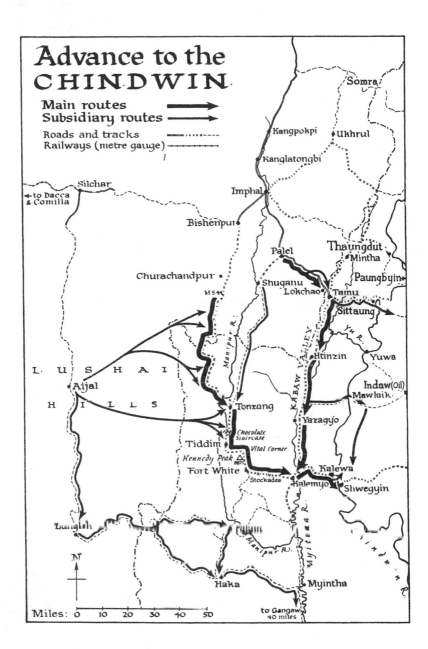

Advance to the
CHINDWIN

Main routes
Subsidiary routes
Roads and tracks
Railways (metre gauge)

Somra

Kangpokpi   Ukhrul

Kanglatongbi

Silchar
to Dacca
& Comilla

Imphal

Bishenpur

Palel   Thaungdut
                        Mintha

Churachandpur   Paungbyin

Shuganu   Tamu
MS44   Lokchao

Manipur R.   Sittaung

Htinzin   Yuwa

LUSHAI   Indaw(Oil)
                                Mawlaik
        Aijal
                        KABAW VALLEY
    HILLS   Tonzang

                        Yazagyo

            Chocolate
            Staircase
    Tiddim   Vital Corner
    Kennedy Peak
    Fort White   Kalewa
            Stockades
                Kalemyo   Shwegyin

Lunglah   Manipur R.

N

                        Chindwin R.

            Haka   Myintha

Miles: 0   10   20   30   40   50
                    to Gangaw
                    40 miles

CHAPTER XIII

HOW IT WAS PLANNED

THE great encounter that loomed over the Central Assam front in early 1944, and which was fought out with relentless fury around Imphal and Kohima from March to July in that year, was the first of the two decisive battles of the South-East Asia campaign. Tarauchi, the Japanese Supreme Commander, and Kawabe, their Commander-in-Chief in Burma, both meant it to be decisive—and so did we.

Their daily mounting shipping losses in the Pacific were beginning to tell on the Japanese. Unless they could score some far-reaching strategic success, their armies, strung out on a vast perimeter of conquest, faced slow strangulation. It was to Burma that their slit eyes turned hopefully. Here was the one place they could stage an offensive that might give them all they hoped. If it succeeded, the destruction of the British forces in Burma would be the least of its results. China, completely isolated, would be driven into a separate peace; India, ripe as they thought for revolt against the British, would fall, a glittering prize, into their hands. They were right in thinking that victory in Assam would resound far beyond that remote jungle land; it might, indeed, as they proclaimed in exhortations to their troops, change the whole course of the world war. Burma, for a space, no longer a sideshow in the global struggle, would hold the centre stage.

Kawabe, knowing this, concentrated all his efforts on a great break-through in Assam. To him, the fighting in Arakan was subsidiary; its chief object was to absorb our reserves and thus prevent their use at the vital centre. On the Northern front he was determined to use only the barest forces necessary to slow up the Chinese advances from Ledo and Yunnan. Here he could afford to yield ground because, if he won in the centre, the north would automatically fall to him.

For us, too, it was our great chance. With landing craft and

shipping unavailable, we should have to re-enter Burma overland from the north. We were, in fact, planning to do so. Yet the
topography of the country was so terribly against us and so
limited were the forces we could maintain through the mountains, that any such invasion must be a gamble unless we could
first wear down the Japanese strength. I wanted a battle *before* we
went into Burma, and I was as eager as Kawabe to make it a
decisive one.

At the beginning of 1944, Lieut.-General Scoones was commanding 4 Corps on the Assam front. He was an informed,
thoughtful soldier with a clear mind of the analytical type. My
staff sometimes complained that he produced lengthy appreciations in which all factors and courses of action were conscien-
tiously considered. I always pointed out that these appreciations
could be re-read after the event and found uncannily accurate.
A general whose appreciations can stand this test is not perhaps
as rare as a politician whose speeches can equally bear re-reading,
but such far-sightedness is one of the foundations of real generalship and it not too common a gift. Scoones had, too, a steadiness
in crisis that was, for the battle he was to fight, an invaluable
quality.

In accordance with the current overall plans for the theatre, he
had been given the task of preparing for an advance into Burma.
His 4 Corps, of three Indian divisions, had for several months
been gradually pushing forward to dominate the wide hill area
from the Kabaw Valley, up which we had staggered in the 1942
retreat, to the Chin Hills, some one hundred and fifty miles south
of Imphal. Under cover of this broad arc, roads were being built,
supplies collected, and all preparations made for a limited offensive
across the Chindwin River. The whole layout of 4 Corps area and
the dispositions of its fighting formations were designed with the
idea of our taking the offensive.

The Imphal plain, some forty by twenty miles in extent, is the
only considerable oasis of flat ground in the great sweep of mountains between India and Burma. It lies roughly equi-distant from
the Brahmaputra Valley and the plains of Central Burma, a
natural half-way house and staging place for any great military
movement in either direction between India and Burma. The
aspect of the Imphal plain had greatly changed since we had
sought there in vain for rest and shelter after the Retreat. Instead

of the dripping trees, sodden ground, bombed-out buildings, and muddy tracks that had greeted us, there were now orderly *basha* camps, hutted hospitals, supply dumps, ordnance depots, engineer parks, and wide tarmac roads. Camps of every kind and sort were dotted over the six hundred square miles of the plain, but most were clustered round the villages of Imphal itself and Palel, twenty-five miles south. These administrative establishments had all been sited, as was natural, in the most suitable and accessible spots for their various purposes, with the idea of protection from the air by dispersion, but with no thought of defence against attack by land. As a result they were spread over large areas and were almost invariably overlooked by high ground at point-blank range. In these camps, and scattered along the roads leading north into India and south into Burma, were some sixty or seventy thousand Indian non-combatants, mostly labour. The sprawling railhead base that had been hacked out of the jungle at Dimapur, a hundred and thirty miles north of Imphal, was similarly laid out and manned. As long as our intentions remained offensive and those of the Japanese defensive, Imphal and Dimapur were suitably organized; should the roles be reversed, these widespread bases would become a terrible embarrassment.

Our whole situation on this Central front had another grave tactical disadvantage. Our only line of communication was the road our engineers had so magnificently built from railhead at Dimapur up the hill to Kohima, and on to Imphal. This now forked and we were laboriously extending the two prongs, one down the valley of the Manipur River and the other into the Kabaw Valley. All of these roads ran of necessity north and south, parallel to the Japanese front, and at no great distance from it. They, thus, whether we took the offensive or remained on the defensive, exposed a classic military weakness to an enemy peculiarly fitted and experienced to exploit it to the full.

The three divisions of 4 Corps were deployed with two forward, one at the end of each of the roads to the south: the 17th Division, veterans of the Retreat, on the right about Tiddim in the Chin Hills; the 20th Division, whom I had had in Ranchi, on the left in the Palel-Tamu area. Between these two were eighty-odd miles of jungle mountains. This gap, in spite of the wild country, was, of course, a danger, but the corps had a frontage of some two hundred and fifty miles to watch and guard. Instead

287

of trying to hold a continuous line, Scoones had therefore wisely decided to keep one division, the 23rd at this time, concentrated about Imphal as a striking force. The rotation of divisions between front line and reserve that this enabled him to carry out had excellent results on training and morale. In 4 Corps, also, was 254 Indian Tank Brigade, of two regiments only, one of which, a British unit, was equipped with Lee-Grants, the other an Indian one, with Stuarts. Both these types of tanks were already obsolete, but the Lee-Grant, if well handled, could meet the Japanese medium tanks on equal terms. The Stuart, however, was a light tank, limited tactically both on paddy fields and in jungle, which it was unfair to pit against the enemy mediums. But Cinderella was still at the bottom of all priority lists.

During and after the 1943 monsoon, in a series of patrol clashes and minor actions, we had steadily expanded the territory under our control in the Tamu area. The Kabaw Valley was re-entered; the Chindwin reached and crossed by patrols. Roads were being pushed forward as fast as our meagre resources in excavating machinery permitted and reconnaissances for the eventual offensive being carried out. All was going well here.

It was on the 17th Division front at Tiddim that the more serious encounters had occurred. When we withdrew from Burma in 1942 we left behind in their native hills a small force of Chin Levies with British officers. Here they had held a lone outpost of the Empire until detachments of the 17th Division, advancing again, had reached Tiddim in the December of that year. The whole country is a chaos of jungle-matted, knife-edged ridges, running up to peaks of over eight thousand feet, split by precipitous valleys and pierced from the Indian side only by the fantastic mountain road from Imphal that the troops themselves had built. Here, since May 1943, the 17th Division, at the end of its hundred and sixty miles of precarious road, had fought a small-scale but none the less bitter private war against its old opponents, the Japanese 33rd Division. They were, as of old, well matched, taking it in turns to ambush, raid, attack, and counter-attack one another. For the small forces engaged, casualties were heavy on both sides and the results attained small. The Japanese had up to February 1944 undoubtedly had the better of it. They had not only stopped the 17th Division from pushing on to its goal, the Chindwin at Kalewa, but had forced our troops back to some ten miles south of Tiddim. In January 1944, when the Japanese were preparing their final offensive that was to change the face of the war, our dispositions, on the front they had selected for the decisive blow, were thus two widely separated divisions forward at Tamu and Tiddim and a third many miles behind in Imphal.

We knew the offensive was coming, for throughout January and February, besides the general reinforcement of the Burma theatre by fresh Japanese formations, there were increasing local indications on 4 Corps front. I had not at my disposal the sources of information of the enemy's intentions that some more fortunate commanders in other theatres were able to invoke. We depended almost entirely on the intelligence gathered by our fighting patrols, and the superiority we had developed in this form of activity now paid a high dividend. In spite of the fact that our patrols were finding it more difficult to cross the Chindwin, the newly arrived 15th Japanese Division was identified along the river.

Enemy activity and strength all along 4 Corps front were noticeably increasing. Documents, diaries, marked maps, and even operation orders taken from Japanese killed in these patrol clashes were being brought in almost daily. We had luck and a good haul of documents in one or two bold raids on minor headquarters. All these clues, painstakingly fitted into the mosaic of our intelligence at Corps and Army Headquarters, began to give us a general picture of the enemy's intentions. In spite of our air superiority, the nature of the country and the Japanese habit of moving by night limited the value of air reconnaissance. We did, however, get three very significant items of news from this source. Our pilots reported that the enemy were developing the roads towards the Chindwin from Central Burma. Then they saw large numbers of logs being collected at various places on the east bank of the river and many camouflaged rafts concealed in the lower reaches of the Uyu River opposite Homalin, due east of Imphal. Equally significant, they located great herds of cattle, each several hundreds in number, south of the Uyu and near Thaungdut on the Chindwin. We knew that the Japanese had seized all cattle belonging to the local inhabitants, and it was evident that these herds were being driven to the river as supplies for considerable forces. Our 'V' Force agents also brought us stories of the massing of transport, mechanical and animal, even of elephants.

Piecing all this together with our intelligence staffs, Scoones, whom I visited frequently at this time, and I were agreed that the offensive against him would be delivered by the Japanese Fifteenth Army under Lieut.-General Mutaguchi, with, as a start, three Japanese divisions, the 15th, 31st, and 33rd, an I.N.A. Division, a tank regiment, and other troops. There might be another division, not yet identified, in reserve. It was clear that the Japanese objectives would be, first, to capture Imphal, and second, to break through to the Brahmaputra Valley so as to cut off the Northern front and disrupt the air supply to China. We thought that they would follow their usual tactics of trying to isolate forward formations and then destroy them in detail. We expected they would attempt with a reinforced division to get behind both our 17th Division astride the Tiddim–Imphal road and our 20th Division on the Tamu–Palel road. At the same time other Japanese columns amounting to some two divisions would, crossing the Chindwin near Homalin and Thaungdut, make for Imphal via Ukhrul. A Japanese regiment (three battalions) would, we foresaw, make for Kohima to cut the main Imphal–Dimapur road and threaten the Dimapur base. We calculated the offensive would begin about the 15th March. This was what we expected and, broadly speaking, our forecast proved accurate. The problem was: What should we do to meet it? It was obvious that we could not rely on the present dispositions of 4 Corps, designed as they were entirely for an offensive of our own. The two forward divisions were an invitation to destruction in detail. We could not, as we did in Arakan, tell them to stand fast, although cut off, and we would supply them by air. The second half of the Arakan pattern for victory—the relieving force—was, if not absent, at least not large enough. Our third division could go to the help of only one of the forward divisions and in doing so would leave Imphal wide open to the enemy. There remained three broad alternatives:

(i) To anticipate the enemy offensive by crossing the Chindwin and attacking him first.
(ii) To hold the Japanese 33rd Division in the Tiddim area and fight with all available forces on the line of the Chindwin, hoping to destroy the enemy as he crossed the river, with part of his forces on each bank.

(iii) To concentrate 4 Corps in the Imphal plain and fight the decisive battle there on ground of our own choosing.

The first alternative—to forestall the enemy and attack ourselves—had all the glamour of boldness. Indeed, there were not wanting senior visiting officers who urged me 'to fling two divisions across the Chindwin'. I am afraid they left my headquarters thinking I was sadly lacking in the offensive spirit, but somehow I have never had great confidence in generals who talk of 'flinging' divisions about. 'Fling' is a term for amateurs, not professionals. Besides, I noticed that the farther back these generals came from, the keener they were on my 'flinging' divisions across the Chindwin. Had I accepted their advice the enemy could easily have concentrated, along good communications, a force greatly in excess of any we could maintain east of the Chindwin. We should have fought superior numbers with the dangerous crossing of a great river behind us and with our communications running back through a hundred and twenty miles of the worst country imaginable. Similarly, but to a somewhat lesser extent, if we decided to fight at Tiddim and on the west bank of the Chindwin, we still had this difficult and precarious line of communication behind us. Whatever success we had in those conditions we were unlikely to achieve a decisive result—and it was a decisive success I wanted.

At this stage of the campaign against an opponent as tough as the Japanese and one whose morale was still as high as his was, to gain a decisive success I must concentrate against him a force superior both in numbers and armament. I therefore decided to adopt the third course—to concentrate 4 Corps in the Imphal plain, and fight a major battle there to destroy the Japanese Fifteenth Army. I was tired of fighting the Japanese when they had a good line of communications behind them and I had an execrable one. This time I would reverse the procedure. An important consideration, too, in all my calculations, was that the enemy, if he was to avoid destruction, must win his battle before the monsoon set in. If he had failed by then to occupy the Imphal area he would be in an impossible supply position. Another factor was, of course, our supremacy in the air and the ability it gave me to use air supply. It should be remembered, however, that this would be dependent during the monsoon on the possession of all-weather airfields. The only ones we had were Imphal and Palel; there were none, nor could we construct them in time, on the east bank of the Chindwin.

I realized that from the point of view of morale, a withdrawal was not the best opening for a decisive battle. It would be unpopular with commanders and troops alike. Both the 17th and 20th Divisions were at the time confident, with good cause, that they could not only hold their positions but drive back the enemy. The abandonment of so much British territory would depress our friends and exult our enemies all over the world. It would spread alarm and despondency in India, our base. Yet it was not the hundreds of square miles of jungle mountains that mattered, but the chance to destroy the enemy's forces. That done, territory could easily be reoccupied. I was sure, too, that if commanders explained the design to their men, they would see its soundness, and morale would not suffer.

In war it is all-important to gain and retain the initiative, to make the enemy conform to your action, to dance to your tune. When you are advancing, this normally follows; if you withdraw, it is neither so obvious nor so easy. Yet it is possible. There are three reasons for retreat: self-preservation, to save your force from destruction; pressure elsewhere which makes you accept loss of territory in one place to enable you to transfer troops to a more vital front; and, lastly, to draw the enemy into a situation so unfavourable to him that the initiative must pass to you. It was for this third reason that I now voluntarily decided on a withdrawal. Here was the contrast between the forced retreat of 1942, whose object became merely the preservation of our troops as an intact force, and that of 1944, which was carefully calculated to lead inevitably to our regaining the initiative. Yet so many scrambles to escape have been described as 'withdrawals according to plan' that I was not surprised to find it hard to convince many, especially highly placed civil officials, that it was possible to fight defensively and even to retreat, yet keep the initiative.

Scoones and I discussed the alternatives and we both came independently to the same conclusions—to fight at Imphal. It would be very largely his battle and it was important to have his agreement with the basic ideas on which I wanted it fought. General Giffard also approved my reasoning, and it was a great satisfaction to me to know that his judgment supported me. The plan for what we knew would be the decisive battle was first for Imphal plain to be put into a state of defence. This entailed the concentration of the scattered administrative units and head-quarters into fortified areas, each of which would be capable of all-round defence and completely self-contained in ammunition and supplies for considerable periods. The two all-weather air-fields at Imphal and Palel, vital to the defence both for supporting air squadrons and for air supply, became the main strong-points or 'keeps' in the defence scheme. The garrisons of these fortified areas and keeps were to be found mainly by the administrative troops themselves, so that the fighting units and formations would be free to manœuvre in an offensive role. These preparations were put in hand and throughout February went on at an increasing tempo. Almost every unit in the Imphal plain moved; a large number of strongly defended localities were dug, wired, and stocked. The evacuation of non-combatant and labour units began, while the training of the remaining administrative troops in a fighting role for the defence of their own localities was intensive.

A most important part of the plan was the provision of re-inforcing formations for Assam. Within the army I proposed to pull the 5th Division out of Arakan and move it by air and rail from Chittagong to Dimapur and Imphal. General Giffard had arranged to send a division from India to replace it, and, when that arrived, I contemplated sending the 7th Division from Arakan after the 5th. I also asked for another division to be railed from India to Dimapur, but here there was a difference of opinion between me and the administrative staffs at 11th Army Group, who, with considerable mathematical justification, declared that the already overburdened Assam railway would not be able to compete with the added strain of transporting and then main-taining so large a reinforcement. General Giffard compromised by sending me the Indian Parachute Brigade of two battalions, and by putting in hand arrangements to move the 2nd British Division if it became urgently necessary to do so.

The 4 Corps tactical plan was for the 17th Division to move rapidly back from Tiddim to the Imphal plain, dropping one brigade group some forty miles south of Imphal to block the Japanese advance. The remainder of the division would be in Corps Reserve. The 20th Indian Division was to withdraw from

THE TIDE TURNS

its forward positions in the Kabaw Valley, concentrate in the Moreh area, and, when all 'soft' units on the line of communication had been cleared to Imphal, to fall back slowly on Shenam, which would be held at all costs. The 23rd Indian Division, leaving one brigade group in the Ukhrul area, was to form with 17th Division, the Indian Parachute Brigade, when it arrived, and 254 Indian Tank Brigade, the Corps offensive reserve. The Japanese would thus be allowed to advance to the edge of the Imphal plain, and, when committed in assaults on our prepared positions, would be counter-attacked and destroyed by our mobile striking forces, strong in artillery, armour, and aircraft.

The plan that Scoones and I had hammered out was, I was sure, the right one. It only remained to decide when it should be put into force. The essence of all military planning is timing. A brilliant plan wrongly timed, put into operation too early or too late, is at the best a lame thing and at the worst may be a disaster. When and by whom was the order for the 17th and 20th Divisions to retire on Imphal to be given? It was here I made a mistake. I was, in my own mind, convinced that a Japanese offensive on a large scale against Imphal was coming, and I judged it would begin about the 15th March. On the other hand, it was impossible to be absolutely certain that it would come then, or even that it would come at all. If we pulled back to Imphal and it did not come, not only should we look foolish, but we should have unnecessarily jeopardized the preparations for our own offensive, abandoned much territory, and done nothing to help the Chinese advance in the north. The effect on morale could not but be bad. I therefore decided that all preparations to put the plan into force should be made, but that the word to start the withdrawal to Imphal should be given by the local commander, Scoones, when he was sure that a major Japanese offensive was imminent. What I should have done was to act on my own judgment, and give a definite date early in March on which the withdrawal should begin, and another, some days later, by which the two divisions should be in their new positions. To put the responsibility on local commanders was neither fair nor wise. I was in a better position to judge when a real offensive was coming for I had all their information, and, in addition, intelligence from other sources. Local commanders were bound to be reluctant to retreat without at least a trial of strength; all the hesitations that could

294

assail me would inflict them threefold. There was thus a real risk, that I did not appreciate, of the withdrawal being started too late. Instead of being carried out without interference, it might degenerate into a series of fights to break through involving our reserves and disorganizing the whole plan of battle.

Happily oblivious of the cardinal error I had made and of its possible consequences, I continued preparations to meet the expected onslaught. I was confident that our plans were sound, and I was supported by the knowledge that General Giffard was preparing to send me, should need arise, reinforcements from India. These, added to the formations I proposed myself to transfer from Arakan, would give me the superiority in strength that I wanted to make sure that the invading divisions were not only repelled but destroyed. It seemed that the enemy was about to play into my hands and give me the opportunity I had always hoped for, to cripple his army *before* we re-entered Burma. It was in this rather complacent mood that I awaited the battle. I should have remembered that battles, at least the ones I had been engaged in, very rarely went quite according to plan.

CHAPTER XIV

HOW IT HAPPENED

THE story of the prolonged and hard-fought battle of Imphal–Kohima that developed from the plans of Japanese and British commanders is not easy to follow. It swayed back and forth through great stretches of wild country; one day its focal-point was a hill named on no map, the next a miserable, unpronounceable village a hundred miles away. Columns, brigades, divisions, marched and counter-marched, met in bloody clashes, and reeled apart, weaving a confused pattern hard to unravel. Yet the whole battle can be divided into four reasonably clear phases:

(i) *Concentration*—as each side strained every sinew to bring its forces into the fight.

(ii) *Attrition*—as week after week in man-to-man, hand-to-hand fighting, each strove to wear down the other's strength and to break his will.

(iii) *Counter-offensive*—as gradually, but with increasing momentum, the British passed to the attack, and

(iv) *Pursuit*—when the Japanese broke and, snarling and snapping, were hunted from the field.

The opening moves in the Imphal–Kohima battle took place in the first days of March 1944. Then the 17th Division about Tiddim was at the top of its form. Cowan, who still commanded it, and his men, far from being depressed by the set-backs they had sustained, were thirsting for revenge. He had benefited from experience and was no longer trying to capture the Japanese positions by attacks along the knife-edge ridges of the Chin Hills. In the constant patrol fights, ambushes, and raids that his Gurkhas and the Japanese carried on against one another, the 17th Division was now having very much the better of the exchanges. Cowan was skilfully using the freedom of movement this gave him to

296

begin the systematic isolation and piecemeal reduction of the enemy positions. He had already captured some of the most important of the lost ground, and the whole of it seemed relentlessly falling within his grasp, when the conditions of his local war changed suddenly and completely.

The Japanese offensive began on the 6th March 1944. On that day troops of 214 Regiment of the enemy 33rd Division began a series of attacks on our detachment covering the Manipur River bridge near Tonzang, twenty miles north of Tiddim. Cowan sent a battalion to reinforce our men. The assaults grew in strength, until it was evident the whole 214 Regiment, the equivalent of one of our brigades, was flinging itself against our Tonzang positions. Our defences held stoutly, but were in danger of being overwhelmed. Cowan, therefore, on the 13th, dispatched his 63 Brigade to make sure of this vital position in his rear.

Meanwhile, on the 8th March, another Japanese column, 215 Regiment, crossed the Manipur River from east to west, several miles south of our positions about Tiddim, and moved north by tracks through the hills. Its move was reported, but it was difficult to judge its strength, and neither patrol nor air reconnaissance could keep touch with it in the thick jungle. On the 13th came ominous news. The Engineer officer commanding at Milestone 109, nearly sixty miles north of Tiddim, reported that a Japanese force was in the hills a few miles to the west of his camp. In that camp, except for a few Indian Sappers and Miners, were only administrative units of no fighting value, including some five thousand unarmed labour who had halted there on their way to Imphal. Part of a Jat Indian machine-gun battalion, the only fighting troops within reach, was hurriedly diverted to the camp, which, scattered and low lying, was most difficult to defend. These rather alarming events had been reported to Scoones, and at 2040 hours on the 13th March he telephoned Cowan, ordering him to withdraw his division to the Imphal plain. At 2200 hours Cowan gave out warning orders for the withdrawal of his division the next day.

It was a long column that began to wind through the hills in the afternoon of the 14th. The whole division, including its headquarters, went on foot; transport was kept for stores, ammunition, supplies, and wounded. It took with it two thousand five hundred vehicles, three thousand five hundred animals, and a number of

THE TIDE TURNS

sick. The first day it covered twenty miles, blowing up bridges behind it and sowing mines and booby traps in the camps it had left. The Japanese followed the tail of the column cautiously, with sound tactical sense, concentrating on cutting in ahead and blocking the road.

This they did in two places. The first near Tonzang, where the 214 Regiment made a detour round our detachment while it was heavily engaged, and established itself astride the road on the Tuitum Saddle, two miles north. The second was at the un-happy Milestone 109 camp. As the Japanese 215 Regiment closed in, the small garrison there soon found itself in difficulties, hampered as it was by a mass of non-combatants. On the 14th March the road to Imphal was cut. The 17th Division dealt promptly and effectively with the first block, that beyond Tonzang. On the 16th, Gurkhas with strong artillery support stormed up the Saddle, broke into the Japanese defences with bayonet and *kukri*, and, with surprisingly few casualties to them-selves, chased the enemy off the Saddle. The Japanese would have been wiser to have held it in greater strength, but they were having their difficulties. The road was now open, but only to Milestone 109.

Nor was the Tiddim road the only sector from which danger threatened. By the beginning of March 1944, the Japanese 15th and 31st Divisions were poised along the east bank of the Chindwin, from Tanga in the south to Tamanthi in the north. Apart from patrols, no troops of these divisions crossed the river until on the 14th March a small detachment attacked one of our 'V' Force observation posts, twelve miles west of Homalin, and was repulsed. On the night of the 15th/16th March, however, both divisions began to move in earnest. The 15th Division, to whom had been entrusted the honour of taking Imphal, crossed in three columns about Thaungdut, with orders 'to advance through the hills like a ball of fire'. It was to follow the main axis Myothit–Sangshak–Litan and thence round the north of Imphal. Its task was first to isolate and then capture the town. Its columns moved light and fast. On the 18th March, while one of them was pressing our 20th Division's flank near Myothit, others were approaching Ukhrul and contact was made with them about ten miles south-east of the village, some fifty miles from Imphal. The 31st Japanese Division at the same time crossed the
298

Chindwin in eight columns on a forty-mile front from Homalin to the north. Keeping on the right of their 15th Division, these columns began to push westward like the probing fingers of an extended hand. It was difficult in such close country to discover either their strength or their objectives, but Scoones managed to make a fairly accurate estimate of both. As fighting developed it seemed that one main column, 58 Regimental Group, was to capture Ukhrul and then push for Kohima while another, 60 Regimental Group, turned west on Imphal. Other columns were to cut the main Kohima road north of Imphal, and still more to stream through the Somra Hills towards Jessami, south-east of Kohima. Then the hand was to close, the columns would converge, and, as the Japanese commander described it, they would 'at one fell swoop fall on Kohima and annihilate the British on that front'. Full of confidence in themselves and contempt for their enemy, they plunged forward.

In Imphal I was impressed by the steadiness of commanders and troops. Scoones, in control of the tactical battle on the whole Assam front, had been faced with a difficult and momentous decision. The fog of war had descended. He was deluged with reports and rumours of Japanese columns which seemed to flit in and out of the jungle, now here, now there; little was definite and nothing certain. Two things, however, were clear: first that the 17th Division was cut off, and, second, that a strong threat to Imphal itself from the east was developing. Time was short. The commander of 4 Corps had to make up his mind, there and then, whether he would hold his reserve, the 23rd Division, to meet the thrust at Imphal or send the bulk of it towards Tiddim to help out the 17th Division. Calmly he balanced the risks of each course. Rightly he decided to hold to our plan for the battle and to follow the course which would, if successful, more quickly concentrate his corps in the Imphal plain. He therefore sent, first one brigade, and then a second of the 23rd Division to fight down the road towards the 17th Division.

On how fine a margin the success or failure of these decisions depended can be seen from the history of the Japanese thrust at Imphal from the east. On the 19th March part of the enemy 31st Division surged against the Indian Parachute Brigade and one battalion of the 23rd Division, dug-in to cover Ukhrul. For two desperate days the fight went on, then the brigade was pushed back and Ukhrul fell to the enemy. The three battalions, now considerably weakened, stood again at Sangshak, nine miles to the south. There, from the 21st to the 25th, they resisted desperate night attacks, which were closely supported by the Japanese artillery, while by day snipers and shelling took their toll. With the Japanese came the Jiffs, as we called members of the Indian National Army, who were employed not in direct attacks but in unavailing attempts to confuse and suborn our Indian troops. On the morning of the 26th March the enemy put in an all-out daylight assault. Our losses and theirs were heavy in hand-to-hand fighting. The main positions held, but unfortunately one of the two meagre water-supply points was lost. Throughout the action the R.A.F. had kept up the closest support, and they now attempted, in spite of heavy fire from the ground, to deliver water, but the area held by our troops was so restricted that most of the drops were lost. Almost without water, it was impossible to hold on any longer, and, after dark on the 26th March, what was left of the brigade was ordered to break out and make for Imphal. The ten days' delay and the heavy casualties this small force and the R.A.F. who supported them had inflicted on the enemy were of inestimable value at this critical stage of the battle.

While this savage fighting was going on around Ukhrul and Sangshak, an equally severe action was developing at Litan on the Ukhrul road, about ten miles to the south-west. Here, small detachments from the Parachute Brigade, hurriedly reinforced by a newly landed battalion of the 5th Division, had dug in to block the road to the Japanese advance. Our positions were attacked by superior forces on the night of 24th/25th March and in spite of several counter-attacks the battalion, having suffered heavily, lost its forward localities. Next day the Japanese attempted to cut the road to Imphal in its rear. But now, in the nick of time, the troops of the 5th Division flown from Arakan were coming into action, practically straight from their aircraft. 123 Brigade moved up the road, clearing it to six miles from Litan. The detachment at Litan was withdrawn on 28th, and 9 Brigade of the 5th Division brought up. The Japanese advance from Ukhrul direct on Imphal now met strong resistance, was roughly handled, and, in a week of clashes and ambushes, was held.

While the direct blow was thus parried, the Japanese thrust from Ukhrul against the Kohima–Imphal road broke through, and on the 30th March the enemy blew up a bridge thirty miles north of Imphal and established strong road-blocks. Except for the Silchar track to the west, Imphal was thus cut off by land.

While all this was going on, the 23rd Indian Division, less one brigade, left for the defence of Imphal, had begun its fight on the Tiddim road towards the 17th Division. Major-General Ouvry Roberts, who commanded the 23rd Division, was a good man for such a job. Years before, when I had taught him at the Staff College, he had been marked as likely to become not only a first-class staff officer but a successful commander. He had been my chief staff officer in the 10th Indian Division in Iraq in 1941. There he had done what I have always considered to be one of the best single-handed jobs any officer of his then rank had performed in the war. The Iraq Army was besieging the Royal Air Force base at Habbaniyeh, and, in spite of the gallantry of the pilots of the Flying School, in their obsolete machines, and of Assyrian Levies and airmen on the ground, it looked as if it might fall. At the most critical moment of the siege we flew in Roberts. By his energy, by the direction he imparted to the operations, and by the confidence he inspired, he transformed a somewhat bewildered defence into a successfully aggressive one. Had Habbaniyeh fallen, the results would have been disastrous to the whole Middle East. Now he had transferred those qualities to the command of a division.

The leading units of Roberts's 37 Brigade, with a few light tanks, moving rapidly, drove off a Japanese force which was besieging a small detachment of ours at Milestone 100 on the Tiddim road. Before our troops could push on to the relief of the camp at Milestone 109, the enemy, infiltrating through the jungle, had established a series of road-blocks behind them. They were thus forced to turn and clear the road towards Imphal while the second brigade of the 23rd Division fought south towards them. The situation on the Tiddim road was now for a time as it had once been on the Arakan coast—a Neapolitan ice of layers of our troops alternating with Japanese—but in both training and morale our men were much better fitted to deal with such a confused and harassing business than they had been in 1943.

Still, with relief thus delayed, the situation at Milestone 109 grew critical. Japanese pressure and shelling intensified and in such a restricted area, congested by non-combatants, effective defence

301

became impossible. During the night of the 16th/17th March, these non-combatants were skilfully led out by jungle paths through the enemy positions to join the 23rd Division. The handful of fighting troops held on for two more days and then they, too, broke out and escaped. The Japanese swarming in found much in the way of stores and a number of abandoned vehicles. They at once began to build powerful defences to deny passage to the 17th Division approaching from the south.

Cowan, knowing that the camp at Milestone 109 had fallen, anticipated rightly that the road itself would be strongly held against him. He therefore sent infantry detachments along the high ridges on each side of it, while his main force pressed on up the road. The right column, in a series of hard-fought small actions, cleared the enemy from the crests, and then, during the 21st and 22nd March, closely supported by the fighter-bombers of the R.A.F., 48 Brigade, in heavy fighting, broke through the desperately defended enemy position astride the road a mile south of the camp. The Japanese withdrawing were caught by our western flank detachment and again very roughly handled. To complete their discomfiture they were effectively bombed by the R.A.F. in the area to which they had retired to lick their wounds. After another grim fight the camp was recaptured on the 25th. Much of its contents and most of the lost vehicles were recovered intact and brought out with 17th Division.

While the head of the division was thus effectively dealing with the Japanese 215 Regiment, the rearguard on Tuitum Saddle was nightly beating off fierce attacks from a reinforced 214 Regiment with greatly increased artillery and tank support. A final all-out assault on the 24th, when several enemy tanks were knocked out, was repulsed with heavy loss. On the 26th, the Japanese block at Milestone 109 having been cleared, the rearguard withdrew from Tuitum across the Manipur River and blew up the bridge, while the division resumed its march. Japanese parties were still encountered, on and near the road, but they were easily brushed aside. On the 20th March patrols of the 17th Division and 23rd Division met at Milestone 102. Several small fights were still required to clear the road to the north, but the back of the Japanese opposition had been broken, and they were not, at the moment, capable of another major effort to intercept the 17th Division. Leaving the two brigades of the 23rd Division to hold back the enemy, the 17th Division reached Imphal on the 5th April.

During the later stages of its withdrawal, the division had been maintained by supply dropping from the air. The Japanese Air Force made only one major attempt to attack the long, retreating column and that without serious effect. The enemy's inactivity in the air at this critical time is a measure of what the 17th Division owed to 221 Group R.A.F. Had not our fighters maintained continuous cover and given quick support at call, the withdrawal, if it could have been carried out at all, would have been a much grimmer and more protracted affair, with serious consequences to the main battle around Imphal.

This action on the Tiddim road was, in itself, a considerable success. The 17th Division was now in the Imphal plain, intact with all its transport and wounded. It and the air forces supporting it had inflicted heavier losses on the Japanese than it had suffered. It had beaten them on every occasion in stand-up fights, and, as I saw for myself when I met the division just outside Imphal, its morale was correspondingly high. The 23rd Division had similarly shared in these successes and, in addition, took a slightly mischievous pride in the fact that it had had to come to the rescue of the redoubtable 17th. Yet, looked at from the overall picture of the battle, the fact that the 17th Division had been delayed, and still more that the bulk of Scoones's reserve had of necessity been drawn away at a critical time, might have tragic consequences.

The other forward division of 4 Corps, Gracey's 20th, operating in the Tamu area and at the head of the Kabaw Valley had plenty of excitement in its withdrawal to the Imphal plain, but was never in so difficult a position as the 17th. By the beginning of March, patrols of the 20th Division had penetrated well down the Kabaw Valley and across the Chindwin. A brigade of the 23rd Division had been sent temporarily to the banks of the Chindwin, a few miles north of Sittaung, where it was demonstrating to distract attention from the fly-in by the Chindits then in progress.

The Japanese assembled in the southern Kabaw Valley a force under Major-General Yamamoto the core of which was three battalions of infantry from the 33rd Division, later, in the north of the valley increased by two more battalions. Round this nucleus they grouped considerable bodies of their auxiliaries, the

Burma Traitor Army and the Jiffs. To this somewhat heterogeneous party they entrusted a large part of their available medium
artillery, most of their one tank regiment, and a great deal of
their mechanical transport. Their reason for this was that the
Sittaung-Palel-Imphal road was not only the most direct, but by
far the easiest way by which to bring heavy equipment into the
Imphal plain.

On the 12th March, the Japanese began to push up the Kabaw
Valley in two columns covered by a wide, and to our men,
confusing screen of Burmans and Jiffs, whom it was most difficult
for our men to distinguish from the local inhabitants and our own
troops. Nevertheless our patrols frequently penetrated this screen
and inflicted casualties on the Japanese. On the 17th, after a severe
three-day fight which momentarily halted the enemy, the forward
troops on the 20th Division's southern sector fell back slowly
under orders on Tamu, holding successive positions while the
'thinning out' process behind them continued. The Japanese made
several minor attacks and one serious one, supported by medium
tanks. All these were beaten off and the withdrawal continued at
our own pace. Throughout, the Japanese showed their usual
fanatical courage, on one occasion attempting to rush and destroy
our guns with pole charges and magnetic mines. This party was
lured into an ambush, set round evacuated gun pits, and wiped
out. Three Japanese, all wounded, including an officer, were the
only survivors. They were the 20th Division's first prisoners and
of great value to our intelligence.

During the 16th March, Japanese of the forces which had
crossed the Chindwin a few miles north of Thaungdut began to
threaten the division's flank. As pressure increased, the order to
fall back to the defended locality of Moreh, two miles north of
Tamu, was given. On the 20th, one of the few tank versus tank
actions of the campaign took place, between a troop of the
3rd Dragoon Guards and Japanese medium and light tanks. The
enemy armour was routed, with the loss of four tanks destroyed
and one captured, which, to the great satisfaction of the Dragoons,
they were able to bring back. After dark on the 22nd March the
Japanese heavily attacked our Moreh positions, but were repulsed
and lost more tanks.

By now the threat of the main Japanese advance on Imphal
from the east was growing more menacing, and Scoones was

compelled to look for a reserve to replace the brigades of the 23rd Division that had gone to the rescue of the 17th. He could only find this by drawing on the now heavily pressed 20th Division, and to provide it he had to order Gracey to evacuate Morch and come back to Shenam and Tengoupal, about nine miles from Palel. On the 2nd April, 32 Brigade was, therefore, withdrawn into Corps Reserve, leaving only two brigades to cover Palel and hold the south-eastern approaches to the plain.

Within a week of the start of the Japanese offensive, while the 17th Division was still fighting its way out, it became clear that the situation in the Kohima area was likely to be even more dangerous than that at Imphal. Not only were enemy columns closing in on Kohima at much greater speed than I had expected, but they were obviously in much greater strength. Indeed it was soon evident that the bulk, if not the whole, of the Japanese 31st Division was driving for Kohima and Dimapur. I had been confident that the most the enemy could bring and maintain through such country would be one regimental group, the equivalent of a British brigade group. In that, I had badly under-estimated the Japanese capacity for large-scale, long-range infil-tration, and for their readiness to accept odds in a gamble on supply. This misappreciation was the second great mistake I made in the Imphal battle.

It was an error that was likely to cost us dear. We were not prepared for so heavy a thrust; Kohima with its rather scratch garrison and, what was worse, Dimapur with no garrison at all, were in deadly peril. The loss of Kohima we could endure, but that of Dimapur, our only base and railhead, would have been crippling to an almost fatal degree. It would have pushed into the far distance our hopes of relieving Imphal, laid bare to the enemy, the Brahmaputra Valley with its string of airfields, cut off Stilwell's Ledo Chinese, and stopped all supply to China. As I contemplated the chain of disasters that I had invited, my heart sank. However, I have always believed that a motto for generals must be 'No regrets', no crying over split milk. The vital need was now to bring in reinforcements, not only to replace the vanished reserve in Imphal but, above all, to ensure that Dimapur was held. To achieve this I bent all my energies.

I had available for the purpose under my own command the 5th Indian Division, and 3 Special Service Brigade, composed of one army and one Royal Marine commando. Both these formations were in Arakan. Plans had already been made for the move of the 5th Division, either by road and rail or by air, to Assam. As time was short I ordered it to begin to fly at once. Here I found a serious difficulty. The need for speed had increased and was desperate, but Troop Carrier Command had only eight Dakota squadrons, four British and four American, which, with the demands already on them, could not lift the division at anything like the rate I now demanded.

At this time large numbers of transport aircraft were employed on the Hump route, carrying supplies to China from India. If we lost the Imphal-Kohima battle the Hump route would be closed. It seemed obvious therefore that it would be madness not to divert some of the China lift to the vital needs of Fourteenth Army. Unfortunately not even the Supreme Commander himself had the authority to do this—only the American Chiefs of Staff in far-off Washington could give the word. However, Baldwin and I seized the opportunity of a meeting with Admiral Mountbatten on the 13th March to press hard for such a transfer. He saw the urgency at once, and, on his own responsibility, ordered thirty Dakotas, or their equivalent in other aircraft, to join Troop Carrier Command—a decision which earned my gratitude and played a major part in the result of the battle.

The fly-in of the 5th Indian Division began on the 17th March. By the 20th its first brigade, 123, had deplaned in Imphal. On the 24th, Divisional Headquarters was complete and by the 27th the divisional troops and a second brigade, 9, were also in. Their transport was limited to mules and jeeps, but the officers and men, fresh from their Arakan triumphs, were in fine form. The third brigade, 161, I diverted to Dimapur. I disliked breaking up a division, but the Japanese pressure on Kohima made the quick arrival of help imperative. I had warned Christison in Arakan to get the 7th Indian Division to Chittagong, ready to follow to Assam with all speed. 3 Special Service Brigade later, in early April, I sent by rail to Silchar to guard the Bishenpur–Silchar track, the western entrance to the Imphal plain, and from it to threaten the flank of any Japanese move round Imphal.

I asked General Giffard, who was, as always, a tower of strength in emergency, to let me have Wingate's 23 Long-Range Penetration Brigade, which was still in India. He agreed to rail it to

Jorhat, where I could place it as a mobile force to cover the railway to Ledo, and, if necessary, use it against the flank of an attack on Dimapur. He also sent from India, as previously arranged, the new 25th Indian Division to replace the 5th Division in Arakan. This, being largely a sea move, did not increase the extreme pressure of traffic which now fell on the Bengal and Assam railway system or add to the air transport problem. I asked General Giffard also to send to my help 33 Corps Headquarters and the 2nd British Division from his reserve in India. He at once agreed. He and Auchinleck had already, before I asked, begun preparations for this move. There was still considerable anxiety as to whether, if we did receive these substantial reinforcements, we should be able to maintain them, especially in heavy fighting which would increase greatly demands for supplies and replacements of all kinds. The risk was there but I declared my willingness to accept it and my belief that it could be overcome. My experience has always been that British administrative staffs, like British engineers, work to such safety margins that there is always quite a lot in hand. We continued to evacuate non-combatants from Assam at the rate of thousands a week by air, road, and rail, so that without increasing the Imphal ration strength we could replace them by fighting men. Snelling, my Chief Administrative Officer, nobly supported me. We could, he declared, maintain the extra fighting formations, although if the Imphal road were cut, as he somewhat ruefully admitted, we should be hard put to it. On the 18th March, General Giffard ordered the 2nd Division to move to Fourteenth Army. Its original destination was to have been Arakan, as a relief for the 7th Division, but this was changed, at my request, to Dimapur, as the situation there was becoming more threatening. I sent Fourteenth Army movement staff officers to work out details with their opposite numbers in India. Lieut.-General Stopford, 33 Corps Commander, reported to me at my headquarters on the 23rd.

Even when these moves were in hand my anxiety was hardly lessened. They would take time—and time was so short. It was a race between the Japanese onrush and the arrival of our reinforcements. As I struggled hard to redress my errors and to speed by rail and air these reinforcements I knew that all depended on the steadfastness of the troops already meeting the first impetus of the attack. If they could hold until help arrived, all would be well; if

not, we were near disaster. Happily for the result of the battle—
and for me—I was, like other generals before me, to be saved from
the consequences of my mistakes by the resourcefulness of my
subordinate commanders and the stubborn valour of my troops.

Pushed out some thirty miles to the east, to cover the approaches
to Kohima, was one battalion, the newly formed Assam Regiment, with detachments of the Assam Rifles, the local armed
police. The main weight of the enemy advance fell on this
battalion, in the first battle of its career. Fighting in its own
country, it put up a magnificent resistance, held doggedly to one
position after another against overwhelming odds, and, in spite of
heavy casualties, its companies although separated never lost
cohesion. The delay the Assam Regiment imposed on the 31st
Japanese Division at this stage was invaluable.

Behind this screen, desperate efforts were in hand to make
Kohima Ridge into a great road-block to bar the way to Dimapur.
Non-combatants and hospital patients had already been evacuated,
and, under the energetic and determined leadership of Colonel
Richards, commanding Kohima, the men in the convalescent
depot, some five hundred of them, were issued with arms,
organized into units, and allotted to the defences. Every man
who could be scraped up from administrative units was roped in
to fight. More trenches were dug, dressing stations prepared,
defences manned, but it was a very miscellaneous garrison of
about a thousand who stood-to as the covering troops were
forced slowly back, and it was a grim prospect they faced as
fifteen thousand ravening Japanese closed in on them.

I had flown to Dimapur, and with Imphal in grave danger of
being cut off and with the battle there by no means going
according to plan, I realized I could not expect Scoones properly
to control what would be tactically a separate battle at Kohima.
I therefore placed Major-General Ranking, who commanded the
base and rear areas of Assam, known as 202 Line of Communication Area, in control of all operations in the Kohima-Dimapur-
Jorhat theatre, until the arrival of 33 Corps. It was for him a
sudden plunge from administrative duties in a peaceful area into
the alarms and stresses of a savage battle against desperate odds.
And it would be against odds. In front of Kohima, Ranking had
the Assam Battalion; in Kohima, besides the convalescents, he had
a raw battalion of our allies, the Nepalese Army, and a couple of

independent companies of the Burma Regiment. The only fighting unit he had in hand was a battalion of the Burma Regiment. Not much, all told, with which to meet a full-strength Japanese division. I admired the way in which he and his subordinate commanders faced their peril. In Dimapur I had asked the brigadier commanding the base what his ration strength was. 'Forty-five thousand, near enough,' he replied. 'And how many soldiers can you scrape up out of that lot?' I inquired. He smiled wryly. 'I might get five hundred who know how to fire a rifle!' But, as at Kohima, everything that could be done to put the sprawling base into a state of defence was being done. As I walked round, inspecting bunkers and rifle pits, dug by non-combatant labour under the direction of storemen and clerks, and as I looked into the faces of the willing but untried garrison, I could only hope that I imparted more confidence than I felt.

During the last days of March, 161 Brigade of the 5th Indian Division completed its fly-in from Arakan. Never was a reinforcement more welcome. Reports now showed that the whole of the Japanese 31st Division was ten to twenty miles from Kohima and that our covering force could not hope to delay them seriously, still less hold them. Even if the Assam battalion managed to fall back reasonably intact, it was doubtful if Kohima could hold out. The immediate problem was whether to give up Kohima and concentrate on holding the vital Dimapur or to reinforce Kohima with 161 Brigade as it arrived and try to hold the enemy on the ridge until the 2nd British Division came to the rescue.

I discussed the situation with Ranking. Kohima Ridge was an infinitely preferable defensive position to Dimapur, which it covered. If we had not enough troops to hold Kohima, we certainly had not enough to hold Dimapur and, as long as we clung to the ridge, we had some chance of concentrating our reinforcements as they arrived, without too much hostile interference. We decided, therefore, to hold the Kohima Ridge, sending forward for the purpose 161 Brigade to meet the Japanese and stop them, temporarily at least, on or south of it.

Later when in one of the Dimapur offices I held a conference of commanders, it was not surprising that I saw some apprehensive faces turned towards me. I gave them three tasks:

1. To prepare Dimapur for defence and when attacked to hold it.

2. To reinforce Kohima and hold that to the last.
3. To make all preparations for the rapid reception and assembly of the large reinforcements that were on the way.

As always happens on these occasions, as soon as everybody was given a clear task into which he could throw himself, spirits rose and even I began to feel a little better. I took Warren, who commanded 161 Brigade, outside and walked him up and down the path while I gave him, without any attempt to minimize the hazardous task he was being set, a fuller view of the situation, and especially of the time factor. I told him I calculated that the enemy could reach Kohima by the 3rd April and, even if we held there, might by-pass our garrison and be attacking Dimapur by the 10th. I could not expect more than one brigade of the 2nd Division to have arrived by that time, or the whole division before the 20th. Actually the Transportation Services materially improved on these timings. Steady, unruffled, slow-speaking, Warren heard me out, asked a few questions, and went quietly off to get on with his job. I hope I had as good an effect on him as he had on me.

After my talk with him, Warren took his brigade to Kohima on the 29th March, and, such was his energy, that the next day one of his battalions was in action with the enemy, over twenty miles south, while the rest of the brigade was disposed to cover the withdrawal of the Assam Battalion. I had meanwhile left Dimapur and sent Ranking my written directive, in which I stressed that his main task was to safeguard Dimapur base. There were at this time reports and rumours of Japanese forces within striking distance of Dimapur, and he decided that the situation necessitated troops for the close defence of the base if he was to carry out this task. He, therefore, much to Warren's annoyance, ordered 161 Brigade back to the Nichugard Pass, eight miles south-east of Dimapur, to be in position there by the evening of the 31st March. In taking this action Ranking was, I think, influenced understandably by the stress I had laid on his primary task—the defence of Dimapur base. The reports proved untrue, and the withdrawal of the brigade was an unfortunate mistake. Had it remained south of Kohima, Warren would almost certainly have at least delayed the Japanese advance on Kohima for several days. That would have put a very different aspect on the battle which followed.

Japanese pressure towards Kohima was mounting. With the withdrawal of 161 Brigade, the covering troops were in grave difficulties as the enemy outflanked and enveloped them. The Assam Battalion, still fighting stubbornly and losing heavily, was split in two. Half of it, about two hundred strong, made its way into Kohima and joined the garrison; the rest evaded encircling Japanese and, in good order but exhausted, reached the main Dimapur road behind 161 Brigade.

I have spent some uncomfortable hours at the beginnings of battles, but few more anxious than those of the Kohima battle. All the Japanese commander had to do was to leave a detachment to mask Kohima, and, with the rest of his division, thrust violently on Dimapur. He could hardly fail to take it. Luckily, Major-General Sato, commander of the Japanese 31st Division, was, without exception, the most unenterprising of all the Japanese generals I encountered. He had been ordered to take Kohima and dig in. His bullet head was filled with one idea only—to take Kohima. It never struck him that he could inflict terrible damage on us without taking Kohima at all. Leaving a small force to contain it, and moving by tracks to the east of Warren's brigade at Nichugard, he could, by the 5th April, have struck the railway with the bulk of his division. But he had no vision, so, as his troops came up, he flung them into attack after attack on the little town of Kohima. I have said I was saved from the gravest effects of my mistake in underestimating the enemy's capacity to penetrate to Kohima by the stubborn valour of my troops; but it needed the stupidity of the local enemy commander to make quite sure. Unfortunately, at the time, I did not know this was to be supplied, or I should have been saved much anxiety. Later, when it was evident, I once found some enthusiastic Royal Air Force officers planning an air strike on Sato's headquarters. They were astonished when I suggested they should abandon the project as I regarded their intended victim as one of my most helpful generals! But the time to indulge in such frivolities was not yet.

Lieut.-General Montague Stopford, commander of 33 Indian Corps, with some of his staff, had reached my headquarters at Comilla on 23rd March. I knew him and had every confidence in him as a commander, but his corps headquarters had not previously operated and, indeed, had done little training. They would have to shake down and gain experience as they fought—

never an easy thing to do. The success and speed with which they overcame their teething troubles were a measure of their ability and their commander's leadership.

I had at first considered Silchar as the location for 33 Corps Headquarters. It was central, had certain advantages in approach to Imphal and in communications; but the unexpected seriousness of the threat to Dimapur made it imperative to get not only the bulk of the reinforcements but Corps Headquarters also into that area. I also decided that Kohima at this stage must have priority over Imphal. Stopford himself urged this and I agreed with him. I gave Stopford as his objects:

1. To prevent Japanese penetration into the Brahmaputra or Surma Valleys or through the Lushai Hills.
2. To keep open the Dimapur–Kohima–Imphal road.
3. To move to the help of 4 Corps and to co-operate with it in the destruction of all enemy west of the Chindwin.

These tasks were not changed throughout the battle, and remained the overall directive for 33 Corps. I gave him tactical freedom in the methods he chose to carry them out, and he, therefore, deserves the credit for accomplishing them.

On the 3rd April, Stopford arrived at Jorhat on the Assam railway, some sixty-five miles north-north-east of Dimapur, and established his headquarters there. Next day he took over control of operations from Ranking. In the ten days that had passed since Stopford had received his original orders the Kohima situation had developed, but not, alas, to our advantage, and I decided that his immediate tasks had now become:

(i) To cover the concentration of his corps as far forward as practicable.
(ii) To secure the Dimapur base.
(iii) To reinforce and hold Kohima.
(iv) To protect, as far as possible without jeopardizing (i) to (iii), the Assam railway and the China route airfields in the Brahmaputra Valley.

The 33 Corps plan to achieve these ends was:

(a) To concentrate the corps as it arrived north-east of Dimapur. This would avoid its becoming immediately involved in an enemy attack on the base and would place it advantageously to deliver a counter-stroke. It would also automatically protect the railway to Ledo.

(b) To send forward the first brigade of the 2nd Division as soon as it arrived to hold the Nichugard Pass, eight miles south-east of Dimapur, thus covering the base against a direct Japanese advance.

(c) To reinforce Kohima with 161 Brigade of the 5th Indian Division at once.

(d) To use 23 Brigade (Chindits), expected about the 12th April, to strike south on Kohima and to the east of it, with the double object of checking Japanese infiltration towards the railway and of cutting the enemy line of communication to the Chindwin.

(e) To cover the western end of the Silchar–Bishenpur track with another Nepalese battalion which I had made available until the arrival of 3 Special Service Brigade.

(f) To continue to use the newly formed Lushai Brigade to prevent an enemy advance into the Lushai Hills.

Wasting no time, on the evening of the 4th April, Stopford ordered 161 Brigade to move again to Kohima. It left Nichugard the next day, and its leading unit, the 4th Battalion, The Royal West Kent Regiment, joined the garrison late the same day, just after the first Japanese night attack had overrun some of our positions. The rest of the brigade, warned of the congestion in Kohima, halted and dug in for the night. Early on the morning of the 6th, a company of Rajputs got into Kohima and one platoon of it brought out two hundred walking wounded and non-combatants. During the morning, however, the Japanese closed round the town, and the brigade was unable to gain the ridge. The road behind was soon afterwards cut by a strong enemy detachment who established a block between the brigade and Dimapur. The situation at Kohima was thus: its garrison of about three thousand men closely invested by superior forces, 161 Brigade cut off five miles to the north, a detachment holding the Nichugard defile south-east of Dimapur, and the base itself in no state to resist a serious attack. A decidedly unpleasant situation, but there were not wanting more hopeful signs.

At the end of March, the 2nd British Division had been dispersed in training in Southern India. Such was the rapidity of its move, carried out by the Movement Staffs of G.H.Q. India and of General Giffard's headquarters, that on the 2nd April its leading elements were arriving at Dimapur, two brigades and the Divisional Headquarters were on the way by air, and one brigade by rail. A regiment of tanks and later 268 Indian Motorized Brigade were also thrown in for good measure by General Auchinleck.

As I shuttled between Dimapur, Imphal, and my headquarters at Comilla, I was beginning to see light. We had hard days ahead of us, but everywhere our troops, unperturbed by events, were steady and full of fight. We had lost nothing vital.

CHAPTER XV

ATTRITION

ON the Assam front the first week of April had been an anxious one. Thanks to my mistakes the battle had not started well; at any time crisis might have slipped into disaster—and still might. We were in tactical difficulties everywhere. The Japanese were pressing hard on the rim of the Imphal plain; they still threatened the Dimapur base, while the Kohima garrison was in dire peril; and they had cut the Kohima–Imphal road, which was certainly no part of *my* plan. Yet for their gains they had paid a higher price in dead and wounded, and, above all, in time, than they had calculated on in *their* plan. Now our air forces, tireless and bold, dominated the skies. Under their wings our reinforcements were flowing in more smoothly and rapidly than I had hoped. As I watched the little flags, representing divisions, cluster round Imphal and Kohima on my situation map, I heaved a sigh of relief. As the second week of April wore on, for all its alarms and fears I felt that our original pattern for the battle was reasserting itself.

In my visits to formations I tried to impart this feeling, and I found it shared by commanders and troops. By the beginning of April when the 5th Indian Division, less the brigade sent to Dimapur, had arrived, Scoones at Imphal would have the best part of four divisions, and under his steady leadership I was confident the tide would turn. It was on the Kohima side of the picture that I looked the more anxiously. Here it would take all Stopford's energy and optimism to right the battle. Not only were the defenders of Kohima in desperate case, but it was still open to the Japanese 31st Division to sidestep them and go for Dimapur. I therefore decided that the Kohima battle should have preference over that at Imphal for reinforcements, supplies, ammunition, indeed for anything 33 Corps required, and that even at the cost of skimping Scoones I must nourish Stopford. Luckily Sato

315

continued to limit himself to frontal attacks on Kohima, first by day and then, as the toll exacted by the garrison and by the swift retaliation of our aircraft in daylight proved too high even for Japanese stomachs, by night. Throughout the day and in the intervals between these night attacks, the enemy artillery, mortars, and machine-guns hammered relentlessly at our positions on Garrison Hill. British and Japanese trenches were within yards of one another, every move brought a shot, rest was impossible. Sheer exhaustion rather than the enemy threatened to vanquish our men. Then came the worst blow of all. During the night of the 5th/6th April the Japanese gained possession of the water supply, and thirst was added to the other horrors. The R.A.F., regardless of fire from the ground, swept over at tree-top level to drop motor-car inner tubes filled with water. By good fortune a small spring was found inside our lines, yet, even with this to supplement the air force contribution, the water ration dropped to less than a pint a man and a little more for the wounded. Gradually the area we held was squeezed until, from a rough square with sides of a thousand yards, it became a meagre five hundred by five hundred. Into this confined space the enemy rained down a pitiless bombardment; against its haggard, thirsty garrison they hurled attack after attack.

But help was at hand. By the 11th April, headquarters and two brigades of the 2nd Division had reached Dimapur; the third was following close behind, and next day the Chindit 23 Brigade arrived at Jorhat. We had thus drawn about level with the Japanese in numbers, and, as soon as the 7th Indian Division, now under orders from Arakan, could be got in we would be on the way to superiority.

Immediately it was available, Stopford sent the leading 5 Brigade of the 2nd Division up the road towards 161 Brigade, now held up short of Kohima. The first enemy road-block encountered was rushed, but the second, six miles farther on, repulsed an un-supported infantry attack. Next day the divisional artillery and some tanks arrived. A second attack broke through, but the Japanese counter-attacked. They were beaten off and the column pushed on. During the next few days several positions barring the road were taken in stiff fighting until, on the 15th April, 5 Brigade and 161 Brigade joined hands. The next brigade (6) of the 2nd Division was then brought up and freed 161 Brigade for its

ATTRITION

advance to relieve Kohima. On the 18th, the brigade, with tank, artillery, and air support, launched an assault astride the main road and along the ridge on its right. Progress was at times slow, as the enemy reacted with fierce local counter-attacks, but Warren's men finally broke through and joined up with the hard-pressed garrison, clinging grimly to their smoking hill-top. A Punjabi battalion was the first to enter, and at once took over part of the perimeter from the exhausted defenders. Kohima was relieved.

After dark the wounded were brought out under fire and carried to ambulances that had crept close up under such cover as could be found. Next day, the 19th, 161 Brigade continued its attack, but failed to take Kuki Piquet, though some advance was made. Throughout the day, the road back was kept open, and by it Kohima was restocked, so that many of the garrison got their first full meal since the siege began. On the 20th, 6 Brigade of the 2nd Division moved in under cover of artillery and relieved the rest of the original garrison. At six o'clock on that morning Colonel Richards handed over the command he had so gallantly held and collected his men. Three hours later they marched out, and, just below what had been the hospital, they found lorries waiting to take them from the dust, din, and stench of death in which they had lived for eleven days.

They had endured much. Forced into an ever contracting circle by the relentless assaults of vastly superior numbers, their casualties had been severe. There had been no evacuation for the wounded, and men were hit again and again as they lay in the casualty stations. Thirst was not the least of the trials of these devoted men. Sieges have been longer but few have been more intense, and in none have the defenders deserved greater honour than the garrison of Kohima.

Although the small force that had been cut off on Garrison Hill had now been relieved, most of Kohima Ridge itself remained in hostile hands. With their centre on the town, the Japanese held an immensely strong position, some seven thousand yards long, astride the main Imphal–Dimapur road. The natural defensive strength of a succession of steep, wooded ridges had been improved by the Japanese genius for inter-supporting field works and concealment, until it was as formidable a position as a British army has ever faced. Its flanks, extending into high and most

317

difficult country, were protected by inaccessibility. The enemy also had detachments dug in well forward on tracks which led through dense jungle to the main road and railway. There was thus the constant threat of infiltration and of movements against our rear. It was always a wonder to me why Sato did not attempt a bold stroke of this kind. It would have been typically Japanese, and he had, even at this stage, enough troops for it if he cared to take some risk at Kohima itself.

Our own build-up was proceeding rapidly. The concentration of the 2nd British Division was practically complete—too complete as far as its transport was concerned, for its lorries, parked nose to tail, threatened to turn the two-way main road into a one-way track. An attack by twelve Oscars on a mass of this useless transport, jammed into a village, lent point to my exhortations to 33 Corps to get it out of the area. Luckily the R.A.F. maintained such a degree of air superiority that we did not pay the heavy penalty that should have been exacted. Relieved of this excessive transport, the division found, like others in Burma, that it could move faster and more freely without it. The leading brigade (33) of the 7th Indian Division had arrived, also by air, from the Arakan fighting, and 23 Chindit Brigade was already advancing in several columns south-east from the railway. One of these columns had its first serious and successful brush with the enemy on the 16th April. On the 22nd it attacked a strongly held village but was repulsed. Within the next few days, in co-operation with a well-directed air strike, it again attacked and this time took the village.

Stopford, commanding 33 Corps, whose headquarters was established at Jorhat, was rightly urging the 2nd Division to advance, but the terrain and the type of warfare were new to British troops, while the unavoidable arrival of the division piecemeal made the task of Grover, the divisional commander, a difficult one.

His plan was for one brigade of the 2nd Division, supported by the bulk of the artillery, to keep up heavy pressure against the Japanese centre at Kohima while the two remaining brigades, one on each flank, carried out turning movements to seize high ground behind the Japanese front line. 161 Brigade was placed centrally as a General Reserve, and 33 Brigade of the 7th Division was held back to cover Dimapur. The columns of 23 Chindit Brigade were

318

to continue their thrust south-east towards Jessami to cut the Japanese supply routes from the Chindwin. When the two flank brigades had reached their objectives it was intended to launch the main attack in the centre.

Starting on 21st April, the leading battalion of the left brigade (5) crossed the valley by jungle tracks to the east of the main road and climbed two thousand feet to a track running along the ridge due north from Kohima. Here it found a large Japanese position prepared for defence but unoccupied. During the next few days, hampered by rain on the slippery ascent and dependent entirely on animal and porter transport, strange to British troops, the rest of the brigade joined them. On the 29th, an attack on further Japanese positions, this time occupied, failed; and the brigade was held up well short of its final objective.

Meanwhile the other flank brigade (4) had scrambled up steep ridges towards the enemy left, meeting little opposition, but owing to rain and the difficulties of movement and supply it did not make progress as fast as had been expected.

The centre brigade (6) was, on the night of the 22nd/23rd April, heavily attacked on the shambles of Garrison Hill. In fierce hand-to-hand fighting the Japanese were beaten off, but for the next two days our men were under constant pressure and bombardment, much as the original garrison had been. On the 22nd, an attempt with infantry and tanks to relieve the pressure failed, as the tanks were held up by difficult ground. Then, on the night of the 27th a more formidable assault—the first of a series of attacks and counter-attacks—was launched on the Deputy Commissioner's Bungalow. This had once been a charming house in a delightful garden, but was now a heap of rubble in a devastation with one chimney only standing, black and twisted against the sky. This attack, after desperate fighting, succeeded in reaching and holding, not only the site of the house but the bluff in the garden, which overlooked the Kohima crossroads and denied them to the enemy—a very valuable tactical success. On the night of the 29th/30th the Japanese made a final attempt, in an all-out counter-attack, to regain possession, but failed with heavy loss. Each side was left holding part of the garden, with the tennis court as a no-man's-land between them, and with hand grenades shuttling back and forth in the place of tennis balls.

As neither flank brigade could make the progress hoped for and

319

as the centre brigade was hard pressed opposite Kohima itself, the divisonal plan was changed. The wider turning movements were abandoned, and it was decided to deliver a more concentrated attack on the Japanese position so that all three brigades could act in close tactical combination and in turn have the full support of the divisional and corps artillery.

This set-back was disappointing, but the 2nd British Division was now complete, the 7th Indian was coming in well and would be followed by 268 Indian Motorized Brigade. I should soon have here the two-to-one superiority over the Japanese that was my aim at both Kohima and Imphal, but I was determined not to push Stopford, at this stage, beyond the pace he considered wise. He was the last commander to drag his feet, and his 2nd Division, the spearhead of his attack, while as brave as troops could be, was inexperienced; its very dash rendered it liable to heavy casualties unless its attacks were deliberately prepared with all possible support. So, although I continued to divert artillery ammunition, petrol, and air strikes, badly needed on other fronts, to 33 Corps, I did not nag at them to hurry. The corps had to win its first battle; 4 Corps, comparative veterans, could wait.

There were not wanting at this time those who, crediting from a distance the alarmist reports that always circulate at such moments, urged me at all costs to 'break through and relieve Imphal'. I had no intention of yielding to pressure; Imphal was in no danger of falling. It is not the easiest task of a superior commander to stand between such pressure and his subordinate commanders, but at times it is his duty. General Giffard, who understood the situation well, increased my debt to him by the firmness with which he did this now.

The battle of Kohima was a bloody one. The first full-scale assault by the 2nd Division under the new plan was so delayed by rain that it was not until the 3rd May that deployment was complete. The plan was for 4 Brigade on the right to capture G.P.T. Ridge, advance to Jail Hill, and link up with 6 Brigade in the centre, which by then, having broken out from Garrison Hill, should have taken Kuki Piquet and F.S.D. Ridge. 5 Brigade on the left was to occupy Naga village and dominate the Treasury area. The attack was to be supported by tanks and by all available guns, firing time-concentrations in support of each brigade in turn. The attack began in the early morning of the 4th May.

320

4 Brigade, delayed by undiscovered Japanese bunkers, reached G.P.T. Ridge, but was unable to secure the whole of it, nor to approach Jail Hill. By nightfall on this part of the field the enemy positions and ours were inextricably mingled. 6 Brigade failed to take Kuki Piquet and, although its tanks reached F.S.D. Ridge, the infantry, subjected to devastating fire from other enemy positions, could not dig in or remain. A portion only of the ridge was held by nightfall and here again British and Japanese were mixed up together. 5 Brigade entered Naga village, but during the night of the 4th/5th May were counter-attacked heavily and pushed back to the western edge of the village, which they managed to hold. The Treasury area remained firmly in enemy hands.

During the 5th May both sides were exhausted. The British could attempt no more than local consolidation, and, luckily for us, the Japanese launched no counter-attacks. On the 6th, all brigades made attempts to improve their positions by local attacks, but only minor adjustments at the cost of considerable casualties were achieved. Stopford now handed over his Corps Reserve, 33 Brigade of the 7th Indian Division, to Grover who, on the 7th May, used one of its battalions to attack Jail Hill, from which on previous days heavy and accurate machine-gun fire had hampered both 4 and 6 Brigades. The attack with great gallantry reached its objective, but was unable to dislodge the enemy from his deep bunkers, and we were again forced to abandon Jail Hill.

After four days' bitter fighting with heavy casualties, the assault had little to show. While the 31st Japanese Division certainly lacked initiative, it had all the enemy's fanatical stubbornness in defence. Our troops were again discovering that it was one thing to reach a Japanese bunker, another to enter it. Nor had artillery bombardment and accurate attacks by Hurricanes and Vengeance bombers on the limited areas engaged had much result. The most effective weapon proved to be the tank, firing solid shot at point-blank range; but the wooded terrain, its steepness, and the wet that made tanks churn everything into liquid mud, restricted their use. It was clear that the battle would be prolonged and savage.

During the 8th, 9th, and 10th May, while its forward troops remained in close contact with the enemy, 33 Corps prepared to renew the attack. A main feature of the plan for the fresh attack, on which the corps commander insisted, was to be a generous use of smoke to screen the attacking troops from the enfilade and long-range machine-gun fire that had proved so damaging.

The main objectives in this attack, Jail Hill and the D.I.S., were allotted to 33 Brigade of the 7th Division, but as both these were enfiladed from G.P.T. and F.S.D. Ridges, 4 and 6 Brigades of the 2nd Division were to clear the latter features before 33 Brigade reached its objectives. The attack began on the night of the 10th/11th May, but that of the 2nd Division was only partially successful. When dawn came the enemy still held several bunkers on the reverse slopes of G.P.T. Ridge and a strong-point on F.S.D. Ridge. The main attack by 33 Brigade fared better. Probing forward in the darkness, a Punjabi battalion found Pimple Hill unoccupied and promptly dug in on it. The Queen's Regiment, after a stiff fight, was, soon after dawn, in possession of most of Jail Hill; and a second Punjabi battalion, although they suffered considerably, had cleared the D.I.S. area. As the light strengthened, both these battalions were attempting to dig in on their gains, but were being greatly hampered, not only by fire from the front but by accurate enfilade from automatic weapons on G.P.T. and F.S.D. Ridges, not yet free of enemy. The situation of the two battalions, hanging on with great determination in the mud and rain but losing men fast, was relieved by a heavy smoke-screen put down at 8.45 a.m. by our artillery for several hours. The Japanese did not appear to have laid out any fixed lines of fire, and the effect of their machine-guns was reduced to such an extent that our men were able to dig in.

During the 11th, both battalions were reinforced, and after dark, with the help of Indian Sappers, they cleared a mine-field in the cutting between Jail Hill and the D.I.S. area, which up to then had prevented tanks from joining them. The fight was resumed on the 12th, when in the afternoon, aided by tanks, further progress was made on Jail Hill and in the D.I.S. area, but little elsewhere. At dawn on the 13th, in the face of our pressure, the surviving Japanese in both places fell back, and mopping-up was completed by midday. Seeing that the key-points of Jail Hill and the D.I.S. area were lost, the enemy evacuated G.P.T. Ridge, F.S.D. Ridge, and Kuki Piquet, which were occupied by the 2nd Division.

While this considerable action was going on, our other positions all along the front were being cleared up and extended by local operations. Typical of the Japanese resistance was the last phase of the prolonged struggle for the Deputy Commissioner's Bungalow, where, although cut off, some enemy in deep bunker continued to fight stubbornly. Sappers made a track up which a tank could climb and the Dorsets then attacked with its support. Each bunker was engaged in turn by the tank's 75-mm. guns, whose effect at thirty yards was decisive. Japanese attempting to escape were bayoneted or shot; none tried to surrender. The few remaining bunkers were demolished by pole charges thrust through their loopholes and, by the afternoon of the 13th May, the Deputy Commissioner's Bungalow, his garden and tennis court, which had acquired an almost ritual significance, were all finally in our hands at remarkably low cost in casualties.

Treasury Hill was the next objective of 33 Brigade. A Gurkha battalion was concentrated on Garrison Hill during the 14th for a deliberate attack next day, but from patrol reports the brigadier concluded that most of the enemy were pulling out and he ordered an infiltrating attack in the dark. By first light on the 15th, the Gurkhas, meeting practically no resistance, had occupied the whole of Treasury Hill.

The gains thus made in a few days since the 10th May changed the whole picture around Kohima. The most satisfactory feature was the failure of the Japanese anywhere to counter-attack— evidence of their increasing disorganization under these heavy blows. There followed on this part of the battlefield a short lull while both sides regrouped themselves for a renewal of the struggle.

Meanwhile, on the Imphal front fighting as bitter but more diffuse had been claiming my attention. It was not without its moments of anxiety, for Scoones was being hard pressed.

Like unevenly spaced spokes of a wheel, six routes converged on to the Imphal plain to meet at the hub, Imphal itself:

(i) From the north, the broad Kohima road.
(ii) Also from the north, the foot-path down the Iril River Valley.
(iii) From the north-east, the Ukhrul road.
(iv) From the south-east, the tarmac Tamu–Palel road.
(v) From the south, the rugged Tiddim highway.
(vi) From the west, the Silchar–Bishenpur track.

It was by these that the Japanese strove to break into the plain. The fighting all round its circumference was continuous, fierce, and often confused as each side manœuvred to outwit and kill. There was always a Japanese thrust somewhere that had to be met and destroyed. Yet the fighting did follow a pattern. The main encounters were on or near the spokes of the wheel, because it was only along these that guns, tanks, and vehicles could move. The Japanese would advance astride the route, attack our troops blocking it, and try to outflank or infiltrate past them. We should first hold, then counter-attack, and the struggle would sway a mile or two, one way and the other. All the time our airmen, who played so vital a part in these battles, would be daily in sortie after sortie delivering attacks at ground-level and hammering the enemy's communications right back into Burma. Gradually we should prevail, and, driven from the spokes of the wheel, the Japanese would take to the hills between them. Relentlessly we would hunt them down and when, desperate and rabid, they turned at bay, kill them. This pattern repeated itself along each of the spokes as, on one after the other, we passed from defence to offence.

Our casualties in this kind of fighting were not light. The infantry, as usual, suffered most and endured most, for this was above all an infantry battle, hand-to-hand, man against man, and no quarter. Our heaviest losses were among the officers, not only in the infantry who in this close fighting could not fail to be conspicuous, but among the artillery observation officers who to give accurate support pushed on with the leading troops, and among the young tank commanders who, regardless of safety, kept their turrets open or moved on foot so that they could guide their tanks through the jungle.

To deal briefly with the events on each spoke of the wheel is probably the clearest way to give a picture of this battle, but it should be remembered that encounters on all the spokes were going on simultaneously. At no time and in no place was the situation, either to commanders or troops, as clear even as I can make it now. Into Scoones's headquarters, from every point of the compass, day and night, streamed signals, messages, and reports, announcing successes, set-backs, appealing for reinforcements, demanding more ammunition, asking urgently for wounded to be evacuated, begging for air support. His was the task of meeting or withstanding these appeals, of deciding which at the moment was the place to which his by no means over-generous reserves should be allotted. It was impossible for him to satisfy all his commanders. It needed a tough, cool, and well-balanced commander to meet, week after week, this strain. Luckily Scoones *was* tough, cool, and well balanced.

To take first the actions on the Iril Valley and Ukhrul road spokes. By the beginning of April, the leading troops of the 5th Division, who had gone into action on the Ukhrul road almost straight from their aircraft, had with the remaining brigade of the 23rd Division pushed back the imminent threat to Imphal until the Japanese were held just west of Litan. But the enemy were now round Imphal on the north, and our troops on the Ukhrul road were menaced in the rear by a Japanese force which on the 6th April attacked Nungshigum, a great hill which dominated the Imphal plain and gave direct observation over the main airstrip at a range of five or six miles. The fighting for this hill was typical of a hundred actions that went on at this stage round the edges of the plain.

Nungshigum has two peaks, a north and a south. The Japanese attack drove our men off the northern, but we clung to the southern. On the 11th April, after several attempts, the enemy gained that too. On the 12th we retook the southern summit, but lost it again. On the 13th, while Hurribombers, their guns blazing, dived almost into the tree-tops, and tanks, winched up incredible slopes, fired point-blank into bunker loopholes, our infantry stormed both peaks—and held them. The Japanese grimly defended their positions until the last men still fighting were bombed or bayoneted in their last foxholes.

In this fight, so difficult was the country and so dense the jungle that the tanks of the Carbineers had to go into action with turrets open if their commanders were to see enough to help the infantry. The young officer and N.C.O. tank commanders unhesitatingly took this risk of almost certain death and, alas, a high proportion of them were killed.

When the 5th Division had secured Nungshigum, it was relieved by the 23rd Division of all responsibility for the Ukhrul road and proceeded to clear the Iril Valley. Between the 16th April and the 7th May there was heavy fighting to eject the Japanese from their positions on the big Mapao Spur which divides the Iril Valley from the Imphal–Kohima road and gives observation over the north-western portion of the plain. Our attacks, which met fierce Japanese counter-attacks, were only partially successful. We drove the enemy from the southern parts of his position but he still held to the northern, though he no longer presented a serious threat to Imphal.

1 Brigade of the 23rd Division, having combed the hills to the south of the Ukhrul road and chased the headquarters of the 15th Japanese Division through the jungle, turned north and cleared the road to within fifteen miles of Ukhrul. The enemy headquarters escaped, but to say the least its operational efficiency was not increased. 37 Brigade of the 23rd Division soon afterwards moved up the road and made contact with 1 Brigade. The division then, during the first half of May, kept up pressure on the enemy over the whole Ukhrul road front. By the middle of the month the situation both in the Iril Valley and on the Ukhrul road could be considered stabilized.

On the Palel road spoke of the wheel at the beginning of April, the 20th Division, having lost one brigade taken for Corps Reserve, was with the two remaining brigades, 80 and 100, holding a twenty-five-mile front running from Tengoupal, ten miles south-east of Palel, through Shenam to Shuganu, fifteen miles south-west of Palel. The country is a criss-cross of steep ridges and deep *nullahs*, all tree-covered, with in parts dense jungle. Gracey's troops could not, of course, maintain a continuous line; they had to content themselves by holding the most important heights and the passes by which the main road and the most usable tracks approached Palel and the Imphal plain. Between these tactical points they strove to dominate the country and prevent Japanese infiltration by constant and aggressive patrolling. In this, luckily, they had already obtained something of a mastery over the enemy, but it was a long and vulnerable front which, throughout this phase of the battle, was a source of anxiety to Scoones.

The Japanese commander here, Major-General Yamamoto, was under great pressure from his superiors to break into the Imphal plain. The tanks and artillery which constituted a large part of his force were urgently wanted by Mutaguchi, the Army Commander, to reduce our defences around Imphal. So Yamamoto launched attack after attack to crash through the

ATTRITION

20th Division defences on the Shenam Pass. These assaults, supported more heavily than usual for the Japanese by armour and artillery, were constant throughout April.

Some of the bitterest fighting was around Tengoupal which directly covered the main road up which Yamamoto was trying to blast his way. Between the 4th and the 11th April the Japanese attacks were continuous and made some progress. On the 11th April, a counter-attack in which the Devons distinguished themselves retook lost ground, but on the 15th and 16th fanatical enemy assaults on a young Indian battalion which had relieved the Devons regained portions of the position and were continued during the two succeeding nights. On the night of the 19th/20th April, three separate attacks with medium tanks were beaten off, but our men, never very thick on the ground, were becoming exhausted from want of rest. On the 22nd April, after very heavy fighting, parts of our position were overrun; but the enemy had suffered too heavily to be able to continue and the attacks died down. Shenam, on the other side of the road, had not been heavily attacked, which was lucky, as part of the brigade here had to be sent to reinforce Shuganu, threatened by the reported approach of Japanese forces.

The Indian National Army's Gandhi Brigade was on this front, and, towards the end of April, parties of Japanese, accompanied by Jiffs disguised as local inhabitants and as our sepoys, infiltrated towards Palel. There were numerous patrol clashes and we staged several successful ambushes, but it was impossible in such wild country to intercept every hostile group, and on the night of the 29th/30th April a small Japanese party actually attacked the Palel Keep. No damage was done and the signal reporting the occurrence ended, 'enemy now being slain'. This attempt was a stout-hearted effort in contrast to the abortive 'attack' made on one of our positions by the Gandhi Brigade on the night of the 2nd/3rd May, in which a large party of Jiffs was ambushed and scattered as it approached. After this, considerable numbers of these unfortunate Jiffs appeared to be wandering about the country without object or cohesion. They had suffered a good many other casualties at the hands of our patrols and during May were surrendering in large numbers, but our Indian and Gurkha soldiers were at times not too ready to let them surrender, and orders had to be issued to give them a kinder welcome. The

327

Gandhi Brigade took no further appreciable part in operations and what was left of it the Japanese in disgust used mainly as porters.

However, Japanese patrols were in the hills north and east of Palel, and their presence might interfere with the regular use of the airfield. This could not be risked, and Scoones sent 48 Brigade of the 17th Division between the 6th and 8th May to comb that part of the country. When this brigade moved on to other tasks, he replaced it by 1 Brigade of the 23rd Division which completed the comb-out and chased the headquarters of the Japanese 15th Division to the north over the Ukhrul road as already described.

This infiltration of Japanese parties into the area north-east of Palel coincided with a final effort by Yamamoto to break through on the main road. On the nights of the 6th/7th and the 7th/8th May fierce Japanese attacks on the Tengoupal front were repulsed, but on the 8th May they broke into our positions. Counter-attacks, most gallantly supported by the R.A.F's fighter bombers, failed to recover lost ground and we made a partial withdrawal. There were further Japanese attacks on the nights of the 9th/10th and the 10th/11th May during which we again lost some of our positions. A rather anxious situation was restored on the 12th by a most gallant counter-attack, and for the moment both sides were too exhausted to undertake further attacks or counter-attacks. The 20th Division had successfully withstood very heavy assaults and continuous pressure for over two months, and to ease the strain on it Scoones now relieved it on the Palel front by Roberts's 23rd Division at its full strength of three brigades. On this spoke of the wheel, too, by mid-May we could consider the situation stabilized.

It was along the Tiddim road and the Silchar–Bishenpur track, the southern and western spokes of the wheel, that some of the heaviest fighting of this Battle of Attrition took place. When the 17th Division reached Imphal after its withdrawal along the Tiddim road, Scoones left behind it, to hold off the Japanese 33rd Division which was pressing towards Imphal, two brigades, 37 and 49, of Roberts's 23rd Division. 37 Brigade was quickly recalled to join its division, and 49 Brigade on the 9th April was attacked in its positions south of Bishenpur at Milestones 30 and 35 on the Tiddim road. These attacks were repulsed and a Japanese detachment that had audaciously inserted itself between the forward battalion and the rest of the brigade was completely destroyed. In the short lull which followed, Scoones pulled out 49 Brigade so as to complete the 23rd Division and replaced it by his Corps Reserve, 32 Brigade of the 20th Division. The brigadier of 32 Brigade realizing the danger of encirclement from the west that threatened the old 49 Brigade position, decided to pull back to Bishenpur, where he commanded both the Tiddim road from the south and the Silchar track from the west.

It was well that he did so. Repulsed on the Tiddim road, the enemy, reverting to his favourite tactics, concentrated in the jungle west of the road, and made for the Bishenpur–Silchar track, hoping to break into the Imphal plain from the west. In the second week of April, Japanese patrols reached the track and encountered ours, but by then our 32 Brigade was in position covering Bishenpur. On the night of the 14th/15th April the Japanese 33rd Division, which had now received reinforcements, attacked towards Bishenpur, but was again repulsed. While this attack was developing the enemy succeeded in blowing up the bridge at Milestone 51 on the Silchar track. This was a three-hundred-foot suspension bridge over an eighty-foot deep gorge and its destruction made a complete break in the track. The demolition was a typical Japanese suicide operation. While skirmishing was going on in darkness near the bridge, three Japanese eluded the engineer platoon guarding it and placed the explosive charges. One Japanese jumped to his death in the gorge; the other two went up with the bridge. Having failed to dislodge our troops covering Bishenpur, the enemy then attempted to pass a strong column into the plain round the north-west of the village. Heavy fighting lasting several days resulted, and there were alarms and excursions throughout the area as Japanese detachments probed forward towards Imphal.

The threat from the west had caused Scoones to pull back the 17th Division, which had been operating north of Imphal, and give it the task of securing this line of approach. He also left under Cowan's Command 32 Brigade, now fully engaged and under heavy pressure. On the 19th April, just in time, the leading troops of the 17th Division began to arrive and went straight into action north-west of Bishenpur. To the south of that village the enemy occupied the straggling hamlet of Ninthoukhong in force. A first attempt by 33 Brigade to eject them failed on the 23rd April and so did a second by troops of the 17th Division two days later. In these attacks we suffered heavily and lost seven medium tanks. The valour of our troops had been equalled by the tenacity of the Japanese. Very bitter fighting continued and cost both sides many casualties; the Japanese advance into the plain was halted, but they held the village and remained a dangerous threat.

Again the fighting on the Silchar track west of Bishenpur flared up. The Japanese were under orders to break through at all costs and 32 Brigade from the 20th Division were under equally emphatic orders to prevent them. The savage struggle surged backwards and forwards along the track and across it. Our casualties were alarmingly heavy, especially in British officers of the Indian Army who could not fail to be picked out in such close fighting. These officers, many of them in their early twenties, made me proud to belong to the same army. One young lieutenant-colonel, commanding a battalion that had already lost three-quarters of its officers and who had himself been severely wounded in the stomach by grenade fragments, was again hit while leading his men. When asked why at this second wound he had not gone back at least as far as the Field Ambulance to have his wounds properly dressed, he admitted that the grenade in the stomach was a nuisance as it made getting about rather difficult, but he could still keep up with his men so there was no need to go back. As to the second wound, 'The bullet', he explained, 'has passed straight through my shoulder so it causes me no inconvenience!' No wonder the Japanese never broke through. When, a little time afterwards, I wished to promote this very gallant officer to command of a brigade, I found to my grief that he had been killed later in the battle.

Heavy attacks on the 26th April were thrown back, although our forward troops remained cut off from Bishenpur for some time until the track was reopened. Fighting continued, and, having failed in direct assaults, the enemy resorted to large-scale infiltration. In the first half of May, too, the Japanese Air Force made some of its rare appearances in strength. Besides bombing and strafing our airfields, about twenty-five Zeros attacked Bishenpur on the 6th and again on the 10th May. On the latter day our anti-aircraft guns took heavy toll and the visits were not repeated. The Japanese had managed to get into Potsangbam—the 'Pots and Pans' of the British soldier—only two miles south of

Bishenpur. Potsangbam, like many villages in the plain, was intersected by high banks and belts of trees, which hampered tank movement and provided admirable positions for defence. Heavy fighting by 32 and 63 Brigade was needed, with lavish air support from the fighters of 221 Group and the bombers of Strategic Air Force, before our men were able on the 15th May to winkle the enemy out. We lost twelve tanks and it was here for the first time the Japanese used their ten-inch mortars, one of which we captured. The situation around Bishenpur was still confused. The Japanese 33rd Division was living up to its reputation for being always dangerous, but it had suffered heavily. Deserters who came in reported that at the end of April one of its regiments was reduced from some three thousand to a strength of only eight hundred. The fact that even two or three deserters had appeared was a new and encouraging sign. We believed, however, that the division had since received further reinforcements and would again attempt something. It was not possible to say here, as we could on other sectors of the Imphal front, that the situation was stabilized.

On the Imphal–Kohima road, the last and most important of the Imphal spokes, the Japanese 31st Division had cut the road thirty miles north of Imphal on the 30th March. While some of the enemy turned north and moved on Kohima, a strong detachment of their 15th Division came south towards Kanglatongbi, where we had a large supply depot. 63 Brigade of the 17th Division, newly arrived in Imphal, after its arduous withdrawal from Tiddim, was at once rushed up to the north to stop any further hostile advance. The depot was rather hurriedly evacuated but, on the 9th April, a fighting patrol with armour escorted lorries removing arms and ammunition; then the Japanese occupied it and large quantities of such items as clothing fell into their hands. In a series of attacks between the 11th and 15th April, in which our tanks, much to the surprise of the enemy, forced their way on to a steep narrow ridge covering Kanglatongbi, the Japanese were deprived of their forward positions. Gradually the enemy were pushed back, fighting all the time, and on the 23rd April Kanglatongbi was raided. On the 7th May the brigade was relieved by the 5th Division, as part of the re-sorting that Scoones was carrying out to reassemble his divisions with their original brigades, and joined its own

331

17th Division, to take part in the even harder fighting already described about Bishenpur.

Briggs, as usual, wasted no time. His 5th Division now had with it 89 Brigade of 7th Division, which I had flown in to Imphal to compensate for his 161 Brigade that went so urgently to Dimapur. His original plan had been a wide right hook, with 123 Brigade from the Iril Valley to cut the main Kohima road well behind the Japanese; but the continual rain caused heavy floods which held this up, and, with his accustomed adaptability he abandoned it. Leaving 9 Brigade, on the east of the road, to hold Mapao Spur that had been such a hard nut to crack when he had attacked from the Iril Valley, he used 89 Brigade in a series of short hooks behind the enemy, while 123 Brigade, brought in by the direct route, pushed north along the main road. After brisk fighting, the supply depot, with a great deal of its original contents, was finally retaken on the 21st May and both brigades began to push north up the road. The situation on this spoke was well in hand.

By the middle of May 1944, therefore, my worst anxieties were over. At Kohima the Japanese had been thrown definitely on the defensive; on the Imphal–Kohima road the advance had begun; around Imphal, Scoones could feel assured that, unless the enemy were greatly reinforced, danger from the north and east was unlikely. The Japanese 15th Division had been well hammered and was losing cohesion. To the south and west, where the redoubtable 33rd Japanese Division was being reinforced from both their 53rd and 54th Divisions, there was still the prospect of a last attempt by the enemy. Our command of the air over the whole battlefield was virtually unchallenged and, thanks to this and to the daring of our patrols, the enemy supply system was falling into confusion. Most significant, too, the monsoon was almost upon us.

The more satisfactory turn that events had taken did not pass unnoticed in other circles than Fourteenth Army. The number of visitors at my headquarters notably increased. In the opening stages of the battle most of my visitors had been rather gloomy, a state of mind perhaps understandable, as India was full of rumours of disaster. Now, except that they believed Imphal was starving, they tended to optimism. They were particularly anxious that I should 'relieve Imphal before it was too late'.

Neither General Giffard nor I was as anxious as they appeared about Imphal's power to hold out; we knew that 4 Corps would shortly take the offensive. The supply situation there, though tight—certain rations had already been reduced—would not become difficult until about the middle of June and not desperate until at least a month later. I therefore stuck to my date, the date I had consistently given for the opening of the road, the third week in June. There were not wanting suggestions from many sources as to how the relief of Imphal might be hastened. They did not all show a practical realization of the problem. One staff officer, not on my headquarters, proposed that I should push an armoured column, escorting supply lorries, rapidly along the road to replenish Imphal 'as the Royal Navy had revictualled Malta'. I replied that to send a convoy of merchantmen, escorted by destroyers, down a canal both banks of which were held by the enemy and in which at frequent intervals there was no water—for the bridges on the road would be down—should not, I thought, appeal to naval tacticians, however gallant.

All the same, the time had now come for the Fourteenth Army to pass from the vigorous offensive-defensive it had been conducting to a full offensive on the Assam front. Although the road would have to be opened within the next five or six weeks, the immediate object of this offensive would be not so much the relief of Imphal—that would be incidental—but the destruction of the Japanese Fifteenth Army. No one could have been more eager to launch this offensive than my two corps commanders.

The problem for Scoones was whether to make this offensive on all sectors of his front simultaneously or to strike first on one and then on another. He would have found it difficult to stage large-scale attacks all round the plain because, not only was he limited in ammunition and I had cut him heavily in petrol to save air-lift, but the amount of animal transport that would be needed in such extensive operations could not be provided. The monsoon was also upon us. When this came, although it would handicap the enemy more than us, it would, as far as we were concerned, halve the rate of movement off the few main roads and make air supply hazardous. Our offensive could, therefore, be on only part of 4 Corps front. Scoones decided, with my full agreement, to launch it against the weakened Japanese 15th Division in the north and north-east, with his 5th and

333

20th Divisions, while he continued for the moment the wearing-down process on the Palel and Bishenpur fronts, with the 23rd and 17th Divisions. This plan had the advantage that not only did it attack the enemy in his weakest link, but by operating along the Kohima road it helped to reopen our line of communication to Dimapur.

On the Palel sector of 4 Corps front the relief of the 20th by the 23rd Division began on the 13th May and continued, a battalion at a time, until the end of the month. During this time both divisions refrained from major undertakings, although I Brigade of 23rd Division continued the clearing of the country east of Palel begun by the 20th Division. The 23rd Division had consolidated its positions, when, from the 16th to the 20th May, the Japanese fiercely attacked the Shenam Pass in the Palel area. Some of our defences were temporarily lost, but counter-attacks regained them all. The enemy resumed his attacks from the 9th to the 12th June and lost heavily, for no appreciable gains. At Shuganu attacks and counter-attacks alternated, and, as a result, the 23rd Division advanced slightly and improved its positions. We had been considerably inconvenienced during the first half of May by the intermittent shelling of the Palel airfield by Japanese medium artillery. The advance of I Brigade, which combed the hills for ten miles to the east of Palel, put a stop to this nuisance. It also disposed finally of the Jiffs of the Gandhi Brigade, large numbers of whom, urged by leaflets dropped from the air, hastened to surrender. Minor activity continued through-out the area, but very few Japanese patrols managed to evade our forward troops. One enemy party of an officer and seven other ranks did, however, as late as the night of the 3rd/4th July succeed in reaching Palel airfield. As a farewell gesture they destroyed eight parked aircraft with magnetic mines and Bangalore torpedoes, and escaped unscathed—a very fine effort.

In mid-May, on the Bishenpur sector the 17th Division was fighting hard to hold the Silchar track with 32 Brigade which it had borrowed from the 20th Division; its own 63 Brigade had just captured Potsangbam. It was typical of our 17th and the Japanese 33rd Divisions that at this time each of them was plotting a bold surprise stroke against the other.

The Japanese plan was, by a series of sudden thrusts at night, to pierce deep into the defences of Bishenpur and then to disrupt the 17th Division from within. Cowan's plan, instead of penetration, was a wide turning movement with one brigade to come in on the Tiddim road behind the 33rd Division and crush it between this brigade and his two brigades in the north. 48 Brigade of the 17th Division had been taken as Corps Reserve and from the 4th to the 8th May had been engaged in cleaning up enemy parties which had infiltrated north-east of Palel. It was thus well placed, when Scoones returned it to Cowan, to begin the turning movement.

On the 15th May, 48 Brigade set out. Moving rapidly across country, two days later it struck the Tiddim–Imphal road at Milestone 33 and dug in. During the 17th the Japanese hurriedly collecting all available troops, including those of the administrative services, twice attacked this road-block with tanks. They failed to dislodge our troops and suffered heavily. A more serious attack was delivered by troops of the 15th Japanese Division on the evening of the 19th, but this too was repulsed. In these attacks the enemy lost several tanks, three of which were captured and blown up, and left three hundred counted bodies in front of our positions, besides many more in the tall elephant grass. In accordance with the plan, 48 Brigade then moved north up the road to Moirang. The village was taken in two days' fighting and another road-block established. It was now that the other two brigades of the 17th Division should have come south on a wide front and driven the Japanese 33rd Division against 48 Brigade. Unfortunately the Japanese counter-attack had already been delivered, and 32 Brigade by itself failed to make enough progress. 48 Brigade was therefore ordered north and, fighting its way from village to village against considerable opposition, entered Potsangbam on the 30th May and thus rejoined the 17th Division. This turning movement had inflicted many casualties on the enemy at comparatively light cost to itself, but it had failed in its object—the destruction of the Japanese 33rd Division.

The reason for this failure was that on the night of the 20th/21st May the enemy had launched his penetration attacks on our Bishenpur positions. One strong column pierced our defences and attempted to seize a hill only a few hundred yards from 17th Division Headquarters. A small Indian piquet on the hill held out for several hours against fanatical assaults. Cowan stoutly refused to move his headquarters, but was compelled to call on the 20th Division for help, and also to divert troops who should have been co-operating with the 48 Brigade turning movement. Scoones hurriedly organized a small force, about a brigade in strength, under the headquarters of 50 Parachute Brigade, and with this reinforcement the enemy was first pinned down and then surrounded at the foot of the hill. In five days' hand-to-hand fighting they were almost annihilated, a few only escaping back into the hills to the west. Visiting the site of the battle a little later, I was struck by the way in which several Japanese gun crews had obviously been shot and bayoneted while serving their pieces in the open at point-blank range. While this was going on, another party of the enemy in darkness broke into 63 Brigade area at Bishenpur and entrenched themselves in the mule lines. Our troops surrounded them and, with the help of tanks in several days' fighting, wiped them out. The slaughter of Japanese, and, unfortunately, of mules also was heavy. Bull-dozers had to be employed to bury both.

It was here that some Gurkhas were engaged in collecting Japanese corpses from the corners inaccessible to bulldozers when one Japanese, picked up by a couple of Gurkhas, proved not to be as dead as expected. A Gurkha had drawn his *kukri* to finish the struggling prisoner when a passing British officer intervened saying, 'You mustn't do that, Johnny. Don't kill him!' The Gurkha, with his *kukri* poised, looked at the officer in pained surprise, 'But, sahib,' he protested, 'we can't bury him *alive!*'

A third, but minor, Japanese attempt was made in a suicidal attack on our guns just north of Bishenpur. The enemy party was killed to a man. These penetration attacks were remarkable in their boldness and in the desperation with which the enemy fought to the death. They failed in their object—to break through the 17th Division into the Imphal plain—and they lost heavily, but they did prevent us from reaping the results of our turning movement. There can have been few examples in history of a force as reduced, battered, and exhausted as the 33rd Japanese Division delivering such furious assaults, not with the object of extricating itself, but to achieve its original offensive intention.

The order, signed by Major-General Tanaka, on which the 33rd Division launched these forlorn hopes is worthy of reproduction, showing as it does the attitude of the Japanese commanders and the stark way in which they dealt with their troops:

> Now is the time to capture Imphal. Our death-defying infantry group expects certain victory when it penetrates the main fortress of the enemy. The coming battle is the turning point. It will denote the success or failure of the Greater East Asia War. You men have got to be fully in the picture as to what the present position is; regarding death as something lighter than a feather, you must tackle the task of capturing Imphal.
>
> For that reason it must be expected that the division will be almost annihilated. I have confidence in your firm courage and devotion and believe that you will do your duty, but should any delinquencies occur you have got to understand that I shall take the necessary action.
>
> In the front line, rewards and punishments must be given on the spot without delay. A man who does well should have his name sent in at once. On the other hand, a man guilty of any misconduct should be punished at once in accordance with the military code.
>
> Further, in order to keep the honour of his unit bright, a commander may have to use his sword as a weapon of punishment, exceedingly shameful though it is to have to shed the blood of one's own soldiers on the battlefield.
>
> Fresh troops with unused rifles have now arrived and the time is at hand—the arrow is ready to leave the bow.
>
> The infantry group is in high spirits: afire with valour and dominated by one thought and one thought only—the duty laid upon them to annihilate the enemy.
>
> On this one battle rests the fate of the Empire.
>
> All officers and men fight courageously!

Whatever one may think of the military wisdom of thus pursuing a hopeless object, there can be no question of the supreme courage and hardihood of the Japanese soldiers who made the attempts. I know of no army that could have equalled them.

To turn now to those sectors of 4 Corps front, to the east and to the north, on which we passed to the offensive. On the Ukhrul road and in the Iril Valley, the 23rd Division had kept up its pressure on the Japanese, and under cover of this, the change-over with the 20th Division from the Palel sector was carried out during the second half of May, and the front taken over by 80 and 100 Brigades. 32 Brigade of the 20th Division was still in the Bishenpur area with the 17th Division. No sooner were the troops of the 20th Division in their new positions covering Kameng and Nungshigum when it was discovered that the Japanese were building up their forces in the Sangshak area,

337

with the obvious intention of launching further attacks astride the Ukhrul road. A considerable concentration of mechanical and animal transport and increased movement was observed on their line of communication right back to the Chindwin. A good deal of sparring for position and heavy patrol activity now began on both sides. As part of the 4 Corps offensive, on 3rd June the 20th Division was ordered to advance with the object of destroying that part of the Japanese 15th Division east of the Iril River and of establishing a brigade group in Ukhrul.

The right wing of the division's offensive astride the Ukhrul road was at once counter-attacked by two reinforced regiments of the enemy 15th Division. The fight swung backwards and forwards as positions changed hands in local but severe fighting. Indeed at one time the Japanese pressure became so threatening that on the 11th June the 4 Corps reserve of two battalions was moved up. However, on the evening of that day, the 20th Division successfully retaliated, and by the 13th, all lost ground had been regained. During the following week our troops pushed back the enemy still farther and there were definite signs of his resistance cracking on both sides of the Ukhrul road.

Meanwhile the other brigade (80) of 20th Division had on the 7th June struck out north from Nungshigum up the Iril Valley and, in spite of the difficulties of continuous rain, flooded streams, and deep mud that made all movement a desperate labour, had reached a point twenty miles north of Imphal. From there it raided the main east and west lateral communications of the enemy. These raids were most successful and increased the already evident dislocation of the Japanese 15th Division. By the 20th June, 80 Brigade had pushed still farther north and was astride this enemy line of communication. The Japanese 15th Division had suffered heavily. Its supplies were dwindling rapidly, its replenishment routes were cut and now the monsoon made it impossible for the enemy to use other tracks. In this sector the 4 Corps offensive was, at the end of May, going well and with increasing momentum.

On the other northern approach to Imphal, the main Kohima road, we had also made progress. Here the 5th Division, after retaking Kanglatongbi on the 21st May, had pressed north on both sides of the road, aided by a series of short hooks coming in behind the Japanese positions. On the 3rd June 4 Corps orders

338

for intensifying the offensive were received, telling the 5th Division to destroy that part of the Japanese 15th Division west of the Iril River and to open the Kohima road to Karong, some thirty-five miles north of Imphal. Here we must leave the 5th Indian Division preparing in the rain and mud for a further push against the still stubborn but weakening Japanese 15th Division, and move to the other end of the road, to Kohima, where great things had been happening.

After our successes in mid-May and the short pause that followed for reorganization, the Kohima battle entered on its second phase. Although we now had the initiative, our situation was not a particularly good one. We had the town, or rather where the town had been, for the whole area in mud and destruction resembled the Somme in 1916; but the Japanese on the left were still holding the dominating Naga village position and the surrounding hills, while on the right they were along the great Aradura Spur. From both these, they commanded Kohima at close artillery range and, of course, dominated and closed the Imphal road. 4 and 5 Brigades of the 2nd British Division were, therefore, ordered to press on and capture the Japanese positions on both flanks. These were formidable tasks, but it was hoped that, after their defeat on the 13th May, the enemy resistance would be crumbling. These hopes were dashed The second phase of the battle was to be as hard fought as the first. The capacity of the ordinary Japanese soldier to take punishment and his fanatical will to resist were unimpaired. It was in the enemy higher control that weaknesses were first to appear.

During the five days of reorganization, units had some short periods of rest and 268 Indian Brigade took over part of the forward area. Patrolling and minor attacks by both sides were constant. On the 19th May, 5 Brigade made their final attempt to clear Naga village. After initial success the attack was held up by the usual skilfully concealed Japanese bunkers and by mortar fire from reverse slopes. Casualties were heavy and the attack was called off.

Meanwhile the headquarters of the 7th Indian Division, with its 114 Brigade, had arrived from Arakan and taken its own 33 Brigade and 161 Brigade of the 5th Division, both already in the area, under its command. On the 20th May, the division took over the left sector of the Kohima front, which included Treasury

Hill and Naga village. 268 Brigade held Garrison Hill, leaving the main Kohima–Imphal road sector and all to its right to the 2nd Division. 33 Brigade then took up the struggle for Naga village where the 2nd Division had left it. Between the 24th and 30th May an Indian battalion delivered two attacks on the centre of the enemy defences. Twice they occupied them but suffered terribly and were unable to hold on. Medium artillery was then brought up to fifteen hundred yards' range while a Gurkha battalion infiltrated on to Gun Spur in the enemy's rear and dug in. At the same time a British battalion skilfully infiltrated in thick mist on to Church Knoll, the highest point in Naga village; the enemy, who still held positions on the reverse slopes, had little fight left in him and did not counter-attack. 33 Brigade was then relieved by 114 Brigade which kept up the pressure until, on the 2nd June, the Japanese gave them best and abandoned Naga village, leaving large numbers of dead in the shattered bunkers and foxholes. Meanwhile 161 Brigade, north of the village, had also made considerable gains against opposition. The northern half of the Japanese position at Kohima was in fact now ours.

On the southern sector, as the enemy outposts fell back before them, the 2nd British Division moved to the attack on the formidable Aradura Ridge. On the 26th May, in spite of heavy rain, 6 Brigade reached a point half a mile west of the ridge. The next day 4 and 5 Brigades established themselves on a line running along the front of the northern face of the ridge to mile 48 on the main road, while 6 Brigade continued its climb to the Crest. During the afternoon, 4 and 5 Brigades came under very heavy fire from the reverse slope of Aradura Ridge and were compelled to withdraw to their start line. 6 Brigade under heavy fire had closed up by evening and were digging in south and west of the Crest. The advance up rain-sodden slopes for three thousand feet had been almost as much an ordeal as the enemy fire. Here, owing to the desperate defence of the enemy, his well-sited and concealed positions, and the extreme difficulty of movement on these slippery, steep jungle slopes, a position of stalemate developed.

The corps commander in these circumstances decided to transfer the attack from the western and northern slopes of the Aradura Ridge to the eastern, a method now made possible by our capture of Naga village. The redispositioning of the troops for the new attack, and the necessary patrolling and reconnaissance, occupied some days. The attack proper began with an attempt by 5 Brigade to take Big Tree Hill, some two thousand yards north-east of Aradura. This attack was held up towards evening, but was resumed next day with tank support and was successful. The whole brigade then advanced to the west of the road, cutting the Japanese supply routes to their troops high up on the Aradura Ridge. This was the end of the enemy resistance. As our troops advanced, the Japanese pulled out and the Aradura Ridge was ours.

The successes that the 2nd and 7th Divisions had been able to achieve in the last month had been helped in no small degree by the skilful and mobile operations of 23 L.R.P. Brigade in the very difficult and roadless Naga country on the left of 33 Corps. Through the jungle and over the hills, by tracks, passable only on foot or at the best by pack animals, the columns of the brigade, air supplied, thrust round the enemy flank and struck at his communications from the Chindwin. Apart from the enemy resistance, the mere physical exertion of slipping and sliding, heavily loaded, up and down these soaking tracks was a test that only tough, well-trained, and determined troops could have passed.

Columns circled the right flank of the Japanese main position and took Kharasom, a nodal centre of enemy supply tracks, about twenty-five miles due east of Kohima, against considerable opposition. The action of these columns achieved a threefold success. They cut the main northern Japanese supply route at the most awkward time for him, they constituted a threat to his rear whose strength he found it difficult to assess, and they stimulated the active support of the local tribesmen. These were the gallant Nagas whose loyalty, even in the most depressing times of the invasion, had never faltered. Despite floggings, torture, execution, and the burning of their villages, they refused to aid the Japanese in any way or to betray our troops. Their active help to us was beyond value or praise. Under the leadership of devoted British political officers, some of the finest types of the Indian Civil Service, in whom they had complete confidence, they guided our columns, collected information, ambushed enemy patrols, carried our supplies, and brought in our wounded under the

341

THE TIDE TURNS

heaviest fire—and then, being the gentlemen they were, often refused all payment. Many a British and Indian soldier owes his life to the naked, head-hunting Naga, and no soldier of the Fourteenth Army who met them will ever think of them but with admiration and affection.

It was clear now, at the beginning of June, that on the Kohima front the enemy was breaking and pulling out as best he could. While he still fought stubbornly as an individual, the cohesion of his units and the direction of his forces were obviously failing. The time had come to press on and destroy what was left of the 31st Japanese Division. The Supreme Commander, on the 8th June, issued a Directive that the Kohima–Imphal road was to be opened not later than mid-July, and I was grateful to him for not being stampeded by more nervous people into setting too early a date. I intended that the road should be open well before mid-July, but I was now more interested in destroying Japanese divisions than in 'relieving' Imphal.

So was Stopford. His plan was for the 2nd Division, with the bulk of the corps artillery and tank support, as his main striking force, to push down the Imphal road. The 7th Indian Division was to advance south-east in pace with the 2nd Division through the country to the left of the road, thereby protecting the flank of the British division and cutting off an enemy attempting to disengage to the east. Simultaneously, 23 L.R.P. Brigade was called on for further exertions in an advance on Ukhrul. This would exploit the special qualities of each formation; the hitting power of the 2nd Division group; the ability of the 7th Division to operate on pack transport away from roads, with little artillery support and on a lighter supply scale; and the extreme mobility of 23 Brigade on air supply. It was hoped that the 2nd Division would force the enemy off the road to their destruction at the hands of the 7th Division and 23 Brigade. In any other type of country, this should have been easy. 33 Corps now had superiority in numbers, artillery, and armour, and absolute domination in the air; but here the jungle, the hills, the single road, and, over all, the monsoon clouds and pelting rain made the development of our strength slow and its employment difficult. Small rear-guards were able to delay our advance while larger parties slipped away, but only in great disorganization and at the expense of abandoning much of their equipment.

342

On the 6th and 7th June, the 2nd Division, after mopping up in the Aradura area, pushed on towards the 55th Milestone on the Imphal road. There was some sharp fighting with Japanese rearguards before this was reached, and it is typical of the difficulties encountered that on the latter day the Royal Engineers with the leading troops had to clear three landslides and five road-blocks, pick up numerous mines, and replace two sizeable bridges. Luckily, in most instances the enemy, while he blew up the spans, neglected to destroy the abutments, and our engineers, who had shown the forethought to provide themselves with the original blueprints of all bridges, were able to calculate and carry well forward what was required for replacement of the spans.

The first serious opposition was met at Viswema at about Milestone 60. Here the enemy held a strong rearguard position on a great ridge across the road, covered by mine-fields, artillery, and interlocking machine-guns. Our leading troops were held up, and, during the evening of the 8th June, forced to fall back a little. Next day a strong flank-attack was directed against the ridge but, in the thick jungle, mist and rain, mistook one hill feature for another and missed its objective. The error, so close and broken was the country and so stiff the enemy resistance, was not discovered until the 11th June. The attack was then reorientated and went in finally on the 14th. It was successful, and many enemy were killed as they attempted to withdraw. About four miles were gained along the road, but then delay was again caused by a blown bridge. This and another enemy rearguard slowed the advance and only a few miles were covered, so that, by the evening of the 16th, the leading troops were halted about a mile short of Mao Songsang.

Mao Songsang was the crest of the watershed between Kohima and Imphal. It offered another—the highest—of the ridges running roughly at right angles across the road. All our information was to the effect that the Japanese intended to hold this very strong position in a final attempt to bar the advance of 33 Corps on Imphal. Viswema had been a covering position to be held for some days while Mao Songsang was prepared. During the 17th June, many enemy positions located on the Mao Songsang ridge were heavily bombarded by night, while encircling movements round both the east and west flanks were launched. To everyone's surprise the enemy abandoned his positions and slipped away.

343

This was, I think, the first time in the Burma campaign that such a position had been surrendered without a fight—a most significant change in Japanese mentality.

The 2nd Division pushed on hard at the heels of the enemy during the 18th and made its best advance up to that time—some fourteen miles—but was then held up a few miles short of Maram as the Sappers rebuilding a bridge were heavily mortared.

Meanwhile the 7th Division had advanced on a wide front east of the road, meeting at first no opposition, but pressing hard on the retreating Japanese, who abandoned guns, mortars, and equipment of all kinds. Contact was regained on the 6th June some ten miles south-east of Kohima, and, on the night of the 7th/8th, an indecisive attack was put in on a Japanese position on the Kekrima Ridge a few miles farther east. After a number of encounters among the broken hills, a detachment managed, after a nightmare march of some days through pathless and dripping jungle, to outflank the position and the enemy, having delayed our advance until the 13th, pulled out. On the 16th, the 7th Division reached and cut the main Japanese east-west supply route, the Tuphema–Khorasom–Somra track, at the same time threatening Mao Songsang from the rear. On the 17th they fought to within a mile of the village. There is no doubt that the action of the 7th Division decided the Japanese to abandon that position, which they could have expected to hold for a considerable time against attack from the north.

The maintenance of the 7th Division was now becoming a problem and, its immediate task completed, it was concentrated east of Mao Songsang to operate by fighting patrols against the remaining tracks used by the enemy and to round up stragglers. The main supply line of the division was first a twelve-mile twisting ribbon of mud along which jeeps skidded and slithered, their wheels spinning, and then along a pack animal and porter track.

All this time, the columns of 23 L.R.P. Brigade had pushed on wide to the east. Mountains and rain were their chief opponents, but in a series of small, scattered encounters in dripping jungle they ambushed bewildered Japanese mule trains, inflicted casualties, took prisoners, still rather a novelty, and completely dislocated the enemy line of communication. Again, the contribution of 23 Brigade to 33 Corps' advance was real and effective.

To my great annoyance at this time I was laid up in hospital in Shillong for some days, by an attack of malaria with some unpleasant complications. My annoyance was twofold. First, because I could not visit the front at this very interesting moment, and, second, because I had always preached that to get malaria was a breach of discipline. I had delivered what I felt to be some very effective exhortations to the troops on this theme and I felt now it would be a little difficult to repeat them. In fact, I had only proved on my own body the truth of my contention. Troops were forbidden to bathe after sunset and I had disobeyed my own orders. Returning very muddy and dirty late one evening I had washed in the open and been well and deservedly bitten by mosquitoes. However, I was attended while in hospital by my American Deputy Chief of Staff, Colonel Burton Lyons, and a small tactical headquarters. With his usual cheerful efficiency he soon had everything organized, and I was closely in touch from my bed with all that went on.

It was indeed going very well. Torrential rain was slowing up operations on all sectors of the Assam front, but in spite of it, by the 18th June, 4 Corps' 5th Division was, by attacks along the Kohima road and short hooks to each side of it, slowly approaching Kangpokpi. Although Scoones had ordered this division to advance to Karong, I had later told him not to let it go beyond Kangpokpi. I did this because reports were then coming in of considerable reinforcement of the Japanese forces south and east of Imphal. I expected, even at this stage, some further trouble from them, and I did not wish the 5th Division to get too far away from the 17th. Besides, 33 Corps was making satisfactory progress south. I should, I think, have been wiser instead to have urged Scoones to push on along the Kohima road as far and as fast as he could. I exaggerated the danger of renewed attacks on Imphal, and, by what was in effect slowing up the 5th Division, I allowed a considerable number of Japanese to escape between it and 33 Corps towards Ukhrul and the Chindwin. It was largely because of this that Ukhrul proved later to be so well defended.

By the 18th June, the spearheads of my two corps were some forty miles apart on the Kohima road, the 2nd Division approaching Maram and the 5th nearing Kangpokpi. Although he had given up the much stronger defences of Mao Songsang, the enemy attempted to hold against the 2nd Division another rearguard

345

position at Maram, about eight miles farther south. The weight of our artillery preparations and air-strike, combined with the rapidity of the 2nd Division's deployment and infantry attack, was such that, instead of holding for the ten days ordered, this rearguard was overrun and mostly destroyed in a matter of hours. This was the last serious attempt the enemy made to delay the advance of 33 Corps. It was now evident that the 31st Japanese Division was disintegrating and the enemy higher command no longer controlled the battle. In Karong, for instance, our troops captured the almost complete equipment, maps, and documents of the 31st Divisional Infantry Headquarters, and at Milestone 92, the double-span bridge, although prepared for demolition, was rushed before the enemy Sappers could fire the charges.

On the 22nd June, after a brush with fleeing enemy at the Kangpokpi Mission Station—a Japanese headquarters as it had been mine two years before—the tanks of the 2nd Division met the leading infantry of the 5th Division at Milestone 109. A convoy, which was waiting for this moment, was at once sent through, and 4 Corps had its first overland supply delivery since the end of March.

The Imphal–Kohima battle, the first decisive battle of the Burma campaign, was not yet over, but it was won.

CHAPTER XVI

PURSUIT

AT Fourteenth Army we were now out for much more than the mere expulsion of the invaders, or even their destruction. Evidence was coming in to me daily of the extent of the Japanese defeat, of their losses in tanks, guns, equipment, and vehicles, and of the disorganization of their higher command. In spite of the enemy reinforcements that were being sent into Burma, I calculated that after the defeats he had suffered on all three Burma fronts, Kawabe, the Japanese Commander-in-Chief, would desperately need time to regroup and refurbish his battered forces. There was no hope of any considerable amphibious operation against Southern Burma; we had not got the landing craft, and, even if we had, the Japanese battle fleet, now returned to Singapore, so dominated the Indian Ocean as to make such attempts too hazardous. I believed, more firmly than ever, in spite of the doubts of so many, that, if we were to regain Burma, it must be by an overland advance from the north. For the first time this now seemed a practical proposition. If we could drive the enemy over the Chindwin, establish bridgeheads on its east bank, and be ready to push a considerable force into the plains of Central Burma immediately the monsoon ended, we could strike Kawabe's main force in front of Mandalay before it had recovered. This now became the object of all our efforts.

General Giffard, with the same thought in mind, had already, in the second week of June, directed me:

(a) To re-establish communications between Dimapur and Imphal.

(b) To clear the Japanese from the area Dimapur–Kohima –Imphal plain–Yuwa–Tamanthi.

(c) To be prepared to exploit across the Chindwin in the Yuwa–Tamanthi area, i.e., along a stretch of some hundred and thirty miles of river.

347

The first of these three tasks Fourteenth Army had now completed; the second we were about to undertake; the third I had begun to plan as much more than mere exploitation. It was to be a second and final decisive battle. To fight it I must have, by the time the monsoon ended:

(i) The necessary divisions, replenished, trained, equipped, and placed ready to move.
(ii) A vastly improved system of communications to the Chindwin, an adequate land and air transport organization, and enough supplies collected well forward.
(iii) Bridgeheads, firmly held, across the Chindwin.

Fourteenth Army Headquarters, wholeheartedly backed by 11th Army Group, set to work at once on the first two of these requirements, which represented a colossal labour, especially for the administrative, technical, and training staffs and services. I snatched time from all this to visit most forward formations to congratulate them on what they had achieved and to spur them on, weary as they were, to an all-out pursuit. The troops responded magnificently. In spite of every difficulty of climate and terrain, the pursuit was pressed with relentless vigour right through the monsoon. I had asked for the impossible—and got it.

I allotted the task of clearing the enemy roughly north of the line Kangpokpi-Ukhrul and eastward to 33 Corps, and all south and west of that to 4 Corps. This was based on the existing positions of formations, but as it entailed a joint attack on Ukhrul by the 7th Division of 33 Corps and the 20th Division of 4 Corps, it was not a very good boundary. I soon realized this and transferred the 20th Division to 33 Corps, so that the attack on Ukhrul should be co-ordinated by one commander.

Ukhrul was the rallying point for the Japanese 15th and 31st Divisions and for all detachments and stragglers, east and north of Imphal. The enemy hoped that Mutaguchi's Fifteenth Army, shielded by the weather and the ground, would be able to receive a large part of the reinforcements that were coming into Burma at a rate of six or seven thousand a month. Optimistic even still, the Japanese Command seemed to have decided to fight on to keep a hold in Assam.

By the 1st July, Ukhrul was encircled. The 7th Division attacked from the west and north, the 20th Division closed in from the

348

south and south-east, and 23 L.R.P. Brigade repeated its old role
of cutting the escape routes to the east. Two days later, after
overcoming stubborn resistance on all lines of advance, our troops
were fighting in the outskirts of the village. Although these
enemy detachments had suffered heavily and stragglers and small
parties were daily being mopped up all over the area, it was not
until the 8th July that the whole of Ukhrul itself was finally in
our hands. Even then a considerable force of Japanese, cut off
on the Ukhrul–Imphal road, held out until the 14th, when it was
encircled and wiped out, all its guns and transport being captured.
What was left of the enemy 15th and 31st Divisions was now in
rapid retreat for the Chindwin, still covered by small but tenacious
rearguards.

The physical difficulties of the pursuit were great. A typical
entry from the War Diary of one of the brigades engaged reads:

*Hill tracks in a terrible state, either so slippery that men can hardly walk or
knee-deep in mud. Administrative difficulties considerable. Half a company
took ten hours to carry two stretcher cases four miles. A party of men without
packs took seven hours to cover five miles.*

On the day Ukhrul fell I transferred another division, the 23rd,
from 4 Corps to 33 Corps, and made Stopford responsible for all
operations east of the Manipur River. He was thus entrusted
with the pursuit on the Palel–Tamu axis, while 4 Corps, in
addition to cleaning up the Bishenpur track area and south of it,
where formed bodies of the enemy still held out, continued to
control the advance on the Tiddim road. It was on these two
routes into Burma, the Tamu road and the Tiddim road, that
fighting and interest now mainly centred.

Roberts's 23rd Division was deployed on a twenty-mile front
across the main Tamu road, facing Yamamoto's force of about
two Japanese regiments (brigades) made up from the 33rd and
15th Divisions, supported by a very depressed I.N.A. Division.
The main enemy strength was entrenched in the hills covering
the road. The weather was appalling; continuous heavy rain,
low clouds shrouding the hill-tops, and every little stream a
torrent. In such conditions, although constant pressure by patrols
and minor probing attacks forced the enemy to withdraw from
several features, preparations for the real advance were slow.
To speed matters up and give weight to the push, Stopford

reinforced the 23rd Division with a brigade (5) of the 2nd Division and 268 Indian Brigade.

Roberts's plan was a heavy assault by a brigade (37) in the centre, covered by all available corps artillery and some tanks, combined with an attack by another brigade (1) which was intended to roll up the enemy from the right and strike the road behind him. Meanwhile a third brigade (49) on the left was to carry out a wide turning movement through the hills to cut in on the main road about ten miles behind the Japanese positions. The attack on the centre was timed for the 24th July, but the left flank column, starting earlier, was well behind the enemy and had reached its objective on the road by the night of the 22nd/23rd July. Next day it found the Lokchao bridge position, a Japanese tank and artillery harbour, heavily defended. The attack on the centre made good progress against stiff resistance throughout the 24th and 25th, while that from the left also pushed on against less opposition. By the 27th the right flank brigade had completed its turning movement and made contact with the left at the Lokchao bridge, from which the enemy withdrew. He had suffered considerable losses in men, guns, vehicles, and some tanks and tractors.

I visited the 23rd Division on this day and reached the forward troops, by jeep and on foot, only with difficulty. Whole sections of the road had vanished in landslides; the troops, soaked and filthy, were struggling forward across steep slopes through mud with the consistency of porridge half-way up to their knees. It was campaigning at its hardest, but everyone was cheerful. The litter of the Japanese rout was everywhere; their corpses shapeless lumps in the mud. Luckily, our casualties had not been heavy and devoted efforts were being made to get them back by bearers or jeep ambulances where the road was possible. Their sufferings from wet, cold, and jolting during these interminable journeys were grim, but those I spoke to all assured me in their various languages that they were all right, when quite obviously several of them were, alas, far from it. It struck me then, as so often, that I had very brave soldiers. So had the enemy. A Japanese officer with a horribly shattered leg was brought back roughly bandaged in a jeep ambulance. A British officer was shocked to see the wounded man's hands were bound. He stopped the jeep, and ordered the Indian guards to untie him. They explained that the prisoner had several times torn the bandages from his leg. Even now, with his hands tied, he had attempted to rip them off with his teeth. The Japanese soldier, even in disaster, retained his one supreme quality—he chose death rather than surrender.

After their obstinate defence astride the road, the surviving Japanese, abandoning much equipment, escaped by jungle paths, and a brigade (5) of the 2nd Division passed through to occupy Tamu without opposition.

It was always a disappointment in the Burma campaign to enter a town that had been a name on the map and a goal for which men fought and died. There was for the victors none of the thrill of marching through streets which, even if battered, were those of a great, perhaps historic, city—a Paris or a Rome. There were no liberated crowds to greet the troops. Instead, my soldiers walked warily, alert for booby traps and snipers, through a tangle of burnt beams, twisted corrugated iron, with here and there, rising among the squalid ruins, the massive chipped and stained pagodas and chinthis of a Buddhist temple. A few frightened Burmans, clad in rags, might peer at them and even wave a shy welcome, but at the best it was not a very inspiring business and more than one conquering warrior, regarding the prize of weeks of effort, spat contemptuously.

In Tamu he had other reasons for spitting. The place was a charnel house, of a macabre eeriness hard to describe. Five hundred and fifty Japanese corpses lay unburied in its streets and houses, many grouped grotesquely around stone Buddhas which looked blandly out over the sacrifices huddled at their feet. Dozens more, over a hundred, lay in indescribable filth, dying of disease and starvation, among the corpses. It was not only in Tamu itself that such evidences of the collapse of the enemy administration were found. Along all routes leading to the Chindwin, whether from Ukhrul Imphal, Tamu, or on the Tiddim road, were found such grisly reminders of the fate of a retreating army. More than once, small field hospitals were found where the patients lay on their stretchers, all dead, neatly shot through the head, killed by their comrades who had no means of evacuating them and preferred this—as no doubt the patients themselves did—to their capture. From these and other signs it was increasingly clear that the Japanese Fifteenth Army had suffered an even more disastrous defeat than we had at first realized. The likelihood of our achieving our objects by the end of the monsoon was promising.

With the capture of Tamu, the time had come to press on with the regrouping and resting of my formations, which General Giffard had wisely urged on me and which I agreed was necessary if I was to be ready for a major offensive within a few months. I was at this time anxious about the health of the troops. They had endured a great deal and showed it. The infantry especially, who as ever had borne the brunt of the fighting and the worst of the hardships, were very fined down. They were too thin to my mind, a state which was not improved by the jaundice yellow of all our complexions as a result of the daily dose of mepacrine. They were cheerful enough and pleased with themselves, as well they might be, but as fighting died down, sickness rose. I told my doctors to select several battalions, British, Indian, and Gurkha, who had come out to rest, and give them a mass examination. The results perturbed me. A very large proportion of men were suffering from malnutrition, the disease that had killed thousands of Japanese. It was not that our men had not had enough to eat. Although ration scales had at times been lowered, as at Imphal, and at others had been irregular, there had never, thanks to the efficiency of the supply and transport services and the extreme devotion of the air forces, been a serious shortage. Unavoidably, however, there had been depressing monotony in the diet and practically no fresh meat or vegetables. In addition, I was informed, the constant mental strain of fighting in the jungle had of itself reacted on the metabolism of the men's bodies, so that often food passed through them without the normal amount of nourishment being extracted from it. Obviously rest, freedom from strain, a more varied diet, and some amenities were imperative if these formations were to be keyed up for the winter campaign; and they would have to be, for most of them would be engaged in it.

4 Corps Headquarters had been in action much longer and had had a harder time than 33 Corps. I was anxious that it should be taken right out and given a rest, so on the 31st July it closed down in Assam, and 33 Corps took over the whole Central front. During August, 4 Corps Headquarters returned to India.

General Giffard had sent me the 11th East African Division under Major-General Fowkes, which impressed me very favourably when I inspected it. I thought, like the West African Division, it had too many British Officers and N.C.O.s and I was given the same reasons why they were necessary. Again I was not convinced, but, as before, this was no time to make changes which at best could now only be long term. This division I gave to Stopford to replace the 23rd Division which was pulled out to recuperate in India. The 17th Division also gathered at Imphal en route for India. The 2nd and 7th Divisions were concentrated on the road north of Imphal and about Kohima, and the 20th Division south of Imphal, where, beyond a little mild patrolling to round up solitary, moribund Japanese, these divisions could devote themselves to recuperation. 3 Commando Brigade was returned to Arakan for projected amphibious operations. This gave 33 Corps five divisions, a couple of infantry brigades, and a tank brigade to command, but as only two divisions and one brigade were actively engaged the burden was mainly an administrative one. I should have liked to have got more divisions to India. That was a real change, but time and the limited railway capacity forbade it. However, most men of the remaining divisions were given leave, while the army and corps staffs, and above all the divisions themselves, did remarkably well in producing amenities and amusements out of our very limited resources. I am afraid our armies in Europe and North Africa would have smiled at what seemed not too bad to us, but the troops realized the difficulties and made the best of what we could get them. Health, appearance, and general well-being improved weekly.

On the 6th August, my fifty-third birthday, I sent orders to Stopford, now in control of all operations on the Central front:

(i) To pursue the enemy with not less than one brigade group on each of the routes:
    (a) Imphal–Tiddim–Kalemyo–Kalewa.
    (b) Tamu–Kalewa.
    (c) Tamu–Sittaung.
(ii) To occupy Sittaung and deny the Chindwin to enemy shipping.
(iii) If opportunity offered, to seize Kalewa, and prepare to establish a bridgehead.

353

In accordance with these instructions the 11th East African Division, having relieved the 23rd Division, began a two-pronged advance from Tamu towards Sittaung on the Chindwin, thirty-six miles by road to the east, and into the Kabaw Valley on Kalemyo, some hundred miles south.

This was the East African introduction to war in Burma; they signalized it by several successes in minor encounters. On the 16th August, their leading brigade (25) crossed the Yu River, then in high flood and very rapid. On the 18th they had their first serious clash, and drove a Japanese detachment from its position. For the rest of the month they advanced slowly, partly because of the need constantly to brush aside the resistance of small rearguards, but mainly because of the difficulties of the track. On the 4th September, Sittang was occupied and found to be a second Tamu. Among some hundreds of corpses only two men were living, one Japanese and one I.N.A. sepoy. On the 10th September, a small bridgehead was formed on the east bank opposite Sittang. The enemy was too disorganized to counter-attack, but many clashes took place as African patrols from this bridgehead pushed out and met enemy ones.

The main body of the East African Division entered the Kabaw Valley, of ill omen. I have heard it said that in Burma we often selected particularly disease-ridden spots in which to fight the Japanese because our scientific safeguards against malaria, scrub typhus, and other jungle ills were so much better than theirs. I certainly never deliberately did this. When we were retreating in 1942, and our men were dispirited, undernourished, and exhausted, our sickness rate was vastly higher than the enemy's; when they in turn retreated in 1944 and their men were in that state, the position was reversed. But at most periods of the campaign, even after our anti-malaria discipline had improved and our superior remedies were available, I do not think our casualties from sickness were any lower than theirs. I always believed—and this I confirmed later by the observation of large bodies of Japanese prisoners—that both British and Indian troops were more susceptible to these diseases than were the enemy. I always acted on that belief, and, had I been able, would have fought the Japanese in the healthiest, and not the most disease-ridden, areas I could find. We entered the Kabaw Valley because it was the most practicable route for our purpose. I was therefore very interested to be told that, while East Africans are by no means immune from malaria, they are much more resistant to it than either Europeans or Indians, and that when they do develop the disease its attacks are less virulent. It was partly in the hope that this was true that I gave the East Africans to Stopford for the Kabaw Valley advance. Whether there is scientific support for this theory, I think those who held it can claim that it received considerable confirmation. The African malarial casualties were not light, but I doubt if any other of our troops would have kept them as low.

The leading brigade (26) of the 11th East African Division was approaching Htinzin in the Kabaw Valley and was thirty miles south of Tamu on the 21st August 1944. It had met with little opposition, but had picked up a great deal of abandoned enemy equipment, including lorries, several of which it put in running order, although this was only in the pious hope that when the monsoon ended they might be used on the road. The rate of advance was not fast if judged by the map, but on the ground it represented a real achievement. At this time all available air supply for the division was wanted on the Sittang axis and consequently the Kabaw road had to be made up to a jeep standard, often by corduroying it, as the troops advanced. At least two large bridges and innumerable small ones had to be built, often only to be washed away by spates. Rain fell without stopping for three weeks at an average of five inches a day. Mud, water, mosquitoes, and back-breaking labour were the order of the day.

The first serious resistance in the Kabaw Valley was encountered on the 27th September when a strong enemy position blocking the road was carried by assault, a number of the enemy killed, and the advance resumed to Yazago forty-five miles south of Htinzin.

On the 11th September, a battalion had been pushed out to the east from the road to work through the hills and take Mawlaik, a small but valuable river port on the Chindwin. This battalion was held up by enemy covering the approaches to the town, and after three weeks had made no further headway towards its objective. Other units of its brigade (21) were then moved up and on the 20th October attacked the positions covering Mawlaik from the north. This attack failed, but another, next day, had more success, although, in spite of excellent air strikes, the Japanese resistance was not fully overcome, and they still clung to the tops of the vertical cliffs which are a feature of the local landscape. It was not until the 10th November, after a series of small but fiercely contested assaults in which the enemy suffered considerably, that Mawlaik was at last in our hands. Under cover of this fighting, the 1st Battalion of the Assam Regiment, from 268 Brigade on loan to the 11th Division, slipped across the Chindwin, and, by vigorous patrolling, established our second bridgehead on the east bank opposite Mawlaik. The East Africans then pushed south along the west bank from Mawlaik towards Kalewa.

Meanwhile with the help of many accurate strikes by the R.A.F., the main advance in the Kabaw Valley had, in spite of increasing opposition, by the 2nd November, reached a point on the road about twelve miles from Kalemyo. Here it struck, as expected, a strong Japanese position, much photographed from the air. The leading brigade became involved in front of this, but the next brigade by-passed it and, on the 12th, reached a point only five miles from Kalemyo. From here it shelled the routes passing through the town and next day sent out patrols which cut into the Kalemyo–Fort White road, just west of Kalemyo. Here one of these patrols made contact with a patrol from the 5th Indian Division advancing on the Tiddim road and the two, sepoys and askaris together, entered the town.

This joint entrance might at first sight appear a dramatic and fitting ending to the parallel advance of these two fine divisions, but in hard fact it would have been better had the 11th Division reached Kalemyo while the Japanese were still locked with the 5th Division on the Tiddim road. I could not, however, reproach the 11th Division for slowness, as I had seen for myself the climatic and natural obstacles that, more than the enemy, delayed them. Their advance was a great achievement, which a year before would almost universally have been proclaimed impossible.

Now to turn to the simultaneous advance of the 5th Indian Division, which had been going on in conditions equally difficult and against stronger opposition. During July, after its drive north to link up with the 2nd Division from Kohima, the 5th Division, turning about, joined the 17th Division in pushing back the enemy astride the Tiddim road south of Imphal. By the third week of

356

July the Japanese, after determined resistance, were driven out of the last portion of the Imphal plain in which they had a footing, and began their long withdrawal. The Japanese retreat on the Tiddim road was under better control than on any other part of the front. The rearguards of the reinforced 33rd Japanese Division which had been made up to ten battalions, a tank regiment, artillery, and engineer units, only withdrew under pressure, stubbornly contesting ridge after ridge astride the road. Although our troops inflicted serious losses on them, including the capture of most of their tanks, and the climatic condition were of the hardest, there was less evidence of disorder, such as littered the tracks of the other enemy columns. Again the 33rd Japanese Division was living up to its reputation of being the toughest division in Burma.

By the end of July the 17th Division was on its way to a well-earned rest. It had been actively engaged since December 1941, that is, for three years and eight months, and almost all that time in direct contact with the enemy. A record, I should think.

On the 18th July, the 5th Division, relieving the 17th, had taken over operations on the Tiddim road, and by the 31st its leading brigade (9) had reached a point forty-two miles south of Imphal. Many of the Japanese rearguard positions were of great natural strength and all were stubbornly defended, but our troops ejected the enemy from each in turn. The method followed a pattern. As soon as the position was located, it was shelled and strafed from the air. While this preparation was going on, a wide outflanking movement would be launched through the hills to strike behind the enemy. Then, in co-ordination with this, a frontal attack with tank support would be launched. In this way, by the 23rd August, the brigade had reached the 85th milestone from Imphal. It had advanced at an average rate of two miles a day. That alone—with the road disappearing before and behind it in landslides—would have been no mean achievement, without opposition, but it had had some hard fighting. It had counted over 300 Japanese dead, besides many graves, captured 18 prisoners, 11 tanks, 15 field guns, 19 mortars, 33 machine-guns, and over 200 lorries. All this would have been impossible without the incredibly efficient air support the division enjoyed even in the worst weather. Our troops for their part suffered the inevitable casualties of a monsoon

357

campaign. The figures are instructive. This brigade in 26 days had only 9 killed and 85 wounded, but lost 507 from sickness.

The engineer resources of the Fourteenth Army did not permit both the Tiddim road and the Kabaw Valley route to be made and maintained at the same time. I had already decided in favour of the Kabaw Valley, which was not only a much easier road to make but, with fewer curves and none of the terrible gradients of the other, was obviously much better suited to the heavy traffic expected in the dry weather. The result of this decision, however, was the abandonment of the Tiddim road as a line of communication; it was allowed to fall away behind the troops as they advanced. As it was impossible in the hills to build any landing strips, the 5th Division became completely dependent on air dropping for all its requirements. It also relied for direct fire support largely on the fighter bombers of 221 Group, R.A.F. What this regular air supply and support meant in skill and strain to the aircrews only those who have flown among these shrouded hills can judge. Yet throughout the whole of this monsoon the fighters of Air Marshal Vincent's 221 Group flew over our troops every single day. I do not think such devotion has ever been surpassed in any air force, and I doubt if it has been equalled.

One result of the decision to abandon the road was that casualties could not be evacuated. They must either accompany the division or be dumped in native villages, in either event an unhappy prospect. I was particularly worried about the victims of scrub typhus, a disease that was proving lamentably fatal without really good nursing, so I had asked for a few nurses to volunteer to accompany the division. The only difficulty was to pick the handful required from the numbers who eagerly volunteered for what could only be a dangerous and hard task. These devoted women not only saved many lives, but were a morale-raiser to the whole division.

It was at this period that a formation that had, up to now, been lurking discreetly in the wings, took the stage in no mean part. The Lushai Brigade, it will be remembered, had been hurriedly improvised from certain spare Indian battalions and some local levies to prevent Japanese infiltration through the Lushai Hills. Its headquarters, under Brigadier Marindin, whom I had known well as a battalion commander in the Retreat of 1942, was at Aijal, in roadless country over a hundred miles south-west of

Imphal. As an orthodox infantry brigade it left something to be desired. There had been very little indeed in the way of equipment or transport to give it; its signals were improvised, it had neither engineers nor artillery. I am told, though I do not vouch for this, that when it went into action, so scant was the equipment of its headquarters, that staff officers could be heard politely saying to one another, 'May I please have the map for a moment?' And that when the brigade was not in action 'the' map served as cloth to the brigader's camp table. It certainly had vermouth stains on it on the one occasion I used it! But what it lacked in equipment the Lushai Brigade made up in initiative.

As the Japanese showed no signs of coming to the Lushai Brigade, I thought that the brigade had better go to them. At the end of June I gave Marindin an order which might have made many a brigadier look a little doubtful, but which seemed to please him mightily. It was: '*Completely to dislocate Japanese traffic on the road Tiddim–Imphal from Tiddim northwards, and render it useless to the enemy as a line of communication.*' I told him that he could not rely on air support. I would give him what I could, but it would not be much. If he got into trouble, no one could help him; he would be too far away. And, as generals always do on these occasions, I wished him luck. I placed the brigade under the 5th Division with which they were soon in close co-operation.

The brigade of four Indian battalions, the Lushai and Chin Levies and some 'V' Force detachments, was scattered over a wide area. It took time to collect them, organize their transport, most of it local mules and porters, and start on the march to the Tiddim road. Marindin's plan was to deploy the brigade on as wide a front as possible, giving each battalion a sector with orders to raid the road at least once a day somewhere in that sector. He spread three of his battalions along the west of the road from Milestone 44 to Tiddim, not continuously, but with gaps of from ten to fifteen miles between the sectors. With his fourth battalion —my old friends the Bihar Regiment from Ranchi, who were so proud of their womenfolk—and the Levies he improved on my orders. He launched them on a drive into the Chin Hills to capture the local capitals, Falam and Haka, fifty miles south of Tiddim, and to rouse the Chins, who in the main had remained loyal throughout their occupation by the Japanese. The Chin Levies were overjoyed at the prospect of liberating their own

THE TIDE TURNS

country. They took with them their families, rather like the Children of Israel trekking out of Egypt, dumping them in their own villages as they recaptured them one by one. The whole brigade when deployed was thus operating vigorously against the Japanese line of communication and rear areas on a front of over one hundred miles.

The two most northerly battalions were in position by the end of July after most difficult marches of eighty and one hundred and twenty miles, over mountains five thousand feet high, and across flooded rivers. They wasted no time. The Japanese soon found movement by day or night was harried, not only from the air, but by stealthy ambushes and sudden bursts of fire. They were compelled heavily to piquet the road. At least five or six hundred Japanese were tied up in this static defence; over two hundred were killed, many wounded, and numbers of vehicles destroyed; all at the cost of twenty or thirty casualties to our troops.

It was, however, Marindin's third battalion, which, getting into position somewhat later, made the biggest bag. This battalion concentrated on a small sector of eight miles where the Japanese road ran on the east bank of the Manipur River through a precipitous gorge. Our men on the west bank, protected by the raging torrent, could keep this road under constant fire at ranges from one hundred and fifty to five hundred yards. The enemy could not build a diversion to his road through the gorge, and, unless he staged a major operation to bridge the river elsewhere and send a considerable force to deal with the Lushai Brigade, he faced two alternatives. Either he could run the gauntlet or, abandoning his vehicles, take to the hill-sides to the east. This battalion, keeping the road under Bren and mortar fire day and night, accounted for several hundred Japanese and destroyed over one hundred vehicles. Lorry traffic on this sector ceased.

Helped by these actions of the Lushai Brigade, the main advance on the Tiddim road was taken up by a fresh brigade (161) of the 5th Division. Its operations followed the pattern of the brigade it relieved, continually ejecting Japanese rearguards from their positions by air strikes, flanking hooks, and frontal attacks, bridging streams and clearing landslides. On the 14th September the leading troops reached the west bank of the Manipur River, a hundred and twenty-six miles from Imphal.

Evans, who commanded the 5th Division, had expected that

the enemy would put up a strong resistance at the Manipur River, which now, in flood, was a most formidable obstacle. All available intelligence supported him in this belief. He had, therefore, obtained Stopford's agreement to sending back his rear brigade (123), not yet committed, by lorry through Imphal to Shuganu and thence down the east bank of the Manipur River, to come in behind any enemy barring the advance of the 5th Division. The brigade, with a mountain battery and a field company of Sappers and Miners, collected at Shuganu in the first week of September and moved south. It was completely on a pack basis and maintained entirely by air. By the 14th September, as the 5th Division was reaching the river, this brigade, pushing on rapidly, seized the high ground opposite it on the east bank. The enemy, realizing that he was in imminent danger of being cut off, contented himself with shelling our crossing place, and gave up the defence of the river line.

Even with the Japanese driven from its banks, the crossing of the Manipur was no easy operation. The river, one hundred yards wide, was in full spate, flooding through its gorge at a speed of ten to twelve knots, hurling itself against boulders in fountains of spray, and bringing down tree trunks in full career. Its roar, audible for miles, was like that of a great football crowd. Not without difficulty the engineers got a rope across, and a flying bridge—a ferry attached to a cable—was built. The first boat to attempt the crossing was capsized by the fury of the stream. All its occupants were lost. But the cable held and next day, the 16th September, the ferry was working, though a crossing was still a hazardous and nerve-testing experience. Ferrying, in these conditions, was a slow business, but by the 19th a road-block had been placed behind the Japanese rearguard whose shelling, particularly that of some 155-mm. guns, had been thoroughly unpleasant. Next day the rearguard was attacked. An attempt by the enemy to break through the road-block after dark failed, and they took to the jungle, abandoning ninety dead and the objectionable 155-mm. guns.

Without pause, Warren who had replaced Evans, a victim of climate and exhaustion, in command of the division, pushed on for Tiddim with the troops already across, while tremendous efforts were made to get the remainder of the division over the river as the road behind it collapsed in mud and landslides. The leading brigade (123), in spite of the difficulty of the country, advanced on a wide front so as to overlap the frequent but small Japanese rearguards. By the 1st October our troops were in the hills some miles due east of Tiddim, in contact with the enemy who still covered the town and held the main road approach. The advance was a succession of minor engagements in which the Japanese 33rd Division still fought well and put in frequent counter-attacks. The outflanking tactics of our troops paid, and even the formidable 'Chocolate Staircase' position was turned in this way and abandoned by the enemy after little resistance. Chocolate Staircase was the name given to the Tiddim road where in seven miles it climbed three thousand feet with thirty-eight hairpin bends and an average gradient of one in twelve. The road surface was earth, and marching men, animals, and vehicles soon churned it into ankle-deep mud. The hill-side, and with it the road itself, often disappeared in thunderous landslides; then every available man had to turn to with pick and shovel to shape a track again. No soldier who marched up the Chocolate Staircase is ever likely to forget the name or the place. The enemy made several more desperate attempts to block the road to Tiddim but the constant threats to his line of retreat, his fear of losing guns and vehicles, the accuracy of 221 Group's air strikes even in this country, and the unquenched *élan* of our troops in direct attack had their effect. Tiddim was occupied on the 17th October.

As 'Vital Corner' and Kennedy Peak were approached the Japanese resistance became more stubborn. The 8,800-foot Kennedy Peak was the highest point passed on the Tiddim-Kalemyo road, and there they were expected strongly to bar our way. To outwit their defence, Warren staged two wide turning movements. One, on the right, by a brigade (161), aimed at the road junction two miles south of Fort White; the other, on the left, by a battalion to strike into the Kalemyo road in the Stockades area, some ten miles east of the Fort. The brigade reached its objective, but the battalion was held up in the hills about twelve miles east of Kennedy Peak. While these flanking moves were taking place, the remainder of the division with its tanks pushed steadily up the main road. Its leading brigade (9) sent a battalion in a close left hook round the mountain, to cut the road just south of the Peak, where it established a road-block.

In several days' fighting and after very accurate softening up by the R.A.F. and Mitchell bombers of the U.S.A.A.F., the enemy positions covering Vital Corner, well dug and backed by concealed artillery, began to give way to our frontal assault. On the 3rd November resistance crumbled. The Japanese, attempting to withdraw by the main road, ran into the battalion of 9 Brigade. After frantic and costly efforts to force a way through, they broke up into small parties and, abandoning everything except their small arms, took to the surrounding jungle. Our troops and tanks took heavy toll as they followed up the disorganized enemy, many of whom were intercepted by the battalion which had been sent on the wide left turning movement. On the 4th November, Kennedy Peak was ours. The Japanese losses were heavy and their dispersal almost complete, yet as our advance continued they were able temporarily to throw it back by a counter-attack on the night of the 6th. This was their last effort. On the 8th, Fort White was entered by our patrols and junction made, as planned, between 9 and 161 Brigades. A rapid advance followed against light opposition and in the afternoon of the 13th November, as already related, a patrol of the 5th Indian Division met a patrol of the 11th East Africa Division and together entered a deserted Kalemyo.

The 5th Indian Division had completed a remarkably fine feat of arms and endurance in its advance from Imphal to Kalemyo. The carefully checked figures for enemy casualties, excluding those inflicted by the Lushai Brigade—and only fresh bodies on the ground were allowed to count—were 1,316 killed and 53 prisoners. The division's own battle casualties in the same period were 88 killed, 293 wounded, and 22 missing. The contrast is a fair measure of the skill this experienced Indian division had now reached in the art of killing Japanese. The division, after clearing its area of enemy stragglers, collected in Kalemyo, and was flown out to refit in the Imphal plain.

The Lushai Brigade throughout had maintained its galling pressure on the enemy rear areas. By mid September, its activities had been extended and the Lushai Scouts and Levies were operating towards the main Tiddim–Fort White road and even east of Fort White. In October, the brigade was given the role of protecting the right flank of the 5th Division in its advance and of breaking into the Myittha Valley with the ultimate object of seizing and holding Gangaw, seventy-five miles south of Kalemyo.

363

This was something of a tall order for the brigade, but, unperturbed, it proceeded on a hundred-mile front, ambushing, raiding, infiltrating, to carry it out. On the 18th and 19th October, it occupied the Chin capitals of Falam and Haka amid great rejoicings and reunions of the loyalist tribesmen, not a little enlivened by the free distribution of rice and stores captured from the Japanese.

The small enemy detachments in the Chin Hills withdrew, skirmishing, as the columns of the brigade advanced eastward. On the 15th November, our troops reached the Myittha River, forty-five miles south of Kalemyo, but a Japanese detachment still held Gangaw and there were many small parties and stragglers scattered along the river. The Levies and Scouts pushed on eastwards and, by the end of November, were on the Chindwin, twenty miles south of Kalewa, and raiding the east bank. The main force of the brigade pushed south up the Myittha Valley towards Gangaw. By mid-December, when greater events were impending, the Lushai Brigade had patrols on the east bank of the Chindwin, had cleared the whole country west of the Myittha River, and was closing in on the last Japanese foothold in the Myittha Valley at Gangaw.

There is no doubt that the enterprise and dash of this improvised and light-hearted brigade was a very real contribution to the pursuit to the Chindwin. It had operated for six months on pack transport, supplemented by an unavoidably meagre air supply, across two hundred miles of jungle mountains, against the enemy flank and rear. Considering the paucity of its equipment and resources, it gave one of the most effective and economical examples of long-range penetration.

Another independent brigade which had played a less spectacular, but none the less helpful, part was 268 Indian Infantry Brigade, under Brigadier Dyer, a commander whose resource and cheerfulness became renowned throughout the army. Formed originally as a motorized brigade to work with armoured formations, all its regular battalions were withdrawn in August 1944, and it was reconstituted with one Nepalese and three newly-raised Indian infantry battalions, all then untried in battle. Its task was, during September, to clear the wild jungle country on the west bank of the Chindwin north of Sittaung of Japanese patrols and Indian National Army stragglers. In combing out this area, it uncovered several concealed Japanese supply and arms dumps, from which the enemy hoped to support themselves when, as they frequently attempted to do, they re-infiltrated across the river. At the beginning of October, 268 Brigade also took over from a brigade of the 11th East African Division the Sittaung area itself, including the newly-established bridgehead. Our patrols on the east bank then pushed deeper into the screen that the Japanese were now building against our penetration, and enlarged the bridgehead.

While all these diversions on the flanks had been going on, the main advance of the 11th East African Division to establish a bridgehead across the Chindwin at Kalewa continued. The road to Kalewa enters the gorge of the Myittha River five miles east of Kalemyo, and the Japanese held the entrance in some force. A road-block was placed behind the enemy position and maintained in spite of counter-attacks. In a series of assaults, supported most accurately by air strikes, the Africans gradually forced their way through the defile against stubborn opposition. On the 2nd December they entered Kalewa which had been reduced to ruins, largely by our air bombardment, and was deserted.

Meanwhile a brigade (21) of the 11th Division, moving south from Mawlaik, scattered a Japanese detachment that attempted to bar its path, and, on the 24th November crossed the Chindwin on tarpaulin rafts, about twelve miles north of Kalewa. It then bore down on the enemy holding the east bank opposite Kalewa.

The time had now come to establish the permanent bridgehead. Fowkes, commanding the 11th Division, planned with the help of his brigade already on the east bank to put another brigade (25) over the river just north of Kalewa and then to pass his third brigade (26) through to seize all tactical features within artillery range of the bridgehead. The crossing took place on the night of the 3rd/4th December according to plan. The enemy's opposition developed during the day and he shelled the ferries, but the bridgehead was firmly established by nightfall. Next night the follow-up brigade began crossing and pushed on down the Pyingaing road. Stiff opposition was encountered. Throughout the establishment of the bridgehead R.A.F. fighter bombers gave constant and close support which, in several instances, led to the Japanese abandoning positions even before our troops attacked them. It was not until the 8th December that the enemy, under pressure from both the bridgehead itself and the brigade coming down from the north, began to give way, and to withdraw on Shwegyin.

On the 10th December our engineers completed a floating Bailey bridge over the Chindwin. Its length was 1,154 feet, then the longest Bailey bridge in the world. The Indian Sappers and Miners assembled the spans in the Myittha River under cover, floated them in to the Chindwin, and put the bridge in position in twenty-eight hours. It was an obvious target for air attack, and so we brought from Calcutta barrage balloons no longer needed there. Two days later an attack was made on the bridge, but luckily without success, and our anti-aircraft fire brought down two aircraft. For several days the bridgehead was expanded by minor advances and clashes, until, on the 13th December, Shwegyin was occupied, and the area around it cleared. The 11th East African Division by mid-December thus occupied a firm bridgehead east of Kalewa extending to about eight miles by twelve, and the pursuit that had begun at Imphal had now set the stage for the next act.

The Imphal-Kohima battle which now ended was the last and greatest of the series that had been fought continuously during the past ten months on all the Burma fronts. They had achieved substantial results; the Japanese Army had suffered the greatest defeat in its history. Five Japanese divisions (15th, 18th, 31st, 33rd, and 55th) had, at any rate temporarily, been destroyed as effective fighting formations, while two other divisions, an independent brigade, and many line of communication units had been badly mauled. Fifty thousand Japanese had been killed or died, and their bodies counted on the Arakan and Assam sectors. Allowing only half that number for badly wounded—and a very high proportion of their wounded died or were maimed—the enemy had lost permanently some seventy-five thousand men. Add to this fifteen thousand casualties suffered on the North Burma sector of N.C.A.C., and the total irrecoverable losses inflicted in operations under Fourteenth Army command were some ninety thousand men. The Japanese themselves later estimated their casualties in these battles at this figure. In addition, there were the four or five thousand Japanese accounted for by the Yunnan Chinese.

A most remarkable feature of the fighting had been the few

prisoners we had taken. Some six hundred had been captured, and of these I do not believe that more than a hundred and fifty were physically capable of further resistance; the rest were either grievously wounded or in the last stages of exhaustion. This proportion of prisoners to killed, about one in every hundred, is notable compared with that in European or African theatres, and is an indication of the fanatical nature of Japanese resistance.

Japanese losses in equipment were also high. Nearly all the tanks and most of the vehicles that the enemy brought into Assam were destroyed or captured. Over two hundred and fifty guns were taken, besides those thrown into rivers or buried by the Japanese themselves. Of course, given time, these losses both in men and material could be made good, and the divisions would fight again; but whether, even if we allowed them that time— and I had no intention of doing so—they would ever become once more the same aggressive, arrogant fighting formations was another matter.

Our own losses, as was to be expected in such fighting, had not been light. The Fourteenth Army, alone, had suffered some forty thousand battle casualties, killed and wounded. Many of the latter would recover and return to fight again, but losses had been heaviest where they were hardest to replace, in the officers and N.C.O.s of the fighting units. We had yielded only a handful of prisoners; of these the wounded had almost invariably been murdered or left to die. We had lost no guns. An area of Burma more than twice the size of Ireland had been liberated. We had done well.

If you are a general, whether your army has won a great battle or lost it, it is hard not to slur over your own mistakes, to blame others for theirs; to say, if you lost, what bad luck you had, and, if you won, how little luck had to do with it. My army had indubitably won *this* battle and I look back now on its conduct with considerable personal satisfaction, allowing myself, in the warm glow of success, a good deal more credit, no doubt, than I deserved. Yet the plan of the Imphal battle had been sound and we had adhered to it. Basically, it had been to meet the Japanese on ground of our own choosing, with a better line of communication behind us than behind them, to concentrate against them superior forces drawn from Arakan and India, to wear them down, and, when they were exhausted, to turn and destroy them.

N*   367

All this we had done in spite of my mistakes in mistiming the withdrawal of the 17th Division from Tiddim and underestimating the strength of the Japanese thrust at Kohima. These errors would have been disastrous but for the way in which, supported by the Supreme Commander and General Auchinleck, General Giffard sent so speedily to my rescue reinforcements from India. They and the fighting qualities of my troops saved me in the first days of the battle.

We had proved right in our reliance on the air forces, British and American, first to gain control of the air, and then to supply, transport, and support us. The campaign had been an air one, as well as a land one. Without the victory of the air forces there could have been no victory for the army, and, when it came, the shares of the soldier and the airman were so intermingled that it was a joint victory. Air supply and close support by fighters and bombers had been carried out with precision and effect in full view of the army, but far beyond the range of its sight the enemy's line of communication and administrative installations had been kept under almost constant attack by the Allied bombers. The cumulative effect of this was immense; his river craft, his motor transport and railway trains slunk along haltingly only at night. The air forces never stopped him moving his formations, but they slowed them up, destroyed their vehicles, and disrupted their communications. In future we knew it would be safe to put even greater reliance on our air arm.

Our estimate of the Japanese mentality and generalship had also proved right. Kawabe and his subordinates showed the over-boldness, the rigidity, and the disregard of administrative risks that I had expected and which gave me my opportunity. We had learned how to kill Japanese; how to use tanks in any country that was not a swamp; how to build roads and airfields with little equipment and strange materials. Our troops had shown them-selves steadier, more offensive, and better trained than ever before. They did not now accept any country as impassable, either for the enemy or themselves. They refused to be jittered by encircle-ment; they were as ready as the enemy to strike out into the jungle and to infiltrate. We had by degrees become better in the jungle than the Japanese. Most important of all, every British, Indian, African, and Chinese division that had served under Fourteenth Army had met picked Japanese troops in straight, bitter fighting and had beaten them. Our troops had proved themselves in battle the superiors of the Japanese; they had seen them run. This was the real and decisive result of these battles. They had smashed for ever the legend of the invincibility of the Japanese Army. Neither our men nor the Japanese soldier himself believed in it any longer.

Shortly after we had recaptured it, I visited Shwegyin. There, still lying in the amphitheatre of hills on the river bank, were the burnt-out and rusted tanks that I had so reluctantly destroyed and abandoned in the Retreat, two and a half years before. As I walked among them, resavouring in imagination the bitter taste of defeat, I could raise my head. Much had happened since then. Some of what we owed we had paid back. Now we were going on to pay back the rest—with interest.

BOOK V

The Decisive Battle

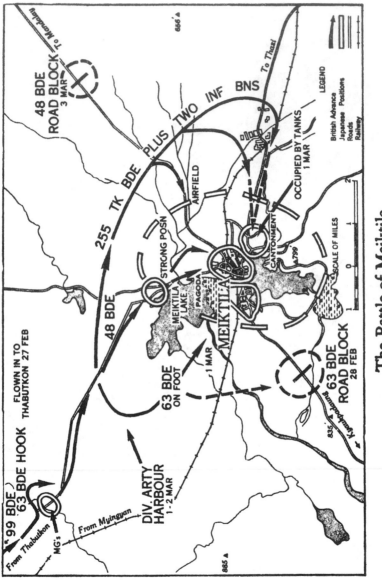

The Battle of Meiktila

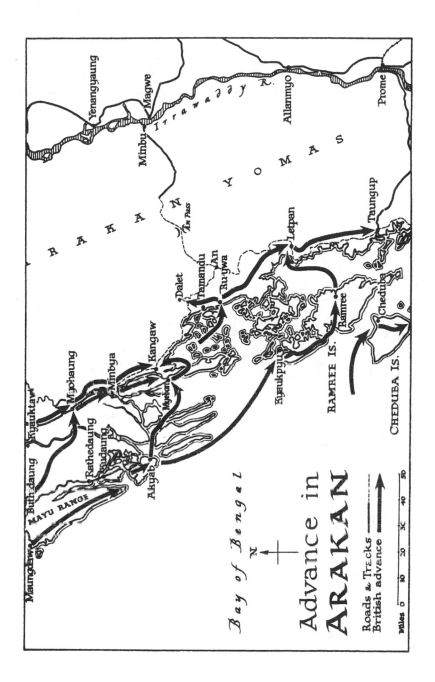

Bay of Bengal

N

Advance in
ARAKAN

Roads & Tracks - - - - -
British advence ⟶

Miles 0   10   20   30   40   50

Maungdaw

Buthidaung

MAYU RANGE

Rathedaung

Baudaung

Akyab

Myohaung

Minbya

Myebon

Kangaw

Kyaukpyu

RAMREE IS.

Ramree

CHEDUBA IS.

Cheduba

Dalet

Tamandu

An

Buywa

Letpan

Taungup

Kyauktaw

Yenangyaung

Magwe

Minbu

Irrawaddy R.

Allanmyo

Prome

A R A K A N   Y O M A S

Ta Pass

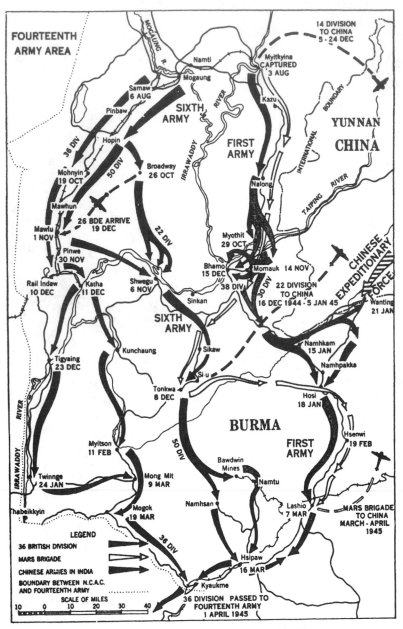

NORTHERN FRONT, AUGUST 1944—MARCH 1945

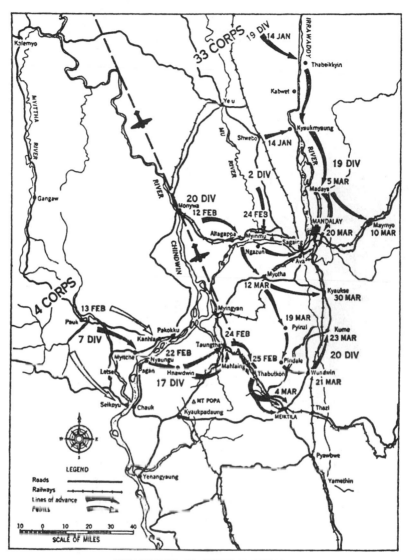

THE BATTLE OF CENTRAL BURMA

CHAPTER XVII

APPROACH TO THE IRRAWADDY

IT often happens that, when the first phase of a hard-fought campaign has been successfully completed and the second is in full swing, the commander will be as much occupied in preparations for the next stage as with the actual fighting in progress. This was so with me during the pursuit to and over the Chindwin. My mind and my time were largely filled with plans and preparations for the great battles that must follow the establishment of our bridgeheads over that river.

Nor was I the only one so employed. As soon as it was clear that the Imphal battle would end in decisive victory, an orgy of planning broke out at all levels. On the 2nd July, with Baldwin, commander of the Third Tactical Air Force, I met Admiral Mountbatten to discuss future operations. His headquarters was at this stage examining various alternative plans. I gave it as my opinion that an offensive would require no greater manpower than would be needed to hold a defensive line in North Burma, and that my army could be ready to begin such an offensive on the 1st November. The Supreme Commander, like the rest of us, was determined on an offensive as soon as possible after the monsoon, but its overall plan had not yet been decided upon. Baldwin and I returned to our headquarters, and at once got down to planning what we hoped would be our share in it.

A month before, the Chiefs of Staff in London had issued a directive for Burma. In it they laid down the objects of the next campaign as:

To develop, broaden and protect the air link to China, in order to provide maximum and timely flow of POL (Petrol, Oil, Lubricants) and stores to China in support of Pacific operations. So far as is consistent with the above, to press advantages against the enemy by exerting maximum effort, ground and air, particularly during the current monsoon season, and in pressing such advantages to be prepared to exploit the development of overland communications to China. All these operations must be dictated by the forces at present available or firmly allocated to S.E.A.C.

This directive was plainly a compromise between British and American views, with the American predominating. To me it seemed much too modest. I believed that the best and quickest way to secure worth-while communications with China was to clear the enemy out of Burma, and use Rangoon. The extent of the Japanese defeat at Imphal, which did not seem to have been appreciated, made this now feasible. I was sure that Admiral Mountbatten would be more ambitious in his plan. I, therefore, set my staff to work on plans for the capture of the Mandalay area, but always with the intention that this would at once be followed by an advance south on Rangoon. Indeed, we ran an unofficial private Fourteenth Army plan to effect this, which my Chief of Staff, Tubby Lethbridge, christened 'Operation Sob'— Sea or Bust.

Meanwhile, above us in S.E.A.C. Headquarters three alternative plans were being prepared:

Plan X. Stilwell's N.C.A.C., reinforced by more British and Indian divisions from Fourteenth Army, to be the main striking force, and to secure up to the line Katha–Mongmit–Lashio, while the Yunnan Chinese pushed to join up with them about Lashio. The reduced Fourteenth Army to conduct a limited offensive across the Chindwin.

Plan Y. The Fourteenth Army to be the main striking force, and to secure the Mandalay area. The N.C.A.C. and Yunnan Chinese to stage an offensive from the north, and join up with Fourteenth Army about Maymyo.

Plan Z. The capture of Rangoon by an amphibious and airborne operation, followed by a drive to meet our forces coming from the north.

I was heartily in favour of Plan Y. Apart from the fact that it allotted the major role to my army, it seemed to me to offer the best prospect of making the Japanese fight a battle with their main forces on ground favourable to us, and so giving us a chance of really smashing them before the next monsoon. I did not at this stage favour Plan Z. It was strategically most attractive, but I doubted if we could get in time either the equipment or

374

forces that would be required for an amphibious attack on a defended Rangoon. I thought our 'Operation Sob' would get us there at least as quickly.

However, when the Supreme Commander shortly afterwards issued his overall directive, allotting each part of the South-East Asia forces its task, we discovered that both Plans Y and Z were to be attempted. The plan for the offensive, to be known by the code word 'Capital', was:

(i) An advance across the Chindwin by Fourteenth Army, supported by 221 Group R.A.F., to occupy the area between that river and the Irrawaddy. Success to be exploited to include the capture of Mandalay.

(ii) A complementary advance by N.C.A.C. and the Chinese Yunnan Force, supported by the 10th and 14th U.S.A.A.F., to the line Thabeikkyin–Mogok–Lashio.

(iii) A limited advance in Arakan by 15 Corps, supported by 224 Group R.A.F., to secure our forward positions and to prevent interference with our airfields.

(iv) As these operations progressed, a sea and airborne assault (code name 'Dracula') to seize Rangoon some time before the 1945 monsoon, i.e. about March 1945.

If I had been doubtful of our ability to carry out Plan Z ('Dracula') with the forces available, I was still more so at the prospect of attempting both Z and Y simultaneously. I felt we were likely to fall between two stools and be strong enough neither in the south nor the north. Of course, if new divisions and air squadrons were to come from Europe, it would be a different matter; but that was obviously improbable until Germany was defeated—and optimistic views on the imminence of this were beginning to fade. However, I cheered myself with the thought that I was in no position to judge such high-level matters, and that there had, so far, been no suggestion to take away any of my troops.

When General Giffard came to see me on the 28th July 1944, he confirmed this. Plan Y, he said, was possible with what we had; Plan Z would require outside resources. Whether these would be available could not be known until September at the earliest. Meanwhile, he directed me to prepare plans for my share in Plan Y, which I was to carry out in three phases:

(i) The occupation, by a land advance and an airborne operation, of the Kalewa–Kalemyo area.
(ii) An overland and airborne advance to secure the Shewbo plain.
(iii) The liberation of Burma, as far south as the line Pakokku–Mandalay, where Fourteenth Army would make a junction with N.C.A.C. about Maymyo.

I was happy to be able to tell him that our Fourteenth Army plan was in essentials the same as Plan Y. It differed only in my intention to maintain my forward formations as they advanced mainly by air, and the consequent necessity to keep all supply aircraft for this purpose, rather than for the airborne operations suggested. I explained that, not only did I think that I could advance faster in this way and inflict heavier losses on the Japanese, but that it would simplify my line of communications problem and reduce the amount of road-making required to something practicable. He agreed to my continued preparation on these lines. I had to confess, however, that my estimate that my army would be ready to begin the great offensive on the 1st November was too optimistic; the 15th November was now the earliest date.

One reason for this was that manpower, especially in British infantry, was becoming an anxiety. The flow of reinforcements from home was not nearly enough to keep my British units up to strength. As a result of dwindling numbers, British battalions in Indian divisions were becoming so weak that they could not be used equally with Indian units. This led to adverse comment from the Indians, who had to take a greater strain. Then, too, it was not possible to reinforce British battalions with men of their own regiments. This gravely detracted from the regimental spirit, which has always been the strength of the British soldier, and morale was affected. So serious was the situation that divisional commanders were now calling for Indian battalions in place of British. I asked that reinforcements from home should be speeded up, and that the several thousand British anti-aircraft artillerymen, locked up in the defence of rear airfields now unlikely to be seriously attacked, should be drafted into the infantry. I found that Admiral Mountbatten had this already in hand. In due course, the anti-aircraft gunners came, proving themselves to be worthy infantrymen. Even so, the strength of British infantry continued to fall, and I was more and more compelled to substitute Indian for British battalions in my divisions.

In spite of this and other worries, our current operations and our preparations for the offensive were going well, when in August both were momentarily jeopardized. The suggestion was then made that, to make sure the forces required for the amphibious assault on Rangoon would be really available and not locked up in fighting in North Burma, the Fourteenth Army should withdraw to Imphal. Generals Giffard and Stilwell, who was Acting Supreme Commander, opposed the idea most strongly, and it was dropped. I heard no more of troops being taken away from me, although we had to spare some aircraft for the training of parachute regiments in India. Fourteenth Army, throughout September, pushed on with its preparations to carry out General Giffard's three-phased directive to me.

As the autumn of 1944 turned to winter, and one by one we established bridgeheads—at Sittaung, east of Tamu, at Mawlaik, fifty miles farther south, and at Kalewa—the first phase was completed. I was particularly pleased I had done it, as I had planned, without an airborne operation. At this time I paid a good many visits to the forward troops, but more to the divisions in the rear to see their training for open warfare and river crossings. There was no doubt about their keenness and their desire to close with the enemy again—the hall-mark of high morale. I grew increasingly confident.

The Japanese higher command had played into our hands. We had inflicted on them in the Imphal battle the major defeat that I had always felt would be necessary before we could with assurance break into Central Burma and meet their main army on its own ground. The extent of that defeat became clearer from the sights that greeted our pursuing troops on the heels of the Japanese. Abandoned guns and tanks, bogged down vehicles, scattered equipment, and, everywhere, corpses lying singly beside the track, sitting grotesquely in cars, propped against trees, huddled together in miserable huts, floating in every stream—the whole horror of retreat in the monsoon, the ultimate beastliness of war. It is true that we had crushed only a portion of Kawabe's Burma army, but it would be disorganized, diseased, and almost starving remnants of some of his best divisions that would scramble across the Chindwin. He would need time to re-form and re-equip these shattered formations.

It is of interest that our estimates of enemy casualties in the Imphal–Kohima battle were, as we discovered after their final surrender, very close to the figures the Japanese themselves calculated. These were:

Formation	Strength Before Battle	After Battle	Losses
15th Division	20,000	4,000	16,000
31st Division	20,000	7,000	13,000
33rd Division	25,000	4,000	21,000
Army troops Administrative units	50,000	35,000	15,000
Totals	115,000	50,000	65,000

Our battle casualties at Kohima–Imphal were over 15,000, but to these must be added a much larger number evacuated sick during the monsoon campaign and pursuit. Including these we had probably a rather higher total than the Japanese, but the great bulk of our casualties recovered; most of theirs died on the retreat from lack of medical care, exposure, and exhaustion.

The more I considered the enemy situation and our own, the more I was sure that here was our opportunity. My orders were to drive the enemy out of a considerable part of Northern Burma and take Mandalay, but more important than the occupation of any area or any town, was the destruction of the Japanese Army. A second great defeat for that army, properly exploited, would disrupt it and leave, not Mandalay, but all Burma at our mercy. It, therefore, became my aim to force another major battle on the enemy at the earliest feasible moment.

With this General Giffard was in complete agreement. He did not underestimate the difficulties, especially logistically, but he did everything in his power to overcome them for me. Recognizing how important it was that I should be able to concentrate my attention on the vital Central front, he relieved me, not only of the Arakan front, but of the vast line of communication area

378

that I had up to then controlled, and which had made me look back almost as often as forward. I had a sentimental pang at parting from my old 15 Corps, but my gratitude for the relief was great. I had already handed back the N.C.A.C., so now I was free to devote all my energies to the forthcoming battle.

It posed innumerable problems of supply, transportation, air support, medical arrangements, engineering, communications, reinforcement, reorganization, and training; but three questions dominated all our considerations:

(i) How and where could we bring the enemy main forces to battle with the greatest advantage to ourselves?
(ii) What would be the greatest strength we could maintain east of the Chindwin for the battle?
(iii) What would be the Japanese strength?

I wanted to fight the battle on ground where our superiority in the air and in armour would have its greatest scope, that is, in comparatively open country. The obvious place was the Shwebo plain, a great loop of land enclosed between the Irrawaddy and the Chindwin, immediately north-west of Mandalay. This is part of the 'dry belt', the central plain of Burma. Here the country is generally flat or undulating, covered in cultivation with some scrub patches, easily passable, sprinkled with villages, criss-crossed by many cart tracks and some roads. Over considerable areas it is so open and, except in the rainy season, so dusty, as to offer something like desert conditions. It would suit us admirably.

But it was one thing to decide we would like to fight there, another to persuade the Japanese to do so. If they did, the enemy commander would know full well what disadvantages he was accepting. He would fight with the river loop around him— difficult when all his supplies would have to be brought over it under air attack, disastrous if he had to retreat. Yet I was quite sure he *would* fight in the Shwebo plain. I relied on my knowledge of the Japanese and on the mentality of their high command as I had known it. I knew there had been changes in that command. In October reports had reached me that Kawabe had been sent back to Japan in disgrace and replaced by a General Kimura, of whom not a great deal was known, except that he was regarded by the Japanese as one of their best men. Even so, I expected him to conform to type, to be over-bold, inflexible, and reluctant to change a plan once made. In spite of the Imphal lesson, he would, I thought, be confident that he could beat me on his own ground and, even if he were not, he would never dare to lose face by giving up territory without a struggle. He would see the Chindwin behind us; not the Irrawaddy behind him. I did not believe it was in the Japanese nature to let Mandalay go, or even be brought into the front line, without a pitched battle. He might try to hold us on the Chindwin or even to throw our bridgeheads into the river, but he had largely lost his chance to do that. In fact, I was prepared to back my judgment that he would choose to fight a defensive battle, with his main strength, north of Mandalay. If he won this, he could then leave the difficulties of maintenance in the monsoon to force us to withdraw; he might even hope to restage an offensive of his own into India after the rains. The Japanese were always military optimists.

Our problem, therefore, was to get as many divisions and as much armour as possible, and as quickly as possible, into the Shwebo plain, and there fight an army battle. The answer, as almost all answers in war and particularly in Burma, depended on supply and transport. True, we held three bridgeheads over the Chindwin, notably the one at Kalewa; the difficulty was not to cross the river, but to maintain a large force once it was over. I had available for the battle six and two-thirds divisions and two tank brigades (2nd, 5th, 7th, 17th, 19th, 20th Divisions, 268 Brigade, 28 East African Brigade, 254 and 255 Tank Brigades), and I could, I knew, obtain another division, or perhaps two, from General Giffard if I could use them. Yet, scheme as we might, take risks to the limit of reason, we could not with our transport resources, air and road, maintain in battle trans-Chindwin more than four and two-third divisions and the two tank brigades. Even that would perhaps be optimistic. We should be four hundred miles from railhead, and of that distance two hundred and fifty would be earth road only, liable, unless we made it all-weather before the monsoon, to become impassable. Our air-lift was strictly limited and based mainly in the Comilla and Chittagong areas, two hundred and sixty and two hundred and forty miles away. Even the forward airfields around Imphal were two hundred miles distant and not served by rail. In whatever way we worked out our maintenance calculations, the best answer we could get was always the same—four and two-thirds divisions and two tank brigades.

What was this force likely to meet? The total enemy strength in Burma, as far as we knew in December 1944, was:

Ten infantry divisions
One tank regiment
Two independent mixed brigades
100,000 Japanese line of communication troops
Two Indian National Army divisions (about 6,000 each)
The Burma National Army (seven battalions)

Several of the divisions were under strength still, but the Japanese had for some time been bringing in reinforcements to Burma at the rate, we estimated, of seven thousand a month. The line of communication troops, though not as skilful as those in divisions, could be relied on to fight defensively with equal desperation, and Japanese morale, while not at the supreme pitch it had attained before the Imphal defeat, was still of the last man and the last cartridge standard. The individual Japanese soldier remained, as I had always called him, the most formidable fighting insect in history. The I.N.A. divisions had little fighting value; the B.N.A., judging by our experiences of 1942, might be more of a nuisance, but it was likely to be kept for internal security duties.

This total was a considerable force, but it was not to be expected that the whole of it would oppose Fourteenth Army. I relied on Northern Area Combat Command and the Yunnan Chinese to hold two Japanese divisions in the north; 15 Corps to keep one and a third in Arakan; and our deception schemes, with their threats of amphibious attack, to tie down a further one and a third in the south. This would leave against Fourteenth Army, five and one-third Japanese divisions, one independent mixed brigade, one tank regiment, some thirty or forty thousand line of communication troops and the two I.N.A. divisions. It would always be possible, of course, for the Japanese, by taking risks on other sectors, to increase their forces in the Mandalay area, but I hoped that if we kept up the pressure elsewhere this was not very likely. There was also the possibility that further enemy formations would be brought from Siam and Indo-China. I did not think any would come from Japan or overseas, as the American successes in the Pacific and against Japanese shipping made it unlikely. Indeed, I hoped the enemy would find it hard to replace any further losses we could inflict on him in Burma. A constant anxiety in all our plans was the amount of air-lift we could rely on getting. Even with optimistic estimates of what we could bring forward by road and by river, we should still need thousands of tons daily by air. After much discussion, a firm allotment of our minimum requirements in air-lift was made to Fourteenth Army for the forthcoming operations, and on this we made our plans.

All the same, four and two-thirds British and Indian divisions, a river behind them and at the end of this precarious line of communication, was not the odds I should have liked with which to attack five and a third Japanese divisions in their own selected positions. A year ago I would not have looked at the proposal. Even now, it was not so much our advantage in the air, in armour, in greater mobility in the open, which gave me confidence to go on with my plan, but the spirit of my troops, my trust in their experienced commanders and in the high fighting value and hardihood of them all.

It will be noted that my plan was based on three foundations:

(i) The firm intention of the enemy commander to fight with his main forces north of Mandalay.
(ii) The ability of other sectors of our Burma front to hold off from us during the battle some four or five Japanese divisions.
(iii) A definite air and road maintenance lift on which I could rely.

The first was a matter of my own judgment in which, perhaps rashly, I had at that time considerable faith. The second, I thought, should be safe enough, as 15 Corps in Arakan would have two Indian, two West African divisions, an East African and a commando brigade, and a tank brigade, i.e., four and two-thirds divisions and armour. Sultan's N.C.A.C. would have one British, three (later five) Chinese divisions, Mars Force (a Sino-American formation the equivalent of a weak division), and a Chinese tank brigade—the equivalent of five or six divisions. It looked at first sight as if these flank forces, one nearly as large, the other larger than mine, were out of balance. The fact was

382

that my force was as big as maintenance would allow. It is true that a reduction in the N.C.A.C. strength, if it had meant an increase of air-lift for Fourteenth Army, would have helped me a great deal and left them enough for their tasks. It was more likely, however, that any spare American air transport would have gone to China, and if, as I hoped, the Chinese divisions pushed hard down the east of the Irrawaddy, well south of Lashio, they would take a big weight off me at Mandalay.

To have reduced 15 Corps in Arakan would not have helped me. It was maintained largely by sea, its rail and road communications with India were separate from mine, and it now used comparatively little air transport. On the other hand, 15 Corps could be of the greatest help to Fourteenth Army, when, after a successful battle in the Mandalay area, we pushed south. My air supply bases were, as I have said, two hundred to two hundred and fifty miles from where the battle would, I hoped, be fought. Two hundred and fifty miles was, with Dakotas, the limit of economical air supply; after that distance is exceeded delivery falls off rapidly and more and more aircraft are needed for the same lift. We had no more aeroplanes, so, if the Fourteenth Army was to exploit a success by moving south of Mandalay, the only answer was to bring our air supply bases nearer. These, if they were to support large operations, would have to be accessible by either rail or sea. There were no sites with rail access, but the islands, Akyab, Cheduba, and Ramree, all in Japanese hands, off the Arakan coast, would, if taken quickly, provide excellent airfields within the necessary two hundred and fifty miles radius of most of Burma south of Mandalay. I pressed very hard that, in addition to holding down the largest possible number of Japanese formations in Arakan, 15 Corps should establish air bases in these islands to supply Fourteenth Army.

As we in Fourteenth Army Headquarters worked hard at our plans, and as our divisions reorganized, regrouped, and began to move into their assembly areas, above us in Supreme Headquarters, change and reorganization were in the air. In mid-October, Stilwell was recalled. The Generalissimo had insisted on it, and, in spite of pressure from Washington and from Admiral Mountbatten, had refused to yield. The only thing that was surprising was that the open breach had not come sooner.

Stilwell, although Chiang's Chief of Staff, had never bothered to hide his contempt for 'The Peanut', as he usually called him in private and in public. The American had no confidence in the Chinaman's military judgment or political integrity, and announced it. He believed that the Generalissimo was more interested in using American Lease-Lend money and equipment to secure his own personal position in China than in fighting the Japanese. Stilwell, who overestimated his own indispensability to Chiang and the extent to which the American Government would go in his support, was surprised and deeply hurt. In Fourteenth Army and, I think, throughout the British forces our sympathies were with Stilwell—unlike the American 14th Air Force who demonstratively rejoiced at his downfall. To my mind he had strange ideas of loyalty to his superiors, whether they were American, British, or Chinese, and he fought too many people who were not enemies; but I liked him. There was no one whom I would rather have had commanding the Chinese army that was to advance with mine. Under Stilwell it *would* advance. We saw him go with regret, and he took with him our admiration as a fighting soldier. He was replaced by three generals who divided between them his half-dozen jobs. The command of N.C.A.C. went to his loyal second-in-command, Lieut.-General Dan Sultan, whom I already knew and liked. Wedemeyer, Admiral Mountbatten's American Deputy Chief of Staff, replaced Stilwell in China as Chiang Kai-shek's adviser, but I gathered that the idea of building up a great American-led Chinese army to march to the sea vanished with Stilwell. General Wheeler became Deputy Supreme Commander, an excellent appointment.

One advantage did come from Stilwell's departure. It became easier to set up a reasonable land command in South-East Asia in the place of the, to say the least, illogical organization that had been tried up till then. Admiral Mountbatten at last was able to persuade the Combined Chiefs of Staff to accept an Allied Land Forces commander with an integrated Anglo-American Headquarters. A.L.F.S.E.A., Allied Land Forces South-East Asia, would control Fourteenth Army, N.C.A.C., 15 Corps and Line of Communications Command. We welcomed this, but a sad blow fell on Fourteenth Army when we learned that General Giffard was not to continue to command. He had

APPROACH TO THE IRRAWADDY

seen us through our efforts to become an army and through our first and most desperate battles. Fourteenth Army owed much to his integrity, his judgment, his sound administration, his support in our darkest hours, and to the universal confidence he inspired among us. We saw him go with grief. I and others built on the foundations he laid. He was succeeded on the 12th November 1944 by Lieut.-General Sir Oliver Leese, who had commanded the Eighth Army in Italy.

General Leese, whom I had already known when he was an instructor at the Quetta Staff College, I found easy to serve under. His military judgment was eminently sound. Indeed, in this I differed from him only once—on the need for a sea and airborne operation against Rangoon—and then he was right and I was wrong. His staff, which he brought with him and which replaced most of our old friends at General Giffard's headquarters, had a good deal of desert sand in its shoes and was rather inclined to thrust Eighth Army down our throats. No doubt we provoked them, for not only were my people a bit sore at losing General Giffard, but, while we had the greatest admiration for the Eighth Army, we also thought that the Fourteenth Army was now quite something. However, almost all the new men were experienced and able staff officers—some like Bastyan, the Chief Administrative Officer, were outstanding—and our staffs soon settled down to working together. The new Commander-in-Chief approved the plans which I had worked out under his predecessor and which were in fact already under way.

During September and October there was great activity throughout the Fourteenth Army back areas. For two years our formations had fought in jungles and amongst hills; they were now about to break out into open country with unobstructed views and freedom of movement away from tracks. Not only would the laborious tactics of the jungle have to be replaced by speed, mechanization, and mobility, but commanders and troops would have to adjust their mentality to the changed conditions. This was especially so in the use of armour and artillery. Instead of one or two tanks, surrounded by infantry, carefully nosing forward along a narrow jungle track, we might hope to use powerful, rapidly moving, armoured formations on extended fronts. Artillery would fire at longer ranges, change position more frequently, and have to be ready to answer calls

385

from the air more quickly. In the same way, our supporting airmen would have to be ready instantly to come to the help of infantry. In all the divisions not engaged in actual fighting, training to meet these new conditions proceeded vigorously. It says much for the energy and skill of corps and divisional commanders that, in the short time available, and in spite of constant moves, so much was accomplished to fit the troops for their new role.

When General Giffard relieved me of the Line of Communication Command and of Arakan, it meant that the airfields and supply depots from which our air maintenance came would no longer be in the Fourteenth Army area or under its control, as up to then they had been. The air supply organization had, therefore, passed from me to General Giffard. The combined Army, R.A.F., and U.S.A.A.F. staffs which had proved so successful during the Imphal battle were expanded into a new organization, comprising the Anglo-American Combat Cargo Task Force (C.C.T.F.) with a British Army component known as Combined Army Air Transport Organization (C.A.A.T.O.). The American Brigadier-General Evans commanded the air component and Brigadier Dawson from my staff went to command the army portion. At first, especially during the concentration of 4 and 33 Corps forward for the Chindwin crossings, the new organization suffered from teething troubles. Complaints, especially from 33 Corps, of irregular and incorrect deliveries were frequent. It had obviously been easier and simpler for Fourteenth Army to control its own air supply, but, now that A.L.F.S.E.A. was itself directly commanding several formations besides my army, it was no longer possible for us to do it. The new organization, however, quickly found its feet. It was able to obtain more signal units, and thus to strengthen what had always been our weakest link—communications. We provided more F.A.M.O.s (Forward Airfield Maintenance Organizations) mainly from beach groups now not required for amphibious operations, and in a short time air supply to Fourteenth Army was working better than ever. C.A.A.T.O., Brigadier Dawson, and his men expanded the Fourteenth Army system of air supply, and it later became the accepted organization for the whole British Army. They made a major contribution to the ultimate victory.

In my own army, too, there were some changes. The 17th Division, which was resting in India at Ranchi, began to change its standard mixed animal and mechanical transport organization for a new one we had invented, in which all the division, except one brigade group, was completely mechanized. The remaining brigade was to be entirely air transportable. To achieve this, all its vehicles were jeeps and its twenty-five-pounder guns were fitted with the narrow 'Jury' axle which would allow them to be wheeled in and out of a Dakota aircraft. The scale of baggage, supplies, and ammunition carried was cut down, reliance being placed on quick replenishment by air. Incidentally, this re-organization was only completed in a last-minute rush after the division had rejoined at Imphal. When the 5th Division, having recaptured Kalemyo, was brought back to Kohima, and later Jorhat, to rest, it was reorganized in the same way. These changes were made because I intended, if things went well, to use these two divisions in a very mobile role in Central Burma. Even if, because of maintenance difficulties, it meant substituting them at some stage of the campaign for standard divisions, I believed it would be worth it.

Another change affected me personally very closely. Steve Irwin, who from the formation of Fourteenth Army had been my Chief of Staff and to whose loyalty, brilliance, and im-perturbable common sense I owed so much, was promoted Major-General and left me to be Commandant of the Quetta Staff College. If there he turned out staff officers approaching his own standard of devotion and ability, no man could have served his country better, but, selfishly, I was very sorry to see him go. I was again very fortunate as I was able to get in his place Brigadier 'Tubby' Lethbridge, a Sapper who combined the typical clear-headedness of an engineer with a broad humanity that made him a pleasure to work with or under. His sense of humour, which thank Heaven all my principal staff officers have had, and, wonderful to relate, retained, was perhaps more rumbustious than Steve Irwin's, but equally unquenchable. He entered at once into the partnership with Snelling on which so much, including myself, depended. The experience he had gained during a long visit to the Australian Army in New Guinea made the conditions of our war familiar to him.

On the 1st October, I had issued orders for the advance over the Chindwin. Throughout the month, while the 11th East African and 5th Indian Divisions were battling to gain Kalemyo, the two corps, 4 and 33, were assembling for the crossing. My own Headquarters moved from Comilla to Imphal, where we set up a joint headquarters with Air Vice-Marshal Vincent's 221 Group R.A.F. Headquarters.

4 Corps Headquarters during October returned from India to Imphal, but Scoones, who had stoutly held Imphal, was soon afterwards promoted to a command in India. I was allowed to replace him, at my urgent request, by Frank Messervy from the 7th Division, who had the temperament, sanguine, inspiring, and not too calculating of odds, that I thought would be required for the tasks I designed for 4 Corps. The 19th Indian Division, as yet untried in battle arrived under Major-General Pete Rees and moved up towards the Chindwin in the Tamu–Sittang area. To Messervy's 4 Corps I had allotted the 7th and 19th Indian Divisions and 255 Tank Brigade; to Stopford's 33 Corps, the 2nd British, and 20th Indian Divisions, 268 Brigade and 254 Tank Brigade. 4 Corps I had ordered to break into the Shwebo plain through the Sittaung bridgehead and seize, by an airborne operation if necessary, the Japanese airfields in the Ye-u–Shwebo area. 33 Corps was to cross by the Kalewa bridgehead, when it was in our hands, and advance on Ye-u–Shwebo. If 33 Corps reached this area before 4 Corps, then the latter would be flown in to the captured airstrips. As soon as the two corps made contact, 255 Tank Brigade would be sent through 33 Corps to join 4 Corps. The Lushai Brigade and the newly-arrived 28 East African Brigade would push down the west bank of the Chindwin on Gangaw to protect the right flank of 33 Corps and our main line of communication to the bridgeheads. The 11th East African Division, as soon as 33 Corps had crossed at Kalewa, would be flown out to India.

I was particularly anxious, if possible, to avoid having to seize Shwebo by an airborne operation. I judged it would be attended by considerable risk and would absorb a high proportion of our allotted air-lift, so badly needed for ordinary maintenance. I therefore told the R.A.F. and 4 Corps to reconnoitre closely the northern routes from the Chindwin to the railway, to discover if it seemed possible to move large forces on this axis. The reports were favourable and, on Messervy's recommendation, I agreed to the whole of the 19th Division being committed to advance by these tracks. At the same time, I instructed him not

to engage the 7th Division east of the Chindwin without my permission as I still thought it might have to be flown into the plain.
The Fourteenth Army offensive began on the 3rd December
1944, when a brigade of the 20th Division led the 33 Corps
advance by crossing the Chindwin through the Mawlaik bridgehead, thirty miles north of Kalewa. As this brigade splashed south-
eastwards through waterlogged fields, the 11th East African
Division was fighting hard to extend its bridgehead at Kalewa.
It was not until the 18th that the remainder of the 20th Division
were able to follow by that bridgehead. Next day the 2nd
Division passed through, moving eastward on Pyingaing, the
'Pink Gin' of the Retreat. Almost simultaneously, 4 Corps in
the north had begun their advance. On the 4th December, the
19th Division broke out from the Sittaung bridgehead with
orders to take Pinlebu, some sixty miles to the east.

To meet these invading columns, we believed the Japanese
had in the river loop four divisions, the 53rd in the Rail Indaw
area, where it was opposing the advance of the 36th British
Division of N.C.A.C. down the Railway Corridor, the 15th
some way south of Indaw, the 31st in Shwebo and north of it,
and the 33rd opposite Kalewa. The last three had all been badly
smashed in the Imphal battle, but strenuous efforts had been
made to re-equip and bring them up to strength. Our intelligence
estimated, correctly I believe, that their strengths were now:
15th Division, five to six thousand; 31st Division, eleven thous-
and; 33rd Division, over six thousand. There were, besides, a
number of army units and line of communication troops, giving
a probable total in the loop, exclusive of the 53rd Division, of
some twenty-five thousand.

Parallel to the Chindwin and about twenty-five miles to the
east of it, running from the north to opposite Kalewa, was a
well-defined line of hills from two thousand to two thousand
five hundred feet high, the Zibyu Taungdan Range. When the
enemy made no serious attempt to hold us in our northern
bridgeheads, I expected him to meet us with covering forces on
the defiles through this range, while behind it he continued to
reconstitute his divisions and to bring in others. I looked for a
hard fight on the Zibyu Taungdan.

The 19th Division made surprisingly rapid progress. Two of
its brigades followed a northerly track; the third, one roughly

parallel but more to the south. Both routes would pass through the Zibyu Taungdan Range to turn south on Shwebo. This was the first time the division had been in action, but the troops, a high proportion of whom were prewar regulars, advanced with the greatest dash, led literally by their dynamic commander, Pete Rees, known to his British troops as the 'Pocket Napoleon', a reference to his size and his success in battle. What he lacked in inches he made up by the miles he advanced. Whether he was hailooing on his troops from the roadside or leading them in his jeep, he was an inspiring divisional commander. The only criticism I made was to point out to him that the best huntsmen did not invariably ride ahead of their hounds.

On the 12th December, Rees's headquarters was forty-five miles north-east of Sittaung, on the 16th, he had taken Banmauk, forty-odd miles farther east, and pushed a patrol on to Rail Indaw where it met the 36th Division, thus forming, for the first time, a connected front from the Indian Ocean to China. On the same day his southern column captured Pinlebu. The 19th Division was now well through the Zibyu Taungdan, and, while the Japanese rearguards had fought well, the irresistible rush of our men had swept them away.

I had, a week before, begun to suspect that I had misread the Japanese commander's intention. Now I realized I had. If he had meant to fight in the Shwebo plain, he would undoubtedly have held on to these hills with more determination. Since the beginning of the month, too, I had been getting reports, confirmed by air reconnaissance, that the general direction of Japanese movement in the river loop was back across the Irrawaddy, not forward. Then, too, the defensive positions captured by the 19th Division in the defiles did not seem designed for prolonged resistance, but for delay only. We had surprised the enemy by the speed with which we had mounted our offensive over the Chindwin, and by its strength and swiftness. It was borne in upon me that, either because of this, or because I had all along mistaken the enemy's intention, he was not going to do what I had expected—fight a major battle north of the Irrawaddy. It looked as if this battle, like so many of mine, was not going to start quite as I intended. It was time for me to use a little of that flexibility of mind that I had so often urged on my subordinates.

The fact that the first foundation on which I had built my plan had collapsed was, to say the least, disconcerting. The idea of crowding the whole of Fourteenth Army into the river loop, if the enemy were not going to wait for me there, was obviously not a good one. It could only lead to frontal assaults across the Irrawaddy, with the whole Japanese army free to dispose itself in superior force to resist, or, if we did get over, to attack us in our inevitably weakened state. My object remained the destruction of the Japanese army; I could never achieve it that way. Luckily, 4 Corps had only one division committed across the Chindwin, so I still retained fluidity; but any major alteration, to be effective, must be quick, and would in any case throw a terrific burden on the administrative staffs. The first thing to do was to discover, or at least re-estimate, what was now the Japanese intention.

After the Imphal battle, there had been a great shake up in the Japanese High Command. A number of senior officers besides the Commander-in-Chief, Kawabe, had been removed. I knew that Kimura had replaced him, but, partly through wishful thinking and partly through lack of information about the new man, I had concluded he would have much the same characteristics and faults as his predecessor. In this I was wrong. General Kimura was to prove himself a commander with a much higher degree of realism and moral courage. An artilleryman, regarded with some justification as one of the most brilliant officers of the Japanese Army, Kimura was transferred straight from Imperial General Headquarters in Tokyo to Burma. Within a fortnight of his arrival he had completely recast the plans for the defence of Central Burma. About the time Kimura took over, the Japanese forces in Burma were, to the best of our knowledge, organized in three armies, or, as we should have called them, corps:

(i) *Twenty-Eighth Army,* under Lieut.-General Sakurai, already well known to us, was responsible for the Arakan front and, although we only learnt this later, the Irrawaddy Valley, up to the Yenangyaung oilfields. It had the 54th and 55th Divisions and the newly raised 72nd Independent Mobile Brigade.

(ii) *Fifteenth Army,* under Lieut.-General Katamura (late commander of the 54th Division, who had replaced Mutaguchi, removed) consisted of the 15th, 31st and 33rd Divisions and, we thought, 24th Independent Mobile

Brigade. It was responsible for the Central front, including the Railway Corridor.

(iii) *Thirty-Third Army*, under Lieut.-General Honda, which held the North-eastern front, facing N.C.A.C. and the Yunnan Chinese, had consisted originally of the 18th and 56th Divisions, but we had also identified in this area units of the 53rd and 2nd Divisions. We were not sure if these divisions were complete in the area.

(iv) *Burma Army Area Reserve*, we thought to be the 49th Division in South Burma, about Pegu.

Kimura decided he could not, in their present state, risk the three battered divisions from Imphal in a battle in the open plain. He therefore ordered a gradual withdrawal behind the Irrawaddy, leaving only light covering forces behind to delay our advance, while he prepared for what he called the 'Battle of the Irrawaddy Shore'. In that battle, by concentrating his maximum strength against the Fourteenth Army, he hoped, not without reason, to cripple us as we struggled to cross the river, and then, with the help of the monsoon, to destroy us as we limped back to the Chindwin. As part of his preparations, he reduced the Thirty-Third Army considerably by sending the 2nd Division back to Meiktila and transferring the 53rd to Fifteenth Army. He also removed 24 Independent Brigade to Moulmein. The 2nd Division and 24 Brigade came into his General Reserve which up to now had contained only the 49th Division. This Reserve could be moved north again by rail or road when required, and served as a precaution against possible British amphibious operations in Southern Burma. Later, Marshal Tarauchi ordered the removal of the 2nd Division to Indo-China and it was en route when our offensive across the Irrawaddy developed. It was an inexplicable order and Tarauchi must have reproached himself for it. Kimura was able to make these reductions in his Thirty-Third Army and in the Railway Corridor, as he intended in the north-east to remain completely on the defensive and, if forced, to withdraw slowly before the advance of our 36th Division, Sultan's Chinese, and the Yunnan Force.

Of course, the full extent of these alterations in Japanese plans and organization was not known to me for a long time, but the 19th Division's advance had brought us the usual harvest of captured Japanese diaries, letters, and orders. From these and air reports we could piece together, reasonably accurately, what the enemy intended. My suspicions were confirmed; it was obvious that, wisely, they had decided to fight behind, instead of in front of, the Irrawaddy. My problem was now to cross the river first and defeat them afterwards—a much harder one than to defeat them and then cross.

My staff and I, before preparing our original plan, had naturally studied several alternatives. Amongst them had been a project to pass a considerable force up the Gangaw Valley to seize a bridgehead over the Irrawaddy near Pakokku and then, striking east, appear south of Mandalay. This idea I had discarded because I was sure the Japanese would remain north of Mandalay and I should require 4 Corps there if I were to defeat their main force. The route to Pakokku was long and most difficult, but, after some hard thinking, I reverted to this scheme in a modified form.

My new plan, the details of which were worked out in record time by my devoted staff, labouring day and night, had as its intention the destruction of the main Japanese forces in the area Mandalay–Thazi–Chauk–Myingyan. It was based on 33 Corps, with the 19th Division transferred to it, forcing crossings of the river north and west of Mandalay, thus drawing towards itself the greatest possible concentration of Kimura's divisions. Meanwhile 4 Corps, moving secretly south up the Gangaw Valley, would suddenly appear at Pakokku, seize a crossing, and, without pause, strike violently with armoured and airborne forces at Meiktila.

Meiktila, with Thazi twelve miles to the east, was the main administrative centre of the Japanese Fifteenth and Thirty-Third Armies. In this area were their chief supply bases, ammunition dumps, hospitals, and depots. There were also five or six airfields. Road and rail routes from the south-east and west converged on Meiktila and Thazi, to spread out again to the north like the extended fingers of a hand, whose wrist was Meiktila. Crush that wrist, no blood would flow through the fingers, the whole hand would be paralysed, and the Japanese armies on the arc from the Salween to the Irrawaddy would begin to wither. If we took Meiktila while Kimura was deeply engaged along the Irrawaddy about Mandalay, he would be compelled to detach large forces to clear his vital communications. This should give me not only the major battle I desired, but the chance to repeat our old hammer and anvil tactics: 33 Corps the hammer from the north against the anvil of 4 Corps at Meiktila—and the Japanese between.

Time was pressing. The more units of 4 Corps that crossed the Chindwin, the more difficult it would be to get the corps on to its new axis. At a table outside Messervy's caravan, near Tamu, I explained my new plan to both corps commanders. At this conference I made clear my intention that the forthcoming battle would be followed by a dash south to take Rangoon before the monsoon. This project, the taking of Rangoon, had been in all our minds at Fourteenth Army Headquarters for some time, and a good deal of examination and planning for its achievement had been carried out. It was first issued to subordinate formations in the Operation Instruction issued on the 19th December, after our meeting. In it I gave as my intention:

(i) In conjunction with N.C.A.C., to destroy the enemy forces in Burma.
(ii) To advance to the line Henzada–Nyaunglebin.
(iii) To seize any opportunity to advance from that line and capture a South Burma port.

I did not specify Rangoon because, while Rangoon would ultimately be necessary, I was inclined to consider Moulmein might be a better initial strategic objective. There would be plenty of time to decide later which we should attempt.

I allotted formations to corps thus:

4 *Corps*
 7th and 17th Divisions
 255 Tank Brigade (Sherman tanks)
 Lushai Brigade
 28 East African Brigade

33 *Corps*
 2nd, 19th, and 20th Divisions
 254 Tank Brigade (Lee-Grants and Stuart tanks)
 268 Brigade

The 5th Division, reorganizing on its mechanized and airborne establishment I held in Army Reserve.

394

The two corps commanders accepted these changes without fuss and with the determination that, however difficult, the new plan would be made to succeed. Stopford in 33 Corps proceeded to revise his plans; Messervy in 4 Corps completely to remake his.

For success it was essential that both the blow that was being launched from Pakokku and its strength must be concealed from the enemy until the moment it fell upon him. A scheme was therefore prepared, which, it was hoped, would persuade Kimura that 4 Corps was still moving complete into the Shwebo Plain, on the left of 33 Corps, and that any movement in the Gangaw Valley was merely a demonstration to distract his attention from our attack on Mandalay from the north. To achieve this, a dummy 4 Corps Headquarters, using the same wireless channels, had to be substituted at Tamu for the real one when it moved out. All signals from 33 Corps to the 19th Division had to be passed through this dummy headquarters. The real 4 Corps was to keep wireless silence until control of operations in the Gangaw Valley necessitated breaking it; even then they were limited to simulating only the headquarters of the withdrawn 11th East African Division. 'Indiscreet' conversations in clear between staff officers and operators were arranged, news broadcasts made slightly inaccurate references to formations engaged, and many ingenious devices were employed to mislead the simple Japanese, while the volume of traffic was made to conform to having both corps concentrated in the Shwebo plain. Operationally this signal deception scheme was a real annoyance to corps and divisional commanders and its enforcement a test of patience and discipline, but it paid an excellent dividend. The enemy was completely deceived.

I had been tempted to make the seizure of Meiktila a wholly airborne operation in its first stages, but I had to abandon the idea, partly for lack of parachute troops, but mainly because the air-lift allotted to Fourteenth Army would barely cope with maintenance alone. It was as well I did so. At dawn on the 10th December I was awakened in my headquarters at Imphal by the roar of engines as a large number of aircraft took off in succession and passed low overhead. I knew loaded aircraft were due to leave for 33 Corps later in the morning, but I was surprised at this early start. I sent somebody to discover what it was all about. To my consternation, I learnt that, without warning, three squadrons of

American Dakotas (seventy-five aircraft), allotted to Fourteenth Army maintenance, had been suddenly ordered to China, where Stilwell's prophecy had been fulfilled, and the Japanese, galled by Chennault's air attacks on shipping, had begun to overrun the forward American airfields. Passing overhead were the first flights bound for China. The supplies in the aircraft, already loaded for Fourteenth Army, were dumped on the Imphal strip and the machines took off. The noise of their engines was the first intimation anyone in Fourteenth Army had of the administrative crisis now bursting upon us.

For it was a crisis. It meant that the second foundation—a firm allotment of air-lift—on which all our plans had been based, was swept away. The loss threatened to bring operations to a standstill. The proposed move of 4 Corps, which I was then contemplating and on which Fourteenth Army staffs were already working, was most affected; but even in 33 Corps, whose arrangements were less difficult, the build-up of supplies and stores for the advance would now be dangerously slow. What this would mean in additional anxiety and work for all administrative staffs could hardly be exaggerated. I was especially sorry for those of Fourteenth Army and 4 Corps Headquarters. They were wrestling with a complete change of plan and the diversion of half the army to Meiktila; now all the calculations of air-lift and all timings would, with the loss of seventy-five aircraft, have to be worked out again. When they tackled this problem, their resiliency, ingenuity, and refusal to be beaten by anything, filled me with admiration.

Thanks to the great efforts of A.L.F.S.E.A. and S.A.C.S.E.A. and to drastic reductions in the air-lift for 15 Corps in Arakan, the lost tonnage was eventually restored from various sources, but not until there had been a serious retardation in our plans, which at a fair estimate was from a fortnight to three weeks. The effects were felt throughout the ensuing operations for two reasons: first, this slowing-up gave the Japanese extra time to recover and react to our moves, and, second, it left less time before the monsoon to complete our tasks.

Even before the unexpected reduction in our allotted air-lift, it had been obvious that the new plan would strain all our resources to the utmost. The administrative risks were great. First there was the move of 4 Corps from Tamu to Pakokku,

396

a distance of three hundred and twenty-eight miles by a very rough earth road, which in rain was impassable mud and in dry weather almost impassable dust. To move a corps of two or three divisions and a tank brigade over the curves and gradients of this track, to build up resources for a major opposed river crossing at the end of it, to place all the petrol and ammunition required for the dash to Meiktila, and to do all this within two months, without the enemy being aware of it, would require no mean effort of skill and determination.

Little maintenance transport could run on the road while the actual move was in progress, and 4 Corps had, therefore, to be supplied, and its casualties evacuated, by air. This entailed the building of numerous landing strips capable of taking the heavy C46 transports, and of other airfields for the fighters that must be brought forward to give essential cover—a vast task in itself. The crucial factor was, as so often, the adequacy of our air supply. Snelling and his staffs calculated that, if all went according to plan, our reduced air-lift, allowing for a slower build-up and rate of advance, would be just enough to maintain both corps and to build up the minimum reserves of ammunition and equipment needed for the river crossings and the subsequent battle. This made no allowance for serious enemy interference with our aircraft or for weather, both factors, which, as we already knew, could completely throw out our plans. While air transport would be our main method of maintenance for the forward formations, it alone could not possibly suffice. It had to be supplemented by every other available means. Rear formations of the army would have to be placed on supply by road, rail, or river at the earliest possible moment, and divisions moving forward would have to ferry in their own transport.

As far as roads were concerned, the need for considerable engineering resources on the track by which 4 Corps was to move to the Irrawaddy, especially on the hilly section from Gangaw to Pauk, compelled us to abandon ideas of making the road from Kalewa to Ye-u up to all-weather standard. The roads to Tiddim and Sittang had already disappeared from our plans. We had to limit all-weather construction to one stretch of road only, that from Tamu to Kalewa. This alone, with the lack of road metal and of road-making machinery, would have been impossible had not Bill Hasted, my Chief Engineer, and one of the heroes

397

of the campaign, made a revolution in road building by using 'bithess'. The earth formation of the road was levelled and packed tight, largely by hand-labour; deep ditches, with frequent spill ways, were dug along each side, and the surface covered by overlapping strips of Hessian cloth, dipped in bitumen. As long as no holes appeared in the waterproof cover all was well, and even when, as was inevitable, they did, repairs, like patching a tyre, were quickly and easily made. For over a hundred miles this novel surface proved able to take a thousand vehicles a day when the monsoon came. All the same, I had some uncomfortable moments when I thought of what depended on this one road.

The Japanese railways which we hoped to take over as we advanced would be badly damaged both by our own bombing and by demolitions. We should be very lucky if we got any serviceable locomotives, although we might pick up a little repairable rolling-stock. However, in spite of all our bombing efforts, the Japanese were working their railways, and if they could, we should be able to restore any lengths of line that fell into our hands. We therefore planned to concentrate on getting the lines Alon–Ava and Myingyan–Meiktila into operation at the earliest opportunity. It is not easy to fly in, or bring by road, railway locomotives, but from various sources we collected in India miscellaneous light engines which later we flew in in pieces or even brought whole on tank transporters. For the rest, the incomparable jeep, converted to rail, would have to serve.

In our difficulties we turned our eyes hopefully to water transport. We now held a stretch of the Chindwin and hoped soon to be on the Irrawaddy. Apart from the perils of navigation, especially on the Chindwin, there was one serious obstacle to the use of these rivers as our line of communication—we had no boats. Most of the shipping on the Chindwin we had sunk ourselves during the Retreat and since by air attack; the remainder, the Japanese had destroyed or removed downstream to the Irrawaddy. One hot day at the beginning of the advance, I took Bill Hasted, my quiet-spoken Chief Engineer, a little upstream of Kalewa and said, 'Billy, there's the river and there are the trees,' pointing to the great forests within half a mile of the bank. 'In two months I want five hundred tons of supplies a day down that river.' He looked thoughtfully at the river and the trees, and then at me. 'The difficult we will do at once; the impossible will take

398

a little longer,' he quoted from a saying in frequent use in the Fourteenth Army, and added with a grin, 'For miracles we like a month's notice!' 'You're lucky,' I answered, 'You've got two!'

But it was I who was lucky, lucky to have such a Chief Engineer. A few weeks later when I revisited the site, along the river bank, humming with activity, there was a mass production boat-building yard. Hasted's engineers, reinforced by I.W.T. construction companies flown in from India and by local Burmese labour, were turning out boats by the dozen from teak logs dragged in from the forest by 'Elephant Bill's' Fourteenth Army elephant companies. The boats were not graceful craft; they looked like Noah's Arks without the houses, but they floated and carried ten tons each. Three of these, lashed together and decked, made a very serviceable raft that would carry anything up to a Sherman tank. Building these dumb barges was no mean achievement—we launched several hundred of them—but the real problem was to provide power craft to tow them. A.L.F.S.E.A. came to our rescue by flying in outboard engines, marine petrol engines and even small motor tugs in parts which were put together on the river bank. Tank transporters, borrowed from our armoured units, went back and brought motor launches from railhead at Dimapur—a nightmare drive, described by an indignant tank commander as 'the prostitution of transportation'. Kalewa, its quays rebuilt, was restored to its former position as a considerable river port.

Some of the most spectacular feats of our I.W.T. services were the salvaging, with most inadequate and improvised equipment, of many comparatively large vessels, Japanese landing craft, heavy steel floats, tugs, and even small steamers, from the bottom of the river. These formed a considerable proportion of the tonnage eventually available. My especial pride, however, was the warships we built for the Royal Navy in our Kalewa shipyards. They were two wooden, punt-like vessels, with lightly armoured bridges, which steamed twelve knots, and were armed with one Bofors gun, two Oerlikons, and a couple of double Browning light automatics mounted for anti-aircraft fire. I claimed to be the only general who had designed, built, christened, launched, and commissioned warships for the Royal Navy. One I called *Pamela*, after Admiral Mountbatten's younger daughter, and the other *Una*, after our own daughter. The sequel to the double christening, which I effected with a couple of bottles of wine of doubtful quality, came in the form of a dignified rebuke from Their Lordships of the Admiralty who pointed out, more in sorrow than in anger, that only Their Lordships themselves were authorized to suggest names for His Majesty's ships of war. I hope they forgave me, for H.M.S. *Una* and H.M.S. *Pamela* brought the White Ensign, and all it meant to us soldiers, back to the Chindwin and the Irrawaddy. The little ships and their navy crews maintained the real Nelsonian tradition of steering closer to the enemy. They were often in action and both suffered damage from enemy shot. In their day they swept the seas, or at least the rivers. It was fun to have our own navy again.

The line of communication on which Fourteenth Army operations would, apart from direct air supply, depend as soon as the monsoon began in May, was thus a varied one, and would run:

(*a*) By the all-weather road from railhead at Dimapur, via Imphal to Tamu—206 miles. Then by,

(*b*) the fair-weather road which, by expedients like 'bithess', we hoped to make all-weather, to Kalewa—112 miles.

(*c*) Across the Chindwin by Bailey bridge and a fair-weather road to Shwebo; thence by a very bad, but all-weather, road to Mandalay and 33 Corps—190 miles.

(*d*) The river link, with our home-built or assembled boats, from Kalewa to Myingyan—200 miles—serving 4 Corps.

(*e*) Finally, from Myingyan partially by all-weather road, and, it was hoped, rail to Meiktila—59 miles.

To carry out the opposed crossing of a great river and fight a major battle at the end of such a line of communication, between five hundred and six hundred miles from railhead, would have been difficult enough had we been granted ample time, but the monsoon, to be expected in early May, meant that within five months or less we had to make this line of communication fit for bearing traffic in all weathers. If by that time we had not done so, unless we had the use of a port in South Burma, the Fourteenth Army could hardly hope to maintain itself. We were certainly going to have a busy five months.

As it emerged from the hills, 19th Division's drive gained

momentum and the enemy rearguards broke before it. On the 19th December, our men swept through Wuntho and, having turned south, by the 23rd were some twenty-five miles beyond it. This advance of nearly two hundred miles in twenty days was an astonishing feat, not so much because of the opposition overcome—although that was by no means negligible—but because of the difficulty of the country. For most of the distance there was no road; the earth track built through the hills by the Japanese for their invasion of Assam had largely disappeared during the rains. The 19th Division, with very little road-making equipment, had to cut the track anew. Most of the division went on foot, but guns and lorries had often to be winched and man-hauled up steep slopes, and in one place the only way to get the track round a cliff was to cantilever it out on timber supports. It was vastly exhilarating to fly over the division in a light aeroplane. Through gaps in the treetops that screened the hills below, I could see on every rough track files of men marching hard with a purposefulness that could be recognized from five hundred feet. Behind them gangs, stripped to the waist, were felling trees and hauling them to make rough bridges across the numberless streams and gullies that cut the route, while guns waited to move on again the moment the last log was in position. Dust rose in reddish clouds as whole companies with pick and spade dug into banks to widen the road and let the lorries pass. These men hacking out a road, dragging vehicles, pushing on with such fierce energy to get to grips with the enemy, were a heartening sight. When I came down on their hurriedly-prepared airstrips and talked to them, and to Pete Rees, who was as usual in the van, my spirits soared. The 19th Division had waited long enough to get at the enemy and nothing was going to stop it now.

Also under 4 Corps, 268 Brigade had crossed the Chindwin south of Sittang, and, advancing by jungle paths, had seized Oil Indaw, broken through the hills, and reached the Mu River which flows south into the Shwebo plain. It was now moving south on the right of the 19th Division. On the 26th December, in accordance with the new plan, I transferred both 268 Brigade and 19th Division from 4 Corps to 33 Corps*, which from that date became responsible for the tactical direction of all operations

---

* 286 had been temporarily operating under 4 Corps since 11th November and now reverted 'in situ' to 33 Corps on 19th December (see p. 394).

on the northern part of Fourteenth Army's front.

While the 19th Division had been sweeping south, the eastwatd advance of the 20th and 2nd Divisions of 33 Corps from Mawlaik and Kalewa continued. The Japanese were obviously pulling out ahead of our troops along the Shwegyin–Ye-u road, leaving it blocked by mines and felled trees. These took some time to clear and it was not until the 23rd December that the leading troops of the 2nd Division passed through Pyingaing, which, contrary to our expectation, the enemy did not attempt to hold. The first resistance was met some miles to the east, where next day a Japanese rearguard was in position astride the road. It held on obstinately, but on the 22nd, a Gurkha battalion from the 20th Division, moving south-east, came in behind the Japanese position and placed road-blocks and ambushes on the road. For five days the battalion hung on and in that time accounted for the greater part of the enemy. The 2nd Division then arrived on the 27th and attacked the gorge frontally, driving what was left of the enemy rearguard on to the Gurkha bayonets. The advance was pressed on against a little opposition and a small mechanized column made a dash for the Kabo weir. This controlled the irrigation of the Shwebo plain and its destruction would have led to eventual famine over a wide area. The column arrived just in time to forestall and drive away a Japanese demolition party. It was evident that the rapidity of our advance here also was taking the enemy by surprise, and his only reaction was some abortive raids by his fighter aircraft. The leading troops of the 2nd Division seized Ye-u and its airfield on the 2nd January 1945 and during the next day and night crossed the Mu River, both north and south of the town, against slight opposition. The Sappers then began to build a bridge to replace the old trestle one destroyed by the Japanese, and by the 5th, the 2nd Division, covered by effective air support, had established a firm bridgehead. It had also, about Kabo, made touch with the approaching 19th Division.

Then ensued a race between the 2nd and the 19th Divisions for Shwebo. The reconstructed Japanese 15th Division, which had abandoned any further attempt to hold our 19th Division, was now in full retreat to the Irrawaddy. Its place had been taken by a regiment of the Japanese 31st Division which put up a stubborn fight at Kanbalu throughout the 2nd January to cover the withdrawal. The 19th Division broke through, and its leading troops, marching a hard fifty miles to Shwebo, reached the town on the 7th. During the 8th they placed a series of stops to the east and south of the town and proceeded to mop up the Japanese garrison. On the 9th troops of the 2nd Division, after clearing minor opposition on the north-eastern approaches, entered without meeting resistance, for the enemy had that morning attempted to escape, only to be intercepted and very roughly handled by a battalion of the 19th Division some miles south of the town.

The brigade of the 20th Division, which, as already related, had crossed the Chindwin at Mawlaik early in December and moved south-east to surprise the Japanese holding up the 2nd Division east of Pyingaing, struck south from there. With all pack transport it marched by tracks through the forest, until on the 6th January it emerged and surrounded the strongly entrenched enemy communication centre of Budalin, twenty miles north of Monywa. The town fell after bitter fighting against a Japanese garrison of only a hundred, who resisted most gallantly. Only a dozen or so Japanese escaped, but our casualties were over sixty in this small but typical action. The main body of the 20th Division had followed this brigade and now began to close in on Monywa.

As 33 Corps proceeded so vigorously to clear the Shwebo plain and establish its divisions along the Irrawaddy, Messervy's 4 Corps was on its long march to Pakokku to deliver what we hoped would be the decisive stroke at Meiktila. I had transferred to Messervy's command the Lushai Brigade, already in the Myittha Valley over fifty miles south of Kalemyo, and 28 East African Brigade, which had recently come into Army Reserve. The Lushai Brigade had been in contact with the Japanese for a long time and 28 Brigade might be mistaken for the 11th East African Division, now being withdrawn after its strenuous monsoon campaign. If these two brigades were used to cover the advance of 4 Corps, I hoped they could create the illusion that only the original 33 Corps formations were in the Gangaw Valley, and 4 Corps still far away on the left of Fourteenth Army. Accordingly, Messervy ordered the Lushai Brigade to take Gangaw and 28 East African Brigade to close up on it. Behind them he turned all the engineer resources I was able to provide—

and they were not very great—to supplement his own in improving the track for the 7th Division which was to follow. By the 6th January, the bulk of this division, after a hundred miles march from Tamu, was concealed in the forests ten miles south of Kalemyo, with every available man working to improve the road.

The administrative skill of 4 Corps staff at this period, and indeed throughout the campaign, was taxed to the utmost. Not only had their complete plan been suddenly changed, when I switched them from the left of the army to its extreme right, but they had to arrange the three-hundred-mile march of the whole corps by a very inferior fair-weather track winding through hills. For miles at a time they had, in fact, to make the track. It was difficult enough to get three-ton lorries over it, but when it came to passing through the tank brigade with its fifty-ton load of tank and transporter, coaxing their long wheel bases round tight bends with one edge over a sheer drop, constantly reversing and going forward again, the march became a nightmare in slow motion. The gradients and the dust were at times such that the tanks had to tow their own transporters. Traffic control was a major problem. Imagine the scene if a tank transporter, loaded with a big motor launch, grinding up a hill on the way to Pakokku, met another returning empty, sliding in the dust down the same one-way track above a precipice. That such encounters occurred only at prepared crossing places was one of the things the road control had to watch. How effective that control was can be judged by the fact that there were no major hold-ups.

The loss of our allotted air-transport squadrons fell heavily on all our moves. What would have gone by air now had to go by road, adding to the congestion and the time. The air forces, British and American, were magnificent. The transport planes that remained to us flew incredible hours. They identified themselves completely with the army. It was as much a point of honour with them as with the soldiers that, not only the troops, but all the thousands of tons of supplies and gear required, should get through in time. Airmen, too, realized as well as we did that the whole success of the coming battle depended on the secrecy of 4 Corps' move. A single Japanese reconnaissance plane, investigating too closely a cloud of dust, might sight a line of tanks moving slowly towards Pakokku, and realize what that meant. Vincent's 221 Group R.A.F. was responsible that no enemy plane got close enough to do this, and he discharged his responsibility with unsurpassed thoroughness. Throughout daylight his fighters patrolled over the route, and, as far as I know, no Japanese scout ever penetrated his screen without being shot down for his daring. Vincent and his men piled up our debt to them until we could never repay it, and 221 Group R.A.F. had as big a share in our victory, when it came, as any army formation. We were proud to serve with them, but I could not help thinking that sometimes the army recognized their achievements more readily than some of the higher Air Force headquarters.

Gangaw proved rather a tough nut to crack. Messervy did not want to deploy too many troops against it, as that would arouse Japanese suspicions. The lightly-armed Lushai Brigade probed hard, but the Japanese, as ever, resisted stubbornly in well prepared positions. The problem was solved by laying on an 'Earthquake', that is, a really heavy—for the Burma front—air bombardment. We called in to our aid the bombers of the Strategic Air Force and a most imposing demonstration of air power was promised. To view it, the corps commander, a couple of air marshals and some other senior officers rather light-heartedly set out with me on the 10th January in a flight of light planes for Gangaw. Guided in the leading plane by a most distinguished air officer, we flew low over very attractive country. Neither my pilot nor I was concerned with navigation; we followed our leader. However, I suddenly realized we had been flying for a long time; I consulted my watch and with a start realized that unless we had travelled in a circle, which we did not seem to have done, we must for about the last half hour have been flying steadily south over Japanese-held territory. I began to take an intense interest in the country below. True enough, we were well beyond Gangaw. I signalled wildly to my companions; my pilot quickly gained height and turned back. The rest followed, we flew north again and after a little circling we found the Gangaw airstrip. Those assembled there to greet us had watched us fly steadily past them to the south, their feelings a mingling of astonishment, alarm, and—I regret to add, amongst the more junior—amusement. The air marshal's chagrin and the comments on his ability as a navigator were luckily offset by the success of the 'Earthquake'. The airmen dropped several tons of explosive for every Japanese in the position but, what was better, they dropped them *on* the position. Then cannon and rocket-firing fighters went in just ahead of the assaulting troops, the last wave, so close to our men that to keep the enemies' heads down, it had to be a dummy run. Gangaw was taken by the air force and occupied by the Lushai Brigade—a very satisfactory affair. Soon afterwards the gallant Lushai Brigade was assembled and I bade its officers and men farewell. They were then flown out to a well-earned rest in India, after a year of the most strenuous and effective long-range penetration operations. Their place was taken by 28 East African Brigade which continued to cover the concentration and screen the advance of the 7th Division close on their heels.

The divisions of the Fourteenth Army were now, in the second week of January, approaching—or, in the case of the 19th Division, were actually on—the Irrawaddy along a front of over two hundred miles, from Wuntho in the north to Pakokku in the south. The Japanese, as far as we knew, were still unaware of our change in plan and of the stealthy march of 4 Corps; their eyes, we hoped, were still fixed on Mandalay, not Meiktila. The stage was set for that most dramatic of all military operations—the opposed crossing of a great river.

CHAPTER XVIII

CROSSING THE IRRAWADDY

THE Irrawaddy, which the Fourteenth Army now approached, is one of the world's great rivers. It runs through Burma for thirteen hundred miles, a thousand of them navigable from the sea by sizable steamers. From time immemorial it has been the main highway of Burma; trade and war have followed its course. The waters of the Irrawaddy rise with the rains from March to September, when they are at their highest, and then subside again, while the river's current, like its width, varies with the season, from one and a half miles an hour to five or six. Thus, in January, the water was low and the current at its slowest.

Nevertheless, as an obstacle the Irrawaddy was most formidable. In the northern part of the Fourteenth Army area, where it confronted the 19th Division, it ran, first through forest and then for twenty-five miles between low hills, which narrowed it to some five hundred yards. As the country flattened out, the river widened to an average of two thousand yards, with a maximum of well over four thousand at its junction with the Chindwin. In the narrower parts the banks shelved steeply; in the broader stretches, through flat, arid country, they were low and the stream was frequently divided and obstructed by islands and sandbanks, which changed position with every flood. In many places, as the water had fallen, it had left behind broad stretches of soft sand into which vehicles sank axle deep, thus limiting the approaches to the river. Navigation was always difficult, especially when, as now, the water was low, and the selection of a crossing place could only be made after detailed reconnaissance.

By the 9th January, patrols of the 19th Division of 33 Corps had reached the Irrawaddy about Thabeikkyin, and found the enemy on both sides of the river. This energetic division at once began vigorously to clear the west bank, meeting with considerable opposition. The 2nd British Division was in the Shwebo area, moving south, while the 20th Division was sweeping down on Monywa. 4 Corps had begun its long march to Pakokku, and the Lushai Brigade was about to attack Gangaw to clear the way, while the head of the 7th Division was stealthily closing up behind it. The 17th Division had returned to Imphal from India, and was re-equipping on the new mechanized and airborne establishment; the 5th Division, completing the same re-organization, had recently moved to Jorhat and was in Army Reserve. The advance of the Fourteenth Army was going well.

On Fourteenth Army's left flank the N.C.A.C. was pushing south, on the east of the Irrawaddy, in a three-pronged drive against weakening opposition. Sultan had in December lost his 14th and 22nd Chinese Divisions, as these had been flown out to China in answer to urgent appeals for help. Stilwell's forecast had come true; the Japanese army was advancing, and already some American airfields had been overrun and more were threatened. In spite of this reduction in his forces Sultan continued his three advances. On his right the 36th British Division, under Festing, after making contact with our 19th Division, had on the 20th December, crossed to the east of the river at Katha and pushed south in two columns. The right column followed the river bank and was now about forty miles north of Thabeikkyin; the left, moving roughly parallel up the Shweli River Valley was some thirty miles to the east. Sultan's second prong, the 50th Chinese Division, was a little ahead of this and a further thirty miles to the east. His third prong, the 30th and 38th Chinese Divisions, having captured Bhamo in mid-December, was about to make contact with the Chinese Yunnan Force at Wanting, one hundred and twenty miles east of Katha.

To meet this menacing and broad-fronted Allied advance from the north and west, Kimura was regrouping his forces. Gradually, by piecing together intelligence from all sources, we located his divisions—with reasonable accuracy, as it proved. Honda's Thirty-third Army, consisting of the 18th and 56th Divisions, the latter temporarily reinforced by a regiment from the 49th Division and another from the 2nd Division, was south of Bhamo opposing the Yunnan Chinese and the Chinese divisions in the two eastern prongs of Sultan's advance. Katamura's Fifteenth Army, made up of the 15th, 53rd, 31st, and 33rd Divisions, was along the line of the Irrawaddy in that order from north to south. The bulk of the 53rd Division, which during December had opposed the 36th British Division in the Railway Corridor, had, our intelligence believed, been withdrawn to the Mandalay area. Identifications of Japanese dead showed that it had been replaced by detachments of the 18th and 56th Divisions, drawn from the formations opposite the Chinese. On the Fourteenth Army front, the 15th and 53rd Japanese Divisions, widely spread, faced the threat of our 19th Division; the 31st garrisoned the Sagaing Hills and the Irrawaddy line to the west, while the 33rd Japanese Division covered Monywa and the Gangaw Valley. In Arakan and South Burma the enemy had his 54th and 55th Divisions. Somewhere behind his front, we calculated, were the rest of his 2nd and 49th Divisions, a couple of strong independent brigades, and the surviving I.N.A. formations, some of which we suspected were on the river bank well west of Mandalay.

The enemy knew we were about to attempt crossings, and, realizing that it was impossible to hold two hundred miles of river line continuously and effectively in strength, he did not attempt to do so. Instead, he wisely concentrated his defences at the most likely crossing places, watched the intervening spaces, and held his reserves, especially artillery and tanks, mobile and well back, until our intentions were clearer. He left certain detachments on our side of the river in the Sagaing Hills and around Kabwet, some sixty miles north of Mandalay, to impede our advance, to give him observation, and if necessary to form sally ports across the river. He also organized small suicide penetration units to raid on our bank, and, by interfering with our preparations, to delay and confuse us. Generally speaking, Kimura's dispositions to meet our assault from the north were suitable, and after his tour of inspection, he probably felt that, while he might not be able to stop us crossing in some places, he should be able to destroy such forces as did manage to get over. His shortage of air support and reconnaissance was, of course, a great handicap, and must have worried him a great deal, but he made arrangements to use what he had more freely and more boldly.

If Kimura was not without anxieties, I certainly had mine. One of the greatest was shortage of equipment. I do not think any modern army has ever attempted the opposed crossing of a great river with so little. We had few power craft, and those we had were small, old, and often damaged by the long journey over execrable roads. Our handful of military boats and rafting stores had seen months, even years, of hard use and rough handling. All our equipment was very much 'part worn'. We were especially weak in outboard engines, on which we should have to rely to a great extent; most, even of those available, were underpowered for their tasks and almost all were unreliable. We tried to eke out our own equipment with a number of captured pontoons, but these were of poor type and really suitable only for bridging. Burmese country boats, of which we obtained a few, were good cargo carriers, but, to the uninitiated, extremely awkward to navigate. We strained every nerve to produce more amphibious equipment, but it was simply not there. My headquarters found all the equipment, technical units and help it possibly could, but, strive as we would, I could not provide my corps commanders with more than a fraction of what I should have liked or of what they might reasonably demand. Apart from its deplorable quality, I could not give them equipment enough to allow of more than one division at a time crossing in each corps, and, even for that one division, far too many trips would be required, the boats and rafts having to ferry back and forth many times. I was, as I said at the time, asking them to cross on 'a couple of bamboos and a bootlace'. They knew the risks quite as well as I did, but neither they nor the divisional commanders made unnecessary protests. They realized no more was available; what was lacking in material they made up in ingenuity, skill, organization, and determination. The only equipment my army had in full supply was, as ever, brains, hardihood, and courage.

There was, however, one way in which I could help them—in the air—and I appealed for a greater allotment of air power to Fourteenth Army for the forthcoming operations. Stratemeyer, the American general commanding Eastern Air Command, responded nobly. In January he placed the United States 12th Bombardment Group at the orders of Vincent's 221 Group R.A.F., and this he followed by instructions to Major-General Davidson's 10th U.S. Army Air Force, to the Strategic Air Force, and to 224 Group R.A.F. in Arakan, to give all support possible to Fourteenth Army on demand. This gave Vincent a really formidable strength, which, helped by closest co-operation between our staffs, he handled brilliantly throughout the whole operation.

I had already moved my headquarters to Imphal. It had been a relief to get away from Comilla at last. At Imphal, not only was the climate preferable but the whole atmosphere was better for a fighting headquarters. As neither Vincent nor I intended to stay so far back when the battle moved on, he at once began to make the headquarters of his 221 Group mobile and jungle-worthy. From that time onwards, our two headquarters lived side by side, worked and moved as one. To see Vincent's Chief of Staff, the huge 'Tiny' Vass, and my stocky 'Tubby' Lethbridge, both stripped to the waist, working out their intricate, dovetailed programmes of day and night air reconnaissances, patrols, strafes, supply drops, bridge bustings, and bombardments, was a lesson in good temper and inter-Service co-operation. The Allied air forces ranged all over Burma as far south as Rangoon, on a plan designed almost entirely to help Fourteenth Army. Enemy fighter squadrons were driven farther and farther back, his com-munications harried all round the clock, his movement by day made perilous and by night delayed. Our attacks were preceded by devastating 'earthquake' bombardments; our bridgeheads as we clung to them screened by fire from the air. Never, I believe, was air co-operation closer, quicker or more effective; never was it more gratefully appreciated than by the Fourteenth Army and its commander.

Major problems that faced me were the timing and location of the crossings, notably the relation between those of 33 Corps and 4 Corps. In what order should the divisions cross and where? It would, of course, have been nice to have crossed everywhere simultaneously and thus have confused and spread out the opposition, but this was out of the question. We lacked not only the equipment but also the supporting arms to allow more than one division in each corps to cross at a time. The broad plan was to persuade Kimura to believe that the main crossings would be north and immediately west of Mandalay, so that, when he was thoroughly committed in desperate fighting in that area, the decisive blow at Meiktila would catch him off balance.

Obviously the first crossing should, therefore, take place north of Mandalay. If the 19th Division got over here, it would look as if it was meant to join with the British 36th Division, already on the east bank, in a strong drive on Mandalay from the north. This would draw enemy formations to meet it. The 19th Division was, therefore, ordered to snatch a crossing as quickly as possible, well above Mandalay. There would then inevitably be a pause while the rest of 33 Corps drew up to the river and prepared to cross. 4 Corps, with much farther to go and more unknown perils to meet, might be later in arriving on the river about Pakokku. Would it be better to let the next division of 33 Corps cross west of Mandalay before 4 Corps farther south? If it did, it should strengthen the idea that our main thrust was in the north and might attract and pin down still more Japanese formations in that area. On the other hand, I was very nervous that Kimura would realize that the southern crossing was in strength. The longer Messervy's divisions hesitated on the bank or were assembled near it, the greater the risk of discovery. I decided, therefore, that the first 4 Corps crossing should take place as soon as Messervy was in position to launch it. This would mean that it would probably be either simultaneous with, or a little after, the 33 Corps crossing west of Mandalay. As soon as possible after the establishment of its bridgehead, 4 Corps would deliver the mechanized and airborne blow at Meiktila.

Once these decision were made, I left it to corps commanders to select the exact locations for their crossings, to choose which divisions should make them, and to prepare the best tactical plans and arrangements that the meagre resources I had allotted them would permit. It was a busy time for all of us. Corps and divisional commanders were immersed not only in the daily control of the fighting, but in the immensely complicated build-up and preparation for the crossings. Unless one has been engaged in the actual staff work of such operations, it is impossible to realize the vast amount of detail and the accurate timing on which, by the narrowest margins, success may depend. Nor is it easy to realize the burden of an anxiety that may not be shown, but which all commanders must carry. I had again moved my and 221 Group Headquarters, this time into the jungle just north of the Kalemyo-Kalewa road, and I paid frequent visits by air to both corps; but my main responsibility at this time was to see that the transportation resources of the army brought forward smoothly and steadily the great tonnages of supplies, ammunition, and equipment required for the crossings and for the new battles that would follow.

I really believe that the heroes of this time were the men who kept the wheels turning and the wings flying—the Indian drivers who, two to each three-ton lorry, drove night and day in shifts over hundreds of miles of crumbling roads; the Sappers who built up those roads almost between the passing wheels; the R.I.E.M.E. men who worked incredible hours to turn the worn vehicles round again; the Air Force mechanics, stripped to the waist, who laboured in the sun by day and the glare of headlights by night to service the planes. All of them were magnificent to watch. They identified themselves utterly with the troops ahead; they were and felt themselves to be a part, and a vital part, of the team. They had the pride and bearing of fighting men, for they were one with them.

Yet sometimes, even when I was in the midst of these splendid men or with the forward divisions, doubt and fear slunk in upon me. I was asking so much of them—was it too much? In no other theatre would an army have been launched on such a task with so pitiful an equipment. Success depended on what? Luck? A Japanese pilot streaking the tree tops in his Oscar, an enemy agent with a wireless set crouched above the track counting tanks, or a prisoner tortured until he talked—and Kimura's divisions would move, the muzzles of his guns swing towards our crossing places. Imagination is a necessity for a general, but it must be a *controlled* imagination. At times I regained control of mine only by an effort of will, of concentration on the immediate job in hand, whatever it was. And then I walked once more among my soldiers, and I, who should have inspired them, not for the first or last time, drew courage from them. Men like these could not fail, God helps those who help themselves. He would help us.

I drew comfort, too, at this time from quite another thought. I had, more than once, in two great wars, taken part in the forcing of a river obstacle, and I had on every occasion found it less difficult and less costly than expected. I had also read some military history, and, although I cudgelled my brains, I could not call to mind a single instance when a river had been successfully held against determined assault. As the time drew near for the first crossings, I hugged this thought to me. Historically, the odds were in my favour.

When on the 9th January 1945 the 19th Division had first reached the Irrawaddy, they had slipped a British patrol across by night near Thabeikkyin. This patrol located some Japanese positions on the east bank and got back safely. By the 11th, Rees's troops were probing up and down the west bank, and on that day got more patrols across, ten miles south of Kyaukmyaung. A battalion, at the same time, bumped into the well dug-in and fiercely defended enemy position on the west bank near Kabwet. A brisk little action ensued, in which our troops cleaned up a part of the position, but it became clear that the Japanese had, and intended to keep, a bridgehead of their own on our bank. Rees detailed troops to contain and to reduce this position, which, being in the middle of his stretch of river bank, was a considerable nuisance. During the next few days the 19th Division continued to draw up to and clear the west bank. Then, on the 14th, an infantry company crossed by stealth near Thabeikkyin, to be followed by one of the remaining companies each day, until a whole battalion was over. At first they met only slight opposition from patrols, but were soon held up just south of the village, where a small bridgehead was formed. During the night of the 14th/15th January the main 19th Division crossing began about Kyaukmyaung, twenty miles south of Thabeikkyin. Here the Japanese held no posts on the river bank, and the first battalion to cross remained concealed until the next night, when another joined it and there were some patrol clashes.

A third battalion crossed on the night of the 16th/17th and, for the first time, on the 17th, the enemy, realizing that a serious attempt at crossing was in progress, collected his rather scattered troops and attacked heavily. This he continued at intervals throughout the day, but all these attacks were beaten off. By the 19th, the whole of 64 Brigade was in the Kyaukmyaung bridgehead, and was steadily expanding it against increasing opposition. On the night of the 20th/21st, after heavy artillery preparation, the Japanese put in several determined attacks, which were again repulsed with heavy loss after hand-to-hand fighting. In spite of mounting resistance and growing casualties, the brigade pressed outwards and seized a ridge of scrub-covered rock, eight hundred feet high, parallel to the river, three miles inland, and a bare peak rising abruptly from the river bank, two and a half miles south of the original crossing. These successes deprived

the Japanese of direct observation over the bridgehead, blinded
their artillery and thus, in fact, ensured its retention. Farther north,
the bridgehead at Thabeikkyin had been reinforced just in time
to throw back a series of savage counter-attacks.

The Japanese, confused by numerous feints and patrol crossings
elsewhere, had not been quick to decide which were the real
crossings, and even then they took some time to concentrate
against them. Every hour of this delay was invaluable to the
sweating 19th Division, ceaselessly ferrying men and supplies
across the river on almost anything that would float. Yet, once
they had begun to assemble, the enemy reacted swiftly and
violently. As I had hoped, Katamura, commander of the 15th
Japanese Army, responsible for the river line here, took these
crossings to be an attempt to join up with the 36th British
Division, as a preliminary to an advance down the east bank on
Mandalay by the whole of our 4 Corps, which he still thought
was on the Fourteenth Army's left. He called up his 15th and
53rd Divisions and added artillery units from his other divisions,
the 31st and 33rd. Kimura, who himself believed, as did his army
commander, that this was the expected British 4 Corps attack,
transferred to Katamura a strong force of additional artillery and
some of his few remaining tanks. This was a formidable force
with which to overwhelm the two brigades of our 19th Division
newly across the river, but Katamura, luckily for us, instead of
building up a strong, well-prepared attack, committed the
common Japanese error of launching his troops into the assault
piecemeal as they arrived. Covered by the heaviest artillery
concentration that our troops had as yet endured on so small a
front, he put in attack after attack, some by direct suicide assault,
some by infiltration. These were kept up almost daily and nightly
for three weeks. Gradually, as the enemy dead piled up, the edge
was taken from the attack and, in the beginning of February, for
the first time, there was a lull for two days and two nights. Tanks
had now been ferried over, and preparations were begun for the
break-out.

I had visited the bridgeheads and seen something of the bitter
struggle to retain them. The fighting had been severe, the
casualties to our men considerable and the strain of fighting in
these restricted places with their backs to the river no light one.
The troops looked fine-drawn and thin, but were in good heart.

I was able to visit my own old battalion, the 1/6th Gurkha Rifles, in which I had served for many happy years. It was good to see them again and to be told by their divisional commander that they had done well in the bridgehead fighting. I spoke to Gurkha officers whom I had first known twenty-odd years before, when I was Adjutant and they were chubby recruits straight from the Nepal hills. Now they were subadars, commanding companies and platoons on a hard-fought field, wise soldiers and real leaders. The British officers whom I had known as junior subalterns—some, the sons of my friends, even as babies—were now seasoned battalion or company commanders, among them General Cowan's son, a most gallant and promising young officer. I felt proud—and a little conscious of my fifty-odd years—as I looked at them.

They were all loud in their praises of Vincent's airmen who supported them. He had moved fighter squadrons to strips within a few miles of the river and the answer to a call for help from the bridgeheads came in a matter of minutes. When I visited these airmen I saw pilots leaving for their fifth or sixth sortie of the day. Their part in holding the bridgeheads was a great one. They became particularly effective in locating and silencing the Japanese artillery, and in shooting up his tanks.

After the lull, the Japanese renewed their attacks on the bridgehead, but their assaults were neither in the same strength nor pressed with the same resolution. They were attempts to hold rather than to evict. The fact was, that during February, our increasing pressure nearer to Mandalay was preventing further reinforcement of the Japanese facing the 19th Division. While the enemy thus weakened, our men in the bridgehead gathered strength as replacements for casualties, tanks, transport, and supplies were ferried over to them. They, in their turn, passed to the attack. Day by day, night by night, they pushed back the enemy, a hundred yards here, a quarter of a mile there, as in bitter local actions we drove them out of villages and off high ground. Steadily the bridgehead grew in area and in security.

While 19th Division fought hard to gain and hold its footing over the Irrawaddy, the 20th Division, under Gracey, drew near to Monywa. The town had been largely destroyed during the Retreat in 1942 and it had since then been subjected to numberless air bombardments, so that it was now a mere skeleton, but it had remained the chief Japanese river port and administrative centre on the Chindwin. We knew that it had been extensively fortified, and we did not expect it to be given up without a struggle. Nor was it. From the 14th to the 16th January, Gracey's men were engaged in clearing its approaches and the surrounding country of enemy parties who withdrew on the town. The assault proper began by heavy attacks on the defences by fighter bomber and rocket aircraft. The enemy positions were of exceptional strength, comparable to those at Kohima, and were held by part of a regiment of the Japanese 33rd Division, who, as was their habit, made us pay for every strong-point we took. On the 22nd January the last resistance was overcome, the survivors of the garrison faded away, and Monywa was ours.

As soon as Monywa was securely in our hands, I moved my Tactical Headquarters there as it was admirably placed to control both my corps. On the 8th February my main headquarters with the Headquarters 221 Group joined me there, and we set up a complete and very comfortable joint headquarters, partly in the jungle and partly in some of the least battered houses on the outskirts. The Japanese had left behind a number of booby traps which were disconcerting, but my chief frights came from snakes which abounded in the piles of rubble. They seemed specially partial to the vicinity of my War Room which lacked a roof but had a good concrete floor. It was my practice to visit the War Room every night before going to bed, to see the latest situation map. I had once when doing so nearly trodden on a krait, the most deadly of all small snakes. Thereafter I moved with great circumspection, using my electric torch, I am afraid, more freely than my security officers would have approved. It seemed to me that the risk of snake bite was more imminent than that of a Japanese bomb. Paying one of my nightly visits, moving slowly, and, as I was wearing rubber-soled shoes, silently, I lifted the blanket which served as a door. On the other side of the room, seated before the situation map, lit by a shaded light, were the officer on duty and a younger colleague who had recently joined the headquarters. The older officer was speaking in the voice of assured authority. He placed his finger firmly on the map. 'Uncle Bill,' he announced, 'will fight a battle here.' 'Why?' not unreasonably asked the youngster. 'Because,' came the answer, 'he always fights a battle going in where he took a licking coming out!'

On the day Monywa was taken, other troops of the 20th Division, pressing on, reached the Irrawaddy at Myinmu. Near here, a few days later, there was a fight with a large Japanese party attempting to withdraw over the river. Resisting stubbornly, the enemy had been almost annihilated, when the last survivors, in full equipment and with closed ranks, under the astonished eyes of our men, marched steadily into the river and drowned. For the next ten days the division searched for a crossing place. Daring reconnaissances were carried out and our patrols, constantly pushed across the river, maintained a reign of terror and thuggery among the Japanese posts on the southern bank.

During this period I visited Gracey's units, and, on one occasion, attended a performance of some well-known Ensa artistes near Allagappa, not far from the river bank. I thought what a tribute it was to our Air Force that in broad daylight we could collect several hundred men to watch a show almost within artillery range of the enemy. It was a good show, too, and I was sorry I should have to leave before it was over to get back to the airstrip. However, just when I was due to leave it was whispered to me that a Japanese raiding party was across the road I should have to travel, so I was able, with a clear conscience, to continue my enjoyment while the intruders were chased away, and afterwards to thank the artistes, one of whom was a lady.

At this time the Japanese commander, Kimura, realized that his attempts to delay us in the Chindwin–Irrawaddy loop had for all practical purposes failed. He still retained a footing on the north bank at Sagaing, where he was so strongly dug in among the hills that it would have been very expensive to eject him. His other holds on our bank at Kabwet, in the midst of our 19th Division, and in our 20th Division sector, had by now been wiped out. Although he had failed to drive the 19th Division bridgeheads back into the river, and he must have known we were about to attempt crossings in the stretch of river west of Mandalay, Kimura did not waver in his determination to hold the line of the Irrawaddy, and at all costs prevent us entering Central Burma.

His dispositions were made solely to meet the threat from 33 Corps, for as yet he had no knowledge of our projected main stroke at Meiktila with 4 Corps. The activity towards Pakokku he regarded as demonstrations by minor forces. He hoped to contain the 19th Division in its bridgeheads with his 15th Division; his 31st Division would hold Sagaing and the southern river bank as far west as Ngazun. The impending crossing by our 20th Division he would meet in the first place with his 33rd Division, strengthened by a regiment of his 4th Division, additional artillery, and the bulk of what was left of his 14 Tank Regiment. He had, indeed, already moved troops from Pakokku northward. His 53rd Division he would place centrally, just south of Myotha, as a mobile reserve to strike as required when the battle for the crossings developed. Though we did not discover this until a week later, he brought one regiment of his 2nd Division from Meiktila to reinforce the west of Mandalay. In addition, he proposed to withdraw troops from his 18th Division on the Lashio sector to Mandalay. Kimura exhorted his troops to stand fast and promised them victory in what he called the 'decisive battle of the Irrawaddy Shore'. The length of the river line he had to defend and his shortage of troops he tried to counteract by preparing many more positions than he could expect to hold simultaneously. He moved bodies of troops from one to the other to deceive us and hoped when our plans were clearer to be able to occupy the appropriate ones in time.

Gracey, meanwhile, searched for crossing places. He had a couple of weeks in which to do this, as at least that time was needed to build up in 33 Corps area the supplies and equipment that would be required for the Irrawaddy battle. This build-up was not easy. I gave preference in transport and air-lift to 4 Corps, who not only had the more difficult and hazardous operation, but would, I hoped, be the decisive factor. This meant some restriction on the operations of 33 Corps, before the crossings, and a slowing up of its preparations, which were very galling to them, but which were unavoidable if the Pakokku crossing was not to risk discovery. 33 Corps, which up to now had been the favoured child in the Fourteenth Army, found some of these things hard to bear, especially as its troubles were added to by some ominous creaking in the new air transport machine as it got into top gear. However, in spite of several minor crises, the whole forward concentration of the corps, including its tank brigade, and the assembly of the stores and equipment allotted to it for the battle, were completed in time.

The actual 20th Division crossings, covered by several feints, began on the night of the 12th/13th February. There were two—a main one by 100 Brigade just west of Myinmu, and a subsidiary by 32 Brigade about seven miles downstream. Firm ground led down to the water and there was some cover for forming up, but the sites were selected mainly because reconnaissance had shown that there were no Japanese permanently posted to cover them and their patrolling was not frequent. The spot chosen for 32 Brigade crossing was also on the exact boundary between the Japanese 31st and 33rd Divisions as shown by captured maps. Experience had taught us that to attack at such a point was always an advantage, as the Japanese rarely seemed properly to interlock their junction points.

At 0400 hours on the 13th February the leading flight of 100 Brigade, the Border Regiment, pushed off in silence. The night was dark but throughout the evening the wind had freshened and it now proved troublesome to heavily laden and underpowered boats. The river here was fifteen hundred yards wide, but obstructed by partially submerged sandbanks, between which ran strong currents. Several boats grounded and there was difficulty in getting them off. At first there was luckily no opposition, and it was not until some time after the first troops had landed that light and ill-aimed small arms and mortar fire was directed against them. Once the first landing had been made, the rest of the brigade followed rapidly, and by eight o'clock the whole of it was over—an excellent piece of organization. A well-directed and heavy air strike on the Japanese artillery that was likely to cover the crossing places had been put down the previous day, and the enemy guns were in process of moving or taking up new positions at the critical time. A few 75-mm. shell burst on the beach with little effect. The landing could be claimed as a complete surprise and practically unopposed. By dusk on the 13th February, 100 Brigade had established a small bridgehead.

32 Brigade had a longer water crossing and suffered greater difficulties from wind, currents, and sandbanks. The outboard motors were, as usual, unreliable and very difficult and noisy to start. However, here also the crossing was a surprise and by dawn the first battalion, the Northamptons, were over and

digging in. All ferrying at both crossings stopped at daylight, but neither bridgehead was seriously attacked through the day. Again the Japanese were slow to recognize main crossings and to collect their troops to attack. Real opposition did not begin until the 15th when Japanese aircraft straffed the beaches, damaging a number of boats but inflicting few casualties. This was followed by a heavy night attack on 100 Brigade, during which the Japanese landed by boats behind our men and used flame throwers. The attack was repulsed and, pushing on, our troops extended their bridgehead until it was over three miles long by half a mile deep.

Fighting now became fiercer as each enemy reinforcement arrived, to be thrown in, as usual, piecemeal. By the 15th February, in spite of pressure, our bridgehead was six miles by two, so that on the 16th we were able to start ferrying by day and our build-up rapidly increased. There followed a series of suicide attacks, mainly on 100 Brigade, by waves of Japanese infantry supported by tanks, but the two bridgeheads had now joined up and they held firm. The enemy losses were heavy; five of their attacks were in daylight, and on several occasions our aircraft caught them as they assembled for the assault. Rocket-firing Hurricanes proved our most successful anti-tank weapon, and their best day was the 20th February, when they knocked out thirteen medium tanks. The fiercest fighting with the heaviest casualties on both sides occurred between the 21st and 26th February. When the Japanese counter-attacks were finally thrown back and they recoiled exhausted, on one sector of our defences five hundred enemy corpses were buried by bulldozers and on another over two hundred. The commander of the Japanese 33rd Division, Tanaka, said later that during this period two of his battalions delivered an attack with a strength of twelve hundred men, only to lose nine hundred and fifty three. By the 27th February, fighting strongly, the 20th Division had expanded its holding to eight miles by two and a half in depth. Some of the hardest fighting of the campaign had taken place in this narrow bridgehead.

While these events were happening on 33 Corps front, 4 Corps, to the west of the Chindwin, had been collecting and driving south towards the Irrawaddy at Pakokku. When on the 10th January the Lushai Brigade captured Gangaw, the 7th Indian

Division, leading the secret 4 Corps advance, was stretched out over three hundred and fifty miles of road from there to Kohima. By the 18th practically the whole division was collected in the Kan area, one hundred and sixty miles from its objective, Pakokku. Messervy, the corps commander, and Evans, the divisional commander, appreciated the need for speed, as I had given the 15th February as the last date acceptable for the crossing. They feared that even small Japanese rearguards on the difficult main track through the hills could cause fatal delay, and so they planned the advance on a wide front to outflank enemy holding the track. Ahead, as advanced guard, was to go 28 East African Brigade to conceal the arrival of other troops in the area; behind them would follow at a respectful distance one brigade (114) and the headquarters of the 7th Division. 89 Brigade, all on pack transport, was to push out by jungle tracks on the left flank and then swing in on the main route again at Pauk, only forty miles from Pakokku. It was hoped that this would cut off the Japanese rearguards facing the East Africans, or would at least make them withdraw. Out to the left towards the Chindwin, 4 Corps sent the Lushai Scouts and Chin Hills Battalion to guard the flank of the marching columns, and farther still on the west bank of the river itself a Punjabi battalion formed a link with 33 Corps now approaching Monywa on the other bank. On the right of the 7th Division the Falam Scouts moved through the hills to cover that flank. One brigade (33) was to remain at Gangaw, and ferry forward later as transport became available.

This advance, which began on the 19th January, went well. The Japanese rearguards astride the main track, which were small and obviously under orders only to delay, relied largely on obstructions and mines. In one stretch of three miles through the hills they felled across the path several hundred trees. With the help of the 'Quads', gun-towing vehicles of the field artillery, and ten elephants, the divisional engineers cleared this in one day. Half way through the march a Japanese force counter-attacked the Falam Scouts out on the right and drove them in towards the column. For the moment there was some alarm, but an Indian battalion, hurriedly sent out, stiffened the Scouts and held off the enemy, who proved to be not in great strength. 89 Brigade carried out its hook without meeting any opposition until on the 28th January it seized Pauk, and had a skirmish to gain the high ground across the main track fifteen miles farther on, over-looking the Irrawaddy Valley. Here 4 Corps got its first distant view of its objective.

At Pauk the 7th Division took over the lead. 114 Brigade passed through 89 Brigade on the 3rd February to attack Pakokku, the approaches to which were known to be strongly defended on the west bank. The East African Brigade was sent south to make a feint at crossing opposite Chauk, forty miles downstream from Pakokku, and 33 Brigade was brought forward to Pauk. The march had been a trying one. When I saw the troops at Pauk their jungle green uniforms and their faces were red from the dust, and the jungle itself on each side of the track was red too, every leaf thick in dust. But there was no rest, even for the units halted at Pauk. Every available man was turned out to build airstrips and to improve the road so that tanks, heavy lorries, and transporters carrying the precious boats for the crossings could come forward.

Throughout the march, daily planning conferences had been held at 4 Corps Headquarters and later at Divisional Headquarters, when the most thorough instructions were issued for the crossings. The exact sites would, of course, have to wait on actual recon-naissance, but Messervy had already decided that they would be in the neighbourhood of Nyaungu, at the narrowest part of the river. He realized that because of this, Nyaungu was rather an obvious place, but the slowness and fewness of his power craft and the need to build up quickly on the far bank forced him to choose a short crossing. Even here the river was a thousand yards wide. Deception was essential. He planned to divert the enemy from his real crossing place by having, in addition to that of the East Africans at Chauk, two other demonstrations—a main one at Pakokku itself and another at Pagan, six miles south of Nyaungu. So much depended on these deceptions that they were elaborately and carefully prepared. I longed to be able to give Messervy a battalion or two of parachute troops, who would have simplified his problem a great deal, but we had none.

Daily photographic air reconnaissance along the Irrawaddy, combined with other sources of intelligence, gave us a fairly complete idea of the Japanese dispositions on the sector which 4 Corps was approaching. The enemy had no suspicion that a major crossing was about to be attempted here. His troops were strung out along the river. On the west bank in the Letse area, fifteen to twenty miles north-west of Chauk, he had 153 Regiment. The four battalions of 72 Independent Mobile Brigade with the 2nd Indian National Army Division, whose strength was variously reported as between five and ten thousand, held a wide stretch from Chauk to Nyaungu. Farther north about Pakokku was 214 Regiment. For some fifty miles of river this was not much. The enemy were thin on the ground, and, if we could draw them away from our crossings, we might hope to have a substantial grip on the far bank before they could collect force enough to oust us. One advantage of Messervy's choice was that, like the 20th Division, he was crossing at the junction of two Japanese formations. 214 Regiment at Pakokku was the extreme left of the Japanese Fifteenth Army and 72 Independent Brigade was the right of Twenty-eighth Army; the boundary between the two ran practically through Nyaungu.

4 Corps' threefold advance to the river was pushed with determination. 114 Brigade, approaching Pakokku, soon ran into strong opposition, eight miles west of the town, where the enemy were well dug in on high ground at the Kanhla crossroads, and seemed determined to fight it out. Our first immediate assault failed, and it was not until the 10th February that a deliberate attack by the brigade with tanks drove the Japanese out and inflicted severe casualties on them in the open. The brigade was then given the tasks of clearing the west bank of stragglers and preventing any interference with the crossings from Pakokku which appeared to be held in force. 89 Brigade reached the west bank opposite Pagan, and by night slipped a patrol of Sikhs across, who reported by wireless that the south end of the town was unoccupied. This patrol remained hidden on the east bank and continued to send back most valuable reports of the enemy movements around it. Three or four large country boats with Burmese crews were captured near Pagan, and this, together with the reports of the patrol, decided Evans to turn the feint at Pagan into a subsidiary but real crossing. The plan was for one company to cross silently in the country boats, to be followed by the rest of the battalion. 28 East African Brigade also reached its objective, Seikpyu, without serious opposition, and began realistically to stage the first moves of a crossing. 33 Brigade, selected to make

the main crossing at Nyaungu, occupied Myitche and, under cover of the village, made its preparations.

The most thorough reconnaissance possible with the enemy on the opposite bank was made to select the actual crossing places. The water had again dropped in February and it was found that the river had considerably changed its bed. New sandbanks had appeared, and no direct crossing was possible. The oblique courses that had to be followed were from fifteen hundred up to two thousand yards long. In fact, one of those eventually used was just over two thousand, the longest opposed river crossing attempted in any theatre of the Second World War. Soundings were made by night by men of the Special Boat Section and frogmen who painstakingly charted the only practicable channels. The west bank was low and cultivated with rice fields at practically river level; the east bank, a line of rugged cliffs one hundred feet high, broken by eroded gullies, completely overlooked it. Defences could be seen in places along these cliffs, but as the days passed no increase in them showed on our air photographs. On the other hand, more digging appeared opposite those places where we were making feints.

It had originally been intended to make a daylight crossing with full artillery, air, and tank support to overwhelm opposition, but the shortage of air lift and the difficulties of road transportation made it impossible to dump the ammunition required in the time. The idea of a completely silent night crossing was then explored, but there would be no moon and it was thought that boats would be unable to find the tortuous channels in the dark, and this method was abandoned. Finally it was decided that the first flight would be silent just before dawn and would be followed up immediately by the remaining flights in power craft under all available covering fire. It was calculated that, even if all went well, a brigade could not be ferried over in the equipment available in less than seven hours.

Eventually it was decided that the operation should be in four phases:

(i) An assault crossing, the first flight of which was to be silent and at night, launched from points on the west bank, one and a half to three miles upstream of Nyaungu, to seize four beaches and the cliffs one mile north-east of the village on the east bank. The South Lancashire Regiment was loaned for the assault crossing from another brigade as they had had experience in boat work and had taken part in the landing at Madagascar.

(ii) A rapid follow-up in daylight of the three battalions of 33 Brigade and some tanks, under all available covering fire, to build up the bridgehead.

(iii) A rapid advance from the bridgehead to capture Nyaungu and with it the eastern end of the shortest river crossing, which would be organized and put into operation at once.

(iv) Expansion of the bridgehead to take the 17th Division which would cross as soon as possible by the direct Nyaungu route.

On my visits to 4 Corps I had completely approved Messervy's and Evans's plans. I was much impressed by the skill and energy with which they overcame the obstacles that confronted them at every step in their preparations and which would have daunted any but the most forceful commanders. As the moment of this all-important crossing approached, on which the whole fabric of my battle plan rested, I devoted myself mainly to doing what I could to support Messervy.

One of the anxieties I had was to ensure that the 17th Division was ready to cross the moment the bridgehead was gained. For surprise, we must strike at Meiktila without delay. I had taken Cowan, still the divisional commander, and his senior officers now at Imphal, completely into my confidence and explained their role to them. They seized the opportunity to study the country they would operate over and to conduct sand-table exercises based on the forthcoming operations. The move from Imphal to Pauk caused anxiety, as the transport shortage, both road and air, was still acute, but, ferrying itself a part at a time in its own transport, the division, less its airborne brigade which dropped off at Palel, was concentrated in Pauk by the 12th February—just in time. Much of the divisional artillery and engineers had already gone forward to help the 7th Division in its crossing.

The night chosen for the 7th Division crossing was the 13th/14th February. The Engineers could not begin to bring up their equipment until the enemy had been evicted from the Kanhla crossroads, and this did not take place until the 11th. Even after that, movement could only be at night. Time was short. Yet to drag these cumbersome loads along sandy, uneven tracks in complete darkness, with the least possible noise, and to have every trace of the feverish activity of the night hidden before daylight from prying eyes that overlooked every yard of our bank, was not only a vast labour but a great feat of organization. Yet by dawn on the 13th February, all the troops and the equipment were assembled in concealment within reach of the crossing points. Here they spent a day in final preparations and in a wait for zero hour, that anyone with a glimmer of imagination must have found trying.

Six miles downstream, the Sikhs of 89 Brigade were similarly and with equal stealth preparing for the subsidiary crossing, while still farther south the East Africans were more openly staging a false crossing.

As soon as darkness fell, equipment, boats, and all the paraphernalia for the main crossing began to move down to the water. Assembly areas were marked and the troops tramped slowly and silently from their bivouacs. The Special Boat Section made a final reconnaissance of the far bank to see if it had been occupied, and in doing so met two Japanese swimming in the river. To prevent their escape they had to be shot and it is possible that the noise put the enemy on the alert.

The night was pitch dark, a strong wind was blowing and there was a distinct lop on the water, as at a quarter to four, the leading company of South Lancashires got into their boats and started the long paddle across. At last their boats grounded on the opposite bank. With as little splashing as they could, they waded ashore and scrambled up the cliffs, while the boats turned and made back. By five o'clock on the morning of the 14th February the company had reached the cliff top, so far without meeting any enemy. There they disposed themselves for defence and awaited the rest of their battalion.

On the west bank the remainder of the South Lancashires moved down according to programme and began to embark just as the first faint light of dawn was tinting the sky. The channels to be followed had been marked behind the first flight and things had indeed gone well, but from that moment they began to go wrong. In spite of their past experience, the Lancashire men fumbled badly at the embarkation and there was a good deal of delay and confusion. Because of noise, it was not possible to start up the outboard engines until the men were in the boats, and when the time to do so eventually came several motors failed to start. Some of the boats also were found to leak badly, having been damaged in transit. More delay resulted. Eventually the commanding officer, realizing that a start must be made, ordered the boats that were ready to move off, irrespective of whether they were in their correct flights or not. The result was that the reserve company, which should have been last, found itself when daylight came in midstream ahead of the first wave. Even then, all might have been well had the boats made straight for the east bank, but the reserve company decided it would circle to take its proper place behind the others. The strong current and the wind were too much for the feeble engines and the reserve company, in confusion, began to drift downstream. The remaining boats, seeing them go and not realizing what was happening, turned to follow them. At this moment the enemy opened fire with rifles from the cliffs and with machine-guns from the water's edge. Two company commanders and the engineer officer were quickly killed, casualties grew, and several boats, including that of the commanding officer were sunk. The guns on our bank and some of the tanks waiting to embark now opened fire, but owing to secrecy they had not registered, and at first their shooting was perforce slow. Within a short time aircraft from the cab rank were called in and under this combined cover the boats made back to our bank. The crossing, except for the isolated company, now in great danger, had failed.

Nor was this the only failure. The subsidiary crossing by 89 Brigade had met with initial disaster. The gallant patrol hidden on the east bank in Pagan had, during the night, reported that the enemy had reinforced the town and the whole of it was now occupied. The assaulting company, however, stoutheartedly decided to set out in its native craft. As they approached the far bank they came under fire and the Burmese boatmen, not unnaturally, panicked. The clumsy boats got out of control and in spite of the Sikhs' efforts were swept downstream. At last the boatmen, urged by the sepoys, regained control and brought them back to the starting point. It would have been suicide to

428

have tried to cross in daylight in these slow, awkward boats, and there the crossing rested.

To watch across the great river as dawn breaks over ancient Pagan is to hold one's breath at so much beauty. Pagan, once the capital of Burma, was in all its glory at the time of the Norman Conquest; now, silent, ruined, and deserted, it is still noble—and very beautiful. Its twelve hundred temples, madder red or ghostly white, rise, some like fantastic pyramids or turreted fairy castles, others in tapering pagoda spires, from the sage green mass of trees against the changing pastel blues, reds, and golds of sunrise. As a foreground flows the still dark yet living sweep of moving water. Yet as the officers of 89 Brigade gazed disconsolately towards Pagan in the chill of early morning, they are to be forgiven if the beauty of the scene was somewhat lost to them. They had other and less pleasant things to think about: their attempt at crossing had definitely failed. Then suddenly, to their surprise, they saw a small boat bearing a white flag put off from the opposite bank. In it were two Jiffs, who, when they came ashore, said that the Japanese had marched out of Pagan and moved hurriedly up river, leaving only troops of the Indian National Army to garrison the town. Their one wish, now the Japanese were gone, was to surrender. Quickly a platoon of the Sikhs with a British officer crossed in the only available boats. True to their word, the garrison of Pagan marched out and with smiles laid down their arms. By evening most of the Sikh battalion was established in the outskirts of Pagan. This incident was, I think, the chief contribution the Indian National Army made to either side in the Burma War.

Back at the main crossing, while all this was going on at Pagan, the engineers were working feverishly to repair the returned boats for a new crossing. The South Lancashire Company on the east bank reported it was now firmly dug in and had not so far been attacked. It was, therefore, decided to make a second effort to reinforce it. The Brigadier judged it would take too long to reorganize the South Lancashires, so he ordered a Punjabi battalion to make the crossing as soon as possible. The 4/15th Punjabis, with great calmness and in excellent order, embarked on what promised to be a most hazardous enterprise. At 9.45 a.m. their leading company set out under the heaviest covering fire that could be provided by artillery and air. As the boats chugged slowly across they were hardly fired on at all; it seemed that there were still no Japanese at the actual crossing and that even those downstream, who had taken such toll of the South Lancashires as they drifted past, had withdrawn. Some of the boats grounded on sandbanks but the men waded or swam ashore. The whole company reached the beaches intact and swarmed up the cliffs. The curtain of covering fire moved ahead of them and swept their flanks. As soon as the boats were available the rest of the battalion began to cross, and throughout the afternoon heavily laden craft continued to go to and fro practically unmolested. By nightfall three battalions were over, and ferrying had stopped as the risk of losing boats in the treacherous current in the dark became too great.

33 Brigade for the night formed a small but well-defended bridgehead and stood-to, expecting savage counter-attacks. None came; only a few jitter parties prowled about the perimeter. We even succeeded in getting a patrol along the river bank to the Sikhs at Pagan. At dawn on the 15th, the crossing was resumed with increasing tempo. All day long men, mules, tanks, guns, and stores poured across, and again no enemy opposed them. By evening, the South Lancashires and most of 89 Brigade were in the bridgehead. The Japanese, who had now collected in some strength, were driven into caves near Nyaungu where they held out desperately in a sort of catacomb. Its entrances were blown in and sealed off, the defenders left to die inside. During the day another company of the Indian National Army surrendered. By the 16th, Nyaungu village was in our hands and the main bridge-head, now about four miles by three, had joined up with the Sikhs at Pagan. We were over.

This sudden success after a shaky beginning was something of a surprise as well as a relief. It was due, first, to the fact that the enemy command was concentrating on the crossings of 33 Corps to the north and regarded all river bank activities from Pakokku southward as mere demonstrations. A captured Japanese intelligence officer later explained that they did not believe that there was more than the East African division in the area, and that it was directed down the west bank towards Yenangyaung. Even when crossings appeared to be threatened, the enemy considered they would not be in force and that if any actual attempts were made they would be at Pakokku and Chauk. They therefore pulled their troops away to meet these threats, leaving only small detachments and the Indian National Army to watch the Nyaungu sector. In fact, as the 7th Division made its crossings the enemy was hastily marching away to the north and south from the sites—a happy result brought about by Messervy's able deception measures.

These deception measures had indeed drawn off the Japanese, as those engaged in them discovered. As 114 Brigade of the 7th Division closed in on Pakokku, the Japanese hurried in reinforcements from the river line and put up a stubborn struggle. Even after being driven out of the town, the remnants of the garrison, now convinced that a crossing was about to be attempted here, dug themselves in on an island in the river a little to the south, while other Japanese hurriedly strengthened their positions on the opposite bank. Having cleared the town and west bank, we kept the enemy pinned here by making faces at him, until he realized from the seriousness of the Nyaungu crossing that he was wasting his time.

The feint at a crossing opposite Chauk by 28 East African Brigade was so convincing that it brought prompt and violent retaliation. The Japanese here were able to counter-attack in some strength, as they had collected a force on the west bank to meet the expected advance of a division of ours towards the Yenangyaung oilfields. The East African Brigade was driven back some miles and Messervy had to send it reinforcements of all arms to prevent a threat to the route from Pauk to Nyaungu developing. After some sharp exchanges this Japanese counter-attack was held at Letse, twenty-five miles south of the road, before any delay to the main operations could be caused.

Meanwhile, in the 7th Division bridgehead there was great activity. Patrols and air reconnaissances were pushed out in all directions to give warning of the hourly expected Japanese attacks. Yet it was not until the 17th February that the enemy acted. Several air attacks were delivered on our crossing places and the enemy troops, driven across the river out of Pakokku, marched against the left flank of 33 Brigade's bridgehead at Nyaungu, where they were roughly handled by that brigade as it pushed outwards to gain elbow room. On the 19th February, 89 Brigade, doing the same to the south of Pagan, met troops of

72 Japanese Independent Brigade coming north from Chauk after the withdrawal of the East Africans. Realizing at last that the crossing at Pagan was in strength, but still not appreciating what was in store, the local enemy commander ordered all troops in the neighbourhood to concentrate against it, and drive the Allied forces back into the river and annihilate them. As a result, there was delivered against our bridgehead and its approaches a series of savage counter-attacks.

Messervy's original intention had been to expand the bridgehead sufficiently to hold two divisions before the 17th Division assembled in it, but he shared my anxiety that the blow at Meiktila should not be delayed. He therefore decided to pass over the 17th Division before the bridgehead was large enough to receive it, and to let it collect outside. During the 16th and 17th February, the 17th Division, less the brigade left at Palel, moved by night into the vicinity of the crossing and between the 18th and 21st was ferried over to its assembly areas on the east bank. As soon as any of its units were across, the division began to push out patrols, which had some skirmishes, but as far as could be ascertained the Japanese had no idea that a fresh division was now in the bridgehead.

To turn north again for a moment to 33 Corps. The 20th Division crossing, which was a direct threat to Mandalay, had, as I hoped, attracted Kimura's attention from our activities about Pagan, but I could not expect to conceal much longer our strength there. I was increasingly anxious, therefore, to push the 2nd Division over the Irrawaddy, still nearer to Mandalay, just as Kimura must begin to realize the threat to Meiktila, and thus make him hesitate to detach troops from the Mandalay front for the new battle. It was not easy to stage the 2nd Division crossing in time for this, as the equipment for it had to be collected from that used by the other divisions, a process not helped by the fact that much of it had been damaged, and a considerable portion of it had to be left with them as ferries at the crossings already made. However, Stopford and Nicholson, commanding the 2nd Division, were prepared to attempt the crossing on the 24th February, a date which suited my plans admirably.

Although the enemy must have been expecting an attempt at crossing by our 2nd Division, they had used so many of their troops in the attacks on 20th Division bridgehead and to hold the Sagaing Hills on the north bank, that for the fifteen miles of river to the west of Sagaing they had only a regiment, which could do little more than watch and patrol, with detachments at the most likely crossing places. They had, however, in several places prepared strong defensive positions and they obviously hoped, as soon as our intentions were evident, to occupy these with such reserves as they could muster. A good deal of patrol activity went on as both sides pushed scouting parties across the river and the 2nd Division nibbled into the Sagaing defences. On the 21st February Stopford, in order to allow the division to concentrate for its crossing, sent 268 Brigade to take over the Sagaing sector of its front. By constant pressure this brigade occupied the Japanese garrison, which could have been much better employed if it could have withdrawn to the southern bank.

On the moonlit night of the 24th/25th February, the 2nd British Division began its crossing at the village of Ngazun, about ten miles east of 20th Division's bridgehead. The leading battalion of 6 Brigade pushed off on the fifteen-hundred-yard crossing at 2200 hours; but the enemy were alert, and opened heavy machine-gun and mortar fire. Although our casualties were not heavy, many assault boats were holed, others damaged, and some sunk. Of the first battalion, a portion reached an island in midstream and dug in there under fire. A second battalion came under heavy fire in its boats and was forced to return to the north bank. A third battalion whose boats had been pushed somewhat downstream by the current, succeeded, less a company, in gaining the opposite bank and establishing itself precariously there. The crossing, if not a failure, was near to becoming one. Nicholson and his staff rose to the occasion. In spite of the inevitable confusion on the beaches, they reorganized the scattered 6 Brigade, brought up fresh troops, and during the 25th, under cover of smoke from all available guns of 33 Corps, disregarding heavy enemy fire, passed a battalion over the river and also completed the battalion on the island. By the morning of the 26th February, 5 and 6 Brigades were all on the south bank with some tanks. The recovery, after the initial set-back, was a fine feat of leadership and organization.

After his first resistance on the beaches, the enemy was strangely passive at this beachhead. Unlike his reaction at the others he delivered little in the way of counter-attacks, interfering with our build-up only by shelling and minor air action. Kimura was in fact pausing to regroup for a final effort on the Irrawaddy shore. He did not know it, but the real storm had not yet broken on him.

CHAPTER XIX

THE VITAL THRUST

A S the last week of February 1945 began, Kimura could—and did—contemplate the Burma scene, if not with confidence, at least with hope. On his Central front, which he recognized as the decisive one, the picture he saw was that both corps of our Fourteenth Army were in the Chindwin–Irrawaddy loop; 4 Corps on our left, with a bridgehead forty-five miles north of Mandalay, and 33 Corps with a foothold over the river thirty-five miles west of the city. Both these bridgeheads he had so far managed to contain; they were isolated and their build-up should be slow. A third division of ours had just begun another crossing nearer to Mandalay, but this, too, he could hope to hold for a time. The British 36th Division, which he had expected to continue south to join our 4 Corps, had, rather surprisingly, suddenly turned east, and was at the moment fighting a desperate battle to maintain the small bridgehead it had gained over the Shweli River at Myitsun. It seemed clear that this division was definitely committed to the American-Chinese drive on Lashio, and need not, for the present, be taken into account in the Mandalay battle.

To Kimura, the situation on his north-eastern front cannot have been reassuring. Sultan's Chinese divisions had by now joined up with the Yunnan Chinese near Wanting, and had, in addition, cut the Wanting–Lashio road some fifty miles north of Lashio. Still, the Japanese 56th Division and other troops had successfully extricated themselves and were falling back south in good order. They could be relied on to slow up the Allied advance long enough to let Kimura fight the decisive battle. In Arakan, too, things had not gone well with the Japanese. There, their 54th Division had been roughly handled by our 15 Corps, and the latest British landing on the coast at Ru-ywa threatened to cut his Arakan forces in two. However, Arakan was not a vital front, and as

435

long as the two passes, An and Taungup, between the coast and Central Burma were held, the British forces in Arakan, large as they were, could do little real damage. The threat of a seaborne invasion, that had for so long hung over Japanese heads, did not appear to Kimura imminent. To weaken forces held to meet it was a risk, but a risk that he could take.

There remained to be considered the British crossing of the Irrawaddy at Pagan. Kimura, thanks to our deception measures and the failure of his air reconnaissance, still assumed that we had in this area little more than one division, of which the bulk was on the west bank, pinned down by his troops at Pakokku and opposite Chauk. It followed that the Pagan crossing could not be in force. He was, in fact, satisfied that all our operations in that area were merely a demonstration against the oilfields to distract his attention from the main attack by our two corps on Mandalay. His formations already in the Pakokku–Chauk sector could, he felt, deal with this division, at least until he fought his main battle.

Mandalay, Kimura realized, was the decisive sector. His object must be to collect here the greatest force he could, as quickly as he could, and hurl it against the Fourteenth Army while it was split by the Irrawaddy and its divisions on his bank of the river were isolated. If he could defeat the Fourteenth Army, the loss of Lashio and Arakan would be a trifle and only temporary at that.

The situation, if it were to be retrieved, called for drastic measures. He took them. At one stroke he decided to withdraw the bulk of his forces on all other sectors of the Burma front and to bring them against the Fourteenth Army in the Mandalay area. Everything must give way to the Battle of the Irrawaddy Shore. It was a sound and soldierly decision. From Thirty-third Army, which held his northern front against N.C.A.C., he withdrew the bulk of his 18th Division and one regiment of his 49th Division, leaving only the 56th Division to face Sultan's three Chinese divisions, the Mars Brigade, and the mass of the Yunnan Chinese, while one regiment of the 18th Division delayed the 36th British Division. From Arakan, the Japanese 54th Division, dropping rearguards on the two passes, was to march with all speed eastwards and concentrate north of Yenangyaung. From Southern Burma were ordered to Mandalay the remainder of the 49th and one regiment of the 55th Division. A regiment of the 2nd Division was on its way to Siam; it was turned back at Pegu and hurried to Central Burma. The arrival of these formations, added to the four and two-thirds Japanese divisions already opposing Fourteenth Army, would give Kimura a force the equivalent of eight Japanese and one and a third Indian National Army divisions. Some of the Japanese divisions were battered and below strength and the I.N.A. formations of little fighting value, but even so these nine divisions, against the estimated British five, straddled across the river, should be enough. The Battle of the Irrawaddy Shore could yet be won!

Considering the state of his communications after two and a half years of Allied bombing and that our practically complete command of the air compelled him to make most moves by night, Kimura carried out this large-scale regrouping by road, rail, and river with surprising speed. I did not, of course, at this time, know the full extent of these transfers, but I soon began to get indications of it from many sources and to realize that the odds against me would be heavier than I had calculated.

It will be remembered that I had originally based my plan for the battle of Central Burma on the three assumptions that:

(i) The Japanese would fight in the Shwebo plain north of Mandalay.
(ii) My allotted air transport lift would not be reduced, and
(iii) Pressure on the other Burma fronts and the threat of seaborne landings would prevent the Japanese from seriously reinforcing their formations opposing my army.

The first of these, the Japanese had disposed of by withdrawing behind the Irrawaddy; the second, the Combined Chiefs of Staff in Washington and London had shattered by sending a substantial part of my American squadrons to China; and now the third had gone after the other two. War is like that.

I did what I could about it. I urged that everything should be done to increase the pressure on the other Burma fronts, especially that 15 Corps should thrust with the greatest maintainable strength from Taungup towards Prome. I was even willing to give up sixty tons a day of my precious air-lift to help with this. I also asked that the 36th British Division should be returned to Fourteenth Army, but only if its American air maintenance

could come with it. Both Admiral Mountbatten and General
Leese were sympathetic to this request, but it would naturally
take some time to return the division and its removal must
interfere with Sultan's operations. The only positive action
I could take was to bring in my last division, the 5th Indian, now
at Jorhat. I had always meant to have it for the battle. It was being
reorganized, like the 17th Division, on an airborne and mechanical
transport establishment to take part in the dash for Meiktila and
the subsequent advance—which would indeed be another dash—
on Rangoon. I had intended, if it were forced upon me by the
supply situation, to hold back or even return to India another
division so that I could use the 5th with its special mobility. Now,
when it looked as if the five divisions I had would be faced with
considerably more than that number of Japanese, it became
imperative to have the 5th Division, in addition, to make at
least six.

This, on paper, seemed to be one of those demands for a miracle
that even a month's warning would not make possible. Our
supply services were already strained; our transport aircrews
had for some weeks been flying at intensive rates, that, according
to all experience, could not be demanded for more than a few
days. There was a limit to human endurance and they must be
near it. Yet I had to have the 5th Division. It was again a question
of which risk I took—the tactical one of losing my battle through
lack of troops, or the administrative one of having the troops and
the battle collapsing because I was unable to supply them. I
decided to accept the administrative risk because, if I had the
additional division, I felt sure, in spite of developments, that I
could win the battle of Central Burma and, if I won that,
I believed I could get to Rangoon. I was strengthened in this
decision by the fact that, thanks to the efforts of Admiral
Mountbatten, our deficiency in aircraft was being slowly made
up mainly from British sources outside Burma. Besides, Hasted's
boats, built in the Chindwin shipyard, promised to give us a good
lift as soon as we could secure an Irrawaddy port, and we might
hope as we advanced to make some use of the Japanese railways.

Snelling's staff and that of Combat Cargo Task Force were
splendid. As was their duty, they pointed out the dangers, but
they knew the need, and once the decision had been made they
worked the miracle. Throughout the battle we were never without

acute anxiety on the supply and transport side. Almost daily there was a crisis of some kind. The reserves of some basic ration would fall frighteningly low, guns would be silent for want of ammunition, river craft out of action for want of spares, wounded collecting in some hard-pressed spot with no means of evacuating them. Petrol was always desperately short. Yet we got over all these difficulties and a thousand others, by juggling between formations with the limited transport available and by cruelly overworking the men who drove, flew, sailed, and maintained our transport of all kinds. Time and again, and just in time, the bare essentials for their operations reached those who so critically needed them. Very rarely had any formation more than its basic needs. If it had, it meant that some officer in it, with the understandable but selfish desire to be able to say, 'Thanks to me, our chaps are better off than other troops,' had somehow got hold of more than his fair share, while his neighbours, or more probably those ahead of him, went short. It was a natural failing, and the Army staff soon came to know who were the greedy ones, individuals and formations.

There was no difficulty, apart from maintenance, about calling in the 5th Division. Throughout January it had been preparing and, at the beginning of February, I had called its commander, Warren, to my headquarters to explain as fully as I could what would be required of him. Warren had succeeded Evans, who had fallen sick during the monsoon advance on Kalemyo in the previous September. I always found it stimulating to do business with Warren. He did not waste time or words, but asked questions on essentials, nor was he one of the selfish sort. If I told him I could not give him everything he wanted, I knew that, realizing it was not there for me to give, he would, without moaning, get on without it. As I said good-bye to him when he left me to fly back to his headquarters, he had strengthened my confidence in success. I never saw him again. Somewhere, in the two hundred and fifty miles of jungle hills between his headquarters and mine, he lies with his comrades. His loss, just when his division, which had implicit trust in him, was about to undertake difficult and arduous operations was a severe blow. He was not easily to be replaced and I feared the effect on the division. Only a month before, I had appointed Bob Mansergh, the Chief Artillery Officer of the 5th Division, to command the 11th East African Division.

He was an exceptionally able young officer whom I had marked for advancement and, above all, he was known in the 5th Division which he had served well. The 11th East African was not likely to be engaged in the near future, and there would still be time for them to settle down under a new commander. I therefore put Mansergh in Warrens' place, and I do not think I could have made a better choice. I consoled the disconsolate East Africans by giving them Brigadier Dimoline from the 28th East African Brigade. He had had much experience with East African troops and was very popular with them. Orders were issued for the 5th Division, leaving behind its airborne brigade, to move up to the Pakokku area. I watched it pass through Monywa, full of ardour, but by the time that happened the battle for Meiktila was in all its fury.

Between the 18th and the 21st February, the 17th Division and 255 Tank Brigade were brought over the river into the 7th Division bridgehead, which they expanded for their own assembly area. The advance on Meiktila began on the 21st, while the last units of the 17th Division were still crossing. 48 Brigade followed the main track east, while the tank brigade, which had left one regiment on the west bank for the Pakokku fighting, moved parallel to the south. The first resistance was soon met astride the road, but the tanks coming in from the flank, it was easily brushed aside. In the afternoon, a point some fifteen miles from the river was reached, where the road split into three; the direct continuation to the east going to Welaung, the northern fork to Kamye, and the southern to Seiktein. Reconnaissance showed that the Welaung track would be most difficult for vehicles while the other two were passable. Next day, the force therefore divided, 63 Brigade Group taking the southern route to Seiktein, while a detachment made all speed to seize some high ground eight or nine miles along the Kamye track. It was hoped that this would facilitate a pincer movement on Taungtha and perhaps, by the southern trend of the main force, give the idea that the movement was directed on the oilfields. During the day, 63 Brigade had a brisk fight with a Japanese delaying party and destroyed it, capturing two guns. On the 23rd February this brigade, turning north along the main road to Taungtha, got within two miles of Welaung against increasing opposition, again capturing two guns. Simultaneously, the rest of the 17th

Division pushed on to Kamye against little resistance, although there was an attack on the column from the air and a few vehicles were destroyed.

All that night under cover of outposts, work went on to make passable the half-mile wide sandy *chaung* west of Taungtha. Bales of brushwood and stretches of wire netting were put down, and by dawn on the 24th a passage was ready. Both columns then converged on Taungtha. 48 Brigade with the tanks easily broke through from the south-west against light opposition, but 63 Brigade from the south fought all the way against tougher defences. After the town was taken, the whole division and the tanks moved across country on a wide front, overrunning scattered parties of Japanese, to an assembly place east of Taungtha on the main road and railway to Meiktila. Before the division could settle down for the night, however, the whole of what it named 'Snipers' Triangle' between the Welaung and Meiktila roads had to be cleared of enemy suicide squads. Over a hundred snipers were flushed from their concealment and killed.

On the 25th February there was skirmishing with Japanese coming down from the north, but the division and tanks, leaving behind 48 Brigade to deal with this and to collect a supply drop, advanced fifteen miles and took Mahlaing, twenty miles from Meiktila. Next day the rest of the division, having duly collected the precious supply drop, reached Mahlaing, while the tank brigade rushed Thabutkon airstrip, ten miles farther on. As soon as it was secured, work began and was continued all night to repair damage done by the retreating Japanese. Next morning, the tank brigade was compelled to halt for a petrol drop and for maintenance, but the fly-in of 17th Division's airborne 99 Brigade began, while 63 Brigade continued the advance along the road. Eight and a half miles from Meiktila, it encountered a well-dug and wired position astride the route. This was the strongest and most determined attempt yet made to hold us up. There was very heavy machine-gun and light automatic and considerable artillery fire; the *chaung* in front of the position was well mined and the bridge over it destroyed. Without delay, 63 Brigade made a wide hook to the north, and came in behind the enemy where the position was less formidable, while the replenished tank brigade arrived and delivered a simultaneous frontal assault on a wide front. The Japanese had had no experience of these massed

441

armoured attacks and seemed quite incapable of dealing with them. The position was rapidly overrun. Its considerable garrison was hunted into the open, and there was a good killing. 63 Brigade then advanced to within five miles of Meiktila and harboured for the night. Patrols in darkness, probing the western defences of the town, reported that they were strongly held and appeared most formidable. All night, explosions could be heard and flames seen at various points over the countryside, as the enemy destroyed his supply and ammunition dumps. Cowan and his force of a division and a tank brigade had covered eighty miles over difficult tracks and against opposition. We had arrived before Meiktila; we now had to take it.

Major-General Kasuya, commanding the Meiktila area, as senior Japanese officer, had at the first alarm taken control of all enemy troops in and around the base. These totalled some twelve thousand men, but they were scattered in several detachments, protecting dumps, airfields, and communications. In addition, he had about fifteen hundred miscellaneous base troops in Meiktila and a number of hospital patients. Kasuya had only a few days in which to prepare the defence of Meiktila, but he realized its importance and was determined to hold it to the last. He displayed the greatest energy, collecting his administrative units, improvising infantry companies from odds and ends, ceaselessly digging defences and organizing his perimeter into sectors and reserves. Every available man went into the fighting line, including any patient in hospital who could stand, even if only on one leg with crutches. The Ordnance Depots were opened and automatic weapons with ample ammunition issued to almost every man. Kasuya called in two airfield defence battalions and some anti-aircraft batteries from airfields he knew he must abandon, sighting the guns for anti-tank and perimeter defence. He had one piece of luck. The bulk of a regiment of the 49th Division had just arrived in Meiktila on its forced march to join Fifteenth Army under Kimura's redistribution plan, and Kasuya held it there.

The actual strength return, later captured, of the Japanese in the town itself showed a total of three thousand two hundred, with a large number of guns. Dug in under houses, in the banks of lakes, in concrete and earth covered timber strong-points, sitting among its piled up rice sacks and its ammunition dumps, Meiktila's garrison presented a formidable defence. Much more formidable in fact than that of either Myitkyina or Bhamo, smaller towns with smaller garrisons, that had taken so long to overcome. Meiktila had another great advantage for defence; its approaches from the west and south were covered by wide lakes, so that the entry roads were in effect causeways, easily closed by artillery and allowing no chance for manœuvre. From these lakes also ran deep irrigation channels and ditches into the surrounding country, which would slow up all movement and greatly restrict that of armour.

We had now reached the critical phase of the battle for the destruction of the Japanese army. Kimura's great drive against 33 Corps, which he believed to be the whole Fourteenth Army, was beginning. From all sides his forces converged on the Mandalay area. Now was the time to seize Meiktila quickly, and then, when he reacted as he must to that vital threat, to launch from the 33 Corps bridgeheads an all-out offensive. Every division of Fourteenth Army was committed; all except one, the 5th, were engaged in full battle. Our expenditure of petrol and ammunition was rising with the increasing area and tempo of the struggle; our supply line lengthening and becoming more precarious. We were unavoidably, once more, putting heavier demands on our air transport squadrons, and the administrative side of the battle began to look more like a gamble than I relished. The formidable concentration of enemy strength, the struggle for Meiktila ahead of us, and the need for speed had all narrowed our margins for success.

The administrative and tactical anxieties inseparable from a savage and fluctuating battle turned to real alarm when a completely unexpected blow fell on me. On the 23rd February, the 17th Division drive was well on the way to Meiktila and the Irrawaddy crossing of the 2nd Division just about to begin, when Marshal Chiang Kai-shek demanded the return, without delay, of all United States and Chinese forces in the N.C.A.C. They were required to take part in a projected offensive in China. He also insisted that, pending their departure, they should in no circumstances advance south of the line Lashio–Hsipaw–Kyaukme, eighty miles north-east of Mandalay. Kimura would thus be at liberty to transfer almost the whole of his troops on the N.C.A.C. front to mine, while I should, when the Chinese divisions were withdrawn, become responsible for the protection of the newly-won

Burma–China road. I had relied on Sultan's forces co-operating in the advance on Rangoon by moving parallel to me beyond my eastern flank; any hope of that was now at an end. Worst of all, I gathered it was proposed that the American transport squadrons supplying the Chinese should be used to fly them out, while the aircraft allotted to me would take on the supply of the British 36th Division and of the Chinese awaiting transfer.

All these horrors I did not learn until some days after the strike at Meiktila had been launched. The withdrawal and halting of the Chinese forces was bad enough, but the loss of the aircraft would have been fatal to my operations. General Leese and I protested vehemently. Admiral Mountbatten flew to Chungking to argue with the Generalissimo, but to no avail. He insisted on the withdrawal, and advised Admiral Mountbatten to halt the Fourteenth Army at Mandalay. Throughout the next crucial days the threat of this disaster hung over me. I could not if I wished—and I had no intention of doing so—now call off the battle; I could only more urgently force it to a conclusion. Yet I confess that, while this uncertainty lasted, I was hard put to it to maintain before my own staff, commanders, and troops that appearance of freedom from anxiety so essential in an army commander. Luckily, I was not kept under this strain too long. On Admiral Mountbatten's representation, backed by the British Chiefs of Staff, the United States Chiefs of Staff agreed to leave the bulk of their transport squadrons in Burma until either we had taken Rangoon or until the 1st June, whichever was the earlier. This removed my immediate anxiety, so that, although orders for the rapid withdrawal of the Mars Brigade from N.C.A.C., to be followed later by the Chinese divisions, went out on the 11th March, I felt very much better.

I put out of my mind the fact that if my army had approached but not taken Rangoon by the 1st June, when the monsoon would be in full blast, the withdrawal of American air squadrons would leave us in a disastrous maintenance situation. Sufficient for the day was the evil thereof!

To revert to the 17th Division and 255 Tank Brigade, poised for the attack on Meiktila. The reports Cowan was receiving warned him that the garrison of the town would be stronger than first estimated, and that, while the outer defences extended in an oval some three miles by four and a half all round Meiktila, those on the west, where the two large lakes covered much of the front, would be the most difficult to attack. He knew, also, that considerable bodies of Japanese were roaming the neighbourhood and closing in on the town. The need to seize Meiktila and the airfield on its eastern outskirts, before the enemy could come in strength to the rescue, was urgent. He decided, therefore, to block the main approaches with detachments a few miles out, and using mobility, armour, and air support to the utmost, put in his main attacks from the north and east.

Cowan's moves were bold and flexible. On the morning of the 28th February, leaving all but essential fighting transport behind at Thabutkon, 63 Brigade, brushing aside light opposition, marched to an area about two miles north-west of Meiktila. From there it pushed on its forward troops until they were in close contact with the western defences, while a strong road-block was placed across the main road from Chauk. At the same time the divisional artillery, with one battalion to help in their protection, came into action about two miles farther back, in a position from which the guns could support attacks on the town from any direction. 48 Brigade, moving astride the road from Thabutkon, struck at Kasuya's northern defences, but was held up until nightfall by one of the strongest enemy positions around a monastery on the edge of the town.

255 Tank Brigade, with two infantry battalions and a self-propelled twenty-five-pounder battery under its command, moved rapidly by bounds round the north, north-east, and east of Meiktila. The roads to Thazi and Pyawbwe were blocked, and, after a most exhilarating ten-mile sweep across country, the tanks and their infantry regrouped to the east of Meiktila. Cowan put the bulk of his artillery and air support at their disposal and well co-ordinated, accurate, and heavy bombardment and air-strikes preceded the tanks as, with the infantry on their tails, they roared to the assault. This armoured onrush was met by very heavy artillery, anti-tank, and machine-gun fire from a deep screen of mutually supporting bunkers and fortified houses. Snipers, concealed everywhere, picked off our infantry, as they forced their way into the streets. The attack penetrated well into the town as far as the railway station, killing many enemy and destroying several guns. Resistance was fanatical and to the death. Wounded Japanese and small pockets of survivors still fought on

desperately in the area we had overrun. In the late afternoon it became clear that mopping-up and consolidation could not be completed before dark. Cowan, fearing with justification, to leave his tanks among the ruins for the night, in spite of protests pulled the attacking force back to harbour two miles outside the town, leaving only strong patrols to hold our gains. During the night the Japanese infiltrated back into some of the areas they had lost and a fierce point-blank fight went on throughout the darkness.

That day I had been on the Mandalay front where the break-out of 33 Corps, led by the 19th Division, was beginning in earnest, and I was anxious that it should be well timed with the 4 Corps operation. On my return in the evening to my headquarters at Monywa, I studied reports from Meiktila. These gave the impression that the attack was held up, and I decided I ought to go there. We could not risk a second Myitkyina. I would fly in next morning. I was very angry when the R.A.F. informed me, with the utmost politeness but equal firmness, that they would not fly me to Meiktila—it was too dangerous! The airstrips had not yet been properly repaired, they were frequently under fire, and Japanese fighters were reported. It was no use pointing out that a whole brigade had been landed on these same airstrips, that they were being used every hour of daylight by unarmed R.A.F. and U.S.A.A.F. transports and that if they were being shot up that was not an R.A.F. responsibility as it was my soldiers who should protect them from ground attack. I was told that the R.A.F. would be delighted to fly any of my staff anywhere at any time, but not me, not to Meiktila, not now. This idea of my value was flattering, but extremely annoying. I was about to have it out with Vincent, when luckily, for the sake of our friendship which I valued, I had another idea.

There had just arrived at my headquarters a visiting American general with his own Mitchell bomber. I asked him if he would like to come with me and see something of the Meiktila battle. As I hoped, with characteristic American generosity, he suggested we made the trip in his aircraft. I gratefully accepted and early on the morning of the 1st March we set out—I feeling rather like a schoolboy who had dodged his masters and was playing truant for the day. We flew to 4 Corps Headquarters on the river bank opposite Pagan, picked up Messervy, and went on to one of the airstrips now in operation near Thabutkon. It was quite peaceful, though there was a little popping not far away and a few dead Japanese on the edge of the field. We were offered a second breakfast, and I ate my first Japanese-provided meal—biscuits and tinned food from a captured store. It was not very good. I gained more mental gratification from it than nourishment. Punch Cowan had sent a couple of jeeps to meet us, and we bounced merrily along the road to his battle headquarters just outside Meiktila. He soon put Messervy, me, and our American friend in the picture of the fight, which judging by the noise, smoke, and constant zooming of aircraft diving on their targets, was no skirmish. Indeed, this day, the 1st March, saw the bitterest fighting of the battle. Cowan's troops were slowly biting into Kasuya's defences, tough though they were. 63 Brigade had begun an attack on Meiktila from the west, and, in spite of restricted approaches, were into the outskirts of the town. 48 Brigade with some tanks had resumed their assault on Meiktila East from the north, and were making progress against the most resolute opposition. 255 Tank Brigade and its infantry had seized a steep, heavily defended hill, which rose abruptly to five hundred feet on the edge of the South Lake, near the south-east corner of Meiktila, and gave observation over the whole area. Here bitter fighting was going on, as tanks and infantry clawed into the defences of the town itself.

Cowan's conduct of this difficult and divided battle was impressive. With his main attention fixed on the various assaulting brigades, he had at frequent intervals to glance over his shoulder as ground and air reports of Japanese movements in the surrounding country were brought to him. He had, too, all the anxieties of an air supply line, which rested on precariously held landing strips, at a time when ammunition and petrol expenditure was at its highest. Not least, he was very short of sleep and remained so for several days. Yet throughout he was alert to every change in the situation on any sector, and swung his air and artillery support to meet and take advantage of it. His firm grip on his own formations and on the enemy never faltered. To watch a highly skilled, experienced, and resolute commander controlling a hard-fought battle is to see, not only a man triumphing over the highest mental and physical stresses, but an artist producing his effects in the most complicated and difficult of all the arts. I thought as I watched what very good divisional commanders I had.

After speaking on the 'blower' to a brigade commander and listening in on the tank net—always an interesting and often a worth-while thing to do in an action—I left Cowan conducting his grim orchestra. Assured that the battle was in competent hands at the top, I thought I would go a little closer and see how it was being handled lower down. I chose 48 Brigade as, at the moment, they seemed to be cracking a particularly tough nut. We went by jeep round the north of the town and then moved forward on foot somewhat more cautiously. We had a word with various subordinate commanders on the way; all very busy with their own little battles and all in great heart. One of them told us the best place from which to see anything was a massive pagoda that crowned a near-by rise. We reached it along a path screened from the enemy by bushes, and crouching below the surrounding wall, crossed a wide terrace, where already in occupation were some Indian signallers and observation parties. Peering cautiously over the wall, we found on our right the end of the North Lake, placid and unruffled. To our left front, about a thousand yards away, the main road entered Meiktila between close-built houses, now crumbling in the dust, smoke, and flame of a bombardment. We were, I knew, about to assault here, but it was the scene immediately below and in front of us which gripped the attention.

The southern shore of the lake, for nearly a mile, ran roughly parallel to the northern edge of the town. Between them was a strip about half a mile wide, of rough, undulating country, cut up by ditches and banks, with here and there clumps of trees and bushes. Three hundred yards from us, scattered along water cuts, peering round mounds, and lying behind bushes, were twenty or thirty Gurkhas, all very close to the ground and evidently, from the spurts around them, under fairly heavy fire. Well to the left of these Gurkhas and a little farther forward, there was a small spinney. From its edge more Gurkhas were firing Bren-gun bursts. A single Sherman tank, in a scrub-topped hollow, lay between us and the spinney, concealed from the enemy but visible to us. In the intervals of firing, we could hear its engine muttering and grumbling. The dispositions of our forces, two platoons and a tank, were plain enough to us, but I could see no enemy.

Then the tank revved up its engine to a stuttering roar, edged forward a few yards, fired a couple of shots in quick succession, and discreetly withdrew into cover again. I watched the strike of the shot. Through my glasses I could see, about five hundred yards away, three low grassy hummocks. Innocent enough they looked, and little different from half a dozen others. Yet straining my eyes I spotted a dark loophole in one, around which hung the misty smoke of a hot machine-gun; I could hear the *knock-knock-knock*, slower than our own, of its firing. Searching carefully, I picked up loopholes in the other mounds. Here were three typical Japanese bunkers, impervious to any but the heaviest shells, sited for all-round defence, and bristling with automatics—tough nuts indeed. The tank intervened again. Without shifting position it lobbed two or three grenades and a white screen of smoke drifted across the front of the bunkers. One of the Gurkhas below us sprang to his feet, waved an arm, and the whole party, crouching as they went, ran forward. When the smoke blew clear a minute or two later, they were all down under cover again, but a hundred yards nearer those bunkers. A few small shells burst in the water at the lake's edge. Whether they were meant for the tank or the Gurkhas, they got neither, and the enemy gunners made no further contribution.

When I looked for it again, the tank had disappeared, but a smoke-screen, this time, I think, from infantry mortars, blinded the bunkers again. The Gurkhas scrambled forward, dodging and twisting over the rough ground, until some of them must have been hardly thirty yards from the enemy. Somewhere behind the spinney, the tank was slowly and methodically firing solid shot at the loopholes. Spurts of dust and debris leapt up at every impact.

As the fight drew to its climax, we moved out of the pagoda enclosure to a spot a little forward and to the right where, from behind a thick cactus hedge, we had a clearer view. The tank reappeared round the spinney's flank and advanced still shooting. Gradually it worked round to the rear of the bunkers, and suddenly we were in the line of its fire with overs ricochetting and plunging straight at us.

One army commander, one corps commander, an American general, and several less distinguished individuals adopted the prone position with remarkable unanimity. The only casualty was an unfortunate American airman of our crew, who had hitch-hiked with us to see the fun. As the metal whistled over his head he flung himself for cover into the cactus hedge. He was already stripped to the waist and he emerged a blood-stained pin cushion. However, he took his misfortune very well and submitted to what must have been a painful plucking with fortitude.

After this little excitement, the tank having, to our relief, moved again to a flank, we watched the final stages of the action. The fire of Brens and rifles swelled in volume; the tank's gun thudded away. Suddenly three Gurkhas sprang up simultaneously and dashed forward. One fell, but the other two covered the few yards to the bunkers and thrust Tommy-guns through loopholes. Behind them surged an uneven line of their comrades; another broke from the spinney, bayonets glinting. They swarmed around the bunkers and for a moment all firing ceased. Then from behind one of the hummocks, appeared a ragged group of half a dozen khaki-clad figures, running for safety. They were led, I noticed, by a man exceptionally tall for a Japanese. Twenty Gurkha rifles came up and crashed a volley. Alas for Gurkha marksmanship! Not a Japanese fell; zigzagging, they ran on. But in a few seconds, as the Gurkhas fired again, they were all down, the last to fall being the tall man. The tank lumbered up, dipped its gun and, with perhaps unnecessary emphasis, finished him off. Within ten minutes, having made sure no Japanese remained alive in the bunkers, the two platoons of Gurkhas and their Indian-manned tank moved on to their next assignment which would not be far away. A rear party appeared, attended to their own casualties, and dragged out the enemy bodies to search them for papers and identifications. It was all very business-like.

If I have given more space to this one incident, that was being repeated in twenty places in the battle, than I have to much more important actions, I plead some indulgence. It was the closest I had been to real fighting since I had been an army commander, and it was one of the neatest, most workmanlike bits of infantry and armoured minor tactics I had ever seen. There is a third reason. The men who carried it out were from a Gurkha regiment of which I have the honour to be Colonel.

Back at Cowan's headquarters, we followed the general progress of the assault on Meiktila. It had not everywhere gone as smoothly as the fight we had watched. The enemy had not wasted the few days allowed him for preparation. Every house was a strong-point, every water channel had its concealed bunkers, every heap of rubble its hidden machine-gun or anti-tank gun. Snipers lurked in every ruin. It was costly fighting, and jeep ambulances shuttled between the battle and the airstrips carrying the wounded to quick and merciful evacuation. Progress if slow was, however, steady.

Throughout the 1st March and the following night, there was hand-to-hand fighting as savage as any yet experienced in a theatre where close combat was the rule rather than the exception. By evening, when we left for Monywa, our troops were well into the town, but the Japanese resistance showed no signs of breaking. They died where they fought, and as darkness fell, even in the sectors we had gained, survivors emerged from cellars and holes to renew the battle.

On the 2nd March in Meiktila East, 48 Brigade with artillery, tank, and air support slowly forced the enemy from house to house, until they were penned in the southern end of the town with their backs to the South Lake. 63 Brigade, in two strong attacks, cleared the whole of Meiktila West with great loss to the enemy. During the 3rd, after intense fighting, Meiktila East was finally cleared by a series of converging attacks. Enemy 75-mm. guns engaged our tanks and infantry at point-blank range, but were gradually eliminated, one by one, until the last fifty Japanese jumped into the lake and were drowned or killed. The slaughter had been great. In one small area of the town alone, which measured only two hundred by one hundred yards, eight hundred and seventy-six Japanese bodies were collected. Meiktila was a shambles, but, by six o'clock on the evening of the 3rd, it was ours.

All day while the fight in the town had gone on, our tanks and infantry had been clearing the area to the east of numerous enemy parties. The country here was covered with villages, many of which ran into one another to form large groups of houses. In them and among them, along ditches, on the butts of a rifle range, and in the broken ground, the Japanese fought with the same grim fierceness as in the town. But it availed them no more; the slaughter was heavy. During the 4th and 5th March, wider sweeps with the closest air support were made to clear all sides of the town. The main airfield was secured, and was in full operation, though still at times under fire, by the 5th. Cowan's whole force then concentrated in and around Meiktila.

The capture of Meiktila in four days and the annihilation of its garrison—for, as the Japanese themselves admitted, hardly a man escaped—was a magnificent feat of arms. It sealed the fate of the Japanese army in Burma, and it came as a terrible surprise to Kimura. He had been completely misled as to the location of our 4 Corps and as to the strength and intentions of our troops in the Pakokku area. At first he had no idea what this force, which had struck such a grievous blow at his vitals, was, but he did realize at once the fatal danger he would be in if he could not quickly recover Meiktila. Kimura, unlike many Japanese commanders, had always reacted speedily and boldly to changed situations. Once again he did so. The plan to concentrate all his resources against our 33 Corps was abandoned. Reinforcing formations, moving to the Mandalay area from every part of Burma, were diverted to Meiktila. Even some of the troops already engaged against the Mandalay bridgeheads were pulled out of the fight and put into reverse to meet this new danger. All were urged to greater speed, and every available method of transport strained to move them quickly.

The task of recapturing Meiktila was entrusted to Lieut.-General Honda with his Thirty-third Army Headquarters, and he was left in no doubt as to its urgency. Under him were placed the 18th Division (less one regiment) from the north, one regiment of the 53rd Division from Mandalay, and one regiment of the 33rd Division, hurriedly pulled in from the Pakokku area. From the south, having travelled the two hundred and eighty miles from Pegu in under a fortnight, came the 49th Division (less a regiment), while army units, artillery, including heavy artillery, and what was left of the tank regiment were added. A regiment of the 2nd Division also took part in the later stages of the battle. Somewhat earlier, two battalions and other troops from the 55th Division arrived at Mount Popa to stiffen up the Indian National Army formation in the area, and two more infantry and one artillery battalion of the 54th Division, also from Arakan, reached Yenangyaung, crossed the Irrawaddy, and reinforced the troops facing our 28 East African Brigade on the west bank. Honda thus had the equivalent of a corps of two divisions for his task. His plan to retrieve the Meiktila disaster was a two-fold one. He intended

to cut our communications to Meiktila on both sides of the
Nyaungu bridgehead. On the west, the East Africans were to be
driven back some fifteen miles until the road was cut there, and,
on the east, converging attacks from the north on Taungtha and
from the Mount Popa area in the south towards the bridgehead
were to reach the Meiktila road. With our only artery to the 17th
Division thus squeezed out, strong Japanese forces would attack
Meiktila. The plan was probably about as good a one as could
be made but, like so many Japanese plans, it did not take into
account certain realities. The enemy's total forces directed to the
Meiktila battle, formidable as they were in numbers, were
arriving piecemeal, drawn from many formations, and from all
directions. Complete divisions were not being engaged. It would
be difficult to co-ordinate and concert their common action,
especially as their transport losses mounted daily and we had
practically complete control of the air. Even so, there might have
been some hope for Honda's plans had not our commanders and
troops shown themselves so aggressively active.

At this stage, everyone in Fourteenth Army realized the need
for speed and for the boldest offensive action over the widest area.
The enemy had chosen, in spite of the disadvantages of his situation, to fight us on the Irrawaddy and in the Central Burma plain.
This was our opportunity finally to break up the Japanese army.
Both corps and every division must strike at any enemy forces
within reach. Especially must they, with air, armour, and
mechanized units, fall on the scattered Japanese columns marching
to the battle and destroy them before they could unite. An
important element in our plan was to disrupt the Japanese
command organization. In my headquarters at Monywa, I now
had a very efficient wireless interception and location unit which
was able with considerable accuracy to identify and locate the
various Japanese headquarters. With the help of air reconnaissance
and informers, we were even able to pin-point some of the more
important. On them we directed, not only constant and heavy
air attacks, but raids by our columns. We followed them when
they moved, and bombed and harried them when they halted.
Gradually their signals grew fewer, they were forced to longer
periods of silence, and the orders their commanders issued lagged
further and further behind a rapidly moving battle.

From Meiktila, Cowan's 17th Division struck in all directions.

Infantry and tanks went out daily to hunt, ambush, and attack approaching Japanese columns of various sizes in a radius of twenty miles of the town. So successful were these actions, that attempted enemy concentrations were broken up and large-scale attacks prevented or at least delayed. Nevertheless, the pressure on Meiktila increased as the hostile forces built up. The enemy's chief aim was to take the airstrip, some two miles from the town, on which, as the road to the bridgehead was now closed, all our supplies were landed. Could he succeed in denying this to us for any length of time, we should be compelled to rely entirely on dropping, and our situation would become precarious. The struggle for the airfield was savage and continuous but the 17th Division still continued to push out in all directions, killing hundreds of Japanese and capturing many guns.

Cowan had not enough troops to spare for the complete perimeter defence of the airfield, and the enemy had, by mid-March, dug in so close to the strip that by night our troops disputed with his patrols in the no-man's-land of the actual runway. At dawn each day, before aircraft could land, a sweep had to be carried out to drive back enemy infiltration and to clear the ground of mines. The fly-in of the airborne brigade of the 5th Division began and was completed by the 17th March. The last part of this brigade was landed while the strip was under direct artillery fire, and it says much for the gallantry of the American and British aircrews that every sortie, without exception, was completed, even though machines were being destroyed after landing. The losses in troops during this operation were surprisingly small. Only those who have landed in such circumstances can realize how quickly it is possible to empty an aeroplane of passengers.

Soon after the brigade's arrival, the Japanese by a great effort reached the edge of the airfield. All landings ceased, there was a great reduction in supplies, petrol grew short, reinforcements could not be brought in nor wounded evacuated except by an occasional light plane from a small strip inside the town. Not for the first time, Cowan found himself cut off in a savage battle. This time, to the anxieties of such a situation was added a deep personal sorrow. He learnt, in the midst of the battle, that his son, the splendid young officer I had met with my old regiment in the 19th Division bridgehead, had died of wounds received in the taking of Mandalay. We lost too many of our generals' sons; the cruellest thing about war is that it takes the best.

It was imperative to regain the use of the main strip. North of it, where the Japanese were dug in, was difficult and broken country, intersected by deep gullies which were tank obstacles. The enemy had brought up many anti-tank guns, and was freely using mines which he drew from the many local dumps. When these ran out, he grimly replaced them by human mines. A Japanese soldier with a 100-kilo aircraft bomb between his knees, holding a large stone, poised above the fuse would crouch in a foxhole. When the attacking tank passed over the almost invisible hole, he would drop the stone—then bomb, man, and, it was hoped, tank would all go up together. Luckily the device was not very effective and accounted for more Japanese than tanks. In spite of the fiercest resistance, our infantry, supported where possible by tanks, and almost always by fighter-bombers placing their loads within a hundred yards of our troops, gradually forced back the enemy from the airfield. Even then, for days after the area near the strip had been cleared, Japanese medium artillery dominated it, and it was not until the 29th March, that the enemy was driven from the last of the broken ground in which his guns were concealed. Beaten in this hand-to-hand fighting, his scattered remnants fell back, leaving behind in our hands nearly all their guns and having suffered disastrous casualties.

While these grim battles to take and hold Meiktila were raging, the rest of 4 Corps was not idle. Soon after our troops had passed through on their way to Meiktila, Honda's counter-attack from the north had reoccupied the hills around Taungtha and dominated the road. The 7th Division, at the beginning of March, was stretched on an arc from Letse on the west bank, held by 28 East African Brigade, then across the river south of Pagan, through the bridgehead—now ten miles deep—and finally curving round to twelve miles upstream of Nyuangu. Inside the bridgehead had collected the 'tail' and supply column of Cowan's force, some five thousand soft vehicles in all. Messervy had three important and immediate tasks:

(i) To capture Myingyan. Until this was in our hands as river-head, we could not use our Chindwin shipping to relieve the strain on our communications.

(ii) To reopen the road to Meiktila.
(iii) To prevent the enemy pressure, now developing from the
south on both banks of the Irrawaddy, from cutting the
road again.

He at once pushed out columns, supplied by air, across the flat
sandy plain towards Myingyan. Every move by day was betrayed
by dense dust clouds, and opposition was continuous from enemy
rearguards well furnished with artillery. Fighting all the way,
our troops reached a deep dry chasm at right angles to the
advance, four miles from Myingyan. Here, the Japanese were
strongly dug in, and the first assault only gained the forward
trenches before it was held.

At this moment Messervy's second task, the clearing of the
Taungtha hills to open the Meiktila road, became urgent.
Masking Myingyan, therefore, he swung the weight of his attack
in this direction. His plan was for an armoured column from
Cowan to open the road to Taungtha, while the 7th Division
drove the enemy out of the hills. Taungtha was captured without
much difficulty, but it was not until the 7th March, that a footing
in the hills was gained, only to be lost to a Japanese counter-attack.
Another week of tough fighting was required before the heights
overlooking the road were taken, and contact made with the
column from Meiktila. At this juncture, the first brigade of the
5th Division to come by road arrived in the bridgehead, and
completed the task of clearing the Taungtha area, while the troops
of the 7th Division turned again to the capture of Myingyan.

The first attack on Myingyan failed but, after heavy fighting,
our tanks and infantry had forced a way into the outskirts by the
night of the 18th. Four more days of continuous struggle were
needed to take the rest of the town; the Japanese delivering
suicide counter-attacks until the last. Their losses in men and
guns—the enemy 15th Division lost most of its remaining
artillery here—were large, and the survivors, attempting to
escape, were caught in the open by our pursuing columns. Few
got away. The capture of Myingyan was greeted with a sigh of
relief by the Fourteenth Army administrative staffs, for time to
get it working again as a port was short. The building of wharves
began at once, almost under fire, and in a surprisingly short time
boats from our Kalewa shipbuilding yard were unloading at

them. An energetic start was also made to get the Myingyan–
Meiktila railway running. Bridges were rebuilt, and even some
of the captured and wrecked engines were patched up to clank
and rattle precariously over the rusty permanent way.

While our assault on Myingyan was in full swing, Honda's
push from the south came in. On the east bank, the I.N.A.
formations in the Kyaukpadaung area, with a stiffening of
Japanese troops, were directed north-west on Nyaungu. They
met columns of the 7th Division striking in the opposite direction
and collided head on. The Jiffs had little stomach for the fight and
fled or surrendered; the Japanese were killed. Simultaneously,
another brigade of the 7th Division advanced down the east bank
of the Irrawaddy on Chauk. They, too, encountered Japanese
advancing to meet them, and stiff fighting took place, especially
some six or seven miles north of Chauk, where the Japanese clung
desperately to strong positions. These were taken, a short further
advance made, and the troops dug in. Here they remained, on the
edge of the most northerly oilfield, as news of more Japanese
concentrations in the Mount Popa area decided Messervy not to
push farther south for the moment. Honda's counter-attack from
the south on the east bank had proved abortive, largely because
the I.N.A., who formed an appreciable part of it, had no wish
to fight. This was as well, because the other half of his thrust from
the south, that came in on the west bank and was composed all
of Japanese, produced temporarily a critical situation.

The Japanese had for some time been harrassing 28 East African
Brigade Group in the Letse neighbourhood, and a Punjabi
battalion had been sent to stiffen it. When reinforcements reached
the enemy, they launched on the 20th March determined attacks,
and began to surround and push back the Africans. A British
battalion was hurriedly transferred from the east bank and
joined them. With them and the Punjabi battalion, in close
fighting, it got the better of the enemy and slowly drove them
back. Any threat to the Nyaungu bridgehead and the road to
Meiktila was now, after some anxious days, relieved.

By the last week in March, the Battle of Meiktila had been
won. It had been intended as the decisive stroke and I had subordinated everything to its success, yet it had been only half of
the great Battle of Central Burma. That other half had been fought
out simultaneously around Mandalay.

CHAPTER XX

THE BATTLE
OF THE IRRAWADDY SHORE

BEFORE following the course of the battle which, simultaneously with that for Meiktila, was waged about Mandalay, it would be well to glance at events on the flanks of the Fourteenth Army, for these had their effect on the main battle and its subsequent development. On the right, Christison's 15 Corps in Arakan and, on the left, Sultan's N.C.A.C. had each been actively engaged.

When, towards the end of 1944, our thoughts began to turn more optimistically to widening the scope of operations in South-East Asia, the situation in Arakan was strategically unsatisfactory. Here, we had four divisions locked up by the threat of a Japanese force much smaller than our own. The wise thing to do, as General Giffard had recognized, was to push back the enemy until they were no longer in a position easily to restage an offensive, and then, leaving say one division to contain them, free the other three for use elsewhere. If we were to take Akyab, secure the mouth of the Kaladan River, and hold the country to the east of it as far south as the Myebon Peninsula, we should be able to do this. Now that the divisions from Europe promised for South-East Asia did not seem likely to materialize, it became increasingly desirable to free our own formations from Arakan. 15 Corps had for some time been planning an offensive to achieve this. Christison had under him four divisions, the 25th and 26th Indian, the 81st and 82nd West African, with 3 Commando Brigade and 50 Indian Tank Brigade. He was supported by 224 Group R.A.F. and a naval task force, most of whose landing craft had been left in Burma waters as too worn out to be of use in Europe. Opposing Christison was Lieut.-General Sakurai Seizo, commanding the Twenty-eighth Army, who had under him in Arakan a regiment of the 54th Division and part—we were not sure at the time what part—of the 55th Division. Actually the bulk of the 55th Division had already moved into Southern Burma. This Sakurai was not the Sakurai Tohutaro, who had commanded the abortive Japanese Arakan offensive, but the names caused us some confusion.

The offensive began on the 12th December 1944 and three days later the 82nd Division, under Major-General G. S. Bruce, took much fought-over Buthidaung and once again opened the last few miles of the road from Maungdaw to the Kalapanzin. In the many creeks around the tiny port of Maungdaw had been collected over six hundred river craft, which in five days were carried by road through the Mayu Range and launched in the Kalapanzin River, to help in the maintenance of the advance south. Meanwhile, the 81st Division under Major-General Loftus-Tottenham, advancing for the second time down the Kaladan Valley, by-passed Kyauktaw, where nine months before it had met with disaster. Moving wide to the east through thick hill jungle, it struck at the Japanese communication centre of Myohaung which, on the 25th January, was taken by a converging movement of the 81st Division from the north and the 82nd from the west. After considerable fighting, the Japanese extricated themselves and withdrew. While this was going on, the 25th Division, under Major-General G. Wood, supplied from the sea, advanced on the 26th December to Foul Point, the tip of the Mayu Peninsula, and then occupied Kudaung Island, north of Akyab, and separated from it by only a narrow channel.

Akyab Island had been garrisoned by a Japanese regiment of three battalions, but the unexpectedly rapid advance of the West Africans in the Kaladan Valley had caused Sakurai, or perhaps Miyazaki, commander of the 54th Division, to transfer two of these battalions to meet the threat there. In December our intelligence learnt of the departure of one of these battalions but not of the second. On the 2nd January 1945 an artillery officer flying over the island in a light aeroplane, seeing the local inhabitants making friendly signs, boldly landed on the airstrip and single-handed captured Akyab—the last Japanese battalion had pulled out forty-eight hours earlier. Our troops, who were on the point of delivering a full-scale attack, ferried peacefully to the island. It is pleasant to think that the fall of Akyab was to a considerable extent due to the Kaladan advance of the 81st Division, which thus redeemed its earlier set-back.

The Japanese in Arakan were now in general retreat to the south. Their only route of withdrawal for guns and vehicles was by the road that ran, a few miles from the sea, down the whole Arakan coast, meeting the new An Pass road from the Irrawaddy at Tamandu and the old road from Prome at Taungup. Christison's aim was to trap the Japanese forces by cutting the coastal road ahead of them. Command of the air and sea and his landing craft, even if decrepit, gave him the power to do this. He planned to seize the Myebon Peninsula, thirty miles east of Akyab, by sea-borne assault, and then, in a second amphibious operation, to strike at Kangaw, eight miles farther east. There he would cut the road before the retreating Japanese had reached the town. Kangaw was approachable from the sea only by narrow *chaungs* which were commanded from Myebon, so it was necessary to secure that place before attempting the second operation. Not only was 15 Corps likely to meet stout resistance at both places, but the naval difficulties of a landing were extreme. The Arakan coast south of Akyab is screened by mangrove swamps and cut by muddy, shallow *chaungs*, uncharted and unpredictable. There are no beaches worthy of the name; only a few small stretches of sand, often soft, overlooked by jungle hills, where men might wade ashore. To discover these possible landing places, and to plot a way to them, called for the greatest daring and skill from the Navy. As ever, these qualities were forthcoming; small boat parties and frogmen took soundings and examined beaches. On the 12th January 1945 a commando brigade landed by surprise against slight opposition. During the next few days, a brigade of the 25th Division followed, and the Japanese, hurriedly collecting their forces, counter-attacked in strength. They were beaten off and our troops, fighting hard, proceeded to clear the whole peninsula.

The next step was the second landing by 3 Commando Brigade, on the 22nd January near Kangaw, under cover of heavy sea and air bombardment. The Japanese were more prepared here, and the commandos clung to a small beach-head under fierce attack until the next night, when a brigade of the 25th Division was landed. The brigade was plunged at once into bitter hand-to-hand fighting, as the Japanese, realizing the threat, collected all available troops and flung them against the bridgehead.

The attack was so fierce and sustained, and supported by such heavy artillery fire that, at the time, it was thought the Japanese were using nearly a whole division. Actually, their force was much less and nearer a brigade in strength. Our men fought back and, on the 29th January, turned to the attack. They took Kangaw village and established a road-block south of it that finally closed the Japanese escape route. Two days later the enemy, reinforced, put in his fiercest counter-attack—and his last. This battle was the crisis of the Arakan operations. It lasted for a day and a night. The attack was delivered with great determination against the commando brigade in positions which, if they had fallen into Japanese hands, would have endangered all our forces then ashore. When the attack was finally repulsed, the enemy left over three hundred dead in the area.

Meanwhile a brigade of the 25th Division, pushing north-east from the Myebon Peninsula, gained touch with the leading brigade of the 82nd Division, pressing on for Kangaw. Caught between these and our troops already at Kangaw, the Japanese scattered and, in the first half of February, took to the hills to the east, leaving behind them over a thousand dead, sixteen guns, many vehicles, and great quantities of equipment. This series of actions, so aggressively and skilfully conducted by Christison, was a first-rate example of combined operations by all three Services. The Royal and the Royal Indian Navies had performed wonders of navigation, covered all landings, and, perhaps most marvellous of all, kept their scrap-iron landing craft at work. Their last service, which strained their resources to the utmost, was to maintain the force at Kangaw until the 11th February, when the Army was able to take over this task. The air forces, British and American, had been tireless in providing accurate and continuous covering fire. At Kangaw they dropped seven hundred and fifty tons of bombs in a successful attempt to silence and mask the enemy's artillery.

Less spectacular than the capture of Kangaw, but from my point of view even more valuable, was the seizure of the islands of Ramree and Cheduba, for these would provide the sea-supplied airfields that could nourish my army in a dash for Rangoon. Ramree is an island of considerable size, being fifty miles long by twenty at its widest part—a large area in which to play hide and seek with a small, but typically stubborn, Japanese garrison. A brigade of the 26th Division assaulted Kyaukpu at its northern end on the 21st January, but it was not until six weeks later that the last enemy fugitives fell victims to the naval patrols—and the sharks—as they attempted in small craft or on rafts to reach the mainland. Cheduba, a smaller island to the south of Ramree, was occupied by Marines without opposition on the 26th January.

About this time, General Leese ordered Christison to:

(i) Develop Akyab and Ramree as air-supply bases for the Fourteenth Army.
(ii) Clear North and Central Arakan.
(iii) Seize a bridgehead at Taungup, over fifty miles south of Akyab.
(iv) Open the Taungup–Prome road, if possible, before the monsoon.

The first of these tasks was to take precedence over the other three. This was all, and perhaps more, than I could expect, and I was grateful, but I did not rely on the opening of the Taungup road to provide my army with another line of supply, certainly not before the monsoon. To do that would require considerable engineering resources and time, but I did hope that a determined push up the road from the coast would detain Japanese forces that would otherwise be used against me. I urged that Christison should also press hard against the An Pass, as well as up the Taungup road.

By the end of January, the badly battered Japanese 54th Division was in two widely separated groups—one about An, blocking the road east over the pass, the other at Taungup, covering the road to Prome. The Japanese 55th Division, which had taken little part in these operations, had already moved east and now had its main body in the Prome–Henzada area with some detachments in South Burma. The only hope of preventing that division being used against me was such pressure on the Taungup road that it would be compelled to face west again.

The maintenance of 15 Corps, in spite of all Christison's ingenuity, was now becoming increasingly difficult. To ease it, the 81st Division and the bulk of 50 Tank Brigade were withdrawn from the corps, to be followed by other formations later, but this did not deter Christison. He planned to deal with the enemy at An first, then, moving down the coast road to Taungup, to destroy the Japanese there, and finally to advance towards Prome. I applauded his resolution and urged speed—nothing would embarrass Kimura more than to have 15 Corps' spearhead pricking him in the posterior while I punched his nose.

For the An operations, Christison's first step was, on the 4th February, to send the 82nd West African Division, less a brigade, up the water-course of the Dalet Chaung to approach the pass from the north-west. His second, on the 16th February, to land a brigade of the 25th Division near Ru-ywa, thirty miles south of Kangaw and twelve west of An. Naval and air support was on this occasion supplemented by a medium battery secretly landed on a small island off shore. Next day, the village of Ru-wya was captured, but on the 19th the enemy put in the usual savage counter-attack, at the same time heavily shelling the beach-head. This attack was thrown back with difficulty, but further brigades were landed and preparations begun to encircle the enemy at An. In the first week of March, these moves were in full swing and going well when, as so often happened in Burma, they had to be called off for reasons beyond the immediate commander's control.

Around An, the country was the worst jungle hill type, and the supply of our encircling columns, hacking their way forward, could only be by air drop. At this moment the Meiktila–Mandalay battle was approaching its highest intensity, and its success, too, depended on air supply. My difficulties, as I brought more formations into the field in Central Burma, increased; so did my clamour for more aircraft. General Leese decided, therefore, that it was necessary drastically to reduce the allotment of air supply to 15 Corps and to transfer its aircraft to the main front. There was no doubt as to the wisdom of this decision, but it meant the abandonment of the An operations at once and of others later. All brigades of the 82nd Division were ordered back to the coast and the 25th Division to Akyab.

In spite of this undeserved disappointment, Christison valiantly tried to carry out his remaining tasks with the transport, mainly sea, remaining to him. He landed a brigade of his 26th Division at Letpan, some thirty-five miles north of Taungup. This brigade, followed by 22 East African Brigade, pushed south down the coast road, but was held up, five miles short of Taungup, by strong positions astride the road in difficult country. Christison knew as well as I did, the cost and futility of narrow frontal attacks on such positions, and again he had not the air-lift to supply jungle columns in outflanking marches. The Japanese, with a strong block on each, thus remained in control of both the roads from the coast to the Irrawaddy, and were free to collect, behind these detachments, what they could from the remains of their Arakan garrison and send it to join their forces opposing the Fourteenth Army.

In actual fact, the enemy reinforcements thus set free did not amount to as much as I feared at the time and, in any case, it would not have been Christison's fault if they had. He had skilfully and loyally done all he could to aid me; above all, he had secured the essential airfields which would enable me to go south. At Akyab, Ramree, and Cheduba he at once began to lay in the stocks my army would require and to build the airfields. All-weather strips would be required, and it was at first intended to make only this type, but it was found that, with their slower construction, they could not be ready until the first half of May. This would not allow for supply during my advance, so, while pressing on simultaneously with the all-weather fields, 15 Corps built a number of fair-weather strips. This greatly increased the work but ensured my supply up to the end of April when the all-weather landing grounds would take over for the monsoon. As may be imagined, I watched the progress of these airfields with anxiety, which changed to relief when I saw how steadily and rapidly 15 Corps was building them.

On the Fourteenth Army's other flank, the left, Sultan, although the return to China of all his American and Chinese formations had been demanded and two of his divisions had already gone, continued his advance. But it was necessarily at a slower pace and gave the Japanese the chance, which they took, to retire in good order and to divert troops to oppose the Fourteenth Army. As the action on the N.C.A.C. front was obviously slowing up, I asked General Leese in mid-February to let the 36th British Division revert to my command, so that I could use it in the Mandalay battle. He refused, on the sensible grounds that the loss of this active division would still further upset Sultan's plans and there would be difficulties about bringing its American air contingent with it. However, in an Operation Instruction of the 27th February, he ordered Sultan to take the Kyaukme–Lashio line, co-operate in the Mandalay battle, and then exploit south towards Loilem. If all that were done, I should be very satisfied.

Meanwhile, Festing was pushing along his 36th Division. On the 9th February, in the face of determined resistance, he forced the crossing of the five-hundred-yard-wide Shweli River at Myitson, and, with the help of most efficient American fighter and light bomber cover, held his bridgehead against all assaults, including attacks by flame-throwers. After nearly a month of these attempts, and having suffered heavy casualties, the Japanese gave up the struggle and fell back south, contenting themselves with attempts to delay. The division went on to clear the Mong-mit area, to take Mogok with its famous ruby mines, and, on the 30th March, to join up with the American Mars Brigade which had reached Kyaukme.

On the 1st April my request for the return of the 36th British Division was granted, and it bade farewell to the N.C.A.C. with whom it had served so effectively and in such good comradeship with both Chinese and Americans. Festing and his division, besides a good fighting job, had done a great deal to dispel the cloud of uninformed criticism that at one time threatened to darken Anglo-American relations. Instead of only hearing second-hand and often malicious stories, the soldiers of both nations had now seen one another fighting the enemy. The result was mutual respect. The division was given a great farewell by its American friends as it turned south-west to Maymyo to rejoin the Fourteenth Army. I ordered it to fly one brigade into Mandalay in its maintenance aircraft at once, and to concentrate the rest of the division as quickly as possible to relieve the 19th Division, in such clearing up operations as were still going on in the area Mandalay–Maymyo–Myittha–Ava. Unfortunately the 36th Division's American transport aircraft were to be withdrawn on 1st May, and therefore the division would, before that date, have to be flown out to India. My use of this division could only be very temporary. Actually, I managed to keep one brigade in action until the 10th May.

On the 7th March, the Chinese I Army, under my old friend Sun, captured Lashio, the Japanese falling back in good order in front of it. A few days later, the first regiment of the Mars Brigade was ordered to China, to be followed later by the rest of the brigade. The loss of the Mars Brigade, its only American formation, would greatly weaken N.C.A.C., but its maintenance by air in mobile operations required a greater effort than that needed for a much larger Chinese force, and Sultan therefore wisely let it go first. On the 16th March, Hsipaw, on the railway thirty-five miles south-west of Lashio and about a hundred from Mandalay, was occupied. The Chinese then sat down on the line they had reached, while the Japanese, who had withdrawn intact before them, now broke all contact and, leaving only a few scattered detachments to watch them, transferred their forces south directly to oppose the Fourteenth Army or into the Shan Hills to threaten its flank. When the Chinese halted, some two thousand five hundred local tribesmen under American officers took over responsibility for the safety of the Stilwell road against possible marauders.

From now on, the Chinese for all practical purposes, ceased to take any part in the Burma War. To me, of course, this was most disappointing, as I had hoped that a Chinese push towards Loilem would have engaged at least some enemy and helped to protect my very vulnerable left flank. However, there seemed to be nothing that I, or apparently anyone else, could do about it, except to remember our motto, 'God helps those who help themselves', and to get on with the war without the Chinese. So with little hope of help on either of my flanks, I continued the main battle.

When, in the last days of February 1945, 4 Corps gripped Meiktila in a stranglehold, the divisions of 33 Corps were poised in their bridgeheads along the Irrawaddy to the north and west of Mandalay ready to strike. The 19th Division, forty miles north of the city, after its struggle, first to hold and then to extend its bridgeheads, was straining at the leash for a dash down the east bank on Mandalay. The 20th Division, fighting without pause, had a deep, firmly held eight-mile stretch of the southern shore of the river, forty miles west of Mandalay, in which it was collecting to break out. The 2nd British Division had been left almost unmolested in the last gained bridgehead, some twenty-five miles west of Mandalay, and was now drawing up its tail across the river.

The crisis of the great battle was at hand. Kimura's gaze was fixed on Mandalay and its neighbourhood, his troops faced north and were marching hard to meet us there, yet he could not fail within a few days, perhaps hours, to awake to the danger behind him at Meiktila. When he did, I must prevent him, as far as I could, from reinforcing that area until Messervy had firmly established 4 Corps across the Japanese rear—the anvil to meet the hammer from the north. To do this, Kimura, just as he began to realize what the loss of Meiktila meant to him, must be struck about Mandalay till he reeled, so that he could detach forces from there only at grave peril to his Irrawaddy line. Then as disruption spread outward from Meiktila, 33 Corps must be loosed in an all-out offensive to the south—the hammer to the anvil. It was not Mandalay or Meiktila that we were after but the Japanese army, and that thought had to be firmly emplanted in the mind of every man of the Fourteenth Army.

On the 27th February, an A.L.F.S.E.A. Operation Instruction was issued directing Fourteenth Army to:

(i) Destroy the Japanese forces in the Mandalay area.
(ii) Seize Rangoon before the monsoon.

As orders, based on the Fourteenth Army Operation Instruction of the 19th December 1944, to achieve these objects had already been given to corps two months previously, no changes in our plans or dispositions were necessary. Operations continued at an increasing tempo.

Rees's 19th Division was the first to be slipped. On the 26th February one of its brigades (64) broke out from the Kyaukmy-aung bridgehead and bit into the foothills to the east, gaining elbow room for the second brigade (62), which next day thrust through the Japanese lines on the river bank. The two brigades then drove south, like a rush of waters over a broken dam. The enemy were swept away, leaving a few crumbling islets of resistance, to be engulfed later, as the third brigade (98) raced from the northern Thabeikyin bridgehead to catch up with the rest of the division. By the 3rd March, the 19th Division was in tankable country; on the 4th, Rees was able to report that the wretched 15th Japanese Division, that had been first shattered at Imphal, then bled white again in the attacks on his bridgeheads, had now disintegrated and was incapable of further organized resistance. Leap-frogging his brigades, next day he crossed the Chaungmagyi River, eighteen miles north of Mandalay and the last natural obstacle before the city. The Japanese had prepared strong positions about Madaya, just south of the Chaungmagyi, where the railway from Mandalay ended, but a motorized column of Rees's men swept into their trenches with or before the enemy trying to occupy them, and went on to clear the town in street fighting. As Mandalay was approached, opposition stiffened but was still unco-ordinated, and, by dawn on the 8th March, one brigade (64) was fighting two miles east of Mandalay Cantonment, while another (98) with its motorized column had reached the northern outskirts of the city. Japanese resistance outside Mandalay was now reduced to small parties, roaming the countryside with little knowledge of what was happening around them, but in two places the defence was still strong and well organized— on Mandalay Hill and in the city itself at Fort Dufferin.

Mandalay Hill is a great rock rising abruptly from the plain to nearly eight hundred feet and dominating the whole northeastern quarter of the city. Its steep sides are covered with temples and pagodas, now honeycombed for machine-guns, well supplied, and heavily garrisoned. Throughout the day and night of the 9th March, the fiercest hand-to-hand fighting went on, as a Gurkha battalion stormed up the slopes and bombed and tommy-gunned their way into the concrete buildings. Next day two companies of a British battalion joined them, and the bitter fighting went on. The Japanese stood to the end, until the last defenders, holding out in cellars, were destroyed by petrol rolled down in drums and ignited by tracer bullets. It was not until the 11th March that the hill was completely in our hands. When, shortly afterwards, I visited it, the blackened marks of fire and the sights and stench of carnage were only too obvious, while distant bumps and bangs and the nearer rattle of machine-guns showed that the clearing of the city was still going on. Through all this noise and the clatter of men clearing a battlefield, came a strange sound— singing. I followed it. There was General Rees, his uniform sweat-soaked and dirty, his distinguishing red scarf rumpled round his neck, his bush hat at a jaunty angle, his arm beating time, surrounded by a group of Assamese soldiers whom he was vigorously leading in the singing of Welsh missionary hymns. The fact that he sang in Welsh and they in Khasi only added to the harmony. I looked on admiringly. My generals had character. Their men knew them and they knew their men.

The other Japanese stronghold, Fort Dufferin in Mandalay

City, was a great rectangular, walled enclosure, containing one and a quarter square miles of parkland, dotted with official residences, barracks, and other buildings including the fantastic, teak-built Royal Palace of Theebaw, the last Burmese king, its upturned eaves rich with carving, vermilion, and gilding. The crenellated, twenty-foot-high outer walls of the fort were faced with thick brickwork and backed by earth embankments seventy feet wide at their base. All round lay the moat, over two hundred feet wide, water filled and studded with lotus—a picturesque but hampering weed. Fort Dufferin, an immense edition of the toy fortress I used to play with as a boy, manned by Japanese, was a very formidable object to a lightly equipped army in a hurry.

For the next few days, Rees's battalions fought their way street by street through the city, suffering heavily, especially in officers, from snipers, until on the 15th the Fort was completely surrounded. The attack on Fort Dufferin might well have been a scene from the Siege of Delhi in the Indian Mutiny. Medium guns were brought up within five hundred yards to breach the walls, rafts and scaling ladders prepared, storming parties detailed, and an attempt made to enter through the great pipes that ran into the moat. On the night of the 16th March, in attacks on the north-west and north-east corners of the Fort, 'Forlorn Hopes' were repulsed by heavy automatic fire, and our men withdrew, after most gallantly rescuing their wounded. On the 18th and 19th, four separate attempts to cross the moat failed. Such attacks threatened to become expensive, so a more modern aspect was given to the siege by aircraft attacks on the walls. The interior of the Fort had been bombed on the 13th, and serious attempts to breach the walls with 500-pound bombs began on the 16th. The bombs, like the 5.5-inch shells, only damaged the outer face; the great bank of earth behind was unbreached. Recourse was then had to skip bombing, when Mitchell bombers, flying low, tried to drop 2,000-pound bombs on the waters of the moat so that they would bounce into the walls. After several days of these attacks a small breach some fifteen feet wide, up which troops might scramble was made, but the assault would have been hazardous and certainly costly. I was, therefore, against it, as we could now by-pass the Fort, and its eventual capture was in-evitable, more indeed a matter of news value than military advantage. I was prepared to wait.

However, during the night of the 19th/20th March there was extra activity in and around the Fort, and, after the morning air strike, a group of Anglo-Burmese waving white flags and Union Jacks appeared at one of the gates. The garrison, they reported, had during darkness crept through drains from the moat into the southern part of the town. Many were intercepted by our troops, others who hid in deserted houses were hunted down during the next few days, only a handful escaped into open country. Our men entering the Fort found large dumps of Japanese stores and ammunition, a number of European and Anglo-Burmese civilian prisoners, and a fair sprinkling of booby traps. Rees himself, as was proper, hoisted the Union Jack again over Fort Dufferin and revisited Government House, now sadly battered, where years before in more peaceful days he had served as Military Secretary. To our great regret, Theebaw's Palace had been burnt down, whether fired by our shelling and bombing, although we had tried to avoid it, or by the Japanese to destroy the stores they had in it, I do not know. A day or two later, I staged a more formal ceremony at which both corps and all divisional commanders were present, when I hoisted the Union Jack over Mandalay. The capture of Mandalay had been as much the result of operations at Meiktila and elsewhere as of those around the city itself. Every one of my divisions had played its part; it was an Army victory. I thought it would be good for everyone to have that fact demonstrated.

While these dramatic events had been taking place in Mandalay, the 19th Division had achieved another triumph of daring and mobility. As early as the 6th March, one of its brigades (62) had been pulled out of the race for Mandalay when still twenty miles north of the city, and next day struck off south-east for Maymyo, the summer capital of Burma in the hills twenty-five miles east of Mandalay. Marching for four days by smugglers' tracks, across two mountain ranges, and through a deep valley, the brigade suddenly burst into the quiet of that lovely hill station to the utter surprise of its Japanese garrison and the numerous administrative troops located there. Some fled north in a train that, luckily for them, happened to be standing with steam up in the station, but the majority were wiped out among the pleasant bungalows and along the flower-bordered roads. An enemy convoy, trying to slip away in the night, was ambushed and yielded

470

a gun and forty or fifty lorries which proved a valuable supplement to the pack transport of the brigade. The capture of Maymyo cut the road and railway, which were the only direct and effective lines of communication from the Japanese supply depots of Central Burma to their troops still opposing Sultan's forces. It also did much to secure my left, which, now far ahead of his Chinese, had been something of an anxiety to me. Leaving a battalion to block any hostile move from the north-east and to collect the Japanese stragglers and vehicles that still hopefully made for Maymyo, the remainder of the brigade marched to Mandalay and rejoined their division. Since reaching the Irrawaddy, in ten weeks of hard fighting and rapid movement, the 19th Division had not only cleared the enemy out of Mandalay, Maymyo, and a large area, but had counted six thousand Japanese killed on its battlefields.

The other Indian division of Stopford's 33 Corps, the 20th under Gracey, had needed no urging when in turn it was launched in the general offensive. The prolonged and fierce fighting in the bridgehead, when Japanese casualties had been so heavy, had weakened the enemy and sapped his powers of resistance. Gracey's troops pushed rapidly east, clearing village after village, and expanding their bridgehead towards that of the 2nd Division. On the 2nd March, the two divisions made contact along the river. Throughout the 3rd and 4th fighting went on, the Japanese artillery being particularly active, but their infantry were losing some of their tenacity and the bridgehead was steadily enlarged to the south-east. On the 5th March, the two bridgeheads of the 20th Division linked up. From then onwards the expansion of the bridgehead was more rapid; the enemy were obviously breaking. They had already suffered a decisive defeat on the Irrawaddy line and another about Meiktila, although at this time they still showed no signs of abandoning the attempt to retake that town. They had lost heavily in guns, much of their armour had been destroyed or captured. It was not easy in the then fluid state of the battle to be certain what Kimura's plan was, but, as far as we could deduce, it was to halt us on a line running south-west from Kyaukse, with its bastions at Kyaukse itself, Myingyan, Taungtha, Mount Popa, Kyaukpadaung, and Chauk. The Japanese Fifteenth Army was to hold the right, the Thirty-third the centre, and the Twenty-eighth the left. Whether this was with the object of holding us off from the north, while another attempt was made to retake Meiktila, or to cover a reorganization and a general withdrawal to the south, we did not know. I hoped the former; the longer the enemy stayed in Central Burma the better chance we had to destroy him. It was plain, however, that, after the losses he had suffered, the enemy was in no condition to hold such a line; his increasing shortage of artillery alone would have made it impracticable. What was needed now to complete the Japanese confusion was to cut lanes through them, striking at their command and communication centres both by land and air, so that the already weakening grip of their commanders on the situation would be completely broken. Speed was the keynote, both to prevent the Japanese rallying and to give us time before the monsoon for the advance to Rangoon. The moment had come to strike boldly, and no one was more fitted to do it than Gracey and his men. I had never seen troops who carried their tails more vertically.

Gracey's plan was for two of his brigades (32 and 80) to converge on Kyaukse from the north and north-west, while the third (100) carried out a wide encircling movement, through Pyinzi to take Wundwin on the main railway sixty miles south of Mandalay. This brigade, which was spearheaded by an armoured and motorized column, had the double object of cutting off the Japanese retreating in front of the other brigades and of linking up with 4 Corps from Meiktila.

On the 8th March, the 20th Division broke out into a rocky undulating country interspersed with villages, mango groves, and small banana plantations. The armoured column lunged first at Myotha, a communications junction fifteen miles from the river. Resistance was disorganized, but in places stubborn, and it was not until the 10th that Gyo, a village half-way to Myotha, was taken by 80 Brigade after brisk fighting, in which the enemy suffered severely and lost seven guns. Two days later this brigade fought through Myotha, south of which large hostile concentrations were reported, and some days were spent in clearing the surrounding country. On the 19th, another brigade, 100, struck south-east for twenty-five miles and seized Pyinzi, following this up by a further fifteen miles to Pindale. On the 21st March, after meeting stiff opposition, it reached Wundwin, surprising the Japanese line of communication troops there who fled, leaving over two hundred dead. Wundwin was the administrative centre of the Japanese 18th Division; here were its headquarters, depots, supply dumps, and hospitals. Its capture disrupted the divisional command and supply systems, and resistance became even more disjointed.

From Wundwin, the armoured column struck north for thirty miles, spreading consternation among the Japanese installations on both sides of the railway. Several hundred Japanese were killed, a few light tanks destroyed, guns and mechanical transport taken, and great quantities of documents collected. Among the captures were a train full of arms and ammunition, a tank and tractors, and a complete convoy of lorries loaded with assault boats and outboard engines. In one place a small hospital was seized before the staff had time to kill the patients, and fifty-three sick and wounded prisoners were taken—the largest single bag yet obtained. On the 29th March, the brigade made touch south of Kyaukse with other troops of the division attacking the town.

While 100 Brigade was playing such havoc with the Japanese around Wundwin, 80 and 32 Brigades struck east and south-east on Kyaukse and Myittha. They were opposed by small but tough enemy parties in every village, but on the 13th March they were half-way to the Mandalay–Rangoon railway, and on the 16th some of our columns reached it, twenty miles south of Mandalay. Next day, 32 Brigade was approaching Kyaukse, ten miles farther south. This town was of the greatest importance to the Japanese, for not only was it their chief supply centre for a large part of their army, but it was the bastion behind which Kimura hoped to restore some order in his shattered units. It was easily defensible, and already considerable numbers of Japanese, fleeing from the north and west, had rallied there, so that it took several days of stubborn fighting to drive the enemy out of their positions. To the last they clung to the town itself, in the effort to save at least some of the great quantities of stores it contained, and it was not until the 30th March that it fell. When our troops reached the railway station, they found a wrecked train fully loaded with the last stores the Japanese had hoped to get away, medical equipment, photographic supplies, sewing machines, and, strangely enough, books and magazines.

This break-out of the 20th Division was a spectacular achievement which only a magnificent division, magnificently led,

473

could have staged after weeks of the heaviest defensive fighting. In three weeks the division had swept clear of the enemy an area forty-five miles by forty and was across the Rangoon–Mandalay railway on a fifty-mile stretch. The Japanese had left two thousand dead and fifty guns behind them. Their 15th and 31st Divisions were now little more than groups of fugitives seeking refuge in the Shan Hills to the east. It is interesting to note that the 20th Indian Division was the only formation of Fourteenth Army to have been trained since its inception for war in Burma. It had been well trained. Nor did it rest on its laurels, but in every direction continued with mobile columns to strike at any Japanese groups located, and to surprise and slaughter them.

In all these operations, and particularly in those aimed at the disruption of the enemy command, the Allied air forces played a notable part. As soon as a Japanese divisional or army headquarters opened up, our wireless location unit, recognizing their call signs and even the mannerisms of their individual operators, quickly pin-pointed their positions. Then American and British light bombers and ground support aircraft were on them like terriers on to rats, while a motorized and armoured column often followed before the dust had settled. The life of a Japanese general and his staff in these days was not a happy one.

The 2nd British Division, which on the 25th February had been the last to cross the Irrawaddy, at once began to extend its bridgehead. Although it did not meet the strong opposition that had faced the 19th and 20th Divisions and indeed was never seriously counter-attacked, the resistance of small Japanese parties in villages, supported by artillery, made the advance somewhat slow. By the 6th March, troops of the division were five miles south of the Irrawaddy and the bridgehead was expanding to both the east and west along the river bank. On the 11th, the small town of Kyauktalon was taken by the eastern advance and two days later Myinthi, twelve miles to the south-east, was occupied. The advance east along the river bank continued and, after a stiff fight on the 17th March, Ava Fort was cleared of the enemy. Next day a Japanese detachment holding the southern end of the Ava bridge was driven out. The great bridge which we had destroyed in the 1942 Retreat was of course still down, but its northern end had already been occupied by our 268 Independent Brigade.

On the same day, the 18th, troops of the 2nd Division met patrols of the 20th sweeping far round their southern flank. On the 20th March, Nicholson's men occupied Amarapura, the great railway workshops seven miles south of Mandalay, now largely destroyed by our bombing and by Japanese demolition, and on the 21st made contact with patrols of the 19th Division pushing south. The casualties inflicted on the enemy in the 2nd Division's break-out had not been severe, but a great deal of booty fell into our hands including much needed engineer stores and, most valuable of all, some serviceable rolling stock.

Although all offensive action, either by N.C.A.C. on our left or by 15 Corps on our right, had ceased and the Fourteenth Army alone faced practically the whole of the Japanese forces in Burma, our position was now, I thought, very favourable. Both banks of the Irrawaddy from Mandalay to Chauk and the main road and railway to Rangoon as far south as Wundwin were in our hands. Meiktila was firmly and finally held, the road to it from Myingyan was open, and we were steadily expanding our grasp over the surrounding country. The enemy formations, although still fighting stubbornly, had lost almost all their armour, a large proportion of their guns, and much of their transport. Everywhere they were in great and growing confusion. Kimura's only hope, now, was to extricate himself, fall back to the south, and collect what troops he could to hold us off from Rangoon. *Our* best hope was to rush him off his feet before he could regain balance—and to pray for a late monsoon.

BOOK VI

Victory

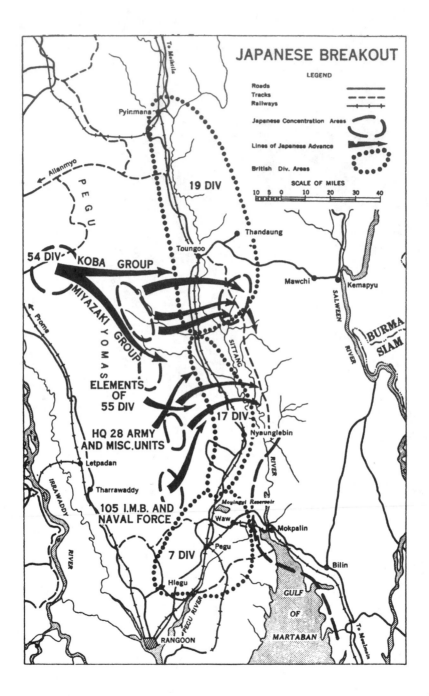

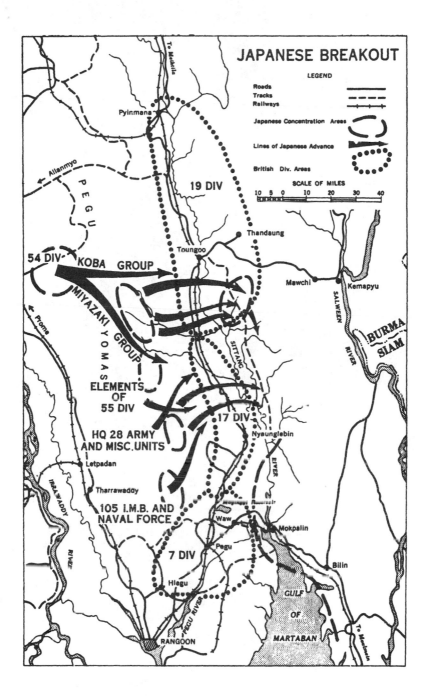

JAPANESE BREAKOUT

LEGEND

Roads	——————
Tracks	– – – –
Railways	+–+–+–+
Japanese Concentration Areas	
Lines of Japanese Advance	▬▬▶
British Div. Areas	::::::

SCALE OF MILES

10 5 0 10 20 30 40

To Meiktila

Pyinmana

To Mandalay

Allanmyo

P E G U

19 DIV

Thandaung

Toungoo

54 DIV — KOBA GROUP

MIYAZAKI GROUP

Y O M A S

Mawchi

Kemapyu

SALWEEN RIVER

BURMA
SIAM

Prome

ELEMENTS
OF
55 DIV

17 DIV

HQ 28 ARMY
AND MISC. UNITS

Nyaunglebin

SITTANG

RIVER

Letpadan

Tharrawaddy

105 I.M.B. AND
NAVAL FORCE

Moyingyi Reservoir

Waw

Mokpalin

IRRAWADDY RIVER

7 DIV

Pegu

Bilin

Hlegu

PEGU RIVER

GULF
OF
MARTABAN

To Moulmein

RANGOON

CHAPTER XXI

THE RACE TO RANGOON

IN mid-March 1945 the Battle of Central Burma was drawing to its close, yet Kimura still obstinately refused to admit defeat—an admirable trait in a commander, but one which he was in danger of carrying to excess. His divisions, especially those of Katamura's Fifteenth Army, were in a bad way; they had lost not only guns, transport, and equipment but were now losing their cohesion. If he wished to avoid destruction, Kimura could not fight much longer anywhere north of a line from Yenangyaung to Pyawbwe, and I did not intend he should fight long on that line. The time had come to take our next step—Rangoon.

Our own divisions, although they had been operating strenuously and continuously for several months without rest, were still in great heart. Our casualties, despite the amount of close fighting, had not been unduly heavy, and, as far as Indian units were concerned, had been largely replaced. British reinforcements, as so often in this theatre, lagged behind casualties, and owing to their numerical weakness I had again to replace British battalions by Indian. The state of our road transport, too, caused anxiety. We had lost neither guns nor vehicles to the enemy, but much of our motor transport was on its last legs, and replacements were short. There could be no pause either in operations or in the movement of supplies by road, so that time for overhaul was scant. In spite of heroic efforts to make all possible vehicles serviceable for the next phase, we could only hope that, with forward formations largely on air supply and with an increasing use of river and railway, we should just manage to keep enough lorries running. In the event, we saved the situation only by taking all serviceable vehicles from formations going out of Burma and issuing them to those remaining.

The state of our armour worried me even more. Our striking power, and with it our speed, would depend, beyond anything, on the armoured spearheads of our advance. Yet our Shermans, Lee-Grants, Stuarts, and armoured cars were all obsolete and mostly long overdue for replacement. They had been used hard, and it was only the skill and determination of their crews, British and Indian, backed by the devoted I.E.M.E. and I.A.O.C. men, that had kept them on the road up to now. With daily demands on our armour, opportunities for the extra maintenance so badly needed were not easy to find. I visited the tank and armoured car units to thank them for their magnificent efforts in the past battle and to impress on them how much I should rely on them for the next. I told them that, when I gave the word for the dash on Rangoon, every tank they had must be a starter, and that every tank that crossed the start line must pass the post in Rangoon. After that they could push them into the sea if they wanted! But they had to get to Rangoon!

It would be a race, and a stern one, against two tough competitors, the enemy and the monsoon. The Japanese, in spite of the hammering we had given them, were still numerous and formidable; the shadow of the monsoon loomed over us, only seven or eight weeks away. If we did not take Rangoon before it broke, we should, with landing grounds out, even dropping hazardous, roads dissolving and health deteriorating, find ourselves in a desperate situation with the prospect of a disastrous withdrawal. It was now the middle of March; a normal monsoon would break somewhere about the 15th May. Before we could begin the drive south, we had to finish the present battle, clear the large areas to the north of Meiktila and Yenangyaung, rearrange our forces, and break the crust of any new line of Japanese resistance. We could not expect to do all that before the first week of April. Then, with luck, we should have some forty days to reach—and take—Rangoon. From Meiktila, by the railway route, Rangoon is three hundred and twenty miles; from Chauk, via the Irrawaddy Valley, three hundred and seventy. We should have to move at an average of eight or ten miles a day. That, against opposition and demolitions, was fast. There would be no time to stage elaborate attacks; positions that could not be taken by quick assault would have to be by-passed. Even when they were taken, there could be no pause for thorough mopping-up, nor could we wait to deal with the very large bodies of Japanese already driven into the hills on the flanks of both routes.

Inevitably large enemy masses would be left behind us. As soon as we had got Rangoon, the troops would have to turn in their tracks, come north again, and hunt them. Thinking of that, I hoped that my armoured units would not take too literally my permission to push their tanks into the sea at Rangoon.

The possibility that alarmed me most, however, was that the Japanese would, as they had in other towns, put a suicide garrison into Rangoon that would keep us out for the monsoon. I could not contemplate with anything but dismay a repetition of the Meiktila battle, around Rangoon at the end of a most precarious supply line, in the midst of the rains. I therefore urged that when the Fourteenth Army approached within striking distance of Rangoon from the north, an amphibious and airborne assault— our old friend 'Dracula'— should be put in from the sea. I had always opposed 'Dracula' if it were to be done at the expense of the Fourteenth Army, but now, when divisions were being released both from Arakan and from my army, I believed we had enough troops to stage it without seriously affecting my offensive. Air support for the actual assault would, I realized, have to be at my expense, but our air superiority was so marked that I was prepared to accept that. The naval position had improved and we now had the landing craft necessary for a limited operation. The original 'Dracula' had been planned to take Rangoon while the Fourteenth Army was still far to the north; the new one would be, I hoped, a hammering on the back door while I burst in at the front. It could, therefore, be on a reduced scale and within our means.

The 'Dracula' project had had a chequered career. Both Generals Giffard and Leese had, like me, opposed it when it meant reducing the Fourteenth Army. Later when it became possible to contemplate an amphibious operation with resources from elsewhere, General Leese had still condemned it. Even more confident than I was that the Fourteenth Army could take Rangoon unaided, he recommended that the forces now available for an amphibious operation should be used to seize the island of Phuket off the Kra Isthmus, as a preliminary to the reconquest of Singapore, rather than to help in the capture of Rangoon. Otherwise, he contended, there would be considerable and unnecessary delay in the next step after Burma, the reconquest of Malaya. On the 23rd February, Admiral Mountbatten had agreed. The decision was taken to discard 'Dracula' and prepare for the operation off the Kra Isthmus—Operation 'Roger'—to be carried out not later than 1st June. For this a new corps, numbered 34, was formed in India of the 23rd Indian and 81st West African Divisions and 3 Commando Brigade, all withdrawn from Burma. I was delighted that Roberts, who had led the 23rd Division so well at Imphal, was given the new command. I had now seen him go from Colonel on the staff of my division in 1941 to Lieutenant-General in 1945, and I felt rather complacent about the report I had written on him at the Staff College ten years earlier.

All the same, I was not happy about the decision to abandon the sea attack on Rangoon. I felt that, with all the risks we were taking, the extra insurance would have been wise. However, I did not let it worry me unduly, for I judged that, unless the luck of the weather were heavily against us, we ought to keep to schedule and manage alone. So confident of this was I, that I had already, on the 18th March, issued detailed orders for the advance on Rangoon, to carry out the Operation Instruction I had issued to corps commanders on the 19th December 1944.

We had, in fact, been making plans quietly at Fourteenth Army Headquarters for the capture of Rangoon since the previous July, and in November, when our bridgeheads over the Chindwin were either achieved or about to be achieved, we settled down to serious planning. The last edition of Operation 'Sob', our Fourteenth Army private plan to reach the sea, envisaged a double advance, by the railway and by the Irrawaddy, with a full corps and a tank brigade on each. The Japanese would not, I calculated, be able to produce enough troops to stop us on both; if they held one corps, the other would break through. However, the state of our transport and shortage of supply aircraft soon ruled that plan out. We had, at the moment, seven divisions operating in Central Burma, but of these the 36th must leave the theatre almost at once as its American air transport was about to be removed. If we were to advance at all south of Meiktila and Yenangyaung, another division would have to go back to India— probably the 2nd British as its strength was falling and it was more difficult to supply than an Indian. This would leave five divisions, and of these, only three, with the two tank brigades, could be maintained by air in a rapid advance far to the south. Against these comparatively small striking forces the Japanese might still bring superior strength, and it was clear that we should have to concentrate our main effort on one axis. The question was, which?

The nearness of the monsoon made me decide that the essential characteristic of our advance must be speed, and that presupposed a wholly mechanized force on the main axis. The strength of this should be at least a corps of two divisions and a tank brigade, and it was necessary, therefore, to choose the better route for a completely mechanized corps. We were leaving behind the open motorable country of Central Burma; whichever route we took there would be a single road, off which, even in dry weather, it would be difficult to deploy. When the rain set in, the movement of both wheeled and tracked vehicles off the metalled road would be impossible. There was little to choose between the northern half of either axis, but the farther one went south on the Irrawaddy line, the more numerous became the water channels that had to be crossed. All bridges would be blown, and, even if we carried an inordinate quantity of Bailey bridging, there would be serious delays—delays which we could not afford. In distance, too, the railway route had an advantage of some fifty miles. Most important of all, the farther east we drove through the Japanese, the more of them would be cut off in the roadless jungles of the Yomas, to struggle out as best they could during the monsoon—a second retreat with, I hoped, even more disastrous consequences to them than that from Imphal. There were, of course, disadvantages to the railway route. On it we should meet the stronger enemy group, and we should be liable to counter attack in flank from the Shan and Karen Hills, where increasing hostile concentrations were being daily reported. In spite of these disadvantages, I chose the railway axis for my main advance. At the same time, to engage the enemy on as wide a front as possible, to split his forces and distract his command, I would push down the Irrawaddy Valley the maximum mobile force I could maintain. If we were held on the railway, I would at least have a second string to my bow.

The choice of formations for the two lines of advance was not difficult. The 5th and 17th Divisions of 4 Corps were both on the new mechanized and airborne basis, and in addition, the bulk of that corps was collected in the Meiktila area, some fifty miles south of the general location of 33 Corps. It was obvious, therefore, that 4 Corps should follow the railway axis and be the main striking force. This did not mean that 33 Corps on the Irrawaddy route would be idle. Stopford could be relied on to push his divisions hard. Indeed, with less Japanese opposition, it was not beyond the bounds of possibility that he might reach Rangoon first. On the railway axis, all troops south of Toungoo would have to be completely on air supply; those north of it, as far as possible, on road and perhaps rail. For 33 Corps, on the river, there would be air supply for one division and part of the tank brigade only; the rest would have to manage on road and water transport.

While we had been planning, a development had taken place which promised some embarrassment to the Japanese and consequently some advantage, even if no great one, to us. As early as 1943, we had heard that Aung San, the Burman whom the Japanese had made a Major-General and Commander-in-Chief of their puppet Burma National Army, was disappointed with his masters. In November 1944, we dropped near Pegu a member of the B.N.A., whom we had captured on the Chindwin, and through him and other agents kept touch with the various nationalist bodies inside Burma. We were soon getting wholesale demands from the Communist Anti-Fascist Organization for money, arms, and supplies. Then, in early March 1945, we got news that on the 16th of that month the Japanese were sending the B.N.A. to the front, but that Aung San and his men were ready to defect to us. On the 20th March, an officer of Force 136, the clandestine organization which engineered all these contacts, was parachuted in but failed to get any clear indications of the Burmese leaders' intentions. However, on the 26th March, the B.N.A. rose, surprising and killing some Japanese officers and certainly adding to the anxieties and confusion of the enemy.

There was at this stage a difference of opinion between Force 136 and our Burma Civil Affairs Organization. Force 136 wanted to foster and support the mutinous B.N.A. in all respects; Civil Affairs, claiming with a good deal of reason, that the B.N.A., especially after the liberation of Burma, would be more trouble than use, opposed any support of it. My opinion was that the B.N.A., prowling on their lines of communication, could not fail to be a nuisance to the Japanese and give them an uncomfortable feeling on dark nights. If they were not with us, as well as against the Japanese, we should end up by having to fight them, too. There was a lot to be said politically for having the only Burmese Nationalist armed force actually fighting on our side. I, therefore, recommended we should help Aung San, with arms and supplies, and try to get some tactical control of his forces to make them fit into the general plan. Admiral Mountbatten, quite apart from any arguments of mine, had come to the same conclusion and decided that Aung San should be supported. I did not expect the B.N.A., to exert any serious influence on the campaign, but I hoped they would—as in fact they did—occasionally cut up stragglers, harrass small parties, and ambush vehicles, but I made no changes in my plans because of any help expected from them.

It was very plain to me—and if it had not been, plenty of people were willing to enlighten me—that this dash for Rangoon by a mechanized force, confined to one road, thrusting against time through superior numbers, was a most hazardous and possibly rather un-British operation. I knew the risks and the penalties of failure but, as I checked over the final plans, I was ready to accept them. Whatever the risks, we were winning. We had kicked over the ant-hill; the ants were running about in confusion. Now was the time to stamp on them. My soldiers were out for Rangoon, and anyone who was with them and had seen them fight could not doubt that they would get there. Once more the exhilaration running through the army was a tangible thing that could be seen and felt. I shared it.

In my Operation Instruction of the 18th March, I gave as my main intention, 'the capture of Rangoon at all costs and as soon as possible before the monsoon'. I divided the operation into three Phases:

(1) The present battle.
(2) An interim period for mopping up and regrouping.
(3) The advance south.

I hoped that Phase 1, which by the destruction of Kimura's armies in Central Burma would make Phase 3 possible, would end shortly. In the Second or Interim Phase, which I hoped would also be a rapid one, Messervy's 4 Corps, with the 5th and 17th Divisions and 255 Tank Brigade, would strike at the Japanese about Pyawbwe and prepare for the thrust south. Stopford's

33 Corps, with the 2nd British and 20th Divisions, would clear the area Mandalay–Maymyo–Wundwin–Mahlaing–Myingyan, freeing all its roads and railways for our use. The 7th Indian Division, already on the Irrawaddy, would then replace the 2nd British and the corps would position itself for the advance south. The 19th Division would, as the 2nd and 20th moved west, take over the security of the area from Mandalay to Meiktila. In Phase 3, 4 Corps would push down the railway axis and take Rangoon. 33 Corps, moving on both banks of the Irrawaddy, would capture Chauk and cut off Yenangyaung by a flanking movement on Magwe. Then in turn, Yenangyaung, Prome and finally Rangoon, if possible before 4 Corps could reach it, would be occupied. At the start of Phase 3, the 19th Division would come under direct Fourteenth Army control and would be used to protect the left flank and communications of 4 Corps.

Towards the end of March 1945, Kimura at last accepted defeat in the great battle of Central Burma, but before doing so he had used up every reserve available to him. He had run true to Japanese form; he had left it until too late. None the less, in spite of his plans and his armies crumbling about him, he prepared resolutely and energetically to deny us the two routes to the south.

The line from Kyaukse to Chauk, on which he had hoped to halt our onrush, was gone. Katamura's Fifteenth Army, with its 15th, 31st and 33rd Divisions, had disintegrated, and, with the fall of Kyaukse now imminent, any chance of reorganizing and re-equipping it in the forward area had vanished. Fugitive and scattered, it was now scrambling into the foothills to the east, but in those very Shan Hills the Japanese 56th Division in reasonably good order was arriving from the moribund Chinese front. Kimura ordered the shattered Fifteenth Army to collect on this division, and then to make for Toungoo, where, given time, he hoped to re-form it, and thus provide himself with a much needed reserve. His other armies, the Twenty-eighth and Thirty-third, though battered and short of artillery, transport, and much else, were still capable of fighting, especially defensively, with all the savage tenacity of the Japanese soldier. Kimura's thoughts, like mine, must have turned to the advent of the monsoon; his with hope, mine with dread. If he could hold somewhere well north of Rangoon until the rains, he would at least gain the respite

486

he so desperately needed. To this end he placed an army to bar each of our routes.

On the railway axis, Honda's Thirty-third Army, with the 18th, 49th and 53rd Divisions, was ordered to hold us about Pyawbwe, astride the road and railway to Toungoo. In addition, Kimura planned to use the 56th Division, now in the Shan Hills, not only to cover the collection of what was left of the Fifteenth Army, but to threaten and perhaps counter-attack in flank any advance of ours to the south along the railway.

Sakurai's task with the Twenty-eighth Army was to prevent our advance down the Irrawaddy at or north of Yenangyaung, while blocking any attempts by our forces to break eastward through the passes from Arakan. Under him were seven infantry and three artillery battalions in Yamamoto's Force, the 54th and 55th Divisions and the 2nd Indian National Army Division. Like most plans drawn up by generals, Kimura's was neat enough on paper. What it would look like on the ground was another matter.

As March drew on, I found that with Kyaukse still holding out—it did not fall until the 30th—Phase 1 of my Operation Instruction was taking longer than I had intended. Time was running out, and the spectre of a Japanese stand in Rangoon began to haunt me more and more. It was difficult to get information of Japanese intentions, but there was certainly at this time no evidence that they would on our approach evacuate the city. My view was that, however desirable it might be to hasten the liberation of Malaya, it was more important to make sure of Rangoon. Apart from my own interest in the matter, I felt that a failure in Burma would be a strong brake on any invasion of Malaya. So I renewed my pressure for the modified 'Dracula'. The British Chiefs of Staff unknowingly came to my assistance by saying that the attack on Phuket Island should not be attempted until it was quite certain we were about to take Rangoon. Partly because of this, on the 2nd April, the earlier decision was reversed, and Admiral Mountbatten gave orders that an amphibious assault on Rangoon by one division, with a drop by a battalion of parachute troops, should be prepared for not later than the 5th May. I was glad of this, even when, having failed to get them from any other source, S.E.A.C. took two Dakota squadrons from me to practice the Parachute Battalion. Their loss at once threw a heavier burden on Snelling and his overtaxed staffs. They grappled with it, as they had with all the impossibilities I had already demanded—and got—from them.

I was all the more anxious to make the Second Phase of operations now beginning a rapid one. In the large block of Central Burma, between Myingyan–Mandalay–Wundwin–Chauk, there still remained many scattered but sometimes strong parties of Japanese who were either with dull ferocity holding out or trying, mostly by night, to escape south and east. I took advantage of the regrouping necessary for the advance on Rangoon to comb this area, whose roads and railways were essential to us, by what I called a 'Union Jack' manœuvre. This entailed passing strong columns diagonally through it; part of the 5th Division with other troops from the north-west to the south-east, and the 20th and 2nd Divisions from north-east to south-west. My corps and divisions were well trained in the staff work of rapid movement, and I gave them this rather complicated pattern of moves across each others' communications with little fear of confusion as the quickest way to sweep the area.

I was so eager to hurry things up that I pressed 33 Corps to begin their 'Union Jack' moves of Phase 2, while they were still fighting hard to end Phase 1 around Kyaukse. Stopford was able to make a successful start with 268 Brigade on the clearing operation on the 20th March, but it was not until the 26th that two brigades of the 2nd Division were able to join in. By sweeps through and across the area in several directions, which produced many clashes with small enemy groups, the greater part of the area was cleared, and the 2nd Division, with the exception of 5 Brigade, was withdrawn to fly out to India. The most serious resistance, it was then discovered, remained to be dealt with. It was centred on Mount Popa, an extinct volcano which rises majestically and abruptly nearly five thousand feet above the plain. Here, five or six hundred Japanese with several guns, including mediums, clung most tenaciously to the slopes of the mountain. At the end of March, 5 Brigade began operations to dislodge them, but although some enemy were killed and two guns captured, little progress had been made in a fortnight's rather cautious skirmishing. To hurry things up, Stopford then reinforced 5 Brigade with that most useful maid-of-all-work, 268 Brigade, now reduced to two battalions and an Indian artillery regiment. After a series of brisk fights in rugged country, 268 Brigade by the 19th April had forced the enemy to withdraw from Mount Popa. Several of the groups into which the retreating Japanese split were intercepted, but the bulk of them got away without further serious loss.

The rest of Phase 2 on 33 Corps front had gone better. On the 12th April, a brigade of the 7th Division had, after a fight, captured Kyaukpadaung, the road centre where three years before I had argued with the Chinese commander. Next day, Gwegyo, of unhappy memories, was cleared. Enemy casualties were considerable in both these actions. By the 17th, the brigade turning west had its patrols in the southern outskirts of Chauk. Another brigade of the 7th Division, fighting down the east bank of the Irrawaddy, had already got a foothold at the northern end of Chauk. On the 18th, the two brigades squeezed the enemy out of the town, and Chauk with five guns, forty lorries, and much other booty was ours.

While these events had been taking place in the Mount Popa–Kyaukpadaung area on the east bank, activity was boiling up on the west side of the Irrawaddy. Here, after its failure in the attempt to cut 4 Corps' communications, Yamamoto Force, much weakened, had reverted to the defensive. Its task was to hold our 28 East African Brigade about Letse and thus cover the withdrawal of the Japanese 54th Division from Arakan. This withdrawal was now well under way and, as it progressed, the enemy strength on the west bank steadily increased. The East African Brigade was to return to India as part of our programme for reducing supply demands, and in the second week of April it was relieved by 114 Brigade of the 7th Division from the east bank. The substitution took some little time, and as a result our advances on the east and west banks were not level. Towns on the eastern bank were usually taken several days before the corresponding places on the other side. This led to large bodies of the enemy, cut off from retreat on the east, escaping to the west bank, and again swelling the numbers who could oppose our advance there. The estimated enemy strength on the west bank north of Prome at this time was nine to ten thousand, and our intelligence reported that the main concentrations were in the Salin area sixteen miles north-west of Yenangyaung, and a larger one about Padan, twenty-eight miles south-west of Magwe, where 54th Division troops from the An Pass were collecting. Numerous smaller parties were scattered along the west bank, but it appeared that the general object of all Japanese forces in the area was to retreat south under cover of rearguards, until they could recross to the east either at Allanmyo or, if this town had been lost, at Prome.

With the idea of cutting off the gathering at Salin and the enemy opposing 114 Brigade, Evans, commanding the 7th Division, on the 24th April sent his 89 Brigade across the river to the west bank opposite Yenangyaung. It formed a bridgehead and rapidly spread out north and south against minor opposition. Meanwhile, 114 Brigade continued to press south, clashing on the way with scattered parties of rather bewildered Japanese. On the 26th, Salin, evacuated by the enemy, who withdrew south-west to avoid 89 Brigade, was occupied. The two brigades made contact, and pushed south together, 114 Brigade on the right finding resistance stiffening as it approached Padan. On the river bank, 89 Brigade entered Minbu, opposite Magwe, on the 29th against slight resistance but 114 Brigade had a stiff fight, ten miles north of Padan, in which the Japanese rearguard counter-attacked three times, and another determined action nearer Padan on the 29th. After this fight, patrols failed to gain contact as the enemy was in full retreat to the south. The Japanese had contrived to cover the withdrawal of the 54th Division from Arakan, but their whole situation on the west of the Irrawaddy had now become perilous, not only from the pressure of our two brigades on that bank, but because the rapidity of our 20th Division's advance on the other, constantly compelled them to seek farther and farther south for a crossing to the east.

While the rest of 33 Corps had been moving in the 'Union Jack' manœuvre over the Irrawaddy, the 20th Division had been left behind to deal with the last stubborn resistance of the Japanese at Kyaukse. Then, having taken Kyaukse on the 30th March and harried the last of Katamura's unhappy divisions into the hills, it handed over to the 19th Division and collected south of Meiktila. There, with characteristic energy, Gracey flung himself into preparations for Phase 3. With serviceable vehicles from the 2nd Division, which was about to fly out to India, he was able rapidly to reorganize two of his brigades on a motorized establishment. On the 11th April, the conversion complete, he set out with all speed to take part in the 33 Corps advance south. His task was to strike at the Japanese rear at Magwe and Allanmyo.

Sakurai, commander of the Japanese Twenty-eighth Army, entrusted with the defence of the Irrawaddy Valley, was facing north and east. His main communications, road and river, ran south, but his link with the Thirty-third Army, eighty miles away on the railway axis, bent east at Magwe and went through Taungdwingyi. The latter town could be either a bastion to defend his right rear or a threat to it. Everything depended on who occupied it. Sakurai was short of troops, no British were nearer to Taungdwingyi than Meiktila, the country between was waterless and the road unfit for motor transport; there would be time enough for warning. Sakurai, therefore, concentrated his Japanese troops at places nearer to our forces and on our direct lines of approach; he left Taungdwingyi mainly to Indian National Army units and to his administrative troops. In this he made a fatal mistake—he miscalculated the speed at which we could move. On the 11th April, no British forces were within sixty miles of Taungdwingyi; on the 14th, one of Gracey's mechanized brigades had seized it. The blow was so sudden that for some days the Japanese command did not realize what had happened, and continued to send convoys via Taungdwingyi to the great profit and entertainment of the 20th Division. Small parties of Japanese and larger ones of Jiffs were encountered by our patrols in the neighbourhood, but the only serious hostile action was an attempt to collect a force to hold a position about ten miles south on the road to Allanmyo. On the 18th April, a small armoured column from Taungdwingyi reached the Irrawaddy, eleven miles south of Magwe, and sank three boatloads of Japanese trying to escape across the river. The other mechanized brigade, which had halted at Natmauk, thirty miles north of Taungdwingyi, advanced from there and occupied Magwe, against light opposition, on the 19th April. In clearing up the town, thirteen guns and a hundred and twenty Jiffs were captured and a little later a complete battalion of the Indian National Army, over six hundred strong, was collected in batches from the roadside, where it was waiting to surrender. At Magwe, as at Taungdwingyi, enemy convoys, which included a complete field ambulance, continued to arrive and were promptly and efficiently dealt with. The

VICTORY

Japanese retaliated by shelling Magwe from the west bank, but took no other action.

On the day Magwe fell, the 7th Division was pushing from the north down both banks of the Irrawaddy. On the east bank, a brigade encircled Yenaungyaung, and on the 22nd occupied the town and oilfield against intermittent, but at times fierce, opposition. The Japanese were bewildered by the speed, strength, and direction of the 20th Division's thrust. Their whole plan for the defence of the oilfields had collapsed; even their retreat was cut off. As we held the main roads, they were forced in their efforts to escape south either to take to side tracks, abandoning their vehicles and heavy equipment, or to cross the river westwards, hoping ultimately to recross farther downstream. Sakurai's only chance of collecting any appreciable portion of his forces again was, by hook or by crook, to hold us north of Allanmyo. This he tried to do, but the most he could produce to block our 20th Division columns, advancing from Taungdwingyi on Allanmyo, were small, hurriedly assembled parties who, while they fought gallantly, could not do more than cause us some delay at the cost of practical annihilation to themselves. Allanmyo was entered on the 28th April, and cleared against the hopeless resistance of a devoted rearguard from the 55th Divisional Cavalry, who lost five guns and most of their number killed. By now, however, this high morale was no longer universal among Japanese troops. As our brigade from Magwe pushed down the east bank to link up with the one at Allanmyo, patrols discovered a large enemy party resting in a village. An air strike was immediately laid on. The Japanese scattered in panic and on the site were afterwards found abandoned four guns, wireless sets, grenade dischargers, many rifles, and six officers' swords. Morale was certainly not what it had been, but Japanese savagery remained, for the bodies of six villagers tied to trees and bayoneted were also found.

By the 1st May, 33 Corps Headquarters was established at Magwe, and the 7th Division, with two of its brigades on the west bank, was also there. 268 Brigade was collecting in Allanmyo, about to cross for operations on the west side of the river, while the 20th Division was just starting its advance from Allanmyo on Prome and Rangoon.

By the end of March, 4 Corps with its headquarters at Meiktila, was gathering for the main drive south. Grouped round the town were the 17th Division, the 5th Division, with one brigade still to arrive, and 255 Tank Brigade. In addition, the headquarters and one brigade of the 19th Division were there, ready to take over as soon as the corps left, while the remaining brigades of this division were along the Mandalay road to the north. I found a rather noticeable jam of headquarters in Meiktila, and I decided I should have to wait for some of them to move before I brought mine there. I felt, too, that perhaps the Japanese were a little close as yet for an Army Headquarters in Meiktila to be really comfortable.

In fact, the Japanese were still a good deal in evidence, and it became daily plainer that Honda would try to regroup his divisions on the good defensive position astride the main road at Pyawbwe. His 49th Division, detailed to hold the centre, was already in place digging hard, his 18th, about Thazi, was to occupy the right, and the 53rd, coming in from the north-west, to take up the line on the left. Given a little time, the Japanese position could become most formidable and, if we were seriously delayed by it, our chances of getting to Rangoon would be slight. On the other hand, if we really smashed Honda's army, it was unlikely that Kimura could produce another force capable of holding us farther south. Honda's stand so far north should be all to our advantage, but we must crush him and quickly.

On the 30th March, Messervy's 4 Corps with the 17th Division and 255 Tank Brigade, set about doing so. Cowan, the divisional commander, was in tactical control of the battle and his plan was for a converging attack. His 99 Brigade was to move first east to take Thazi then, turning south, to seize the high ground south-east of Pyawbwe. 48 Brigade was to strike straight down the main road from Meiktila, while 63 Brigade was to swing round Pyawbwe on the west and occupy the rising ground south-west of the town. A fourth tentacle of envelopment would be an armoured and motorized infantry column, which, driving still wider on the west, would cut the Rangoon road south of Pyawbwe. Having gained these positions, the whole force would close in on the main defences and assault them from all sides.

No sooner had the various advances gained contact, than it became clear that the Japanese, while surprised by the speed with which we had mounted our attack, were determined at all costs

493

to halt us. Scattered over the country around Pyawbwe were many villages, some large, some small, and almost all of these had been made into strong-points, mutually supporting and self-supplied from dumps within them. The enemy thus held a wide defensive zone which had to be fought through before his main positions could be reached. It would have been difficult to devise a scheme of defence more suited to the Japanese soldier or more calculated to delay us.

The first hitch in our proceedings occurred when 99 Brigade found a strong garrison firmly embedded in Thazi to which the enemy clung as cover for the escape route into the Shan Hills. Direct assault would, at the best, be costly; any other form of attack would necessarily be slow. Similarly, on the Meiktila road, 48 Brigade was soon fighting its way forward from village to village—a dogged process. Whether these Japanese had been caught by our advance before they could fall back on to positions nearer Pyawbwe, or whether it was the policy of their Higher Command to hold in such depth, I did not know, but they fought like cornered wild cats. When you knew the way—and our men did—they were not difficult to kill, but it took time. And we had not got much time. With this in mind, on the 2nd April, I flew to Meiktila.

I found Messervy and Cowan quite as well aware as I was of the need for speed. Cowan intended to recover the momentum of his advance by leaving a small detachment to contain Thazi, while 99 Brigade, ignoring it, pushed on again. We improved on that by calling in the brigade of the 19th Division from Meiktila to deal with Thazi. This they did a few days later, after some hard fighting. Cowan was confident that, as the result of other steps he was taking, the push astride the road would gather speed. Having seen for myself everywhere the obvious urge to get on and close with the enemy, I left feeling much happier than when I had arrived as so often happened after contact with the forward troops.

For some days 99 Brigade forced its way through the villages south of Thazi, until on the 7th April, it drew level with 48 Brigade which was held up opposite Yindaw, a large village ten miles from Pyawbwe. Both brigades had advanced with determination, killing several hundreds of the enemy and capturing guns, but Yindaw, which they now faced, one on the north, the other on the east, was the toughest nut their teeth had yet met in this battle. It was part of the Japanese permanent defences, with a strong garrison, estimated at about a thousand, who had orders to hold to the last. It had, also, great natural strength, as on one side it was protected by a lake and on others earthen banks and water channels restricted all approaches, limiting those for armour practically to the road itself. It was our tanks that the enemy feared most, and his defences were generously covered by anti-tank guns, obstacles, and mines. For three days, Yindaw was bombarded from the ground and the air while our troops broke into some of its outer defences. Then on the 8th, remembering our decision at Thazi, our brigades were ordered to by-pass it on both sides and leave it to be dealt with by the 5th Division, which was following the 17th. Next day, 99 Brigade reached the high ground just north of Pyawbwe. Fighting strongly, 48 Brigade on the road was closing in from the north-west, and 63 Brigade, having completed its sweep round the town and inflicted many casualties, was on the rise to the south-west. While the brigades were thus pushing forward, the armoured column fought its way to the Rangoon road and, on the 9th, cut it south of Pyawbwe. It even sent a reconnaissance to Yamethin, twelve miles farther south. During the night of the 9th/10th April, three Japanese medium tanks were rash enough to approach ours. A brisk action ensued in the light of our searchlights, and all three enemy tanks were destroyed in the only night tank-versus-tank encounter of the campaign.

On the 10th, the heart of the Japanese position, Pyawbwe itself, was attacked. Here the defences were most thoroughly prepared and the 49th Division, which held them, fought grimly. 99 Brigade's first assault, in spite of its gallantry, failed to take the heavily bunkered waterworks position. Another of its attacks took a full day of close fighting to clean up a maze of nullahs and dug-outs on the outskirts of the town. Mortars and the point-blank fire of pack-guns eventually drove the last of the garrison into the open, where some three hundred were accounted for by our tanks. 48 Brigade, in hand-to-hand fighting, cleared the cantonment quarter, and carried by assault the heavily defended railway station and railway embankment areas. Throughout the day, the armoured column drove northward on a broad front against increasingly disorganized opposition, knocking out guns, overrunning supply dumps, and killing many Japanese as they began to break south. It was this armoured attack in rear which finally cracked the enemy resistance. By dawn on the 11th, the whole of Pyawbwe was in our hands. Such defenders as survived had made off south and east in the darkness, many of them only to be hunted down by our mobile patrols which at daylight began to scour the country.

The skill with which Messervy and Cowan had handled the battle was matched by the dash and resource of their troops. Nearly two thousand enemy dead were picked up in Pyawbwe and the surrounding villages, many more were killed about Thazi. Thirty-one guns, eight tanks, many vehicles, and great quantities of stores and ammunition in scattered dumps fell into our hands. It was a thorough and costly defeat for the enemy. The Japanese 49th Division, which had clung so desperately to its defences, had been destroyed in them. The 18th Division, in Thazi and the villages to the south, had been unmercifully hammered until it broke up. The 53rd Division had been caught by our troops west of Pyawbwe, as it tried to move back to take up its positions on the Japanese left, and had been thumped and banged out of the ring before it could reach them. It was no longer a fighting formation, but a collection of fugitives. For its size, Pyawbwe was one of the most decisive battles of the Burma war. It shattered Honda's army, but it did more—it settled the fate of Rangoon.

Now the straight, all-out drive on Rangoon could be loosed. Early on the morning of the 11th April, as the 17th Division cleared the battlefield and hunted down enemy stragglers, the 5th Division went through. They were off! I stood beside the road outside Pyawbwe and saw them go. Three hundred miles and, with luck, some thirty days before the monsoon to do it in. It would be a close thing, but, after yesterday's battle, I was sure 4 Corps would pull it off. They certainly meant to, and they looked like it; there was an air of purpose about every truck that rolled dustily by. Mansergh, commanding the 5th Division, drew his to one side, stopped and got out to greet me. Fresh, alert, and eager, he somehow, for a flash, made me think of the start of a dawn duck shoot in India, but we spoke of more serious business, before he, too, moved on. I watched vehicle after vehicle pass, loaded with Indian soldiers grasping their weapons, and on their faces was the same look as on their commander's, alert and eager. I had begun the war as a brigadier in this division in 1939, and I was proud of them. We should get there all right! A dull roar above made me look up. That noise, three years ago, would have sent us all diving for cover. Now, I was the only one to raise my head, and see our fighters streaking south across the sky. We took them for granted, yet it was they who made possible this swift move of soft vehicles, almost nose to tail, down one road. I went back to Cowan's headquarters and found him grimly cheerful, as a commander who had won such a battle might well be. With Messervy we discussed on the map the way the advance would go.

We had often talked of this before; now we were to see if the methods we had devised would be the right ones. The leading division, at the moment the 5th, would move with an armoured and motorized infantry group ahead. There would be a bound forward, as rapid as possible, to seize an airstrip or a site for one, the fly-in to it of airfield engineers, and the quick follow-up of the air transported brigade. Then, while that brigade held the air base, cleared the surrounding country, kept open the road, or, if necessary, reinforced an attack, the rest of the division would make its next bound. Each division would lead in turn, reach its objective, halt, and let the other through. There must be no pause. Airstrips would be required at least every fifty miles, but preferably, to save road transport, at more frequent intervals. The rate of our advance would be in direct ratio to the speed with which they could be brought into operation. In fact, after the first day or two we put airfield engineers with the tanks at the head of the column, so as to start work on airstrips at the earliest possible moment.

The armoured group ahead of the 5th Division quickly covered the twelve miles to Yamethin, drove through the town, and pushed on. When darkness fell, however, a Japanese suicide party some three or four hundred strong with anti-tank guns infiltrated into the town from the east and dug in among the houses. At dawn next day they commanded the only road and the soft vehicles, which had halted for the night north of Yamethin, were held up. The intruders proved extremely difficult to dislodge, and it was not until the 14th that the last of them was exterminated and vehicles could pass freely. Angry at the delay, the 5th Division pushed rapidly on for thirty miles to Shwemyo, which it occupied on the 16th. Just beyond the village, the road runs through a deep valley with the Shwemyo Bluff, a ridge some seven hundred feet high, completely dominating it for several miles, and forcing it to pass through narrow defiles. There is no other way for wheels past the Bluff, and we had always feared that we might be held up there. For a time it looked as if we should.

The Japanese had rushed up from South Burma a fresh regiment of their 55th Division, which was now hurriedly digging in on the Bluff. Pressing in front with his leading brigade, Mansergh debussed his second and sent it by a forced, outflanking march, deep through hills and jungle, to take the enemy in rear. On the 18th, our men suddenly fell upon them, still digging, and flushed them from their half-completed entrenchments at the bayonet point. Meanwhile, to save air transport which was urgently needed to bring in supplies, especially petrol, several lorry loads of which had been destroyed by Japanese fighters in an attack on our armoured group, the air transported brigade was brought by road to the landing ground at Shwemyo. That night our leading troops harboured two hundred and forty miles from Rangoon.

On the 19th, the armoured group, still in the lead, rumbled twenty miles down the road, to find Pyinmana strongly held. While the main column was catching up, the tanks bulldozed a by-pass road round the town, went ten miles farther, and seized the airfield at Lewe—a more valuable prize than the town. In a matter of hours the airstrip was repaired and troops and stores were being steadily flown in.

Lieut.-General Honda, commanding the Japanese Thirty-third Army, with several of his staff, was visiting Pyinmana when our troops were suddenly reported on its outskirts. Luckily for him, his staff car was faster than our tanks. Leaving one mechanized brigade to clear Pyinmana, the other, with its armoured group from 255 Tank Brigade, swept on. The situation at this stage had in it an element of comedy. 4 Corps was charging south down the road and railway, while, driven off these, in the hills on each flank, faint but pursuing, enemy parties of all sizes were marching hard in the attempt to reach Toungoo before us. If Radio Tokyo had announced, 'Our forces are pursuing the enemy rapidly in the direction of Rangoon', it would have been nearer the truth than usual.

All eyes were now on Toungoo. Japanese and British alike were converging on it in desperate endeavours to forestall one another. We must occupy it before the enemy could concentrate there, if we were to avoid the long delay of clearing the town house by house. There was another reason. Its group of airfields, some of the best in Burma, were the most northerly within good fighter range of Rangoon and, if the amphibious landing there were to be practicable, we must have them as bases for its air cover. The landing was now scheduled for the 2nd May; on naval advice it could not be later owing to weather. This date provided us with our last and, I was beginning to think, the most formidable competitor in the race. We were beating the Japanese, there was as yet no sign of the monsoon, but, if we were to beat 'Dracula' too, we should have to step up our time-table. We had eleven days to be in Rangoon, and over two hundred miles to go—twenty miles a day. That put us on our metal!

Kimura was driving his men as hard as Messervy and I were driving ours. He had ordered all troops in the Shan Hills to get to Toungoo with sleepless speed. Their roads were the fair-weather hill-tracks that ran roughly parallel to our route, sixty or seventy miles to the east. Opposite Toungoo and about seventy miles from it, this track turned abruptly west and joined the Rangoon road in the town. Led by the partly reorganized 15th Division, the Japanese, ferrying fast in any kind of vehicle left to them, made for Toungoo, and it looked as if they might beat us to it. But I still had a shot in my locker for them. As they drew south, their way led them through the country of the Karens, a race which had remained staunchly loyal to us even in the blackest days of Japanese occupation, and had suffered accordingly. Over a long period, in preparation for this day, we had organized a secret force, the Karen Guerrillas, based on ex-soldiers of the Burma Army, for whom British officers and arms had been parachuted into the hills. It was not at all difficult to get the Karens to rise against the hated Japanese; the problem was to restrain them from rising too soon. But now the time had come, and I gave the word, 'Up the Karens!' Japanese, driving hard through the night down jungle roads for Toungoo, ran into ambush after ambush; bridges were blown ahead of them, their foraging parties massacred, their sentries stalked, their staff cars shot up. Air-strikes, directed by British officers, watching from the ground the fall of each stick of bombs, inflicted great damage. The galled Japanese fought their way slowly forward, losing men and vehicles, until about Mawchi, fifty miles east of Toungoo, they were held up for several days by road-blocks, demolitions, and ambuscades. They lost the race for Toungoo.

Still leading 4 Corps' advance, the 5th Division, brushing aside disjointed opposition, in three days covered fifty miles and, on the 22nd April, with a final spurt, our armour crashed into Toungoo. Although we had heavily bombed the town the day before, the arrival of our ground forces was a complete surprise. The signals of a protesting Japanese military policeman on point duty were disregarded, and the first tank went over him. Panic reigned as our tanks roamed the streets, the enemy flying in all directions, intent only on escape. They left behind them only fifty dead, so fast did the living make for the jungle to swell the numbers trudging south. Honda had established his army headquarters in Toungoo and had issued the usual optimistic orders that it was to be defended to the last. He staged another hurried flight, but this time he abandoned most of his headquarters equipment and it was several weeks before he recovered any control over the remains of his army. We had not expected so swift a victory at Toungoo. Now it was one hundred and sixty miles to go and eight days left. The race between 4 Corps and 15 Corps, which was to make the Rangoon landing, promised a close finish. Betting at this stage was three to one on 4 Corps, but even the most optimistic of its supporters would have liked a 31st April in the calendar.

Without a pause the 5th Division, sweeping aside Japanese fugitives, next day reached Pyu, over thirty miles south of Toungoo. Here, although the important bridge had been de-molished, the site was undefended and the construction of a new bridge was quickly in hand. On the way, the 1st Division of the Indian National Army was encountered. It surrendered *en masse*, with its commander, one hundred and fifty officers, and over three thousand men. They were just in time to begin work on the captured airfields. On the 24th April, the 17th Division, close up and ready, was due to pass through and take the lead, but the 5th, its blood thoroughly up, went on another twenty miles to Penwegon. Here, when our first armoured car crept up, the

Japanese demolition party was already in position at the bridge—but asleep. They never woke. In the 17th Division, indignation battled with consternation when the 5th thus overran their mark. We were now one hundred and fourteen miles from Rangoon with seven days to the 2nd May.

I knew that with the loss of Toungoo, Kimura must realize that the situation in South Burma was critical. He was probably out of touch with his army commander, now a fugitive, and he could not have much left in the way of reserves. We learnt, on the 24th, that he was moving his headquarters to Moulmein, but whether this meant that Rangoon would be abandoned or whether, as I had always feared, he would leave a garrison there, I could not tell.

I did not think he would risk running the gauntlet of our Navy and Air Force in an evacuation by sea. Whatever he did, he would have to hold Pegu as it covered his last withdrawal route to the east, and all our intelligence confirmed that the enemy were concentrating for its defence. Although, of course, we did not know it at the time, Tarauchi, the Japanese Supreme Commander, had ordered Kimura to hold South Burma at all costs and, if possible, Rangoon too. Kimura decided that to hold Rangoon was not possible. He again showed energy in crisis, and called every man and unit to the defence of Pegu. Disregarding the possibility of a sea landing, which in any case he believed we should not attempt so near the monsoon, he brought 24 Independent Mixed Brigade from Moulmein, and hastily formed two new brigades, each under a Major-General, from the miscellaneous units of the Rangoon garrison and the lines of communication. One of these brigades contained several anti-aircraft batteries and they brought with them their guns to be used in an anti-tank role. Into these improvised brigades Kimura swept shore-based naval units, fishermen, and civilians. By the 28th April, this force of three brigades, with numbers of fugitives from the north, was collected at Pegu, and, apart from a handful left to carry out demolitions, no Japanese were in or south of Rangoon. I calculated that Kimura would try to hold Pegu throughout the monsoon if it were only to allow his troops in the Irrawaddy Valley to escape over the Salween River. We could expect bitter resistance.

On the 25th April, the 17th Division took the lead. After some twenty miles, its armoured spearhead ran into a Japanese rear-guard, many of whom were horsed cavalry, and ploughed through them, killing some and scattering the rest. On the 26th, Daiku was reached—eighty miles from Rangoon with five days to go and Pegu in between. Next day, where fifteen miles farther south the road passed through a defile between the six mile wide Moyingyi Reservoir on the east and swampy ground on the west, more serious resistance was met. Here, the enemy had laid a considerable mine-field, which took toll of our tanks and was defended by suicide parties of Japanese engineers and infantry. By evening a way had been forced through the mine-field, in which the defenders left three hundred dead. All night skirmishing went on and, next morning, the 28th, our advance again met stiff opposition ten miles north of Pegu. After heavy air bombard-ment, at the approach of our troops the Japanese pulled out, but it was not until evening that our armour reached the outskirts of Pegu to find the town strongly held.

That morning, another of our armoured and infantry columns had hooked round the Moyingyi Reservoir and cut the Japanese escape road to the east of it, compelling their retreating vehicles to be abandoned or to take to cross-country tracks farther south. A Jiff officer who surrendered reported that over four hundred British and American prisoners of war were in a village some distance away. They were being escorted from Rangoon towards Moulmein, when their Japanese guards, hearing the road ahead was cut by our rapid advance, abandoned them and fled. Patrols were at once sent out to locate the party and did so, unfortunately not before some of our aircraft seeing a column of men in khaki, as distinct from the green all our troops wore, had dived and straffed them, killing and wounding several. Some of the officers and men rescued were from the 17th Division, captured in the 1942 fighting, and now found themselves back with their old formation.

The troops of 4 Corps were already on reduced rations, having given up food for petrol and ammunition, but the knowledge that they were only forty-seven miles from Rangoon and that the Japanese at Pegu were the only obstacle between them and the capital, spurred them on. The town of Pegu stands on both banks of the winding Pegu River. The road to Rangoon crosses the river by the main bridge in the town itself; the railway crosses twice, by two bridges to the north. The Japanese were cunningly entrenched in the town and covered both railway bridges which they had demolished. Cowan's plan was first to clear the part of the town on the east bank by a double assault, delivered by a brigade from the north and his armoured column from the east and south-east. On the morning of the 29th April, both these attacks were launched. The northern attack broke into the town, but was held short of the road bridge. The armoured column, hampered by mine-fields and canals, was unable to use its tanks to the full and although the infantry pushed on alone they were not, unsupported, able to penetrate far among the houses where Japanese resistance was desperate.

Undismayed, Cowan now extended his operations to the west bank. In a series of small dog fights the approaches to the railway bridges on the east were cleared and attempts to cross made. These were held back by heavy fire, until a platoon of Indian infantry, crawling over the wrecked girders of the southern bridge, succeeded most gallantly in gaining the west bank. With the bayonet they cleared the nearest Japanese trench and held out until more of their battalion, swimming, rafting, and scrambling over the wrecked bridge, joined them. We now had a footing, even if a somewhat precarious one, on the west bank. While this was going on, our troops on the east bank, against bitter opposition, overran almost the whole of the northern residential area of Pegu, but at nightfall on the 30th the enemy still covered the intact road bridge.

I had spent the 29th April at my headquarters, now established in Meiktila, where I had received rather alarming reports of a Japanese counter-attack directed down the Mawchi road against our line of communication at Toungoo. I was told the main Rangoon road was already under Japanese artillery fire. We had only one brigade of the 19th Division to hold this attack and it might prove very embarrassing if the enemy made any further headway, so on the 30th I flew to Toungoo. As I drove down the main road towards Rees's headquarters, I had convincing evidence of the accuracy of at least one item of my intelligence report—the Japanese were quite noticeably shelling the road. I found Rees as usual cheerful and unalarmed, though at that moment superior enemy forces were pressing on his brigade not very far to the east of us. His troops had dug in among the hills astride the road and he was confident they would hold. I visited some of his units, and stayed to watch a battery firing at Japanese reported to be collecting for an attack. One of the gunners, stripped to the waist, his bronzed body glistening with sweat, was slamming shells into the breach of a twenty-five-pounder. In a lull in the firing I stepped into the gun pit beside him. 'I'm sorry,' I said, 'you've got to do all this on half rations.' He looked up at me from under his battered bush hat, 'Don't you worry about that, sir,' he grinned, 'Put us on quarter rations, but give us the ammo and we'll get you into Rangoon!' I did not doubt it; with men like that who could?

The Japanese on the Mawchi road tried hard to carry out their orders and cut our communications, but my gunner and his comrades were too good for them. Helped by the Karens, who clung to the Japanese coat-tails, Rees was able in the days that followed, not only to hold them, but to push them back farther into the hills, until the Rangoon road, at any rate, was no longer under their fire. An unspectacular task, out of the limelight of the race for Rangoon, but essential and carried out, as were all 19th Division's tasks, cheerfully, promptly, and with no little grief to the enemy.

During the night at Toungoo, reports of the Pegu fighting had come in which made me eager to see what was happening there. Accordingly on the morning of the 1st May, taking with me Messervy and two or three others, including Major Robert Fullerton one of my American staff officers, I set off by air. As we approached Pegu I committed a very foolish and culpable act. I told my pilot to fly on south as I wished to see for myself what the country over which the 17th Division would have to operate was like. Sitting beside the pilot I had just seen, far away in the direction of Rangoon, tall columns of smoke—which might be bombing or perhaps evidence of evacuation—when we came under considerable anti-aircraft fire. We received several hits, one of which exploded against Fullerton's leg. My pilot with great skill and coolness took evasive action in clouds and landed us on a newly-made advanced strip just north of Pegu. There was a dressing station alongside the airfield and by the greatest good fortune John Bruce, the consulting surgeon of the Fourteenth Army, happened at that very time to be visiting a forward surgical team. Bruce, one of the foremost British surgeons, saved

504

Fullerton's life, but nothing could have saved his leg. I felt—and still feel—very guilty about this. I had no business as Army Commander to go where I did, and, if I was so stupid as to go, I had no excuse for taking Messervy or the others with me.

After this unhappy introduction to Pegu, I found that during the night the situation had improved. We had kept our hold on the west bank and, on the east, patrols probing forward in the dark had reported the enemy thinning out and the sound of motor transport driving away. At dawn our troops had advanced to the attack, but found the whole of Pegu on the east bank clear, except for mines and booby traps. Leaving his air-transported brigade to deal with the west bank and the small parties of Japanese roaming the countryside, Cowan prepared for the final stage of the advance on Rangoon. If the only delay was to come from the Japanese, he could have pushed through the remaining forty miles in the next two days and reached Rangoon some hours ahead of the landing party. Unfortunately, it was not.

On the afternoon of the 1st May, a great misfortune befell 4 Corps. Pegu was in our hands and the advance resumed, when a torrential storm burst over the whole area, followed throughout the night by continuous heavy rain. The monsoon was on us—a fortnight before its time! By morning much of the country was waterlogged, airstrips going out of action, and the Pegu River rising ominously. As a precautionary measure, all 4 Corps was immediately placed on half rations.

The troops slipped, splashed, and skidded forward, but all streams were in spate and all bridges down. On the evening of the 2nd, when news of the successful landing south of Rangoon and of the Japanese evacuation had been received, the 17th Division was halted in drenching rain forty-one miles by road from its goal. More heavy rain during the night swept away approaches to bridges already built, and a whole brigade found itself marooned on what had suddenly become an island. The leading infantry, soaked, hungry, but still full of ardour, wading and often swimming, tried to push on. They were delayed by two miles of heavily mined road, while the side tracks were often submerged and, like the road, mined. They were still struggling to reach Hlegu, when, late on the 3rd May, they heard 15 Corps had occupied Rangoon.

In spite of their disappointment at losing the race, the 17th Division, having lifted the mines, pushed on with determination.

On the 4th, a battalion, having long ago left all transport behind, swam and rafted itself across a wide and rapidly flowing *chaung* to reach Hlegu, twenty-eight miles from Rangoon. It was here, on the 6th May, that a small column of the 26th Division from Rangoon linked up with 4 Corps, meeting the 1/7th Gurkha Rifles who, in January 1942, had fired the first shots of the Burma War.

The landing south of Rangoon on the 2nd May had gone smoothly. I had always wanted it to be a little later, but naval advice was unanimous—and as it proved right—that the 2nd was the latest date the weather would allow. It had been a great achievement by Rear-Admiral Martin, Lieut.-General Christison, and Air Vice-Marshal the Earl of Bandon, the responsible commanders, to have had all ready for D Day. The Assault Force, mounted at Akyab and Ramree Islands, sailed in six convoys, slowest first, between the 27th and 30th April. It was covered on passage by 224 Group fighters and a naval carrier force of four escort carriers. Twelve bomber squadrons, British and American from Strategic Air Force, were allotted to the operation. The naval covering force of one British and one French battleship, two escort carriers, two British and one Dutch cruiser, and six destroyers put to sea from Trincomalee in Ceylon on the 30th April. Its duty was to prevent any interference by Japanese naval forces, and it cruised south of Rangoon and east of the Andamans, filling in time by bombarding those islands and Car Nicobar. A destroyer force was also in position south of Rangoon and, on the 30th April, it intercepted eleven enemy craft, escaping with about a thousand troops from Rangoon to Moulmein, and sank nine of them.

The overture to the landing was on D—1 Day, the 1st May, when a heavy bombing attack was delivered on all located defences on both sides of the Rangoon River. Some hours later, a battalion of the 50th Indian Parachute Brigade dropped at Elephant Point. A party of about thirty Japanese, either left for observation or just forgotten, offered resistance to the Gurkha paratroops. One wounded Japanese survived. Early on the same morning a pilot, flying over Rangoon, saw written in large letters on the gaol roof the words, '*Japs gone. Exdigitate*'. The R.A.F. slang was not only evidence of the genuineness of the message, but a gentle hint to speed up operations. However, it was determined, wisely

I think, to continue according to plan. Early on the 2nd, the weather became worse and there was some doubt whether the small landing craft could face the sea. However, it was decided to risk it and by skilful seamanship all reached and entered Rangoon River. A brigade of the 26th Division, under Major-General Chambers, was landed on each bank and the advance began. Within a few hours a deluge of rain descended making all movement arduous. Nevertheless the troops advanced several miles, and by nightfall the eastern brigade was within twelve miles of Rangoon.

While the 26th Division was thus plodding forward, the pilot of a Mosquito aircraft of 221 Group, flying low over Rangoon and seeing no signs of enemy, decided to land on Mingaladon airfield at the Cantonment, about eight miles north of the city. The strip was in bad repair and he crashed his aircraft in landing, but, undismayed, he walked into Rangoon, visited our prisoners at the gaol, and assured himself that the Japanese had really gone. In the evening, commandeering a *sampan*, he sailed down the river and met the advancing 26th Division. We were rather pleased about this in Fourteenth Army. If we could not get to Rangoon first ourselves, the next best thing was for someone from 221 Group, which we regarded in all comradeship as part of the Fourteenth Army, to do it. On this confirmation of the Japanese flight, further bombing was called off and the build-up by sea, that was to follow the landing of the 26th Division, was cancelled.

It was not until the evening of the 3rd May that the brigade on the east bank, struggling through waterlogged country, appeared on the Hlaing River, immediately south of Rangoon. It was ferried over and entered the town. The population in thousands welcomed our men with a relief and a joy they made no attempt to restrain. We were back!

CHAPTER XXII

THE LAST BATTLE

A BURMAN once told me that the name Rangoon means 'The End of the War'. Whether that is so or not, it certainly was not its end for us. Fresh problems rolled in. To begin with, Burma was by no means clear of the Japanese; our intelligence staffs estimated that there were still between sixty and seventy thousand west of the Salween, to say nothing of large forces in Siam and Indo-China which could be used to reinforce them. Although the complete expulsion of all enemy from Burma thus threatened to be a considerable operation, it now took second place in our thoughts. The major task, in which we were at once plunged, was planning, re-equipping and regrouping for the imminent invasion of Malaya and the capture of Singapore. Already Fourteenth Army divisions had been withdrawn to India to prepare for this, others were to follow, and of those left in Burma, some would soon have to be taken out of the fighting so as to be ready to sail from Rangoon with the invading force. We pursued the two projects—the clearing of Burma and the preparation of the Malayan invasion—simultaneously, finding at times one antagonistic to the other, but, when that happened, giving preference to the new campaign.

The tactical situation in Burma was unusual. Kimura's armies had been broken and scattered over a wide area, so that there was hardly a district south of Meiktila where Japanese groups of various sizes and in varying degrees of disorganization did not roam. My map showed blue Japanese and red British formations interspersed and intermingled as if they were coloured counters spilt haphazard over the sheet. Our double dash for Rangoon had cut through the enemy, leaving two long gashes across his body. Our 4 Corps advance, the easterly of these gashes, formed what has been described, justly, I think, as the longest and narrowest salient in history. It was over three hundred miles long, with an average width of less than a couple of miles, and often not more than a few hundred yards on each side of the road. In the Irrawaddy Valley, 33 Corps had driven a similar though much broader salient for over two hundred miles. Both these slender strips were true salients, for they projected into enemy territory with hostile forces on both sides of them, and, as we required to use the roads through them, they had to be held throughout their lengths. It was, of course, quite impossible to stretch unbroken lines of troops for such distances; detachments were stationed at intervals along the routes, and the gaps between patrolled, while columns thrust out and tracked down Japanese parties in the country on each side. In the sweltering, soaking monsoon weather, it was a strenuous and exhausting role for troops. In addition to these two long north to south corridors from Toungoo to Pegu and from Yenangyaung to well south of Prome, the 19th Division was driving two west to east corridors along the Meiktila–Taunggyi and the Toungoo–Mawchi roads. The newly landed 26th Division, in and around Rangoon, had gained touch with 4 Corps and was about to do so with 33 Corps, thus completing the incisions which severed the Japanese from north to south.

The Japanese, as far as we could judge at this time, were in, or trying to collect in, four main groups:

(i) *In the Irrawaddy Valley*, where on both banks of the river, the Japanese Twenty-eighth Army had, north of Prome, the 54th Division with units from the 49th and 55th Divisions, what was left of 72 Independent Brigade and the 2nd Indian National Army Division. Farther south, and mainly in the hills of the Pegu Yomas, were parts of the 55th Division and a considerable body of line of communication troops. We estimated their total strength in the Irrawaddy Valley at about fifteen thousand men, all engaged in trekking east to cross the Meiktila–Rangoon road and join forces with the enemy east of the Sittang.

(ii) *In the Shan Hills east of Meiktila*, the 56th Division and what was left of one regiment (brigade) from each of the 15th, 18th, and 53rd Divisions, about six thousand in all, were making their way south.

(iii) *East of the Sittang River, opposite our cordon from Toungoo to Nyaunglebin*, were the remnants of the Thirty-third Army, containing a hotch-potch of units from the 2nd, 18th, 49th, 53rd, and 55th Divisions, and, farther east still in the Salween Valley, the battered 31st and 33rd Divisions, with a large number of line of communication troops. In this double group we reckoned the enemy had some twenty-five thousand men.

(iv) *In the area Mokpalin–Moulmein east of the mouth of the Sittang and on the east coast of the Gulf of Martaban*, Kimura had collected round him 24 Independent Brigade, the evacuated Rangoon garrison, survivors from the Pegu battle and numbers of line of communication units, a total, we thought, of about twenty-four thousand troops.

There were also, of course, the many small groups and stragglers not included in the main concentrations, who brought the enemy estimated grand total up to some sixty or seventy thousand. In actual fact, we found later that we had considerably under-estimated the enemy numbers. All hostile formations were dis-organized, lacking transport, supplies, and equipment, but if they could, as they evidently intended, concentrate east of the Sittang, they might again become formidable. Difficult as we might find the monsoon conditions, they would be worse for them and, in spite of the weather, the fatigue of our troops, and the demands of future Malayan operations, we must allow no respite to the enemy in Burma.

My intention, therefore, was now:

(i) To intercept and destroy as many as possible of the enemy as they attempted to reach the east bank of the Sittang.

(ii) To prevent the Japanese concentrating and reorganizing in the Moulmein area.

(iii) To advance on Moulmein and destroy the enemy who had already collected there.

To these ends I issued orders:

(a) *To 4 Corps*
(i) To destroy all enemy attempting to cross the Pegu Yomas from west to east.
(ii) To take Mokpalin.

(iii) To advance with the 19th Division, which now reverted to 4 Corps, as far as Thaudaung twenty miles east of Toungoo and thus secure our line of communication.

(b) *To 33 Corps*
    (i) To destroy all enemy in the Irrawaddy Valley.
    (ii) To open the road and railway from Prome to Rangoon.
    (iii) To capture Bassein.

(c) *To the 26th Division*
    (i) To secure Rangoon and its area.
    (ii) To effect a junction with the 20th Division, south of Prome.

The Japanese, at this time, did not seem to be bothering so much about the east bank of the Irrawaddy, where they had only the battered remnants of the 55th Division and the 2nd Indian National Army Division, as about the west bank. There they still had a considerable part of the 54th Division, in reasonable order, and Yamamoto's force of seven battalions and artillery, a total we estimated as still about ten thousand men. On the west bank, Sakurai appeared to have organized his troops into two groups, a northern consisting of Yamamoto's force to hold up our 7th Division, and a southern, the 54th Division, concerned mainly in getting intact across the Irrawaddy into the Pegu Yomas. If he failed in this, the division would waste away west of the river, but if he succeeded, it might fall on the flank of our forces advancing down the Prome road on Rangoon, or, at the worst, escape east through the Yomas.

The efforts of 33 Corps to prevent the Japanese forces on the west bank from regaining the east resulted in two considerable engagements. The first, some thirty-five miles north-west of Allanmyo, lasted from the 11th to the 15th May. In it, troops of the 7th Division destroyed Yamamoto's rearguard, and, what was perhaps more important, captured seventy-five of the enemy's rapidly diminishing stock of lorries. The main body of Yamamoto's force then made for Kama, a village on the river, about twenty miles above Prome, where the 54th Division had formed a bridgehead on the east bank, and were hurriedly beginning to cross. The second action, at Kama, on both sides of the river was a more serious affair. On the west bank, the two brigades of our 7th Division and 268 Brigade closed in on Kama from the

VICTORY

north and north-east; on the other bank the third brigade of the division, with some units of the 20th Division, encircled the Japanese bridgehead on the east with two cordons, an inner and an outer.

West of the river, our troops in severe fighting destroyed most of what was left of Yamamoto's battalions. On the east bank, from the 21st to the 30th May, the enemy 54th Division made constant and reckless efforts to break out from the bridgehead. Our inner cordon was holding in thick jungle, and although almost all attacks on its positions were repulsed, the enemy was able to infiltrate between our posts, and, in spite of considerable casualties, to assemble between the two cordons. Evans, commanding the 7th Division, then brought troops from the west to the east bank to thicken up the outer cordon, attacks on which had begun on the night of the 27th/28th May. These attacks were continued on the following nights. The Japanese, with fanatical courage, repeated their methods against the inner cordon, assaulting simultaneously several of our positions while other parties tried to slip between them and make for the hills. Many of these groups were intercepted and badly knocked about, but considerable numbers of the 54th Division, in small parties, did reach the cover of the Pegu Yomas. Fourteen hundred Japanese bodies were counted, many more lay unseen in the jungle, and seventy-four prisoners were taken—a further sign that enemy morale was not what it had been. The 54th Division after this action, having lost all its transport and most of its guns, was no longer capable of serious counter-attack and concentrated on escape to the east. The dispersal of the Japanese forces in the Irrawaddy Valley, which amounted to two-thirds of the Twenty-eighth Army, by 33 Corps was a brilliant piece of major tactics by Stopford, his commanders, and their troops.

In addition to operations against the Japanese, we had in Burma other problems that demanded rapid solution. As the monsoon grew in intensity, so did the difficulties of our maintenance by air and road increase. Apart from the weather, we were rapidly losing our American transport squadrons, and our own R.A.F. ones were terribly in need of rest and maintenance before they would be required over Malaya. It was essential, therefore, for supply reasons alone, to reopen the port of Rangoon at the earliest possible moment. This would also be required very soon for the reception and loading of ships for the Malayan expedition. All available engineers and labour were, therefore, at once turned on to restore the docks which had suffered very severely from our bombing. This was a tremendous task as it included, not only the rehabilitation of the wharves, but the construction or repair of the innumerable facilities of a modern port—railway sidings, warehouses, power stations, cranes and road approaches. The three least damaged berths were ready to receive ships almost at once, the river was swept of mines by the 8th May, and a few days later more berths were in action. In six weeks, we had three thousand tons of stores coming over the wharves daily, and the maintenance crisis was past. Considering the shambles the docks had been when we took them and the paucity of our resources for their repair, this was a splendid achievement by our Engineer and Embarkation Units. No less splendid, and even more arduous, was the feat of our transport staff and units in keeping up a constant flow of supplies by road, rail and river from railhead at Dimapur, nine hundred miles away, to augment air-lift, until the docks were open. The roads, hundreds of miles of which were unmetalled, were falling to pieces under the battering of thousands of lorries, tank-transporters and guns, and, above all, under the ceaseless downpour of rain of projectile force. Such short lengths of railway as we had been able to bring into use were ramshackle in the extreme, and almost devoid of rolling stock. For river craft we still depended on the products of our own Kalewa shipyards and the wrecks we had been able to salvage. Officers and men, who through such difficulties brought us our rations and supplies, would deserve gratitude. Add to that the fact that on the line of communication for a great part of its length convoys were liable to run into parties of desperate Japanese making east across the road or lurking beside it, then no tribute to their determination, skill, and courage could be too high. Their achievements were only possible because they had developed the same high spirit as reigned in the combat units of the army.

Another problem which, with startling suddenness, loomed upon us was that of the care and administration of the civil population. We had, almost overnight, acquired most of Burma, and with it eighty per cent of its inhabitants—some thirteen millions of them. There was no civil government for us to take over; it had completely disappeared. Insecurity and dacoity were rife. Great acreages had gone out of cultivation, while trade had vanished with the breakdown of communications and the loss of security. The almost complete absence of consumer goods had spun the Japanese paper currency into wild inflation. The whole population was short of clothing, necessities, and above all of food. Indeed, large sections of it were on the verge of starvation. Towns had been burnt and many were deserted, their inhabitants having taken to the jungle where they lived hazardously in miserable destitution. The Japanese throughout their occupation had done little or nothing to meet the essential needs of the civil population. Even where bombs and battles had spared them, public utilities, water supplies, and roads had, through Japanese indifference, deteriorated to a shocking degree.

Almost without exception our return was welcomed. It was only in those areas on the north where the liberating troops were Chinese, and memories of their behaviour in the 1942 Retreat still lingered, that there was an element of nervousness. With the vast majority of the Burmese the trouble was that they expected us to bring them an immediate return to the carefree conditions of happy Burma before the war. This, alas, we could not do at once.

The first necessity was to restore the framework of government throughout the country, but we were hampered by an acute shortage of qualified officials who could be installed in the civil districts which we rapidly, one after the other, liberated. Of the original British civil servants, some had in the past years vanished into other services or joined the armed forces. Too many, it seemed to me, were held in India under the exiled Burmese Government. Our own Civil Affairs staff were all allotted to the parts of Burma already in our hands before the last advance. As they retreated, the Japanese had taken with them many of the Burmese officials, who, mostly unwillingly, had served under them, while those who supported Ba Maw's puppet government had fled, to avoid their own countrymen as much as to escape us. Gradually, Burmese civil officials of all ranks began to come out of hiding and report for duty; others were located and persuaded to return; but all had to have their records checked before they could be reinstalled. However, in a surprisingly short time considering all the difficulties, a civil administration, somewhat skeleton in form, was set up and, with increasing efficiency, functioning.

It was an even more difficult matter to get the economic life of the country running again. Not only were we lacking many requirements for the army, but outside Burma there was a world shortage of the articles most needed to supply the desperate necessities of the civil population—notably cotton goods. Even were imports from abroad obtainable, they would not relieve the situation until communications within Burma were restored, and the ports, especially Rangoon, operating again. Nevertheless, even before we got the army back to full rations, we diverted some of its supplies and part of our precious air-lift to succour the most distressed areas.

Parallel with this problem of the civil administration, was a smaller Burmese politico-military one. How to treat the Burmese National Army, originally Japanese sponsored, but now in arms against them? I had all along believed they could be a nuisance to the enemy but, unless their activities were closely tied in with ours, they promised to be almost as big a nuisance to us. It seemed to me that the only way satisfactorily to control them was to get hold of their Commander-in-Chief, Aung San, and to make him accept my orders. This, from what I knew of him and of the extreme Burmese nationalists, I thought might be difficult, but worth trying.

Aung San had had a chequered career. In 1930 as an under-graduate at Rangoon University, like most Asian students, he took an active, and at times a rather violent, interest in politics. By 1939, he was the secretary of the extremist Nationalist Minority Group and served a seventeen-day prison sentence for his activities. About this time he was contacted by Japanese agents, who saw in the energetic and able young nationalist a promising tool for their own ripening designs. It thus happened that, when, in 1940, Aung San's organization was proscribed, he and some thirty others of its members were able to evade the police and reach Japan. Here, they were given military training in a Japanese officers' school and were indoctrinated with the belief that Japan would shortly drive the British out of Burma and bring freedom to its people. When the invasion did occur, Aung San and his companions came with it. The Japanese used them as a nucleus round which to collect irregular Burmese forces and to organize a Fifth Column throughout the area of operations. They were undoubtedly a help to their masters in many ways and, on one or two occasions during the Retreat, fought bravely against us, though their chief combat duties were the ambushing and murdering of stragglers.

Aung San, whose intelligence and courage had brought him to the fore, showed anxiety to set up a Burmese Government, but the Japanese, although they wanted a puppet government, were not prepared to accept him as its head. Perhaps they had already sensed he would not be the pliable and submissive dupe they required, and in any case they had Ba Maw, who was much more what they wanted. Instead, they appointed Aung San Commander-in-Chief of the Burma Defence Army, later the Burma National Army, that was set up under the closest Japanese control.

It was not long before Aung San found that what he meant by independence had little relation to what the Japanese were prepared to give—that he had exchanged an old master for an infinitely more tyrannical new one. As one of his leading followers once said to me, 'If the British sucked our blood, the Japanese ground our bones!' He became more and more disillusioned with the Japanese, and early in 1943 we got news from Seagrim, a most gallant officer who had remained in the Karen Hills at the ultimate cost of his life, that Aung San's feelings were changing. On the 1st August 1944 he was bold enough to speak publicly with contempt of the Japanese brand of independence, and it was clear that, if they did not soon liquidate him, he might prove useful to us. Force 136 through its agents already had channels of communication and, when the revolt of the Burma National Army occurred and it was clear Aung San had burnt his boats, it was time to deal directly with him. With the full approval of Admiral Mountbatten, the agents of Force 136 offered Aung San on the 21st April a safe conduct to my headquarters and my promise that, whether we came to an understanding or not, I would return him unharmed to his own people. He hesitated until the 15th May, but on that day it was reported to me that he and a staff officer had crossed the Irrawaddy at Allanmyo, and were asking to meet me. I sent an aircraft, which flew them to my headquarters at Meiktila the next day.

The arrival of Aung San, dressed in the near Japanese uniform of a Major-General, complete with sword, startled one or two of my staff who had not been warned of his coming. However, he behaved with the utmost courtesy, and so, I hope, did we.

516

He was a short, well-built, active man in early middle age, neat and soldierly in appearance, with regular Burmese features in a face that could be an impassive mask or light up with intelligence and humour. I found he spoke good English, learnt in his school and university days, and he was accompanied by a staff officer who spoke it perfectly, as well he might, if it were true as I was told that his father had been a senior British official who had married a Burmese lady.

At our first interview, Aung San began to take rather a high hand. He was, he said the representative of the Provisional Government of Burma, which had been set up by the people of Burma through the Anti-Fascist People's Freedom League. It was under this Provisional Government that he and his National Army served and from whom they took their orders. He was an Allied commander, who was prepared to co-operate with me, and he demanded the status of an Allied and not subordinate commander. I told him that I had no idea what his Anti-Fascist People's Freedom League was or represented. As far as I and the rest of the world were concerned, there was only one Government of Burma and that was His Majesty's, now acting through the Supreme Commander, South-East Asia. I pointed out that he was in no position to take the line he had. I did not need his forces; I was destroying the Japanese quite nicely without their help, and could continue to do so. I would accept his co-operation and that of his army only on the clear understanding that it implied no recognition of any provisional government. He would be a subordinate commander, who would accept my orders and see that his officers and men also obeyed them and those of any British commander under whom I placed them. He showed disappointment at this, and repeated his demand to be treated as an Allied commander.

I admired his boldness and told him so. 'But,' I said, 'apart from the fact that you, a British subject, have fought against the British Government, I have here in this headquarters people who tell me there is a well substantiated case of civil murder, complete with witnesses, against you. I have been urged to place you on trial for that. You have nothing in writing, only a verbal promise at second-hand, that I would return you to your friends. Don't you think you are taking considerable risks in coming here and adopting this attitude?'

517

'No,' he replied, shortly.

'Why not?'

'Because you are a *British* officer,' he answered. I had to confess that he scored heavily—and what was more I believe he meant it. At any rate he had come out on my word alone. I laughed and asked him if he felt like that about the British, why had he been so keen to get rid of us? He said it was not that he disliked the British, but he did not want British or Japanese or any other foreigners to rule his country. I told him I could well understand that attitude, but it was not for us soldiers to discuss the future government of Burma. The British Government had announced its intention to grant self-government to Burma within the British Commonwealth, and we had better limit our discussion to the best method of throwing the Japanese out of the country as the next step towards self-government.

We resumed in good temper, and I asked him to give me the strengths and present dispositions of his forces. This he was either unwilling or unable to do—I thought a bit of both. I pressed him in this, but could get nothing definite. I had the impression that he was not too sure what his forces were, where they were, or what exactly some of them were doing. I said I had had reports that there were many bands of armed Burmans roaming about, claiming to belong to his army, who were no better than dacoits preying on their own countrymen. Rather to my surprise, he agreed and said he hoped we would both of us deal severely with these men, who were no troops of his. He went on to say that, at first, he had hoped the Japanese would give real independence to Burma. When he found they would not, but were tightening the bonds on his people, he had, relying on our promises, turned to us as a better hope. 'Go on, Aung San,' I said. 'You only come to us because you see we are winning!'

'It wouldn't be much good coming to you if you weren't, would it?' he replied, simply.

I could not question the truth of this. I felt he had scored again, and I liked his honesty. In fact, I was beginning to like Aung San.

I told him that after the war we should revive the old regular Burma Army, under British officers, on the basis of the Burma Rifles battalions which still existed, and that there would then be no place for any other army—his would have to go. He at

518

once pressed that his forces should be incorporated in the new army as units. This was obviously not altogether the solicitude of a general for his men, but the desire of a politician to retain personal power in post-war Burma. I answered that I thought it most unlikely that the Burmese Government would accept them as units, but that I saw no reason why they should not, subject to a check of their records, be enlisted as individuals on the same terms as other recruits. He persisted in pressing for incorporation as units, but I held out no hopes of this. He then asked me if I would now supply and pay his units in the field? He was obviously finding this beyond his powers, and I knew that, if we did not accept the responsibility, his men would be reduced, as many were already, to living by exactions from the people—as dacoits in fact. I said I would not consider paying or supplying his troops unless he and they were completely under my orders. In our final talk, he had begun to take a more realistic view of his position, but he still would not definitely commit himself. Before he accepted the role of a subordinate commander, he said, he must consult with his 'government', and he asked to be returned, suggesting that he should meet me again in about a week's time. I agreed, warned him of the consequences of refusing terms which, in view of his past, were most generous, shook hands, and sent him off by air again.

I was impressed by Aung San. He was not the ambitious, unscrupulous guerrilla leader I had expected. He was certainly ambitious and meant to secure for himself a dominant position in post-war Burma, but I judged him to be a genuine patriot and a well-balanced realist—characters which are not always combined. His experience with the Japanese had put his views on the British into a truer perspective. He was ready himself to co-operate with us in the liberation and restoration of Burma and, I thought, probably to go on co-operating after that had been accomplished. The greatest impression he made on me was one of honesty. He was not free with glib assurances and he hesitated to commit himself, but I had the idea that if he agreed to do something he would keep his word. I could do business with Aung San.

Operations against the Japanese were continuing over wide areas, and I wanted to get the role of Aung San's forces clear before clashes occurred between them and our troops. Having reported to my superiors the results of our interview and my views on his reliability, I therefore, instead of waiting for him to come in again, sent him, a few days later, definite proposals.

I would employ and ration all units of the Burma National Army then in action, provided they reported to and placed themselves unreservedly under the orders of the nearest British commander. I would recommend that suitable individual members of the B.N.A. should be allowed to volunteer for recruitment in the future Burma defence forces. Aung Sang accepted these terms without haggling, asking only that he should be consulted on major decisions on the employment of the B.N.A. and on the enlistment of its members into the regular forces. On the 30th May, my Deputy Chief Civil Affairs Officer told Aung San that I had informed the Supreme Commander of our arrangement and that it was in force. Accordingly, somewhat to their surprise, our troops began to meet parties of Burmese in Japanese uniforms, who marched in, and whose officers stated they were reporting for duty with the British. They were regarded with considerable suspicion at first but, almost without exception, obeyed orders well. They proved definitely useful in gaining information and in dealing drastically with small parties of Japanese. Aung San had kept his word. I have always felt that, with proper treatment, Aung San would have proved a Burmese Smuts.

In our preparations for the invasion of Malaya, which were pushed on simultaneously with all these activities in Burma, a factor which had already caused us anxiety rapidly assumed serious proportions and threatened to cripple all our plans. This was the repatriation of British troops. Many of my British soldiers and officers had served continuously for four or five years in the East, most of them in the often heart-breaking conditions of the Burma front, without in all that time a sight of their homes. In danger and discomfort, keyed up under strain, they suffered the soldiers' dumb pain of separation. Letters were late and sometimes irregular; time and distance seemed to make strangers of those they loved. In their months' old newspapers from home they read of the unfaithfulness of soldiers' wives, and saw pictures of English girls gambolling in the harvest fields with Italian prisoners. They heard that men on other fronts got home leave. Their own newspaper, *Seac*, was full of articles and letters urging the return home of men with long service in South-East Asia.

They heard of protests and read of promises by distant politicians that their experience and their common sense made them doubt. There was a danger that 'Repat' would become an obsession. When I asked a man in his foxhole or sitting beside the track what he was, he would often, instead of answering, 'I am a Lancashire Fusilier', 'an F.O.O.'s signaller', or 'the Bren Gunner of this section', say 'I am four and two', or 'Three and ten'. He meant that was the number of years and months he had served in the East, and the unspoken question in his eyes was, 'How many more?' I could not answer him. The British officers, N.C.O.s, and privates who had served longest were our key men. If we sent them home without replacement, neither our British nor our Indian formations could continue to fight efficiently.

It was not for want of representations by their commanders, from the Supreme Commander downwards, that these men remained; their replacement was out of our hands. That being so, it would have been wiser and kinder if we had confined ourselves to doing all we could to speed up repatriation—as indeed we did— and everything possible to discourage so much talk about it. Yet, when all was said and done, we still had men with four and even five years in the East without leave home, and that is trying a man higher than he should be tried. The British soldier is accustomed to longer periods of overseas service than any other, yet it is not surprising that, under this growing spate of repatriation talk, among some of them the *élan* which they had shown for so long began to fade. To their honour, my British soldiers, officers and men, endured to the end; never did they shirk duty or hesitate to enter battle, but the strain was telling on them.

The War Office had decided, some time before, that the period of unbroken service in the East for officers and men of the British Army should be four years. In Burma we had many who had served longer than that, but whose repatriation had been delayed for one cause or another. In 1945, the period was reduced from four years to three years eight months and, although we did our best to get men home, for reasons of transportation and partly because replacements were not forthcoming for key men, the backlog of those overdue for repatriation began to pile up. This reduction to three years eight months removed the framework of units and made considerable alterations necessary. There was much reorganization and retraining, and almost all British and many Indian and African units lost battle-worthiness. This forced the postponement of the planned date of the landing in Malaya to the 9th September. Then without warning, on the 7th June, the Supreme Commander was told by the Secretary of State for War that next day he was announcing in Parliament that the period of service in the East was reduced to three years four months, and that the men affected would be sent home as soon as possible without waiting for their replacement.

This news was a bombshell that shattered all the plans we had been making. The number of men affected was very large; one-third of the British officers and men in S.E.A.C., and those the most experienced with a high proportion of N.C.O.s, would have to be returned to the United Kingdom before the 1st October. Admiral Mountbatten and Generals Auchinleck and Leese at once cabled protests, pointing out that, unless they were authorized to carry out this crippling reduction gradually and in accordance with operational necessity, all Malayan operations would have to be postponed indefinitely. Nevertheless, the Secretary of State duly made his statement without any of the suggested qualifications, and it was broadcast throughout South-East Asia. Every man in the army now knew when he was due for repatriation, and thousands were already overdue. The Secretary of State considered that in his statement there was provision for retaining men on the grounds of 'operational necessity', but certainly no soldier so detained would think other than that a clear promise had been broken. It would have been not only unfair to land such men on the Malayan beaches, but unwise. Supported by all his senior commanders, Admiral Mountbatten refused to do this. The only alternatives then were to postpone indefinitely, that is until reinforcements were received from Europe, the Malayan invasion, or to take the grave risk of carrying it out with much reduced and less experienced forces. There were many advantages in holding to the September date for the landing; delay would certainly mean increased Japanese preparation and resistance. Both General Leese and I were in favour of taking the risk and Admiral Mountbatten agreed. So the resorting of units began all over again as the long-service men were sent to India to await passage home. Some key men, mostly officers, had to be retained under the operational necessity clause, and they took their fate philosophically. Others, with more thought for their regiments and their men than for themselves, volunteered to stay. We pressed on, both in India and in Burma, in greater urgency than ever with our preparations.

Meanwhile a considerable reorganization of the higher army command in South-East Asia had been going on and was completed in the next few weeks. I had moved my Fourteenth Army Headquarters to Rangoon. It was now sent to India to plan the Malayan campaign, and the Fourteenth Army ended its long and not uneventful connection with Burma.

I had been chosen to succeed General Leese as Allied Land Forces Commander, and my place at Fourteenth Army in India was temporarily taken by Christison until Lieut.-General Sir Miles Dempsey, who had brilliantly commanded the Second Army in Europe, could come out to replace him. There was no one to whom I would more willingly have entrusted my Fourteenth Army than Dempsey. A new army, the Twelfth, was formed under Stopford to control all land operations in Burma. He had under his command 4 Corps, with the 5th, 17th, and 19th Indian Divisions, 268 Brigade and 255 Tank Brigade. He had also under his operational control the 7th and 20th Indian, 82nd West African Divisions, 22 East African Brigade, and Aung San's Burma National Army. Of these, the 5th Division was to be returned almost at once to India and the 7th and 20th mounted, with numerous other troops, from Rangoon for the Malayan invasion. Headquarters 33 Corps now brought to an end its most distinguished career, and was disbanded to form the basis of the new Twelfth Army Headquarters.

I had not seen England for over seven years, and I seized this opportunity to ask for leave for a short visit home, before embarking on new campaigns which I thought might be long and arduous. My leave was granted perhaps the more readily because, outside a narrow military circle, I was quite unknown to the authorities in England. I had never met the Prime Minister, and I suspect he may have wanted to see what I was like before confirming me in so important an appointment. I saw planning well under way at Delhi, and then, with my wife, flew home. There we had a hectic, but happy month.

While I was on leave, the last battle of the Burma Campaign, the Battle of the Break-Out, was fought. It was obvious that, unless they were reconciled to dying of exposure, disease, and starvation in the Pegu Yomas, Sakurai's Twenty-eighth Army must sooner or later break out from the hills, cross the Mandalay–Rangoon road and make a desperate attempt to rejoin the rest of Kimura's forces east of the Sittang River. Sakurai's men were in a bad way. They had been very roughly handled by 33 Corps, for transport they were reduced to a few pack animals and such bullock carts as they could seize from the villagers. Their remaining supplies were meagre in the extreme, and they subsisted mainly by foraging from the wretched Burmese. Of artillery they had only a few light guns and of armour none. The monsoon was in full blast, every *chaung* was in spate, the rain was ceaseless, and they had little shelter. The sick received scant medical attention; they could only be left to die. Few armies in their situation would have thought of anything but surrender. Yet, when our aircraft showered the areas in which they were with leaflets inviting surrender and promising good treatment, there was no response. Instead, Sakurai collected his men and prepared to break out.

Our troops were, like the Japanese, hampered by the water-logged ground, especially in the flatter country between the Mandalay–Rangoon road and the Sittang. This would not have been so great a handicap had not air transport been greatly reduced by the withdrawal of all American aircraft from South-East Asia by the 1st June. At the same time, several squadrons of our own left Burma to prepare for the Malayan operations. 4 Corps, under Lieut.-General F. I. S. Tuker, who was temporarily replacing Messervy on leave, had its two divisions, the 19th and 17th, strung out in a thin line from Pyinmana to Pegu. Patrols from these divisions and from 'V' Force thrust into the hills, but the Japanese were too far west for more than minor contacts with enemy reconnaissance parties. A few prisoners were, however, taken and from these we began gradually to trace out the pattern of enemy concentrations. Sakurai had managed, deep in the Yomas hills, to collect his army in five groups:

(i) The 54th Japanese Division farthest north.
(ii) 72 Independent Mixed Brigade.
(iii) Twenty-eighth Army Headquarters, with various other units and line of communication troops.
(iv) The 55th Division, less about one regiment.
(v) 105 Independent Mixed Brigade.

Our surmises as to his intentions were confirmed when, on the 2nd July, a long-distance patrol from our 17th Division captured an order of the Japanese 55th Division giving full details of the enemy's plan. All that was lacking was the date of its proposed execution. Sakurai proposed, in several columns, to break out across the Rangoon road on a front of one hundred and fifty miles between Toungoo and Nyaunglebin. The state of the ground would limit his exits from the hills to certain major tracks; these with the forces allotted to them were all given in the captured order. The bulk of the enemy escape routes led through the 17th Division sector, and it was clear that our cordon must be strengthened.

With this intention, Stopford, commanding the Twelfth Army, transferred considerable reinforcements, mainly from the Irrawaddy front, to Tuker's 4 Corps. The 7th Division, which had already replaced the 5th, received a brigade headquarters and four battalions from the 20th Division, and the 17th Division a brigade headquarters and four battalions from the 19th Division and three battalions from the 20th. Five battalions, each about four hundred strong, of Aung San's army, now called the Patriot Burmese Forces, also joined 4 Corps. These reinforcements enabled Tuker and his divisional commanders to thicken their lines and to arrange their troops in depth. First came patrols pushed into the hills on tracks that the Japanese were expected to use. Then strong-points, with artillery and armour, blocking the routes as they debouched from the hills to cross the road. Farther east, in the plain between the road and the Sittang, were columns to intercept such enemy as managed to cross the road. On the west bank of the river were located some regular units and the battalions of the P.B.F., to catch the Japanese as they tried to get over the river. Finally, even beyond this on the east bank, were lurking patrols of Force 136 and parties of the P.B.F. to ambush any survivors who did contrive to cross. It was a severe gauntlet Sakurai would have to run.

The first main moves in the Battle of the Break-Out came from the Japanese Thirty-third Army, with its main force of some six to seven thousand men on the east of the Sittang and about three thousand holding three bridgeheads on the west bank. The enemy's object was, by counter-attack aimed at Waw which would threaten, if not cut, our rail and road communications north from Rangoon, so to distract our attention and draw off our troops that their Twenty-eighth Army would be able to break through between Toungoo and Nyaunglebin. To meet this expected attack, the 7th Division had one brigade forward, facing east covering the Japanese bridgeheads from Mokpalin to Myitkyo, a front of twelve miles. The remaining two brigades were stretched out on a fifty-mile line, facing west, watching the exits from the Pegu Yomas. Units were much below strength as, in the British, repatriation had taken heavy toll and, in Indian, men had been sent on leave.

On the night of the 3rd July, the Japanese counter-attack began with fierce assaults on three of our positions in the eastern brigade area. All held, and, as more Japanese crossed the Sittang an extraordinary battle, which might in more senses than one have been called fluid, began. The whole battlefield was a swamp, in which the only comparatively solid pieces of ground were the railway embankment and the sites of the miserable villages that rose as islands in a waste of water which, averaging two to three feet, was in places, the 7th Division reported, 'too deep for Gurkhas to operate'. Having failed with heavy casualties to take our positions, the Japanese settled down to siege tactics, cut off our posts, and shelled them heavily. The R.A.F. came to the rescue and gave the closest and most valiant support under which our men counter-attacked, but the weather—rain reduced visibility to one hundred yards by day—often made flying impossible. Our casualties mounted and, on the 7th July, our forward troops were ordered to withdraw. This they did by night, wading in a hollow square across the water. They took with them many wounded, and through the long hours of the night the bearers, in the centre of the square, stumbling through mud and water, could never put down a stretcher to rest themselves. Had they done so, the man on it would have drowned. Oddly enough, the Japanese, too, had had enough, and they withdrew at the same time, although later they tried to follow up, and were repulsed decisively. There was one more inconclusive fight, when both sides simultaneously advanced into the 'island' in the loop of the Sittang Old Channel. Then, the Japanese having abandoned all hope of taking Waw, fighting died down, and interest moved farther north, where the long-expected break-out of the Twenty-eighth Army had begun.

Very wisely, Tuker had not allowed the Japanese counter-attack by their Thirty-third Army to distract him from preparations to receive the Twenty-eighth when it broke east. The captured order enabled every escape track to have its standing piquet, and 'V' Force patrols pushed farther west into the hills. There would thus be ample warning of the break-out, which was expected on the 20th July. Actually it began the day before, with an attack by about one hundred Japanese on a platoon post of the 17th Division. This was followed almost daily by enemy parties, of from two to five or six hundred strong, emerging from the Yomas and trying to force their way across the road. Luckily, they did not arrive simultaneously, and they could be dealt with piecemeal. With typical Japanese tenacity—and stupidity—they followed one another by the same routes, and the numerous encounters that took place followed a uniform pattern. First, the Japanese party would strike our detachment blocking their exit to the road. After suffering heavily in the attempt to destroy it, the enemy would split into several smaller bodies and get past on each side. Pursued by our columns and harried by the planes of 221 Group, the Japanese would take refuge in villages to await darkness. Our men would cut the few tracks, still above water, that led east. Then artillery concentrations would shell the villages, inflicting heavy loss as the water made it impossible to dig trenches. After a day or two's siege, the wretched Japanese in small groups would try to escape under cover of darkness, only to meet our troops on the west bank of the Sittang, and to be stalked and ambushed by the Burmese Patriot Forces and the armed resistance parties we had by now organized in many of the villages. Crossing the Sittang itself was the worst of the enemy's ordeals, and few succeeded. They were surprised as they launched their rafts, shot as they swam and drifted across on logs, or swept away by the rapid current to drown. In a few days, a post of our troops on the river bank counted over six hundred bodies floating down from the slaughter at one of the main Japanese crossing places upstream.

The last Japanese to attempt the break out were 12 and 13 Naval Guard Forces, formed from the Port and Shore Establishments of the Imperial Navy in Burma. They amounted to about twelve hundred men in all and, strangely enough, chose to make their attempt last and alone, on the 31st July. As they struggled across the road, losing heavily in the process, all our forces within reach were turned on them. Rapidly growing fewer, as our troops and artillery took toll, they approached the Sittang, only to find their way blocked by one of our battalions and to be caught between it and another pursuing one. The country was flooded and numerous *chaungs* near the river were in spate. It took nearly a week for an Indian and a Gurkha battalion to close in on the sailors, but of the four hundred to which they were now reduced, as the Japanese themselves afterwards told us, only three escaped. By the 4th August, such Japanese fugitives as had run the gauntlet were over the Sittang, and the last battle in Burma had ended.

Sakurai, lacking transport and communications, and with his troops in the state they were, had indeed done well to stage any sort of organized break-out at all, but his losses were devastating. At the time it was difficult to estimate accurately the Japanese casualties, but over six thousand bodies were recovered by our troops, hundreds were claimed by the Burmese irregulars, and many more lay undiscovered in water and long grass. Of the seventeen or eighteen thousand men of the Twenty-eighth Army who debouched from the Pegu Yomas, the Japanese themselves later stated that less than six thousand, and these starved, exhausted, and diseased, reached the east bank of the Sittang. In addition, between one and two thousand sick, too weak to march, had been abandoned to die in the Yomas.

Throughout this battle, there were two startlingly noticeable features. First, the scale of Japanese surrenders. For the six thousand bodies they had picked up, 4 Corps had taken seven hundred and forty prisoners—an unheard of ratio, at least ten times as high as ever before. Then there was the astonishing smallness of our own casualties. Against the admitted Japanese twelve thousand killed and missing, we had suffered only ninety-five killed and three hundred and twenty-two wounded. We were killing Japanese at a rate of over a hundred to one. The fact was that this final disaster had not only destroyed the Twenty-eighth Army, but had struck a mortal blow at the fighting spirit of the whole Japanese army in Burma.

While I was on leave in England, I had been told of atomic bombs, of their devastating power, and of the intention to drop them on Japan. Opinions differed widely as to whether, even after this, Japanese fanaticism would hold in desperate resistance to the brink of mass national suicide in Japan itself and elsewhere.

On the 6th August, the first atomic bomb destroyed Hiroshima and, on the 9th, the second fell at Nagasaki, so that I was not altogether surprised when my wife and I, flying back to my command, heard in Rome on the 14th that Japan had surrendered unconditionally.

Two days later, I arrived at Headquarters Allied Land Forces, South-East Asia, which were comfortably installed near Supreme Headquarters in Kandy, Ceylon, and there I took over my new and extended command. The staff with the exception of Walsh, who had been General Leese's Chief of Staff and who had left with him and been replaced by Major-General Pyman, was unchanged. Unchanged, but, remembering how they had displaced General Giffard's officers, a little apprehensive that the new broom would in turn brush them away to make room for its own favourites from Fourteenth Army, and a number of sweepstakes were being run on which officers would be dismissed first. However, as I brought with me only my Military Secretary, my aides-de-camp and my Gurkha orderly, Bajbir, who would displace no one, anxiety soon subsided and, although I did make some reductions without replacement, we all got on very well together.

It would have been my fault if we had not, for I found a first-class staff, in excellent running order under Pyman and Bastyan, the Principal Administrative Officer. We soon had our hands full. The area of South-East Asia Land Forces had suddenly expanded to include Malaya, Singapore, Siam, Indo-China, the Dutch East Indies, Hongkong, Borneo, and the Andaman Islands. Each confronted us with special and urgent problems. In two of them, Indo-China and the Dutch East Indies, nationalist movements, armed from Japanese sources, had already seized power in the vacuum left by the surrender, and were resisting the restoration of French or Dutch sovereignty—fighting had already begun or seemed inevitable. In all areas were intact Japanese forces amounting to about half a million men, whose acceptance of the surrender was not certain, and many thousands of British, Australians, Indians, Americans, Dutch, and French, starving and dying of disease in the brutal and barbaric Japanese prison camps. It was obviously vital that we should occupy all Japanese-held territory at the earliest possible moment, not only to enforce the surrender, but to succour these unfortunates.

Appeals from our French and Dutch Allies, cries for help, demands for troops, threats of continued Japanese resistance, apprehensions of wholesale massacre, forebodings of economic collapse, warnings of the starvation of whole populations, poured into our headquarters from every quarter. There were excellent reasons why we should rush to respond to each one. We should have liked to do so, but our shortage of air transport—we had lost over half our former allotment—and the fact that almost all available shipping had already been loaded for the Malayan invasion, hampered and delayed our attempts to move forces rapidly to so many different points. Our first decision, in this welter of conflicting claims, was immediately to carry out the Malayan landing as planned—that is, as if the war were continuing. It would have meant immense confusion had we unloaded and redistributed the troops and stores; besides, at this time, Itagaki, the Japanese commander in Malaya, was breathing defiance, and it was quite possible that resistance would be encountered. In any case, to treat the landing as an operation of war was the quickest way to disembark the force, and, should that go peaceably, we could then direct its later echelons elsewhere.

At the same time, using all available air resources, we prepared to fly the 7th Division from Burma into Siam and, using the Bangkok airfield as a staging station, to lift part of the 20th Division into Indo-China to control Terauchi's Supreme Headquarters in Saigon. The 5th Division, if not required in Malaya, was to sail to Singapore and 3 Commando Brigade to Hongkong. As soon after the occupation of Singapore as possible, the 26th Division was to be landed in Java and Sumatra. All these operations were about to begin, indeed the first ships of the Malayan force were already at sea and all headquarters buzzing with activity, when, on the 19th August, a very considerable spanner was thrown into their busy works.

The British and American Combined Chiefs of Staff had, ignoring Admiral Mountbatten, their Supreme Commander in South-East Asia, entrusted the overall control of the Japanese surrender to General MacArthur, the Supreme Commander in the Pacific. He decreed that the formal surrender in South-East Asia could take place only after it had been ceremonially completed in his own theatre. This, though inconvenient, might not have mattered so much had he not ordered, also, that no landings

in or re-entry into Japanese-held territory would be made until
he had personally received the formal surrender of the Japanese
Empire. This ceremony was fixed for the 31st August, and thus
for twelve days—actually fourteen as it was postponed until
the 2nd September—the forces of South-East Asia had to mark
time.

This delay in the formal surrender of the enemy in South-East
Asia did not prevent preliminary meetings, on our ground,
between our plenipotentaries and theirs, at which, after an initial
tendency to argue, promptly and firmly suppressed, the Japanese
showed a proper submissiveness and readiness to obey orders.
But the delay could have had most serious consequences for our
prisoners in Japanese hands. Admiral Mountbatten, now assured
there would be no resistance, decided, in spite of the ban on
landing, to fly in help to the prisoners. Our men and those of our
Allies were daily dying in their foul camps; thousands were at the
limit of weakness and exhaustion. Had he delayed for even a few
days in sending supplies and relief personnel, many more would
have died pathetically at the moment of rescue. The relief teams
parachuted into the camps with magnificent courage, for they
were by no means sure of the Japanese reaction to their arrival,
but they could not, of course, bring with them great quantities
of stores, medicine, or clothing. All that, and the evacuation of
the prisoners to Burma, had to await the arrival of our troops.
This was held up for a couple of weeks by the delays imposed in
the surrender arrangements, and condemned our prisoners to a
correspondingly longer stay in their camps.

The state of these camps and of their wretched inmates can only
be realized by those who saw them as they were at this time.
Except for derelict huts and *bashas*, the camps were little more
than barbed wire enclosures in which wild beasts might have
been herded together. The Japanese and Korean gaolers, almost
without exception, were at the best callously indifferent to
suffering, or, at the worst, bestially sadistic. The food was of a
quality and a quantity barely enough to keep men alive, let alone
fit them for the hard labour that most were driven to perform.
It was horrifying to see them moving slowly about these sordid
camps, all emaciated, many walking skeletons, numbers covered
with suppurating sores, and most naked but for the ragged shorts
they had worn for years or loin cloths of sacking. The most

VICTORY

heart-moving of all were those who lay on wretched pallets, their strength ebbing faster than relief could be brought to them. There can be no excuse for a nation which as a matter of policy treats its prisoners of war in this way, and no honour for an army, however brave, which willingly makes itself the instrument of such inhumanity to the helpless.

Once the ceremonial surrender to General MacArthur had been staged on the 2nd September, we were free to occupy the Japanese-held territories. On the 3rd, our first detachments, mainly medical units to aid the prisoners, were landed by air near Bangkok, followed by headquarters and a brigade of the 7th Division. On the 11th September, Gracey and a small detachment of his 20th Division were staged through to Saigon and took control of Field-Marshal Tarauchi's headquarters. The situation in Siam was well in hand, as the Regent and his government had for some time during the Japanese occupation been secretly working with us, organizing a resistance movement, and concerting measures for the day of liberation. In Indo-China fighting between local nationalist movements and the French, now released from internment, was already going on, and Gracey was faced with a most difficult politico-military situation in Allied territory, which he handled in a firm, cool, and altogether admirable manner.

The landing of Roberts's 34 Corps over the beaches in the Port Swettenham–Port Dickson area, on the west coast of Malaya, went in on the 9th September as a tactical operation. There was no resistance, and even if there had been I think the operation would have been a success, for the Japanese plans, as we afterwards discovered, were based on our landing elsewhere. The local inhabitants, Malays and Chinese, gave our men a great welcome. When, a little later, I landed myself to see how things were going, the first British soldier I met was a linesman of the Royal Signals, with his rifle slung, holding by one hand a little Chinese boy and by the other a little Chinese girl. Linked with these two grinning youngsters were half a dozen others, all laughing and shouting. The soldier was a little embarrassed to be found patrolling a telephone line with this unofficial escort, but the children enjoyed it immensely. Anyway, soldiers and children always go very well together.

On the 3rd September, Royal Marines from the fleet had taken

532

over Penang Island from its Japanese garrison and, steaming on, the 5th Division had reached Singapore amid great local rejoicing on the 5th. Later the 26th Division, staging from Singapore, landed at Batavia in Java to deal with a very complicated and unhappy situation that had developed in the Dutch East Indies. Hongkong was reoccupied by 3 Commando Brigade on the 10th September. We were then ready to begin the disarming and collection in prisoner of war camps of the five hundred thousand Japanese troops in our area.

I had already, before the receipt of General MacArthur's orders, issued instructions to all my commanders as to how the Japanese surrender was to be conducted in our area. In these I had laid down that all senior Japanese officers were to surrender their swords to appropriate British commanders in front of parades of their own troops. There had been some protests at this from our Japanese experts who averred that:

(i) The Japanese officer's honour was so bound up with his Samurai sword that, rather than surrender it, he would go on fighting.
(ii) Alternatively, as the lawyers say, if he did surrender it before his men, he would never again be able to exercise command over them.
(iii) He would in fact, rather than be so publicly shamed, commit suicide.

My answers to these forebodings had been:

(i) If the Japanese liked to go on fighting, I was ready for them.
(ii) If the officers lost their soldiers' respect I could not care less as I intended to separate them from their men in any case.
(iii) If the officers committed suicide I had already prepared for this by broadcasting that any Japanese officer wishing to commit suicide would be given every facility.

I was convinced that an effective way really to impress on the Japanese that they had been beaten in the field was to insist on this ceremonial surrender of swords. No Japanese soldier, who had seen his general march up and hand over his sword, would ever doubt that the Invincible Army was invincible no longer. We did not want a repetition of the German First War legend of an

533

unconquered army. With this in mind, I was dismayed to be told that General MacArthur in his overall instruction for the surrender had decided that the 'archaic' ceremony of the surrender of swords was not to be enforced. I am afraid I disregarded his wishes. In South-East Asia all Japanese officers surrendered their swords to British officers of similar or higher rank; the enemy divisional and army commanders handed theirs in before large parades of their already disarmed troops. Field-Marshal Tarauchi's sword is in Admiral Mountbatten's hands; General Kimura's is now on my mantelpiece, where I always intended that one day it should be.

In Singapore on the 12th September 1945 I sat on the left of the Supreme Commander, Admiral Mountbatten, in the line of his Commanders-in-Chief and principal staff officers, while the formal unconditional surrender of all Japanese forces, land, sea, and air, in South-East Asia was made to him. I looked at the dull impassive masks that were the faces of the Japanese generals and admirals seated opposite. Their plight moved me not at all. For them, I had none of the sympathy of soldier for soldier, that I had felt for Germans, Turks, Italians, or Frenchmen that by the fortune of war I had seen surrender. I knew too well what these men and those under their orders had done to *their* prisoners. They sat there apart from the rest of humanity. If I had no feeling for them, they, it seemed, had no feeling of any sort, until Itagaki, who had replaced Field-Marshal Tarauchi, laid low by a stroke, leant forward to affix his seal to the surrender document. As he pressed heavily on the paper, a spasm of rage and despair twisted his face. Then it was gone and his mask was as expressionless as the rest. Outside, the same Union Jack that had been hauled down in surrender in 1942 flew again at the masthead.

The war was over.

CHAPTER XXIII

AFTERTHOUGHTS

GENERALS have often been reproached with preparing for
the last war instead of for the next—an easy gibe when
their fellow-countrymen and their political leaders, too
frequently, have prepared for no war at all. Preparation for war
is an expensive, burdensome business, yet there is one important
part of it that costs little—study. However changed and strange
the new conditions of war may be, not only generals, but politicians and ordinary citizens, may find there is much to be
learned from the past that can be applied to the future and, in
their search for it, that some campaigns have more than others
foreshadowed the coming pattern of modern war. I believe that
ours in Burma was one of these.

This may seem a curious claim to make for the struggles of
comparatively ill-equipped men, groping through jungles. Yet
a painters' effect and style do not depend on how many tubes of
colour he has, the number of his brushes, or the size of his canvas,
but on how he blends his colours and handles his brushes against
the canvas. Looking back on the Burma campaign, which presented, at least to me, a strange unity and completeness, I have
many afterthoughts. Of these, I have here chosen a few, not
because they are, perhaps, the most unusual or dramatic, but
because they seem —again to me—to have some interest for the
future.

Higher Direction

For the poor showing we made during the first phase of the
war in Burma, the Retreat, there may have been few excuses, but
there were many causes, most of them beyond the control of
local commanders. Of these causes, one affected all our efforts
and contributed much to turning our defeat into disaster—the
failure, after the fall of Rangoon, to give the forces in the field

535

a clear strategic object for the campaign. As a result, our plans had to be based on a rather nebulous, short-term idea of holding ground—we were not even sure what ground or for what purpose.

When the loss of Rangoon made it impossible to reinforce, or even adequately to maintain the army in Burma, still more when the Chinese divisions began to give way, it was only too plain that the Allies had no immediate hope of driving back the Japanese and very little of even holding them. At this time, those concerned in London and Washington with the conduct of global war, hard pressed as they were on more vital fronts, tended to overlook Burma. Yet a realistic assessment of possibilities there and a firm, clear directive would have made a great deal of difference to us and to the way we fought. Burma was not the first, nor was it to be the last, campaign that had been launched on no very clear realization of its political or military objects. A study of such campaigns points emphatically to the almost inevitable disaster that must follow. Commanders in the field, in fairness to them and their troops, must be clearly and definitely told what is the object they are locally to attain.

The organization of the command in a theatre is, of itself, of the utmost importance. The first step towards ultimate victory in South-East Asia was the setting up of a supreme command, controlling all Allied forces, land, sea, and air, in the area. There will always be difficulties, national and personal, in the creation and working of such a headquarters. In South-East Asia these were greater than in similar commands in Africa, Europe, or the Pacific, because of the underlying difference between the British and American attitudes towards the Burma campaign. The clash of personalities, too, was fierce, and often, as with Stilwell and Chiang Kai-shek, aggravated by distance. There will always be these frictions to a greater or lesser degree in any Supreme Headquarters, but where Allied forces are operating together, there is no effective solution other than a Supreme Headquarters.

The Japanese Army

This was the first time since the Crusades, with the possible exception of some of our Indian wars of the eighteenth and early nineteenth centuries, that the British had fought an Asian or African enemy, whose armament and military organization had been comparable to their own. Like our predecessors, the

Russians in their war against Japan, we found a war against such a foe, at any rate to begin with, an extremely unpleasant and startling experience. Yet, because we possessed certain basic qualities which the Russians of that day did not, we eventually succeeded where they failed.

The Japanese, in the earlier stages of the campaign, gained the moral ascendancy over us that they did, because we never seriously challenged their seizure of the initiative. They bought that initiative, fairly and inevitably, by paying for it with preparation. Our lack of preparation in Burma, military, administrative, and political, made it difficult for our commanders even to bid for the initiative. But we should have tried harder than we did and taken more risks to gain it. Even when weaker, as we were in the earlier stages, to adopt a static defence, to try merely to hold ground, unless relief and reinforcement are at hand, is fatal. The only hope is to take the offensive at least locally whatever the risk and by daring and surprise throw out the enemy's plans. The Japanese were ruthless and bold as ants while their designs went well, but if those plans were disturbed or thrown out—ant-like again—they fell into confusion, were slow to readjust themselves, and invariably clung too long to their original schemes. This, to commanders with their unquenchable military optimism, which rarely allowed in their narrow administrative margins for any setback or delay, was particularly dangerous. The fundamental fault of their generalship was a lack of moral, as distinct from physical, courage. They were not prepared to admit that they had made a mistake, that their plans had misfired and needed recasting. That would have meant personal failure in the service of the Emperor and loss of face. Rather than confess that, they passed on to their subordinates, unchanged, the orders they had themselves received, well knowing that with the resources available the tasks demanded were impossible. Time and again, this blind passing of responsibility ran down a chain of disaster from the Commander-in-Chief to the lowest levels of leadership. It is true that in war determination by itself may achieve results, while flexibility, without determination in reserve, cannot, but it is only the blending of the two that brings final success. The hardest test of generalship is to hold this balance between determination and flexibility. In this the Japanese failed. They scored highly by determination; they paid heavily for lack of flexibility.

The strength of the Japanese Army lay, not in its higher leadership, which, once its career of success had been checked, became confused, nor in its special aptitude for jungle warfare, but in the spirit of the individual Japanese soldier. He fought and marched till he died. If five hundred Japanese were ordered to hold a position, we had to kill four hundred and ninety-five before it was ours—and then the last five killed themselves. It was this combination of obedience and ferocity that made the Japanese Army, whatever its condition, so formidable, and which would make any army formidable. It would make a European army invincible.

Our Forces

In Burma we not only fought against an Asian enemy, but we fought him with an army that was mainly Asian. In both respects not a few of us with little experience of Asians had to readjust many ideas, among them that of the inherent superiority of the white man as a soldier. The Asian fighting man is at least equally brave, usually more careless of death, less encumbered by mental doubts, little troubled by humanitarian sentiment, and not so moved by slaughter and mutilation about him. He is, by background and living standards, better fitted to endure hardship uncomplainingly, to demand less in the way of subsistence or comfort, and to look after himself when thrown on his own resources. He has a keen practised eye for country and the ability to move across it on his own feet. He has not the inherent disinclination to climb hills that the city-bred, motor-riding white man has. Much—I had almost written most—of our fighting in Burma took place at night. Night fighting is, in effect, a form of dispersed fighting because, although men may be close together, they see little and suffer the fears and anxieties of isolation. The more civilized we become, the more we draw our soldiers from well-lighted towns, the more clumsy and frightened shall we be in the dark, and the greater the odds in favour of a more primitive foe.

While field-craft comes naturally to the Asian, he can learn as well as the white man how to handle new weapons, even complicated ones. The European, on the other hand, can at present more readily design and produce such equipment and find the vitally important skilled men to maintain it. He is superior, not so much in natural intelligence, as in education, and thus is able to find a higher proportion of potential officers. He should be able to understand better what he is fighting for, be capable of higher training, and, if it is properly developed, of more sustained morale. Yet with all these advantages, it is foolish to pit white men against Asians and expect them to win just because they are white; to win they must be better trained, better disciplined, and, better led. If they are not, even superior armament will not overcome the numerical and natural advantages of the Asian. We began by despising our Japanese enemy; the pendulum then swung wildly to the other extreme. We built up our enemy into something terrifying, as soldiers always will to excuse their defeats, and frightened ourselves with the bogy of the superman of the jungle. Both attitudes were calamitous to us. It was not until we taught ourselves to take a balanced view of our enemy as a formidable fighting man, who nevertheless had certain weaknesses, and of ourselves as being able with training to beat him at his own, or any other game, that we won.

In an army such as ours, drawn from many nationalities, administration and supply were complicated. In Indian Army formations we began with a proportion of British units among the Indian—about one-third to two-thirds. For a variety of reasons, I came to the conclusion that it was preferable, certainly in infantry brigades, to have either all British or all Indian. Then, each race fought better, supply was greatly simplified, and we could more easily suit divisions to their tasks. My Indian divisions after 1943 were among the best in the world. They would go anywhere, do anything, go on doing it, and do it on very little.

Material

At the beginning of the war there was the greatest contrast between the Japanese and the British logistical outlook, between what they required to operate and what we *thought* we required. They launched their troops into the boldest offensives on the slenderest administrative margins; our training was all against this. The British Army, ever since the terrible lesson of the Crimea, had tended to stress supply at the expense of mobility. The static conditions of the First World War, followed by fast rising standards of living, inevitably increased this bias. In many theatres of the Second World War, the complexity of equipment, the growth of specialized organizations, the expansion of staffs, and the elaboration of communications still further increased the ratio of administrative to fighting strengths and swelled the amount of transport required. In Africa and Europe the decline of the enemy's air power from 1941 onwards and the relative abundance of motorable routes concealed what, in other circumstances, would have been the tactical impossibility of manœuvre with such tail-heavy formations. With us in Burma, from its complete dominance in 1942, the Japanese Air Force became, from 1944, less and less of a danger to movement until it practically disappeared even as a threat. Yet the difficulty of the country with its lack of roads remained and still forced us to limit transport on the ground, while shortage of aircraft compelled the same economy in the air. We discovered that, instead of the four hundred tons a day not considered excessive to keep a division fighting in more generous theatres, we could maintain our Indian divisions in action for long periods, without loss of battle efficiency or morale, on one hundred and twenty. As we removed vehicles from units and formations which joined us on European establishments, they found to their surprise that they could move farther and faster without them. The fewer vehicles on the roads or tracks, the quicker they travelled, and an enforced ingenuity in combining ferrying by lorry with marching covered long distances in remarkably short time. This relation between tactical mobility and numbers of vehicles, between the size of staffs and effective control, will increase in importance in any future war. Unless they are constantly watched and ruthlessly cut down, vehicles and staffs will multiply until they bog down movement.

With us, necessity was truly the mother of invention. We lacked so much in equipment and supplies that, if we were not to give up offensive operations altogether, we had either to manage without or improvise for ourselves. We learnt that if the spirit could be made willing the flesh would do without many things and that quick brains and willing hands could, from meagre resources, produce astonishing results. Our mass production river shipyards, our methods of building roads and airfields, our 'parajutes', our huge market gardens almost in the battle line, our duck farms, our fish saltings, and a hundred other things were gallant and successful efforts by the army in the field to live up to its motto, 'God helps those who help themselves.' My soldiers forced the opposed crossings of great rivers using ludicrously inadequate equipment, stretched brittle communication links to fantastic lengths, marched over the most heartbreaking country on reduced rations, fought disease with discipline and beat it. The Japanese first demonstrated painfully on us that it is not so much numbers and elaborate equipment that count in the tough places, but training and morale. We had to learn this lesson in a hard school before we could turn the tables on them.

New Techniques

In Burma we fought on a lower scale of transport, supplies, equipment, supporting arms, and amenities than was accepted in any other British theatre. Yet, largely because of this lack of material resources, we learned to use those we had in fresh ways to achieve more than would have been possible had we clung to conventional methods. We had not only to devise new tactics but to delve deeply into the motive forces of human conduct and to change our traditional outlook on many things. The result was, I think it true to say, a kind of warfare more modern in essence than that fought by other British forces. Indeed, by any Allied force, with the exception of the Americans in the Pacific. There, their problem, the opposite of ours, was to use the immense resources that became increasingly available to them most effectively in the peculiar circumstances of an ocean war. They solved it brilliantly and evolved a new material technique. We, also in strange conditions, evolved our technique of war, not so much material as human.

Compared with those in Europe, the combat forces used in Burma were not large. Including Stilwell's Chinese, the greatest number of divisions I ever had under my command in action at one time was eighteen. They fought on a front of seven hundred miles, in four groups, separated by great distances, with no lateral communications between them and beyond tactical support of one another. My corps and divisions were called upon to act with at least as much freedom as armies and corps in other theatres. Commanders at all levels had to act more on their own; they were given greater latitude to work out their own plans to achieve what they knew was the Army Commander's intention. In time they developed to a marked degree a flexibility of mind and a firmness of decision that enabled them to act swiftly to take advantage of sudden information or changing circumstances without reference to their superiors. They were encouraged, as Stopford put it when congratulating Rees's 19th Division which had seized a chance to slip across the Irrawaddy and at the same time make a dart at Shwebo, to 'shoot a goal when the referee wasn't looking'. This acting without orders, in anticipation of orders, or without waiting for approval, yet always within the overall intention, must become second nature in any form of warfare where formations do not fight closely *en cadre*, and must go down to the smallest units. It requires in the higher command a corresponding flexibility of mind, confidence in its subordinates, and the power to make its intentions clear right through the force.

Companies, even platoons, under junior leaders became the basic units of the jungle. Out of sight of one another, often out of touch, their wireless blanketed by hills, they marched and fought on their own, often for days at a time. They frequently approached the battle in scattered columns, as they did for the crossings of the Irrawaddy, and concentrated on the battlefield. The methods by which they did this and, above all, the qualities they needed to make these tactics possible and successful repay study. They may be needed again.

Discipline

The more modern war becomes, the more essential appear the basic qualities that from the beginning of history have distinguished armies from mobs. The first of these is discipline. We very soon learnt in Burma that strict discipline in battle and in bivouac was vital, not only for success, but for survival. Nothing is easier in jungle or dispersed fighting than for a man to shirk. If he has no stomach for advancing, all he has to do is to flop into the undergrowth; in retreat, he can slink out of the rearguard, join up later, and swear he was the last to leave. A patrol leader can take his men a mile into the jungle, hide there, and return with any report he fancies. Only discipline—not punishment—can stop that sort of thing; the real discipline that a man holds to because it is a refusal to betray his comrades. The discipline that makes a sentry, whose whole body is tortured for sleep, rest his chin on the point of his bayonet because he knows, if he nods, he risks the lives of the men sleeping behind him. It is only discipline,

542

too, that can enforce the precautions against disease, irksome as they are, without which an army would shrivel away. At some stage in all wars armies have let their discipline sag, but they have never won victory until they made it taut again; nor will they. We found it a great mistake to belittle the importance of smartness in turn-out, alertness of carriage, cleanliness of person, saluting, or precision of movement, and to dismiss them as naïve, unintelligent parade-ground stuff. I do not believe that troops can have unshakable battle discipline without showing those outward and formal signs, which mark the pride men take in themselves and their units and the mutual confidence and respect that exists between them and their officers. It was our experience in a tough school that the best fighting units, in the long run, were not necessarily those with the most advertised reputations, but those who, when they came out of battle at once resumed a more formal discipline and appearance.

Air Power

The fabric of our campaign was woven by the close intermeshing of land and air operations, yet we began in South-East Asia with exaggerated ideas of what air power by itself could accomplish. We discovered, both when it was overwhelmingly against us and equally when it was overwhelmingly with us, that it could not *stop* movement on the ground; it could only impede and delay it. Neither the Japanese air forces nor our own prevented divisions being moved or troops being supplied. They made these things more difficult.

One of the characteristics of air power is its ever-increasing flexibility, but even this has certain limitations. As long as our squadrons, fighter or bomber, could operate from bases within reasonable range of their objectives this flexibility was obvious and marked. When, however, as sometimes happened on a front as wide as ours with distances as great, we had to find another airfield, the flexibility of air power temporarily at least vanished. We built earth landing strips even with little machinery in a matter of hours, but the all-weather airfield capable of acting as a base, of which at least a certain number were required, was a much slower business. During our rapid advances we solved the problem only by making Japanese airfields the primary objectives of our foremost troops. Even then we should have been gravely embarrassed if the enemy had concentrated more thoroughly than they did on destroying runways, road-rollers, equipment, and repair materials.

As we were, compared with most Allied armies, short of artillery (and even if it had been available the country would have hampered its use) we came to rely for close support more and more on the air. We developed our own and adapted other people's methods of calling up air support, of indicating targets and of co-ordinating movement on the ground with fire from the air. We as confidently dovetailed our fire plans with the airmen as with the gunners. Talked in by Air Force officers with the forward troops, our fighters would place their cannon shells and rockets within a hundred yards of our men, and by dummy runs keep down the enemy's heads for the last infantry rush. Quick and accurate co-operation of this sort did not come in a day; it grew with the airmen's and soldiers' mutual confidence, understanding, and pride in one another's achievements. In peace, the function of tactical air support of land operations is apt to fade, but in war its urgency will increase.

A most distinctive aspect of our Burma war was the great use we made of air transport. It was one of our contributions towards a new kind of warfare and I think it fair to say that, to a large extent, we discovered by trial and error the methods of air supply that later passed into general use. We were the first to maintain large formations in action by air supply and to move standard divisions long distances about the fighting front by air. The second Chindit expedition in March 1944, when we landed some thirty thousand men and five thousand animals far behind the enemy's lines and maintained them for months, was the largest airborne operation of the war. The decisive stroke at Meiktila and the advance on Rangoon were examples of a new technique that combined mechanized and air-transported brigades in the same divisions. To us, all this was as normal as moving or maintaining troops by railway or road, and that attitude of mind was, I suppose, one of our main reformations. We had come a long way since 1928 when, as a junior staff officer, I had been concerned with other Indian Army officers in a struggle, not entirely without success, to introduce operational air transport and supply on the North-West Frontier.

Although we moved great tonnages and many thousands of

troops by air, the largest number of transport aircraft we ever had was much less than would elsewhere have been considered the minimum required. It was quite easy theoretically to demonstrate that what we were doing was impossible to continue over any length of time. Yet the skill, courage, and devotion of the airmen, British and American, both in the air and on the ground, combined with the hard work and organizing ability of the soldiers, not only did it, but kept on doing it month after month. As in so many other things, we learnt to revise accepted theories and, when worth it, to risk cutting our margins.

A feature of our airborne operations and movements was that the troops employed were not of some special kind. No soldiers of the Fourteenth Army were taught to believe there was anything mystic, strange, or unusual about air movements or maintenance; to them, of whatever race, these were normal administrative methods. The only exception was parachute jumping. I would, if I had had the aircraft available for practice, have made it an ordinary part of, at least, every infantryman's training. The incidence of serious injury is, I should think, no higher among soldier parachutists than among soldier motorcyclists. Unfortunately, the lack of training aircraft prevented our using parachutists on a large scale, but even so we were undoubtedly the most air-minded army that ever existed. We had to be.

More publicity was given to air transport than to any other feature of the Burma war and, perhaps as a result, certain fallacies about it gained currency. The first was to overlook the fact that our pattern of operations depended, almost entirely, on a very large measure of air supremacy. Until a degree of air superiority, amounting at least locally to dominance, had been secured, neither air supply, movement, nor tactical support could be carried on with the certainty and regularity our operations demanded. The fighter and the bomber between them had to sweep the skies and push back the enemy landing grounds; the air battle had to be won first—and from now on it will always have to be won first. A second fallacy was that air supply is entirely a matter to be arranged by air forces; that the only things required are the aircraft and the men to fly and maintain them. The organization of air supply is as much a job for the army as for the air force. It is as important as flying the aircraft that the immensely varied

545

stores, properly packed, should arrive at the right airstrips for loading at the right time; that they should be sent to the right units, and that on arrival, unloading, distribution, and delivery should be swift and unerring. All these and a dozen other things are the province of the army and entail the most difficult—at least we found it so—of all requirements, a complicated mass of signal communications. Among the most strategically dangerous ideas that half-baked thinking on air supply provoked, was that, even if surrounded, positions could be held for months provided they might be maintained from the air. In fact, troops thus cut off even if fed and maintained, eventually lose heart, and air supply is so easily interrupted; the weather or a few well sited anti-aircraft weapons can easily put a stop to it. Air supply is only half the answer. The other half is an adequate relieving force which, however good the prospect of air supply, must appear in a reasonable time and which the beleaguered garrison must know will appear.

There is one other thing about combined land and air operations —and all operations on land are that. The land and air commanders responsible at each level must not only be in close touch, they should live together as we did. Ours was a joint land and air war; its result, as much a victory for the air forces as for the army.

Special Forces

The British Army in the last war spawned a surprising number of special units and formations, that is forces of varying sizes, each trained, equipped, and prepared for some particular type of operation. We had commandos, assault brigades, amphibious divisions, mountain divisions, long-rang penetration forces, airborne formations, desert groups, and an extraordinary variety of cloak and dagger parties. The equipment of these special units was more generous than that of normal formations, and many of them went so far as to have their own bases and administrative organizations. We employed most of them in Burma, and some, notably the Chindits, gave splendid examples of courage and hardihood. Yet I came firmly to the conclusion that such formations, trained, equipped, and mentally adjusted for one kind of operation only, were wasteful. They did not give, militarily, a worth-while return for the resources in men, material and time that they absorbed.

To begin with, they were usually formed by attracting the best men from normal units by better conditions, promises of excitement, and not a little propaganda. Even on the rare occasions when normal units were converted into special ones without the option of volunteering, the same process went on in reverse. Men thought to be below the standards set or over an arbitrary age limit were weeded out to less favoured corps. The result of these methods was undoubtedly to lower the quality of the rest of the Army, especially of the infantry, not only by skimming the cream off it, but by encouraging the idea that certain of the normal operations of war were so difficult that only specially equipped *corps d'élite* could be expected to undertake them. Armies do not win wars by means of a few bodies of super-soldiers but by the average quality of their standard units. Anything, whatever short cuts to victory it may promise, which thus weakens the Army spirit, is dangerous. Commanders who have used these special forces have found, as we did in Burma, that they have another grave disadvantage—they can be employed actively for only restricted periods. Then they demand to be taken out of the battle to recuperate, while normal formations are expected to have no such limits to their employment. In Burma, the time spent in action with the enemy by special forces was only a fraction of that endured by the normal divisions, and it must be remembered that risk is danger multiplied by time.

The rush to form special forces arose from confused thinking on what were, or were not, normal operations of war. In one sense every operation of war is a special one, whether it is attack, defence, withdrawal, penetration, raids behind the enemy's lines, destruction of his detachments, assault over a beach, river crossings, jungle or mountain warfare, or any of the rest; each has its peculiar requirements. Yet all are and have always been familiar operations of war; any standard unit should expect that, at some time or other, it may be called upon to engage in any of them. The level of initiative, individual training, and weapon skill required in, say, a commando, is admirable; what is not admirable is that it should be confined to a few small units. Any well-trained infantry battalion should be able to do what a commando can do; in the Fourteenth Army they could and did. This cult of special forces is as sensible as to form a Royal Corps of Tree Climbers and say that no soldier, who does not wear its green hat with a bunch of oak leaves stuck in it, should be expected to climb a tree.

I would lay it down that any single operation in which more than a handful of men are to be engaged should be regarded as normal, and should be carried out by standard formations. The only exception I would allow to this is a parachute landing, which, until facilities for training much larger numbers in the drill of jumping are available, must require something of a special force. The absence of such forces does not, of course, mean that ordinary units would not, as they have always done, practise and train for particular operations, but it would avoid having large numbers of picked troops, either waiting long periods to be used for short periods, or eventually being employed for something quite different from that for which they have so long and laboriously prepared. Private armies—and for that matter private air forces—are expensive, wasteful, and unnecessary.

There is, however, one kind of special unit which should be retained—that designed to be employed in small parties, usually behind the enemy, on tasks beyond the normal scope of warfare in the field. There will be an increasing need for highly qualified and individually trained men—and women—to sabotage vital installations, to spread rumours, to misdirect the enemy, to transmit intelligence, to kill or kidnap individuals, and to inspire resistance movements. They will be troops, though they will require many qualities and skills not to be expected of the ordinary soldier and they will use many methods beyond his capacity. Each small party would study and train intensively for a particular exploit and should operate under the direct control of the Higher Command. They should rarely work within our own lines. Not costly in manpower, they may, if handled with imaginative ruthlessness, achieve strategic results. Such units, based on the Army, but drawing on all Services and all races of the Commonwealth for specially qualified men and women, should be an essential component of our modern Armed Forces.

The question of control of these clandestine bodies is not without its pitfalls. In the last war among the Allies, cloak and dagger organizations multiplied until to commanders in the field—at least in my theatre—they became an embarrassment. The trouble was that each was controlled from some distant headquarters of its own, and such was the secrecy and mutual suspicion in which they operated that they sometimes acted in close proximity to our troops without the knowledge of any commander in the field, with a complete lack of co-ordination among themselves, and in dangerous ignorance of local tactical developments. It was not until the activities of all clandestine bodies operating in or near our troops were co-ordinated, and where necessary controlled, through a senior officer on the staff of the commander of the area, that confusion, ineffectiveness, and lost opportunities were avoided.

The Future

In Burma we thus developed a form of warfare, based more on human factors than on lavish equipment, which had certain characteristics. The chief of these were:

(i) The acceptance as normal of the regular movement and maintenance of standard formations by air.

(ii) Great tactical freedom for subordinate commanders.

(iii) The operation, over wide distances in most difficult country, of comparatively small forces in tactical independence but strategic combination.

(iv) Reduced scales of transport and equipment, supplemented by ingenuity and improvisation from local resources.

(v) The high quality of the individual soldier, his morale, toughness, and discipline, his acceptance of hardship, and his ability to move on his own feet and to look after himself.

War in the future may vary in scope from unlimited nuclear war aimed at the complete annihilation of a whole people, to a restricted tactical employment of nuclear weapons, or even to the small war of traditional pattern. Whatever form it takes, especially when nuclear weapons are employed as they will be in any war between great powers, one thing is reasonably certain. Modern war, with its destruction of bases, disruption of communications, and disorganization of control, will, if they are to operate at all, compel armies to disperse.

Dispersed fighting, whether the dispersal is caused by the terrain, the lack of supplies, or by the weapons of the enemy, will have two main requirements—skilled and determined junior leaders and self-reliant, physically hard, well-disciplined troops.

Success in future land operations will depend on the immediate availability of such leaders and such soldiers, ready to operate in small, independent formations. They will have to be prepared to do without regular lines of communication, to guide themselves and to subsist largely on what the country offers. Unseen, unheard, and unsuspected, they will converge on the enemy and, when they do reveal themselves in strength, they will be so close to him that he will be unable to atomize them without destroying himself. Such land operations, less rigidly controlled and more individualistic than in the past, will not be unlike ours as we approached the Chindwin and the Irrawaddy, and stalking terrorists in a Malayan jungle is today, strange as it may seem, the best training for nuclear warfare. The use of new weapons and technical devices can quickly be taught; to develop hardihood, initiative, mutual confidence, and stark leadership takes longer.

The air attacks we sustained and delivered were, compared with what they might be now, feeble things. Yet determined troops, especially in close or broken country, who are prepared to jettison all but fighting essentials and move in small, self-contained formations, will, I believe, make their own way even through the chaos of atomic bombing. In unlimited war, after the first shock of mutual devastation had been survived, victory would go, as it did in our other jungle, to the tougher, more resourceful infantryman. The easier and more gadget-filled our daily life becomes, the harder will it be to produce him. It took us some time to do so in Burma. It can be done in peace; in war there will no longer be so much time.

Until the very horror of modern mass destruction forces men to find some more sensible way of settling national disputes, war will remain, and while it remains it will continually change. Yet, because it is fought between men rather than between weapons, victory will still go, when armaments are even relatively equal, to the side which is better trained and of higher morale—advantages which are obtained neither easily, quickly, nor without the sacrifice of more than money in peace. War remains an art and, like all arts, whatever its variation, will have its enduring principles. Many men, skilled either with sword or pen, and sometimes with both, have tried to expound those principles. I heard them once from a soldier of experience for whom I had a deep and well-founded respect. Many years ago, as a cadet hoping some day to be an officer, I was poring over the 'Principles of War', listed in the old Field Service Regulations, when the Sergeant-Major came upon me. He surveyed me with kindly amusement. 'Don't bother your head about all them things, me lad,' he said. 'There's only one principle of war and that's this. Hit the other fellow, as quick as you can, and as hard as you can, where it hurts him most, when he ain't lookin'!' As a recruit, I earned that great man's reproof often enough; now, as an old soldier, I would hope to receive his commendation. I think I might, for we of the Fourteenth Army held to his Principle of War.

In these pages I have written much of generals and of staff officers; of their problems, difficulties, and expedients, their successes and their failures. Yet there is one thought that I should like to be the overall and final impression of this book—that the war in Burma was a *soldiers'* war. There comes a moment in every battle against a stubborn enemy when the result hangs in the balance. Then the general, however skilful and far-sighted he may have been, must hand over to his soldiers, to the men in the ranks and to their regimental officers, and leave them to complete what he has begun. The issue then rests with them, on their courage, their hardihood, their refusal to be beaten either by the cruel hazards of nature or by the fierce strength of their human enemy. That moment came early and often in the fighting in Burma; sometimes it came when tired, sick men felt alone, when it would have been so easy for them to give up, when only will, discipline, and faith could steel them to carry on. To the soldiers of many races who, in the comradeship of the Fourteenth Army, *did* go on, and to the airmen who flew with them and fought over them, belongs the true glory of achievement. It was they who turned Defeat into Victory.

INDEX

A

'Aberdeen', 258-9, 268, 270

'Administrative Box', 231; Japanese threat to, 235, 237; 7th Division H.Q. in, 239; Japanese capture and lose, 240-1; suicide force near, 244

African forces, too many white men with, 166, 353; response of, to spiritual appeal, 185

'African Way', 224

Agartala airstrip, 234

Aijal, 358

Air: defence weaknesses, 5-9, 116; reconnaissance, 28, 453; support lacking for 1 Burma Corps, 41-2, 50, 116, 120; support for 15 Corps, 127; transport in jungle warfare, 143; transport of Chinese to India, 144; transport for Arakan offensive, 165; evacuation of sick and wounded, 179-80; support for Fourteenth Army, 543-6; transport for Burma campaign, 205; organization of Allied forces, 211-12; supply and transport for Chindits, 217, 219-20, 242, 244, supply of Arakan campaign, 244-6, 234, 242-4; supply of Yunnan forces, 276; supply and support of Imphal-Kohima battle, 357-8, 368; transportable brigade, 387, 497; transport shortages, 395-6, 438, 444, 530; bases on road to Rangoon, 497-9, 500; support of land operations, 544-6; maintenance of formations, 544. See also Royal Air Force, 221 Group; United States Army Air Force.

Air Commando, No. 1, with Wingate's Force, 217, 219, 258-9

Airborne troops, 544-5; in capture of Meiktila, 412, 441, 454; at Palel, 426, 432; in advance on Rangoon, 497. See also Chindits

Akyab, conference at, 4, 9; Air Wing at, 7-8, 41; abandonment of airfield at, 42; Japanese forces in, 226; capture of, 458-9

Akyab Island, withdrawal from, 147; plan to take, 149, 204; Japanese forces in, 226; air base required on, 383, 462; capture of, 459-60; building airfield on, 464; operation 'Dracula' starts at, 506

Alexander, Field-Marshal Sir Harold (Viscount of Tunis), impossible task before, 14, 19, 118; escapes from Rangoon, 14-15; Chinese Armies of, 16-17; Chief of Staff to, 18; conference with, at Prome, 23-4; orders offensive to aid Chinese, 44; at Allanmyo conference, 48; orders holding of Taungdwingyi, 50, 58, 76; courage of, 55-6; sends Chinese Division, 61; discusses disposal of Chinese Armies, 74, 79-80; sends directive for withdrawal, 82; in conference at Ye-u, 95

Alison, Colonel J. R., 217

Allagappa, 84, 89, 418

Allanmyo, conference at, 48; retreat through, 49-50; Japanese withdraw to, 490-1; capture of, 492; action near, 511; Aung San at, 516. Mentioned, 38

Allied Air Command, 211

Allied Land Forces, South-East Asia, 384-6; provides aircraft, 396; provides engineers for boats, 399; orders attack on Mandalay and Rangoon, 467; author in command of, 523, 529; expansion of area under, 529; and Japanese surrender, 530-4

Alon, 96; railway from, 398

Amarapura, 473

American: training of Chinese troops, 144-5; airfield construction, 170-1; railway troops, 170; road construction, 172; attitude to Burma campaign, 249-50, 536; troops in Burma, 255-6. See also United States.

American Combat Engineers, 275

American Field Service Ambulance, 250

American Military Police in Calcutta, 134

American Volunteer Group, Third Squadron, 5, 7, 41-2

Amphibious operations, planning of, 192, 204-5, 213-14; abandonment of, 213-214; off Kra Isthmus, 482; in Arakan, 460-1. See also 'Dracula', operation

An, attack on, 462-3

An Pass, 436; Japanese way of retreat, 460, 462, 490; Japanese retain possession of, 463-4

Andaman Islands, projected operation in, 204, 213-14; bombardment of, 506; included in area of S.E.A.L.F., 529

Anstice, Brigadier J. H., 27, 45, 65

Anthony, mess butler, 26

557

Lushai Scouts, 422
Lushai Hills, 312–13
Lyons, Colonel Burton, 345

M

MacAlevey, Lieut.-Colonel G. M., 98
MacArthur, General Douglas, 530–4
Madaya, 468
Magwe, airfield at, 6, 9, 21–2; Air Wing at, 7–8, 22, 41; Japanese raids on, 41–2; withdrawal to, 50; H.Q. at, 53, 57, 59, 492; Japanese cut road to, 57–8; plan to retake, 60–1, 75; 7th Division near, 489–90; capture of, 491–2
Mahlaing, 80, 441, 486
Maingkwan, 254–5
Maingkwan –Walawbum battle, 254, 257
Malaria, in Kabaw Valley, 106, 354; in Burma Corps H.Q., 114–15; in Arakan, 161; in Fourteenth Army, 177, 354–5; forward treatment of, 178–9; author laid up with, 345
Malaria Forward Treatment Units, 178–80
Malaya, fall of, 37; plan for reconquest of, 481, 508, 512, 520; postponement of landing in, 522; preparation of forces for, 522–3; aircraft taken for operations in, 524, 530; included in area of S.E.A.L.F., 529; landing in, 530, 532
Mandalay, author at, 9, 18; Prome criminals shipped to, 40; air attacks on, 42; Chinese in, 74, 76, 79; withdrawal north of, 80; ferries near, 83; evacuation of, 86–7; air reconnaissances over, 258–9; plan to meet Japanese before, 347, 379–380; plan to capture, 374–6, 393; road to, 400; crossing of Irrawaddy in relation to, 411–12, 432; Japanese concentration for defence of, 418–19, 436–7; 36th Division sends brigade into, 465; launch of attack on, 466–75; capture of, 468–70; civilian prisoners released in, 470
Mandalay Hill, 468
Mandalay–Rangoon railway, 473–4, 482–4
Mandalay–Meiktila battle, 218; planning of, 393–4; disposition of Japanese forces for, 408–9, 418–19, 436–7; building up supplies for, 419–20; around Meiktila, 443–57; on Irrawaddy front, 453, 467–475; Sultan's force co-operates in, 465
Mandalay–Myitkyina railway, Chindits cut, 267
Manipur River, demolition of bridge over, 107; road down valley of, 287; Japanese cross, 297, 302; operations east

of, 349; Lushai Brigade in gorge of, 360; 5th Division reach and cross, 360–1
Mansergh, Major-General E. C. R., 439–440; in advance on Rangoon, 496, 498
Mao Songsang, 343–5
Mapao Spur, 325, 332
Maram, 344–6
Marauders, Merrill's, 254, 257, 270; at Myitkyina, 273–5; exhaustion of, 280
Marindin, Brigadier P. C., 358–60
Mars Brigade, 382, 444, 465
Martaban, Gulf of, 510
Martin, Vice-Admiral Sir Benjamin, 506
Maruyama, Colonel, 274, 281
Mataguchi, General, 326
Matsuyama, Lieut.-General, 276
Maughs, 147, 238
Maungdaw, capture of, 151, 229; Divisional H.Q., 153; abandonment of, 160–1; plan to recapture, 223; restoring port of, 229; Japanese plan to cut road to, 237; held by British, 246; river craft round, 459
Maungdaw–Buthidaung road, 151, 227; British defence of, 157, 159; lost to Japanese, 160; Japanese defences on, 226–8, 244; British reach, 230; capture of tunnels on, 244–6
Mawchi, 73, 500, 503–4
Mawlaik, occupation of, 355–6; bridgehead at, 356, 377; brigade crosses Chindwin at, 389, 403
Mawlu, 267
Maymyo, Army H.Q. at, 9, 10; author at, 10, 14–15, 18; Alexander at, 14–15; air attacks on, 42; Chinese at, 78; Japanese Army H.Q. at, 232; rendezvous of Fourteenth Army and N.C.A.C., 374, 376; capture of, 470–1. Mentioned, 465, 486
Mayu Peninsula, 149, 204, 223, 459
Mayu Range, 149; road running through, 151, 157, 159–60; regarded as impassable, 151, 154; Japanese cross, 156, 239; British battalions on, 159; getting supplies over, 227–8; building road for tanks over, 228–9; Kubo Force destroyed in, 243; getting river craft over, 459
Mayu River, 149, 151, 154, 156
Meiktila, airstrip, 6; air attacks on, 42; Chinese in, 77; withdrawal from, 79–81; Japanese division at, 392; plan for attack on, 393, 395, 411–12, 426, 432, 544; Japanese troops moved from, 419; advance to, 440–2; airfields near, 441, 445–7, 451, 454–5; capture of, 442–52, 467, 475; author visits attacking force at, 446–51; enemies efforts to recover, 452–3, 454–7, 471–2; clearing area

568

Meiktila—*contd.*
round, 480; 4 Corps at, 493; Army
H.Q. at, 503; Aung San in, 516–19. *See
also* Mandalay-Meiktila battle.
Meiktila-Taunggyi road, 509
Mengta, 276
Mergui airfield, 6
Merrill, Brigadier-General F. D., 254, 273–
274. *See also* Marauders, Merrill's
Messervy, Lieut.-General Sir Frank, 145–6;
in Arakan campaign, 223, 226–8, 231,
233, 235; attacks Japanese, 239, 241;
Japanese overrun H.Q. of, 239, 243;
lost hat of, 243; in command, 4 Corps,
388; new plan for, 394–5; at taking
of Gangaw, 403, 405; and crossing of
Irrawaddy, 412, 422–4, 426; at battle of
Meiktila, 446–50, 455–7, 467; and capture
of Pyawbwe, 493–4; and advance
on Rangoon, 497; under anti-aircraft
fire, 504–5
Milestone 109 camp, 297–8, 301–2
Minbu, 490
Mingaladon airfield, 41, 507
Mizukami, Major-General, 274, 281
Mogaung, 251, 255, 278
Mogaung Valley, 253, 270, 278
Mogok, 78, 375, 465
Moirang, 335
Mokpalin, 510, 526
Mong Pai, 73
Mongmit, 374, 465
Montgomery, Major B. F., 25
Monywa, retreat through, 83–4, 89;
Corps H.Q. near, 91–4; Japanese
reported in, 93–4; loss of, 94–6; advance
on, 403; enemy force covering, 409;
capture of, 416–17; Army H.Q. at,
417–18, 446, 453; 5th Division at, 440
Morale, foundations of, 182–96
Moreh, 294, 304–5
Morris, General Sir Edwin, 4, 9
Morrisforce, 275, 277, 280
Moslem League, 128
Moulmein, airfield at, 6; lost to Japanese,
13; Japanese troops in, 392, 510; as
objective of advance, 394, 510; Kimura
moves H.Q. to, 501; evacuation of
Rangoon troops to, by sea, 506
Mountbatten, Admiral Lord Louis (Earl),
Supreme Commander South-East Asia
Allied Command, 168, 201–2; and *Seac*,
190; visits Barrackpore, 191–2; H.Q. of,
200–1; in conference to plan offensive,
201, 203; and General Stilwell, 205–7,
256, 280, 383; unites air forces under one
command, 211; and Wingate, 217–18,
255; at conference on Northern front,
273; seeks command of Yunnan forces,
278; transfers Hump aircraft to Troop

Carrier Command, 306; directive of,
on relief of Imphal, 342; support from,
368, 377; plans of, for Burma campaign,
373–5; and Allied Land Forces commander, 384; and aircraft for supply of
Fourteenth Army, 438, 444; and
operation 'Dracula', 481–2, 487; and
Aung San, 485, 516; and repatriation
problem, 522; and Japanese surrender,
530–1, 534. Mentioned, 242, 251, 438
Moyingyi Reservoir, 502
Mu River, 79, 401–2
Mutaguchi, Lieut.-General, 232, 290, 348,
391
Myebon Peninsula, 458, 460–1
Myingun, 57
Myingyan, transport through, 400; capture
of, 455–7; reconstructed as port,
456; road to Meiktila from, 475. Mentioned, 471, 486
Myingyan-Meiktila railway, 398, 400,
457
Myinmu, 84, 86, 418; bridgehead, 420–1
Myinthi, 474
Myitche, 425
Myitkyina, airstrip at, 6; fall of, 78, 82,
108–9; road through, 172; objective of
Stilwell's offensive, 204, 207, 214, 251,
255, 259, 271–3; Japanese forces at, 232,
252; Chindits move towards, 267;
attacks on, 273–5, 277; siege of, 275; fall
of, 280–1, 443
Myitkyo, 526
Myitnge River, 79, 81, 84–5
Myitsun, 435, 465
Myittha, 465, 473
Myittha River, gorge of, 365
Myittha Valley, retreat through, 82–3,
107; hostile Burmese in, 92, 107;
Lushai Brigade's advance in, 363–4, 403
Myohaung, 459
Myotha, 419, 472
Myothit, 298

N

Naba, 100
Naf River, 147, 151, 223, 229, 238, 246
Naga Village, 320–1, 339–41
Nagas, help build Ledo road, 253; loyalty
and courage of, 341–2
Nagasaki, 529
Nagasang airfield, 6
Natmauk, 60–1, 80, 491
Nepalese troops, 308, 313, 364
Ngakyedauk Pass, building road over,
228–9; troops and tanks cross, 231;
author crosses, 233; Japanese threat to,
235, 237–8; Japanese in, 238, 240
Ngazun, 419, 433–4